The Encyclopedia of the United States Congress

The
Encyclopedia
of the
United States Congress

Edited by

DONALD C. BACON
ROGER H. DAVIDSON
MORTON KELLER

Volume 4

SIMON & SCHUSTER

A Paramount Communications Company

New York   London   Toronto   Sydney   Tokyo   Singapore

Simon & Schuster
Academic Reference Division
15 Columbus Circle
New York, New York 10023

Printed in the United States of America

printing number
1 2 3 4 5 6 7 8 9 10

Library of Congress Cataloging-in-Publication Data
The encyclopedia of the United States Congress / edited by
Donald C. Bacon, Roger H. Davidson, Morton Keller.
p. cm.
ISBN 0-13-276361-3 (set : alk. paper)
ISBN 0-13-307118-9 (v.4 : alk. paper)
1. United States. Congress—Encyclopedias. I. Bacon,
Donald C. II. Davidson, Roger H. III. Keller, Morton.
JK1067.E63 1995
328.73′003—dc20 94-21203 CIP

*Funding for this publication was received from
the Commission on the Bicentennial of the
United States Constitution. The University of Texas
at Austin and the Lyndon Baines Johnson Library recognize
with gratitude this and other assistance rendered by the
Commission in the development of this project.*

Acknowledgments of sources, copyrights, and
permissions to use previously printed materials
are made throughout the work.

This paper meets the requirements of ANSI/NISO Z39.48-1992
(Permanence of Paper).

About the Editors

DONALD C. BACON is a Washington-based journalist specializing in Congress and the presidency. He has served as staff writer of the *Wall Street Journal* and assistant managing editor for congressional and political coverage of *U.S. News & World Report*. A former Congressional Fellow, he holds major prizes in journalism and has written and contributed to numerous books, including *Rayburn: A Biography* (1987) and *Congress and You* (1969).

ROGER H. DAVIDSON is Professor of Government and Politics at the University of Maryland, College Park. He has taught at several universities and served as a Capitol Hill staff member with the Bolling Committee, with the Stevenson Committee, and as Senior Specialist with the Congressional Research Service, Library of Congress. He is author or coauthor of numerous articles and books dealing with Congress and national policy-making, including the standard textbook, *Congress and Its Members* (4th edition, 1994).

MORTON KELLER is Spector Professor of History at Brandeis University. He has been a visiting professor at Yale, Harvard, and Oxford universities. Dr. Keller's books include *Regulating a New Society: Public Policy and Social Change in America, 1900–1933* (1994); *Regulating a New Economy: Public Policy and Economic Change in America, 1900–1933* (1990); *Parties, Congress, and Public Policy* (1985); and *Affairs of State: Public Life in Late Nineteenth Century America* (1977).

Abbreviations and Acronyms Used in This Work

AFL-CIO American Federation of Labor and Congress of Industrial Organizations
amend. amendment
app. appendix
Ala. Alabama
A.M. *ante meridiem*, before noon
Ariz. Arizona
Ark. Arkansas
Art. Article
b. born
c. *circa*, about, approximately
Calif. California
cf. *confer*, compare
chap. chapter (pl., chaps.)
CIA Central Intelligence Agency
Cir. Ct. Circuit Court
cl. clause
Cong. Congress
Colo. Colorado
Cong. Rec. Congressional Record
Conn. Connecticut
CRS Congressional Research Service
d. died
D Democrat, Democratic
D.C. District of Columbia
D.D.C. District Court (federal) of the District of Columbia
Del. Delaware
diss. dissertation
doc. document
DR Democratic-Republican
ed. editor (pl., eds); edition
e.g. *exempli gratia*, for example
enl. enlarged
esp. especially
et al. *et alii*, and others
etc. *et cetera*, and so forth

exp. expanded
F Federalist
f. and following (pl., ff.)
F. Federal Reporter
F.2d Federal Reporter, 2d series
FBI Federal Bureau of Investigation
Fed. Reg. Federal Register
Fla. Florida
F. Supp. Federal Supplement
Ga. Georgia
GAO General Accounting Office
GPO Government Printing Office
GS General Schedule (federal civil service grade level)
H. Con. Res. House Concurrent Resolution
H. Doc. House Document
H. Hrg. House Hearing
H.J. Res. House Joint Resolution
H.R. House of Representatives; when followed by a number, identifies a bill that originated in the House
H. Rept. House Report
H. Res. House Resolution
How. Howard (court reporter)
I Independent (party)
ibid. *ibidem*, in the same place (as the one immediately preceding)
i.e. *id est*, that is
Ill. Illinois
I.L.M. International Legal Materials
Ind. Indiana
J Jeffersonian
Jr. Junior
Kans. Kansas

Ky. Kentucky
La. Louisiana
M.A. Master of Arts
Mass. Massachusetts
Mich. Michigan
Minn. Minnesota
Miss. Mississippi
Mo. Missouri
Mont. Montana
n. note
N.C. North Carolina
n.d. no date
N.Dak. North Dakota
Nebr. Nebraska
Nev. Nevada
N.H. New Hampshire
N.J. New Jersey
N.Mex. New Mexico
no. number (pl., nos.)
n.p. no place
n.s. new series
N.Y. New York
Okla. Oklahoma
Oreg. Oregon
p. page (pl., pp.)
Pa. Pennsylvania
P.L. Public Law
Prog. Progressive
pt. part (pl., pts.)
Pub. Res. Public Resolution
R Republican
Rep. Representative
repr. reprint
rept. report
rev. revised
R.I. Rhode Island
S. Senate; when followed by a number, identifies a bill that originated in the Senate
S.C. South Carolina
S. Con. Res. Senate Concurrent Resolution
S. Ct. Supreme Court Reporter
S.Dak. South Dakota

S. Doc. Senate Document
sec. section (pl., secs.)
Sen. Senator
ser. series
sess. session
S. Hrg. Senate Hearing
S.J. Res. Senate Joint Resolution
S. Prt. Senate Print
S. Rept. Senate Report
S. Res. Senate Resolution
Stat. Statutes at Large
S. Treaty Doc. Senate Treaty Document
supp. supplement
Tenn. Tennessee
Tex. Texas
T.I.A.S. Treaties and Other International Acts Series
U.N. United Nations
U.S. United States, United States Reports
USA United States Army
USAF United States Air Force
U.S.C. United States Code
U.S.C.A. United States Code Annotated
USN United States Navy
U.S.S.R. Union of Soviet Socialist Republics
U.S.T. United States Treaties
v. versus
Va. Virginia
VA Veterans Administration
vol. volume (pl., vols.)
Vt. Vermont
W Whig
Wash. Washington
Wheat. Wheaton (court reporter)
Wis. Wisconsin
W.Va. West Virginia
Wyo. Wyoming

Years of Each Congress

This table provides a simple guide to the dates of each Congress, citing the year in which the following Congress begins as the year in which the previous Congress ends. For the exact opening and closing dates of each session of each Congress from the First Congress to the present, see the table accompanying the entry "Sessions of Congress."

1st	1789–1791	26th	1839–1841	51st	1889–1891	76th	1939–1941
2d	1791–1793	27th	1841–1843	52d	1891–1893	77th	1941–1943
3d	1793–1795	28th	1843–1845	53d	1893–1895	78th	1943–1945
4th	1795–1797	29th	1845–1847	54th	1895–1897	79th	1945–1947
5th	1797–1799	30th	1847–1849	55th	1897–1899	80th	1947–1949
6th	1799–1801	31st	1849–1851	56th	1899–1901	81st	1949–1951
7th	1801–1803	32d	1851–1853	57th	1901–1903	82d	1951–1953
8th	1803–1805	33d	1853–1855	58th	1903–1905	83d	1953–1955
9th	1805–1807	34th	1855–1857	59th	1905–1907	84th	1955–1957
10th	1807–1809	35th	1857–1859	60th	1907–1909	85th	1957–1959
11th	1809–1811	36th	1859–1861	61st	1909–1911	86th	1959–1961
12th	1811–1813	37th	1861–1863	62d	1911–1913	87th	1961–1963
13th	1813–1815	38th	1863–1865	63d	1913–1915	88th	1963–1965
14th	1815–1817	39th	1865–1867	64th	1915–1917	89th	1965–1967
15th	1817–1819	40th	1867–1869	65th	1917–1919	90th	1967–1969
16th	1819–1821	41st	1869–1871	66th	1919–1921	91st	1969–1971
17th	1821–1823	42d	1871–1873	67th	1921–1923	92d	1971–1973
18th	1823–1825	43d	1873–1875	68th	1923–1925	93d	1973–1975
19th	1825–1827	44th	1875–1877	69th	1925–1927	94th	1975–1977
20th	1827–1829	45th	1877–1879	70th	1927–1929	95th	1977–1979
21st	1829–1831	46th	1879–1881	71st	1929–1931	96th	1979–1981
22d	1831–1833	47th	1881–1883	72d	1931–1933	97th	1981–1983
23d	1833–1835	48th	1883–1885	73d	1933–1935	98th	1983–1985
24th	1835–1837	49th	1885–1887	74th	1935–1937	99th	1985–1987
25th	1837–1839	50th	1887–1889	75th	1937–1939	100th	1987–1989
						101st	1989–1991
						102d	1991–1993
						103d	1993–1995

S

SABATH, ADOLPH J. (1866–1952), Democratic representative from Illinois, chairman of the Committee on Rules. A native of Zabori, Bohemia, Adolph Joachim Sabath immigrated to the United States in 1881 and settled in Chicago. He became a naturalized citizen at twenty-one and went into the real estate business, selling and renting to other immigrants. He became a lawyer, police magistrate, and Democratic ward committeeman, rising to prominence as a leader of Chicago's emerging Bohemian American community. Elected to the U.S. House of Representatives in 1906, he campaigned in four languages. Sabath proved to be among the nation's more durable legislators, winning twenty-four consecutive terms from a district that included enclaves of seventeen ethnic groups.

Sabath, who spoke with a heavy accent, never forgot his roots. In his first term, he helped to pass legislation for the expansion of an immigrant station in Philadelphia. "Let us build this building," said Sabath, "to give these worthy foreigners a welcome when they come, and to show them that our country ever extends the warm hand of sympathy and fellowship to the oppressed peoples of the earth." As a member of the Immigration and Naturalization Committee, Sabath fought efforts to restrict immigration, including the National Origins Act, which discriminated against Eastern Europeans and Asians.

During World War I, Sabath advocated the creation of Czechoslovakia and asked President Woodrow Wilson not to negotiate a separate peace with Austria-Hungary. In September 1918, Wilson did recognize Czechoslovakia—a special vindication for Sabath. He was also an early advocate for the creation of Israel.

In 1939 Sabath became chairman of the House Rules Committee, retaining the office for the rest of his life except during the Republican 80th Congress. During his long tenure, Sabath was little more than a figurehead on a committee dominated by southern Democrats and midwestern Republicans.

BIBLIOGRAPHY

Beal, John R. "Adolph J. Sabath: Dean of the House." In *Public Men In and Out of Office.* Edited by John Thomas Salter. 1946.

Boxerman, Burton A. "Adolph Joachim Sabath in Congress: The Early Years." *Illinois State Historical Society Journal* 66 (1973).

Boxerman, Burton A. "Adolph Joachim Sabath in Congress: The Roosevelt and Truman Years." *Illinois State Historical Society Journal* 66 (1973).

STEVE NEAL

ST. CLAIR INVESTIGATION.

Gen. Arthur St. Clair commanded an expeditionary force that suffered heavy losses in a battle with the northwestern Indian confederation on 4 November 1791. He requested a military court to clear his reputation, but it was impossible to constitute a proper tribunal because he was the army's only major general. The best alternative mode of inquiry was a congressional committee. The committee that conducted the St. Clair investigation was the first under the federal Constitution, but the procedure had been used occasionally by the Continental Congress.

St. Clair blamed his defeat mostly on recruiting delays and supply shortages resulting from the lax administration of Secretary of War Henry Knox and Secretary of the Treasury Alexander Hamilton. After a sharp debate on the proper mode of investigation, the House created a select committee, headed by Thomas Fitzsimons of Pennsylvania, to conduct the inquiry.

The committee was authorized to "call for such persons, papers, and records, as may be necessary to assist their inquiries—the essential precedent for all subsequent congressional investigations. It examined reports and correspondence and took testimony from St. Clair, Hamilton, and Knox, as well as a number of officers present at the battle. The investigation, which showed an abundance of administrative delay and confusion, more or less vindicated St. Clair, who escaped personal censure.

Fitzsimons presented the report on 8 May 1792. St. Clair's critics accused the committee of excusing his incompetence, and those judged responsible for administrative failures complained bitterly. When Congress convened in November the report was sharply challenged. Friends of Hamilton and Knox tried but failed to persuade the House to allow them to appear in their own defense—another important precedent, for no officers of the executive branch have ever been allowed to speak directly to the House itself, although they often appear before committees.

After a confused debate the House voted to recommit the report, and the Speaker named the five members of the original committee who were present to form the new committee. The committee submitted its revised report on 15 February 1793, doing no more than correcting a few minor errors. No legislation resulted from the investigation, but the authority of the House to investigate suspected executive misconduct has been beyond serious challenge since 1792.

BIBLIOGRAPHY

Furlong, P. J. "The Investigation of General Arthur St. Clair." *Capitol Studies* 5 (Fall 1977): 65–86.

PATRICK J. FURLONG

SALARIES. Few legislative actions by Congress yield the same degree of anguish and embarrassment as the periodic exercise of setting federal salaries, including those of members of Congress. The constitutional command of Article I, section 6 seems straightforward: "The Senators and Representatives shall receive a Compensation for their Services, to be ascertained by Law, and paid out of the Treasury of the United States." The political reality is quite different. The setting of congressional salaries, as well as those in the executive and judicial branches, has been marked by legislative debates that have been tumultuous, bombastic, and evasive. Rep. Morris K. Udall correctly noted in 1977, "I do not know why it is, but debating this subject always produces more self-righteousness and more passionate oratory and more posturing and more nonsense, if I may say so, than almost any other subject."

The Constitutional Provision. Only one compensation issue was fully resolved at the Constitutional Convention: the source of funds used to pay members of Congress. A move to have members paid by the states they represented was soundly defeated. Because the Articles of Confederation had so enfeebled national powers, it seemed indispensable to make the new national structure independent of the state legislatures. Eight states voted in favor, and only three against, a motion that congressional wages should be paid out of the national treasury.

The Constitutional Convention also considered establishing a fixed and definite compensation for members of Congress. One idea was to select the price of wheat or some other commodity as a proper standard. That plan failed, as did a motion to set the compensation of members at $5 for each day of attendance and for each thirty miles of travel to and from Congress. The specifics of compensation would have to be decided by statute.

On the question of whether to set different pay for senators and representatives, the debates at the Philadelphia Convention are filled with vacillation and uncertainty. Some delegates proposed that senators receive no salary on the assumption that the Senate ought to be composed of persons of wealth. Other delegates thought the salary of senators should be larger than that of representatives. The language of the Constitution was, ultimately, neutral on this issue.

In the original Bill of Rights, James Madison included an amendment that would have delayed any congressional pay raise until after the next election. The purpose was to avoid what seemed to him an "indecorum" when legislators "put their hand into the public coffers [and] take out money to put in their pockets." Congress agreed to propose a constitutional amendment adding these words to Article I, section 6: "No law, varying the compensation for the services of the Senators and Representatives, shall take effect, until an election of Representatives shall have intervened." That language was finally ratified by the states in 1992 and became the Twenty-Seventh Amendment.

Precedents Set by the First Congress. Members of the First Congress debated an issue that has been confronted repeatedly since 1789: how to ensure that compensation would be set neither too high (which would attract profit seekers) nor too low (which would exclude all but the wealthy from serving). Rep. John Page of Virginia told his colleagues in 1789 that low pay "would throw the Government into the hands of bad men, by which the people might lose every thing they now hold dear." Another member of the First Congress, Rep. Elbridge Gerry of Massachusetts, warned that inadequate pay would expose the legislative branch to corruption, a danger that could come from either of two directions: the private sector or the executive branch.

Members of the First Congress considered setting the pay of senators somewhat higher than that of representatives, reasoning that the Constitution requires senators to be older than representatives, to be citizens for nine years (compared to seven for the House), and to serve for six years (compared to two for the House). The effort to give senators greater salaries failed by a considerable margin, however. Congress did pass a compromise measure, giving the members of both houses $6 a day until 4 March 1795, after which senators would receive $7 a day. President George Washington considered vetoing the measure on the ground that the

CONGRESSIONAL "SALARY GRAB." Cartoon contrasting the high pay of members of Congress with the low wages of congressional clerks, whose salaries could not defray the high cost of living in the District of Columbia. Horace Greeley, liberal editor of the *New York Tribune*, stands at left.   LIBRARY OF CONGRESS

bill should have established an immediate difference between the House and the Senate, but finally decided to sign the bill.

Subsequent Changes. After experimenting with a fixed daily rate of compensation, some members of Congress concluded that a per diem system had an unhealthy effect on attendance. Members might dawdle in order to receive additional pay. When the House of Representatives met on 8 February 1796, it considered a bill that proposed paying each member an annual salary of $1,000. Some legislators, however, had misgivings about an annual payment. That method of compensation, they believed, might worsen the problem of declining attendance at the end of a session.

It was not until 1816 that Congress changed the mode of compensation from $6 a day to $1,500 a session. A move to suspend the increase until the next Congress was defeated, and the new salary was made retroactive to the beginning of the session. The increase, coming on the heels of the expensive War of 1812, triggered an angry public debate; a year later, Congress was forced to repeal the act. In 1818, Congress raised the per diem to $8. In 1856, it finally adopted an annual salary schedule, fixing the amount at $3,000 a year. Interestingly, this salary was backdated some eleven months without precipitating protests among voters.

Throughout this early period, congressional salaries were kept below actual expenses, forcing members to draw on their personal wealth or to seek auxiliary sources of income. Members practiced law, engaged in banking, did farming, and entered other trades. By mixing public duty and private income, they subjected themselves to serious conflicts of interest.

The ultimate in retroactive salary increases occurred on 3 March 1873, the day before the 42d Congress adjourned. On that day, Congress raised the annual salary of members to $7,500 and made the increase applicable to the whole of the 42d Congress. Moreover, instead of following the traditional route of raising salaries through a separate legislative bill, Congress added the increase as a rider to an appropriations bill. Under tremendous heat from constituents and the press, Congress within a year repealed what was called the salary grab. When Congress in 1907 did raise compensation to $7,500 a year, it was careful to make the increase effective at the start of the next Congress. By 1955 the annual salary had increased to $22,500.

Salary Commissions. In 1953, the Senate passed a bill to establish a commission that would deter-

BUT ON THE OTHER HAND

PAY-RAISE HAZARDS. Cartoon satirizing the political dangers for members of Congress who wish to legislate congressional salary increases that are typically unpopular with voters. John R. Fischetti, 1953.

LIBRARY OF CONGRESS

mine the salaries of members of the legislative and judicial branches. The House refused to support this delegation of responsibility. In 1967, however, members of Congress used the commission idea to insulate themselves from the emotional issue of pay raises. They created the Commission on Executive, Legislative, and Judicial Salaries, later referred to as the quadrennial commission. Every four years the commission would recommend the rates of compensation to be paid to members of Congress, justices of the Supreme Court and other federal judges, and certain high-ranking executive officials. The president, after receiving those recommendations, would submit to Congress his own salary proposals. Under this plan, the president's proposals would take effect within thirty days unless either house disapproved. Congress could also replace the president's proposals with a different salary schedule. This procedure was very convenient for Congress. Members would not have to vote for a salary increase. All they would have to do

Salaries for Members of Congress

SALARY	DATE OF AUTHORITY ENACTMENT	STATUTORY AUTHORITY
$6 per diem during attendance to 4 March 1795; after 4 March 1795, $7 per diem for senators during attendance at special sessions, and for representatives and senators, $6 per diem during attendance at regular sessions	22 September 1789	1 Stat. 70–71
$6 per diem during attendance	10 March 1796	1 Stat. 448
$1,500 per year; repealed in 1817	19 March 1816 6 February 1817	3 Stat. 257 3 Stat. 345
$8 per diem during attendance	22 January 1818	3 Stat. 404
$3,000	16 August 1856	11 Stat. 48
$5,000	28 July 1866	14 Stat. 323
$7,500	3 March 1873	17 Stat. 486
$5,000	20 January 1874	18 Stat. 4
$7,500	26 February 1907	34 Stat. 993
$10,000	4 March 1925	43 Stat. 1301
$9,000	30 June 1932	47 Stat. 401
$8,500	20 March 1933	48 Stat. 14
$9,000	28 March 1934	48 Stat. 521
$9,500 (effective 1 July 1934)	28 March 1934	48 Stat. 521
$10,000	13 February 1935	49 Stat. 24
$2,500 annual expense allowance (tax free)	3 July 1945	59 Stat. 318
$12,500	2 August 1946	60 Stat. 850
$22,500 ($2,500 annual expense allowance repealed)	2 March 1955	69 Stat. 11
$30,000	14 August 1964	78 Stat. 415
$42,500 (Salary Commission established by P.L. 90-206; salary effective 1 March 1969)	16 December 1967	81 Stat. 642
$44,600 (effective 1 October 1975)	9 August 1975	89 Stat. 421
$57,500 (effective 20 February 1977)	16 December 1967	81 Stat. 642
$60,662.50 (effective 1 October 1979)	9 August 1975	89 Stat. 421
$69,800 (effective 21 December 1982 for representatives, 1 July 1983 for senators)	21 December 1982 30 July 1983	96 Stat. 1914 97 Stat. 338
$72,600 (effective 1 January 1984)	9 August 1975	89 Stat. 421
$75,100 (effective 1 January 1985)	9 August 1975	89 Stat. 421
$77,400 (effective 1 January 1987)	9 August 1975	89 Stat. 421
$89,500 (effective 4 February 1987)	16 December 1967	81 Stat. 642
$96,600 for representatives; $98,400 for senators (effective 1 February 1990)	30 November 1989	103 Stat. 1716

Salaries for Members of Congress (Continued)

SALARY	DATE OF AUTHORITY ENACTMENT	STATUTORY AUTHORITY
$125,000 for representatives; $101,900 for senators (effective 1 January 1991); $125,000 for senators (effective 14 August 1991)	30 November 1989	103 Stat. 1716
$129,500 (effective 1 January 1992)	30 November 1989	103 Stat. 1716
$133,600 (effective 1 January 1993)	30 November 1989	103 Stat. 1716

SOURCE: Adapted from Paul E. Dwyer and Frederick H. Pauls, "A Brief History of Congressional Pay Legislation" (Congressional Research Service, 12 August 1987); Paul E. Dwyer, "Salaries for Members of Congress" (Congressional Research Service, 15 January 1992).

was wait out the thirty days and get the increase when it took effect.

In 1983, the Supreme Court in *Immigration and Naturalization Service v. Chadha* invalidated the legislative veto. To comply with this decision, Congress repealed the one-house veto in the salary act, replacing it with a device that, though it compelled both houses to take action and involved presenting a measure to the president, still allowed Congress to get a pay raise without legislating that raise itself. According to this procedure, the president would propose pay raises and Congress, if it wished to disapprove those raises, would have thirty days in which to pass a joint resolution that the president could sign or veto. If Congress did not act, the salary change would take effect.

This indirect method of adopting congressional pay raises finally backfired in 1989 when President Ronald Reagan recommended a 51 percent increase for members of Congress. At first it looked as if Congress would successfully wait out the thirty days and get the increase, but members soon began to wilt under scathing criticism from the public. Speaker James C. Wright, Jr., proposed that the pay raise be reduced to 30 percent. In a last-ditch effort to preserve the full pay raise, the House tried to adjourn, but Rep. William E. Dannemeyer insisted on a roll call on adjournment. This vote was interpreted as a vote on the merits of the pay raise. More than a hundred Democrats deserted the leadership and voted against adjournment. With one day remaining in the thirty-day period, the two houses passed a joint resolution to kill the pay raise.

Later in 1989, Congress passed legislation that gave members a pay hike of about 40 percent, but this increase was phased in over a two-year period.

To make the salary raise more palatable, Congress added a number of restrictions on outside income, including a ban on honoraria. Under the new legislation, members could no longer get raises by being silent during a thirty-day review period. Both houses would now have to vote affirmatively for future pay increases by passing a joint resolution of approval.

[*See also* Members, *article on* Retirement; Perquisites; Travel; Twenty-seventh Amendment.]

BIBLIOGRAPHY

Davidson, Roger H. "The Politics of Executive, Legislative, and Judicial Compensation." In *The Rewards of Public Service.* Edited by Robert W. Hartman and Arnold R. Weber. 1980.

Fisher, Louis. "History of Pay Adjustments for Members of Congress." In *The Rewards of Public Service.* Edited by Robert W. Hartman and Arnold R. Weber. 1980.

LOUIS FISHER

SANTO DOMINGO. The Caribbean island divided into the countries of Santo Domingo (the present-day Dominican Republic) and Haiti began to attract the attention of U.S. policymakers in the wake of the Civil War. Secretary of State William H. Seward had his eye on Santo Domingo's Samaná Bay as a naval harbor. That country's officials and U.S. entrepreneurs had strong financial interests in a deal, and House Foreign Affairs chairman Nathaniel P. Banks (R-Mass.) proposed to make both Santo Domingo and Haiti U.S. protectorates. But Congress, reflecting popular American disinterest in and/or hostility toward such a step, roundly defeated Banks's resolution.

After he became president in 1869, Ulysses S.

Grant set out to secure a treaty with Santo Domingo as a first step toward annexing the island. He was led to this by his private secretary Orville Babcock, in cahoots with speculators hoping to profit from the island's sugar and tobacco. They sought to secure the Senate's approval by financial inducements and propaganda.

Foreign Relations Committee chairman Charles Sumner (R-Mass.) strongly disapproved because of the taint of jobbery that clung to the scheme and especially because it threatened the future of the black Republic of Haiti.

The treaty failed, as did a proposal for trade reciprocity with Santo Domingo in 1884. After James G. Blaine became secretary of State in 1889, he showed some interest in fostering a U.S. naval and commercial presence on the island. But as before, Congress faithfully reflected the popular disinclination to become involved. Only in the late twentieth century did the Cold War, and more recently immigration from Haiti and the struggle against authoritarian rule there, foster some congressional interest in the island.

BIBLIOGRAPHY

Campbell, Charles S. *The Transformation of American Foreign Relations, 1865–1900.* 1976.
Nevins, Allan. *Hamilton Fish: The Inner History of the Grant Administration.* 1936.

MORTON KELLER

SAVINGS AND LOAN CRISIS.

Growing out of governmental failures on a national and state level, the savings and loan crisis of the 1980s began a transformation of politics and regulatory policy that will be felt in Congress until the end of the twentieth century.

The collapse of more than one thousand savings and loan associations from the mid 1980s through 1993 bankrupted the insurance fund that protected thrift depositors, forcing a wholesale salvage operation for the industry that began in 1989 and cost more than $150 billion before it was completed. Some of that expense was paid by the troubled industry, but most of it was from taxpayers.

The thrift industry, founded to provide a source of ready and cheap money for home mortgages, contracted by more than a third in number of institutions and by tens of billions of dollars in total assets. Ultimately, Congress completely overhauled the regulatory machinery for savings and loans.

Although there were many culpable parties, the crisis reverberated through Congress, which bore a large share of the blame. A few members lost their jobs directly or indirectly as a result. The influence exerted over lawmakers by an industry with deep pockets hastened calls for campaign-finance reform.

Perhaps the most intense political fallout came from a scandal involving Charles H. Keating, Jr., whose California thrift was seized by the federal government in 1989 in one of the most notorious and costly failures. The $2 billion loss associated with the collapse of Keating's Lincoln Savings and Loan Association focused the public's attention on the thrift crisis. Five prominent senators—later known as the Keating Five—were ensnared in the scandal when it was disclosed that Keating and his close associates gave $1.3 million to their reelection campaigns and other political causes and that they had met with federal regulators in Keating's behalf.

It was difficult to pin the collapse of an industry on any one action by Congress. Regulators and legislators approved a host of flawed policy changes in response to a souring economy. In turn, new problems formed and festered in the relaxed regulatory environment, and the industry became ripe for picking by greedy and unscrupulous operators.

Following creation of separate deposit-insurance systems for banks and thrifts in the midst of the Great Depression, thrifts failed only rarely until the 1980s. That changed when inflation surged in the mid and late 1970s. To curb inflation, the Federal Reserve Board held a tight rein on the supply of money in the economy, causing interest rates to soar in the period from 1979 to 1982. At the same time, computer technology enabled the creation of money market funds and other sophisticated financial instruments whose higher yields lured depositors away from thrifts, jeopardizing their survival.

Congress then acted to make thrifts more profitable, and their deposits more competitive. The 1980 Depository Institutions Deregulation and Monetary Control Act was one of two principal federal laws that—in trying to stem losses in the industry—increased taxpayer liability. The 1980 law permitted what was then the federal thrift regulatory agency, the Federal Home Loan Bank Board, to reduce mandatory net worth requirements on savings and loans. The Bank Board did so right away, which made it cheaper for thrifts to grow rapidly once high interest rates abated in 1982.

The 1980 law also dramatically increased the level of deposit-insurance coverage from $40,000 to $100,000 per account. Although the move had the salutary effect of slowing the movement of thrift deposits into money market funds, it greatly increased the liability of the insurance fund.

In the 1982 Garn-St Germain Act, Congress took additional steps to make thrifts more profitable—or at least to make them appear so. Rules limiting investments were greatly relaxed and accounting standards were changed, which enabled thrift operators to disguise or overlook problems on their balance sheets.

Some states went much further than Congress or the Bank Board, opening the door wide for state-chartered thrifts to move into riskier investments or unconventional businesses. A large concentration of failures occurred in those states that had the most lax regulations—notably California and Texas.

Because of federal deposit insurance, depositors managed to escape mostly unscathed. Some had to wait to gain access to their cash; some had accounts larger than the insurance limit of $100,000 and lost a portion of the excess. In Ohio and Maryland, the broad crisis was exacerbated by the existence of state-run deposit-insurance plans that were overwhelmed by thrift failures, sometimes at heavy cost to depositors.

That federal insurance protected depositors meant only that the loss was transferred to the taxpayers tapped to bail out the insurance fund. As a consequence of continued thrift failures, the Federal Savings and Loan Insurance Corporation (FSLIC) became technically bankrupt in 1986 and had a negative net worth of about $14 billion by the time it was dissolved in 1989 (though it still had some cash from deposit-insurance premiums).

A Taxpayer Bailout. Many members of Congress did not accept that there was an impending disaster until long after the FSLIC was insolvent. The Reagan administration proposed a bailout in early 1985, recommending that the industry borrow $15 billion for the FSLIC to use to close insolvent thrifts and cover depositor losses. Industry officials insisted that the problem was not so severe, and their allies in Congress deferred that first bailout for eighteen months. When it was finally enacted in August 1987, the amount funneled to the FSLIC was only $10.8 billion, an amount later judged to be too little too late.

By 1988, steadily mounting losses soaked up all of the FSLIC's cash reserves, and the fund resorted to issuing more than $20 billion in promissory notes to investors who were willing to take over failed thrifts and make good their deposits. Buyers also benefited from generous tax breaks previously enacted to aid the sale of failed thrifts. More than two hundred failed institutions were unloaded in 1988, at a high cost (in excess of $40 billion) that was not fully known until years later.

Although the Reagan administration largely ignored the escalating crisis in the year leading up to the 1988 presidential elections, newly elected president George Bush moved quickly. Before taking office in January 1989, Bush directed Treasury Secretary Nicholas F. Brady to develop a comprehensive solution, which was unveiled on 6 February. In a whirl of legislative alacrity, Congress enacted the sweeping overhaul of thrift regulations coupled to a $50 billion industry- and taxpayer-financed bailout of the deposit-insurance fund. It took barely six months from its unveiling to enactment, and with Bush's signature on 9 August 1989, the bailout began.

A new regulatory structure replaced the Bank Board and the FSLIC. The Office of Thrift Supervision was created to charter and regulate thrifts. A new insurance fund was created as part of the Federal Deposit Insurance Corporation (which previously only protected bank depositors). And the Resolution Trust Corporation (RTC) was created as a temporary agency to take over failed thrifts and dispose of their assets.

It was clear soon after enactment that the $50 billion allotted to the RTC would not be enough. Another $37 billion was given to the RTC and spent. Congress balked at further appropriations, and the bailout effectively shut down in April 1992—with the resulting delay further increasing the cost. Newly elected president Bill Clinton asked Congress in early 1993 for an additional $28 billion for the RTC and $17 billion to capitalize the new Savings Association Insurance Fund. Congress complied by voting in November 1993 to provide an additional $18 billion for the RTC, but no money for the insurance fund, which was to be entirely capitalized by thrift-paid premiums.

The Keating Five. Several key members of Congress were badly tainted by the thrift crisis. House Speaker James C. Wright, Jr., a Texas Democrat, was closely tied to some home-state thrift operators whose institutions failed in dramatic style. Wright was also responsible for delaying action on the 1987 bailout when he thought that regulators were being overly tough on some Texas thrifts. (Wright was driven from office in 1989 for other reasons.)

House Banking, Finance, and Urban Affairs Committee chairman Fernand J. St Germain, a Rhode Island Democrat, also had a special relationship with thrift industry lobbyists. St Germain was absolved by one House ethics investigation and was under the cloud of another when he was defeated for reelection in 1988 in a campaign that focused on his ties to lobbyists.

Even President Bush, who was responsible for moving to resolve the crisis, was touched when it was disclosed that his son, Neil Bush, had been a director of a failed Colorado thrift.

The failure of Keating's Lincoln Savings and Loan, however, was seen as a microcosm of the crisis—the cumulative effect of fraud, inside dealing, regulatory incompetence, and political interference. Ultimately, five senators were the subject of an extraordinary public examination of the thrift's failure and their alleged efforts to fend off federal regulators. The Senate Ethics Committee held twenty-six days of televised hearings in late 1990 and early 1991 to review the possibility that Keating's largess was connected to an April 1987 meeting between the five senators and federal regulators from San Francisco, and to consider whether any of the five had acted improperly.

Of the five senators, only Alan Cranston (D-Calif.) was formally punished for his actions. The Ethics Committee found him guilty of improper conduct and issued a reprimand in November 1991. The full Senate did not act on the Ethics Committee report. Cranston retired at the end of the 102d Congress (1991–1992).

The other four senators were publicly embarrassed by the hearings and attendant publicity. The Ethics Committee found poor judgment but no improper behavior on the part of two of them—John Glenn (D-Ohio) and John McCain (R-Ariz.). Both were easily reelected in 1992. The committee chided the remaining two: Donald W. Riegle, Jr. (D-Mich.) and Dennis DeConcini (D-Ariz.). Its report said that their actions gave the appearance of being improper, but were not cause for punishment. Neither sought reelection when his term expired in 1994.

[See also Depository Institutions Deregulation and Monetary Control Act of 1980; Ethics and Corruption in Congress.]

BIBLIOGRAPHY

Brumbaugh, R. Dan, Jr. *Thrifts under Siege.* 1988.
Cranford, John R. "Keating and the Five Senators: Putting the Puzzle Together." *Congressional Quarterly Weekly Report,* 26 January 1991, pp. 221–227.
Kane, Edward J. *The S&L Insurance Mess: How Did It Happen?* 1989.
Mayer, Martin. *The Greatest-Ever Bank Robbery.* 1990.
Pizzo, Stephen, Mary Fricker, and Paul Muolo. *Inside Job: The Looting of America's Savings & Loans.* 1989.
Strunk, Norman, and Fred Case. *Where Deregulation Went Wrong.* 1988.

JOHN R. CRANFORD

SCIENCE AND TECHNOLOGY.

The Framers of the Constitution, in providing for the three branches of the U.S. government, set the boundaries for congressional action on science and technology. Discussion within the convention ranged over possible powers to support all kinds of "internal improvements," including the establishment of a national university, but in the final document the word *science* appeared only once. Congress should have the power to "promote the Progress of Science and the useful Arts, by securing for limited Times to Authors and Inventors the exclusive Right to their respective Writings and Discoveries." Beyond patents and copyrights, the whole structure of policies and institutions that has grown up to enable the government both to use and to support science and technology is based on many powers distributed throughout the Constitution, not just on a few clauses.

Congress, Science, and Technology in the Early Republic. In the early years of Congress legislative initiatives were relatively undifferentiated: there was no clear division between taxing and appropriation or between provisions for current operations as distinct from the creation of permanent institutions. The two main sources of revenue, tariffs and the sale of public lands, had technological policy implications from the beginning. That tariffs protecting infant industries might affect the relative economic strengths of industrial versus agricultural regions was obvious, and the tariff became a staple issue of sectional politics. The techniques of rectangular survey, laying down nested squares oriented to true north, aided orderly distribution of land but also left a permanent mark on the environment from Ohio westward. In 1798 the act providing for medical care for merchant seamen addressed a purely practical need for a special group of people and at the same time foreshadowed a major institution, the Public Health Service. Not until long afterward, however, were such initiatives, in their technological aspects, guided by active research.

Thomas Jefferson was one of the most scientifically literate of the nation's presidents, but his view of the Constitution led him to doubt the power of

Congress to appropriate money for internal improvements without an enabling amendment. A number of elaborate plans for a national university came to nothing in part because of this doubt. Jefferson did, however, manage the establishment of the U.S. Military Academy at West Point and the Corps of Engineers as a part of the army. He was quick to support exploration and surveys. The Lewis and Clark expedition (1804–1806), dispatched beyond state boundaries and carrying instructions to observe natural phenomena, was a model for many expeditions to come.

A coastal survey was an urgent need of commercial interests but would require the kind of accuracy that only the best scientists of the day could provide. In 1807 an act of Congress created the Coast Survey. On the advice of scientists in Philadelphia, Jefferson appointed the Swiss geodesist and mathematician Ferdinand Rudolph Hassler as its civilian head. Among Hassler's first duties was a trip to England to acquire the best available instruments. All through the hostilities between the United States and Great Britain during the War of 1812 he was busy in London. In 1818, just as he was getting the survey under way, Congress passed an act specifying that only army and navy officers could be employed in the Coast Survey. Unimpressed by Hassler's qualifications and anxious to save money by using personnel already on the payroll, Congress killed the survey by putting economy first and scientific quality second. For the next twelve years the navy operated the survey but produced no charts of value. Clearly Congress had not learned to support science adequately.

When John Quincy Adams returned in 1817 from eight years of diplomatic service in Europe to become President James Monroe's secretary of State, he took up the task of developing a science policy under the general provisions of the Constitution; as secretary of State he had responsibility for home functions in addition to foreign affairs.

Among the unfinished business of setting up the government that awaited Adams was the clause in the Constitution giving Congress the power to "coin Money, regulate the Value thereof, and of foreign Coin, and fix the Standard of Weights and Measures." The coinage had been well provided for back in 1790, when the English system was replaced with the Spanish coin (the dollar) then in general circulation. Nothing had been done at the federal level about weights and measures, however.

Adams undertook a wide-ranging study of the history of weights and measures and the large body of law on the subject held by each state, much of it carried over from the commercial system in use in the British empire. Adams sent his magnificent "Report upon Weights and Measures" to Congress in 1821. His recommendation was that Congress provide for the procurement of "positive standards of brass, copper," or other materials for the various units of measure. The only cost beyond the standards themselves would be a set of duplicates for each federal customhouse and for each of the states.

The accuracy of the work was all-important. In the end it was Hassler who was given the contract, not because he submitted the lowest bid but because he was the best qualified. Adams asked little of Congress in either money or legislation and received only what he requested. The lack of authoritative action by the Congress in response to Adams's suggestions is significant because, after setting standards, Congress left the states and private bodies free to apply and develop their weights and measures to meet their changing needs.

In 1824 Adams became the only president ever elected by the House of Representatives. His administration was thus left without a clear mandate, but Adams nevertheless put forward in his first annual message to Congress a plan for a comprehensive set of institutions of knowledge. He believed that the Constitution gave ample authority for such an initiative; indeed, it seemed by many of its provisions to require it. Adams called for a national university, a national observatory, and a naval academy. A hundred explorations of circumnavigation, he pointed out, would burden the nation less than the cost of "a single campaign in war." He asked for a patent office and a department to plan and supervise scientific projects and other internal improvements. Even Adams's own cabinet was against the plan, and Congress, already rallying to Andrew Jackson for the next campaign, gave the president nothing. The general public jeered at Adams for proposing to use tax money to build "lighthouses in the skies." Defeated at the polls by Andrew Jackson, Adams surrendered the White House in 1829, leaving the whole principle of a science policy in shadow.

Adams's greatest accomplishments in this area, however, lay ahead of him. He was returned to the House of Representatives from his home district in Massachusetts from 1830 to 1848. During this period he shaped an implied science policy for the government that has survived into the late twentieth century. He plunged immediately into a vigorous campaign for an astronomical observatory support-

SCIENCE AND TECHNOLOGY 1761

ed by federal funds. Instead of asking for a permanent institution directly, he supported an act of Congress to reactivate the Coast Survey without specifying that it be headed by a military officer, so that Hassler could return. The authors of the act were so fearful that the survey would become a permanent drain on tax money that they included a specific provision that "nothing in this act . . . shall be construed to authorize the construction or maintenance of a permanent astronomical observatory."

As a theoretically temporary agency that used astronomy and surveying for a practical purpose, the Coast Survey was far from finished with the East and Gulf coasts when in 1848 the Pacific coast was added; the Coast and Geodetic Survey (under that or other names) has been an active agency of government ever since. The support of science was not in question, but the president and Congress accomplished their purposes almost without defining the institutions and certainly without constitutional challenge or much public debate and by supporting operating costs through short-term appropriations. The bias against capital investment and for the support of operating expenses only is a pattern that persists to the present day.

In 1848, when Adams died on the floor of the House of Representatives, most of his great program of 1825 was actually being realized—the naval observatory, the naval academy, the patent office, the coastal survey, the Corps of Topographical Engineers, the exploration of the Pacific Ocean. The president and Congress had an implicit science policy that worked. Since appropriations were not considered reviewable by the judiciary, science policy became (and has remained) largely limited to Congress and the executive branch.

An unforeseen event during Adams's House tenure led Congress to take up the task of spelling out in legislation a major scientific institution. At his death in 1829 James Smithson, an Englishman unknown in America, left his fortune "to the United States of America, to found at Washington, under the name of the Smithsonian Institution, an Establishment for the increase and diffusion of knowledge among men." After years of debate, with Adams spending most of his energy trying to preserve the capital fund of the institution, Congress came up with an elaborate solution. To administer the institution, an act of 1846 created a board of regents including the chief justice, the vice president, three members each of the Senate and House, and six public members elected by a joint resolution of Congress. The effective administrator would be the

secretary of the Smithsonian Board of Regents.

In 1846 that post was filled by Joseph Henry, the nation's outstanding physicist, in response to a resolution calling for a person of "eminent scientific and general acquirements . . . capable of advancing science and promoting letters by original researches and effort." The cumbersome superstructure of the Smithsonian and the Board of Regents was not later imitated, but the specifications for the executive officer set a major precedent.

Bureau Building by Appropriation, 1850–1940. During the 1850s Congress responded to the major scientific activity of the day, the explorations and surveys of the western territories and overseas. The Joint Committee on the Library even tried to administer directly the publication of the results of the Charles Wilkes expedition that had circled the globe (1838–1842). The more usual arrangement was for an executive department, for example the War Department, to conduct the surveys and then submit the scientific results for publication in the congressional series. In 1855 Henry decided to take the Smithsonian Institution out of the library business and to gather the natural history collections from the surveys to form the National Museum as a separate organization under the Smithsonian. Congress responded both by building its own library to function as a national library, and by making direct appropriations to the Smithsonian for the museum.

The secession of the Southern states at the outbreak of the Civil War left the Congress elected in 1860 firmly under the control of the industrial Northeast and the agricultural Northwest. With the departed Southerners went the last substantial doubts about the constitutionality of supporting science and technology. In 1862 Congress passed the Morrill Land-Grant College Act, providing for an agricultural and mechanical college in each state to be funded from the proceeds of the sale of public lands. In the same year, the Department of Agriculture was also created.

An 1863 act of Congress created the National Academy of Sciences by naming fifty incorporators, some the most distinguished scientists in the country (and some not so distinguished), with power over their own rules and membership. When called on to do so by a department of the government, the academy could make a report, with expenses paid from appropriations but with no compensation for the services of the academy members. Without continuing responsibility to the people and without compensation, the academy's accomplishments before World War I were modest.

After the Civil War five different surveying agencies with differing objectives and mapping techniques spread out over the West. Clarence King followed the line of the fortieth parallel; John Wesley Powell focused on the arid regions; F. V. Hayden's natural history survey led to the act creating Yellowstone National Park; the army's Wheeler Survey continued the techniques of the prewar period. The existing Coast Survey triangulated to connect the surveys of the east and west coasts. To eliminate rivalry and duplication, Congress in 1879 approved a consolidation of the four temporary agencies—King, Powell, Hayden, and Wheeler—into the United States Geological Survey, by the simple device of appropriating money for the new agency.

Congress had centralized the appropriation process with the creation of the House Appropriations Committee in 1865. The House had begun by 1880 to give the right to draft money bills, some of which bore on science, to committees other than the Appropriations Committee, especially those responsible for rivers and harbors and for agriculture. With such a system, a few members of each committee were able to specialize and become very well informed in an area, such as agriculture, that represented both a specific science and a political field whose issues transcended any one state or district.

By 1884, continuing charges of overlapping activities and resulting inefficiencies led to the creation of a joint commission, the so-called Allison commission, that extensively examined the organization, administration, and congressional oversight of the Army Signal Service, the Geological Survey, the Coast and Geodetic Survey, and the U.S. Navy's Hydrographic Office. The National Academy of Sciences submitted an extensive report calling for the creation of a department of science. These hearings were among the most comprehensive presentations of science policy in the nineteenth century, and they demonstrated the potential of Congress's investigative powers. In 1885 the further decentralization of the congressional appropriations process signaled the beginning of three decades of gradually mounting expenditures for science.

By the early twentieth century, Congress had increasingly adopted the practice of passing formal organic acts to define the scope and purpose of the scientific bureaus it created. The newcomers—the Bureau of the Census, the National Bureau of Standards, the National Advisory Committee for Aeronautics, the Bureau of Mines, and the Reclamation Service—were better defined than their nineteenth-century predecessors had been. One director of the National Bureau of Standards even carried a copy of his agency's organic act in his billfold and referred to it as if it were a little constitution.

As the exploration of the West gave way to concern for the conservation of natural resources, Congress participated, along with the executive and private interests, in setting aside selected land in the public domain as national forests and parks. By the time of the administration of Theodore Roosevelt, the need for scientific research services as well as for forest management was clear. Strong leadership came from Gifford Pinchot, a friend of Roosevelt and an advocate of resource conservation, who served as the head of the Division of Forestry in the Department of Agriculture. The key legislative act that transferred the reserved forest lands to the Department of Agriculture in 1905 also gave the U.S. Forest Service the right to keep the money received from the sale of forest products or the use of land and resources. According to Pinchot, "That section [of the legislation] gave us, in a way, the power to make our own appropriations." Since opposition to the conservation policies of the Roosevelt administration was high among some western interests, this advantage was important in allowing the Forest Service to develop its research capabilities.

A similar evolution brought protection to the lands set aside as national parks, beginning in the nineteenth century with Yosemite and Yellowstone. To coordinate the many separate natural reservations, the National Park Service was created by organic act in 1916.

Congress participated only minimally in the mobilization of science for World War I. The National Research Council, an arm of the National Academy of Sciences, was created by executive order of President Woodrow Wilson. Such money for war research as flowed to the established scientific agencies usually went to the armed services. By these expenditures the government greatly speeded the transformation of military research from explorations and surveys to the application of physics and chemistry to the design of weapons.

After the war, as the downturn in government spending narrowed the opportunities for creating new institutions for research, Congress recentralized the appropriations process as a part of the Budget and Accounting Act of 1921. The Bureau of the Budget was established by this act, giving the executive a more balanced role in federal funding.

In the 1920s, as Congress largely ceased to form new research institutions, the source of funding shifted outside government to private foundations and to the rapidly growing industrial research laboratories. The leading figure of the period in furthering research in the government, Herbert Hoover, largely contented himself with encouraging voluntary support.

The onset of the Great Depression and the measures of the early New Deal under President Franklin D. Roosevelt did not at first alter the general outlines of the federal research establishment. Plans such as that of Karl T. Compton, president of the Massachusetts Institute of Technology (MIT), for "putting science to work" never reached the stage of legislative action in Congress. After 1935, as New Deal programs became entrenched, there was a significant revival in legislation. Regional systems of laboratories for basic research were created, two in the Department of Agriculture and one in the Bureau of Mines. For the first time the social sciences became strongly represented, for example in the Department of Agriculture's Bureau of Agricultural Economics and the National Resources Planning Board. Military research sharply lagged behind research in agriculture and natural resources in both financial support and intellectual vigor.

The Interrelated System of Science Support, 1940–1960. With the outbreak of World War II and the collapse of France in 1940, four seasoned leaders of the scientific community went to President Roosevelt with a fully developed plan for an organization to foster weapons research. Their leader was Vannevar Bush, president of the Carnegie Institution of Washington and formerly a professor of electrical engineering at MIT. The others were James B. Conant, president of Harvard; Karl T. Compton, president of MIT; and Frank B. Jewett, president of the National Academy of Sciences and of the Bell Telephone Laboratories. Time was too short even to consult Congress, which throughout the war made money available to the National Defense Research Committee (NDRC), through a subcommittee of the Appropriations Committee, so that as many scientists as were required could be hired.

In 1941 the NDRC was put under a more comprehensive organization, the Office of Scientific Research and Development (OSRD), with Bush as director. While the existence of OSRD, which also contained a Committee on Medical Research, was not a secret, it made no public accounting to either Congress or the people. Bush enjoyed direct access to Roosevelt. The established research bureaus continued under their regular budgets, and some laboratories, especially in the armed services, expanded significantly. OSRD did not try to do everything, but carefully chose to emphasize certain lines of research (even if the services did not ask for them) and selected the university and industrial laboratories to do the work.

Specially designed research contracts were made with these institutions, by which the government agreed to provide the money on a fixed-cost no-loss-no-gain basis. The universities agreed to provide research activity, not specific results, and the scientists employed in federally funded research worked for their respective institutions, not the government. Overhead costs that were hard to define in the contracts were paid by the government according to a formula. The decisions to emphasize research in radar and nuclear fission were made in this way, after careful consideration by the outstanding scientists of each field. Later, when emphasis shifted from research and development to procurement of weapons, other agencies took over.

In late 1941 an OSRD committee made the decision to go ahead with research for an atomic bomb and to adopt a policy of close secrecy. Only afterward did control of the rapidly growing project shift to the Manhattan District of the Army Corps of Engineers.

In 1944, foreseeing the end of the war, Bush took the firm and unusual stand that OSRD should go out of existence at the end of the emergency. He gave as his reason the fact that he could not hold on to the scientists, who would want to go back to their university departments. More fundamentally, OSRD leaders recognized the need to bring their new wartime research institutions within the regular organs of constitutional government—Congress and the executive agencies tied together by a budget process open to public scrutiny.

By September 1945, after the almost simultaneous dropping of atomic bombs on Japan and the end of the Pacific war, President Harry S. Truman sent a major message to Congress calling for legislation to convert the research establishment to a peacetime role. OSRD's leaders had already prepared a report, *Science: The Endless Frontier*, calling for a comprehensive national research foundation that would provide federal support for research and graduate education as well as a military and a medical division. In a series of committee hearings going all the way back to 1942, Sen. Harley M. Kilgore of West Virginia had developed another model of a national science foundation that would emphasize patent policy and getting the results of wartime research into the hands of small business.

The quest to find a place in government for nuclear physics research—indeed, for the whole industry that had grown up around the making of the atomic bombs—had begun when the first explosions revealed the existence of the project and its accomplishments. In the summer of 1946 the Atomic Energy Act set up a civilian Atomic Energy Commission (AEC) with citizens as full-time members; the commission itself became the collective administrative head of the agency formed to carry out the act. The separateness of this policy area was emphasized by setting up the Joint Committee on Atomic Energy to oversee it; the act also granted extensive investigative powers to the joint committee.

At the same time an act of Congress gave statutory basis to the navy's program for supporting unclassified basic research in the universities by creating the Office of Naval Research (ONR). Legislation to create a National Science Foundation (NSF) to complete the postwar structure failed to pass in 1946, and President Truman vetoed the version of 1947. Only in 1950 would Congress enact legislation creating the NSF.

As OSRD wound down, its contracts supporting research had to find a home somewhere. Many weapons-research contracts with industry that seemed suitable to continue into peacetime were transferred to the research laboratories of the armed services. The important contracts of the Committee on Medical Research went to the National Institutes of Health (NIH) of the Public Health Service, one of the oldest agencies of the government. An act of Congress in 1944 had given the Public Health Service all the authority it needed to make research grants to universities and hospitals, while its own facilities, staffed with government scientists, were ready to embark immediately on a research program to take advantage of wartime gains in medicine.

As the interrelated system that replaced OSRD grew in the postwar years, the government was able to support research not only in its own laboratories, but in universities and industry as well by using grants and contracts on the OSRD pattern. The budget process already developed for the regular research agencies thus provided the framework by which federal money flowed to the other research sectors. Implicit in this system was the scientific judgment that strong teams in each of the

research agencies brought to bear on the allocations of funds suggested to Congress through the Bureau of the Budget. Once the funds had been appropriated, the agencies then had the responsibility to see that the research was done in accordance with the highest scientific standards. The interrelated system supported research but did not purchase it.

The priorities among fields supported by the interrelated system were strongly influenced by the heritage of the war. The national laboratories, such as that at Los Alamos, New Mexico, supplemented later by the Livermore National Laboratory in California, were direct descendents of the Manhattan Project. The armed services laboratories and their contractors carried on the wartime electronics research. Mathematics, physics, and engineering were as dominant in postwar weapons research as they had been under OSRD. As the Cold War developed, the gap between the priority fields and the rest of science widened. Congress's Joint Committee on Atomic Energy had vast and almost unchecked power over nuclear policy, but its ties to the public and to the scientific community were few. Since Cold War reasoning called for urgent priority in the building of an even more powerful nuclear weapon—the hydrogen bomb—the budget process produced an almost free flow of money to that weapon's developers and thus to the fields of science that had created it.

In the one great shift in postwar priorities—the rise of medical research as a major component of the federal budget—Congress participated significantly. Before World War II the relevant appropriations subcommittees had performed their usual role by cutting the Public Health Service and NIH budgets sent up by the executive. After the war it was a different story. The NIH budget rose from $7 million in 1947 to $70 million in 1953. In fiscal 1948, NIH asked for $23 million and received $26.5 million. By the mid 1950s Sen. Lister Hill (D-Ala.) and Rep. John E. Fogarty (D-R.I.), chairmen of the appropriations subcommittees, regularly asked the directors of the various institutes to give professional opinions as to how much more money they could use than appeared in the budget approved by the Bureau of the Budget. They were able to recommend extraordinary increases in the NIH research budgets in bipartisan bills. Congress had also given the agency wide latitude in the creation of new institutes. Hill and Fogarty were the focal point for vigorous public interest groups backing health legislation. Everyone in the process believed that the

American people wanted health research and would support those who voted for it.

Even medical research in NIH had to emphasize only those parts of the biological and social sciences of interest to the agency's mission. Nonhuman biology was left to the infant and beleaguered National Science Foundation. The social sciences at first had no place in NSF and then achieved only a narrow definition that placed emphasis on those methods used in the social sciences but originating in mathematics and the natural sciences. Some social science research was covertly supported by the mission agencies, including the military services. Most nonhuman biology and geology research was supported by old-line conservation agencies such as the Geological Survey, the Forest Service, and the National Park Service. In the 1960s a few people awakened to the lack of federal support for civilian industrial technology, which the interrelated system largely bypassed. However, military research funded by the government and industrial research within large corporations produced such dramatic results that few noticed the lack of research, public or private, in whole industries such as textiles.

Priority Changes from 1958 to the 1990s. When *Sputnik I*, the first Soviet satellite, circled the earth in 1957, leaders in the U.S. government be-

APOLLO 11 ASTRONAUTS. *Center row, left to right*, Michael Collins, Neil Armstrong, and Edwin (Buzz) Aldrin, honored at a joint meeting of Congress, 16 September 1969. LIBRARY OF CONGRESS

came. aware of America's vast shortfall in science education and felt threatened by the specter of nuclear warheads on intercontinental ballistic missiles. Congress enacted the National Defense Education Act of 1958, which supported students in higher education in many fields of learning in addition to the sciences and placed fellowships in a broader group of institutions than the few large research universities.

President Dwight D. Eisenhower had relied on Lewis L. Strauss, chairman of the AEC, for advice on science policy. Behind Strauss was Edward Teller of the Livermore National Laboratory, who always pushed for more nuclear weapons. In 1957 Eisenhower broke this monopoly of advice by appointing James R. Killian, Jr., the president of MIT, as his science adviser. He also had the President's Science Advisory Committee report directly to the president.

These advisers worked with Congress in designing the National Aeronautics and Space Administration (NASA), which was to be headed by a single administrator, in contrast to the multiheaded arrangements of the early postwar era. The NASA act emphasized civilian control and contained a statutory requirement that information be disseminated as widely as possible. In addition, Congress set up new committees—Aeronautical and Space Sciences in the Senate, and Science and Astronautics in the House—to oversee this new realm of scientific research and technology.

The new space agency sent up a whole series of earth-orbiting satellites that provided a flood of new information about space beyond the earth's atmosphere. As president, John F. Kennedy went beyond the cautions of his experts to set the goal of putting a man on the moon in the 1960s. The decision, gaining the support of the new congressional committees, gave impetus to the rapid buildup of both the manned space program and of NASA itself.

After assuming office President Kennedy promptly moved the science adviser and the President's Science Advisory Committee from the White House into the Executive Office of the President, where Congress could review the budget and summon the adviser before committees. To support this policy mechanism, the Office of Science and Technology was created. The name was a sure sign that research now had a scope much broader than the tightly focused research and development of the wartime period.

From the mid 1960s on, with the start of the Vietnam War and a more intense public interest in the environment, science policy shifted dramatically away from a preoccupation with weapons research and the maintenance of the nuclear industrial complex. The Subcommittee on Science, Research, and Development, chaired by Rep. Emilio Q. Daddario (D-Conn.), held hearings on technology assessment as early as 1967. The Commission of the National Academy of Sciences that recommended the creation of an Office of Technology Assessment (OTA) made the important suggestion that it be placed not in the executive branch but under Congress, in a position comparable to that of the General Accounting Office. The OTA became a reality in 1972 with the sponsorship of Sen. Edward M. Kennedy (D-Mass.). Rep. Daddario, who had left Congress in 1970, returned to become OTA's first director.

Richard M. Nixon's presidency had hardly begun when the science and technology policy structure in the White House began to erode. By 1972 both the office of the science adviser and the President's Science Advisory Committee had disappeared. In each budget cycle the components of the interrelated system continued to be supported, but without clear overall direction, and funding for research leveled off after 1969. The Atomic Energy Commission was abolished by 1977 in favor of the broader Department of Energy and the Nuclear Regulatory Commission. The Joint Committee on Atomic Energy was abolished at the same time.

A major change in the priorities of research support through the interrelated system came when President Ronald Reagan suddenly announced the Strategic Defense Initiative (SDI, popularly known as "Star Wars") for a space-based antimissile defense in 1984. The Department of Defense already had antiballistic missile programs, approved by both the relevant executive agencies and by Congress through the budget process. The Reagan call to the scientists of the country to build a trillion-dollar missile defense on the recommendation of a very few advisers within the White House short-circuited the entire science policy mechanism built up since 1830. The only request to Congress was to open a line-item appropriation, as if the research on the basic idea had already been done. When serious questions were raised about the practicability of the system and many of its components, managers simply changed the design, and critics were left without a forum in either the executive or Congress. The subsequent history of the project demonstrated that SDI used the form and enjoyed the freedom of research contracts while procuring a system that was never defined.

With the precedent set by SDI's de-emphasis of traditional methods of selecting research programs, Congress by the early 1990s increasingly resorted to a budget practice called earmarking. By this practice individual senators and representatives introduce legislation to provide funds directly for research projects and facilities within their states and districts. Since the research institutions created by the old interrelated system are geographically concentrated in a few areas, the practice lets federal research dollars flow to other regions. It also enables universities to get around the old system's bias against investment in capital items such as buildings. Universities, members of Congress, and local communities have a common interest in direct action in a period of stagnant budgets in the research agencies. The judgment of scientific merit is bypassed, not just on individual projects but on the shape and direction of the future research effort. With many members of Congress engaging in earmarking, possibilities for trade-offs multiply.

The potential for earmarking is inherent in the appropriations system itself, as seen in Congress's elimination of Hassler from the Coast Survey in 1818 and the system of civil public works built by the Army Corps of Engineers from the late nineteenth century onward. What has alarmed many spokesmen for the interrelated system is the bypassing of the partnership between government and the scientific community that has played such a major role in the history of both.

The administration of President Bill Clinton early showed a desire for major changes of emphasis in science and technology policy. The appointment as science adviser of John Gibbons, the longtime head of the congressional Office of Technology Assessment, and the strong interest of Vice President Albert A. Gore, Jr., in environmental and industrial policy signaled the change. Secretary of Defense Les Aspin announced the end of the Star Wars program (SDI), and large cuts were recommended for nuclear-energy research and development. Both the proposed nuclear accelerator, the supercollider, and the space station met major opposition in Congress.

Significantly, Clinton's first budget also recommended a 16-percent increase for NSF, showing a desire to support basic science, applied science, and science education on a broad front. The government would share with both industry and universities the responsibilities for keeping U.S. science competitive globally. The congressional authorization and appropriations committees have a clear challenge to recognize the government's changing role in the support of research in both science and technology.

[*For discussion of related policy issues, see* Aerospace; Communications; Energy and Natural Resources; Exploration; Health and Medicine; Nuclear Power; Nuclear Weapons. *See also* Commerce, Science, and Transportation Committee, Senate; Office of Technology Assessment; Science, Space, and Technology Committee, House; Smithsonian Institution.]

BIBLIOGRAPHY

Del Sesto, Steven L. *Science, Politics, and Controversy: Civilian Nuclear Power in the United States, 1946–1974.* 1979.

Dupree, A. Hunter. "Central Scientific Organization in the United States Government." *Minerva* 1 (1963): 454–469.

Dupree, A. Hunter. "The Great Instauration of 1940: The Organization of Scientific Research for War." In *The Twentieth-Century Sciences.* Edited by Gerald Holton. 1972. Pp. 443–467.

Dupree, A. Hunter. "Science Advising and the Founding Fathers: John Quincy Adams." In *The Presidency and Science Advising.* Vol. 7. Edited by Kenneth W. Thompson. 1990. Pp. 3–26.

Dupree, A. Hunter. *Science in the Federal Government: A History of Policies and Activities.* 1986.

Hewlett, Richard G., and Oscar E. Anderson, Jr. *The New World, 1939/46: A History of the United States Atomic Energy Commission.* 1990.

Hewlett, Richard G., and Jack M. Holl. *Atoms for Peace and War, 1953–1961: Eisenhower and the Atomic Energy Commission.* 1989.

National Academy of Sciences. Committee on Science and Public Policy. *Federal Support of Basic Research in Institutions of Higher Learning.* 1964.

Penick, James L., Jr., et al., eds. *The Politics of American Science, 1939 to the Present.* 1972.

Strickland, Stephen P. *Politics, Science, and Dread Disease: A Short History of United States Medical Research Policy.* 1972.

U.S. House of Representatives. Committee on Science and Astronautics. *National Science Policy.* 91st Cong., 2d sess., 1970. H. Con. Res. 666.

U.S. House of Representatives. Committee on Science and Technology. *A History of Science Policy in the United States, 1940–1985,* by Jeffrey K. Stine. 99th Cong., 2d sess., 1986. Background Rept. 1.

A. HUNTER DUPREE

SCIENCE, SPACE, AND TECHNOLOGY COMMITTEE, HOUSE.

The first new committee on an entirely new subject matter created in the House since 1892, when the predecessors of the House and Senate Interior and Insular Affairs committees had been established, the Committee on Science, Space, and Technology was born of an extraordinary combined initiative of the House and Senate leadership only months after the surprise launch of the Soviet satellite *Sputnik I* on 4 October 1957. House Speaker Sam Rayburn and Senate majority leader Lyndon B. Johnson collaborated to create a Select Committee on Astronautics and Space Exploration chaired by House majority leader John W. McCormack of Massachusetts, which produced the National Aeronautics and Space Act of 1958 (also known as the Space Act) and laid the groundwork for the standing committee.

When the Committee on Science and Astronautics was established on 21 July 1958, new jurisdiction was added to that which came from the select committee. House Rules gave the committee jurisdiction over outer space, astronautical research and development, scientific research and development, science scholarships, and legislation relating to federal scientific agencies, especially the National Bureau of Standards (NBS), the National Aeronautics and Space Administration (NASA), the National Aeronautics and Space Council, and the National Science Foundation (NSF).

Seventeen years later, after an examination of the House committee structure and jurisdiction in 1973 and 1974, the committee was redesignated at the beginning of the 94th Congress as the Committee on Science and Technology and given new jurisdiction over civil aviation research and development, all nonnuclear energy research and development, environmental research and development, and the National Weather Service. Later, with the abolition of the Joint Committee on Atomic Energy, nuclear research and development were added, and the committee then had jurisdiction over all energy research and development. In addition to its legislative jurisdiction, the committee received a new special oversight function enabling it to review and study all laws, programs, and government activities involving federal nonmilitary research and development. At the beginning of the 100th Congress, in 1987, the name of the committee was changed again, to the Committee on Science, Space, and Technology.

The committee authorizes programs in NASA, NSF, and the National Institutes for Standards and Technology (NIST, formerly the National Bureau of Standards). However, from the committee's inception in 1958, its leaders understood the need to carve out jurisdiction in areas of science and technology that overlap with such broad categories of jurisdictional concern as national defense or commerce—for example, patent policy, satellite applications, and rocketry. Accommodations must still be reached with other committees when research and development projects are proposed that would be administered by agencies other than those over which the Science, Space, and Technology Committee has clear jurisdiction.

Membership on the committee has increased over the years, reaching fifty-five in the 102d Congress (from thirty members in the 93d Congress). The number of subcommittees has expanded to seven, with the subcommittee jurisdictions and makeup often altered from Congress to Congress. In the early days, for example, there were three subcommittees that dealt exclusively with NASA, while as of 1992 there was only one. The chairman has retained the power to hire staff and to administer the entire committee operation, which gives the committee more homogeneity than most.

The annual authorization of NASA has been a cornerstone for the committee's legislative and oversight practices from the beginning. Strongly advocated by Johnson when he was Senate majority leader, and favored by the House select committee members led by McCormack, the annual authorization procedure established a committee discipline for review of each program activity, funding request, and the cost, schedule, and performance of the ongoing and proposed programs and projects. Acting primarily through its subcommittees, the committee conducted oversight hearings, met with agency officials and contractors, and traveled to the sites where space activities were conducted. These practices schooled the members on agency activities and kept them informed about problems and accomplishments. The committee soon established a record of attention to detail, as new programs and projects were proposed by NASA, which was emerging as a growing and favored agency. The committee has been ever mindful of the continued need for strong public support if the space program were to be successful. If careful examination of NASA's proposed budget revealed items that were not well thought-out or documented, the committee was authorized to reduce their number or to eliminate them entirely if warranted, which gave the committee greater creditability both in the House and with NASA itself.

Twice in the history of the committee, the dangers inherent in space exploration were brought home to committee members: first in January 1967, when the fire aboard *Apollo 1* killed three astronauts who were simulating a launch, and then in January 1986, when the *Challenger* space shuttle came apart, killing the seven astronauts aboard. In both cases, the committee followed a steady course of careful, intense, and thorough investigation. Olin E. Teague of Texas, who was chairman of the Manned Space Flight Subcommittee at the time of the *Apollo* fire, headed up that investigation, making sure that no stone was left unturned, without compromising the future of space exploration. A similar approach was initiated after the *Challenger* accident, with the appointment of ranking member Robert A. Roe (D-N.J.) to conduct the investigation. At its conclusion, the committee's report to the House contained more than one hundred recommendations for NASA, each of which the agency subsequently agreed to.

From the beginning the committee has sought professional staff with technical and scientific skills. In 1964 the committee took a step toward acquiring additional professional staff with the creation of a science policy division at the Congressional Research Service. When the committee's jurisdiction was later expanded, technically qualified professional staff were added for those areas of energy and environment, both on the committee staff and in its support agencies.

Service on this committee has appealed to members. In the early years they found it exciting to be involved in America's growing space program, and later they found it rewarding to deal with cutting-edge science and technology issues. The committee's work has largely proceeded in a bipartisan manner, since disagreements about space, science, or technology policy seldom break down along party lines. After NASA and the standing committee were formed and the space program began to achieve dramatic results, members sensed that this same spirit could be brought to bear in pursuit of other goals. The Space Act of 1958 is an outstanding example of Congress taking legislative initiative. One of its legacies was the committee's creation of the Office of Technology Assessment, the first new congressional support agency since the General Accounting Office was established in 1921. The idea for a technology assessment body began with discussions in 1966 between Charles Lindbergh and Emilio Q. Daddario (D-Conn.), who chaired a subcommittee. The notion was refined and studied through hearings and reports until it was legislated in the Technology Assessment Act of 1972. Another indication of the committee's activity

in science policy matters in the 1970s was the legislated establishment of the Office of Science and Technology in the White House in May 1976.

The committee's pride in its legislative achievements in the technology area stems in large part from its original interest in making sure that federally funded space technology would find application in the private sector. The concept of encouraging private use of federally funded technology was foreign to general practice prior to the Space Act. This new approach slowly took hold, and was the impetus for the 1974 creation of the Energy Research and Development Administration. Several years later the committee joined with the Judiciary Committee to broaden patent laws by extending special provisions for technology development to small businesses, not-for-profit organizations, and universities. After forging these alliances and demonstrating that it had done its homework, the committee worked again with the Judiciary Committee on modifications to the antitrust laws to enable joint research and development ventures to be formed under protection of the Cooperative Research and Development Act of 1984.

Beginning in 1980, as more and more national attention was being focused on the ability of the United States to compete in foreign markets, the committee initiated legislation in technology transfer, scientific education and scholarships, metric conversion, and commercial space launches. It reordered the policy-making apparatus of the Commerce Department to give more emphasis to technology and beefed up the role of technology in the work of the National Bureau of Standards, which was renamed the National Institute for Standards and Technology, with a specific new function to fund advanced technology.

The budget battles of the 1980s and the increasing tendency to lump legislative solutions with major policy implications into omnibus bills have taken a toll on the ability of the committee to articulate its message of the importance of science and technology to the long-term health of the United States. In the 100th Congress, Chairman Robert A. Roe (chairman, 1987–1990; replaced by George E. Brown, Jr., D-Calif.) expressed concern about this tendency, reiterating that continued progress in science, space, and technology was essential for the future economic security of the United States.

[*See also* Commerce, Science, and Transportation Committee, Senate; National Aeronautics and Space Act of 1958; Office of Technology Assessment.]

BIBLIOGRAPHY

Hechler, Ken. *Toward the Endless Frontier: History of the Committee on Science and Technology, 1959–1979.* 1980.

U.S. House of Representatives. *Summary of Activities of the Committee on Science, Space, and Technology.* 101st Cong., 2d sess., 1991. H. Rept. 101-1026.

U.S. House of Representatives. Select Committee on Committees. *Monographs of the Committees of the House of Representatives.* 93d Cong., 2d sess., 1974. Committee Print.

ROBERT C. KETCHAM

SCOTT, HUGH (1900–), Republican representative and senator from Pennsylvania. Hugh Doggett Scott, Jr., was elected to the House of Representatives in 1940, reelected in 1942, defeated in 1944, elected again in 1946, and reelected five more times. In 1958 he was elected to the Senate, where he served three terms, retiring in 1975 at the age of seventy-five. When he retired, he had served in the Congress for thirty-four years and was the first Pennsylvanian to serve three Senate terms and play a leadership role in the Senate—one year as Republican whip, eight years as minority leader. In the House he was a member of the Interstate and Foreign Commerce and Judiciary committees. He also served as chairman of the Republican National Committee during the ill-fated 1948 presidential campaign.

Scott defined himself as a "moderate centrist" or, more colorfully, "as independent as a hog on ice." He was particularly proud when in 1960 the AFL-CIO recorded him as voting "right" on nine out of sixteen issues and the conservative Americans for Constitutional Action agreed with 57 percent of his votes. Earlier in his career he opposed increases in the minimum wage and compared Harry S. Truman's agenda to the program of the Communist party. Yet he became a vigorous supporter of Dwight D. Eisenhower, then a champion of education and of the nuclear test ban treaty. As Pennsylvania political historian Paul Beers has noted, Scott was for and then against gun control, switched from isolationist to internationalist, voted to approve Richard M. Nixon's nomination of G. Harrold Carswell to the Supreme Court and then told black voters he had been wrong on Carswell. He held a potpourri of views on the Vietnam War and was noncommittal on the culpability of Nixon during the Watergate affair. Yet at the time of Scott's retirement, Majority Leader Mike Mansfield paid a florid

HUGH SCOTT. *Left,* with Sen. Howard H. Baker, Jr. (R-Tenn.).   OFFICE OF THE HISTORIAN OF THE U.S. SENATE

tribute to Scott's leadership in the achievement of major civil rights legislation, especially in the areas of voting rights, fair employment practices, and fair housing legislation.

Throughout his career, Senator Scott was admired for his wit and style. Fluent in six languages, he wrote four books, including one on Chinese art.

BIBLIOGRAPHY

Beers, Paul B. *Pennsylvania Politics Today and Yesterday.* 1980.

Neal, Steve. "Can Hugh Scott Tough It Out?" *The Nation,* 29 November 1975, p. 551.

SIDNEY WISE

SCOTT V. SANDFORD (60 U.S. [19 How.] 393 [1857]). The Dred Scott decision was one of the

SATIRE ON THE DRED SCOTT DECISION. The four candidates of the 1860 presidential election dance with caricatures of their supposed supporters while Dred Scott fiddles. *Upper left,* southern Democrat John C. Breckinridge (Ky.) cavorts with his ally Democratic president James Buchanan, depicted as a goat (a reference to his nickname "Buck"). *Upper right,* Republican Abraham Lincoln (Ill.) dances with an African American woman, a reference to his party's abolitionist leanings. *Lower right,* Constitutional Unionist John Bell (Tenn.) dances with a Native American, alluding to his brief attentions to Indian interests. *Lower left,* National Democrat Stephen A. Douglas (Ill.) jigs with an Irishman wearing a cross, possibly referring to Douglas's backing among Irish immigrants and to his own alleged Catholicism. Lithograph, 1860. LIBRARY OF CONGRESS

most important—and disastrous—ever rendered by the Supreme Court. It came as the consequence of Congress's inability to resolve one of the most urgent political issues of the mid-nineteenth century: the question of the expansion of slavery into the territories.

Congress had first dealt with this issue in the Missouri Compromise of 1820, which restricted slavery's spread into the area of the Louisiana Purchase north of Missouri. This quasi-constitutional settlement was upset, however, first by the slave states' anxieties over the internal security of slavery within their borders and then by the rise of the antislavery movement. The Mexican War and the

Wilmot Proviso of 1846 (never enacted into law), which would have prohibited slavery's expansion into any territories acquired as a result of the war, deranged the political equilibrium. Congress anesthetized the problem by the Compromise of 1850, a complex package of legislation that included the so-called Clayton Compromise. This measure, embodied in the Utah and New Mexico territorial organic acts, provided for the direct appeal of slavery questions from territorial courts to the U.S. Supreme Court. This constituted an invitation by Congress to the Court to try its hand at a problem that eluded political resolution.

The uneasy truce of 1850 came undone with the

Kansas-Nebraska Act of 1854, which repealed the Missouri Compromise. This concession to southern ambitions ignited a political firestorm, and Americans became more desperate than ever for a judicial resolution of the problem of slavery in the territories. Chief Justice Roger B. Taney's opinion for the Court in the Dred Scott case provided a solution but one that was extremist, sectional, and antidemocratic.

Dred Scott, his wife Harriet, and their daughters Eliza and Lizzie were African Americans who were held as slaves by a succession of Missouri residents. In 1846, Scott determined to seek his and his family's freedom through a routine freedom suit in Missouri courts, on the grounds that his master had taken him to reside first in the free state of Illinois and then in territory where slavery had been prohibited by the Missouri Compromise. From a federal court judgment in favor of the nominal defendant, John F. A. Sanford (whose name was consistently misspelled in federal court records through clerical error), Scott appealed to the U.S. Supreme Court.

Chief Justice Taney, writing for the Court, held that blacks could not be citizens for purposes of access to federal courts; he thereby assigned Congress ultimate authority over the states on questions of national citizenship and naturalization. The rest of his opinion was selectively nationalist, restricting congressional power to inhibit slavery's spread in the territories yet enhancing congressional power to force them to accept slavery. In holding the Missouri Compromise unconstitutional, Taney denied Congress power over slavery in the territories under the territories clause of Article IV, section 3 and in a strained and implausible interpretation, held that Congress's authority over the territories was derived from a clause in the same section that enabled it to admit "New States . . . into the Union." Finally, in a casual dictum, he suggested that the due process clause of the Fifth Amendment inhibited congressional power to exclude slavery from the territories.

Political reaction to the Taney opinion was violent, but neither the legislative nor the executive branch took steps to diminish the power or jurisdiction of the Supreme Court. Northern Republicans, led by Abraham Lincoln, were determined to overturn the opinion, while southern Democrats demanded that Congress allow slavery in all the territories and protect it there by federal force. But the southern position, and the authority of the Dred Scott case itself, were swept away by the tidal wave of events that followed secession. In 1862, Congress interred the decision by abolishing slavery first in the District of Columbia, then in all territories. Thus, it had the anticlimactic but final word in the most explosive constitutional confrontation between judicial and legislative power in the nineteenth century.

BIBLIOGRAPHY

Fehrenbacher, Don. *The Dred Scott Case: Its Significance in American Law and Politics.* 1978.
Potter, David M. *The Impending Crisis, 1848–1861.* 1976.

WILLIAM M. WIECEK

SEALS. Seals are used by the House and Senate to authenticate documents and to put an official imprimatur on ceremonial or condolence resolutions and on legal documents such as subpoenas, summonses, or warrants. Both chambers use their respective seals sparingly.

The Senate seal in use in 1994 dates from 1886 and depicts a shield surrounded by olive and oak branches and topped with a liberty cap. Two designs were used earlier. The first, from 1798 to 1804, pictured an eagle with talons, while the second, from 1831 to approximately 1876, portrayed three ancient goddesses of freedom, justice, and power. The secretary of the Senate has custody over and supervision of the use of the seal, having been given that authority in 1886 by standing order of the Senate.

The clerk of the House was first authorized by the House to administer a seal in 1794. The existence of an actual seal, however, was not confirmed until 1830. The 1830 seal showed the U.S. Capitol as it appeared then—with the original dome prior to the addition of the Statue of Freedom, and without the extensions of the House and Senate wings. The seal was encircled by twenty-four stars, one for each state. The second version, authorized in 1912, depicted the same scene as its predecessor, except that it was surrounded by forty-eight stars. The 1994 House seal dates from 1963 and depicts the U.S. Capitol from the perspective of the southeast House wing surrounded by fifty stars. The House seal remains in the custody of the clerk of the House, who supervises its use.

BIBLIOGRAPHY

Johnson, Oscar. "The Great Seal Striptease." *Roll Call,* 29 May 1963, p. 5.
Stathis, Stephen. *Seal of the United States House of Repre-*

sentatives. Congressional Research Service, Library of Congress. CRS memorandum. 25 August 1977.

U.S. Senate. Secretary of the Senate. *History of the Senate Seals,* by Emery L. Frazier. 89th Cong., 2d sess., 1966. S. Doc. 89-127.

ILONA B. NICKELS

SECESSION. The secession of eleven Southern states from the Union between 20 December 1860 and 20 May 1861 shattered the federal compact that had been forged at the Constitutional Convention in 1787. Grounded in the constitutional doctrine of state sovereignty, secession marked the climax of a sectional crisis between the free states of the North and the slave states of the South that had reached an impasse over the issue of the expansion of slavery into the federal territories. Congress was unable to break this impasse during the secession winter of 1860–1861. After the postsecession departure of congressmen from the lower South had given the Republicans control of the House (but not the Senate) by late January, congressional Republicans still continued to reject any compromise that would open the territories to slavery.

The election of Abraham Lincoln, the first president from a Republican party pledged to prohibiting the expansion of slavery, triggered the initial phase of secession. Governors in the lower South reacted to Lincoln's election on 6 November 1860 by quickly issuing calls for popularly elected conventions to consider passing ordinances of secession by separate state action. South Carolina, always the most radical of the slave states, was the

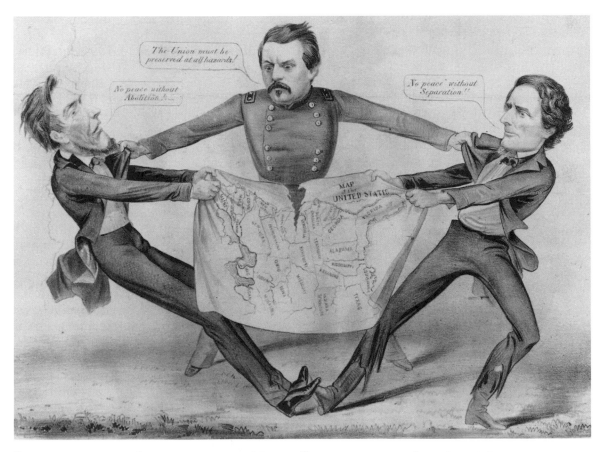

"THE TRUE ISSUE OR 'THATS WHATS THE MATTER.'" Democratic presidential candidate George B. McClellan is portrayed as the intermediary between Union president Abraham Lincoln and Confederate president Jefferson Davis, who are tearing apart a U.S. map in a tug-of-war. Restraining the two presidents, McClellan affirms, "The Union must be preserved at all costs!" Lincoln, holding the northern half of the map, says, "No peace without abolition!" while Davis, pulling the southern half, declares, "No peace without separation!" Lithograph on wove paper, published by Currier and Ives, New York, 1864.

LIBRARY OF CONGRESS

first to leave, on 20 December. It was followed, in order, by Mississippi, Florida, Alabama, Georgia, and Louisiana in January and by Texas on 1 February. In February, at Montgomery, Alabama, delegates from these seven states created a provisional government for the Confederate States of America.

The second session of the 36th Congress proved powerless to arrest the momentum of secession. By the time it assembled in December to hear President James Buchanan's annual message, the machinery for secession in the lower South had already been set into motion. Congress was also operating in a vacuum of leadership. President-elect Lincoln would not be inaugurated until 4 March. Buchanan had lost any popular mandate to rule, and his recommendation for a constitutional convention to yield to all southern demands on slavery was ignored by the Republicans as a sellout to slave interests and by the Democrats as impractical posturing.

Each house of Congress did set up a special committee to deal with the secessionist threat. The Senate, however, remained deadlocked in bitter debate for two weeks before appointing its committee, and the House Committee of Thirty-three (one for each state in the Union) did not meet until 13 December. When it did, the split vote of its Republican members on a resolution to consider additional guarantees for southern rights was seized upon by thirty congressmen from the lower South as final proof that southern interests were endangered within the Union. In a manifesto to their constituency they came out in favor of a southern Confederacy.

A Senate Committee of Thirteen was appointed on 20 December, the day South Carolina seceded, and it proposed a specific plan to save the Union. Named after John J. Crittenden, a Whig from Kentucky, the Crittenden Compromise consisted of six constitutional amendments and four resolutions. Central to the whole package was an extension to the Pacific of the former Missouri Compromise line of 36°30′ north latitude. Slavery was to be recognized and protected south of the line in all territories "now held, or hereafter acquired." Republicans, acting on the knowledge that Lincoln absolutely opposed any expansion of slavery, remained true to party principles by defeating the Crittenden plan in January.

Secessionist victories in the lower South in January convinced congressional Republicans of the need to appear more conciliatory in order to hold the upper South within the Union. Throughout February, the month that secession elections were held in the upper South, Republicans held out the possibility of admitting the territory of New Mexico as a slave state. In addition, most Republicans formally backed the efforts of the "Peace Convention" called by the Virginia legislature. The convention, held in Washington, deliberated for three weeks before backing a modified version of the Crittenden Compromise. This proposal, as well as the statehood bill for New Mexico, was killed by congressional Republicans once Unionist victories had been secured in the upper South. In the end, the Republicans yielded on only one point: about two-fifths of the party voted with Democrats for a constitutional amendment that would have forever prohibited the federal government from interfering with slavery in the states. Before the states could act on this proposed thirteenth constitutional amendment, the nation was in a civil war.

Congress was not in session when war broke out with the Confederate firing on Fort Sumter. In response to Lincoln's call on 15 April 1861 for seventy-five thousand state militia to put down what he called a rebellion, four states in the upper South—Virginia, Arkansas, Tennessee, and North Carolina—joined the Confederacy rather than fight against southern kin.

[*See also* Civil War; Congress of the Confederacy; Secession; Sectionalism.]

BIBLIOGRAPHY

Potter, David M. *The Impending Crisis, 1848–1861*. 1976.
Stampp, Kenneth M. *And the War Came: The North and the Secession Crisis*. 1950.

WILLIAM L. BARNEY

SECRECY OF CONGRESS. The Continental Congress and the Constitutional Convention met in secret, and the Senate, in writing its first rules, never considered opening its sessions to the public. Most senators believed that the body's role in providing advice and consent to the executive branch and in acting as a "council of revision" for measures coming over from the House compelled it to conduct its business behind closed doors. The absence of a gallery in the Senate chamber in the building in New York City where the Senate first met no doubt contributed to this viewpoint as well.

Not until 1794 did the Senate agree to open its legislative sessions to the public. The initial impetus for this decision was public interest in the challenge to seating Senator-elect Albert Gallatin. The

Senate opened its sessions to the public during debate on Gallatin's credentials, and later acted to open its legislative sessions to the public beginning in December 1794.

The Senate kept its doors closed during consideration of so-called executive business (debate on treaties and presidential nominations). Although these sessions were not open to the press or public, and debate transcripts were released to the public much later, senators frequently passed information about the proceedings to the press. In June 1929, at the suggestion of Sen. Robert M. La Follette, Jr. (R-Wis.), the Senate rules were changed to require that executive business be conducted in public session, while preserving the right of any senator to move for a closed-door session subject to approval by a Senate majority.

The Senate generally receives testimony in impeachment trials in public session, according to a rule dating from the impeachment trial of Justice Samuel Chase in 1805, but the Senate amended the rule before the trial of President Andrew Johnson in 1868 to permit closed-door sessions during deliberations only. During the 1980s, the Senate met in secret session six times to deliberate on verdicts in the impeachment trials of federal judges Harry Claiborne, Alcee L. Hastings, and Walter Nixon.

From the time public sessions on nominations and treaties began in 1929, the Senate has met in secret on all or part of forty-one days, including 25 February 1992, when it considered President George Bush's proposal to grant most-favored-nation trading status to the People's Republic of China. Thirty of these secret sessions occurred after 1970, reflecting an increasingly assertive Senate role in policy matters concerning national security. Since 1986, the Senate has held secret sessions in the Old Senate Chamber in the Capitol; the presence of television cameras and other electronic equipment in the Senate chamber can compromise secrecy, so for closed sessions the Senate has returned to this chamber, which it last regularly used in 1859.

The House has a long tradition of holding public sessions. Although it was common for the House to clear its galleries of outsiders to receive a confidential message from the president or some other executive-branch official, closed sessions ceased being commonplace after the War of 1812. The last nineteenth-century House secret session occurred on 27 May 1830, and the House did not meet in secret again until 1979. On 19 July 1983, it met in secret to consider portions of the intelligence authorization bill prohibiting U.S. support for the Contra rebels in Nicaragua.

Under House Rule XXIX, a representative claiming to hold confidential information may move that the House conduct a secret session. The Speaker may permit debate for up to one hour on this motion. If the House concurs in the motion, the galleries are cleared, electronic equipment is turned off, and superfluous staff are excluded from the chamber. Remaining staff are sworn to secrecy until such time as the House should vote to divulge the substance of the secret session. Under an alternative rule (Rule XLVII), the Intelligence Committee may move that the House hold a secret session to determine whether to divulge classified information held by the Intelligence Committee.

Allowing committees routinely to meet in secret session was a long-standing practice of Congress. Committee actions are not official until ratified by the parent chamber, and the feeling was that the preliminary deliberation and action could and generally should be done privately. Also, during the nineteenth century, committee meeting rooms were generally not designed to accommodate an audience. By the early twentieth century, with the construction of the first congressional office buildings, committee rooms became larger, and evidence suggests that more hearings were opened to the public. Business meetings and markup sessions remained closed, however.

In the 1970s, as part of a general movement to open government meetings to public scrutiny at the local, state, and federal levels, proposals were offered in Congress to require that committee hearings and meetings, including markup sessions, be open to the public. However, a committee could vote publicly (in open session, with a quorum present) to close the session for national security or other reasons specified in House and Senate rules.

In a series of rules changes beginning in the House in 1973 and the Senate in 1975, progressively stronger language was added to both chambers' rules to ensure that most committee work would be done in public. The House went even further, requiring that the full House grant its approval before a conference committee could vote to close its meetings. By the end of the 1970s virtually all committee meetings and hearings, except for those dealing with national security issues, ongoing criminal investigations, or matters that might defame an individual, were open to the public. Beginning in the mid 1980s, however, there were press reports that some in Congress were using creative devices to evade the open-meeting requirement, choosing meeting rooms too small to accommodate observers, using only committee staff to conduct preliminary committee activities, or holding private informal gatherings of members.

BIBLIOGRAPHY

Calmes, Jacqueline. "Few Complaints Are Raised as Doors Close on Capitol Hill." *Congressional Quarterly Weekly Report*, 23 May 1987, pp. 1059–1060.

Eckhardt, Bob. "The Presumption of Committee Openness under House Rules." *Harvard Journal of Legislation* 11 (February 1974): 279–302.

"Open Committee Trend in House and Senate." *Congressional Quarterly Weekly Report*, 11 January 1975, pp. 81–82.

Ornstein, Norman J. "The Open Congress Meets the President." In *Both Ends of the Avenue.* Edited by Anthony King. 1983.

Vaden, Ted. "Senate Votes Sunshine Rules for Committees." *Congressional Quarterly Weekly Report*, 8 November 1975, pp. 2413–2414.

PAUL S. RUNDQUIST

SAMUEL ALLYNE OTIS. The first secretary of the Senate. Painting by Gilbert Stuart, oil on wood panel, 1809. Gift of the Honorable and Mrs. Robert H. Thayer.

NATIONAL GALLERY OF ART, WASHINGTON, D.C.

SECRETARY OF THE SENATE. The secretary of the Senate, one of five elected Senate officers, is that body's chief administrative official. The first secretary was elected on 8 April 1789, two days after the Senate achieved its first quorum for business, and from the start the secretary was responsible for keeping the minutes and records of the Senate and purchasing supplies. As the Senate grew, numerous other duties were assigned to the secretary, whose jurisdiction came to encompass clerks, curators, and computers; disbursement of payrolls; acquisition of stationery supplies; training of Senate pages; and maintenance of public records.

The first secretary purchased quill pens, ink, and parchment needed by eighteenth-century senators, while modern secretaries have responsibility for the Senate Stationery Room, whose multimillion-dollar retail operations keep senators' offices supplied. The first secretary took minutes of Senate proceedings, a function today continued by the journal clerk and executive clerk. After the *Congressional Record* evolved into an official publication, the secretary came to supervise the Senate's reporters of debates, as well as those who prepare the *Congressional Record's* Daily Digest. Among other members of the Senate floor staff who report to the secretary are the parliamentarian, bill clerk, legislative clerk, and enrolling clerk. To answer both the immediate and the historical interest in Senate bills, resolutions, hearings, reports, and original records, the secretary oversees the Office of Printing Services, the Senate Document Room, the Office of Senate Security (which maintains classified documents), the Senate Library, the Office of Senate Curator, and the Senate Historical Office.

The secretary maintains the Office of Interparliamentary Services to assist senators participating in international legislative conferences, and the Office of Public Records to collect and provide documents relating to campaign finance, financial ethics, foreign travel, and lobbying. The secretary serves as a member of the Federal Election Commission and keeps senators informed about current election laws and filing requirements.

A seat beside the presiding officer is reserved for the secretary, who examines and signs every act of the Senate. In certain parliamentary circumstances, the secretary may preside. The last such occasion occurred in 1947, when the offices of vice president and Senate president pro tempore were vacant.

This post has attracted a long line of distinguished individuals. Samuel Allyne Otis, the first secretary and a former member of the Continental Congress, served for twenty-five years, never missing a day that the Senate was in session. Two former senators, Walter Lowrie of Pennsylvania and Charles Cutts of New Hampshire, have held the post. In 1985, Jo-Anne L. Coe became the first woman to serve as secretary of the Senate. In 1994 Martha S. Pope became the second woman to hold the office and, as a former sergeant at arms, the first person to have held the Senate's two major administrative posts.

It has not been unusual for secretaries to devote their entire careers to the Senate. Several secretaries began as pages, including Edwin A. Halsey, who served throughout the New Deal years; Leslie Biffle, a confidant of President Harry S. Truman; Carl A. Loeffler and J. Mark Trice, secretaries during the Republican majorities of the 80th (1947–1949) and 83d (1953–1955) Congresses; and Walter J. Stewart, secretary from 1987 to 1994.

With a budget of $13 million (fiscal year 1992), the secretary directs a staff of approximately 225 persons. In 1991, Congress established the annual salary of Senate officers, including the secretary, at $123,000.

[*See also* Clerks; Historians of the House and Senate; Pages; Parliamentarian, *article on* Senate Parliamentarian; *and table on following page.*]

BIBLIOGRAPHY

Byrd, Robert C. *The Senate, 1789–1989: Addresses on the History of the United States Senate.* Vol. 2. 1991.
U.S. Senate. *Report of the Secretary of the Senate* (semiannual, 1823–).

WALTER J. STEWART

SECRETARIES OF THE SENATE. From 1945 through 1965. *Left to right,* J. Mark Trice, Leslie Biffle, Felton M. Johnston, and Carl A. Loeffler.   LIBRARY OF CONGRESS

Secretaries of the Senate

NAME	START OF SERVICE	END OF SERVICE
Samuel Allyne Otis	8 April 1789	22 April 1814
Charles Cutts	12 October 1814	12 December 1825
Walter Lowrie	12 December 1825	5 December 1836
Asbury Dickins	13 December 1836	15 July 1861
John W. Forney	15 July 1861	4 June 1868
George C. Gorham	6 June 1868	24 March 1879
John C. Burch	24 March 1879	28 July 1881
Anson G. McCook	18 December 1883	7 August 1893
William R. Cox	7 August 1893	31 January 1900
Charles G. Bennett	1 February 1900	13 March 1913
James M. Baker	13 March 1913	19 May 1919
George A. Sanderson	19 May 1919	24 April 1925
Edwin Pope Thayer	7 December 1925	9 March 1933
Edwin A. Halsey	9 March 1933	29 January 1945
Leslie Biffle	8 February 1945	4 January 1947
Carl A. Loeffler	4 January 1947	3 January 1949
Leslie Biffle	3 January 1949	3 January 1953
J. Mark Trice	3 January 1953	5 January 1955
Felton M. Johnston	5 January 1955	30 December 1965
Emery L. Frazier	1 January 1966	30 September 1966
Francis R. Valeo	1 October 1966	31 March 1977
J. Stanley Kimmitt	1 April 1977	4 January 1981
William F. Hildenbrand	5 January 1981	2 January 1985
Jo-Anne L. Coe	3 January 1985	6 January 1987
Walter J. Stewart	6 January 1987	14 April 1994
Martha S. Pope	15 April 1994	—

SECTIONALISM. The pattern of enduring, large-scale geographical alignments that have shaped congressional policy coalitions and voting blocs throughout American history is known as sectionalism. Along with party loyalty, constituency interest, ideological predispositions, and institutional structure, sectionalism has thus been one of the principal organizing features of political conflict in the national legislature. American sectionalism originated in the uneven development of regional economies in the nineteenth century, particularly in the fundamental differences between what became the industrial Northeast and the agrarian, cotton-producing South. It has been distinguished from the sectionalism of most other nations in that ethnic and religious hostility has not, for the most part, shaped regionally patterned political conflict.

North versus South alignments played a very large (though often shifting) role in antebellum congressional policy-making, especially during the 1850s. But sectional political competition assumed a comparatively rigid and persistent form as a consequence of the American Civil War and Reconstruction. During the ensuing period, congressional policy-making was organized by a national party system that sent an almost solid bloc of Democrats to represent the white majority in the South and a slightly less solid bloc of Republicans from the heavy industrial regions of the North. During the 1930s, the New Deal significantly reshaped this alignment of the national party system by strengthening the Democratic party, primarily through the addition of northern industrial workers to what became known as the Roosevelt coalition. Some three decades later, the reenfranchisement of southern blacks through passage of the 1965 Voting Rights

Act substantially changed the Civil War alignment once again. The addition of millions of new African American voters to Democratic party ranks in the South was more than matched, at least in presidential races, by the loss of white voters to the Republicans. The net result of both the New Deal and black reenfranchisement was to weaken intrasectional cohesion and to change the way in which sectionalism found expression through the party system, without, however, altering the basic North-South polar axis of regional competition.

The Civil War to 1930. Sectional competition arising out of the national political economy created by the American Civil War was the primary influence on the national party system and congressional policy formation between 1860 and 1930. In the decades preceding the turn of the century, southern separatism in the form of secessionist demands and insistence on separate political and economic development repeatedly threatened national unity. While the Union victory in 1865 turned away the most serious challenge—secession—reunification did not relieve the hostility of former Confederates to federal rule. In order to strengthen national loyalists in the former Confederate states, northern Republicans in Congress enacted a number of policies that could, if aggressively implemented, have reconstructed the southern political economy by weakening or even overturning the dominant position of white plantation owners in the region. These programs, however, ultimately failed to protect loyalists (primarily black freedmen) from a violent reimposition of white dominance, institutionalized primarily through the Democratic party. By 1900, the federal government had withdrawn from any active role in protecting the political rights of southern blacks, and the Democratic party had become the almost exclusive vehicle for the expression of southern (albeit white) interests in national politics.

During this period, and inseparably intertwined with conflict over southern separatism, the United States underwent an extremely swift process of industrial and territorial expansion that was supported by both the consolidation of a national market and rapid capital accumulation into large industrial trusts. The emergence of these trusts, particularly in the form of the "modern business enterprise" that so distinguished U.S. industrialization, was sustained by a northern, Republican developmental program that rested on several policies: (1) adherence to the international gold standard, (2) tariff protection for almost all manufactured products,

(3) government subsidies to transportation projects connecting the western frontier to the entrepôt cities of the East, and (4) strong opposition to proposals either to break up trusts through national legislation or to regulate their operations through state or local governments.

Southern and western agrarians, including large landowners, yeoman farmers, and tenants, found common interest in opposition to this Republican program. While the battle their representatives in Congress fought against the excesses of industrialization and its consequences for the national political economy was largely unsuccessful, the Interstate Commerce Act in 1887 and the Sherman Antitrust Act in 1890, along with the Populist party insurgency in 1892 and William Jennings Bryan's campaign for free silver in 1896, stand as political monuments to agrarian disaffection with northeastern, Republican-led development. In these legislative struggles, Senators John Sherman of Ohio and Nelson W. Aldrich of Rhode Island were often aligned against southern Congress members such as Texas representative (later, senator) John H. Reagan (former postmaster general of the Confederacy) and Tennessee senator Isham G. Harris.

By 1900, the entry of the United States into international politics, particularly the race for colonial possessions, partially shifted the locus of sectional competition to imperialism and, a decade and a half later, to U.S. intervention in the European battleground of World War I. Southern and, to a lesser extent, western agrarians opposed both as military adventures that undercut the republican basis of national government (particularly states' rights) and carried benefits only for the industrial interests and financial commitments of northeastern metropolitan centers.

On the domestic side, the congressional alliance of southern Democrats and agrarian Republicans from the West and Midwest enacted a "progressive" program that placed corporate trusts, the railroads, and the national financial system within the ambit of central state regulatory authority. Beginning with the targeting of railroad rates in the Mann-Elkins Act in 1910, the major legislative achievements of this drive to impose political regulation on the industrial and financial giants of the twentieth century included passing the Clayton Antitrust Act in 1914, creating the Federal Reserve System in 1913, regulating commodity futures and warehouses between 1914 and 1916, and dramatically lowering duties in the Underwood Tariff of 1913. Enacted over the fervent opposition of Republicans in the manufacturing belt, this regulatory program built on and consolidated the factional divisions within the Republican party that had previously sparked the overthrow of Speaker Joseph G. Cannon (R-Ill.) in 1910. The defection of western and midwestern Republican "progressives" from party regularity in the Cannon revolt ended a period of strong party rule in the House of Representatives that had begun in 1861 and been reinforced by Speaker Thomas Reed in 1890. The weakening of the speakership that followed Cannon's defeat transformed the House, over the ensuing two decades, into an institution in which a strong, decentralized committee system came to dominate legislative deliberations.

Although U.S. entry into World War I abruptly terminated the expansion of central state regulatory authority that characterized the Progressive era in national politics, sectional conflict in the decade following the Versailles agreement still aligned the agrarian South and West against northeastern and midwestern advocates of unrestrained corporate expansion. With the Republican landslide in the 1920 general elections, the Democratic party returned to what had become a traditional minority role in national politics. Even though the Republicans controlled Congress and the executive branch through the 1920s, they were plagued by schism as western agrarians weakly resisted the policy leadership of northeastern and midwestern regulars. Industrial workers played only a minor role in congressional decision making in this decade, sometimes allying with northern Republicans on monetary policy and the tariff and less frequently coalescing with southern Democrats on labor legislation. For most of this interwar period, a self-consciously organized farm bloc, led by senators such as Robert M. La Follette of Wisconsin and Charles L. McNary of Oregon and representatives such as Gilbert N. Haugen of Iowa and Lister Hill of Alabama often proposed innovative and ambitious changes in the national political economy.

The legislative politics and policy-making of the 1920s was organized by strong political parties, both within and outside Congress, often strengthened in the Republican party by close executive-legislative cooperation. This cooperation, in turn, was reinforced by the very close interdependence between congressional and presidential election returns in the North, the regional base of the Republican party. During this period, as in every administration from Andrew Johnson's to Herbert Hoover's, an often dominant, always strong Congress set the domestic agenda of the nation; the executive branch usually played only a reactive and administrative role in policy-making.

Sectionalism and the New Deal. The economic distress that accompanied the Great Depression allowed the Democratic party to recapture the White House and end the interwar Republican consolidation of northern corporate power in the national political economy. From 1931 through 1994, the Democrats controlled the House of Representatives in all but four years. Because the party already represented almost all the districts of the South, it was enduring Democratic gains in the North that initiated this long era of party dominance. Among the factors that turned these northern gains into permanent additions to party ranks were the sustained prostration of northern industrialists and financiers during the Depression, the exploitation of the congressional committee system as the institutional basis for adjusting factional disputes between southern agrarians and northern labor, and the erection of decentralized programs that allocated benefits between coalition partners without threatening the interests of the southern plantation economy or undermining federal protection of industrial workers in the northern manufacturing belt. Seen from the broadest historical perspective, the New Deal coalition was institutionalized within the congressional committee system, which in turn became the central policy-making arena of the national Democratic party. During these decades, the West both rapidly expanded and was the site of vast federally sponsored projects that shaped the region as a new and independent force in national politics.

Franklin D. Roosevelt's New Deal coalition added industrial labor to the coalition of the northern Democratic party, even as the southern wing further reduced the already insignificant Republican presence in the South to a small handful of representatives from mountain districts in the Appalachians. The New Deal Democratic coalition of northern labor and ethnic minorities with southern whites (and a slowly increasing number of southern blacks) rested on a highly political process through which otherwise conflicting regional interests were brokered by party leaders in Congress and, when the Democrats controlled the presidency, the executive branch. Over the subsequent thirty-year period, in which the New Deal coalition dominated national elections and legislative decision making, this sectional alliance dramatically expanded the central state bureaucracy and forcefully extended federal power in both domestic and foreign affairs. When John F. Kennedy entered the White House, this coalition was at its zenith and the new administration was immediately forced to come to terms with old guard Democrats whose careers had been built on compromise—men such as Speaker Sam Rayburn of Texas, Senators Carl Hayden of Arizona and John J. Sparkman of Alabama, and Representatives Carl Vinson of Georgia and Richard W. Bolling of Missouri.

Even while supporting many policies that depended on or necessarily entailed an expansion of federal power, the New Deal coalition combined social groups and interests that remained highly suspicious of central state authority. For southern whites, in particular, continued allegiance to the national Democratic party rested on the party's often tacit but sometimes contentious acceptance of racial segregation in the South. For northern workers, on the other hand, federal regulation of labor relations was often viewed as a double-edged sword that could just as easily be—and sometimes was—used to impose discipline on the industrial labor force as to liberate workers from corporate oppression. Loyalty to the party coalition, for both of these great sectional interests, depended greatly on the party's continuing ability to contain integrationist sentiment while at the same time pursuing social welfare and labor policies benefiting the lower classes of the North.

The hard bargaining through which these and other conflicting interests within the New Deal coalition were resolved can be seen in the debates over the effectiveness and redistributive impact of agricultural commodity programs in the 1950s, as well as the often hypocritical stance that the congressional party adopted toward civil rights initiatives until the early 1960s. During the thirty-five years in which the New Deal coalition organized the social base of the Democratic party, national politics was characterized by a slow decline in the strength of political parties, starkly accentuated by an increase in ticket splitting between congressional and presidential races by voters throughout the country, but most particularly by southern whites. In Congress, the already strong committee system increasingly consolidated legislative policy-making into the decentralized recesses of the committee system, and thus into the hands of members whose constituencies benefited from the federal programs that fell within their jurisdiction. While these committees delegated wide bureaucratic discretion to the federal agencies that implemented these programs, committee members often sought to use their institutional positions to influence agency decisions of importance to their individual districts. Nowhere was this influence more strongly felt than in the military establishment, the interests of which were advanced by the strong and cohesive Senate and House Armed Services committees led by Sen. Richard B. Russell of Georgia and Rep. L. Mendel Rivers of South Carolina. Backed by a conservative coalition of southern Democrats and midwestern Republicans after northern Democrats bolted the fold, even reactionary chairmen could prevail over liberal insurgencies that had the support of a nominal majority of the Democratic party.

The Civil Rights Movement and Collapse of the New Deal Coalition. Between 1933 and 1965, the viability of the New Deal coalition was slowly undercut by several demographic and political trends. One of the most important was the migration of millions of previously disenfranchised southern blacks to northern urban centers. Spurred by the national mobilization during World War II and the industrial prosperity of the 1950s, this movement created a strategic voting bloc in the large states of the manufacturing belt, for whom destruction of the segregationist institutions of the South was a high and uncompromising priority. Somewhat related to this migration was a shift in Democratic party strength toward the North, particularly toward metropolitan constituencies in which organized labor steadily consolidated a position of dominance arising out of federal intervention and regulation of collective bargaining agreements and union shop organizing. By 1960, the North often elected as many Democrats to Congress as did the South, and it was conceivable that, for the first time in U.S. history, the party could control the presidency and national legislature while losing a majority of the states and districts of the South. By demonstrating this potential change in sectional base, Lyndon B. Johnson's victory over Barry Goldwater in the 1964 election provided momentum for a wide-spectrum assault on southern segregation. This assault in turn marked the termination of the often tacit understandings and agreements that had underlain the New Deal coalition.

Passage of the Civil Rights Act of 1964 swung the federal bureaucracy, particularly the departments of Justice and Health, Education, and Welfare, behind primary and secondary school desegregation. One year later, the Voting Rights Act of 1965 sent federal registrars into the former states of the Confederacy, where they suspended restrictive suffrage provisions and added hundreds of thousands of African Americans to the voting rolls. While almost all of these new voters were Democrats, their entry into the electorate led many southern whites to leave the party in presidential and, to a lesser extent, congressional elections.

In Congress, the demise of the New Deal coalition was evident in the bitter balkanization of the Democratic party as southern conservatives sought both temporary voting alliances and more enduring working arrangements with Republicans. As the years passed, however, the increasingly competitive party system in the South, reinforced by change in the racial composition of the Democratic party in the region, encouraged the replacement of these conservatives with even more conservative Republicans or moderate Democrats. Thus, while the immediate impact of these civil rights measures was a dramatic decline in Democratic cohesion in legislative voting, in subsequent decades the unity of the party on congressional roll calls actually rose, as those whites alienated by liberal policies associated with the national Democratic party were assimilated into southern Republican party constituencies. In later years, the increasing cohesion among Democratic members both strengthened congressional party organizations and the party leadership and, in relative terms, reinforced the declining importance of the committee system in policy-making.

In the 1970s and 1980s, the decreasing prestige and influence of the committee system was reflected in bitter floor fights over the formulas that distributed federal funds to different regions of the country and over regulatory standards that promised to influence the direction and pace of regional economic growth. These fights covered a wide spectrum of national policies, such as the allocation of fuel subsidies to the poor, public works jobs, federal education funds, defense contracts, and land conservation. Additional floor struggles further undermined the traditional prerogatives of legislative committees as regional, cross-party alliances such as the Northeast-Midwest Advancement Coalition sought to reallocate regional shares in federal budget authorizations and appropriations.

Although this broad and sweeping overview of sectionalism in national politics and policy-making can only sample the range and influence of regional competition in Congress, the persistent, historical alignment of the American political system along a Northeast–Deep South axis can still be seen in the changing characteristics and social bases of the major parties, the institutional organization of legislative institutions, and the devices through which the executive and legislative branches influence each other's decisions. While many observers have speculated that a "nationalization" of political culture and economic activity has permanently undermined the bases of sectionalism as a force in U.S. politics, these deductions from modernization theory may seriously understate and misinterpret the enduring impact of continuing regional differences within the national political economy.

[See also Blocs and Coalitions; Civil War; History of Congress, article on Sectionalism and Nationalism; Political Parties; Secession; States' Rights.]

BIBLIOGRAPHY

Bensel, Richard Franklin. Sectionalism and American Political Development, 1880–1980. 1984.
Bensel, Richard Franklin. Yankee Leviathan: The Origins of Central State Authority in America, 1859–1877. 1990.
Key, V. O., Jr. Southern Politics in State and Nation. 1949.
Sanders, Elizabeth. "Industrial Concentration, Sectional Competition and Antitrust Politics in America, 1880–1980." In Studies in American Political Development I, edited by Karen Orren and Stephen Skowronek. 1986.
Turner, Frederick Jackson. Sections in American History. 1932.

RICHARD FRANKLIN BENSEL

SECURITIES ACTS. [The following article focuses on the Federal Securities Act of 1933 (48 Stat. 74–95) and the Securities Exchange Act of 1934 (48 Stat. 881–909)]. When the stock market crashed in 1929 and the Great Depression descended on the United States in the early 1930s, it became politically unacceptable that Wall Street remain all but unregulated. The revelations following the crash —of insider trading and suspect relationships between banks and brokerages—spectacularly presented by the Pecora Wall Street investigation in early 1933, ensured that regulation of the securities market would be high on the agenda of the early New Deal.

The first bill to come before Congress was the work primarily of Huston Thompson, former chairman of the Federal Trade Commission (FTC). This Wilsonian states' rights Democrat was as hostile to strong federal regulation as he was to big business, and so he proposed a weak system of securities oversight to be handled by the FTC.

Opposition arose in hearings before the Senate Banking and Currency Committee from various banking and business interests on one side, and on the other from the rising body of New Deal lawyer-regulators who wanted something more substantial. David Lilienthal, later to head TVA, called the bill "a pretty amateurish piece of drafting."

Sam Rayburn, who then chaired the House Interstate and Foreign Commerce Committee, offered an alternate bill, the work of brain trusters Raymond Moley, Felix Frankfurter, James M. Landis, Benjamin Cohen, Thomas Corcoran, and House legislative counsel Middleton Beaman. It drew much from the British Companies Act of 1928–1929 but went far beyond that law in its disclosure, registration, and enforcement provisions.

The House quickly passed Rayburn's bill. (Cohen told Landis: "Rayburn did not know whether the bill passed so readily because it was so damned good or so damned incomprehensible.") Senate majority leader Joseph T. Robinson preferred the Rayburn to the Thompson bill, and a House-Senate conference committee agreed on what was essentially the Rayburn measure. President Franklin D. Roosevelt signed it on 27 May 1933.

In 1934 Landis, Corcoran, and Cohen turned their attention to the creation of a regulatory agency to administer the Securities Act, one that would not be under the influence of the financial community. The resulting bill, sponsored by Rayburn and Sen. Duncan U. Fletcher, initially relied on the FTC to oversee the securities exchanges. But the Federal Reserve Board (which opposed FTC control over margin requirements), state banks, businessmen, and especially the smaller regional exchanges opposed this arrangement. Finally, Rayburn and Sen. Carter Glass of Virginia (who watched paternally over the FTC) agreed on a small Securities Exchange Commission (SEC), ultimately composed of five members. The Federal Reserve Board was left with control over margin requirements. The bill became law on 6 June 1934.

The SEC and the act it administered turned out to be one of the most successful and long-lasting achievements of the New Deal. Law professor William O. Douglas initially dismissed the Securities Act as a "nineteenth-century piece of legislation," but he changed his mind as an SEC commissioner from 1934 to 1939. He and Landis did much to make the SEC a generally effective guardian of the probity of the American securities market.

[See also Banking Act of 1933; New Deal; Pecora Wall Street Investigation.]

BIBLIOGRAPHY

Landis, James M. "The Legislative History of the Securities Act of 1933." *George Washington Law Review* 28 (1959): 29–49.
McCraw, Thomas K. *Prophets of Regulation.* 1984. Chap. 5.
Parrish, Michael E. *Securities Regulation and the New Deal.* 1970.

MORTON KELLER

SECURITIES EXCHANGE ACT. *See* Securities Acts.

SEDGWICK, THEODORE (1746–1813), Federalist leader, senator and representative from Massachusetts, Speaker of the House, lawyer, judge. Active in the American Revolution and a member of the western Massachusetts elite, Sedgwick entered politics in 1780, as a representative and then senator in the Massachusetts legislature. Influenced by the ideals of the Revolution, he successfully defended a slave, Elizabeth Freeman, by establishing the unconstitutionality of slavery in Massachusetts. As a delegate to the Continental Congress in 1785, Sedgwick promoted an energetic national government. He was an active opponent of Shays' Rebellion and enthusiastically supported the Federal Constitution in the Massachusetts ratifying convention of 1788.

Sedgwick was elected to the First Congress, where he allied with Alexander Hamilton, endorsing his public credit plans and the national bank. He chaired several committees and shaped much early legislation. Intensely partisan, he condemned the Jeffersonian Republicans as favoring French revolutionary anarchy and defended Jay's Treaty and a pro-British foreign policy. In June 1796, Sedgwick was elected to the Senate and became the Federalists' chief spokesman there. During the French crisis of 1798, he advocated war, breaking with President John Adams over sending a diplomatic mission to France. He supported the Alien and Sedition Acts, resisting Republican efforts to repeal them.

Sedgwick served briefly as president pro tempore of the Senate in 1798 and completed his term in 1799, when he returned to the House as a representative. He was chosen Speaker in the Sixth Congress, having been promoted by the Hamiltonian wing of the Federalist party. Unable to use the position to his party's advantage, he found his tenure frustrating. He joined Federalist efforts to deny President Adams reelection and staunchly supported Aaron Burr when the election of 1800 was thrown to the House. Sedgwick left Congress in 1801, remaining embittered about Jefferson's triumph. He was a powerful congressional debater and an influential and tireless promoter of the Federalist cause.

BIBLIOGRAPHY

Welch, Richard E. *Theodore Sedgwick, Federalist.* 1965.
Elkins, Stanley, and Eric McKitrick. *The Age of Federalism: The Early American Republic, 1788–1800.* 1993.

WINFRED E. A. BERNHARD

SEDITION ACTS. *See* Alien and Sedition Acts.

SELECT COMMITTEE. *See* Committees, *article on* Select and Special Committees. *For discussion of particular select committees, see* Aging Committee, House Select; Children, Youth, and Families Committee, House Select; Ethics Committee, Senate Select; Hunger Committee, House Select; Indian Affairs Committee, Senate; Select; Intelligence Committee, House Permanent Select; Intelligence Committee, Senate Select; Narcotics Abuse and Control Committee, House Select.

SELECTIVE SERVICE. *See* Conscription.

SENATE. [*This entry includes three separate articles providing a general analysis of the Senate as a legislative body:*

An Overview
Daily Sessions of the Senate
Senate Rules and Procedures

For comparable treatment of the House, see House of Representatives. *For broad discussion of congressional powers and practices, see nine articles under* Congress. *See* History of Congress *for eight articles that survey the history and development of Congress from its origins to the present.*]

An Overview

The very first provision of the U.S. Constitution states: "All legislative powers herein granted shall be vested in a Congress of the United States which shall consist of a Senate and a House of Representatives." Those "legislative powers," as they have been elaborated, interpreted, exercised, and preserved, have made Congress the most powerful national legislature in the world. It is bicameral in structure, with its lawmaking power equally divid-

THE GREAT TRIUMVIRATE. The Senate has historically been the forum where vivid personalities voice and argue the leading issues on the nation's policy agenda. The "Great Triumvirate" of Henry Clay of Kentucky, John C. Calhoun of South Carolina, and Daniel Webster of Massachusetts—their names here used in an advertisement for a cigar maker—held center stage during the 1812–1852 period and for many Americans epitomized sectional views on nationalism, slavery, and economic policies.   OFFICE OF THE HISTORIAN OF THE U.S. SENATE

ed between House and Senate. Each chamber, acting separately, must approve of each piece of legislation before it can become law. The equality of the Senate within the bicameral arrangement has made it—from the start—independent and powerful as a legislative institution.

In its basic institutional features, the Senate reflects the circumstances of its origins. The Framers of the Constitution were in total and early agreement that there should be two chambers—distinct, different, and equal. After all, eleven of the thirteen state legislatures already had a bicameral arrangement, and nine of the eleven had labeled one chamber its "Senate." This bicameral agreement of 1787 was grounded in a philosophy widely shared among the Framers that power ought not to be concentrated anywhere in government, especially not within that institution of government most likely to predominate—the legislature.

As James Madison explained during the ratification debate (in *Federalist* 51),

> In republican government, the legislative authority necessarily predominates. The remedy for this inconveniency is to divide the legislature into different branches; and to render them, by different modes of election and different principles of action, as little connected with each other as the nature of their common functions and their common dependence on the society will admit.

The debate at the Constitutional Convention over the exact content of those differences, however, was lengthy, bitter, and nearly fatal for the new constitution.

Four Basic Institutional Features. Having agreed that members of the House should be apportioned among the states according to population, the Framers became deadlocked, in Madison's words, by "the opposite pretensions of large and small states" regarding their representational strength in the Senate. The ultimate compromise provided that two senators would be apportioned to each state, regardless of population. Voting equality in the Senate was the price the large states paid to get what they wanted—a new union.

The apportionment decision was a victory for the small states. It fixed two basic institutional features of the Senate—both of which gave advantages to the small states. First, every senator was given a statewide constituency. While these Senate constituencies might vary widely in population, the voting strength of the smallest state would equal that of the largest state. In 1990, senators from the twenty-six smallest states represented only 18 percent of the nation's population, yet they held a majority of the votes in the Senate. Conversely, the nine largest states contained a majority of the nation's population but held only 18 percent of the Senate's votes.

The apportionment decision also guaranteed a second institutional feature: that the Senate would be relatively small in size—twenty-two members at the beginning, one hundred members today. For nearly a century, the Senate has been only one-quarter the size of the House. In the smaller body, each member has a greater opportunity to be heard. And successive generations of senators have nurtured an array of parliamentary procedures to guarantee that opportunity.

The Framers of the Constitution had certain other ideas about the Senate, and they translated them, too, into permanent features of the institution. They pictured the more popularly elected House as especially liable to succumb to transient public passions and to be in need, therefore, of another body, whose members would provide a brake, a second look, a longer-run view, and a well-deliberated decision. "The use of the Senate," said Madison in his *Notes on Debates in the Federal Convention of 1787*, "is to consist in its proceeding with more coolness, with more system and with more wisdom, than the popular branch."

In the most famous anecdote about the Senate, Thomas Jefferson asks George Washington why he consented to the idea of a Senate. "Why did you pour that coffee into your saucer?" asks Washington. "To cool it," replies Jefferson. "Even so," replies Washington, "we pour legislation into the senatorial saucer to cool it." In Madison's words, that saucer would consist of "enlightened citizens, whose limited number and firmness might reasonably interpose against impetuous councils."

From this set of views came two other fundamental institutional features of the Senate. To promote "coolness" and to ensure the election of "proper characters," the Framers provided some electoral insulation from the popular mood. Senators would be elected for six-year terms. Their terms would be staggered, with only one-third of the membership up for election under one single set of circumstances and pressures. And they would be chosen by their state legislatures. This latter piece of insulation was removed—gradually in practice, and formally in 1913—when the Seventeenth Amendment to the Constitution mandated the popular election of senators.

The staggered six-year terms still provide some continuity. But the longevity of senators has become every bit as tenuous—in fact, more so—at the hands of the electorate as that of House members. And such "coolness" as Congress exhibits is more the result of the two-chamber lawmaking sequence than of any especially dispassionate steadiness on the part of the Senate.

In the expectation, however, that the Senate would be a calm, deliberative body, the Framers gave to the Senate a set of special policy prerogatives. In foreign policy, they granted the Senate the power to ratify treaties and to confirm the appointment of ambassadors. The wise and stable Senate, they believed, would be the best guardian of the nation's reputation in foreign affairs. They also bestowed on the

Senate the power of "advice and consent" to presidential nominations of top-level executive department officials and to the federal judiciary. These various provisions placed the Senate uniquely in a position to exercise an extra increment of influence over the executive and judicial branches.

Each of these four basic institutional features—statewide constituency, small size, six-year terms, special policy prerogatives—differentiates the Senate from the House of Representatives. Taken together, they constitute the starting point for any understanding of the Senate; all of the characteristic properties or behaviors now associated with the modern Senate are the derivatives of one or more of the original four.

Constituency makeup and small size combine, for example, to make the Senate a uniquely favorable arena for small states to band together to protect their common interests. At various points in U.S. history, slave states in the South, agricultural states in the Midwest, and water-poor states in the Far West have relied upon their disproportionate voting strength in the Senate to protect their interests. But more broadly and more importantly, today the Senate's special body of internal rules and procedures grants the same institutional advantages to all sorts of minority interests and diverse viewpoints—provided only that some senator gives voice to them.

For this development, the small size of the Senate has been crucial. It permitted the early acceptance of a less formal, more flexible set of rules than was possible in the larger House—rules conferring no prerogatives upon a presiding officer, no previous question rule to shut off debate, no germaneness rule to prevent irrelevant or pernicious attachments to legislation. Senate party leaders have far fewer procedural resources with which to promote the orderly processing of business than do their counterparts in the House. Taken together, these procedural features guarantee individual senators a high degree of independence in advancing their personal goals.

Above all, the Senate's rules preserve the right of every individual senator or small group of senators to talk at length and at will—to filibuster—so as to stop all activity and kill legislation they oppose. It was not until 1914 that the Senate imposed upon itself a cloture rule to make it possible to stop debate. But the procedures related to its imposition, and the extra majority (now three-fifths of the membership) required to invoke it, have made cloture difficult to carry out.

The cloture rule, as it protects the right of every individual senator to talk or threaten to talk or to exact a price for silence, is the quintessential procedural bulwark of the modern Senate. It is every member's ultimate weapon. And its presence has necessitated a whole series of ad hoc devices to keep Senate business flowing—unanimous consent agreements and multitrack scheduling, for example. The Framers of the Constitution got what they wanted—a deliberative legislative body. But subsequent procedural developments within their small-sized, state-based institution have sometimes produced deliberation unto obstructionism unto paralysis.

Media Spotlight on the Senate. A fifth distinctive feature of the Senate—institutional in its impact and permanence—must be added to the original four. It is the amount and the kind of media attention that senators attract. By every measure, senators command more media attention than House members—more on the nightly newscasts, more in the national press, more during their campaigns at home, and more on weekend talk shows in Washington. Two years after the House had begun to televise its floor proceedings, the Senate in 1986 followed suit. Given the advent of a new communications technology that has made possible mass media attention to public figures, the phenomenon of media attention to senators and their business can be seen as a derivative of the four basic features previously discussed.

As a matter of logistics, the relatively small size of the body makes it more tempting, if not easier, for reporters to cover than the House. Furthermore, in the smaller body personalities stand out, and the media—especially television—prefer to deal with personalities rather than with the numerology of coalition building so essential to understanding the House. A senator's six-year term gives members of the press an added incentive to invest their time in establishing contacts with the chamber's newcomers.

Because of their huge work load and small numbers, senators tend to spread themselves across numerous committees, subcommittees, and policy areas. While this means that they specialize less than House members, it also means they are better prepared to talk to the press about a wide range of subjects. And the Washington-based press has an insatiable appetite for commentary on all subjects of the moment. In addition, their statewide constituencies have forced most senators to concern themselves with the fullest range of national policy

SENATE

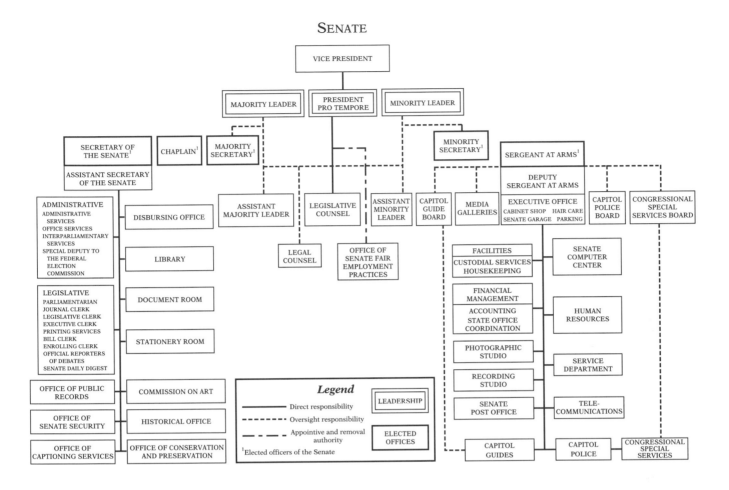

problems. Their election campaigns, too, tend to demand more of an emphasis on national policy matters than do House campaigns.

Finally, by virtue of their special prerogatives, senators get propelled into the national spotlight whenever foreign policy matters or presidential appointments are matters of dispute. From Woodrow Wilson and the Versailles treaty or Lyndon B. Johnson and Vietnam on the foreign policy side, to Ronald Reagan and Robert Bork or George Bush and Clarence Thomas on the nominations side, the Senate has frequently found itself at the center of national controversy. Some such controversies have been highly partisan, some not. But in all cases, Senate investigations, debates, and votes have been widely publicized and intensively followed. And a few senators have become prominent media figures in the process.

This media-Senate attraction is fully mutual. From the senator's point of view, media attention is a resource to manipulate in order to achieve their own goals. Most of them want media attention and they work hard to get it. They hire staff people

whose only job is to get it for them. Most prominent among the publicity seekers are senators with presidential or vice presidential ambitions. For almost all of its history, the Senate has been a major incubator of presidential candidacies. Ambitions for higher office can always be found in various stages of development within the Senate, most actively among members of whichever party lacks an incumbent president eligible for reelection.

As presidential nominations have become tied increasingly to public participation in primaries, media attention has become the indispensable ingredient of senatorial success in pursuit of higher office ambitions. Estes Kefauver pioneered this path by parlaying his televised hearings on organized crime into a string of primary victories in 1956. In every election since, one or more senators have turned media attention into a bid for the presidential nomination. Typically, this attention comes by way of some highly publicized senatorial performance (Howard H. Baker, Edward M. Kennedy), a leadership role in the senatorial party (Lyndon B. Johnson, Bob Dole), or association in the Senate with an issue of absorbing national concern (Barry Goldwater, George McGovern).

The opportunity to publicize one's issue positions and to be recognized by the media on a given issue is, of course, available to all senators as they work to fulfill other personal goals—reelection, making good policy, or developing a reputation for effectiveness in the Senate. Committee or subcommittee chairmanships and party leadership positions provide the greatest opportunities in this respect. At any point in time, therefore, a minority of senators will figure prominently in the public eye. Their presence, as it focuses the media's attention on the Senate, enhances the opportunity for other members to take their turn in the spotlight.

The Changing Senate. Our addition of media attention to the four original features of the institution indicates that the Senate has changed as the national context has changed. Historians have charted its ups and downs as a national force. In the earliest years, it struggled to achieve functional parity with the House. And in the pre–Civil War period, it enjoyed what has been called its "golden era," the time when the institution best lived up to the Framers' idea of a deliberative assembly. In that time of national peril, conflicting philosophies and strategies were articulated and debated, at length and single-mindedly, by senators of exceptional talent. Their ability has been memorialized by their successors, with John C. Calhoun, Henry Clay, and Daniel Webster being named by the Senate as three of its five "outstanding senators."

While there is, among today's senators, some nostalgia for that era of great debate—and occasional traces of the deliberative impulse—the modern Senate does not command any such superlatives. But it has maintained its parity within the bicameral system. As such, it remains the most powerful second legislative chamber in the world.

In the contemporary period, there have been two dominant characterizations of the Senate as an institution. The Senate of the 1950s and 1960s has been described in largely *communitarian* terms—as a club or small town, as self-contained, self-regulating, inward looking. The Senate of the 1970s and 1980s has been described in largely *individualistic* terms— as a gathering of prima donnas or movie stars, as entrepreneurial, publicity seeking, outward looking. The differences are, of course, matters of degree. But they are measurable. And they are both distinctively senatorial descriptions. Neither would serve very well to describe the House.

In the communitarian Senate, behavior was heavily influenced by informal, member-to-member un-

derstandings about apprenticeship for newcomers, committee-based specialization for everyone, and self-restraint in the use of procedural advantages for obstructive purposes on the Senate floor. These norms helped to restrict participation, regulate the internal distribution of influence, and dampen internal conflict. They made members sensitive to the benefits of collegial approval and, thereby, helped to buffer and modulate the divisive impact of external influences. It was an arrangement that tended to keep the legislative policy agenda small, and for that reason, it was kept in place by policy conservatives.

In the individualistic Senate, the basic understanding among members is that everyone plays whenever, wherever, and however he or she wishes. And all senators now have the necessary resources to become players. Every senator holds a position of leadership on at least one subcommittee, in addition to which the jurisdictional lines separating subcommittees are more easily breached. Senate staffs, which exploded in size from 1,115 in 1957 to 3,593 in 1979, have made possible a greater breadth of participation and a greater independence for each senator. And publicity opportunities have, as noted, increased apace. With these resources at hand, collegial approval has lost the importance it once had. Senators who wish to pursue reputations and cultivate constituencies outside the Senate are enabled and encouraged to do so.

This atomized and hyperactive Senate is much more difficult to lead than the more collegial one that preceded it, and recent majority leaders have found it impossible to duplicate the 1950s success of Johnson. The Senate floor, the special province of the party leadership, has become more important as a decision-making arena and, at the same time, a more unruly cockpit. The decline of self-restraint in exploiting Senate rules for individual or partisan advantage is symbolic of the institutional change that has taken place in the last quarter of a century.

This change can be explained as the indirect result of changes in the external context and as the direct result of changes in Senate membership. Among the changes in context that had indirect effects, we would include: a change in the policy agenda that brought issues like civil rights, environmentalism, consumerism, and women's rights to the fore; an explosion of private special interest groups battling for or against these causes; the revolution in communications and the onset of public relations politics; the Watergate scandal and the resulting clamor for openness in government; the decline of party organizational influence in controlling nominations and the subsequent rise of self-starting candidates; and the increased costs of electioneering and the nationalization of campaign financing. Taken together, these changes encouraged greater issue activism and more highly personalized coalition-building methods both electorally and legislatively.

More directly, however, the Senate changed when new members were elected to it, bringing with them from the outside new policy commitments and new values with regard to their participation in policy-making. The modern turning point was the Senate election of 1958, which brought an especially large cohort of activist, liberal Democrats into the chamber. It took several more elections, bringing in some activist Republicans as well as Democrats, plus the sixteen years of benign, egalitarian leadership by Mike Mansfield (1961–1977), to make the individualistic pattern secure and to register—as in the field of civil rights—some distinctive changes in national policy.

Within the constraints fixed by its five basic institutional features, we can expect the Senate to change whenever new, politically relevant external conditions arise and whenever elections produce a new group of senators large enough and committed enough to make changes in chamber procedures or policies. The Senate remains distinctive and identifiable in its core characteristics. But it also remains an ever-changing institution within an ever-changing context.

BIBLIOGRAPHY

Baker, Ross. *Friend and Foe in the U.S. Senate.* 1980.

Byrd, Robert C. *The Senate, 1789–1989: Addresses on the History of the United States Senate.* 2 vols. 1988, 1991.

Evans, Lawrence. *Leadership in Committee: A Comparative Analysis of Leadership Behavior in the U.S. Senate.* 1991.

Fenno, Richard. *The United States Senate: A Bicameral Perspective.* 1982.

Hibbing, John, ed. *The Changing World of the U.S. Senate.* 1990.

Matthews, Donald. *U.S. Senators and Their World,* 1960.

Sinclair, Barbara. *The Transformation of the United States Senate.* 1989.

RICHARD F. FENNO, JR.

Daily Sessions of the Senate

Prior to the sound of the bells that signal the start of a Senate session, reporters huddle around the majority leader's desk on the Senate floor in the morning ritual known as the dug-out to receive his briefing on that day's anticipated floor action. The Senate is then called to order by its presiding officer, officially the vice president of the United States, but in his frequent absence, the president pro tempore. That position is held by the most senior majority-party senator, although in his absence other majority-party senators also serve as presiding officer, rotating approximately every hour throughout the day.

After the prayer offered by the Senate chaplain, the majority leader and minority leader each receive ten minutes of "leader time." The majority leader usually announces the planned agenda for the day during his allotment of time; the minority leader may react to the agenda or may address other pertinent legislative or political issues. Sometimes the leaders reserve their time for use later in the day or yield it to other senators.

The Senate will then normally go into a period of "morning business," during which bills are introduced, committee reports are filed, messages are received, and senators may be granted unanimous consent to give "morning business speeches," usually five minutes in length, on any topic they wish. The duration of the morning business period on any given day varies widely, ranging from a few minutes to an hour or more.

The Senate will then take up a piece of legislation or an item of executive business, such as a nomination or a treaty. Whether legislative or executive business, the Senate must first agree to call a matter up before the matter can receive consideration. This is usually done through prior negotiation, and then agreed to by the unanimous consent of all present on the floor at the time. Alternatively, when negotiations to obtain unanimous consent to take up the matter have failed, the majority leader may make a motion to proceed to the consideration of a bill or executive item. The motion to proceed may precipitate extensive debate, even a filibuster, if the measure itself is strongly opposed. If a vote does occur on the motion to proceed, a simple majority suffices for adoption.

Once a measure is before the Senate, the debate on the legislation and the amendments that may be offered to it are normally unlimited. Except in certain parliamentary circumstances, amendments to a bill in the Senate need not be relevant, or germane, to the content of the bill. Therefore, it is usually difficult to predict the length of time the Senate will spend in consideration of a specific measure. The majority and minority leaders strive to mitigate this uncertainty by negotiating unanimous consent agreements that restrict the debate time and structure the number and nature of amendments to be offered. These agreements, commonly referred to as "u.c." or "time" agreements, provide the blueprint for a bill's consideration.

When legislation is considered on the Senate floor without a unanimous consent agreement, attempts might be made during its consideration to negotiate terms for the remainder of the debate and amending process. Most often these negotiations take place in the cloakrooms or in the leaders' offices. Quorum calls are used to permit senators to leave the floor and participate in the negotiations. The clerk of the Senate reads the call of the roll quite slowly, an indicator that the purpose of the quorum call is not to command the actual presence of a majority of Senators on the floor, but rather to suspend formal action while the process continues informally, off the floor. It is a common pattern to have the Senate's proceedings punctuated with the interruption of frequent quorum calls. When senators are ready to resume floor action, the quorum call is "rescinded" or withdrawn.

Voting on final passage of a bill or an amendment can either be by the "yeas and nays" or by voice vote. If the yeas and nays are ordered, the clerk of the Senate reads each senator's name in alphabetical order and each vote is recorded. In a voice vote, the judgment of the chair determines the outcome, and no names or positions are recorded.

No day in the Senate is truly typical. The Senate may work on one bill for most of a day and well into the evening, it may temporarily suspend a bill's consideration and turn to another piece of legislation, or it may switch back and forth among several measures during the same day. This flexibility reflects the Senate's emphasis on arranging business through informal negotiations that can accommodate the schedules of the senators who are key to the legislation under consideration. It also allows the opportunity to mediate political conflicts as they arise.

The Senate's floor schedule is also difficult to predict because each senator recognized to speak has the right to extend debate and keep the floor for as long as desired, thus preventing or delaying a vote. Senators also enjoy the right to offer "non-germane" amendments. Known as "riders," such amendments allow a single senator to introduce subject matter for floor consideration, sometimes contrary to the wishes of the party leaders. Both extended debate (which may become filibusters) and non-germane amendments are an integral part of

the Senate's tradition of offering individual senators considerable procedural autonomy.

After the vote on final passage of the measure, or after the majority leader in consultation with the minority leader has concluded that no more progress can be made on legislation that day, the Senate turns to a series of routine actions known as the wrap-up. This might include a recitation of a series of unanimous consent requests for minor internal procedural arrangements (e.g., permission for committees to meet while the Senate is in session). Noncontroversial bills that have been cleared for passage through both party cloakrooms then are called off the calendar by the clerk of the Senate, and passed by unanimous consent or voice vote, usually with little or no debate. Finally, a motion is made by the majority leader or his designee to either recess or adjourn the Senate until its next scheduled meeting time, thus ending the daily session.

BIBLIOGRAPHY

Congressional Quarterly Inc. *How Congress Works*. 2d ed. 1991.

Green, Alan. *Gavel to Gavel: A Guide to the Televised Proceedings of Congress*. 1991.

Oleszek, Walter J. *Congressional Procedures and the Policy Process*. 1989. Pp. 177–238.

ILONA B. NICKELS

Senate Rules and Procedures

The U.S. Senate has forty-two standing rules that have been adopted to control its day-to-day functions. These brief rules are supplemented by thousands of precedents filling several dozen volumes and dating back to the 1800s. In current practice, the rules are often waived by unanimous consent. These unanimous consent agreements themselves, however, rely on the precedents for interpretation. As a result, the actions that the Senate has previously taken are often more important than the actual rules in determining procedure.

Moreover, the evolution of the positions of majority and minority leaders, a twentieth-century development, has made the rules less relevant. Because they have the prerogative of introducing unanimous consent agreements, these leaders, especially the majority leader, set the pace and course of floor action in the Senate. Despite this centralization of power, a single senator who knows the rules of the Senate and chooses to use them can significantly affect Senate action.

History of the Rules. In April 1789, one day after a quorum of the Senate had first been achieved, a special committee to prepare a system of rules was created. The committee was composed of some of the new Senate's most experienced legislators: one committee member, Richard Henry Lee of Virginia, had been president of the Continental Congress; another, Caleb Strong of Massachusetts, had been a delegate to the Constitutional Convention.

The twenty "standing rules" finally adopted by the Senate in 1789 were similar to the 1778 rules of the Continental Congress. Debate over the rules was intense. William Maclay of Pennsylvania, for instance, proposed a rule that would have allowed four senators to force a vote on any question on which debate was becoming "tedious." The Senate rejected this course, moving instead toward a set of rules allowing unlimited debate.

The Senate has remained organized with its rules in force without interruption since 1789. Because only a third of the Senate is newly elected every two years, it is considered a continuing body whose rules require no readoption from one Congress to the next. As a result the Senate's standing rules have been subjected to fewer and less dramatic changes over time than have the House rules, which have been held not binding on a newly elected House unless readopted, frequently with certain revisions—usually but not always a perfunctory procedure.

The person who had the most influence on Senate rules and procedures was Thomas Jefferson of Virginia. As vice president of the United States, Jefferson served also as president of the Senate (1797–1801), and it fell to him to interpret the newly adopted standing rules. He created a manual of precedents, *The Manual of Parliamentary Practice*, to guide the Senate in implementing the rules. His publication, which is still used today, contained fifty-three sections covering the range of Senate activities, from the order of business to motions for debate, and even included information on such esoteric areas as impeachment. Jefferson prefaced his manual with the following observation: "It is much more material that there be a rule to go by than what that rule is. . . . It is very material that order, decency, and regularity be preserved in a dignified public body."

During the nineteenth century, the Senate continued to revise and expand its rules, recodifying them in 1806, 1820, 1828, 1868, 1877, and 1884. The Senate did not adopt another new codification until 1979, when it incorporated many provisions of the legislative reorganization acts of 1946 and 1970 into its rules. One of the primary thrusts of the 1979 recodification was to provide detailed new provisions that took into account the greatly expanded Senate committee structure.

The Senate as a Deliberative Body. Through all their changes and permutations, the rules have always been designed, first and foremost, to allow the Senate to be a deliberative body. The rules protect the rights of the minority to debate and delay. Many bills have been killed through the use of the filibuster—that is, the technique of debating a bill endlessly to prevent its coming to a vote. Prior to the adoption, in 1917, of Rule XXII, which allows two-thirds of the Senate to invoke cloture or limit debate, a single senator could filibuster and defeat a bill. Despite this change in the rules, a minority of the Senate—two-fifths of its members—can still prevent a majority from working its will. This emphasis on minority rights differentiates the Senate rules from those of the House of Representatives, where a simple majority of the members can vote to end debate.

Interpreting Rules and Precedents. As the rules and precedents of the Senate became more complex, the Senate established the office of parliamentarian. Charles L. Watkins was named the first parliamentarian in 1937; he served until 1964. The Senate parliamentarian is charged with maintaining the precedents and advising the chair on procedural matters. The parliamentarian sits below the presiding officer and whispers advice, which is then repeated by the chair. The parliamentarian is appointed by the secretary of the Senate after consultation with the majority leader.

Committee Rules and Procedures. The major change in the Senate rules in the second half of the twentieth century was the 1979 inclusion of many specific rules controlling committee activities. Among its other provisions, Rule XXVI allows the committees to adopt their own rules and procedures as long as they are consistent with the standing rules of the Senate. Rule XXVI has, however, only one enforceable stipulation involving committee procedures: the requirement that a physical quorum be present when any measure or matter is reported. Under the rule, the presence of such a quorum is "deemed to be a ratification by the Committee of all previous action." The presence of a quorum means that no point of order can be raised against the measure on the Senate floor based on any previous action by the committee. Thus, despite their detail, Rule XXVI and the committee rules themselves are nonbinding.

Committees usually have regular meeting days, but a committee may meet at the call of its chair or, at other times, on the request of a majority of its members. Matters on the committee calendar are usually the order of business during a committee meeting, but any matter within the committee's jurisdiction may be considered. Most committees have standing subcommittees to which they may refer pending bills. Ad hoc subcommittees are frequently appointed to study and report on particular bills or subjects of interest. The chairman, or some designated member of the committee, reports bills to the Senate, where they are placed on the Senate calendar of business unless unanimous consent is given for immediate consideration.

In practice, most committees reflect the interests and temperaments of the chairman, who is usually selected by virtue of seniority. The style of the chairman, rather than the rules, often establishes the procedures of the committee.

Floor Procedures. Generally speaking, procedures on the Senate floor are controlled not by the rules but by the majority and minority leaders. Although designed to establish a regime for handling legislation, nominations, and treaties—the three major responsibilities of the Senate—the rules are routinely ignored. Instead, legislative business usually is considered under ad hoc unanimous consent agreements.

The majority and minority leaders implement and direct the Senate's legislative schedule and program. Most measures are passed on the call of the calendar or by unanimous consent procedure. The more significant and controversial bills are usually considered under a unanimous consent agreement limiting debate and controlling the introduction of amendments. These agreements allow the Senate to transact its business under rules that provide for unlimited debate.

First and second readings. The Senate rules require that, before passage, every bill and joint resolution must have three readings, each on a different legislative day. Two of these readings must occur before the bill or resolution is referred to committee. Bills are seldom read in full, however, since all bills and resolutions are available in printed form. These readings are most commonly dispensed with by unanimous consent. The requirement that readings occur on different legislative days is rarely invoked and usually only when there are procedural conflicts. This requirement, however, can still be

forced on the Senate by a single senator. After the second reading of a bill, it is referred by the presiding officer to that standing committee that in his or her judgment has jurisdiction of the subject matter. The Senate rules require action by the joint leadership or unanimous consent to refer a bill jointly or sequentially to two or more committees.

Once a bill has been introduced or reported by a committee, it is placed on the Senate calendar. Placement on the calendar does not guarantee consideration by the full Senate, however, and this is the point where an understanding of the rules and procedure can be very significant. A bill may be brought to the floor by a simple majority vote if it has been on the calendar for one legislative day. Again, it is the majority leader who normally makes the motion to proceed to consideration of a bill. Since the motion to proceed is a debatable motion, it is usually made after negotiation with possible opponents and when a unanimous consent agreement has been successfully formulated.

On very controversial matters, the Senate frequently has to resort to cloture, or limiting debate, to work its will. Under Rule XXII, three-fifths of the Senate (sixty senators) can vote to limit debate. Once cloture is invoked, debate is limited to one hour for each senator, with a maximum of thirty hours unless that time limit is increased by a three-fifths vote.

Amendments. Once a bill or resolution is before the Senate, it is subject to amendment, both by the committee reporting it and by individual senators. With one exception, committee amendments take priority over those introduced by individual senators and are considered in the order they appear in the printed copy of the measure before the Senate. Once the committee amendments have been disposed of, any senator may propose amendments to any part of the bill not already amended. While such an amendment (called an amendment in the first degree) is pending, an amendment to that amendment (an amendment in the second degree) is in order. Much of the action on controversial bills involves the amending process, and the procedure can be very technical, involving amendments in the first and second degree. Each of these procedures has its own set of rules and governing precedents, which differ from those of the House of Representatives. Moreover, there are special procedures for amendments to certain types of bills—general appropriations and budget bills, for example. Nongermane amendments are prohibited in certain cases—for example, general appropriations bills, bills upon which cloture has been voted, and concurrent resolutions considered under the Congressional Budget and Impoundment Control Act of 1974. Otherwise, there is no requirement of germaneness.

In most instances proposed amendments need not be germane to pending legislation. The right of every senator to offer nongermane amendments, except as noted above or unless constrained by a unanimous consent agreement, has long been a distinguishing feature of Senate procedure. It provides individual senators, or groups of senators, a range of options through the amending process. A senator may introduce nongermane amendments to (1) alter dramatically or effectively kill legislation proposed by a committee, (2) bypass committees entirely by bringing new issues directly before the Senate, or (3) prolong debate and thus deter a final vote as a statement of opposition to pending legislation.

Third reading and vote. When all committee amendments and individual floor amendments have been disposed of, a bill is ordered "engrossed" and is read for a third time. This reading is by title only. The senators then vote on the bill, which is passed by majority vote. Even at this point, senators can use certain procedures to kill or avoid further proceedings on a bill. For example, at any time before final passage, a bill can be "laid on the table," or postponed indefinitely. It can be referred back to committee (or to another committee). It can even be displaced by a majority vote to move action to another bill.

Most bills are passed by a voice vote only, although any senator can request a roll-call vote. A roll-call vote is taken if one-fifth of the senators demand it. Even after passage of a bill, a senator who voted with the majority or did not vote can move to "reconsider" the bill. A majority vote determines questions of reconsideration. It is extremely unusual for the Senate to reconsider a vote, and these motions are routinely tabled by unanimous consent.

Unfinished Business. Congress measures itself by *sessions* of varying duration, up to one year, and *Congresses,* which last for two years. Bills and resolutions started on their way to enactment but left unfinished at the end of one session of a Congress are carried over to the next session. Bills pending at the end of a final session of a Congress, however, do not carry over and must be reintroduced if they are to be considered again.

Executive Matters. In addition to its legislative responsibilities, the Senate is charged with the executive functions of providing "advice and consent" on nominations and treaties. These functions are handled separately from legislative business, and executive business is governed by unique rules and procedures.

Treaties. To discuss treaties, the Senate moves into executive session—a special period during which the Senate considers those matters that it shares only with the executive branch of government and not with the House of Representatives. The Senate may decide to consider a treaty in closed or secret session, and it has sometimes done so when classified material was being discussed. Most often, however, treaties are considered in open session.

Rule XXX, which governs the procedures involving treaties, requires a two-thirds majority to ratify a treaty. Unlike ordinary legislation and nominations, treaties do not die at the end of a Congress. For example, the Genocide treaty was submitted by President Harry S. Truman in 1949 and remained before the Senate for thirty-seven years until it was finally ratified in 1986.

Nominations. A presidential nomination requiring advice and consent must be approved by a majority vote of the Senate. After a nomination is received, it is referred to the appropriate committee, which holds hearings and votes to recommend or reject confirmation. If approved by the committee, the nomination is reported back to the Senate for debate and vote. If the nomination is confirmed, a resolution of confirmation is transmitted to the White House and the appointment is then signed by the president.

Presidential nominations may be made during Senate recesses. The Constitution authorizes the president to "fill up" vacancies that may occur during such recesses "by granting Commissions which shall expire at the end of the next session." Such nominations are thus valid only for the current session of the Senate and must be renewed again with full advice and consent when the session ends. The use of recess appointments to the Supreme Court troubled senators enough that on 29 August 1960 they passed a sense of the Senate resolution stating that "such appointments . . . should not be made except under unusual circumstances and for the purpose of preventing or ending a demonstrable breakdown in the administration of the Court's business."

Unlike treaties, nominations that are not acted on in a session die and must be resubmitted to the Senate at the next session. Nominations that are not confirmed before a recess of more than thirty days are also returned to the president and must be resubmitted.

[*The preceding article is designed to provide an overview of rules of procedure in the Senate. The encyclopedia includes numerous other entries on particular rules and procedures, which can be found by consulting the Synoptic Outline of Contents, the Glossary, and the Index in the back of volume 4. See also* Manuals of Procedure, *article on* Senate Manuals; Parliamentarian, *article on* Senate Parliamentarian; Precedents, *article on* Senate Precedents; Rules and Administration Committee, Senate. *For comparable discussion of the House, see* House of Representatives, *article on* House Rules and Procedures.]

BIBLIOGRAPHY

Haynes, George H. *The Senate of the United States: Its History and Practice.* 1938.

Oleszek, Walter J. *Congressional Procedures and the Policy Process.* 2d ed. 1984.

Rothman, David J. *Politics and Power: The United States Senate, 1869–1901.* 1966.

Tiefer, Charles. *Congressional Practice and Procedure.* 1989.

U.S. Senate. Committee on Rules and Administration. *Rules and Manual of the United States Senate.* 102d Cong., 1st sess., 1992. S. Doc. 102-1.

U.S. Senate. *Senate Procedure, Precedents, and Practices,* by Floyd M. Riddick. 97th Cong., 1st sess., 1981. S. Doc. 97-2.

Wilson, Woodrow. *Congressional Government.* 1885.

ROBERT B. DOVE

SENATOR.

The term *senator* (which in Latin means "old man") derives from ancient Rome, whose senators were at first elected by patricians and later appointed to posts that combined legislative and administrative duties. Article I, section 3, paragraph 3 of the Constitution requires that a senator be thirty years of age, a U.S. citizen for nine years, and an inhabitant of the state from which he or she is chosen. Under the terms of one of the entrenched clauses of the Constitution (Article V), each state is guaranteed two senators, a right that cannot be taken away without the state's consent.

The Constitution also specifies that the Senate be divided into three classes and that one-third of the Senate be chosen every second year. This provides a six-year term for each senator and accounts for the continuity of the Senate, that is, the fact that two-thirds of its membership carries over from one Congress to the next.

The popular election of senators was established in 1913 with the ratification of the Seventeenth Amendment. (Before that, senators were named by their respective state legislators.) Unlike members of the House of Representatives, senators may be appointed by governors when vacancies occur because of death, resignation, or disqualification. No senator may be appointed during his or her term to any other civil office in the United States.

Senators have every legislative power available to members of the House of Representatives except the power to originate revenue bills, and they have the additional power to "advise and consent" on nominations and treaties. Further, senators sit in judgment on impeachments voted by the House of Representatives.

BIBLIOGRAPHY

Davidson, Roger H., and Oleszek, Walter J. *Congress and Its Members.* 2d ed. 1985.

ROBERT B. DOVE

SENATORIAL COURTESY.

An old and traditional practice, senatorial courtesy permits individual senators, under some circumstances, to prevent the confirmation of a presidential appointment. The practice has evolved over time, but its roots are traceable to the First Congress.

In 1789, George Washington nominated Benjamin Fishbourn to be the naval officer of the port of Savannah, Georgia. Fishbourn had had a successful military career and had served in the state government in Georgia. By any applicable standard, he was qualified for the federal post. But Fishbourn did not have the support of William Few and James Gunn, Georgia's two senators. They had a candidate of their own for the position. Out of courtesy to their colleagues from Georgia, the other members of the Senate declined to confirm Washington's nomination of Fishbourn. Thus was born the tradition of senatorial courtesy.

The custom evolved in subsequent years to include several important dimensions. With few exceptions, a senator may seek the courtesy of colleagues in rejecting nominees only for positions whose jurisdiction falls within the state represented by that senator—for example, U.S. marshals, U.S. attorneys, and federal district court judges. To exercise a claim of senatorial courtesy, a senator must usually be a member of the same political party as the president. Until the early 1930s, a senator only needed to inform his colleagues that he found a nominee "personally obnoxious" to receive their courtesy in withholding confirmation. Since then, senators have been expected as well to state their reasons for opposition to a nominee.

The evolution of senatorial courtesy turned the appointment process on its head for those positions that have jurisdiction within the confines of a single state. Typically, the senator or senators of the president's party representing a state where such an appointment is to be made select a candidate for the position and recommend that person to the president. In most cases, the president nominates the person recommended and the Senate routinely confirms the appointment. For example, if there was a district court vacancy in the state of New York and one of that state's senators was a member of the president's party, the senator would normally select a candidate for the judgeship and pass the recommendation on to the president. The Justice Department would investigate the candidate's suitability, and, assuming that no potentially embarrassing information was turned up, the president would nominate the candidate proposed by the senator.

The custom of senatorial courtesy is occasionally violated. Presidents do not always accept recommendations received from senators. Sometimes senators who are not members of the president's party are permitted to select candidates for positions in their states—usually when the president is seeking their support on legislation or other matters. And sometimes, though rarely, the Senate will confirm a nominee even after a colleague has declared the nominee "personally obnoxious."

Senatorial courtesy has become a less significant component of the appointment process in recent years because the number of presidentially appointed positions with jurisdiction in a single state has diminished, recent presidents have more jealously guarded their control over their appointments than ever before, and the decline of political parties generally and of senators' attachment to their state parties has reduced the importance of patronage appointments as part of the political rewards system.

[*See also* Advice and Consent.]

BIBLIOGRAPHY

Harris, Joseph P. *The Advice and Consent of the Senate: A Study of the Confirmation of Appointments.* 1968.

Mackenzie, G. Calvin. *The Politics of Presidential Appointments.* 1981.

G. CALVIN MACKENZIE

SENIORITY. The rank of a member of Congress is determined by seniority. Although seniority is not part of formal chamber or party rules, it is a well-established tradition in both houses of Congress. Rank in the House or Senate chamber is known as *chamber seniority;* rank on a committee—based on length of service on that panel—is called *committee seniority.*

Chamber Seniority. The formal starting date of a member's service—usually 3 January, the official beginning of a new Congress—determines his or her chamber seniority. When a senator fills an unexpired term, the date of appointment, certification, or swearing in determines the official date. In the House, the date of the new member's election determines the starting date.

For members sworn in on the same date, prior experience is a factor in determining seniority. In the Senate, prior Senate, House, and gubernatorial service, in that order, count toward seniority. The most senior member of the Senate of the majority party is usually designated the president pro tempore. In the House, only prior House service counts toward seniority. In both chambers, if members still have equal rank, seniority is determined by listing members alphabetically. Until 1980, a senator could gain several days' seniority if his or her predecessor resigned before the end of his or her term and the new member was then sworn in early. In that year, both parties eliminated the practice of giving these new senators an edge in seniority for obtaining committee assignments.

Chamber seniority is important in bidding for room assignments, gaining access to patronage appointments, and, in the House, floor recognition. Seniority is also vital to the committee assignment process and therefore to the selection of committee and subcommittee chairmen.

Committee Seniority. Most scholars agree that committee seniority became evident in the Senate by the 1840s, seems to have been followed more strictly in both chambers after the Civil War, and was firmly entrenched in the House by 1910. Prior to 1840, seniority was relatively unimportant, in part because of the high turnover among members that reflected a widely held belief in the concept of the "citizen legislator" (espoused since the earliest days of the nation) as well as the difficulty in traveling to and staying in Washington, D.C., during the congressional session and the relative weakness of political parties. After the Civil War, however, tenure became longer as members began making legislative service a career and political parties gained increased influence. Accordingly, the seniority system gained strength, a development that reflected also the evolution of committees as powerful and autonomous entities and the concomitant growing importance of committee chairmen.

In the House, the year 1910 marks an entrenchment of the seniority system, in part related to the overthrow of Speaker Joseph G. Cannon (R-Ill.). Members made it clear that they wanted stronger adherence to seniority in the selection of committee chairmen, as opposed to allowing the Speaker continued wide discretion in making such appointments. Speaker Cannon, especially, had often bypassed more senior members in selecting committee chairmen in order to appoint members who agreed with his conservative philosophy.

Despite growing adherence to the system, there were some major departures from seniority during its early period in both the House and the Senate. For example, in 1859, Sen. Stephen A. Douglas (D-Ill.) was removed as chairman of the Committee on Territories when he refused to support President James Buchanan on the issue of slavery in the territories. In 1866, three Senate Republican committee chairmen were dropped to the bottom of their committees for failing to vote with the Radical Republicans on overriding a presidential veto of a civil rights bill. In 1871, Sen. Charles Sumner (R-Mass.) was removed as chairman of the Committee on Foreign Relations because of his disagreement with President Ulysses S. Grant over annexation of the Dominican Republic. In 1913, Sen. Benjamin R. Tillman (D-S.C.) was denied the chairmanship of the Appropriations Committee.

In 1882, Sen. Wilkinson Call (D-Fla.) made an unsuccessful attempt to limit members to service on one major committee. In 1919, following the lead of former senator Call, Sen. George W. Norris (R-Nebr.), who earlier had led the revolt in the House against Speaker Cannon, unsuccessfully sought to limit members to seats on two major committees. In 1924, with Republicans in the majority, Sen. Albert B. Cummins (R-Iowa) lost the chairmanship of the Interstate Commerce Committee because he was also president pro tempore. The next-ranking Republican, Robert M. La Follette of Wisconsin, was also passed over. In a rare move, the chairmanship was granted to Democrat Ellison D. Smith (S.C.). In 1925, Rep. John M. Nelson (R-Wis.), chairman of the House Committee on Elections; Rep. Florian Lampert (R-Wis.), chairman of the Committee on Patents; and nine other Wisconsin members were stripped of their seniority and dropped to the bottom of their committees or moved to less influential committees for supporting La Follette's 1924 Progressive Party presidential bid.

With the adoption of the Legislative Reorganization Act of 1946, some committees were abolished or consolidated, giving some of the surviving committees wider jurisdictions. Accordingly, committee chairmen gained greater power and authority. In addition, in the years following World War II, lower turnover among members strengthened the already powerful seniority system, in particular by entrenching Democratic committee chairmen from southern states.

The first assault on the seniority system occurred in the Senate, when in 1953 the Democrats enacted the Johnson Rule (named after Minority Leader Lyndon B. Johnson of Texas), which provided that all Democratic senators be given a seat on a major committee before any Democrat be assigned a second seat on a major committee. The Republican conference informally adopted the Johnson Rule in 1959 and formally adopted it in 1965.

Despite the strong hold of the seniority system, exceptions to it continued to be made. For example, in 1965, the House Democratic caucus censured and stripped of seniority Representatives John Bell Williams of Mississippi and Albert W. Watson of South Carolina for having supported Republican presidential nominee Barry Goldwater the previous year. Both were dropped to the bottom of their committees. For Representative Williams, who ranked second on the Commerce Committee and fifth on the District of Columbia Committee, it was a severe blow.

In 1967, following prolonged ethical and legal battles, the House excluded Rep. Adam Clayton Powell, Jr. (D-N.Y.), from the 90th Congress. The following session, after winning reelection, Powell was seated in the House but was removed as chairman of the Education and Labor Committee and made the lowest-ranking Democrat on the panel.

In 1969, the Democratic caucus stripped Rep. John R. Rarick (La.) of his seniority on the Agriculture Committee for having supported third-party candidate George Wallace in his 1968 presidential bid. (Representative Rarick was the lowest-ranking member of the Agriculture Committee, so the impact was minimal.)

Changes in the Seniority System. The 1970s saw numerous congressional reforms enacted. Many were aimed at decentralizing power to give the large influx of junior Democratic, often liberal, members more of a voice in the workings of their chambers. These new members targeted the seniority system because they believed that limiting its influence was one way they could quickly obtain greater power over the mostly southern and conservative committee chairmen. Electing chairmen by secret ballot and putting limits on the number of chairmanships a member could hold weakened the seniority system and held members more accountable to junior rank-and-file members. Most of the changes made during this period, and indeed after, were made to the respective party rules rather than to chamber rules, since party leaders believed that, were changes to seniority made through legislative vehicles, a bipartisan coalition could hinder the majority's control of the legislative agenda.

In 1970, the House rejected two floor amendments to the Legislative Reorganization Act of 1970 relating to the seniority system. By a teller vote of 160 to 73, the House rejected an amendment offered by Rep. Henry S. Reuss (D-Wis.) that provided that seniority need not be the sole criterion for the selection of chairmen. A second amendment, by Rep. Fred Schwengel (R-Iowa), was rejected 196 to 28. This amendment would have provided that chairmen be selected by committee majority members from among the three most senior members.

In 1971, House Democratic caucus rules were changed so that, first, the Committee on Committees (then composed of Democratic members of the Ways and Means Committee) could recommend chairmen regardless of seniority, and, second, no member could chair more than one legislative subcommittee. Obviously, the latter change especially affected more senior members, forcing them to relinquish such chairmanships. These changes were recommended by the newly formed Democratic caucus Committee on Organization, Study, and Review, created in 1970 to examine party organization and the seniority system. Simultaneously, House Republicans were changing Republican conference rules to allow votes on nominations for ranking minority members, thereby not relying solely on seniority. This change was the product of the Conference Task Force on Seniority headed by Rep. Barber B. Conable of New York.

In 1971 the Senate Democratic caucus modified its rules to allow a caucus meeting to be called by any member and to allow any senator to challenge any Steering Committee chairmanship nomination.

In the same year, Senate Republican conference rules were modified to allow members to serve as ranking member on only one standing committee. Also in that year, both parties established panels to study the seniority system; three Democrats and five Republicans on their two respective partisan panels were charged with the task. On 16 March 1971, however, the Senate tabled a resolution—thereby effectively killing it—that would have permitted committee chairmen to be selected on bases other than seniority.

Notwithstanding the changes discussed, during the 92d Congress (1971–1973), all chairmanships and ranking minority slots in both chambers were held by the committees' senior members. In 1973, the Senate Republicans did make a change affecting the seniority system when they adopted a conference rule that permitted Republican members of each standing committee to elect the ranking Republican and not use seniority as the sole criterion for selection. During the first selection after the change, several senior Republicans were challenged, but none of the challenges were successful.

In October 1974, the House adopted numerous changes to the committee system recommended by the Select Committee on Committees (the Bolling Committee), as modified by the Democratic caucus Committee on Organization, Study, and Review (the Hansen Committee). One month later, with the election of 1974, the so-called Watergate class came to Congress, many of whom had their eyes set on changing the institution, especially the House. More than seventy new Democratic members were elected, and one of their first targets was the seniority system within the new committee structure.

In the House, several changes were made to party rules when the early organizational meetings (authorized by the Bolling Committee) convened to plan for the new Congress. By a relatively close vote of 147 to 116 Democratic caucus rules were changed to make all Appropriations Committee subcommittee chairmen subject to a full caucus vote rather than just a vote of Appropriations Committee Democrats, as had previously been the case. (In 1992, caucus rules were changed again to extend the same requirement to the Ways and Means Committee subcommittee chairmen). An attempt to authorize the caucus to vote on all subcommittee chairmen was, however, rejected. The caucus also voted to authorize a secret ballot on all chairmanship nominations. Also, the new caucus rules allowed competitive nominations if the original Steering and Policy Committee's nominee were defeated.

Perhaps the greatest triumph of the incoming class was the overthrow of three sitting committee chairmen: William R. Poage (Tex.) of Agriculture, F. Edward Hébert (La.) of Armed Services, and Wright Patman (Tex.) of Banking and Currency, all of whom the younger members perceived as too old and out of touch. It is interesting to note that the next-senior members of the Agriculture and Armed Services committees became their chairmen, while the fourth-ranking Democrat, Henry Reuss of Wisconsin, assumed the chairmanship of the Banking Committee. It is also worth noting, and ironic, that the Armed Services chair went to Charles M. Price of Illinois, who lost his chairmanship ten years later to a member then seventh in seniority. Also in 1975, two House committee chairmen were denied subcommittee chairs despite their seniority. This instituted a trend toward removal of chairmen of committees, and especially subcommittees, without regard to seniority that continued to the early 1990s. Other recommendations considered by the caucus were defeated, including one to impose an age limit of seventy on committee chairmen and another to limit the length of time a member could serve as a committee chair to no more than three consecutive Congresses.

The Senate in 1975 adopted no major-party rules changes expressly related to seniority. However, one Democratic change that year—allowing any senator to call a caucus meeting to challenge a nominated chairman—has been interpreted as making committee leaders more accountable.

In 1977, the Senate effected a major reorganization of its committee system that, among other things, opened up many more committee leadership slots to junior members. The committee and subcommittee assignment process was also altered by limiting the number of slots a member could occupy, further diluting the power of the seniority system. Also in 1977, a sitting House Appropriations subcommittee chairman, Rep. Robert L. F. Sikes of Florida, who chaired the Military Construction Subcommittee, was rejected by the Democratic caucus, 189 to 93, following a House reprimand of him the previous year. Two years later, three subcommittee chairmen on the House Commerce and House Government Operations committees were removed and replaced by less senior members.

Later Developments. The reforms of the 1970s democratized the process for selecting committee chairmen and allowed the selection to be based on criteria other than just seniority. Nevertheless, seniority in most cases is still the preeminent factor in determining chairmanships.

Yet in the 1980s several additional nominations for House subcommittee chairman were rejected in favor of more junior members. For example, in 1981, two subcommittee chairmen were rejected and replaced by more junior members. The Senate, however, fervently adhered to the seniority system, even during the six years when the Republicans were in the majority. In 1987, Republican senators Richard G. Lugar of Indiana and Jesse Helms of North Carolina vied for the ranking minority slot on the Foreign Relations Committee. Senator Lugar had chaired Foreign Relations during the previous Congress, but, although they had joined the committee the same day, Senator Helms had served in the Senate longer than Senator Lugar. The position was therefore given to Helms despite the misgivings of many members concerning the latter's policy views.

A number of proposed new caucus rules were defeated during the 1980s. An attempt to impose an age limit of seventy for all chairmen was rejected, as was limiting service to three consecutive terms.

In 1985, Charles Price of Illinois, chairman of the House Armed Services Committee, was unseated at the Democratic caucus meeting. The seventh-ranked Democrat, Les Aspin of Wisconsin, won the chairmanship even though the caucus had nominated the next most senior Democrat, Charles E. Bennett of Florida.

In 1990, two House chairmen, Glenn M. Anderson (Calif.) of the Public Works and Transportation Committee and Frank Annunzio (Ill.) of the House Administration Committee, were deposed, in part because they were perceived as weak, ineffective leaders not protective enough of their committee's jurisdictional prerogatives. Each was replaced by the most senior Democrat available for service.

Proposed Adjustments or Alternatives. Over the years, adjustments in or alternatives to the seniority system have been proposed by organizations calling for reform, by individual members, and by congressional scholars. Some of the most notable options were presented by the liberal Democratic Study Group in 1970. They and others since have suggested the following changes to House rules and practices:

Use the seniority system to nominate chairmen, subject to majority approval by the party caucus (very similar to current practice but not always bowing to seniority)

Have the caucus elect committee chairmen from among the three most senior members of each committee

Authorize the Speaker to nominate chairmen, subject to approval of a majority of the caucus

Authorize the majority members of each committee to nominate the chairmen, subject to caucus approval

Authorize both majority and minority party members of each committee to select the chairmen, subject to full House approval

Establish a special committee to nominate chairmen, subject to majority caucus approval

Impose an age limitation on committee chairmen

Impose a limit on the number of years members can serve as chairmen

Rotate the chairmanships among the three most senior members every two years.

Despite continuing concerns about the seniority system and the recommended changes, Congress still retains it. Perhaps the views of Emanuel Celler (D-N.Y.), former dean of the House during the 92d Congress, are illustrative. He stated that the system survives in part because it is "the least objectionable of all systems for elevation of men to chairmanships."

[*See also* Committees, *article on* Assignment of Members; Leadership; Legislative Reorganization Acts.]

BIBLIOGRAPHY

Aboam, Michael, and Joseph Cooper. "The Rise of Seniority in the House of Representatives." *Polity* 1 (Fall 1968): 52–84.

Goodwin, George. "Seniority System in Congress." *American Political Science Review* 53 (1959): 412–436.

Hinckley, Barbara. *The Seniority System in Congress.* 1971.

Polsby, Nelson W., Miriam Gallaher, and Barry S. Rundquist. "Growth of the Seniority System in the U.S. House of Representatives." *American Political Science Review* 63 (1969): 787–807.

Wolanin, Thomas R. "Committee Seniority and the Choice of House Subcommittee Chairmen: 80th–91st Congresses." *Journal of Politics* 36 (1974): 687–702.

JUDY SCHNEIDER

SEPARATION OF POWERS.

A bedrock concept of the constitutional system, separation of powers is the allocation of authority among the three branches of government as a means to avoid tyranny by ensuring that different parts of the government will be responsive to different constituencies. Advocated in the writings of John Locke and Charles Montesquieu and recognized by the First Continental Congress as a necessity of good government, separation of powers is reflected in the institutional structure of Congress in two ways.

First, Congress's key power of lawmaking is shared with the president, in that the president may propose legislation, inform Congress of the state of the Union, convene special congressional sessions, and veto bills. The courts may pass on the constitutionality of laws through judicial review, and Congress may initiate amendments to the Constitution to change Court rulings.

Second, Congress is a bicameral institution composed of two houses, the Senate and House of Representatives, whose members are elected from different constituencies (states versus districts) and serve terms of different lengths (six years versus two years) and which are also organized differently (two senators from each state versus population-based representation). This arrangement was sought to balance the popularly based House against the more deliberative and elitist Senate, the members of which were originally elected by state legislatures. Thus the two chambers have often found themselves at odds over ideological, partisan, or regional differences. In the 1980s, for example, divided party control between the houses impeded their ability to deal in a unified way with the president on important issues. While in this way losing a measure of institutional efficiency, Congress has gained representational diversity and internal checks.

BIBLIOGRAPHY

Fisher, Louis. *Constitutional Conflicts between Congress and the President.* 1991.

Spitzer, Robert J. *President and Congress: Executive Hegemony at the Crossroads of American Government.* 1993.

ROBERT J. SPITZER

SEQUESTRATION.

The Balanced Budget and Emergency Deficit Control Act of 1985 (more commonly known as the Gramm-Rudman-Hollings Act) established the emergency procedure known as sequestration, in which automatic, across-the-board reductions in spending are made to reduce the deficit.

In 1985, Congress enacted Gramm-Rudman-Hollings because of widespread concern over the federal deficit. The act established declining annual deficit targets leading to budgetary balance by fiscal year 1991. It established sequestration to eliminate any estimated deficit in excess of the annual target for a fiscal year. Sequestration was intended to force the president and Congress to agree on deficit reduction legislation by creating an unacceptable alternative to inaction—large, across-the-board reductions in spending. In 1987, Congress amended Gramm-Rudman to revise and extend the deficit targets through fiscal year 1993 and to restore the automatic triggering feature of sequestration invalidated by the Supreme Court in *Bowsher v. Synar* (1986).

The Budget Enforcement Act of 1990 (BEA) established five-year procedures to enforce the 1990 deficit reduction agreement reached between President George Bush and congressional leaders. It changed sequestration from a procedure for reducing the estimated deficit to a declining annual target into a procedure for preventing new legislation from increasing the deficit further. Under the BEA, it was intended that sequestration would be triggered only if annual appropriations acts breached discretionary spending limits or if mandatory spending or tax legislation increased the deficit. (These requirements have been extended through fiscal year 1998 by the Omnibus Budget Reconciliation Act of 1993.)

BIBLIOGRAPHY

Joyce, Philip G., and Robert D. Reischauer. "Deficit Budgeting: The Federal Budget Process and Budget Reform." *Harvard Journal on Legislation* 29 (1992): 429–453.

U.S. House of Representatives. Committee on Ways and Means. *Description of the Congressional Budget Process and Sequestration Under the Gramm-Rudman-Hollings Act: Overview of Entitlement Programs.* 102d Cong., 2d sess., 1992. Committee Print 102-44.

EDWARD DAVIS

SERGEANT AT ARMS. Both the Senate and the House of Representatives have an officer of that body who carries the title sergeant at arms and who is elected by the respective body at the beginning of each Congress. The responsibilities of the position are defined in the rules of each house, in law, in policies determined by the appropriate House or Senate committee, and in precedents and customs. They or their assistants attend all floor sessions and are the chief law enforcement officers of Congress. They are responsible for maintaining

THE SERGEANT AT ARMS. Bearing the mace in the House of Representatives. Engraving, 1877.
LIBRARY OF CONGRESS

order in the chamber and for the security of the buildings and grounds under the jurisdiction of Congress. Along with the Architect of the Capitol the sergeants at arms comprise the Capitol Police Board and the Capitol Guide Board.

The Constitution enumerates the responsibilities of Congress, but it is silent as to the organization and structure of the legislature. At the convening of the First Congress each body organized itself, electing officers and adopting rules. The House of Representatives elected its first sergeant at arms on 12 May 1789. The Senate selected a doorkeeper but in 1798 expanded the duties and bestowed the title sergeant at arms.

The sergeants at arms are charged with carrying out Article I, section 5 of the Constitution, which authorizes the House and Senate "to compel the Attendance of absent Members" in order to achieve the quorum necessary to conduct business. Although seldom used, this includes the power to arrest absent members and escort them into the chamber.

The sergeant at arms is responsible for maintaining order in each chamber. The Speaker of the first House of Representatives, Frederick A. C. Muhlen-

Sergeants at Arms of the House

NAME	DATES OF SERVICE
Joseph Wheaton	12 May 1789–27 October 1807
Thomas Dunn	27 October 1807–5 December 1824
John Dunn	6 December 1824–3 December 1833
Thomas B. Randolph	3 December 1833–15 December 1835
Roderick Dorsey	15 December 1835–8 June 1841
Eleazor M. Townsend	8 June 1841–7 December 1843
Newton Lane	7 December 1843–8 December 1847
Nathan Sargent	8 December 1847–15 January 1850
Adam J. Glossbrenner[1]	15 January 1850–3 February 1860
Henry W. Hoffman[2]	3 February 1860–5 July 1861
Edward Ball[3]	5 July 1861–8 December 1863
Nathaniel G. Ordway	8 December 1863–6 December 1875
John G. Thompson	6 December 1875–5 December 1881
George W. Hooker	5 December 1881–4 December 1883
John P. Leedom[4]	4 December 1883–2 December 1889
Adoniram J. Holmes[5]	2 December 1889–8 December 1891
Samuel S. Yoder[6]	8 December 1891–7 August 1893
Herman W. Snow[7]	7 August 1893–2 December 1895
Benjamin F. Russell	2 December 1895–4 December 1899
Henry Casson	4 December 1899–4 April 1911
Ulysses Jackson	4 April 1911–22 June 1912
Charles F. Riddell	18 July 1912–7 April 1913
Robert B. Gordon[8]	7 April 1913–19 May 1919
Joseph G. Rogers	19 May 1919–7 December 1931
Kenneth Romney	7 December 1931–3 January 1947
William F. Russell	3 January 1947–3 January 1949
Joseph H. Callahan	3 January 1949–3 January 1953
William F. Russell	3 January 1953–7 July 1953
Lyle O. Snader	8 July 1953–15 September 1953
William R. Bonsell	15 September 1953–5 January 1955
Zeake W. Johnson, Jr.	5 January 1955–30 September 1972
Kenneth R. Harding	1 October 1972–29 February 1980
Benjamin J. Guthrie	1 March 1980–2 January 1983
Jack Russ	3 January 1983–12 March 1992
Werner W. Brandt	12 March 1992–

[1]Served in the House of Representatives from 1865 to 1869.
[2]Served in the House of Representatives from 1855 to 1857.
[3]Served in the House of Representatives from 1853 to 1857.
[4]Served in the House of Representatives from 1881 to 1883.
[5]Served in the House of Representatives from 1883 to 1889.
[6]Served in the House of Representatives from 1887 to 1891.
[7]Served in the House of Representatives from 1891 to 1893.
[8]Served in the House of Representatives from 1899 to 1903.
SOURCE: Office of the Sergeant at Arms, U.S. House of Representatives

Sergeants at Arms of the Senate

NAME	DATES OF SERVICE
James Mathers	7 April 1789–2 September 1811[1]
Mountjoy Bayly	6 November 1811–9 December 1833
John Shackford	9 December 1833–1837[2]
Stephen Haight	4 September 1837–7 June 1841
Edward Dyer	7 June 1841–9 December 1845
Robert Beale	9 December 1845–17 March 1853
Dunning R. McNair	17 March 1853–1861[2]
George T. Brown	6 July 1861–22 March 1869
John R. French	22 March 1869–24 March 1879
Richard J. Bright	24 March 1879–18 December 1883
William P. Canady	18 December 1883–30 June 1890
Edward K. Valentine	30 June 1890–7 August 1893
Richard J. Bright	8 August 1893–1 February 1900
Daniel M. Ransdell	1 February 1900–26 August 1912[3]
Edgar Livingstone Cornelius	10 December 1912–4 March 1913
Charles P. Higgins	13 March 1913–3 March 1919
David S. Barry	19 May 1919–7 February 1933
Chesley W. Jurney	9 March 1933–31 January 1943
Wall Doxey	1 February 1943–3 January 1947
Edward F. McGinnis	4 January 1947–2 January 1949
Joseph C. Duke	3 January 1949–2 January 1953
Forest A. Harness	3 January 1953–4 January 1955
Joseph C. Duke[4]	5 January 1955–30 December 1965
Robert G. Dunphy	14 January 1966–30 June 1972
William H. Wannall	1 July 1972–17 December 1975
F. Nordy Hoffmann	18 December 1975–4 January 1981
Howard S. Liebengood	5 January 1981–12 September 1983
Larry E. Smith	13 September 1983–2 June 1985
Ernest E. Garcia	3 June 1985–5 January 1987
Henry Kuualoha Giugni	6 January 1987–31 December 1990
Martha S. Pope	3 January 1991–14 April 1994
Robert "Larry" Benoit	15 April 1994–

[1]Died in office.
[2]Died in office; exact date of death unclear.
[3]Died in office; date of death presumed to be 26 August 1912.
[4]Duke is the only person to have been elected sergeant at arms for two nonconsecutive terms.
SOURCE: U.S. Senate Historical Office

burg of Pennsylvania, authorized a mace as the proper symbol for the sergeant at arms. On the rare occasions when a member or group of members on the House floor becomes disorderly, the sergeant at arms, on order of the Speaker, lifts the mace from its pedestal and presents it before the offending member or members, thereby restoring order in the chamber. This happened several times in the nineteenth century, but it has not occurred in recent memory, and there is no complete record of such occasions. The Senate has no device that corresponds to the mace.

The sergeants at arms also greet and escort important visitors to the Capitol, handle funeral arrangements for deceased members, and lead formal processions at ceremonial events such as inaugurations. Foremost among the responsibilities of the sergeants at arms is that of law enforcement, most visible in the Capitol Police Force and the security measures and traffic control on Capitol Hill.

In addition, the House of Representatives and the Senate have given their respective sergeants at Arms additional administrative duties, which are delineated in the rules and precedents of each body. The House sergeant at arms keeps the accounts for the pay and mileage of members and delegates and pays them as provided by law. The Senate sergeant at arms supervises the doorkeepers, the service department, the computer center, the telephone and telecommunications services, the recording studio, the post office, the maintenance workers, the surplus office equipment, and the barber and beauty shops.

BIBLIOGRAPHY

Byrd, Robert C. *The Senate, 1789–1989: Addresses on the History of the United States Senate.* Vol. 2. 1991.

Congressional Quarterly Inc., *Congressional Quarterly's Guide to Congress.* 4th ed. Edited by Mary Cohn. 1991.

U.S. House of Representatives. *Constitution, Jefferson's Manual, and Rules of the House of Representatives, 103d Congress.* Compiled by William Holmes Brown. 102d Cong., 2d sess., 1992. H. Doc. 102–405.

U.S. Senate. Committee on Rules and Administration. *Standing Rules of the Senate.* 102d Cong., 2d sess., 1992. S. Doc. 102–25.

CYNTHIA PEASE MILLER

SERVICE ACADEMIES. During the American Revolution, the colonists had few educated military officers. Clearly the new Republic needed a national school for the education of officers. Congress, by an act of 16 March 1802, authorized President Thomas Jefferson "to organize and establish a corps of engineers" that "shall constitute a military academy." On 4 July 1802, ten cadets reported to the school at a site along the Hudson River at West Point, New York. By the 1990s the cadet corps of the U.S. Military Academy at West Point stood at over four thousand.

Similar demands for a naval academy were not answered until 1845. Widespread public concern about brutal and inhumane treatment of midshipmen during training reached a peak in 1842 when a midshipman (the son of the secretary of War) and several others were hanged aboard ship for inciting to mutiny on the brig *Somers*. The introduction of steam propulsion and increased technology compounded the need for better-qualified officers. In 1845 Secretary of the Navy George Bancroft, in a maneuver to bypass congressional approval for funding, succeeded in getting Secretary of War William L. Marcy to transfer Fort Severn at Annapolis, Maryland, to the Department of the Navy. In October of that year, Bancroft ordered midshipmen who were not attached to ships or a staff to gather at Fort Severn to begin a two-year curriculum (later increased to four years). By 1990 cadets at the U.S. Naval Academy at Annapolis numbered four thousand.

To train Air Force personnel, the U.S. Air Force Academy was established in 1955 at Lowry Air Force Base at Denver, Colorado, until construction of a new academy was completed at a site near Colorado Springs. The corps of cadets in the 1990s was composed of approximately four thousand men and women.

Congress plays a dominant role in the appointment of candidates to the three major service academies: congressional appointees account for nearly three-fourths of the academies' combined enrollment. Until 1902, only representatives appointed candidates for admission, the goal being an equal distribution of appointees throughout the nation. Eventually, senators as well as representatives were authorized to have as many as five appointees at each academy at one time. Candidates may also be nominated by the president and the vice president, and a small number of appointments are reserved for active-duty and reserve personnel, members of the reserve training corps, students in service preparatory schools, and children of deceased or disabled Medal of Honor recipients.

The mission of these academies, today under the Department of Defense, is to provide educated, trained, and motivated men and women to serve as career officers. Of the approximately 11,000 applicants annually, 1,200 men and 150 women are chosen for each academy, with some emphasis on recruitment of minorities. All candidates for appointment must be U.S. citizens of good moral character, not over twenty-one years of age, unmarried, and with no dependents. Though candidates are also required to take physical and scholastic tests and pass a medical examination, members of Congress still exercise considerable freedom in making appointments.

The U.S. Coast Guard Academy at New London, Connecticut, established in 1931, and the Merchant Marine Academy at Kings Point, New York, established in 1938, are organized under the Department of Transportation except in time of war, when they become part of the Department of Defense. Admission requirements for these two academies are quite similar to those of the other service academies, but the selection process differs significantly. Members of Congress may nominate up to ten candidates for appointment to the Merchant Marine Academy, but no appointment is guaranteed; candidates are selected from those scoring highest on a nationwide competitive examination. Congress plays no role in admission to the Coast Guard Academy. No political appointment is needed and there are no state or geographical quotas; candidates are selected solely on the basis of a nationwide competitive examination.

The major service academies require five years of postgraduate service, with the naval requirement to be six years after 1996. The Coast Guard and Merchant Marine academies require six years of service after graduation. Graduates of all academies receive a Bachelor of Science degree and a commission as an officer.

BIBLIOGRAPHY

Congressional Quarterly Inc. *Congressional Quarterly's Guide to Congress.* 4th ed. Edited by Mary Cohn. 1991.
Powers, Helen. *Parent's Guide to the Five U.S. Service Academies.* 1986.

PAOLO E. COLETTA

SESSIONS OF CONGRESS. Each Congress meets for a two-year period that coincides with the two-year terms of representatives. To satisfy its constitutional duty to meet at least once a year, Congress has divided its two-year life into sessions. Since adoption of the Twentieth Amendment in 1933, each session corresponds roughly to the calendar year.

Prior to 1934 the terms of the president, vice president, representatives, and senators started on 4 March of the year following their election, but sessions of Congress usually began later. Since 1934, representatives and senators take office at noon on 3 January following election, and the president and vice president at noon on 20 January, as prescribed in the Twentieth Amendment. This amendment also changed the convening date of a new Congress to correspond with the commencement of members' terms, unless Congress by law determines otherwise. Before that year, sessions usually started in December, although among the 169 sessions between 1789 and 1935, 40 began in a month other than December. Since the Twentieth Amendment took effect, Congress has convened in January, except for two three-session Congresses (the 75th and 76th Congresses, 1937–1941).

Before 1935 Congress often held more than two sessions. Of the seventy-three Congresses between

"NATIONAL CAPITAL MOBILIZATION." An eighteenth-century figure representing the District of Columbia watches the rush of members of Congress arriving from Union Station for a session of Congress. Published in the 1930s, the cartoon alludes to the growth of new federal bureaus and the increased activity in Washington during the New Deal. Clifford K. Berryman, *Washington Evening Star,* 1930s.

U.S. SENATE COLLECTION, CENTER FOR LEGISLATIVE ARCHIVES

1789 and 1935, fifty had two sessions, twenty-two held three, and one had four. From the adoption of the Twentieth Amendment through the 102d Congress, all but the two noted have been two-session Congresses.

Prior to the Twentieth Amendment, the Senate met thirty-one times for brief periods in special session following the election of a president to advise and consent on the president's cabinet and other significant nominees. The Senate also held eleven special sessions to consider other executive nominations and four to consider treaties.

The Constitution empowers presidents to call Congress into extraordinary session. John Adams first invoked this clause in 1797 to ask Congress to debate suspension of relations with France; it was most recently done by Harry S. Truman in 1948 to deal with stalled domestic legislation. Of the twenty-seven such sessions thus far, seven dealt with foreign affairs, three with war, eight with revenues, including tariffs, three with appropriations, and six with domestic policy. Extraordinary sessions have become less common because of the practice of

Dates of Congressional Sessions

CONGRESS	SESSION	TERM
1st	1	4 March 1789–29 September 1789
	2	4 January 1790–12 August 1790
	3	6 December 1790–3 March 1791
2d	1	24 October 1791–8 May 1792
	2	5 November 1792–2 March 1793
3d	1	2 December 1793–9 June 1794
	2	3 November 1794–3 March 1795
4th	1	7 December 1795–1 June 1796
	2	5 December 1796–3 March 1797
5th	1	15 May 1797–10 July 1797
	2	13 November 1797–16 July 1798
	3	3 December 1798–3 March 1799
6th	1	2 December 1799–14 May 1800
	2	17 November 1800–3 March 1801
7th	1	7 December 1801–3 May 1802
	2	6 December 1802–3 March 1803
8th	1	17 October 1803–27 March 1804
	2	5 November 1804–3 March 1805
9th	1	2 December 1805–21 April 1806
	2	1 December 1806–3 March 1807
10th	1	26 October 1807–25 April 1808
	2	7 November 1808–3 March 1809
11th	1	22 May 1809–28 June 1809
	2	27 November 1809–1 May 1810
	3	3 December 1810–3 March 1811
12th	1	4 November 1811–6 July 1812
	2	2 November 1812–3 March 1813
13th	1	24 May 1813–2 August 1813
	2	6 December 1813–18 April 1814
	3	19 September 1814–3 March 1815
14th	1	4 December 1815–30 April 1816
	2	2 December 1816–3 March 1817
15th	1	1 December 1817–20 April 1818
	2	16 November 1818–3 March 1819
16th	1	6 December 1819–15 May 1820
	2	13 November 1820–3 March 1821
17th	1	3 December 1821–8 May 1822
	2	2 December 1822–3 March 1823
18th	1	1 December 1823–27 May 1824
	2	6 December 1824–3 March 1825
19th	1	5 December 1825–22 May 1826
	2	4 December 1826–3 March 1827
20th	1	3 December 1827–26 May 1828
	2	1 December 1828–3 March 1829
21st	1	7 December 1829–31 May 1830
	2	6 December 1830–3 March 1831
22d	1	5 December 1831–16 July 1832
	2	3 December 1832–2 March 1833

Dates of Congressional Sessions (Continued)

CONGRESS	SESSION	TERM
23d	1	2 December 1833–30 June 1834
	2	1 December 1834–3 March 1835
24th	1	7 December 1835–4 July 1836
	2	5 December 1836–3 March 1837
25th	1	4 September 1837–16 October 1837
	2	4 December 1837–9 July 1838
	3	3 December 1838–3 March 1839
26th	1	2 December 1839–21 July 1840
	2	7 December 1840–3 March 1841
27th	1	31 May 1841–13 September 1841
	2	6 December 1841–31 August 1842
	3	5 December 1842–3 March 1843
28th	1	4 December 1843–17 June 1844
	2	2 December 1844–3 March 1845
29th	1	1 December 1845–10 August 1846
	2	7 December 1846–3 March 1847
30th	1	6 December 1847–14 August 1848
	2	4 December 1848–3 March 1849
31st	1	3 December 1849–30 September 1850
	2	2 December 1850–3 March 1851
32d	1	1 December 1851–31 August 1852
	2	6 December 1852–3 March 1853
33d	1	5 December 1853–7 August 1854
	2	4 December 1854–3 March 1855
34th	1	3 December 1855–18 August 1856
	2	21 August 1856–30 August 1857
	3	1 December 1856–3 March 1857
35th	1	7 December 1857–14 June 1858
	2	6 December 1858–3 March 1859
36th	1	5 December 1859–25 June 1860
	2	3 December 1860–28 March 1861
37th	1	4 July 1861–6 August 1861
	2	2 December 1861–17 July 1862
	3	1 December 1862–3 March 1863
38th	1	7 December 1863–4 July 1864
	2	5 December 1864–3 March 1865
39th	1	4 December 1865–28 July 1866
	2	3 December 1866–3 March 1867
40th	1	4 March 1867–2 December 1867
	2	2 December 1867–10 November 1868
	3	7 December 1868–3 March 1869
41st	1	4 March 1869–10 April 1869
	2	6 December 1869–15 July 1870
	3	5 December 1870–3 March 1871
42d	1	4 March 1871–20 April 1871
	2	4 December 1871–10 June 1872
	3	2 December 1872–3 March 1873

Dates of Congressional Sessions (Continued)

CONGRESS	SESSION	TERM
43d	1	1 December 1873–23 June 1874
	2	7 December 1874–3 March 1875
44th	1	6 December 1875–15 August 1876
	2	4 December 1876–3 March 1877
45th	1	15 October 1877–3 December 1877
	2	3 December 1877–20 June 1878
	3	2 December 1878–3 March 1879
46th	1	18 March 1879–1 July 1879
	2	1 December 1879–16 June 1880
	3	6 December 1880–3 March 1881
47th	1	5 December 1881–8 August 1882
	2	4 December 1882–3 March 1883
48th	1	3 December 1883–7 July 1884
	2	1 December 1884–3 March 1885
49th	1	7 December 1885–5 August 1886
	2	6 December 1886–3 March 1887
50th	1	5 December 1887–20 October 1888
	2	3 December 1888–3 March 1889
51st	1	2 December 1889–1 October 1890
	2	1 December 1890–3 March 1891
52d	1	7 December 1891–5 August 1892
	2	5 December 1892–3 March 1893
53d	1	7 August 1893–3 November 1893
	2	4 December 1893–28 August 1894
	3	3 December 1894–3 March 1895
54th	1	2 December 1895–11 June 1896
	2	7 December 1896–3 March 1897
55th	1	15 March 1897–24 July 1897
	2	6 December 1897–8 July 1898
	3	5 December 1898–3 March 1899
56th	1	4 December 1899–7 June 1900
	2	3 December 1900–3 March 1901
57th	1	2 December 1901–1 July 1902
	2	1 December 1902–3 March 1903
58th	1	9 Novemer 1903–7 December 1903
	2	7 December 1903–28 April 1904
	3	5 December 1904–3 March 1905
59th	1	4 December 1905–30 June 1906
	2	3 December 1906–3 March 1907
60th	1	2 December 1907–30 May 1908
	2	7 December 1908–3 March 1909
61st	1	15 March 1909–5 August 1909
	2	6 December 1909–25 June 1910
	3	5 December 1910–3 March 1911
62d	1	4 April 1911–22 August 1911
	2	4 December 1911–26 August 1912
	3	2 December 1912–3 March 1913

Dates of Congressional Sessions (Continued)

CONGRESS	SESSION	TERM
63d	1	7 April 1913–1 December 1913
	2	1 December 1913–24 October 1914
	3	7 December 1914–3 March 1915
64th	1	6 December 1915–8 September 1916
	2	4 December 1916–3 March 1917
65th	1	2 April 1917–6 October 1917
	2	3 December 1917–21 November 1918
	3	2 December 1918–3 March 1919
66th	1	19 May 1919–19 November 1919
	2	1 December 1919–5 June 1920
	3	6 December 1920–3 March 1921
67th	1	11 April 1921–23 November 1921
	2	5 December 1921–22 September 1922
	3	20 November 1922–4 December 1922
	4	4 December 1922–3 March 1923
68th	1	3 December 1923–7 June 1924
	2	1 December 1924–3 March 1925
69th	1	7 December 1925–3 July 1926
	2	6 December 1926–3 March 1927
70th	1	5 December 1927–29 May 1928
	2	3 December 1928–3 March 1929
71st	1	15 April 1929–22 November 1929
	2	2 December 1929–3 July 1930
	3	1 December 1930–3 March 1931
72d	1	7 December 1931–16 July 1932
	2	5 December 1932–3 March 1933
73d	1	9 March 1933–15 June 1933
	2	3 January 1934–18 June 1934
74th	1	3 January 1935–26 August 1935
	2	3 January 1936–20 June 1936
75th	1	5 January 1937–21 August 1937
	2	15 November 1937–21 December 1937
	3	3 January 1938–16 June 1938
76th	1	3 January 1939–5 August 1939
	2	21 September 1939–3 November 1939
	3	3 January 1940–3 January 1941
77th	1	3 January 1941–2 January 1942
	2	5 January 1942–16 December 1942
78th	1	6 January 1943–21 December 1943
	2	10 January 1944–19 December 1944
79th	1	3 January 1945–21 December 1945
	2	14 January 1946–2 August 1946
80th	1	3 January 1947–19 December 1947
	2	6 January 1948–31 December 1948
81st	1	3 January 1949–19 October 1949
	2	3 January 1950–2 January 1951

Dates of Congressional Sessions (Continued)

CONGRESS	SESSION	TERM
82d	1	3 January 1951–20 October 1951
	2	8 January 1952–7 July 1952
83d	1	3 January 1953–3 August 1953
	2	6 January 1954–2 December 1954
84th	1	5 January 1955–2 August 1955
	2	3 January 1956–27 July 1956
85th	1	3 January 1957–30 August 1957
	2	7 January 1958–24 August 1958
86th	1	7 January 1959–15 September 1959
	2	6 January 1960–1 September 1960
87th	1	3 January 1961–27 September 1961
	2	10 January 1962–13 October 1962
88th	1	9 January 1963–30 December 1963
	2	7 January 1964–3 October 1964
89th	1	4 January 1965–23 October 1965
	2	10 January 1966–22 October 1966
90th	1	10 January 1967–15 December 1967
	2	15 January 1968–14 October 1968
91st	1	3 January 1969–23 December 1969
	2	19 January 1970–2 January 1971
92d	1	21 January 1971–17 December 1971
	2	18 January 1972–18 October 1972
93d	1	3 January 1973–22 December 1973
	2	21 January 1974–20 December 1974
94th	1	14 January 1975–19 December 1975
	2	19 January 1976–1 October 1976
95th	1	4 January 1977–15 December 1977
	2	19 January 1978–15 October 1978
96th	1	15 January 1979–3 January 1980
	2	3 January 1980–16 December 1980
97th	1	5 January 1981–16 December 1981
	2	25 January 1982–23 December 1982
98th	1	3 January 1983–18 November 1983
	2	23 January 1984–12 October 1984
99th	1	3 January 1985–20 December 1985
	2	21 January 1986–18 October 1986
100th	1	6 January 1987–22 December 1987
	2	25 January 1988–22 October 1988
101st	1	3 January 1989–22 November 1989
	2	23 January 1990–28 October 1990
102d	1	3 January 1991–3 January 1992
	2	3 January 1992–9 October 1992
103d	1	5 January 1993–26 November 1993
	2	25 January 1994–

Congress in uncertain circumstances to adjourn subject to the recall of its chamber leaders.

There are also joint sessions, meetings, or gatherings of Congress. These rarely last longer than part of a day and include such activities as counting the electoral vote, inauguration of the president and vice president, the president's annual state of the union and other major addresses, state funerals, addresses by visiting foreign dignitaries or distinguished Americans, ceremonies, and the bestowal of awards. (A complete list of all sessions and meetings of Congress appears in the "Statistical" section of the *Congressional Directory*.)

During the early nineteenth century, representatives and senators (the latter of whom were elected by state legislatures until 1914) were elected at various times during the course of an election cycle (the first Tuesday after the first Monday in November did not become the uniform day for election of representatives until 1876). To accommodate these variable election dates and to allow time for members to travel from their states to Washington (transportation being arduous and time consuming) regular sessions did not commence until December of the year following the election of a new Congress.

A consequence of this delay was the so-called lame-duck session that occurred after each congressional set of elections but before the commencement of terms (as opposed to commencement of sessions) for the new Congress the following March. Complaints about lame-duck sessions were instrumental in passage of the Twentieth Amendment.

Nowadays congressional leaders set a target date for adjournment of each session and also schedule intrasession recesses, which aid members in planning for trips back to their districts and states. This scheduling also helps chairs and leaders to plan committee and floor work during each session.

[*See also* Adjournment and Recess.]

BIBLIOGRAPHY

Galloway, George. *The Legislative Process in Congress.* 1953.

Luce, Robert. Legislative Assemblies. 1924. Repr. 1974. Chap. 7

U.S. Senate. Senate Historical Office. "Extraordinary Sessions of Congress." Typescript.

FREDERICK H. PAULS

SEVENTEENTH AMENDMENT (1913; 37 Stat. 646). Officially adopted on 31 May 1913, the

Seventeenth Amendment transferred the election of senators from the legislatures of the various states to "the people thereof." It was a product of a long-term American inclination to strengthen representative democracy and, more immediately, of the reformist agitation of the Populist-Progressive era. Designed as a conservative check on the House, the Senate had evolved into a body that many felt had greater potential for representing state, regional, and national perspectives. To do so, however, the selection of its members would have to be removed from the state legislatures, whose rural-dominated, malapportioned character perpetuated minority rule and manipulation by business interests. Moreover, the election process itself had become a major occasion for corruption, and so time-consuming that it frequently overrode legislative business. While the Senate had heard only one bribery case prior to 1866, it adjudicated nine over the next four decades and there were forty-five deadlocks in twenty states between 1891 and 1905.

Popular pressure for direct election began in the 1870s, spearheaded by agrarian associations, organized labor, and assorted radicals and reformers. By 1909, the Populist, Socialist, and Democratic parties had called for direct election, thirty-three state legislatures had memorialized Congress for a constitutional amendment, and twenty-nine states had adopted methods whereby voters could express a senatorial preference. The House of Representatives passed nineteen direct-election resolutions over three decades, including five between 1893 and 1902, only to have them later strangled by the Senate.

The idea of direct election acquired a powerful advocate in publisher William Randolph Hearst, for whom journalist David Graham Phillips wrote a series entitled "The Treason of the Senate" in *Cosmopolitan* between March and November 1906. Receptivity within the Senate itself was enhanced by the growing number of members who had been elected by preference systems. Perhaps the final impetus came from the Senate's handling of the election case of William Lorimer of Illinois, whose selection by the "jackpot legislature" allegedly involved the bribery of fifty-seven members.

On 13 December 1909, insurgent Republican senator Joseph L. Bristow of Kansas introduced a resolution calling for a constitutional amendment. When the resolution finally reached the Senate floor in January 1911, southern Democrats had succeeded in including a provision that only the states could regulate senatorial elections. Standpat (conservative) Republican George Sutherland quickly introduced an amendment sanctioning federal supervision of congressional elections. After standpatters and insurgents joined forces to pass the Sutherland proviso, the former joined several southern Democrats to defeat the proposed amendment. During a special session, the House overwhelmingly passed a resolution calling for a direct-election amendment, after first defeating a Sutherland-type modification. The Senate, on a 64 to 24 vote, countered with a version that contained a federal-control amendment; only eight southern Democrats and the standpat Republicans of New England, New York, and Pennsylvania opposed. After the House refused to accept the Senate version, a stalemate ensued that was broken when the House finally concurred on a 238 to 39 vote, with 110 abstentions, on 13 May 1912.

It took less than a year (until 8 April 1913) for the Seventeenth Amendment to be ratified by the necessary three-fourths of the state legislatures. Ratification was facilitated greatly by the Republican split in the 1912 elections, which allowed Democrats, aided by progressives and insurgents, to gain temporary control over several key state legislatures. Ironically, 1913 was also the high point of senatorial turnover, with 73 percent of the members serving their first term, a development that seemed to prove conservative contentions that the upper chamber was already responsive to the popular will.

BIBLIOGRAPHY

Haynes, George H. *The Election of Senators.* 1912.
Haynes, George H. *The Senate of the United States: Its History and Practice.* 1938.
Fenno, Richard F., Jr. *The United States Senate: A Bicameral Perspective.* 1982.

JOHN D. BUENKER

SEWARD, WILLIAM H. (1801–1872), senator from New York (1849–1861), secretary of State (1861–1869) under Presidents Abraham Lincoln and Andrew Johnson. William Henry Seward played a major role in making slavery a political issue in the North. From the 1840s, when the astute New York politician first expressed his view that the conflict over slavery was "irrepressible," he had a strong impact on northern public opinion.

Seward's political career began in upstate New York. He entered politics in the 1830s just as long-established channels of political power were giving way to new, more democratic forces. His first political affiliation was with the Anti-Masons, and he

WILLIAM H. SEWARD.   LIBRARY OF CONGRESS

drew on the excitement generated by that grass-roots, antielitist movement to catapult himself into the Whig party leadership and the governorship of New York in 1838 at the age of thirty-seven.

Seward's experience as governor left him with the firm conviction that the only way his party could successfully compete with the Jacksonian Democrats was to embrace the antislavery movement. His election to the Senate in 1849 made him one of a new generation of antislavery northern legislators that also included Charles Sumner of Massachusetts, Salmon P. Chase of Ohio, Thaddeus Stevens of Pennsylvania, and Hannibal Hamlin of Maine. Seward gained almost immediate nationwide notoriety when he attacked Henry Clay's plan for the Compromise of 1850. Slavery, according to Seward, hindered economic development, contradicted democratic aspirations, and created a slaveholding class that wielded inordinate power over the federal government. In a speech that was reprinted in newspapers across the North, Seward spoke of a "Higher Law" than the Constitution, thereby insinuating that slavery would eventually fall to more powerful democratic forces. At the same time, however, he categorically refused to join the Liberty and Free-Soil parties in the 1840s, choosing instead to work for change from within the Whig party.

By the early 1850s, however, competing sectional ideologies could not be defused by the normal process of political compromise. Although the Whig and Democratic parties consequently began to unravel, Seward delayed his decision to join the new Republican party until after his reelection to the Senate in 1854. His participation was considered essential to the party's success, since it was universally acknowledged that his decision would influence huge numbers of voters who might otherwise be reluctant to join a third party.

Although Seward was bitterly disappointed when Lincoln was chosen as the standard-bearer of the Republican party in 1860, he became secretary of State in 1861 and was soon the new president's closest adviser. The South had long regarded Seward an extremist, but his behavior leading up to the Civil War was in fact conciliatory. He believed that the Union could be saved without a war and that a policy of delay would prevent the secession of the border states, which in turn would gradually coax the Deep South back. Once the war started, Seward cautioned Lincoln against signing the Emancipation Proclamation in 1863 for fear that it would lead to widespread military desertions. Continuing as secretary of State under Andrew Johnson, Seward sided with the president in his battles with the Radical Republicans over Reconstruction, believing like the president in leniency for the South. Under Johnson, Seward negotiated the purchase of Alaska from Russia.

BIBLIOGRAPHY

Foner, Eric. *Free Soil, Free Labor, Free Men: The Ideology of the Republican Party before the Civil War.* 1970.
Holt, Michael F. "The Anti-Masonic and Know-Nothing Parties." In *History of U.S. Political Parties.* Edited by Arthur M. Schlesinger, Jr. 1973.
Van Deusen, Glyndon G. *William Henry Seward.* 1967.

RICHARD KAZARIAN, JR.

SHADOW SENATORS. The concept of a shadow senator dates to 1796, when legislators in the Southwest Territory, now Tennessee, elected Gov. William Blount and William Cocke to the U.S. Senate. The men reached Philadelphia only to find that Tennessee had not yet been admitted to the Union. They were, however, permitted on the Sen-

ate floor as observers. From their status came the term *shadow senator.* Even after Tennessee was granted statehood, Congress would not seat the two men until they were reelected by the Tennessee General Assembly.

The Senate deviated from the Tennessee Plan in the case of shadow senators from the areas that became Michigan (1837), California (1850), and Minnesota (1858). One of Michigan's shadow senators was already the state's territorial delegate to the House of Representatives; the Senate allowed him and his colleague to occupy "privileged seats" as observers without voting privileges until the state was admitted. In the case of California, the question of privileges for shadow senators was overshadowed by southern hostility to the state's admission as a free state. The same reason may have sparked opposition to observer status for Minnesota's lone shadow senator. The immediate seating of these men after their states gained admission marked another departure from the Tennessee Plan and riled Southerners. No such dispute engulfed the shadow senators elected by the Oregon legislature in mid 1858, eight months before that territory became the thirty-third state.

Alaska chose Ernest Gruening and William A. Egan to the Senate in 1956, three years before the territory attained statehood. Gruening and Egan occupied seats in the diplomatic gallery until Alaska's star was added to the flag; then they, too, had to stand for reelection. Whether they were welcome observers before statehood or seat takers afterward, a majority of shadow senators maintained a low profile while lobbying for their territory's admission to the Union.

The shadow-senator concept was revived in 1990. In that year, District of Columbia voters selected Jesse Jackson to be their agent in promoting statehood for the District.

BIBLIOGRAPHY

Grayson, George W. "Casting D.C.'s Shadows: Statehood-Seeking 'Senators' Are as Old as the Republic." *Washington Post,* 11 November 1990, p. B-5.
Quattannens, Jo Anne McCormick. "Shadow Senators." Paper prepared by the Historical Office, U.S. Senate. 1990. Mimeo.

GEORGE W. GRAYSON

SHERMAN, JOHN (1823–1900), representative and senator from Ohio, cabinet officer, and leading architect of Republican party financial policies in the late nineteenth century. When economic

"BUSTED AGAIN, JOHN!" Published 29 June 1888, soon after John Sherman failed to win the Republican presidential nomination, the cartoon depicts Sherman knocked over by a misfiring rifle, the stock of which reads: "Sherman boom 88," referring to his failed bid. On the ground lie broken gun stocks, labeled "Sherman boom 1880" and "Sherman boom 1884," alluding to his two previous unsuccessful attempts to capture the Republican nomination.   LIBRARY OF CONGRESS

questions such as the currency and the tariff came to dominate congressional policy-making in the post–Civil War decades, Sherman's expertise in these fields brought him prominence in the Senate and the country and made him a leading contender for the Republican presidential nomination. A successful lawyer and businessman and brother of Gen. William T. Sherman, John Sherman first ran for office in 1854, winning a seat in the House on the Anti-Nebraska ticket. (Anti-Nebraskans were Republican forerunners who opposed the extension of slavery into the territories made possible by the Kansas-Nebraska Act.) He was reelected as a Republican three times and served until 1861, when he was elected to the Senate.

During his first term in the House, Sherman was appointed to a special committee to investigate the sectional disturbances in Kansas. His committee report excoriating the proslavery faction there doubled as a Republican campaign document in 1856. In 1859, at the beginning of Sherman's third term, Republicans nominated him for Speaker. But his previous, albeit rather perfunctory, endorsement of southerner Hinton Helper's antislavery book, *The Impending Crisis* (1857), aroused southern representatives to block his election at all costs, despite the plurality of Republicans in the House. After weeks of balloting, the House turned to a compromise choice, Republican William Pennington, who accepted virtually all of Sherman's recommendations for committee appointments. Sherman became chairman of Ways and Means, and his work on the Morrill Tariff Act of 1861 launched his career as a leader in financial policy. In helping to frame this and subsequent tariff measures, Sherman took care to protect the interests of his wool-growing constituents in Ohio.

On entering the Senate in 1861, Sherman took a seat on the Finance Committee, where he played a leading role in formulating wartime financial legislation, including the Legal Tender Act of 1862 creating the so-called greenback paper currency and the National Bank Act of 1863. In 1867 he became chairman of the Finance Committee and for the next thirty years was regarded as the Republican party's preeminent leader on financial questions. Though sometimes tugged from orthodoxy by inflationist elements in his Ohio constituency, he emerged in the 1870s as a leading advocate of a "sound" currency. In 1873 he secured passage of the Coinage Act, which dropped the disused silver dollars from the currency and which silverites later labeled the Crime of 1873. Two years later, he helped frame the Specie Resumption Act mandating the return to specie payments for greenbacks in 1879. As secretary of the Treasury (1877–1881) under President Rutherford B. Hayes, Sherman carefully accumulated a sufficient gold reserve by the appointed date to ensure a relatively calm resumption of specie payments.

Sherman hoped to parlay his achievements at the Treasury into the Republican presidential nomination in 1880, but he failed. In 1884 and 1888, he again unsuccessfully sought the nomination. In 1881, Sherman returned to the Senate. He served as Senate president pro tempore during the 49th Congress (1885–1887) and chaired the Committee on the Library (1881–1887) and the Committee on Foreign Relations (1886–1893 and 1895–1897).

Although during his second stint in the Senate, Sherman no longer chaired the Finance Committee, his interest and influence in that field continued. While never an extremist on the tariff question, he continued to support protective duties, believing that the key to prosperity lay in fostering the American home market even more than in efforts to expand exports abroad. He denounced President Grover Cleveland's 1887 message to Congress calling for substantially reduced tariffs, especially on raw materials. Sherman argued that the sheep farmer of Ohio was as much a laborer deserving of protection from foreign competition as the operative in the woolen mills of New England. During Sherman's tenure in the Senate, the Republican party's devotion to a high protective tariff reached its zenith with the 51st Congress's passage of the McKinley Tariff Act in 1890.

The 51st Congress produced two important laws bearing his name: the Sherman Antitrust Act and the Sherman Silver Purchase Act. Sherman's original antitrust bill aimed to outlaw combinations and trusts in restraint of trade or production. Against fervent Democratic objections that such regulation was the states' prerogative, he stoutly defended Congress's constitutional authority to act and argued that his purpose was to enable federal courts to complement state regulation. Referred to the Judiciary Committee, the bill emerged with the reference to production removed, and it passed in that form. The Silver Purchase Act, an incident in the persistent currency struggle, called for the Treasury to purchase 4.5 million ounces of silver per month, against which it would issue certificates redeemable in gold or silver. The principal author of the bill's final version, Sherman proposed it as a compromise only to avert free coinage of silver. He welcomed its repeal in 1893.

Sherman concluded his public career as secretary of State (1897–1898), a position he resigned because of advancing age and his opposition to the Spanish-American War.

BIBLIOGRAPHY

Burton, Theodore E. *John Sherman*. 1906.
Sherman, John. *Recollections of Forty Years in the House, Senate, and Cabinet*. 1895.

CHARLES W. CALHOUN

SHERMAN ANTITRUST ACT

(1890; 26 Stat. 209–210). The Sherman Antitrust Act, "An act to protect trade and commerce against unlawful restraints and monopolies," was Congress's response to one of the major economic issues of the late nineteenth and early twentieth centuries. It was a piece of legislation that would have sweeping and unexpected consequences.

By the late 1880s there was widespread public concern over the *trusts*, a generic term for big, consolidated business, a new and unsettling development in American economic life. While large corporations had much influence in Congress (particularly in the Senate), the predominant economic interests represented there were small and middle-sized entrepreneurs: farmers, retailers, manufacturers, middlemen. And most members of Congress (and their constituents) had a visceral hostility to monopoly and economic privilege. These attitudes had led to the creation of the Interstate Commerce Commission, charged to regulate railroad rates, in 1887.

Another major factor leading to the passage of the Sherman act was the election of 1888, which gave the Republicans the presidency and a majority in both houses of Congress. The major economic policy goal of the Republicans was a stronger protective tariff. To make it more palatable to those who regarded protectionism as a sop to privilege, the McKinley Tariff Act of 1890 was packaged with other politically attractive bills: the Omnibus Act

JOHN SHERMAN.   *PERLEY'S REMINISCENCES*, VOL. 2

"THE BOSSES OF THE SENATE." Satirical depiction of the influence of big business monopolies on Congress. The Sherman Antitrust Act was intended to prevent the formation of these giant trusts without prompting excessive federal interference in the market economy. Lithograph after a drawing by J. Keppler, *Puck*, 23 January 1889.

THE LIBRARY OF CONGRESS

(1889), which granted statehood to four territories and thus added to Republican senatorial strength; the Sherman Silver Purchase Act (1890), which assured a fixed supply of silver to support the currency; and the Sherman Antitrust Act.

The extent of popular and political support for the measure led to its near-unanimous passage by Congress; it became law on 2 July 1890. Helpful too was its broad (but vague) language. Sen. John Sherman, whose Ohio constituency included many independent oilmen smarting from the rise of Standard Oil, introduced the bill and lent it his name. But much of its text was the work of Senate Judiciary Committee chairman George F. Edmunds of Vermont.

Its key provision was: "Every contract, combination in the form of trust or otherwise, or conspiracy, in restraint of trade or commerce among the several States, or with foreign nations, is hereby de-clared to be illegal." The rest of the act set penalties and gave the attorney general and the federal courts the power to enforce it.

Just what constitutes a "conspiracy in restraint of trade" has generated a century of litigation. American antitrust law has followed an erratic course, at times (as during the Progressive era, the New Deal, and the 1970s) enlivened by an active Antitrust Division in the Department of Justice, and at times (as in the 1920s and the 1980s) characterized by lax enforcement by both the Department of Justice and the courts.

The intention of Congress has long been an important antitrust issue. Did it mean to break up all large combines or just "bad" trusts (to use Theodore Roosevelt's distinction)? Oliver Wendell Holmes thought that it was aimed at common law contracts among firms that led to pools, cartels, and the like and not at mergers creating large new companies.

SEN. GEORGE F. EDMUNDS (R-VT.) Chairman of the Senate Judiciary Committee, who was largely responsible for writing the text of the Sherman Antitrust Act.

PERLEY'S REMINISCENCES, VOL. 2

However, it has been the courts more than Congress that have defined antitrust law since 1890. And it may be that the very imprecision of the Sherman Act, and the frequent changes of course and direction that it has undergone, are in a sense true to its purposes. Both the act and its enforcement reflect the deep American unease with bigness and monopoly. Yet they do not so strongly constrain large enterprise as to dissipate the advantages that come from economies of scale.

[See also Clayton Antitrust Act; Federal Trade Commission Act.]

BIBLIOGRAPHY

Bork, Robert H. "Legislative Intent and the Policy of the Sherman Act." *Journal of Law and Economics* 9 (1961): 7–48.

Letwin, William. *Law and Economic Policy in America: The Evolution of the Sherman Antitrust Act.* 1965.

"Symposium: The Sherman Act's First Century: A Historical Perspective." *Iowa Law Review* 74 (July 1989): 987–1217.

MORTON KELLER

SHERMAN SILVER PURCHASE ACT

(1890; 26 Stat. 289–290). Prior to 1873, the United States minted coins from silver and gold, giving the country a bimetallic currency backing for its paper dollars. For more than half a century, silver and gold had come out of the ground at relatively fixed rates, sixteen silver ounces to one gold ounce, or, as the phrase went, "16:1." Gold had a fixed price of $20 per ounce, however, which made silver nominally worth $1.25 an ounce, but in actuality silver was worth more than that in overseas markets. Its sale to the mints thus grew so weak that Congress abandoned coinage of silver dollars in 1873, which some groups called the Crime of '73.

Soon thereafter, new silver discoveries and increased mine production drove down the price of silver. Western miners wanted a remonetization of silver, as did farmers, who saw it as a means to inflate the currency. Congress in 1878 passed the Bland-Allison Act, authorizing the secretary of the Treasury to purchase $2 million to $4 million of silver each month at market prices and to issue legal tender notes.

Bland-Allison only temporarily restrained the silver advocates. Meanwhile, the price of silver continued to fall throughout the 1880s. By 1890, the silver forces had gained great political influence, as evidenced by the fact that Ohio senator John Sherman lent his name to the act as a means to placate the free-silver advocates within the Republican party.

The Sherman Silver Purchase Act required the Treasury to purchase 4.5 million ounces of silver each month at the market price and to issue legal tender notes redeemable in silver or gold at the option of the Treasury. Although the act in fact meant that the government would purchase virtually the entire national output of silver, it would not do so at the rate desired by the Populists and silver advocates, 16:1. It did, however, touch off a gold drain, based on uncertainties over the nation's commitment to the gold standard, a disequilibrium called the panic of 1893. President Grover Cleveland, a Democrat, called Congress into special session to repeal the Sherman Act, and even though the Democratic party repudiated Cleveland in 1896 to nominate William Jennings Bryan of Nebraska (whose prosilver views were expressed in his "cross of gold" speech), the nation repudiated silver. President William McKinley placed the United States solely on the gold standard in 1900.

[See also Silver Issue.]

BIBLIOGRAPHY

Friedman, Milton, and Anna J. Schwartz. *A Monetary History of the United States, 1867–1960*. 1963.

Hicks, John D. *The Populist Revolt: A History of the Farmers' Alliance and the People's Party*. 1931.

Sharkey, Robert P. *Money, Class, and Party: An Economic Study of the Civil War and Reconstruction*. 1959.

LARRY SCHWEIKART

SILVER ISSUE (BIMETALLISM).

Modern Americans wonder how their forebears could get so aroused over such an abstract concept as the ratio of silver to gold, yet it was perhaps the single most important national issue of the late nineteenth century. The nation had long operated on a de facto bimetallic standard, minting and coining both silver and gold at a consistent ratio (since the early nineteenth century) of 16:1. During the Civil War, the government issued greenbacks, paper dollars not immediately convertible into gold or silver, but bearing a promise by the government to redeem them in gold at some future date. After the war the government reduced the stock of greenbacks. The fixed price of $1.25 per ounce of silver (based on a 16:1 ratio to gold) caused the metal to flow out of the United States since foreign markets paid more than the fixed price. Therefore, Congress decided to stop coining silver altogether. When it passed an act doing so in 1873, the response was hostile, ultimately gaining for the bill the name of the Crime of '73. The Specie Resumption Act of 1875 provided for redemption of fractional paper currency—a bone to the prosilver groups in the West—but pledged that specie payments on greenbacks would resume on 1 January 1879.

New silver discoveries and improved mining techniques soon made silver abundant, so much so that the ratio of silver to gold rose to 17:1. Miners, of course, favored having the government buy and coin all the silver they could dig out of the ground. So they formed one natural constituency for the metal. Farmers added their voices to the chorus calling for "free and unlimited coinage of silver at 16:1," hoping to inflate the economy, and thus shrink the long-term value of their mortgage debt. Organizations such as the Farmers' Alliance joined the miners in agitating for silver, thus forming the basis for the Populist party, which appeared in 1890.

Prosilver legislation began to emerge from Congress. The Bland-Allison Act of 1878 remonetized silver by authorizing the secretary of the Treasury to purchase $2–4 million in silver each month and issue legal tender silver dollars. As silver prices continued to fall and farm agitation grew in the 1880s, western interests placed increased pressure on Congress to purchase and coin more silver. In 1890, Congress passed the Sherman Silver Purchase Act, sponsored by Sen. John Sherman of Ohio, in which the Treasury was required to purchase 4.5 million ounces of silver each month and to issue legal tender notes redeemable in gold or silver at the option of the Treasury.

The 4.5 million ounces were close to the national output of silver. But as more silver flowed into the

"A HORSE OF ANOTHER COLOR." Stuck on the muddy road of "hard times," Uncle Sam's wagon, pulled by the horse "gold," is laden with crates marked "municipal debt," "national debt," "state debt," and "private debt." Silverite senator John P. Jones (R-Nev.) offers the aid of his horse, labeled "silver," to help pull the load of debt. In the caption of the cartoon, Jones says, "Now, let me hitch this nag by the side of old Goldy, and we will snake it up resumption hill in no time. Old Silver has been resting most five years now," referring to Congress's passage of the Coinage Act of 1873, which discontinued the coinage of silver. OFFICE OF THE HISTORIAN OF THE U.S. SENATE

Treasury—used to issue notes, which were then redeemed in gold—gold flowed out of the Treasury.

The fear that the Treasury might abandon the gold standard touched off the panic of 1893. Although the Democrats had shown more sympathy toward the silver movement, President Grover Cleveland, elected in 1892, favored a gold standard. He immediately summoned Congress into a special session to repeal the Sherman Act, which tore the Democratic party asunder. In 1896, the Democrats dropped Cleveland in favor of William Jennings Bryan of Nebraska, who made his famous "cross of gold" speech to the delegates at the convention. The Populists, who had taken the lead on the "free silver" issue, threw their support behind him. The Republicans, meanwhile, had not wavered from their support of the gold standard—"hard money," as they called it. William McKinley, their nominee, won a decisive (some say realigning) victory in 1896, and in 1900 Congress passed an act placing the United States on the gold standard.

[See also Sherman Silver Purchase Act.]

BIBLIOGRAPHY

Barrett, Don. *Greenbacks and the Resumption of Specie Payments, 1862–1879*. 1965.

Friedman, Milton, and Anna J. Schwartz. *A Monetary History of the United States, 1867–1960*. 1963.

Hicks, John D. *The Populist Revolt: A History of the Farmers' Alliance and the People's Party*. 1931.

Nugent, Walter T. K. *Money and American Society, 1865–1880*. 1968.

LARRY SCHWEIKART

SILVER PURCHASE ACT. See Sherman Silver Purchase Act.

SIXTEENTH AMENDMENT (1913; 36 Stat. 184). The Sixteenth Amendment states: "The Congress shall have power to lay and collect taxes on incomes, from whatever source derived, without apportionment among the several States, and without regard to any census or enumeration." Upon completion of its ratification in early 1913, the amendment made it possible to enact an individual income tax, arguably the most significant addition to the power of the federal government in the twentieth century.

The first federal income tax was enacted during the Civil War to ease a desperate shortage of revenue. Constitutional challenges to the tax were delayed because of wartime needs, and it was repealed in 1872.

The income tax reemerged as a highly controversial issue in 1894. After the Civil War the Republican party was dominant. However, it was not exactly "the Party of Lincoln" in terms of regional concerns. If earlier the party had reflected Lincoln's postwar midwestern origins, the Republican party was highly responsive to manufacturing and financial interests in the East and upper Midwest. The South and most of the West were farming regions dominated by agricultural interests. The eastern states had much higher annual incomes, derived from industrial ownership and wages. Eastern banks controlled credit that farmers used to purchase land, seed, and equipment.

Support for various types of taxes reflected economic and geographic divisions. New England and the East favored taxes on land (property taxes) and consumption of products (excise taxes). They also favored high tariffs, especially on manufactured goods from Europe that were competing with their own products. The West and South favored taxes on income (of which they had little) and were adamantly opposed to taxes on land and consumption. The southern states continued their long tradition of opposing high tariffs because they still were exporting high quality cotton and other products to Europe.

An economic depression beginning in 1893 generated political pressure on the reigning Republicans. One source of that pressure was an income-tax proposal supported by southern and western Democrats. The movement was led by Nebraska Democratic representative William Jennings Bryan. Eastern Republicans opposed its passage. William V. Allen, Nebraska's Populist senator, defended it explicitly on sectional grounds: "[I]t is said that an income tax is unjust and sectional. It is sectional because the people of a certain section of this country have incomes which are taxable."

After the delivery of some of the grandest oratory in the history of Congress, the income tax was passed as part of the 1894 Wilson-Gorman Tariff bill on votes that reflected the underlying geographic divisions. It was a modest tax but also one that targeted those with the highest incomes. It provided a $4,000 exemption for families, which excluded all but the most well off. For those with incomes greater than $4,000, the tax was 2 percent on all income.

The tax was immediately challenged in court on

two grounds. The first was that it violated the constitutional provision that all direct taxes had to be levied in proportion to state populations (Art. I, sec. 9). The second ground was a more detailed complaint that the income tax applied to municipal bond interest income, thus infringing on state and local taxing powers. Several cases before the Supreme Court were consolidated in *Pollack v. Farmers' Loan and Trust* in 1895. The Court, in a 5 to 4 decision on the key apportionment issue, ruled the 1894 act unconstitutional. The justices unanimously agreed that the act also was unconstitutional because it taxed municipal bond interest and thus infringed on state and local powers. The Court's action meant that creating a federal income tax would require a constitutional amendment to override the proportionality clause.

An odd set of circumstances in 1909 set the stage for passage of the amendment. Eastern Republicans, led by Senate Finance Committee chairmen Nelson W. Aldrich of Rhode Island, had been increasing tariffs for a number of years. President William Howard Taft thought that tariffs had become too high and in 1909 supported a bipartisan bill in the House that lowered some rates. A concurrent movement in the House, led by young Tennessee Democrat Cordell Hull, sought to reenact the 1894 income tax, excluding only the section taxing municipal bonds. The measure was defeated.

The Senate, under Aldrich's supervision, passed a substitute bill that actually raised tariffs. This set off a political battle, with Democrats and progressive or insurgent Republicans (mostly from the Midwest and West) pitted against the old guard Republicans. In retaliation for the Aldrich bill, the Democrats and insurgent Republicans proposed to add Hull's amendment reenacting the 1894 income tax to the Senate tariff bill.

Aldrich and the eastern Republicans opposed this measure because they opposed income taxes. Taft opposed it because he feared a showdown with the Supreme Court. Together they made a deal with their opponents to support a constitutional amendment allowing an income tax. They also proposed an "excise tax" on corporate revenues. In return the income tax legislation was to be dropped from the tariff bill. The compromise was passed unanimously in the Senate, and there were only fourteen votes against it in the House.

Ratification of the Sixteenth Amendment took four years, with Alabama the first state to ratify in 1909 and Wyoming providing the enabling thirty-sixth approval on 13 February 1913. Within months

of ratification, with Democrats controlling both houses of Congress and the presidency, the income tax was enacted as a simple eight-page amendment to a tariff bill that was more than eight hundred pages long. The legislation was drafted by Cordell Hull.

BIBLIOGRAPHY

Paul, Randolph E. *Taxation in the United States.* 1954.
Seligman, E. R. A. *The Income Tax: A Study of History, Theory, and Practice at Home and Abroad.* 1914.
Waltman, Jerold L. *Political Origins of the U.S. Income Tax.* 1985.

JOHN F. WITTE

SLAVERY. At the commencement of the American Revolution, slavery was legal in all thirteen original states. Between 1776 and 1804, however, the northern states, spurred by the ideals of the Revolution and slavery's limited economic importance, abolished the institution. But south of the Mason-Dixon line, slavery remained a vital economic and social institution. When the Civil War began, slaves were one-third of the southern population and represented the largest capital investment in the country.

As slavery receded nationally, it became the South's "peculiar institution." The political danger posed by the transformation of slavery into a sectional institution was apparent in the constitutional convention, and consequently the Constitution contained some vital compromises on slavery. Among these were the three-fifths clause, by which slaves counted three-fifths in apportioning the House of Representatives, thereby increasing southern representation beyond what its white population would warrant; a prohibition of congressional interference with the African slave trade for twenty years after ratification; and a ban on taxes on exports, which were primarily southern. In addition, fugitive slaves would not become free by virtue of escaping to a free state, but were to be returned to their owners. Most important, the federal government was given no jurisdiction over slavery in the states.

In the years after 1789, slavery eventually became the most important sectional issue in American politics, and Congress was the major arena for this conflict. The origins of the Civil War lay in the inability of the political system in general, and the national legislature in particular, to defuse this controversy.

The slavery issue intruded into congressional affairs almost immediately. Antislavery petitions introduced in the First Congress (1789–1791) touched off a bitter debate in which representatives from Georgia and South Carolina declared that the southern states never would have ratified the Constitution if slave property had not been protected, and warned that emancipation would dissolve the Union. Eventually the House adopted a report denying that Congress had any power over slavery in the states or over the African slave trade. James Madison found this episode a "harrowing experience," so much so that the following year he refused even to introduce a petition condemning the cruelty of the slave trade.

The old Continental Congress, in its final session, had approved the Northwest Ordinance (1787), which prohibited slavery in the area north of the Ohio River. Congress, in turn, passed the Southwest Ordinance in 1789, organizing that region without any prohibition on slavery. Kentucky (1792) and Tennessee (1796) came into the Union with constitutions recognizing slavery; their admission generated little debate.

The tacit agreement to divide the western territories between freedom and slavery along a geographic line was challenged only once in this early period. That occurred in 1798 over the creation of the Mississippi Territory, when a New England Federalist suddenly moved in the House that slavery be prohibited there. This amendment was easily rejected; support for it was confined to northern representatives. Not until the United States acquired territory west of the Mississippi River would the expansion of slavery be seriously challenged in Congress.

The other major question concerning slavery that Congress confronted in its early years was the matter of fugitive slaves. In 1793 Congress enacted the Fugitive Slave Act to implement the Constitution's stipulation (Article IV, section 1) that runaway slaves be returned to their masters. The act, which passed with strong bisectional support, did not work efficiently. Its procedures were inadequate and cumbersome, and it offered little protection to the rights of accused fugitives. Periodic efforts to modify this law produced sharp debate but no change until 1850, when a much more controversial act was passed. The greatest significance of the 1793 law was that it assumed the rendition of fugitive slaves was a federal and not a state responsibility, a position upheld by the Supreme Court in *Prigg v. Pennsylvania* (1842).

The most important action Congress took on slavery in its early years was the prohibition of the African slave trade in 1808, the first year it could do so under the Constitution. The main issue at stake was not the international trade—southerners believed that slavery could survive without importations—but the domestic coastal trade, by which slaves were transported mostly from the upper to the lower South. Southern efforts to exempt the coastal trade from federal regulation failed in the House on an almost straight sectional vote of 63 to 49, and Thomas Jefferson approved the law (1807). While symbolically significant, the law did not close off the international slave trade. It has been estimated that perhaps 300,000 slaves were smuggled into the United States in the years 1808 to 1861, an average of almost 6,000 per year.

Slavery was an issue in Congress during these years only for short periods of time, and the sectional divisions generated did not carry over to other issues. Southerners conceded that slavery was an evil in the abstract that should be discouraged, and that it should be abolished where safe and practical; northerners in turn recognized the property rights of southern slaveholders and left the problem to southerners to deal with as they believed best. With each section roughly equal in area, and the western territories divided between the two sections, the expectation was that the number of free and slave states in the Union would be more or less balanced.

These unspoken understandings were suddenly challenged by the Missouri crisis of 1819 to 1821, which marked the real beginning of the sectional conflict in American politics. As a result, the debate over Missouri's admission to the Union was a major turning point in the history of the slavery controversy in Congress.

Through the Louisiana Purchase (1803), the United States acquired from France the country between the Mississippi River and the Rocky Mountains (except for Texas). Slavery had existed in the region under first the Spanish and then the French, and in 1804 the Senate rejected a bid to prohibit it there. In the absence of any federal prohibition, the number of slaves in the area steadily increased. Louisiana was admitted to the Union with a slave constitution in 1812, and the land north of it was organized as the Missouri Territory.

The South's declining population (and hence its congressional representation) relative to that of the North made southerners sensitive to the need to gain additional slave states and protect slavery in areas of the national domain that were suitable for southern agriculture and slavery. Northerners, on the other hand, increasingly chafed at southern control of the national government. When Missouri sought admission in 1819, there were eleven free states and eleven slave states in the Union. Although virtually all of the proposed state lay north of the Ohio River, there were 10,000 slaves in its population of 66,000, and its citizens, if left to their own wishes, would certainly adopt a slave constitution.

Few members of Congress anticipated any difficulty over Missouri's admission, an assumption that was shattered in February 1819 when Rep. James Tallmadge, Jr., of New York introduced an amendment to the enabling bill imposing a program of gradual emancipation on Missouri as a condition for admission.

Tallmadge was something of a political eccentric, oblivious to party discipline, and seems to have acted largely on his own. Whatever the case, northern members quickly rallied in support of his action, while southerners bitterly denounced it. Some northern members maintained that slavery was incompatible with republican institutions, and cited the Declaration of Independence in support of this position. Southerners responded by insisting that the Declaration upheld only white equality and defended slavery with a frankness not previously seen in congressional debates. Censoring Tallmadge for kindling "a fire which all the waters of the ocean could not extinguish," Thomas W. Cobb of Georgia warned that "it can be extinguished only in blood."

The most important motive for northern support of the Tallmadge amendment was resentment over the South's political power and its control of the national government. Southerners were equally determined to secure an additional slave state in order to protect slavery from federal interference. They increasingly saw the Senate, where each state had equal representation, as a bastion from which to protect southern rights, particularly slavery.

The House passed the Tallmadge amendment by a narrow margin; in a virtually straight sectional tally, only one southern representative voted for it, and only ten northern representatives opposed it. The Senate, however, rejected the amendment, and the Fifteenth Congress (1817–1819) adjourned with the two houses unable to agree.

When the new Congress convened in December 1819, the situation was more complicated because Massachusetts had given its consent for Maine to be divided from it. If Maine were admitted to the Union without Missouri, the balance of states would shift to the North, twelve free states to eleven slave states.

Once again, the two houses deadlocked. Finally, Speaker Henry Clay of Kentucky, who spoke for the border state moderates, took the lead in fashioning a compromise. Under his influence, the House members of the conference committee agreed to drop the Tallmadge amendment and accept the restriction that (except for Missouri) slavery would be prohibited in the Louisiana Purchase north of 36°30′ north latitude; the Senate conferees agreed to separate the Maine and Missouri bills. The resulting Missouri Compromise passed Congress in May 1820.

While there was no likelihood of secession in 1820, the Missouri crisis produced several significant developments for the future of the sectional conflict. The outcome demonstrated that at least unconsciously southerners were committed to the idea that slavery was a permanent institution. Southern members of Congress had voted unanimously (98 to 0) against any restriction on slavery in Missouri, where the institution was not economically vital. Passage of the Compromise also demonstrated that there was a general acceptance of the power of Congress to ban slavery from a territory, which would become an increasingly divisive issue after 1846. Finally, the South's sense of being a conscious minority crystallized during the Missouri debates in Congress.

In the aftermath of the passage of the Missouri Compromise, congressional leaders, fearing that continued agitation would destroy the Union, moved to suppress the slavery issue in national politics. Hoping to reestablish the old Jeffersonian alliance of plain Republicans of the North (farmers and workers) and southern planters, Sen. Martin Van Buren of New York set out to create a new party system that would purposely avoid sectional issues. Van Buren's efforts eventually led to the formation of the Democratic party under the leadership of Andrew Jackson. Ultimately Henry Clay took the lead in creating the Whig party as the major opposition party.

The major issues in the Jacksonian party system were not sectional in nature. On various occasions, however, the slavery controversy intruded into Congress, albeit only temporarily. Until American territorial expansion in the 1840s, Congressional leaders for the most part managed to suppress the slavery issue.

The rise of the abolitionist movement in the North during the 1830s brought the slavery issue back into the halls of Congress. A sharp increase in the number of antislavery petitions greeted the 24th Congress when it assembled in December 1835. Most of these petitions called for the abolition of slavery in the District of Columbia or prohibition of the interstate slave trade. Northern Whigs in particular persisted in introducing them. Southerners resented the petitions' sharply worded condemnation of slavery, and they were alarmed by the idea that Congress could have any jurisdiction over what had always been considered strictly a state institution.

In response to southern demands, both houses adopted gag rules designed to prevent consideration of these petitions. The House rule, which was the more controversial, declared that all petitions dealing with slavery would be automatically tabled without consideration or referral to a committee. This rule had no practical effect because it had been the regular practice in the House simply to bury these petitions in committee; but southern radicals, led by the South Carolina delegation, protested against even receiving petitions dealing with slavery, since in their view Congress had no jurisdiction over the institution.

Abolitionists raised the cry that their civil liberties were being violated in the name of protecting slavery. They found a powerful ally in the House in former president John Quincy Adams, now a representative from Massachusetts. Adams persisted in introducing antislavery petitions each Monday; southern House members would object, a contentious debate would ensue, all business would cease, and the House was kept in a constant uproar.

The House repassed some version of the gag rule on five separate occasions, but by narrower and narrower margins. Northern congressional opposition continued to grow, and in December 1844 the House, on a motion by John Quincy Adams, rescinded the rule. Whereas almost 80 percent of the northern Democrats had supported the rule in 1836, by 1844 the margin was almost precisely reversed, with 77 percent opposed. By repealing the law, which proved to be permanent, members in effect abandoned any hope of suppressing the agitation over slavery. Nevertheless, the antislavery bloc in Congress remained small, and abolitionist petitions were routinely buried in committee.

Eager to unite the South behind his leadership, John C. Calhoun introduced in the Senate a set of deliberately provocative resolutions in December 1837. They declared that under the Constitution the states had "exclusive and sole" control over their "domestic institutions"; that the national government was obligated to respect this power; that any attempt to abolish slavery in the District of Columbia or the territories would be a direct attack on the institutions of the southern states; and that any interference with slavery would threaten the Union. After toning down Calhoun's language, the Senate approved the resolutions.

The furor over antislavery petitions and Calhoun's resolutions was unusual. Most of Congress's time in the 1820s and 1830s was not spent debating slavery. But this situation changed dramatically in the 1840s in response to the annexation of Texas and the Mexican War.

The backdrop for the drive to annex Texas was President John Tyler's break in 1841 with the Whigs in Congress. Hoping to recoup his fallen political fortunes and promote himself as an independent candidate for president in 1844, Tyler opened negotiations with Texas authorities for annexation. His action injected the Texas issue into national politics. The main beneficiary of this development, however, was not the president but James K. Polk of Tennessee, who received the Democratic nomination for president and was elected in November 1844 on an expansionist platform. The Senate rejected Tyler's initial treaty of annexation in 1844, but after the election both houses approved a joint resolution adding Texas to the Union.

Polk wanted to acquire New Mexico and California from Mexico as well, and when all diplomatic efforts failed to achieve this aim he provoked a war with Mexico. Northern Whigs' accusations that the Democratic party, under southern control, was waging the war in order to extend slavery put northern Democrats on the defensive.

Northern Democratic anger finally boiled over in August 1846 when Polk sent a message to Congress requesting a special $2 million appropriation, which he vaguely stipulated was to be used to "facilitate negotiations" with Mexico. Rep. David Wilmot of Pennsylvania, who until then had been a loyal supporter of the administration, shocked the House leadership by introducing an amendment to the bill, modeled on the language of the Northwest Ordinance of 1787, which read: "Provided, that as an express and fundamental condition to the acquisition of any territory from the Republic of Mexico by the United States, neither slavery nor involuntary servitude shall exist in said territory, except for crime, whereof the party shall first be duly convicted."

The Wilmot Proviso passed the House but was stalled in the Senate when Congress adjourned.

Polk was alert to the threat that the Wilmot Proviso posed to both his expansionist program and Democratic unity, so he extracted a promise from Wilmot that he would not introduce the Proviso in the second session of the 29th Congress (1845–1847). Rep. Preston King of New York, however, a Democrat and a member of the original group that drafted the amendment, reintroduced the Proviso on 4 January 1847. King's action heralded the beginning of a sustained struggle in national politics over the expansion of slavery, a struggle that would culminate in civil war.

In 1848 the Senate ratified a treaty of peace with Mexico, by which the United States acquired New Mexico and California, making the question of slavery's expansion no longer hypothetical. The deliberations of the 30th Congress (1847–1849) were dominated by the slavery issue to an extent that was unimaginable even two years earlier. Despaired

Whig senator Thomas Corwin of Ohio, "It meets you in every step you take, it threatens you which way soever you go."

In dealing with the problem of slavery's extension to the new territories, Congress could choose from four possible solutions. The extreme northern position was represented by the Wilmot Proviso—that Congress should prohibit slavery from all the territories. The extreme southern position, largely the work of John C. Calhoun, argued that under the Constitution slavery was legal in all the territories, and only at the time of statehood could it be prohibited. Between these sectional positions were two moderate alternatives. One was to extend the Missouri Compromise line of 36°30′ north latitude to the Pacific and continue the traditional policy of dividing the national domain between freedom and slavery. A number of southern congressmen, including some radicals who believed that Congress

THE UNCERTAIN DEATH OF SLAVERY. Wood engraving that expresses doubt about the ability of various pieces of federal legislation to end slavery in the United States. The illustration includes two newspaper clippings that tell of blacks being whipped and enslaved as punishment for crimes, despite the passage of the Fourteenth Amendment and the Civil Rights Act of 1866. Wood engraving after Thomas Nast, *Harper's Weekly*, 12 January 1867.   LIBRARY OF CONGRESS

HOUSE OF REPRESENTATIVES.   During an impassioned debate over an antislavery petition.   LIBRARY OF CONGRESS

had no power to prohibit slavery from a territory, were willing to accept this solution as fair and equitable. The other moderate proposal, initially suggested by Sen. Lewis Cass of Michigan, but which became most closely identified with Sen. Stephen A. Douglas of Illinois, was to let the residents of the territory decide whether they wanted slavery or not. Advocates trumpeted this doctrine, known as popular sovereignty, as a democratic solution to the vexing problem of slavery's expansion.

Even though the United States had acquired the southern half of Oregon in 1846, the ensuing imbroglio over the slavery issue prevented Congress from organizing that province. The impasse between the sections was the worst crisis since South Carolina's attempt to nullify the tariff in 1832 and 1833. Douglas proposed to extend the Missouri Compromise line to the Pacific. The Senate, with strong southern support, embraced this solution, only to see the northern-controlled House reject it. At this point, Congress passed an Oregon territorial bill prohibiting slavery, and Polk signed it since the region was entirely north of 36°30′ north latitude.

The territorial question became more pressing following the discovery of gold in California in 1848. Rather than going through a drawn-out process of settlement, California within a year had a sufficient population to be admitted as a state. Its admission was unusually important because the number of free and slave states was equal at fifteen each, and the admission of California would break this sectional balance.

With tensions rising and tempers frayed, Henry Clay stepped forward in Congress to propose yet another solution to the sectional crisis. His comprehensive plan, introduced in January 1850, included the admission of California as a free state; organization of the rest of the Mexican cession into the Utah and New Mexico territories under popular sovereignty; fixing the western boundary of Texas at approximately its present limits, thereby giving the disputed region around Santa Fe to New Mexico; assumption of the debt of the Texas Republic by the federal government in exchange for Texas yielding in its boundary dispute with New Mexico; abolition of the slave trade (but not slavery) in the District of

Columbia; a new and more rigorous fugitive slave law to replace the ineffective act of 1793; and a resolution declaring that Congress had no power over the interstate slave trade. In order to reinforce the idea that this was a genuine compromise, Clay united the California, New Mexico, Utah, and Texas boundary proposals into a single omnibus bill.

Congress debated Clay's plan for six months. At the end of July the Senate voted on the omnibus bill, but in the balloting, northern and southern extremists deleted most of its provisions. Clay's gamble that the supporters of compromise were a majority of Congress had failed. Discouraged and physically exhausted, the 73-year-old senator left Washington with his compromise plan in shambles.

At this point, Illinois Democrat Stephen A. Douglas took over floor leadership of the procompromise forces. Realizing that the supporters of compromise were a minority of Congress, Douglas had always opposed the omnibus strategy. He therefore undertook to pass each part of Clay's plan as a separate bill by combining the procompromise forces in Congress with shifting sectional blocs. By mid-September, Congress had individually approved all of Clay's plan, and President Millard Fillmore had signed the bills into law.

The Compromise of 1850 was more an armistice than a true compromise. Only once, in the Senate on the New Mexico territorial bill, did a majority of northerners and southerners vote together on a roll call. The strongest support for the Compromise came from northern Democrats and southern Whigs, but only four senators and twenty-eight representatives, a mere 11 percent of the membership, voted for the entire Compromise. The alignment on the Compromise of 1850 was very different from that on the Missouri Compromise of 1820. In 1820, southerners in Congress had generally supported the Missouri Compromise, while most northern members were opposed. In 1850, in contrast, representatives from the two sections consistently opposed each other.

The armistice of 1850 was suddenly shattered in January 1854 when Douglas, as chairman of the Senate Committee on the Territories, introduced a bill to organize the remaining portion of the Louisiana Purchase west of Missouri and Iowa. Under the terms of the Missouri Compromise, this area had been forever guaranteed to freedom, but under pressure from a small group of southern senators, Douglas agreed to circumvent the Missouri Compromise's ban on slavery.

In its final form the bill created two territories, Kansas and Nebraska, explicitly repealed the Missouri Compromise, and substituted the doctrine of popular sovereignty instead. The precise meaning of popular sovereignty was not made clear; the bill's southern supporters rejected Douglas's notion that the residents of a territory could abolish slavery at any time, which they derisively labeled "squatter sovereignty."

Despite the wave of anger that swept across the North, there was never any doubt, once President Franklin Pierce endorsed the bill as a Democratic party measure, that it would pass the Senate. In March the Senate approved it by a vote of 37 to 14. The real fight was in the House. For two months representatives wrangled over the bill while the administration mounted intense pressure on northern Democrats. Finally, on 22 May, the bill passed the House by a tally of 113 to 100. Northern Whigs unanimously opposed the bill, as did half of the northern Democrats. Only nine southern congressmen, primarily from the border states, voted against the bill. When Franklin Pierce signed the Kansas-Nebraska Act on 30 May, the Missouri Compromise, which for thirty-four years had symbolized the founding generation's approach to the slavery question, was repealed.

Contrary to Douglas's predictions, the Kansas-Nebraska Act heightened the agitation over slavery and deepened the division between the sections. The congressional elections in the fall of 1854 produced one of the sharpest turnovers in American history, as northern Democrats fell victim to widespread popular anger over the repeal of the Missouri Compromise. When the dust settled, the Democratic party retained only 25 of the 91 northern seats it had held in the previous Congress. In addition, the Kansas-Nebraska Act precipitated the formation of a new antislavery party, the Republican party, which took the Wilmot Proviso as its major principle and before long displaced the Whigs as the major opposition party to the Democrats. And finally, popular sovereignty proved a complete failure in Kansas, where fighting soon broke out between proslavery and antislavery forces.

The attention of the 34th Congress (1855–1857) was monopolized by the situation in Kansas. Antislavery settlers soon repudiated the proslavery territorial authorities, established a rival government, and applied for admission as a free state. The Democratic national leadership tried to restore peace in Kansas, but Republicans, who were the largest group in the House, insisted on Kansas's admission as a free state. Sectional animosity was fueled as well by the assault of Rep. Preston S. Brooks of South Carolina on Sen. Charles Sumner of Massachusetts in the Senate chamber in retaliation for an antislavery speech Sumner had delivered on Kansas. After a motion to expel Brooks failed in the House, he defiantly resigned and was triumphantly reelected.

In the national election that fall, Democrats narrowly elected James Buchanan president over the suddenly resurgent Republican party. Two days after Buchanan's inauguration in March 1857, the Supreme Court handed down its long-delayed ruling in the Dred Scott *(Scott v. Sandford)* case. In a sweeping decision, the Court majority declared that Congress had no power to prohibit slavery from any territory, and it went out of its way to strike down as unconstitutional the Missouri Compromise, which had been repealed in 1854 by the Kansas-Nebraska Act. Republicans refused to accept the decision, which contravened all past precedents, as binding, and party members in Congress kept up a steady agitation to prohibit slavery in Kansas and all the territories.

That same year a constitutional convention held in the town of Lecompton, Kansas, drafted a proslavery constitution. With antislavery voters boycotting the election, the Lecompton constitution was approved, and Kansas formally applied for admission as the sixteenth slave state in the Union. Southern members of Congress suddenly confronted an unexpected chance to add one more slave state to the Union, and Buchanan, who sympathized with the South, endorsed Kansas's admission under the Lecompton constitution. This decision was too much for Stephen A. Douglas, the chief advocate of popular sovereignty, and in December 1857, after a stormy interview with the president, Douglas broke with the Democratic party leadership and announced his opposition to the Lecompton constitution.

A titanic struggle ensued in Congress over the admission of Kansas as a slave state. Douglas led the assault on the bill, but on 23 March 1858, after two months of debating, the Senate approved the Lecompton constitution by a vote of 33 to 25. The House then became the arena for one of the fiercest battles in U.S. political history. In an effort to drive the bill through the House, the Buchanan administration pulled out all the stops, including offers of outright bribes to gain the necessary votes. In the end, the House, on 1 April, rejected the Lecompton constitution by a 120 to 112 vote. All 92 Republi-

cans joined 22 northern anti-Lecompton Democrats who followed Douglas's lead and 6 southern Know-Nothings to defeat the bill.

Democratic leaders subsequently worked out a compromise whereby, through indirect means, the voters of Kansas would be allowed to vote again on the Lecompton constitution. On 2 August, with antislavery forces participating, the voters of Kansas rejected the Lecompton constitution by an overwhelming margin. The defeat of the Lecompton constitution terminated the Kansas issue in national politics.

Yet the outcome of the Kansas struggle did not remove the slavery issue from Congress. By now virtually every domestic issue before Congress carried sectional overtones. On New Year's Day 1860, former attorney general Caleb Cushing wrote from Washington after witnessing the debates in Congress: "We seem to be drifting into destruction before our eyes in utter helplessness. The Administra-

NORTHERN VICTORY IN THE HOUSE. On 2 February 1856, Massachusetts Know-Nothing Nathaniel P. Banks was elected Speaker of the House over a South Carolina slaveowner after a nine-week, 133-ballot deadlock. Banks was a former Democrat who had broken with his party over the slavery issue and who later joined the antislavery Republican party. The illustration depicts northerners in the gallery cheering as Banks wins.

NEW YORK STATE HISTORICAL ASSOCIATION, COOPERSTOWN

tion is utterly depopularized; Congress is paralyzed by party spirit; and everybody seems to despair."

In this atmosphere Sen. Jefferson Davis of Mississippi introduced a set of resolutions in January 1860 declaring that the people of a territory could not decide the status of slavery until the time of statehood, and that since slavery was legal during the territorial phase, Congress should pass a slave code to protect slavery in all the territories. The Democratic caucus, under southern control, endorsed Davis's resolutions as a true interpretation of the Constitution. Douglas and other northern Democrats angrily denounced these southern demands as intended merely to foster sectional agitation.

This demand for a congressional slave code split the Democratic party in the 1860 election and helped pave the way for the election of Abraham Lincoln as the nation's first Republican president in November. Even though Republicans were a minority in both houses of Congress, the seven states of the Deep South seceded from the Union between December 1860 and February 1861 in response to Lincoln's election. On 7 February, these states established the Confederate States of America.

Hope for a peaceful solution to the crisis focused on Congress. With Buchanan a repudiated lame duck, leadership fell to the legislative branch almost by default. Once Congress assembled on 3 December, a number of compromise proposals were introduced, but that of Sen. John J. Crittenden of Kentucky, who appropriately held Henry Clay's old seat, received the most attention.

Crittenden's compromise plan was exceedingly complex, and to protect it from legislative interference most of its provisions were in the form of constitutional amendments. But it had two key provisions. First, he introduced an "unamendable amendment" forever guaranteeing slavery in the states where it currently existed. And second, he proposed to extend the Missouri Compromise line of 36°30' north latitude to California, with slavery prohibited in any territory north of the line and legal and protected in all territory south of the line.

Both houses appointed special committees to consider Crittenden's and other compromise proposals. The Senate committee quickly reported that it could not agree on any solution. Attention then shifted to the House, where a committee of thirty-three had been appointed, one member from each state. Of the proposals endorsed by this committee, the most important was the unamendable amendment, which the House approved by the bare two-thirds majority required. Just prior to adjourn-

ment, the Senate concurred. Several states quickly ratified it, but the outbreak of war shortly thereafter ended any chance that it would be adopted.

In the end, despite three months of debate and private discussions, Congress had not come close to finding an acceptable solution to this crisis. Neither of the two groups that had to make a compromise—the Republicans of the North and the secessionists of the Deep South—had any interest in compromise. Also important was the private opposition of president-elect Lincoln, who wrote several Republican members urging them to stand firm. In addition, there was no period of delay as there had been in 1850, and this time secession was not a threat but a reality. In hindsight, it is apparent that there was never any chance for compromise. Indeed, the nation was lucky to have averted another compromise, for if ratified, Crittenden's unamendable amendment would have made it extremely difficult to end slavery.

Six weeks after Congress adjourned, war broke out between the Union and the Confederacy, and four more states, the entire upper South led by Virginia, seceded and joined the Confederacy. Lincoln responded by calling Congress into special session to meet on 4 July 1861.

The 37th Congress (1861–1863) was destined to be one of the greatest and most productive in U.S. history. From the start members confronted the problem of defining the Union's war aims, with southern Unionists especially anxious to secure a declaration that slavery would still be protected. Following the Union disaster at Bull Run, with the loyalty of the border slave states hanging in the balance, Crittenden, who was then serving in the House, introduced the following resolution: "That this war is not waged for any purpose of overthrowing or interfering with the rights or established institutions of these States, but to defend and maintain the supremacy of the Constitution and to preserve the Union." The House approved the Crittenden Resolution by a vote of 117 to 2. The Senate endorsed, 30 to 5, a virtually identical resolution offered by Andrew Johnson of Tennessee.

While Congress, with Lincoln's concurrence, proclaimed that the war was being waged to save the Union and not to abolish slavery, the conflict itself steadily weakened the institution. One problem that immediately arose was what to do with runaway slaves who entered the Union military lines. Congress passed the First Confiscation Act in August 1861, which declared that any slaves who had been used by the Confederacy for military purposes were to be freed. Since the law provided no specific procedure for granting freedom, its ultimate impact was uncertain.

When Congress reconvened in December 1861, the Radical Republicans kept up constant pressure to attack slavery as part of the Union war effort. Evidence that public opinion in the North was shifting could be seen in the House's refusal to approve the Crittenden Resolution when it was reintroduced during this session. Congress passed a series of antislavery measures in this session. It prohibited the army from capturing or returning runaway slaves, including those of owners loyal to the Union. It emancipated the two thousand slaves in the District of Columbia, with compensation of $300 per slave for loyal owners (the only slaveowners compensated for their slave property). And, ignoring the Dred Scott decision, it abolished slavery in the territories.

The most important piece of antislavery legislation passed in this congressional session, however, was the Second Confiscation Act, approved in July 1862. It declared that the slaves of any disloyal person were free if they came into Union custody. In one sense the Second Confiscation Act went beyond the Emancipation Proclamation, for it did not exempt any part of the Confederacy from its provisions.

Despite the growing congressional assault on slavery, Lincoln continued to work for compensated emancipation by state and not federal action. In March 1862 he asked Congress to pass a joint resolution pledging financial aid to any state that abolished slavery. Congress passed the resolution, with Republicans voting unanimously in favor. But border state representatives stubbornly clung to the institution and refused to embrace emancipation.

The Second Confiscation Act authorized the president to use African Americans to suppress the rebellion. The Militia Act, passed at the same time, in July 1862, repealed the long-standing prohibition on enrollment of blacks and authorized the president to accept "persons of African descent" into the military. The law also stipulated that any slave of a disloyal master who served in the military was to be freed, as were his family members (mother, wife, and children). In the following month the War Department authorized the recruitment of blacks into the army, and in issuing the final Emancipation Proclamation on 1 January 1863, Lincoln announced that blacks would be accepted into the Union's armed forces.

The congressional attack on slavery intensified in the 38th Congress (1863–1865). Republicans, who controlled both houses (though with reduced majorities), were less concerned about sentiment in the border states. Under their leadership Congress repealed the Fugitive Slave acts of 1793 and 1850. A law passed in February 1864, amending the Militia Act, emancipated the slaves of owners loyal to the Union who served in the military. And the Wade-Davis bill, which established a program of reconstruction for the states of the Confederacy, provided for the emancipation of all slaves in the Confederacy, which went beyond both the Second Confiscation Act and the Emancipation Proclamation. Lincoln's pocket veto of the bill unleashed a storm of protest from radical members of Congress.

Although the Emancipation Proclamation proclaimed slaves in the areas designated to be in rebellion forever free, its legal status remained murky, as did the status of slaves who were not officially freed during the war by whatever means. Republicans therefore believed that a constitutional amendment was needed to end this legal confusion and make emancipation secure. In 1864 a proposed amendment was introduced in the House abolishing slavery. Modeled on the wording of Jefferson's Northwest Ordinance, it declared: "Neither slavery nor involuntary servitude, except as punishment for crime whereof the party shall have been duly convicted, shall exist within the United States, or any place subject to their jurisdiction."

The amendment passed both the House and the Senate in 1864, but lacked the necessary two-thirds majority in the lower house. On 31 January 1865, after the sweeping Republican triumph in the 1864 election and intense lobbying efforts by the administration, the House passed the proposed amendment by a vote of 119 to 56. It was ratified in December 1865.

The Thirteenth Amendment brought to a close nearly a century of congressional concern over the institution of slavery. That history can be divided into four distinct periods. In the first, which extended from the Northwest Ordinance of 1787 to the Missouri Compromise of 1820, Congress avoided the issue as much as possible in order not to endanger the Union. It treated slavery as strictly a state institution, divided the territories between the North and the South, and frowned on sectional agitation.

In the second phase, extending from 1821 to 1846, national political leaders undertook to sup-

Landmark Slavery Legislation

TITLE	YEAR ENACTED	REFERENCE NUMBER	DESCRIPTION
Northwest Ordinance	1787		Abolished slavery in the Northwest Territory; combined with the Southwest Ordinance, established the policy of dividing the territories between the free states and slave states.
Southwest Ordinance	1787		Opened the Southwest Territory to slavery.
Fugitive Slave Act	1793	1 Stat. 302–305	The federal government assumed responsibility for enforcing the clause of the Constitution mandating the return of runaway slaves to their masters.
Slave Trade Prohibition Act	1807	2 Stat. 426–430	Prohibited the importation of slaves from Africa into any area within U.S. jurisdiction after 1 January 1808.
Missouri Compromise	1819, 1820	3 Stat. 544, 545–548	Continued the policy of dividing the territories between freedom and slavery along a geographic line in the Louisiana Purchase
Compromise of 1850	1850		A collection of bills enacted in an attempt to settle the major disputes between the North and the South; applied the principle of popular sovereignty to the Mexican cession.
Kansas-Nebraska Act	1854	10 Stat. 277–290	Repealed the Missouri Compromise; organized the Kansas and Nebraska territories under popular sovereignty.
Unamendable Amendment	1861		The only part of the Crittenden Compromise to pass, it guaranteed slavery in the southern states but was not ratified.
First Slave Confiscation Act	1861	12 Stat. 319	Emancipated slaves who had been used for military purposes by the Confederacy.
An Act of 16 April 1862	1862	12 Stat. 376–378	Slavery abolished in the District of Columbia.
An Act of 19 June 1862	1862	12 Stat. 432	Provided emancipation in the territories, but without compensation.
Second Confiscation Act	1862	12 Stat. 589–592	Emancipated slaves owned by Confederates who came under Union control. Authorized the president to employ blacks to suppress the rebellion.
Wade-Davis bill	1864[1]		Abolished slavery in the Confederate states as part of a congressional program of reconstruction. It was pocket vetoed by Lincoln.
Thirteenth Amendment	1865	13 Stat. 774–775	Approved by Congress in January and ratified by the required number of states in December, it abolished slavery throughout the United States.

[1]Year of congressional approval

press the slavery issue. National parties avoided sectional issues as detrimental to party unity, Congress tried to prevent debate on the issue, and the two parties sought to isolate sectional spokesmen in Congress. Their efforts were ultimately ineffective: both abolitionists and southern radicals thrust the slavery issue into the congressional arena in the 1830s against the wishes of party leaders. Yet on most other issues, party ties remained strong, frustrating efforts of individuals such as John C. Calhoun to sectionalize alignments in Congress.

A new phase commenced in 1846 with the war against Mexico. From then until the beginning of the Civil War in April 1861, the question of the expansion of slavery was the most important issue in U.S. politics. Congress tried to settle the problem by the Compromise of 1850, but in the long run it was a failure. From the passage of the Kansas-Nebraska bill in 1854 to the defeat of the Crittenden Compromise in 1861, Congress labored unsuccessfully to devise a solution acceptable to both sections. By the end of the 1850s virtually every issue in national politics—economic policy, the Homestead Act, the transcontinental railroad—had become entangled with the slavery issue. Attitudes in both sections hardened, animosities intensified, the spirit of mutual accommodation withered, and in the final crisis that led to war, neither side would compromise.

With the outbreak of the Civil War in 1861, the history of the slavery issue in Congress entered its final phase. From the beginning of the war, antislavery radicals in the Republican party were anxious to attack slavery as part of the Union's war effort. They were initially held in check by more moderate members, but the failure of the Union to quickly win the war strengthened the antislavery forces, who argued that victory was possible only by destroying slavery. Pressed by the radicals, Congress steadily chipped away at the institution. The congressional attack on slavery culminated in passage of the Thirteenth Amendment, which abolished slavery throughout the United States.

Any attempt to deal with the question of slavery inevitably ran athwart the institution's enormous economic importance and the power of racism in the fabric of American life. It fell to Congress to find an acceptable solution to the dilemma of the existence of racial slavery in a republic based on the principles of liberty and equality. But with the South unable to contemplate even a gradual end to the institution, the issue was beyond the power—and the vision—of Congress in the years before 1861. Throughout the sweep of U.S. history, slavery has been the only problem so intractable that it produced a complete breakdown of the democratic process. In the end, it required the cataclysm of civil war to destroy the institution of slavery.

[See also Civil War; Compromise of 1850; Fugitive Slave Act; Gag Rule; Homestead Act; Kansas-Nebraska Act; Missouri Compromise; Scott v. Sandford; Secession; Thirteenth Amendment; Wilmot Proviso.]

BIBLIOGRAPHY

Alexander, Thomas B. Sectional Stress and Party Strength: A Computer Analysis of Roll-Call Voting Patterns in the United States House of Representatives, 1836–1860. 1967.

Brown, Richard H. "The Missouri Crisis, Slavery, and the Politics of Jacksonianism." South Atlantic Quarterly 65 (1966): 52–72.

Craven, Avery O. The Growth of Southern Nationalism, 1848–1861. 1953.

Brock, William R. Politics and Political Conscience: American Dilemmas, 1840–1850. 1979.

Curry, Leonard P. Blueprint for Modern America: Non-Military Legislation of the First Civil War Congress. 1968.

Freehling, William W. The Road to Disunion: Secessionists at Bay, 1776–1854. 1990.

Hamilton, Holman. Prologue to Conflict: The Crisis and Compromise of 1850. 1964.

Moore, Glover. The Missouri Controversy, 1819–1821. 1953.

Potter, David. The Impending Crisis, 1848–1861. 1976.

Randall, James G. Constitutional Problems under Lincoln. Rev. ed. 1964.

Robinson, Donald L. Slavery in the Structure of American Politics, 1765–1820. 1971.

Silbey, Joel H. The Shrine of Party: Congressional Voting Behavior, 1841–1852. 1967.

Sydnor, Charles. The Development of Southern Sectionalism, 1819–1848. 1948.

WILLIAM E. GIENAPP

SMALL BUSINESS COMMITTEE, HOUSE.

Organized by the U.S. House of Representatives to consider legislative issues that affect America's small businesses, the Committee on Small Business is one of twenty-two House standing committees in the 103d Congress (1993–1995). Historically, a variety of panels within the House of Representatives have addressed small business issues. The House in 1941 established the Select Committee on Small Business, which remained in existence until 1974. Like most select committees, it was a study panel only and had no legislative authority.

While the Select Committee on Small Business studied small business issues, legislative authority remained with the Banking and Currency Committee (the predecessor to the Committee on Banking, Finance, and Urban Affairs). During each Congress, the Banking and Currency Committee would traditionally establish a small business subcommittee to consider small business legislation.

In 1974 the House adopted a reorganization plan that changed the jurisdictions of some committees. One change was the creation of a permanent standing Committee on Small Business to replace the Select Committee on Small Business. Jurisdiction over small business issues was moved from the Banking Committee to the new committee.

The Committee on Small Business remains a part of the House committee system in the 103d Congress. The jurisdiction of the committee includes assistance to and protection of small business, including financial aid, and participation of small business enterprises in federal procurement and government contracts. In addition to this legislative jurisdiction, the committee has responsibility for small business–related oversight.

The Committee on Small Business, and the select committee that preceded it, have been closely tied to small business constituencies. The U.S. House of Representatives first organized the select Committee in response to the emergence of small business activists and lobbying organizations such as the National Small Business Union, chartered in 1937. The House continues to be protective of small business interests, and the committee and its members frequently lead the House in these efforts. For example, in 1985 the Small Business Committee was instrumental in the sound defeat of the Reagan administration's attempt to eliminate the Small Business Administration (SBA).

Membership on the Small Business Committee numbers forty-four (only eight House standing committees have more members) and is actively sought by House members because it gives them an opportunity to perform direct services for their constituents. These direct services, which include overseeing the Small Business Administration and examining the impact of general business practices and trends on small businesses, allow these committee members to form special links with small business groups and with the thousands of small business owners in every congressional district of the nation, which in turn can enhance their chances for reelection.

The Small Business Committee actively conducts oversight on a wide range of issues. In the 102d Congress, topics addressed by the committee included: doing business in the Persian Gulf region; effects of wetlands protection regulations on small business; women's business issues; and federal programming assisting small businesses with drug abuse problems.

[See also Small Business Committee, Senate.]

BIBLIOGRAPHY

U.S. Congress. *Congressional Record*. 100th Cong., 2d sess., 19 October 1988. See John J. LaFalce, "Small Business Accomplishments," pp. E3508–E3510.

Victor, Kirk. "Uncle Sam's Little Engine." *National Journal*, 23 November 1991, pp. 2855–2859.

MARY ETTA BOESL

SMALL BUSINESS COMMITTEE, SENATE.

Organized by the U.S. Senate to consider issues concerning small businesses in general, and the Small Business Administration (SBA) in partic-

ular, the Committee on Small Business is one of seventeen Senate standing committees in the 103d Congress (1993–1995).

Since 1950, the Senate has continuously authorized a panel to focus on small business issues. The structure and authority of these committees have varied. When the Senate created the Select Committee on Small Business in 1950, that panel was structured as a traditional select committee; it was authorized to study problems relating to small business, but did not have legislative jurisdiction over small business issues.

A 1976 Senate resolution gave the committee legislative authority over the Small Business Administration, as well as retaining the panel's responsibility to study small business–related problems. Even though the committee obtained legislative responsibilities, it continued to be called the Select Committee on Small Business.

During the 1977 Senate committee reorganization, there were marked differences of opinion about a small business panel. Senators who drafted the committee system overhaul proposal recommended that Select Small Business be eliminated. During floor debate on the reorganization proposal, another group of senators offered an amendment to restructure the select committee, giving it permanent and independent standing committee status. The final outcome was a continuation of Select Small Business structured as it had been prior to the reorganization effort.

In March 1981 the Senate again considered the structure of the Select Small Business Committee. The Senate resolution did not attempt to remove the committee's legislative jurisdiction, but instead gave the panel standing committee status and renamed it the Senate Committee on Small Business.

Thus the Committee on Small Business has remained a part of the Senate standing committee system. It has responsibility for: (1) all proposed legislation, messages, petitions, memorials, and other matters relating to the Small Business Administration; (2) joint consideration with other standing committees of portions of legislation referred to Small Business but related to matters other than the functions of the SBA, or portions of legislation referred to other standing committees but related to functions of the SBA; and (3) studying and surveying, by research and investigation, all problems of American small business enterprises, and reporting thereon from time to time.

The Small Business Committee is closely tied to small business constituencies. Smith and Deering

(1990) found that senators seek appointment to the Small Business Committee for two reasons: to serve constituents and to have an impact on public policy. In terms of constituency services, more than half of America's workers are employed in small businesses. Thus, the authority to investigate problems that affect small business enterprises, coupled with jurisdiction over the vast array of services provided by the Small Business Administration, offer Small Business Committee members many opportunities to serve their constituents. Although small business issues are usually not high on the national policy agenda, these policy issues are of direct consequence to many voters in a senator's home state.

[*See also* Small Business Committee, House.]

BIBLIOGRAPHY

Malbin, Michael J. *Unelected Representatives: Congressional Staff and the Future of Representative Government.* 1980.
Smith, Steven S., and Christopher J. Deering. *Committees in Congress.* 2d ed. 1990.

MARY ETTA BOESL

SMALL BUSINESS LEGISLATION. The U. S. government has historically enacted laws that have protected the American ideals of free markets, free competition, and entrepreneurship. Federal legislation regulating business appeared soon after the Industrial Revolution began. The first antitrust law, the Sherman Antitrust Act of 1890, sought to ensure equal opportunity and to protect against monopolies. The Clayton Antitrust Act of 1914 and the Robinson-Patman Antidiscrimination Act of 1936 were also designed to favor competition and opportunity in a free marketplace and to protect against monopolies.

Following World War I, some individuals realized that federal laws and regulations, which were intended to regulate large companies, were not always advantageous to the small business sector of the economy. Small business owners began to organize and to lobby for laws favorable to small business.

In 1953 Congress passed the first Small Business Act, which declared it the policy of the U. S. government to aid, counsel, assist, and protect the in-

Landmark Legislation

TITLE	YEAR ENACTED	REFERENCE NUMBER	DESCRIPTION
Small Business Act	1953	Title II of P.L. 53-163	The first federal law that specifically protected the interests of America's small businesses; provided the framework for small business policy and created the Small Business Administration (SBA) to administer federal small business programs.
Small Business Investment Act	1958	P.L. 85-699	Provided for state and local development companies called Small Business Investment Companies that, supported by the SBA, assist small businesses.
Amendments to the Small Business Investment Act	1978	P.L. 95-507	Established federal policies and programs for minority business development; included debt and equity capital financing, technical support, and set-asides for minority-owned small businesses.
Small Business Innovation Development Act	1982	P.L. 97-219	To assist small, high-technology firms, this set-aside law requires federal agencies with large research and development budgets to spend a portion of their funding on small business concerns.
Small Business International Trade and Competitiveness Act; Title VIII of the Omnibus Trade and Competitiveness Act of 1988	1988	P.L. 100-418	Provides financial and technical assistance to enhance the ability of small businesses to export, to compete effectively against imports, and to access long-term capital to purchase new plants and equipment used in the production of goods and services involved in international trade.
Women's Business Ownership Act	1988	P.L. 100-533	Seeks to promote small businesses owned and controlled by women, and to identify and remove the discriminatory barriers encountered by women entrepreneurs.

terests of small business concerns. The act established the Small Business Administration (SBA) to administer small business programs.

The arguments of proponents of a federal small business assistance policy in 1953 were similar to the arguments of those who favored antitrust laws earlier in the century. Supporters believed that the ability of small businesses to compete in the marketplace was the measure of a free market system and that the federal government had a responsibility to protect free competition by fostering a climate that encouraged small business development.

In 1958 Congress expanded opportunities for small business owners to receive capital. That year the Small Business Investment Act added a network of state and local development companies to assist entrepreneurs.

Since the 1950s, Congress has continued to reauthorize general small business assistance programs, and to retain the SBA. General programs to assist small businesses include direct loans, disaster assistance, business development training and technical assistance, and assistance in contracting and subcontracting for work with the government and the private sector.

Since the 1970s, lawmakers have also enacted small business legislation directed toward specific populations within the small business community. For example, Congress has sought to foster the development of minority-owned small businesses. Law requires that a portion of contracting work be set aside for minority entrepreneurs; special investment companies have been formed to provide venture capital to minority enterprises; and the SBA operates a multifaceted Minority Small Business and Capital Ownership Development Program authorized by the Small Business Act.

Similarly, legislation has provided specific support to women entrepreneurs. Also administered by the SBA, legislation provides money for demonstration projects and for loans. Federal law also established a National Women's Business Council to recommend to the Congress and to the president ways to improve opportunities for women-owned businesses.

Recent small business legislation has been directed toward specific small business endeavors. The 1982 Small Business Innovation Development Act sought to assist small high-technology firms, and the 1988 Small Business International Trade and Competitiveness Act was designed to assist small businesses engaged in international trade.

[See also Clayton Antitrust Act; Federal Anti-Price Discrimination Act; Regulation and Deregulation; Sherman Antitrust Act; Small Business Committee, House; Small Business Committee, Senate.]

BIBLIOGRAPHY

Droitsch, Roland G. "The Dilemma of Regulating Small Business: The Need for a New Policy Framework." *Villanova Law Review* (November 1988): 971–988.
Thompson, Roger. "Small Business: What's Next." *Nation's Business* (October 1986): 37–39, 42, 46, 48, 50, 52.

MARY ETTA BOESL

SMITH, ELLISON D. (COTTON ED)

(1866–1944), Democratic senator from South Carolina (1908–1944), chairman of the Committee on Agriculture, and advocate for southern cotton growers. Ellison DuRant Smith entered politics in 1890 during an agrarian revolt against Wade Hampton's "aristocracy" and thereafter joined with liberal Democrats and Populists to oppose a protec-

ELLISON D. (COTTON ED) SMITH.

tive tariff, Wall Street, hard money, and big business. He served in the state legislature (1887–1890) but was defeated when he ran for Congress in 1901.

A cotton farmer at Lynchburg, he earned the nickname "Cotton Ed" for his work to organize southern cotton growers. In 1905 he strengthened his political base while a field agent for the Southern Cotton Association; in 1908 he was elected as a Democrat to the U.S. Senate, where he served for thirty-six years. He supported many of President Woodrow Wilson's progressive policies but opposed child-labor legislation and woman suffrage. After World War I, he sponsored the bill that created the Wilson Dam at Muscle Shoals, and opposed the Republican administrations from 1921 to 1933. A supporter of President Franklin D. Roosevelt, he chaired the Senate Agriculture Committee (1933–1944), favoring agricultural price supports but opposing crop controls and such New Deal measures as wage and hour controls that threatened to interfere with the South's economic and social structure. After 1935 he introduced demagogic race baiting into his political campaigns. Roosevelt's attempt to "purge" him from Congress in 1938 failed, and Smith made political hay by walking out of the next Democratic national convention because a black minister delivered its invocation. His opposition to the draft, lend-lease legislation, and other wartime policies—and his age—prevented his renomination in 1944.

BIBLIOGRAPHY

Hollis, Daniel W. "Cotton Ed Smith: Showman or Statesman?" *South Carolina History Magazine* 187 (Oct. 1970): 235–256.

Smith, Selden K. "Ellison DuRant Smith: A Southern Progressive." Ph.D. diss., University of South Carolina, 1970.

Wallace, David D. *The History of South Carolina.* Vol. 4. 1934.

PAOLO E. COLETTA

SMITH, HOWARD W.

SMITH, HOWARD W. (1883–1976), a Democratic representative from Virginia (1931–1967), chairman of the House Rules Committee (1955–1967). Respected and feared as a master of legislative legerdemain, Howard Worth Smith was chief of the powerful conservative coalition of Republicans and southern Democrats in Congress who delayed, but finally could not defeat, the vast expansion of federal authority in social legislation that climaxed with President Lyndon B. Johnson's Great Society.

HOWARD W. SMITH. As chairman of the House Rules Committee, calling the committee to order shortly before an 8 to 4 vote clearing President Lyndon B. Johnson's foreign aid bill for floor action, 23 December 1963.
LIBRARY OF CONGRESS

During his thirty-six years in the House as the representative of a northern Virginia district, "Judge" Smith fought bitterly against bills that he thought would give excessive influence to labor unions, minorities, and free-spending federal bureaucracies and would weaken the states' constitutional rights to control their own domestic affairs, especially in race relations.

Liberals hated him as the reactionary evil genius who bossed the House Rules Committee and controlled the flow of all bills to the floor. He was a vital cog in the bipartisan conservative coalition that emerged in the late 1930s and effectively stymied social legislation in the House for twenty years. Even before he became chairman in 1955, Smith wielded significant influence within the Rules Committee as leader of a narrow majority of Republicans and southern Democrats. Backed by fellow conservatives on the committee, he could delay a bill for weeks or months and would sometimes disappear to his dairy farm in Fauquier County to prevent a vote—hence his nickname: the Fox of Fauquier.

Cartoonists lampooned him as a mean, crusty old codger in a frock coat, wing collar, and pince-nez eyeglasses on a long black ribbon, blocking vital bills intended to benefit blacks, working folks, the elderly, and the poor. His courtly manner masked a razor-sharp mind and a fierce fighting spirit. He looked like a kind Virginia gentleman, but he fought like a guerrilla.

In early 1961, at the outset of his presidency, John F. Kennedy resolved to break Smith's stranglehold on legislation in the Rules Committee by adding two pro-administration Democrats and one Republican to its ranks, thus increasing the committee membership to fifteen and giving the pro-administration forces a precariously slim one-vote majority over the conservative coalition. Speaker Sam Rayburn (D-Tex.) threw his prestige behind the maneuver and the House narrowly approved it, 217 to 212.

In 1940, Congress passed Smith's first major bill, which required all aliens to register and be fingerprinted. The Alien Registration (Smith) Act was later used to convict communists accused of conspiring to overthrow the government. In 1943, Smith and Sen. Tom T. Connally (D-Tex.) cosponsored the Smith-Connally Anti-Strike Act, enacted over President Franklin D. Roosevelt's veto, which was intended to curb wartime strikes. Smith also wrote the section of the 1947 Taft-Hartley Labor-Management Relations Act, which permitted state "right to work" laws allowing workers to hold jobs without joining a union.

After the Supreme Court struck down school segregation, Smith took part in Virginia's "massive resistance" to integration. The Virginia General Assembly repealed the compulsory school attendance laws and provided tuition grants for some students to attend private schools. Also, the governor was authorized to close any school under court order to integrate and to cut off all state funds from any school that tried to reopen in obedience to court orders. Public schools at Norfolk, Charlottesville, and Front Royal were closed in the autumn of 1958. However, the courts nullified the "massive resistance" statutes. Consequently, Smith sponsored an unsuccessful bill to limit the Court's power to nullify state laws.

In a tongue-in-cheek move to scuttle the 1964 civil rights bill, Smith tacked on an amendment barring sex discrimination. It passed, and, ironical-ly, the old conservative is credited with an unintentional boost to the feminist movement.

After federal laws repealed poll taxes and literacy tests for voting, the number of black voters in Virginia and other southern states increased. The Virginia legislature also added many liberals to Smith's constituency in redrawing the lines of his district. As a result, he lost the 1966 Democratic primary to his liberal opponent George Rawlings, Jr., by a few hundred votes.

BIBLIOGRAPHY

Dierenfield, Bruce J. *Keeper of the Rules: Congressman Howard W. Smith of Virginia.* 1987.

FRANK VAN DER LINDEN

SMITH, MARGARET CHASE (1897–), Republican representative and senator from Maine, known for her independent mindedness, courage, and hard work. Margaret Chase Smith was unexpectedly propelled into a political career in 1940. Her husband, Rep. Clyde H. Smith (R-Me.), had not sufficiently recovered from a heart attack to campaign for reelection. He and his supporters convinced his wife—who had served as his chief assistant—to file and campaign in his place; she planned to withdraw when Representative Smith was able to resume his work. However, during her candidacy, Clyde Smith suffered a second, fatal heart attack.

Smith won the June 1940 special election to fill her husband's term. Then she won the September election and served as representative from Maine's Second District for four terms. In 1948 Smith won a seat in the U.S. Senate, a seat she held for the next twenty-four years.

Senator Smith earned many "firsts" during her career. She was the first woman to win election to both the U.S. House and the U.S. Senate, and in 1964 she became the first woman to have her name placed in nomination for the presidency by a major political party.

Another first for Senator Smith was her "Declaration of Conscience," a speech she gave before the Senate on 1 June 1950 denouncing the activities of Republican senator Joseph R. McCarthy. The first Republican to speak out against McCarthy, Smith won the admiration of her colleagues and the nation for her courageous stand.

Noted for her dedication to her work—she never missed a roll-call vote in the Senate—Smith was a moderate whose primary legislative interest was

MARGARET CHASE SMITH. On 11 January 1961.

military preparedness. She served on the House Naval Affairs Committee (1943–1948) and on the Senate Armed Services Committee (1949–1972).

One of the few women of her time in public life, Smith captured the imagination of many Americans. A detail that many felt epitomized her style was the rose that always graced her desk. Known to the citizens of Maine simply as "our Maggie," Smith was defeated in her bid to serve a fifth Senate term in 1972 and returned to her native Skowhegan.

BIBLIOGRAPHY

Gould, Alberta. *First Lady of the Senate: A Life of Margaret Chase Smith.* 1990.
Sherman, Janann. *No Place for a Woman: The Life and Times of Margaret Chase Smith.* Forthcoming.
Smith, Margaret Chase. *Declaration of Conscience.* 1972.

MARY ETTA BOESL

SMITH, SAMUEL (1752–1839), representative and senator from Maryland. Born in Lancaster, Pennsylvania, Smith fought in the Revolutionary War. By the early 1790s he had become one of Baltimore's richest merchants, and in 1793 he was elected to the House of Representatives. A year later he joined the Jeffersonian Republican party and built a powerful political machine based on his wealth and family connections, his popularity among Baltimore's skilled craftsmen, and his position as a militia general. As a congressman Smith represented commercial interests and supported a strong military.

In 1801 Smith proved to be the key figure in resolving the presidential election that had been thrust into the House of Representatives because Thomas Jefferson and Aaron Burr had received the same number of electoral votes. Both men were Republicans, and the party's intent had been to select Jefferson as president and Burr as vice president. Prior to the Twelfth Amendment to the Constitution, however, there was no way for electors to designate their votes by office. The House of Representatives had to choose between the two men, but the opposition Federalist party had sufficient votes to prevent Jefferson's selection, and some Federalists hoped to convince Burr to serve as a Federalist president. For days the House was deadlocked. The nation was plunged into a major political and constitutional crisis, with some Republican state governors threatening to mobilize troops if Jefferson were denied the presidency. Smith, as one of Jefferson's most influential supporters, worked with James A. Bayard, Sr., of Delaware and other Federalists to seek a solution that would break the impasse. Although Smith later denied it, he apparently misled Bayard on Jefferson's willingness, if elected president, to keep several of Bayard's friends employed in federal posts in Delaware. Believing Smith, Bayard made the necessary arrangements to give Jefferson the votes needed to become president.

Smith entered the Senate in 1803 and was chosen president pro tempore in 1805, 1806, and 1807. He led the fight in 1807 for approval of the embargo as an alternative to war with England over the *Chesapeake* Affair. During James Madison's presidency, Smith often opposed the administration's commercial policies. Madison retaliated by dismissing Smith's brother, Robert, as secretary of State and denying the senator access to patronage. Smith's political career then seemed to be over, but during the War of 1812 his military exploits at the Battle of Baltimore reestablished his popularity. In 1816 he returned to the House for three more terms and served as chairman of the Committee on Ways and Means between 1818 and 1822. In 1822 he was elected again to the Senate and soon associated himself with Andrew Jackson. As chairman of the Senate Finance Committee, Smith continued to champion U.S. commerce. He left the Congress in 1833, having served sixteen years in the House and twenty-four years in the Senate.

BIBLIOGRAPHY

Cassell, Frank A. *Merchant Congressman in the Young Republic: Samuel Smith of Maryland, 1752–1839*. 1971.
Pancake, John S. *Samuel Smith and the Politics of Business, 1752–1839*. 1972.

FRANK A. CASSELL

SMITH ACT. *See* Alien Registration Act.

SMITHSONIAN INSTITUTION. The legislation establishing the Smithsonian Institution was passed on 10 August 1846 following ten years of sometimes acrimonious debate. It provided for the erection of a building to contain a museum, a chemical laboratory, a library, a gallery of art, and lecture rooms. To fill the museum, the Smithsonian was given the right to claim the government's scientific and artistic collections in Washington. Beyond these two specifications, however, there was little concrete language concerning the programs of the Smithsonian. Decisions on policy were left to the discretion of the Smithsonian's governing board, the fifteen-member Board of Regents.

Funded through a bequest to the United States by James Smithson (1756–1829), an English scientist, the Smithsonian is not within the federal government. It is a charitable trust, with the government serving as the trustee. Members of all three branches of government sit on its Board of Regents, as do private citizens appointed by joint resolution of Congress. Congressional oversight was initially limited to the six congressional regents—three representatives chosen by the Speaker of the House and three senators by the president pro tempore of the Senate—although the regents are required to submit a report on the operations and expenditures of the Smithsonian to each session of Congress. The chief executive officer is the secretary, an employee of the regents, who does not require congressional confirmation.

During the tenure of Joseph Henry, the Smithsonian's first secretary, from 1846 to 1878, a number of important precedents were established regarding its relationship to Congress. First, the organization committee of the Board of Regents recommended that the Smithsonian serve as a nonpartisan center of scholarly excellence, and the congressional regents acted accordingly. Despite differences in political affiliation, congressional regents almost invariably became strong supporters of the Smithsonian, its programs, and its independence from political partisanship. Second, Congress repeatedly accepted an interpretation of the legislation that gave the regents the authority to decide Smithsonian policy. A corollary was Congress's repeated refusal in the nineteenth century to establish oversight committees for the Smithsonian. Third and most important for the long-term history of the Smithsonian, the institution began accepting federal appropriations to carry out activities on behalf of the federal government. Initially, Henry and the Board of Regents refused to assume responsibility for the government collections specified in the founding legislation. In 1857, however, the Smithsonian accepted the collections, contingent on a congressional appropriation of $17,000 for construction and moving costs and a $4,000 annual appropriation for maintenance costs. By the time of Henry's death, the annual appropriation for the collections had grown to $10,000, nearly a fifth of the total Smithsonian operating budget.

During the tenures of Henry's successors, the annual appropriations increased as the Smithsonian accepted more and more responsibilities on behalf of the government. By fiscal year 1989, the appropriation of over $211 million was 70 percent of the total Smithsonian operating budget. Through its increased appropriations, Congress has gained growing leverage over the operations of the Smithsonian. Nevertheless, the Smithsonian has maintained its nonpartisan nature and a degree of freedom.

The Smithsonian encompasses sixteen museums and galleries, four major research centers, and the National Zoo; it also offers a variety of educational and public service activities. Among its areas of concern are anthropology, astronomy, biology, ecology, art history, history of science and technology, and American history. The collections include over 140 million objects.

BIBLIOGRAPHY

Oehser, Paul H. *The Smithsonian Institution*. 1970.
Rhees, William Jones, ed. *The Smithsonian Institution: Documents Relative to Its Origin and History*. 1901.

MARC ROTHENBERG

SMOOT-HAWLEY TARIFF ACT. *See* Hawley-Smoot Tariff Act.

SNELL, BERTRAND H. (1870–1958), representative from New York and Republican House minority leader during the Depression and New Deal era (1931–1939). A rugged individualist who amassed a fortune in lumber, cheese manufacturing, and electric power and oil production, Snell entered the House of Representatives from the 31st District in New York in 1915 at the age of forty-four. He attained influence within Republican ranks through his close friendship with President Calvin Coolidge and with his appointment to the Rules Committee, becoming its chairman in 1923. In that position, Snell joined with two other Old Guard conservatives, Speaker Nicholas Longworth and Majority Leader John Q. Tilson, in forming the "terrible triumvirate" that ruled the House from 1925 until Longworth's death in 1931.

Snell's election as minority leader resulted from a bitter intraparty battle with Tilson after Longworth died and after the Republican majority in the 72d Congress (1931–1933) evaporated with the deaths of fourteen representatives-elect before Congress convened. Tilson, aligned with President Herbert Hoover, was in effect ousted as minority leader when Snell was designated the party's candidate for the speakership; he lost to John N. Garner (D-Tex.).

As the 1930s progressed, "the fighting lumberjack," as Snell was known, attempted to lead an ideologically divided and dwindling Republican cohort in the House. Termed "ineffectual and disorganized" by one political scientist, Snell's leadership style involved some accommodation with as well as outright antagonism toward the New Deal. Arguably, Snell's strategy of silence during the Court-packing controversy of 1937, which fostered southern Democratic opposition to Roosevelt, helped to promote the formation of the conservative coalition that plagued future liberal Democratic administrations. Recognizing that he would never achieve his long-held goal of attaining the speakership, Snell retired in 1938.

BIBLIOGRAPHY

Barone, Louis A. "Republican House Minority Leader Bertrand H. Snell and the Coming of the New Deal, 1931–1939." Ph.D. diss., State University of New York at Buffalo, 1969.

Ripley, Randall B. *Party Leaders in the House of Representatives.* 1967.

RICHARD C. BURNWEIT

BERTRAND H. SNELL.   LIBRARY OF CONGRESS

SOCIALISM. Two members of the Socialist Party of America have served in the House of Representatives: Victor L. Berger (1860–1929), who represented the German-dominated 5th Congressional District of Wisconsin (1911–1912, 1919, 1923–1928), and Meyer London (1871–1926), who represented the heavily immigrant 12th Congressional District of New York (1915–1918, 1921–1922). They never served in the same session, but together they provided an almost uninterrupted socialist voice in Congress from 1911 to 1928.

Before World War I, the Socialist party was a growing movement that required its elected legislators to shape their measures and votes in accord with party policy. Berger and London, who recognized that they were unlikely to see the triumph of socialism in their time, were revisionist Marxists. While favoring a planned and collectivist economy, they believed that a gradual transformation of the system from capitalism to socialism was possible. They criticized reform measures as basically inadequate but argued that they were necessary under

SOCIALIST RALLY. Anarchist Alexander Berkman addressing the crowd in Union Square, New York City, 1 May 1908.
LIBRARY OF CONGRESS

existing circumstances. For this stance, they were attacked by the left wing of their party.

In Congress, both Berger and London took anti-corporate positions and promoted social legislation and measures promoting political egalitarianism. They viewed many bills before the Congress, such as tariff and taxation reforms, as irrelevant or injurious to the interests of working people. Berger, a newspaper publisher and editor, introduced legislation to improve working conditions, establish public pensions, and socialize major industries. London, a labor lawyer, also sponsored legislation to improve working conditions and institute social insurance.

In foreign policy, both representatives emphasized the international solidarity of workers and criticized U.S. troop movements on the Mexican border. London opposed preparedness measures and voted against U.S. intervention in World War I and against conscription; he also sponsored measures to encourage the wartime nationalization of the food industry. Berger was returned to Congress in the 1918 election but was excluded from his seat

because his opposition to the war had resulted in his conviction under the wartime Espionage Act. Each supported First Amendment rights during the war and the postwar red scare, advocated amnesty for American political prisoners, favored the recognition of the Soviet Union while criticizing Bolshevism, and opposed immigration restriction.

Berger and London believed that their basic responsibility was to publicize socialist ideas rather than fight for unattainable legislation. While they have been the only members of a socialist party to serve in Congress, occasionally other representatives have sponsored proposals reflective of theirs. During the Depression, Progressive Thomas R. Amlie and Democrat Gerald J. Boileau of Wisconsin and Democrats H. Jerry Voorhis of California and Maury Maverick of Texas developed a measure to promote a planned economy, limit individual profits, and share corporate income with the public. Vito Marcantonio of the American Labor Party, representing East Harlem in New York (1934–1936, 1938–1950), offered a class perspective in House debates. In recent Congresses, both Ronald V. Dellums of California, a Democrat, and Bernard Sanders of Vermont, an independent identifying himself as a democratic socialist, promoted national health care, affordable housing, and other social legislation, all very much within Berger's and London's traditions. The support for such ideas at times has been widespread, as seen in the work of Republican Fiorello H. LaGuardia and other representatives and in a variety of progressive and farmer-labor movements.

BIBLIOGRAPHY

Miller, Sally M. *Victor Berger and the Promise of Constructive Socialism, 1910–1920.* 1973.

Rogoff, Harry. *An East Side Epic: The Life and Work of Meyer London, 1871–1926.* 1930.

SALLY M. MILLER

SOCIAL SECURITY ACT (1935; 49 Stat. 620–648). The Social Security Act of 1935 marks the founding of the welfare state in the United States. Based on the report of the Committee on Economic Security—a five-member, cabinet-level committee created by executive order in 1934, with Secretary of Labor Frances Perkins as chair—President Franklin D. Roosevelt recommended the bill to Congress on 17 January 1935. He signed it on 14 August, aptly noting that "if the Senate and the House of Representatives in this long and arduous session had done nothing more than pass this Bill, the session would be regarded as historic for all time."

Designed, in the president's words, to protect individuals against the "hazards and vicissitudes of life," the act was a response to the Great Depression yet was rooted in various social movements that had developed during the Progressive era. Inspired by European examples, these movements had succeeded in laying partial foundations for a system of social legislation at the state level. In particular, the planning of the Social Security Act drew on experience in Wisconsin. Edwin E. Witte, the executive director of the Committee on Economic Security, was a professor of economics at the University of Wisconsin. The staff worked in close collaboration with a Technical Board on Economic Security, drawn from the federal executive branch, that was chaired by Arthur J. Altmeyer, a former secretary of Wisconsin's Industrial Commission. Altmeyer served the Roosevelt administration as assistant secretary of Labor. From 1937 to 1953, he was social security commissioner; in effect, Altmeyer was the executive founder of today's social security program.

The act (P.L. 271, 74th Cong.) consisted of seven substantive titles, followed by four others that dealt with administration, finance, and technical matters. The least controversial were those titles (I, IV, V, VI, and X) that gave grants-in-aid to the states for assisting the needy aged, the blind, and dependent children; for maternal and child welfare; and for work in public health. These functions were not new to state and local governments, and the use of grants-in-aid was not new in intergovernmental relations. The principal innovation lay in extending federal grants to programs of public assistance.

Particularly in regard to grants-in-aid to benefit the aged, the act was thoroughly popular. Indeed, so great was the political appeal of old-age assistance that the designers of the legislation put those grants in Title I, hoping that more controversial titles would ride their coattails. Independent of the president's initiative, many bills authorizing federal grants-in-aid for the needy aged had been introduced in Congress, and one, the Dill-Connery bill, had passed the House in 1934. The congressional rank and file sympathized with the aged and feared the Townsend movement, which was demanding monthly pensions of $200 for everyone over sixty years of age.

Unemployment compensation, contained in Titles III and IX, was more controversial. Among the states, Wisconsin alone had enacted unemployment compensation legislation before 1935, and that only in 1932. The act employed a novel and ingenious "tax offset" technique, foreshadowed in a bill introduced in 1934 by the two chambers' labor committee chairmen, Sen. Robert F. Wagner of New York and Rep. David J. Lewis of Maryland. Congress imposed a payroll tax on employers with the provision that in states where unemployment compensation laws had been passed, employers' contributions for that purpose could be deducted from the federal tax. Thus, the new program remained basically a state responsibility, but responsive to federal inducements.

Old-age insurance, authorized by Titles II and VIII, was the most innovative provision, without precedent at the state level. It was to be a wholly federal program, administered by a three-member, presidentially appointed Social Security Board authorized by Title VII. Members of Congress were dubious about this measure, if only because it imposed a tax on employee wages and employer payrolls beginning 1 January 1937 but would not begin to pay retirement benefits until 1942 (a date that was moved up to 1940 by amendments in 1939). The chairman of the House Ways and Means Committee, Robert L. Doughton of North Carolina, and of the Senate Finance Committee, Pat Harrison of Mississippi, lacked enthusiasm for old-age insurance but loyally supported it after President Roosevelt chose to leave them in charge of the bill rather than seek to have it handled by the committees on labor. Because the bill contained provisions for raising revenue, it was properly under the jurisdiction of the revenue committees.

Republicans in Congress objected to old-age insurance as an illegitimate invasion of the private sphere but were unable to defeat it. Partisans of the private insurance industry, however, did succeed in defeating a provision that would have authorized the government to sell voluntary annuities. Another public-private issue, arising from a proposal by Sen. Joel Bennett Clark of Missouri to exempt from payroll taxes employers having government-approved pension plans, caused a House-Senate deadlock that delayed passage for several weeks. Ultimately, the bill passed without the provision. The vote in the House was 371 to 33, and in the Senate it was 76 to 6—margins that belie the intensity of Republican opposition at earlier stages. Every Republican but one had voted at least once to recommit.

Old-age insurance has been by far the most momentous provision of the Social Security Act. The Supreme Court paved the way for its development by finding the law constitutional in *Helvering v. Davis* (1937). Starting with amendments in 1939, which added benefits for dependents of retired workers and surviving dependents of deceased workers, coverage has frequently been amplified so that social insurance has become a broadly encompassing program, embracing virtually the entire population of workers and their dependents. It is the most costly domestic function of the federal government.

Other important enlargements came in 1950, when coverage was extended to farmers and the self-employed; in 1956, when disability benefits were added; in 1965, when health insurance for the aged (Medicare) was added; and in 1972, when health insurance was extended to the disabled and a very large benefit increase was enacted throughout the program, along with a provision for indexing of benefits—automatic annual adjustments tied to increases in the consumer price index. Until then, Congress had enacted frequent benefit increases ad hoc, typically in election years.

BIBLIOGRAPHY

Derthick, Martha. *Policymaking for Social Security.* 1979.
Lubove, Roy M. *The Struggle for Social Security, 1900–1935.* 1968.
National Conference on Social Welfare. *The Report of the Committee on Economic Security of 1935 and Other Basic Documents Relating to the Development of the Social Security Act.* 1985.
Schlesinger, Arthur M., Jr. *The Age of Roosevelt: The Coming of the New Deal.* 1959.

MARTHA DERTHICK

SOCIAL WELFARE AND POVERTY.

Since the federal government first entered the domain of social welfare and poverty policy in the 1930s, political conflicts have erupted over the type and extent of responsibility government should have for social welfare. In these debates over social policy, Congress has played a dual role. On the one hand, Republicans and conservative southern Democrats have regularly blocked extensions of social welfare policy. On the other hand, once programs have been established and won broad public support, Congress has often taken the lead in making benefits more generous. At the most general level, Congress has played a moderating role, blocking the most activist presidential inclinations either to cut or to extend social welfare benefits.

Although Congress embraced social welfare and poverty policy relatively late in the nation's history, congressional attention to social policy grew rapidly as expenditures rose. By 1990, social welfare expenditures comprised over half the national budget. As federal spending on social welfare grew, so did congressional attention to the organization, financing, and scope of social welfare programs. Because social welfare policies raise questions about financing and taxes, the House Ways and Means Committee and the Senate Finance Committee have played especially important roles in policy development.

New federal social welfare and poverty policy emerged in two great spurts of innovation, the New Deal of the 1930s and the Great Society of the 1960s. In each case, the executive branch set the agenda for reform, but Congress played a significant role in determining the character of the legislation ultimately passed. But the development of social welfare and poverty policy is not only the story of these major episodes of innovation. In the 1950s and again in the 1970s, Congress took the lead in preparing the ground for important extensions of social policy benefits and expanded federal funding.

Federal Policy before the New Deal. The federal government's authority to act in the sphere of social welfare is left ambiguous in the Constitution. Congressional authority over social welfare can be read into Article I, section 8, which gives Congress the power to "provide for the common Defence and general Welfare of the United States." On the other hand, the Tenth Amendment reserves for the states (or to the people) powers "not delegated to the United States by the Constitution, nor prohibited by it to the States"; this suggests that social policy might properly be the province of the states. In practice, social welfare was left to the states in the nineteenth century. Until the turn of the century and the rise of the Progressive movement, Congress took little initiative to enact social policy.

Civil War pensions. The one exception to this early pattern of inaction was pensions for Civil War veterans. Although the initial 1862 law authorizing the pensions covered only Union soldiers injured in battle or the dependents of those killed in the war, eligibility was expanded in the 1880s. With the passage of the Dependent Pension Act of 1890, virtually every northern Civil War veteran and his dependents were eligible for the pensions. Granting the pensions, which were provided by special acts of Congress, became an important congressional activity in the late nineteenth century. In the 49th Congress (1885–1887), 40 percent of the legislation in the House and 55 percent in the Senate consisted of special pension acts. Furthermore, pensions formed a large component of federal spending, reaching 34 percent of the budget in 1890. This highly politicized pattern of social welfare spending reflected the distributive bias and the patronage-based nature of congressional activity in the nineteenth century.

Progressive era initiatives. The wave of governmental reforms enacted during the Progressive era centered primarily on the state level, but several new laws staked out an expanded terrain for federal social welfare activity as well. Legislation focused on two areas: vocational education and rehabilitation measures and maternal and infant health legislation. Federal aid to vocational education and rehabilitation was in part a product of concerns provoked by World War I. With the end of European immigration, fears about shortages of skilled labor overcame congressional resistance to federal support for vocational education. The 1917 Smith-Hughes Act, which provided grants to the states to assist in administering vocational education programs, was the first federal-state grant program. It was followed by a rehabilitation law for veterans in 1918 and a rehabilitation program for civilians, established in 1920.

The Sheppard-Towner Act of 1921 signaled Congress's willingness to support social welfare activities that went beyond war-related measures. In the wake of the Nineteenth Amendment granting suffrage to women and more than a decade of pressure by women reformers, measures to promote child and maternal health were now supported by national law. This new legislation, passed by a Republican Congress, provided funds to the states to establish prenatal and child health centers in which women would be instructed in hygiene and other health matters by other women, generally public health nurses. Despite the spread throughout the country of clinics and visiting nurses sponsored by Sheppard-Towner, Congress terminated the program in 1929. Faced with strong opposition from the American Medical Association, which had earlier paid little attention to preventive care, the supporters of Sheppard-Towner were unable to convince Congress to renew funding.

Thus, on the eve of the Great Depression, social welfare was overwhelmingly the responsibility of state and local governments. Nonetheless, the important precedent of federal grants-in-aid for social welfare purposes had been established.

The New Deal. During the New Deal, a barrage of new social welfare legislation transformed the federal government's social role and opened up new fields of congressional activity. The economic emergency created by the Great Depression spurred newly elected president Franklin D. Roosevelt and the heavily Democratic Congress to consider measures that had been unthinkable only a few years earlier. The central piece of social welfare legislation emerging from the New Deal was the Social Security Act of 1935, which established permanent programs in the areas of old age security, unemployment insurance, and aid to dependent children. Congress's role shifted as the New Deal progressed. Initially eager to gain access to federal resources, Congress overwhelmingly supported early New Deal measures. By 1937, however, a conservative coalition had emerged in Congress. Wary of the growing power of the federal government generated by its new social welfare activities, the coalition blocked significant expansion of the federal social role into the 1940s and 1950s.

Congress's early willingness to support Roosevelt

stemmed in part from the lopsided majorities won by Democrats in 1932. Democrats outnumbered Republicans 311 to 116 in the House of Representatives; in the Senate, Democrats held 60 out of 96 seats. But numbers were only part of the story. Much of Congress's unexpected cooperation stemmed from hunger for federal money. Democrats were starved for patronage; it had been twelve years since a Democrat had sat in the White House. Furthermore, demands on members of Congress were multiplying as states and localities proved unable to cope with the human misery created by the Depression.

Relief measures. The fruit of congressional-presidential cooperation in the early New Deal was a flood of new legislation designed to cope with the Depression. The main thrust of economic recovery policies was regulatory, as embodied in the crop-reduction approach of the Agricultural Adjustment Act and the industrial self-regulation authorized by the National Industrial Recovery Act. Complementing these recovery measures, though, were a variety of new programs that sought to alleviate the suffering of the poor more directly. The Federal Emergency Relief Act of 1933 authorized half a billion dollars to be sent to states to provide relief for the destitute. A second measure set up the Civil Works Administration (CWA), which provided temporary jobs to get the country through the winter of 1933–1934. The CWA paid the prevailing wage and drew half its workers from the relief rolls. Among the relief measures of the early New Deal was also the Civilian Conservation Corps, which sent young unemployed men to work in the nation's forests.

These early measures were officially considered emergency legislation, designed to meet the challenge of the Depression; they were not intended to be permanent features of U.S. social policy. Indeed, despite the great popularity of the CWA, Roosevelt terminated it after only a few months. The president was dismayed by the high cost of providing employment and feared that the program would create a population permanently dependent on the federal government for work.

Similarly, the administration was not enthusiastic about its role as a provider of relief payments to the states. In 1935, Roosevelt declared that the federal government would "quit this business of relief" and proposed a new government jobs program, the Works Progress Administration (WPA). The legislation creating the WPA, the Emergency Relief Appropriation Act of 1935, authorized the president to spend nearly $5 billion on work relief, the single largest appropriation in the history of the nation up to that time. Unlike the earlier experiment with government jobs, the WPA drew its clientele solely from the relief rolls, and it paid a "security wage," which was less than the prevailing wage. Members of Congress sympathetic to the growing labor movement had disputed the latter provision, fearing that it would undercut wage rates. But they ultimately gave the president control over wages, except in construction projects. The size of the WPA appropriation and the discretion it granted the president in spending represented an important movement of power from Congress to the executive.

Social Security. The president also seized the initiative regarding the Social Security Act of 1935, the first piece of permanent social welfare legislation to emerge from the New Deal. Anxious to head off congressional proposals for unemployment insurance and old-age pensions, Roosevelt in 1934 appointed a Committee on Economic Security to consider comprehensive legislation in these areas. The legislation presented to Congress in 1935 called for three new programs: a national system of old-age pensions financed by worker and employer contributions; a federal-state system of unemployment insurance, which gave states the authority to set benefit levels and tax rates; and federal matching grants to provide social assistance to the needy, including children and the elderly. The committee had considered including proposals for health insurance in the legislation; fearing intense opposition from the medical community, however, the panel rejected it as too controversial.

For the most part, Congress responded favorably to the president's legislation. In the House, representatives had been flooded with mail from supporters of the Townsend plan, named after its chief proponent, Dr. Francis Townsend, an unemployed California doctor. The plan called for noncontributory flat-rate pensions for the elderly. But despite the pressure from the Townsend movement, the president's contributory plan was easily approved.

Some changes were introduced in Congress, however, which indicated a desire to stem the power of the federal government. A requirement that states establish a merit system to select the administrative personnel for their social assistance programs was deleted by Congress. As Fred M. Vinson (D-Ky.), a leading member of the House Ways and Means Committee, put it, "No damned social workers are going to come into my State to tell our people whom they should hire." Also, the administration's proposal that the new programs be administered by the Department of Labor was rejected by members of Congress who found the department too liberal and too tied to organized labor. Instead, the programs were housed in an independent Social Security Board.

Southern members of Congress were particularly sensitive to how the new social welfare measures would affect their region's racial caste system. Because of their influence in the Senate Finance and House Ways and Means committees, the panels that considered the social security legislation, they were well-positioned to shape it to their liking. They ensured that the final legislation exempted agricultural and domestic workers from old-age insurance, thus excluding all but 10 percent of African American workers. In addition, southerners blocked the proposed requirement that state old-age assistance programs furnish "a reasonable subsistence compatible with decency and health." Access to such benefits, it was feared, would jeopardize employer control of the southern black labor force.

Thus, although the Social Security Act was a landmark in American social welfare legislation, it was far from a broad declaration of federal support for the poor. Social insurance would not begin to cover a substantial portion of the aged for many years. States and localities exercised considerable control over the two other components, unemployment insurance and assistance to dependent children and the elderly. States enjoyed wide latitude in setting benefit rates and conditions for eligibility in Aid to Dependent Children (ADC) and Old Age Assistance. Most important, Social Security set up a two-tiered system of benefits: a relatively generous system of social insurance benefits for the employed and a less generous, means-tested set of programs for the poor and "unemployable." These categories roughly mirrored a division between popular notions of the deserving and undeserving poor.

Growing congressional conservatism. In the late 1930s, the emergence of a conservative coalition in Congress halted the social reforms of the New Deal. Southern Democrats, wary of growing presidential power and fearful of extensions of federal authority, stymied presidential initiatives after 1937. Republican victories in the 1938 elections strengthened the anti-Roosevelt coalition as southern Democrats and Republicans worked together to put an end to the social experimentation of the New Deal.

This conservative coalition, further strengthened by the 1942 elections, terminated emergency New Deal programs as economic depression gave way to war, and it also blocked most major social policy initiatives of the 1940s. Most notably, Congress rejected a sweeping set of proposals to nationalize and expand social welfare policy put forth in 1941 by the National Resources Planning Board, a nonadministrative agency in the Executive Office of the President. Congressional liberals sought to nationalize unemployment insurance and create a national system of health insurance with the Wagner-Murray-Dingell bills of 1943 and 1945, but like the president's proposals, these were defeated.

When the war ended, fear of a massive depression and widespread unemployment propelled a full employment bill through the House. But as the postwar economy recovered, a far less comprehensive employment act authorizing the president simply to monitor the economy was substituted. The one important piece of social welfare legislation to emerge from the war was the GI Bill of 1944, which offered readjustment allowances for returning soldiers, namely generous education benefits and low-interest mortgages. President Harry S. Truman sought to extend the social agenda of the New Deal but was stymied at each turn by an uncooperative Congress.

The New Deal social policy agenda had stalled, but significant permanent policies had been enacted. Moreover, the 1930s had witnessed the rise of a new breed of urban liberal in Congress who would continue to press for extensions of social policy. Sen. Robert F. Wagner (D-N.Y.) personified this new force. The son of an immigrant janitor, Wagner had close ties to organized labor and throughout the 1930s was a key congressional architect of social legislation.

In the coming decades, the agenda of social policy would be filled by issues and problems, such as health care, that the New Deal legislation had left untouched. But the politics of social welfare would be shaped as well by problems that the designers of New Deal social policy had not anticipated. In particular, their assumption that the need for social assistance would "wither away" proved to be wrong. Instead, many of the most controversial social policy issues would concern the problems of those covered by the lower tier of social assistance, pejoratively known as "welfare."

The War on Poverty and the Great Society. Not until 1964, after the assassination of President John F. Kennedy and the election of the most liberal Democratic Congress since 1934, was Congress ready to extend federal social welfare policies. In

Figure 1
Social Spending as a Percent of Total Federal Spending, 1940–1994

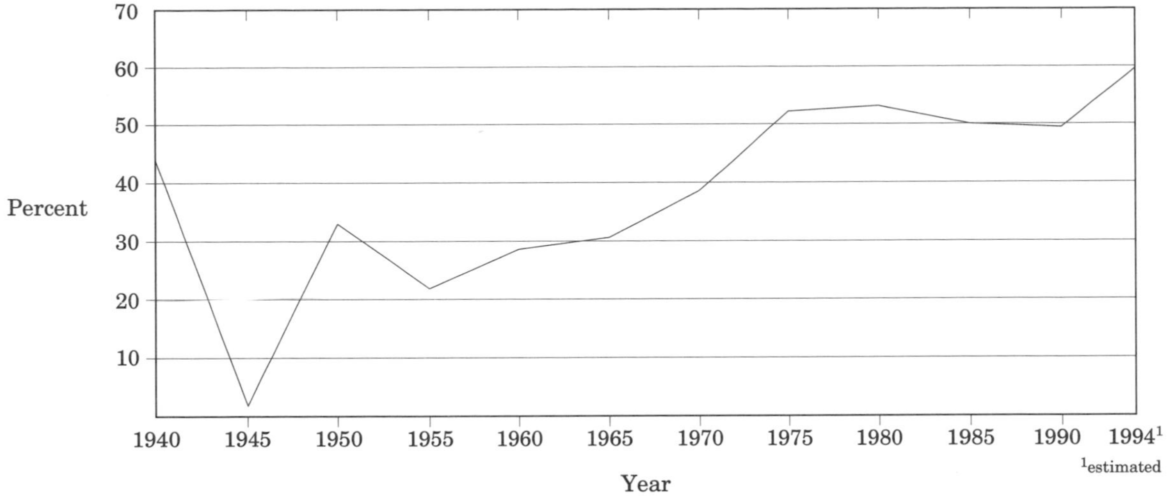

SOURCE: Budget of the U.S. government, fiscal year 1992, Historical Tables, part 7, table 3.1; Budget of the U.S. government, fiscal year 1995, Historical Tables, part 3, table 3.1.

this second "big bang" of innovation, President Lyndon B. Johnson and Congress passed a wave of legislation designed to wage a domestic "war on poverty," provide medical care to the aged and the poor, and revitalize the nation's cities, which had replaced rural areas as home to a majority of the nation's poor. Although these policies were not initiated as a direct response to the southern civil rights movement, the war on poverty came to focus on African Americans, particularly after the urban riots of the 1960s. The poverty programs fell into the lower tier of social assistance, a target of bitter conflict that was infused with racial tension. In contrast, during the 1960s and early 1970s, the upper tier of social insurance programs was quietly expanded with little controversy or public attention.

The postwar decades brought unprecedented prosperity to the United States, but by the 1950s it had became apparent that not all Americans were economically secure. In Congress, members from depressed areas, dependent on declining industries such as coal mining, called attention to pockets of poverty. Unemployment, which crept higher with each cyclical recession, also aroused concern. During the 1950s, congressional liberals (largely nonsouthern Democrats) sought to build support for expanding the federal role to address these social problems. In 1959, House liberals organized into the Democratic Study Group with the express pur-

pose of enacting an activist legislative agenda. Concern about rising unemployment prompted the creation of a Senate Special Committee on Unemployment that toured the country in 1959, listening to the unemployed and collecting information about economic deprivation.

The congressional initiatives of the 1950s had to await the election of Kennedy as president before they could be enacted. Most social welfare measures passed during the Kennedy administration had their origins in those initiatives. Among the most significant were the Area Redevelopment Act of 1961, which sought to channel resources to depressed areas, and the Manpower Development and Training Act of 1962, which offered retraining for unemployed skilled workers. On the other hand, a majority consisting of southern Democrats and Republicans blocked more far-reaching social welfare measures supported by liberal members of Congress.

Kennedy's death and the Democratic landslide of 1964 opened the doors for federal social policy activism on a scale not seen since the early New Deal. Democrats outnumbered Republicans two to one for the first time since the 1930s, and liberal Democrats were able to make changes in House rules that reduced the ability of opponents to block legislation in committee. In addition, President Johnson, a former Senate majority leader, relied on skills gained in his long congressional career to win support for the flood of legislation that would create what he called the Great Society.

The "war on poverty." The newest and most visible element of the Great Society was the war on poverty. The problem of poverty had been "rediscovered" in the early 1960s as national attention was drawn to the poor by such books as Michael Harrington's *The Other America* (1962). Although many of the components of the attack on poverty were not new, the effort to package them into a concerted effort to end poverty was novel. The underlying theme of the poverty program was to prepare the poor to take better advantage of available economic opportunities. Hoping to break the cycle of poverty that they believed was transmitted across generations, the antipoverty planners focused especially on youth.

The charter legislation for the war on poverty, the Economic Opportunity Act of 1964, created programs for youth job training, public service employment for youth, a volunteer national service corps, and a new Office of Equal Opportunity (which operated out of the Executive Office of the President). The most innovative aspect of the war on poverty was the provision for community action agencies, which were established in localities across the country to administer the new programs with the "maximum feasible participation" of the poor. In creating these agencies, the federal government bypassed state and city governments to establish the first direct relationship between community groups and the federal government. The community action component of the war on poverty pioneered a number of special programs such as Head Start for early childhood education, which proved to be durable and popular.

Complementing the war on poverty were a variety of programs meant specifically to address the problems of the urban poor. Model Cities, introduced in 1965, sought to involve poor urban communities in the rehabilitation of their physical environment. Congress, at the president's initiative, created the Department of Housing and Urban Development in 1965 to bring programs that affected cities under one roof and to highlight the national importance of urban affairs. In 1968, Congress passed the National Housing Act, creating two new programs to increase the supply of low-income housing and to facilitate home ownership by the poor.

The war on poverty and urban programs such as Model Cities quickly aroused congressional suspicion and opposition. One source of trouble was big-city mayors, who were angered by challenges from community action agencies and the infusion of federal moneys that they did not control into their cities. The power in the Democratic party wielded by mayors such as Richard J. Daley of Chicago amplified their influence in the White House and Congress. In 1967, Congress passed legislation making the community action agencies subject to mayoral control. The reauthorization process for the poverty program in 1967 revealed just how precarious congressional support for the war on poverty was. Congressional opponents linked the poverty programs to the riots that had broken out in cities across the country, and they opposed further funding as rewarding rioters. In the end, the Economic Opportunity Act was refunded, but in the future it would be under sharp congressional scrutiny.

Food stamps. Congress was far more supportive of the food stamp program, a pilot program of the Kennedy administration that Johnson extended with the Food Stamp Act of 1964. The program, which provided in-kind benefits for the poor, remained small until congressional liberals, notably Senators Robert F. Kennedy (D-N.Y.) and Joseph S. Clark (D-Pa.) took up the cause of hunger in the United States. In 1968, the Senate set up the Select Committee on Nutrition and Human Needs, with George McGovern (D-S.Dak.) as its head. Cooperation between congressional liberals and more moderate members of the House Agriculture Committee laid the basis for program expansion. After the election of Richard M. Nixon as president in 1968, Congress and the White House together greatly expanded the program and set national eligibility standards. Food stamps became widely available to all who qualified, not only those on welfare. By the mid 1970s, food stamps, funded almost entirely by the federal government, had become a central component of social assistance for the poor.

Medicare and Medicaid. Health care, a third major area of social policy innovation during the 1960s, also generated less controversy than the war on poverty. After proposals for national health insurance had been defeated during the Truman administration, congressional supporters began to refocus their efforts on health measures that would serve only the elderly. Throughout the 1950s, bills proposing hospital insurance for the aged were annually introduced and defeated in Congress. The liberal cast of the 89th Congress (1965–1967), however, practically ensured that some health legislation would be enacted.

The Medicare bill, introduced in 1965, at first called only for hospitalization insurance for elderly recipients of Social Security. But the bill that emerged from the House Ways and Means Committee also included voluntary insurance for all medical care for the aged, paid for by the government and the beneficiary. In addition, the bill tacked on a program of medical assistance to the poor, popularly known as Medicaid. This program provided federal matching grants to the states to set up programs to provide care for welfare recipients and the medically indigent. Enacted as titles 18 and 19 of the Social Security Act, the new health programs replicated the two-tiered divide between social insurance and social assistance. The aged recipients of Medicare would be protected by a federal program; the poor and medically indigent would be served by state-level programs with less secure funding and variable levels of coverage.

The "welfare mess." Although the policy initiatives of the Great Society attracted wide public attention and controversy, they never comprised more than one-fifth of social welfare spending. Most expenditures were for the older programs initiated under the Social Security Act, which had begun to grow far beyond their original levels. By the end of the 1960s, social assistance to poor mothers and their children had grown so sharply that talk of the "welfare mess" had become a staple of political debate. Intended for widowed mothers, this program was never envisioned as a major program. Indeed, it was expected to diminish gradually as widows were covered by their husbands' social insurance. But in the 1950s, rising state expenditures on social assistance suggested that something unforeseen was occurring. The number of female-headed families nearly doubled in that decade. This trend was especially troubling because nearly half of these families were poor, and they were disproportionately black.

The Kennedy administration sought to reform the Aid to Dependent Children program by empha-

POOR PEOPLE'S MARCH ON WASHINGTON. Demonstration at the Capitol, summer 1968, part of the Poor People's Campaign in Washington, organized to draw national attention to the needs of the poor.   LIBRARY OF CONGRESS

sizing the rehabilitation of recipients and extending a temporary program that allowed states to offer aid to two-parent families. The program's name was changed to Aid to Families with Dependent Children (AFDC). Alarmed about rising welfare rolls, House Ways and Means Committee chairman Wilbur D. Mills (D-Ark.) spearheaded the drive that created the Work Incentive (WIN) program in 1967, designed to promote work among welfare recipients. The Nixon administration sought the most far-reaching reform of welfare since the 1930s with its proposed Family Assistance Plan, which would have nationalized public assistance and offered aid to working families as well as the nonworking poor. The bill provoked intense conflict in Congress, where both liberals and conservatives found fault with the proposal and ultimately rejected it in 1972. In its place, Congress created Supplemental Security Income, which made social assistance to the aged, blind, and disabled a fully federally funded program. Once again, a more evidently "deserving" category of persons had been folded into the upper tier of federal benefits, leaving recipients of AFDC even more isolated.

As welfare reform eluded policymakers, the number of AFDC recipients continued to grow, from 4.3 million in 1965 to 6.1 in 1969 and 10.8 million by 1974. During the 1970s, however, the value of AFDC payments eroded by one-third as states refused to raise benefits to keep pace with inflation.

Increases in entitlements. For all the attention that AFDC attracted, the most spectacular rises in coverage and expenditure occurred in social insurance, increases in which Congress played a central role. The administrators of Social Security had been extending its reach since the late 1930s. In 1939, survivors of social insurance beneficiaries were granted coverage; disability insurance was enacted in 1956. The greatest increases in the old-age and survivors' insurance trust fund occurred during Richard Nixon's first term as president. As inflation began to rise in the late 1960s and early 1970s, the idea of indexing Social Security benefits to keep pace with price rises began to attract considerable support. Many members of Congress, however, were unenthusiastic about indexing because it meant that future benefit increases would occur automatically, making it difficult for Congress to claim credit.

From 1969 to 1971, Congress failed to act on the president's proposals to index Social Security and instead legislated substantial benefit increases of 15 percent in 1969 and 10 percent in 1971. In 1972,

when Congress finally approved indexing, it also legislated a 20 percent increase in payments. These changes, combined with the increasing number of aged persons covered, made social insurance by far the largest component of American social welfare policy.

Employment legislation. The stagnant economy of the 1970s, combined with the waning of national interest in poverty, halted most social policy innovation. One exception was in the domain of employment. As unemployment soared to rates not seen since the Depression, Congress responded with the first major public jobs program since the 1930s. The Comprehensive Employment and Training Act of 1973 (CETA) initially emphasized job training, but public service employment quickly overshadowed all other components of the act. At its peak in 1978 and 1979, CETA subsidized more than 725,000 jobs.

As inflation rose in the late 1970s, public support for government spending declined. This was reflected in Congress, where CETA was almost eliminated in 1978, being substantially scaled back and targeted to the poor. Beyond that, the antigovernment, antitax movements that rocked politics in the 1970s became the dominant themes in the social policy debates of the 1980s, when Ronald Reagan assumed the presidency committed to reducing the role of government.

Issues of the 1980s and 1990s. Many of the issues that dominated public debate in the 1980s and the 1990s had taken shape in the 1960s and 1970s. One debate revolved around what level of government should be responsible for the design and support of social policy. A second set of issues concerned the relationship between work and welfare. The sharply rising costs of entitlements created a third focus of controversy over social welfare. A final area concerned the gaps in social welfare policy, particularly in health care and the growing problem of child poverty. During the 1980s, Democrats in Congress were able for the most part to defend existing social welfare programs, but, as deficits mounted in the latter part of the decade, new initiatives were rare.

Reagan era cutbacks. The question of where responsibility for social policy should rest remained a controversial question sixty years after the New Deal. President Reagan sought to reverse the trend toward greater federal responsibility in a number of ways. One of the most important was simply to cut social program expenditures. His greatest successes occurred during his first year in office, when

Landmark Social Welfare Legislation

TITLE	YEAR ENACTED	REFERENCE NUMBER	DESCRIPTION
Social Security Act	1935	P.L. 271, 74th Cong.	Provided for federal old-age insurance benefits, federal-state unemployment insurance, federal grants-in-aid for old-age assistance, Aid to Dependent Children (ADC, later AFDC).
Disability Insurance (amendments to Social Security Act)	1956	P.L. 880, 84th Cong.	Established disability insurance benefits.
Economic Opportunity Act	1964	P.L. 88-452	Created community action agencies; provided services and training for the poor.
Medicare (Title XIX of Social Security Act)	1965	P.L. 89-97	Provided health insurance for the elderly.
Medicaid (Title XIX of Social Security Act)	1965	P.L. 89-97	Provided federal-state matching entitlement for medical assistance to the poor.
Supplemental Security Income	1972	P.L. 92-603	Provided federal assistance for the needy aged, blind, and disabled.
Comprehensive Employment and Training Act	1973	P.L. 92-203	Created job training and public service employment.
Earned Income Tax Credit	1975	Internal Revenue Code, sec. 32	Gave tax credit to low-income families.
Omnibus Budget Reconciliation Act	1981	P.L. 97-35	Narrowed eligibility and spending on AFDC and other social spending programs.
Family Support Act	1988	P.L. 100-485	Set up JOBS program for AFDC recipients; provided supplemental services to ease transition to work.

Congress felt controlled by the president's great popularity and his apparent mandate to govern. Most social program cuts were embodied in the Omnibus Budget and Reconciliation Act of 1981 (OBRA). After that, however, Congress resisted most of the social spending cuts proposed by the president. The areas in which spending declined most sharply during the 1980s were in programs targeted at cities. CETA, which localities had used to supplement their local work forces, was eliminated, as was revenue sharing, which provided no-strings-attached revenue for localities. Housing programs were cut by nearly 90 percent. By contrast, social programs that provided individual benefits were spared deep cuts. The president was, however, highly successful in limiting increases in future social spending by instituting tax cuts that reduced federal revenue. As deficits mounted in the 1980s, lack of funds became the dominant factor in deciding social welfare policy.

The president also sought to reduce the federal role in social policy by proposing that categorical grants be transformed into block grants. Since the 1960s, Congress had favored categorical grants, which specified how money should be spent; block grants allowed states and localities more discretion over expenditures. The president's greatest success came in 1982, when Congress agreed to consolidate seventy-six categorical grants in the domain of social welfare into nine block grants. Since that time, however, Congress has resisted further attempts to combine categorical programs into block grants.

Problems of the working poor. A second area of intense controversy in social welfare policy was the relationship between work and welfare. After the failure of Nixon's Family Assistance Plan in 1972, the issue of reforming welfare in ways that would encourage or mandate work remained on the back burner until 1981, when Congress approved a presidential initiative permitting states to experiment with work requirements for welfare recipients. Attention to welfare reform intensified in the 1980s as concern mounted about the emergence of a dependent underclass in the nation's large cities. By the mid 1980s, a congressional consensus emerged around instituting new requirements for work as well as providing training and other benefits, such as short-term child care and medical benefits, to ease the transition to work. These initiatives, based in large part on experimental programs developed by states, became the central features of the Family Support Act of 1988, which required that states have a Job Opportunities and Basic Skills (JOBS) program in order to receive federal monies for public assistance. In addition, the act extended AFDC benefits to two-parent families in all states and set up mechanisms for forcing absent fathers to support their children.

The legislative process that produced the Family Support Act of 1988 was distinctive because of the important role that the National Governors' Association played in designing the legislation and promoting agreement among members of Congress. The leading congressional proponent of the legislation was Sen. Daniel Patrick Moynihan (D-N.Y.), who had been the architect of Nixon's failed Family Assistance Plan.

Although the act was hailed as a significant achievement, many questions about work and welfare remain on the national agenda. President Clinton's promise to "end welfare as we know it" was one of the most popular themes of his 1992 presidential campaign. The president has supported a two-year time limit on receiving welfare, which suggests that future reforms are likely to reinforce work requirements for recipients.

Even with welfare reform, the difficulties of the working poor remain a potent problem. Labor market trends in the late 1980s and early 1990s increased the number of working poor, who were untouched by most federal welfare programs. One of the few programs that did reach this group was the Earned Income Tax Credit (EITC), created in 1975 under the leadership of Senate Finance Committee chairman Russell B. Long (D-La.). The tax credit, available to the working poor with children, was enacted to offset the regressive effects of the Social Security payroll tax and to promote work among the poor. It was gradually raised during the 1970s and in the 1980s, when advocates for the poor, including the Children's Defense Fund, pressed for expansion. Congress and the president agreed to increase it in the 1986 Tax Reform Act and increased it again in 1990. Because the tax credit requires little administration and rewards work, it was able to win bipartisan support. In 1993, Congress approved the president's proposed major expansion of the EITC and extended the credit to families without children for the first time.

Nonetheless, the problem of the working poor remains a thorny issue for U.S. social welfare policy. The social welfare policies inherited from the 1930s and 1960s preserved a distinction between the employed and the unemployable, a distinction that has become more tenuous as the number of female-headed families has grown. Questions about how much mothers should be expected to work and how family and work responsibilities can be balanced are at the frontier of social welfare policy in the 1990s. Congress has responded with some increases in aid for child care, and its proposal for unpaid family leave was signed by President Bill Clinton in 1993 after having been twice vetoed by George Bush.

Successes of aid to the elderly. The one undisputed area of success for American social policy has been old-age pensions. The level of poverty among the elderly declined substantially as Social Security expanded, dropping from 40 percent in 1959 to about 12 percent in 1990. Once the poorest group in the population, the elderly were still below the average poverty rate in 1990.

These successes, however, brought worries about the expense of Social Security and other entitlement programs. Expenses for entitlement programs are difficult to control because eligibility and benefit levels are determined by statutory criteria. Persons who meet those criteria can sue if they are denied benefits. As the American population aged, Social Security expenses grew dramatically, causing Congress to make adjustments in the payroll tax to cover rising costs during the 1970s. Committed to reducing federal social expenditures, President Reagan proposed substantial cuts in Social Security in 1981. Congress, however, easily defeated these proposals. Broadly popular, Social Security became a sacrosanct program with which politicians tampered at their peril. During the 1980s, only minor reforms, including taxes on high-income recipients and delays in cost-of-living adjustments, were ventured.

Child poverty. The effectiveness of Social Security in decreasing poverty among the elderly contrasted with the rise in child poverty. By 1990, one in five American children was poor. Child poverty is, therefore, bound to be one of the key future social policy issues. Congress has shown considerable interest in the issue, reflected in the activities of the House Select Committee on Children, Youth, and Families. Since the late 1980s, the committee has published evaluations of eight federal programs that affect poor children in attempting to win support for higher federal funding. A strong supporter of increased financial support for children's programs, President Clinton proposed a substantial increase in funding for Head Start and universal child immunizations in his 1993 budget. Congress approved scaled back versions of both requests.

Health care. Congress has devoted more concerted attention to the many problems surrounding health care, including rising costs, inadequate coverage for the working poor, and the poor quality of health care available to the poor. The early 1990s saw the introduction of a flurry of legislative proposals on health care. These proposals offered three broad types of solutions. The first, supported by the Senate Democratic leadership, was an employment-based "pay or play" system requiring that employers provide health coverage or pay into a public fund. A second proposal, supported by Democratic liberals in the House and Senate, provided for a single-payer system in which the federal government would act as the lone health care insurer. A final proposal, advocated by Republicans, provided tax breaks to lower- and middle-income uninsured persons and vouchers to the poor.

With the election of Bill Clinton, health care catapulted to the forefront of the social policy agenda. After months of study overseen by Hillary Rodham Clinton, the president unveiled a plan to ensure health care for all Americans. Similar in some ways to the earlier Senate Democratic proposals, the plan mandated that employers pay at least 80 percent of the cost of providing health insurance to their employees. The federal government would assist small businesses, and it would provide insurance for the unemployed and early retirees. The plan endorsed a version of "managed competition," in which consumers would be organized into large regional health alliances that would negotiate rates with health providers on behalf of consumers. The great complexity of the proposed reform means that its provisions will be considered by a number of congressional committees, with the House Ways and Means Committee playing a critical role. Because it aims at comprehensive reform, the health proposal, if passed, would likely be the signature achievement of the Clinton administration.

Homelessness. A final area of emerging social problems was homelessness. Hardly existing before 1980, homelessness became a major problem in most American cities, and the burden of coping with it fell largely to the localities. Congress responded with some assistance in 1987 by approving the McKinney Act, but in the early 1990s the issue remained highly problematic.

The future of social policy. Frustrated by budget deficits and, especially during the Bush administration, the threat of a presidential veto, congressional liberals seeking to expand the federal social role attempted to build public support for social programs by holding hearings and issuing reports on social problems and policies. In addition to the activity around child poverty, congressional Democrats used their control of the House Ways and Means Committee to draw public attention to emerging social problems and governmental responses. The committee's annual review of social policy, published in the "Green Book," became an influential document and target of partisan contention, as it detailed a growing gap between the rich and the poor.

The future of social welfare policy and poverty remained hazy in the early 1990s. Large federal deficits continued to discourage spending on social policy. But other factors pointed to the possibility of renewed federal activism. Most important were President Clinton's efforts to reenergize the federal role in social policy with his emphasis on investing in people. Moreover, congressional reforms enacted during the 1970s broke the lock that conservatives had had on key committees since the 1930s. In addition a strengthened congressional leadership made congressional cooperation with the president more possible. Staff increases in the 1970s enabled members of Congress to enter the policy process with their own technically sophisticated proposals. Such changes suggested that, especially with a Democratic president more committed to expanding the federal social role, the prospects for presidential-congressional cooperation on future social policy innovation were substantial.

[*See also* Children, Youth, and Families Committee, House Select; Economic Opportunity Act of 1964; Family Policies; Health and Medicine; Housing Policy; Hunger Committee, House Select; Labor and Human Resources Committee, Senate; Social Security Act.]

BIBLIOGRAPHY

Abramovitz, Mimi. *Regulating the Lives of Women: Social Welfare Policy from Colonial Times to the Present.* 1988.

Derthick, Martha. *Policymaking for Social Security.* 1979.

Orfield, Gary. *Congressional Power: Congress and Social Change.* 1975.

Palmer, John L., ed. *Perspectives on the Reagan Years.* 1986.

Patterson, James T. *Congressional Conservatism and the New Deal.* 1967.

Robertson, David B., and Dennis R. Judd. *The Development of American Public Policy: The Structure of Policy Restraint.* 1989.

Skocpol, Theda. *Protecting Soldiers and Mothers.* 1992.

Sundquist, James L. *Politics and Policy: The Eisenhower, Kennedy, and Johnson Years.* 1968.

U.S. House of Representatives. Committee on Ways and Means. *Overview of Entitlement Programs: 1993 Green Book.* 103d Cong., 1st sess., 1993. WMCP 103-18.

Weaver, Kent. "Controlling Entitlements." In *The New Direction in American Politics.* Edited by John E. Chubb and Paul E. Peterson. 1985. Pp. 307–341.

Weir, Margaret. *Politics and Jobs: The Boundaries of Employment Policy in the United States.* 1992.

Weir, Margaret, Ann Shola Orloff, and Theda Skocpol. *The Politics of Social Policy in the United States.* 1988.

MARGARET WEIR

SOUTH CAROLINA.

On 23 May 1788, South Carolina became the eighth state to ratify the Constitution. The vote of 149 to 73 was an indication of the strength of the low-country elite that dominated the state's politics and had selected the state's delegates to the Constitutional Convention in Philadelphia.

In the convention the South Carolinians supported the idea of a strong chief executive although South Carolina's experience had been to have a strong legislative branch and a weak executive. They tried unsuccessfully to have members of the House, like the Senate, elected by legislatures instead of the people. And, in a prelude to later confrontations concerning the very nature of the Union, they strongly defended the institution of slavery, arguing that the matter was best left to the southern states.

In the years preceding the Civil War, South Carolinians in both houses of Congress led efforts to preserve and defend the South's "peculiar institution." In January 1830, South Carolina senator Robert Y. Hayne and Sen. Daniel Webster of Massachusetts engaged in one of the more memorable debates ever to take place in the Senate. Each defended his state and section against the other and gave his section's views on the nature of the Union. Hayne championed states' rights and the "Carolina doctrine" of nullification, while Webster spoke for the federal Union.

In 1832, reacting to the passage of the tariff of 1832, South Carolina nullified both that tariff and the tariff of 1828 and threatened to use force to stop customs officials from doing their duty. Just when it looked as if nullification would lead to civil war, South Carolina senator John C. Calhoun and Sen. Henry Clay of Kentucky fashioned the Compromise of 1833 that defused the crisis. That compromise, in which the nation knuckled under to South Carolina's demand for tariff reduction, was itself, however, but a prelude to civil war. In 1836, Calhoun and Rep. Henry L. Pinckney separately proposed the so-called gag rule that for eight years prevented debate on petitions opposing slavery. The caning of antislavery senator Charles Sumner of Massachusetts by Rep. Preston S. Brooks of South Carolina on 22 May 1856 on the floor of the Senate increased the tensions between North and South.

Within a week of Abraham Lincoln's election in November 1860, both of the state's senators withdrew from Congress. On 20 December 1860, South Carolina seceded from the Union, and the delegation's four remaining members withdrew from the House the next day. After the Civil War, those who were elected to Congress before the onset of congressional Reconstruction were denied their seats. In 1868, with the state fully under Radical Republican control and a congressionally approved constitution ratified, South Carolinians were finally allowed to return to Congress.

The political composition and size of the state's congressional delegation have fluctuated over the past two hundred years. From five representatives in 1789 the delegation rose to nine in the early 1800s, then declined to four in 1870. Since 1930 the state's representation has been fixed at six. From 1790 until 1803 the delegation was divided between Federalists and Jeffersonian Republicans. For the next three decades the Jeffersonian Republicans dominated the state's politics. After the nullification crisis, party allegiance in South Carolina declined and was replaced by factional and personal loyalties. Nominally, however, virtually all members of Congress were Democrats. During Reconstruction, between 1868 and 1877, the delegation was entirely Republican and a number of members were African American. Joseph H. Rainey was the first African American to serve in the House. Of the twenty-two African Americans who sat in Congress between 1870 and 1900, eight were South Carolinians. With the end of Reconstruction came the decline of the Republican party in South Carolina, although the state continued to have an occasional

"THE PALMETTO STATE SONG." Cover of sheet music for a song commemorating the signing of the South Carolina ordinance of secession. Lithograph by A. Hoen and Company, published by Henry Siegling, Charleston, S.C., 1861.   LIBRARY OF CONGRESS

black Republican serving in Congress until 1896. From 1896 until 1964 the entire delegation was Democratic. Since 1964 and the revival of the Republican party the delegation has been divided. The 1992 congressional elections resulted in the election of Rep. James E. Clyburn, the first African American to represent South Carolina since 1896.

In the nineteenth century South Carolina's leading congressional figures were James L. Orr, who served as Speaker of the House (1857–1859), and Calhoun, one of the Senate's greatest orators and one of the nation's most original political thinkers. In the twentieth century the most prominent of the state's delegation have been L. Mendel Rivers, chairman of the House Armed Services Committee (1964–1970); James F. Byrnes, point man in the Senate for much New Deal legislation (1933–1941); and Strom Thurmond, States Rights candidate for president in 1948, chairman of the Senate Judiciary Committee, and president pro tempore of the Senate (1981–1987).

For more than two centuries South Carolina has had a somewhat tumultuous relationship with the federal government that has affected the behavior of the state's congressional delegation. Yet no matter how much they might dislike federal policies, South Carolinians, reared in a political tradition of legislative dominance, have used their skills and seniority in Congress for the state's benefit. Because of the caliber and ability of its delegation, South Carolina has wielded an influence in Congress far greater than its size would warrant.

BIBLIOGRAPHY

Edgar, Walter B. *South Carolina in the Modern Age.* 1992.
Wallace, David Duncan. *A History of South Carolina.* 1934.

WALTER B. EDGAR

SOUTH DAKOTA. Lying almost completely within the Missouri River basin, the territory that became South Dakota came to the United States as part of the Louisiana Purchase. It was part of the Dakota Territory established by Congress in 1861 (which included the two Dakotas and Montana) and then of a reduced Dakota Territory when the Montana Territory was organized in 1868.

After several years of agitation in the territory and debate in Congress between "divisionists" favoring separate admission of North Dakota and South Dakota and others who opposed division, Congress passed a statehood act for South Dakota, North Dakota, Montana, and Washington in early 1889. The legislation was signed by the outgoing president, Grover Cleveland. Voters approved a state constitution and elected the state's first governor, Arthur Mellette, on 1 October 1889, and President Benjamin Harrison signed the state's admission proclamation on 9 November 1889.

South Dakota's first congressional delegation consisted of two senators and two representatives. Following the 1910 census, South Dakota received a third House seat, which it kept for twenty years. After 1930, the state's House delegation returned to two, and after 1980, it suffered a reduction to one.

Over more than a century of statehood, South Dakota was predominantly Republican in its congressional delegation. Through the 1992 election, Republicans had won 87 of 110 House elections (79.1 percent) and 26 of 37 Senate elections (70.3 percent). Other elections went to Democrats or, around the turn of the century, Democratic-Populist fusionists.

Some of the Republicans—most notably Senators Richard F. Pettigrew, Coe I. Crawford, and Peter Norbeck—were progressive, antiestablishment, and independent. At least one of the Democrats, Sen. William J. Bulow, was notably conservative and isolationist. Until 1940, the state's congressional Republicans tended to side with the progressive wing of the party; after 1940, South Dakota Republicans were generally conservative.

Major policy interests of the South Dakota delegation have been Missouri River development, the betterment of rural life, protection of farm prices and markets, conservation of natural resources, and Indian affairs. White penetration and settling of the Black Hills, in defiance of U.S. treaties with Native Americans, had occurred in the generation before statehood was achieved, but several early South Dakota members of Congress spoke out in defense of Native American interests.

Senator Pettigrew was a staunch opponent of U.S. imperialism in the Pacific in the 1890s. Senator Crawford's was one of the strongest voices raised against political corruption in the election of U.S. senators by state legislatures, and his ringing denunciations of the election of Sen. William Lorimer of Illinois was a major factor in winning approval of the Seventeenth Amendment for the direct election of senators in 1913. Senator Norbeck chaired the committee that investigated the stock market collapse in 1929, whose work eventually led to passage of the Securities and Exchange Act. Sen. J. Chandler Gurney, who served as chairman of the Armed Services Committee in the 1940s, was a prominent spokesman on the topics of armed forces reorganization, the establishment of the Defense Department, and universal military service. Sen. George McGovern, a major opponent of the U.S. role in Vietnam under President Lyndon B. Johnson, became the Democratic presidential nominee in 1972. In terms of both leadership in major legislative struggles and national political visibility, South Dakota's most noteworthy members of Congress have been McGovern and Norbeck, followed by Crawford, Gurney, and Pettigrew.

BIBLIOGRAPHY

Clem, Alan L. *Prairie State Politics: Popular Democracy in South Dakota.* 1967.

Farber, William O., Thomas Geary, and Loren Carlson. *Government of South Dakota.* 1979.

Fite, Gilbert. *Peter Norbeck: Prairie Statesman.* 1948.

Pressler, Larry. *U.S. Senators from the Prairie.* 1982.

Schell, Herbert S. *History of South Dakota.* 2d ed. 1968.

ALAN L. CLEM

SOUTHERN BLOC. The term *southern bloc* refers to a coalition of southern Democratic senators that transcended party lines to advance mutual legislative interests, primarily but not exclusively to block federal intervention in race relations. The disproportionate share of committee chairmanships held by southern bloc members enhanced its influence.

The southern bloc exemplified southern sectionalism that long united southerners in both houses of Congress. From the beginning of the nation, southern interests had voted together regarding issues of slavery. As recently as 1981 and 1982 several southern House Democrats ("boll weevils") banded together to support Reagan's legislative program. Since the 1930s, the southern Democrats often allied with Republicans against nonsouthern Democrats to form a conservative coalition. The southern bloc and the farm bloc also shared interests, for as V. O. Key, Jr. (1949), noted about Congress in the 1940s: "Between the extreme of urban industrialism and of prosperous, rural Republicanism, the poor, southern Democracy occupies a position in the political center."

Tom T. Connally of Texas was an early leader, and Richard B. Russell of Georgia headed the southern bloc between 1945 and 1969. Prior to the 1960s, almost all southern senators were allied with the bloc. Among those who did not formally ally with it were Lyndon B. Johnson of Texas, Estes Kefauver of Tennessee, and Ralph W. Yarborough of Texas. The 12 March 1956 Declaration of Constitutional Principles ("southern manifesto") assailing the Supreme Court's *Brown v. Board of Education* (1954) decision was signed by nineteen of the twenty-two southern senators (Kefauver, Johnson, and Albert A. Gore, Sr., of Tennessee did not sign) and by eighty-two House members.

Southern senators lacked majority support for voting down federal intervention in race relations. Therefore, as a minority, the bloc relied chiefly upon dilatory tactics permitted by the Senate rules to delay passage of significant civil rights legislation. Successful filibusters by the southern bloc included those against antilynching bills in 1935 and 1938; anti-poll-tax measures in 1942, 1944, and 1946; fair employment practices legislation in 1946; and voting rights in 1960. In 1957, having substantially weakened a civil rights bill, the southern bloc did not filibuster it (except for Strom Thurmond of South Carolina, who filibustered the bill for over twenty-four hours).

Between 1938 and 1963, the southern bloc, in coalition with some western Democrats and Republicans, prevailed on all eleven votes on cloture related to civil rights legislation. (Cloture is a procedure to end debate and vote on the measure being discussed.) Periodic liberal attempts to revise Senate Rule XXII to make cloture easier to secure had the effect of unifying the southern bloc.

On 10 June 1964, after the longest filibuster in history (seventy-four days), the Senate successfully imposed cloture for the first time on a civil rights bill. The Senate also invoked cloture on filibusters against civil rights bills in 1965 (voting rights) and 1968 (open housing).

Since the 1960s, the political constituencies that sustained the southern bloc have been transformed by the growing black vote in the South, increasingly crucial to the election of Democratic senators; Republican inroads into the once solidly Democratic South; and the social and economic convergence between the South and the non-South. In the 1980s, civil rights measures received substantial support from southern Democrats, and the conservative coalition appeared less frequently in congressional voting.

BIBLIOGRAPHY

Fite, Gilbert C. *Richard B. Russell, Jr., Senator from Georgia*. 1991.

Key, V. O., Jr. *Southern Politics*. 1949.

HAROLD W. STANLEY

SOUTHERN MANIFESTO.

Officially known as the Declaration of Constitutional Principles, the Southern Manifesto of 12 March 1956 was a southern, segregationist response to the Supreme Court decision in the case of *Brown v. Board of Education* (1954), which outlawed school segregation. Senators Strom Thurmond of South Carolina and Harry Flood Byrd, Sr., of Virginia proposed the idea, and Sen. Richard B. Russell of Georgia became the principle author.

Attacking the Supreme Court and the *Brown* decision, the manifesto accused the Court of legislating instead of interpreting the law and of violating the rights of the states and the people. According to the manifesto, the Court had clearly abused its judicial power when it overturned a half century of legal school segregation affirmed by the Supreme Court in the *Plessy v. Ferguson* decision of 1896. Forced school integration, the senators wrote, was not only unconstitutional but would cause "chaos and confusion" in the southern states. It would bring "revolutionary changes" in southern education and in race relations. The document called on the south to use all "lawful means" to resist implementation of the *Brown* decision. The manifesto was signed by nineteen senators and eighty-two House members.

The Southern Manifesto received wide publicity. Many newspapers carried the full text with the names of the signers. It was a clear statement by southerners who were trying to block the growing civil rights movement, but it did not slow down the judicial, congressional, and administrative drive that would soon break down the barriers of legal segregation.

BIBLIOGRAPHY

Fite, Gilbert C. *Richard B. Russell, Jr.: Senator from Georgia*, 1991.

GILBERT C. FITE

SPACE ACT OF 1958.
See National Aeronautics and Space Act of 1958.

SPANISH AMERICAN WAR.

Following the Civil War, repeated scandals and allegations connected to foreign ventures restrained American policy and stymied territorial expansion. This pattern was reversed in 1898, and Congress was the crucible for the portentous change. Populists and silverites suspicious of both the president and financial interests helped impel the United States into a war against Spain over Cuba. The results were greater presidential power and the acquisition of Puerto Rico, the Philippines, Hawaii, and Guam.

Cubans had repeatedly revolted against Spanish misrule. In 1895 widespread banditry by displaced peasants became islandwide insurrection. Spain responded in kind to the insurgents' scorched-earth warfare and concentrated civilians in disease-ridden camps. By 1898, 50,000 Spanish soldiers had perished, as had 200,000 Cubans. The struggle became deadlocked. The insurgents would obtain independence or leave Cuba in ashes. Spain would not abandon her investment of blood, honor, and money.

Reports of death and devastation stirred sympathy in Congress for the Cubans. The first to react was Sen. William V. Allen (Populist-Nebr.), who advocated recognition of Cuban belligerency and independence in December 1895. Both houses of Congress soon passed a concurrent resolution in favor of recognizing Cuban belligerency. President Grover Cleveland disagreed, preferring Spanish sovereignty with local self-government.

During the election of 1896, Democrats were preoccupied with the silver issue, but their Populist allies called for a "free and independent Cuba." Republicans praised "the Cuban patriots." When Republican William McKinley became president, he appealed for contributions to the Red Cross for humanitarian relief for the island, pursued diplomatic concessions from Spain, and explored buying Cuba.

Historians once contended that social-Darwinian thinkers created an intellectual climate for expansion and that yellow journalism aroused public opinion and swept the government into war. There is little evidence for such an interpretation. The intellectuals largely opposed the war and expansion, while the papers of Democratic publishers Hearst and Pulitzer rather reflected public opinion and had no perceptible influence on McKinley. Congress relied on its own sources of information and counsel in dealing with the distressing events in Cuba.

In March 1898 respected Sen. Redfield Proctor (R-Vt.) convinced many colleagues of Cuba's desolation by describing his recent visit. Republican leaders then secured a $50 million military appropriation and backed McKinley's careful actions, including his calm report on the emotional but secondary issue of the sinking of the *Maine* in Havana harbor. In the Senate, however, Democrats, Populists, and silver Republicans called for Cuba's freedom, accused the president of resisting war at the behest of financial interests, and demanded recognition of the Republic of Cuba to invalidate millions in Cuban bonds issued by Spain.

By 1 April 1898, McKinley had concluded that Madrid was not negotiating in good faith. On 11 April, he asked Congress for authority to help the Cubans and halt the fighting but not for a declaration of war; he also asserted that recognizing a Republic of Cuba was improper and would hamper U.S. freedom of action. After a sharp House debate, the Republican majority voted to let the president use force as necessary and establish a stable government. In the Senate, Democrats, Populists, and

DESTRUCTION OF THE *MAINE*. President William McKinley's message about the destruction of the battleship is read in the Senate on 25 March 1898. Drawing by W. A. Rogers, *Harper's Weekly*.
OFFICE OF THE HISTORIAN OF THE U.S. SENATE

silverite and other dissident Republicans added the Turpie-Foraker amendment recognizing the "Republic of Cuba" and the resolution of Sen. Henry M. Teller, a silver Republican from Colorado, disclaiming U.S. "sovereignty, jurisdiction or control" over Cuba to avoid potential financial responsibility for Spain's Cuban bonds.

The president threatened a veto on the grounds that the Senate measure invaded his prerogatives and prematurely granted recognition to Cuba. Speaker Thomas B. Reed and House Republicans supported McKinley. The fight in the Senate was close, but the president prevailed by 42 to 35. The final resolution upheld the executive's primacy in foreign affairs. It gave him authority to use military force to end the "abhorrent conditions" in Cuba and included part of the Teller resolution but did not recognize the Republic of Cuba. Spain broke diplomatic relations, then declared war. Congress proclaimed on 25 April that a state of war existed, and McKinley readied the navy for combat.

Commodore George Dewey destroyed the Spanish Pacific fleet in Manila Bay on 1 May, but a Spanish army remained. McKinley thus sought to obtain Hawaii, which had coal and water required for steamships and was preferable to the alternative Aleutian route for transporting troops to the Philippines. The Senate had blocked a treaty to annex the Republic of Hawaii in 1897. Even with the impetus of war, securing a two-thirds vote on a treaty was impossible, so the president sought a joint resolution. In the subsequent debate, supporters of the war and expansion engaged antiexpansionists and moderates, who believed annexation premature. Speaker Reed himself opposed the president. McKinley again lobbied House members, Reed yielded for wartime unity, and the House concurred by 209 to 91. On 6 July the Senate provided the required majority, but with only 42 in favor, 21 against, and an ominous 26 not voting.

Congress aided the president in his skillful direction of the war by passing the Hull bill to expand the army to 60,000 soldiers. A nearly uninterrupted series of military victories followed in Cuba, the Philippines, and, finally, Puerto Rico. There was great logistical confusion in hastily sending a volunteer army overseas. The troops in Cuba suffered from bad food and disease and came home in woeful condition. McKinley deflected a congressional investigation by establishing the independent Dodge Commission.

The fact that almost one-third of the senators had not voted on Hawaiian annexation worried the president. He meant to take no chances on the peace treaty, when every vote would count, and so he appointed three senators to the commission to negotiate with Spain: expansionists Cushman K. Davis (R-Minn.) and William P. Frye (R-Maine) and antiexpansionist George Gray (D-Del.). McKinley ignored the protest of another Republican member that it was unconstitutional to name senators, since they would vote on their own handiwork.

In the fall elections, the Republicans gained six seats in the Senate but still lacked the necessary two-thirds majority. Opponents of the administration, however, again were divided. Some Democrats favored modifying the treaty. Others opposed it outright. A number of silver Republicans, including Teller, and western Democrats were expansionists who wanted to obtain the Philippines, Puerto Rico, and even Cuba. Silver's spokesman and the likely Democratic party nominee in 1900, William Jennings Bryan, reflected their views and undercut the treaty's opponents when he urged prompt ratification and the postponement of unresolved problems.

Reports of fighting between American troops and Filipinos sharpened the need for a resolution of differences. McKinley used patronage to win over southern Democrats John L. McLaurin of South Carolina and Samuel D. McEnery of Louisiana. Their defections made possible the final bare margin of 57 to 27. Other resolutions opposing Philippine annexation or promising eventual independence failed.

Congressional Populists and silverites helped bring war and Cuba's eventual freedom. The war led to acquisitions in the Caribbean and Pacific that had eluded previous expansionists, but neither the public nor Congress thirsted for new foreign adventures or even for expanded trade. McKinley's steady direction of Congress, the war, and peacemaking not only aided his political triumph in 1900 but also ensured that the presidency dominated national politics.

[See also Platt Amendment.]

BIBLIOGRAPHY

Gould, Lewis L. *The Spanish-American War and President McKinley.* 1982.

Holbo, Paul S. "The Convergence of Moods and the Cuban-Bond 'Conspiracy' of 1898." *Journal of American History* 55 (1968): 54–72.

PAUL S. HOLBO

SPARKMAN, JOHN J. (1899–1985), Democratic representative and senator from Alabama, chairman of the Senate Banking and Currency and Foreign Relations committees, Democratic vice presidential candidate in 1952. Sparkman, who came to Congress in 1937 as President Franklin D. Roosevelt began his second term, embodied Roosevelt's southern progressive constituency. He was a Morgan County farm boy who had worked his way through college and law school to become a teacher and practicing attorney. Over four decades, one in the House and three in the Senate, he first supported New Deal legislation and then continued to cre-

JOHN J. SPARKMAN.

ate facsimiles of such even after the founder of the New Deal was long dead.

Small farmers, small businessmen, and small bankers were among his early and abiding legislative concerns. Once in the Senate, he formed a working partnership with his senior colleague from Alabama, Lister Hill, that became legendary for its effectiveness. Joined by their fellow progressives in the Alabama House delegation, Sparkman and Hill, through federal programs sometimes of their own design, helped to bring their largely rural and generally poor home state into the modern age economically and technologically. They did so despite a growing tendency of Alabama governors to attack the national government, a trend that reached its peak with George Wallace in the 1960s.

As an internationalist, Sparkman supported most presidential proposals for U.S. initiatives, from Harry S. Truman's Marshall Plan to Lyndon B. Johnson's military action in Vietnam. Sparkman was a member of the U.S. delegation to the fifth General Assembly of the United Nations in 1950. He served on the Senate Foreign Relations Committee and in 1975 became its chairman, albeit a less assertive one than his immediate predecessor, J. William Fulbright of Arkansas.

His other committee chairmanships included: the Select Committee on Small Business (81st, 82d, 84th–90th Congresses); the Committee on Banking and Currency (90th–91st Congresses); and, as cochairman, the Joint Committee on Defense Productions (91st–93d Congresses).

John Sparkman was liberal on virtually every issue save one, racial equality. He was in many ways a natural choice as Illinois governor Adlai E. Stevenson's 1952 vice presidential running mate; it was specifically hoped that he would bring Alabama back into the Democratic column after the state's defection to Strom Thurmond's Dixiecrat ticket in 1948. He did so, but Dwight D. Eisenhower was nonetheless elected president, presaging the future in being the first Republican since Reconstruction to carry some southern states. Sparkman continued in the Senate, serving five more terms and finally retiring at the close of the 95th Congress in January 1978 at the age of seventy-eight.

The last twenty-five years of his congressional service were much more difficult than the first fifteen. The Supreme Court's unanimous 1954 *Brown v. Board of Education* decision outlawing school segregation (in which Alabaman justice Hugo Black joined) effectively destroyed the old states' rights argument of southern conservatives. Ironically, it also pushed Sparkman and other white southern liberals and moderates into more conservative postures on any policy question that was even remotely related to racial integration. Sparkman, however, maintained his internationalist commitments and his conviction that government has a fundamental obligation to help those most in need.

BIBLIOGRAPHY

Preston, Nathaniel, ed. "The Role of the Senate in Determining Foreign Policy." In *The Senate Institution*. 1969.
Sparkman, Ivo Hall. *Journeys with the Senator*. 1977.

STEPHEN P. STRICKLAND

SPEAKER OF THE HOUSE. Drawing on British and colonial precedent, the Framers created the position of the Speaker of the House of Representatives as that body's presiding officer. For many centuries British Speakers were under the influence of the monarchy. In 1376 Peter de la Mare became the first Speaker to have been elected by the Commons, but it was not until the seventeenth century that the British speakership emerged from crown control. When the colonial governments were established in the seventeenth century, colonial speakers were under the influence of royal governors. By the century's end, they too had emerged as the voice of the legislative body, playing an independent political role in addition to serving as presiding officers. It was this hybrid political and parliamentary model that shaped the Founders' perceptions of the office. Consequently, the American speakership has always been a political and a parliamentary office, and it remains so today.

Formal Duties. The Speaker is elected by a majority vote of members and need not be a member of the House. His constitutional responsibility is to preside over the House. He is empowered by the rules of the House to administer the oath of office to members, to call the House to order, to maintain order and decorum, to recognize members for the purpose of speaking or making motions, to rule upon the propriety of motions under the Constitution and the Rules of the House, to refer bills to committee, to put questions to a vote of members, to declare a quorum, to count and declare all votes, to receive and transmit formal messages to the Senate and to the president, to appoint all select and conference committees, to appoint House members to conferences, and to sign all bills passed by the House. Such formal duties define the Speaker's role while the House of Representatives is in session, that is, on the House "floor." When the House meets in the Committee of the Whole, the Speaker does not preside but names a member to chair the Committee of the Whole. In addition, the Speaker may appoint a member as Speaker pro tempore during floor sessions.

Political Functions. These formal duties pertinent to the legislative process capture the main aims of the Framers but only hint at the meaning of the office as it has developed over time. From its earliest days, the speakership has been an irreducibly political office. While its parliamentary role continued and, especially prior to the Civil War, predominated, the speakership evolved as one of the most powerful political offices in the nation. The political role of the Speaker of the House results from the fact that the speakership is controlled by the political party that controls a majority of seats in the House. The Speaker is, therefore, the leader of his congressional party and has further powers deriving from party rules. While the rules of the Democratic and Republican parties vary somewhat, in general the Speaker participates in making his party's standing-committee assign-

REP. JOSEPH G. CANNON (R-ILL.). Speaker of the House (1903–1911).   LIBRARY OF CONGRESS

ments, influences the flow of legislation to the floor (currently by nominating the chairman and majority members of the Rules Committee), makes recommendations on legislation to the party caucus, can authorize members' travel, appoints members to party task forces, makes political appearances on behalf of members, and in recent times has been influential in raising and distributing campaign funds.

Administrative Duties. To the Speaker's parliamentary and political functions has been added, especially in modern times, a vital role as chief administrator of the House. The Speaker is responsible for the offices of sergeant at arms, clerk, doorkeeper, House counsel, House parliamentarian, and the Capitol Police on the House side of the Hill. He is responsible for office assignments, all travel not delegated to individual members or to committees, and appointments to special boards and commissions. These administrative duties place the office under a heavy burden and are often sources of institutional stress. They have, however, expanded the Speaker's leverage over members and hence his power. In 1992 the House, in response to scandals in the House Bank and House Post Office, created the positions of Director of Non-Legislative and Financial Services and House Auditor and Inspector General. These offices are to be filled on recommendation of the Speaker and the majority and minority leaders. These employees are accountable to the House Administration Committee and are removable by the Speaker alone. In 1993 these new offices were being implemented and the extent to which they will affect the Speaker's power is yet to be determined. One result of the expansion of the Speaker's administrative powers in the post–World War II era has been a dramatic expansion in the Speaker's staff. Whereas Speaker Sam Rayburn had a personal staff numbering fewer than a dozen people in the 1950s, Speakers Thomas P. (Tip) O'Neill, Jr., James C. Wright, Jr., and Thomas S. Foley have had staffs numbering in the dozens in the 1980s and 1990s. This bureaucratization of the speakership brought about fundamental change in the office, with more and more responsibility delegated to core staff. It seems unlikely that the new administrative offices created in 1992 will lessen the Speaker's need to rely on staff.

The political role accorded Speakers by their party membership greatly enhances the powers given to the office under the Constitution and House Rules, and the political and institutional powers work reciprocally to strengthen the Speaker's hand. At the same time, the dual role of presiding officer (requiring fairness) and party leader (requiring political commitment) creates a tension in the office that has provided its distinctive character. Although the Speaker need not be a member of the House, all Speakers to date have been. Thus, Speakers have obligations as representatives of their constituencies that place further claims on their loyalty. The speakership is, then, a multifaceted office that appears somewhat splintered to observers from parliamentary regimes in which the speakership has become a nonpolitical office.

History of the Office. The evolving character of the speakership has meant that Speakers of differ-

EVERY LITTLE MOVEMENT WILL HAVE A MEANING OF IT'S OWN.

SPEAKER JAMES BEAUCHAMP (CHAMP) CLARK (D-MO.). Although the powers of the Speaker were curtailed after the 1910 revolt against Speaker Joseph G. Cannon, the position was still viewed as a path to the White House. As the cartoonist predicted, Clark did make a run for the presidency, seeking the Democratic nomination for the 1912 presidential election. He lost to Woodrow Wilson, then governor of New Jersey. Clifford K. Berryman, *Washington Evening Star*, c. April 1911.

U.S. SENATE COLLECTION, CENTER FOR LEGISLATIVE ARCHIVES

ent periods have played different roles. During the pre–Civil War period, for example, the party system was unstable and often fragmented, and so the Speaker of the House could not easily emerge as a powerful party leader. The most famous antebellum Speaker was Henry Clay of Kentucky, who was elected to the office on his first day in the House as the leader of the congressional War Hawks. Clay was a charismatic national leader who used the speakership to further his presidential ambitions. While no student of parliamentary procedure, he used the power of recognition to his own political purposes and won the respect of members by his firm command from the chair. His parliamentary encounters with his nemesis, John Randolph of Roanoke, were notorious, yet the House backed

Clay in all of his rulings from the chair. He served off and on as Speaker from 1811 until 1824, when he moved to the Senate. Other Speakers of this period served much shorter tenures, and none could be said to have been a national leader in the Clay mold, although one, James K. Polk of Tennessee, was later elected president, something Clay never achieved.

Peak of power. After the Civil War, the United States welcomed a strong two-party system. During the fifty years following the war, Congress was relatively strong, the presidency relatively weak, and the Republican party mostly predominant. The speakership reached its peak of power, and both Republican and Democratic Speakers were strong party leaders and major players on the national stage. Among Democratic Speakers, the two most effective were Samuel J. Randall of Pennsylvania, who was responsible for the adoption of major rules reforms in 1880, including the creation of the Rules Committee, and John G. Carlisle of Kentucky, who later served as a U.S. senator and as secretary of the Treasury in the second administration of Grover Cleveland. These two Democrats were not as effective, however, as the best of the Republican Speakers of this period, including James G. Blaine of Maine, the "Plumed Knight" who led his party for almost two decades; Thomas B. Reed of Maine, who revolutionized the House by the adoption of the Reed Rules in 1890; and Joseph G. (Uncle Joe) Cannon of Illinois, who ruled the House with an iron hand from 1903 until his power was undermined by the great revolution of 1910 in which the Speaker lost control over the Rules Committee.

These Republican Speakers distinguished themselves in several ways. Each was responsible for major innovations in House Rules. Blaine developed the "Speaker's list" for floor recognition and used the power of committee appointment to maintain control over the House agenda. Reed broke the back of the disappearing quorum and dilatory motion, clearing the way for majority governance in the House for the first time. Cannon gathered the various reins of power into his hands and demonstrated how they could be used. He stood toe to toe with Presidents Theodore Roosevelt and William Howard Taft and made the House the dominant force in the government. All three Republicans were serious presidential candidates. Blaine left the House for the Senate, and as senator he competed for the presidential nomination in 1884. Reed was the main rival of William McKinley for the Republican nomination in 1896. Cannon sought the nomination in 1908.

The "feudal" House. After the revolt against Cannon in 1910, the speakership began its slow transformation to a new and very different kind of office. Beginning at the turn of the century, membership tenure began steadily to lengthen, especially among southern Democrats. The power that had been taken away from the speakership devolved upon the standing committees and their chairmen. Over time the committees became the real locus of power in the House. The Democrats flirted with caucus governance during the speakership of James Beauchamp (Champ) Clark of Missouri (1911–1918), and the Republicans offered a reasonably strong speakership under Nicholas Longworth of Ohio (1925–1931). But by the time of the Great Depression and New Deal, the committee barons had taken full control of the House. Since the Democrats controlled the House for all but two Congresses between 1933 and 1970 (the year when average congressional tenure reached its peak), they most shaped this system; and since the most senior

REP. THOMAS S. FOLEY (D-WASH.). Speaker of the House (1989–). OFFICE OF SPEAKER THOMAS S. FOLEY

Speakers of the House of Representatives

Congress	Name	Date Elected	Congress	Name	Date Elected
1st	Frederick A. C. Muhlenberg (Pa.)[1]	1 April 1789	28th	John W. Jones (D-Va.)	4 Dec. 1843
2d	Jonathan Trumbull (F-Conn.)	24 Oct. 1791	29th	John W. Davis (D-Ind.)	1 Dec. 1845
3d	Frederick A. C. Muhlenberg (Pa.)[1]	2 Dec. 1793	30th	Robert C. Winthrop (W-Mass.)	6 Dec. 1847
4th	Jonathan Dayton (F-N.J.)	7 Dec. 1795	31st	Howell Cobb (D-Ga.)	22 Dec. 1849
5th	Jonathan Dayton (F-N.J.)	15 May 1797	32d	Linn Boyd (D-Ky.)	1 Dec. 1851
6th	Theodore Sedgwick (F-Mass.)	2 Dec. 1799	33d	Linn Boyd (D-Ky.)	5 Dec. 1853
7th	Nathaniel Macon (R-N.C.)	7 Dec. 1801	34th	Nathaniel P. Banks (R-Mass.)	2 Feb. 1856
8th	Nathaniel Macon (R-N.C.)	17 Oct. 1803	35th	James L. Orr (D-S.C.)	7 Dec. 1857
9th	Nathaniel Macon (R-N.C.)	2 Dec. 1805	36th	William Pennington (R-N.J.)	1 Feb. 1860
10th	Joseph B. Varnum (R-Mass.)	26 Oct. 1807	37th	Galusha A. Grow (R-Pa.)	4 July 1861
11th	Joseph B. Varnum (R-Mass.)	22 May 1809	38th	Schuyler Colfax (R-Ind.)	7 Dec. 1863
12th	Henry Clay (W-Ky.)	4 Nov. 1811	39th	Schuyler Colfax (R-Ind.)	4 Dec. 1865
13th	Henry Clay (W-Ky.)	24 May 1813	40th	Schuyler Colfax (R-Ind.)	4 Mar. 1867
	Langdon Cheves (R-S.C.)	19 Jan. 1814		Theodore M. Pomeroy (R-N.Y.)	3 Mar. 1869
14th	Henry Clay (W-Ky.)	4 Dec. 1815	41st	James G. Blaine (R-Maine)	4 Mar. 1869
15th	Henry Clay (W-Ky.)	1 Dec. 1817	42d	James G. Blaine (R-Maine)	4 Mar. 1871
16th	Henry Clay (W-Ky.)	6 Dec. 1819	43d	James G. Blaine (R-Maine)	1 Dec. 1873
	John W. Taylor (R-N.Y.)	15 Nov. 1820	44th	Michael C. Kerr (D-Ind.)	6 Dec. 1875
17th	Philip P. Barbour (R-Va.)	4 Dec. 1821		Samuel J. Randall (D-Pa.)	4 Dec. 1876
18th	Henry Clay (W-Ky.)	1 Dec. 1823	45th	Samuel J. Randall (D-Pa.)	15 Oct. 1877
19th	John W. Taylor (R-N.Y.)	5 Dec. 1825	46th	Samuel J. Randall (D-Pa.)	18 Mar. 1879
20th	Andrew Stevenson (J-Va.)	3 Dec. 1827	47th	J. Warren Keifer (R-Ohio)	5 Dec. 1881
21st	Andrew Stevenson (J-Va.)	7 Dec. 1829	48th	John G. Carlisle (D-Ky.)	3 Dec. 1883
22d	Andrew Stevenson (J-Va.)	5 Dec. 1831	49th	John G. Carlisle (D-Ky.)	7 Dec. 1885
23d	Andrew Stevenson (J-Va.)	2 Dec. 1833	50th	John G. Carlisle (D-Ky.)	5 Dec. 1887
	John Bell (W-Tenn.)	2 June 1834	51st	Thomas B. Reed (R-Maine)	2 Dec. 1889
24th	James K. Polk (D-Tenn.)	7 Dec. 1835	52d	Charles F. Crisp (D-Ga.)	8 Dec. 1891
25th	James K. Polk (D-Tenn.)	4 Sept. 1837	53d	Charles F. Crisp (D-Ga.)	7 Aug. 1893
26th	Robert M. T. Hunter (W-Va.)	16 Dec. 1839	54th	Thomas B. Reed (R-Maine)	2 Dec. 1895
27th	John White (W-Ky.)	31 May 1841	55th	Thomas B. Reed (R-Maine)	15 Mar. 1897

[1]Nonpartisan

Democrats were from the deep South, it was the southern wing of the party that gained most of its benefits. Committee appointments on the Democratic side were made by the Democratic members of the Ways and Means Committee, which was typically controlled by senior southerners. The path of legislation to the floor passed through the standing committees, which met at the call of chairmen, who were typically southern Democrats. From there, legislation went to the Rules Committee, chaired by southern Democrats and controlled by a coalition of southern Democrats and Republicans. By controlling the legislative process the Conservative Coalition was able to throttle liberal legislation.

While the southern wing of the Democratic party had always had influence due to its size and seniority, it was only after President Franklin D. Roosevelt's Court-packing scheme in 1937 and the retribution he sought against some southern Democrats in the 1938 elections that the Coalition emerged as a regular voting block. With southern Democrats controlling most major committees, with the Rules Committee in the hands of the Coalition, and with the Coalition active on the floor, the liberal Democratic political agenda was placed in abeyance until the Lyndon B. Johnson administration and its Great Society.

By far the strongest Speaker of this period was

Speakers of the House of Representatives (Continued)

Congress	Name	Date Elected	Congress	Name	Date Elected
56th	David B. Henderson (R-Iowa)	4 Dec. 1899	80th	Joseph W. Martin, Jr. (R-Mass.)	3 Jan. 1947
57th	David B. Henderson (R-Iowa)	2 Dec. 1901	81st	Sam Rayburn (D-Tex.)	3 Jan. 1949
58th	Joseph G. Cannon (R-Ill.)	9 Nov. 1903	82d	Sam Rayburn (D-Tex.)	3 Jan. 1951
59th	Joseph G. Cannon (R-Ill.)	4 Dec. 1905	83d	Joseph W. Martin, Jr. (R-Mass.)	3 Jan. 1953
60th	Joseph G. Cannon (R-Ill.)	2 Dec. 1907	84th	Sam Rayburn (D-Tex.)	5 Jan. 1955
61st	Joseph G. Cannon (R-Ill.)	15 Mar. 1909	85th	Sam Rayburn (D-Tex.)	3 Jan. 1957
62d	James Beauchamp (Champ) Clark (D-Mo.)	4 Apr. 1911	86th	Sam Rayburn (D-Tex.)	7 Jan. 1959
63d	James Beauchamp (Champ) Clark (D-Mo.)	7 Apr. 1913	87th	Sam Rayburn (D-Tex.)	3 Jan. 1961
64th	James Beauchamp (Champ) Clark (D-Mo.)	6 Dec. 1915	88th	John W. McCormack (D-Mass.)	9 Jan. 1963
65th	James Beauchamp (Champ) Clark (D-Mo.)	2 Apr. 1917	89th	John W. McCormack (D-Mass.)	4 Jan. 1965
			90th	John W. McCormack (D-Mass.)	10 Jan. 1967
66th	Frederick H. Gillett (R-Mass.)	19 May 1919	91st	John W. McCormack (D-Mass.)	3 Jan. 1969
67th	Frederick H. Gillett (R-Mass.)	11 Apr. 1921	92d	Carl B. Albert (D-Okla.)	21 Jan. 1971
68th	Frederick H. Gillett (R-Mass.)	3 Dec. 1923	93d	Carl B. Albert (D-Okla.)	3 Jan. 1973
69th	Nicholas Longworth (R-Ohio)	7 Dec. 1925	94th	Carl B. Albert (D-Okla.)	14 Jan. 1975
70th	Nicholas Longworth (R-Ohio)	5 Dec. 1927	95th	Thomas P. (Tip) O'Neill, Jr. (D-Mass.)	4 Jan. 1977
71st	Nicholas Longworth (R-Ohio)	15 Apr. 1929	96th	Thomas P. (Tip) O'Neill, Jr. (D-Mass.)	15 Jan. 1979
72d	John Nance Garner (D-Tex.)	7 Dec. 1931	97th	Thomas P. (Tip) O'Neill, Jr. (D-Mass.)	5 Jan. 1981
73d	Henry T. Rainey (D-Ill.)	9 Mar. 1933	98th	Thomas P. (Tip) O'Neill, Jr. (D-Mass.)	3 Jan. 1983
74th	Joseph W. Byrns (D-Tenn.)	3 Jan. 1935	99th	Thomas P. (Tip) O'Neill, Jr. (D-Mass.)	3 Jan. 1985
	William B. Bankhead (D-Ala.)	4 June 1936			
75th	William B. Bankhead (D-Ala.)	5 Jan. 1937	100th	James C. Wright, Jr. (D-Tex.)	6 Jan. 1987
76th	William B. Bankhead (D-Ala.)	3 Jan. 1939	101st	James C. Wright, Jr. (D-Tex.)	3 Jan. 1989
	Sam Rayburn (D-Tex.)	16 Sept. 1940		Thomas S. Foley (D-Wash.)	6 June 1989
77th	Sam Rayburn (D-Tex.)	3 Jan. 1941	102d	Thomas S. Foley (D-Wash.)	3 Jan. 1991
78th	Sam Rayburn (D-Tex.)	6 Jan. 1943	103d	Thomas S. Foley (D-Wash.)	5 Jan. 1993
79th	Sam Rayburn (D-Tex.)	3 Jan. 1945			

Sam Rayburn of Texas, who led the Democrats from his first election as Speaker in 1941 until his death in 1961, a period interrupted by Republican control of the 80th (1947–1949) and 83d (1953–1955) Congresses. Many regard Rayburn as the most powerful Speaker in the history of the House, but he was never as powerful as his late nineteenth-century predecessors. Instead, he was a man whose personality and political circumstances were ideally suited to the conditions of the House during its "feudal" era. Rayburn had been an effective chairman of the Committee on Interstate and Foreign Commerce during the 1930s, and as Speaker he respected the prerogatives of the committees and

their chairmen. He made himself the broker among these titans rather than seek power over them. In this way, he positioned himself so that his stature enhanced his ability to influence events when it was important to him to do so. Because the arrangements of the baronial House suited his purposes well, he resisted any change in them until 1961, when he led the successful effort to "pack" the Rules Committee in order to break the back of the conservative coalition's control over it. That victory and Rayburn's death heralded the end of an era in the history of the House and its speakership.

Reforms. The 1960s and 1970s were a time of tremendous change in the House. The liberal wing of the Democratic party was pressing for social and economic legislation that was resisted by conservative Democrats and Republicans. To enact their programs, the liberal Democrats sought to change the rules that permitted conservative control of the congressional agenda. Led in the House by the liberal Democratic Study Group, the reformers sought further to abridge the power of the committee chairmen, to open up the legislative process to public scrutiny, to redistribute power from committees to subcommittees, and to strengthen the office of Speaker, which liberal Democrats expected to control. The Legislative Reform Act of 1970 and subsequent reforms adopted by the Democratic caucus transformed the House. Among the most significant changes were those that provided for recorded (later electronic) votes, opened committee meetings to the public, empowered committee majorities to call meetings, required caucus votes to approve committee chairs, transferred the power of committee assignments to the Democratic Steering and Policy Committee from the Ways and Means Democratic caucus, and gave the Speaker the power to nominate Democratic members of the Rules Committee. Especially significant was the adoption of a "subcommittee bill of rights," which provided staffing and required all legislation to be referred to subcommittee before being considered by the full committee. These changes revolutionized the House, diffused power within it, and greatly strengthened the office of Speaker. The two Speakers who presided over these changes were Democrats John W. McCormack of Massachusetts (1962–1971) and Carl B. Albert of Oklahoma (1971–1976). These Speakers confronted the most difficult period in the history of the House since before the Civil War, as the country was torn apart by domestic strife over the civil rights movement and the Vietnam War. Both were protégés of Rayburn. Of the two, Speaker Albert was more receptive to the changes that followed in the wake of political upheaval.

The "post-reform" House of the period since 1975 has suffered from a malady that is both similar to and different from the malady of the old House. In the "pre-reform" House, conservatives controlled the parliamentary machinery and used that control to thwart the liberal agenda. When Congress failed to act, it was often because those in control did not want action. In the post-reform Congress, legislation has frequently bogged down even when everyone has agreed that legislation is needed. Power has been so diffused that it is difficult to forge consensus. The inherent difficulty in gaining agreement among 435 autonomous members was exacerbated by divided government. Except during the administration of Jimmy Carter (1977–1981), Republicans were in control of the White House and Democrats in control of at least one house of Congress from 1969 through 1992 (Republicans did control the Senate from 1981 through 1986, during Republican Ronald Reagan's presidency). This condition contributed to a paralysis in public policy.

Under these circumstances, the speakership of the House changed again. Democratic Speakers emerged as public spokesmen for their party and as policy leaders in ways not seen since the turn of the twentieth century. As his party's highest elected officeholder, Speaker Tip O'Neill of Massachusetts (1977–1986) was especially prominent in leading the Democratic opposition to the policies of President Reagan. His successor, Jim Wright of Texas, sought to use the powers of the speakership to forge a legislative program in both domestic and foreign policy. His heavy-handed tactics caused disgruntlement within the ranks of his own party and attacks from Republicans, notwithstanding his considerable legislative success in the 100th Congress. When, in the 101st Congress, ethics charges were brought against him, he lacked the legislative support to survive and was forced to resign. Speaker Tom Foley of Washington (1989–), assumed a much more conciliatory role.

Thus, the speakership of the House is, on the one hand, defined by its parliamentary, administrative, representative, and partisan roles, which have evolved over time; on the other, the speakership's character has changed with the changing character of the party system, the distribution of power between the two major parties, and the character of individual Speakers. It is unique among all American political creations, reflecting as it does the fragmentation of power under the Constitution and the diversity of the American political system.

BIBLIOGRAPHY

Cheney, Richard B., and Lynne V. Cheney. *Kings of the Hill: Power and Personality in the House of Representatives.* 1983.

Follett, Mary Parker. *The Speaker of the House of Representatives.* 1896.

Kenon, Donald R., ed. *The Speakers of the U.S. House of Representatives, 1798–1984.* 1986.

Peters, Ronald M., Jr. *The American Speakership: The Office in Historical Perspective.* 1990.

Sinclair, Barbara. *Majority Party Leadership in the U.S. House.* 1983.

RONALD M. PETERS, JR.

SPECIAL COMMITTEE. *See* Committees, *article on* Select and Special Committees.

SPECIAL ELECTIONS. Special elections to Congress are used to fill vacant seats in both the Senate and House of Representatives. Voter participation in these elections usually falls well below normal levels, except when they are held concurrently with regular general elections. Special elections occasionally produce prominent figures, particularly in the contemporary Senate, where Democrats Edward M. Kennedy (Mass.) and Sam Nunn (Ga.) and Republicans Ted Stevens (Alaska) and Strom Thurmond (S.C.) first gained their seats through special elections.

For Senate vacancies, the Constitution authorizes state legislatures to empower governors to make temporary appointments "until the people fill the vacancies by election as the legislature may direct." Forty-nine states provide for temporary appointments, but Arizona requires special elections for all Senate vacancies. Most states provide for nomination by primary or party convention, and they usually require that special elections be held at the next statewide election, unless the seat becomes vacant after a statewide election but before the end of the term, in which case the appointee serves until the term expires.

All House vacancies are filled by special elections, with authority over scheduling and nomination procedures delegated to the states. Most states provide for nomination by primary or other party action. For House vacancies that occur during a Congress's first session, all states mandate a special election; for second-session vacancies, the special election is usually held at the same time as the regularly scheduled election for the seat. Some states do not provide for a special election under these circumstances: the seat remains vacant until the next Congress convenes.

BIBLIOGRAPHY

Sigelman, Lee. "Special Elections to the U.S. House: Some Descriptive Generalizations." *Legislative Studies Quarterly* (1981): 577–588.

Studlar, Donley T., and Lee Sigelman. "Special Elections: A Comparative Perspective." *British Journal of Political Science* 17 (1987): 247–256.

THOMAS H. NEALE

SPEECH OR DEBATE CLAUSE. The speech or debate clause of the Constitution, Article I, section 6, clause 1, confers immunity upon members of Congress with the words: "For Speech or Debate in either House, they [the Senators and Representatives] shall not be questioned in any other Place." That clause covers both what members of Congress do on the floor of the House or Senate—debating, motions, and voting—and what they do in other areas of the legislative process, such as bill preparation, investigations, committee work, and oversight of departments and agencies. It protects members from criminal prosecutions or civil suits against them and from being questioned as witnesses in suits against others. Thus, for example, when a senator prepares and offers an amendment to a tax bill in committee to confer a benefit on a particular company, his preparation and his offering of the amendment could not be questioned in a civil case or even in a criminal indictment. Speech or debate immunity gives protection against depositions and subpoenas, which are frequent in modern civil cases. The immunity protects congressional staff when they function as the "alter egos" of members on legislative matters.

This speech or debate immunity serves as a pillar of the government's separation of powers by keeping disputes about Congress out of the courts and by requiring executive officials and private individuals alike to deal with members of Congress politically rather than through legal assault. Speaking broadly, since World War II, presidents have often been of one political party while one or both houses of Congress have had a majority of the other political party. Yet during this time presidents have not generally attempted to use Justice Department prosecutions or civil lawsuits to fight issues with Congress because the speech or debate clause prevents such lawsuits. When President Ronald Reagan tried to file such a lawsuit in 1983, entitled *United States v. House of Representatives,* the court agreed with lawyers for the House that the case had to be dismissed. Charges by the president or anyone else against Congress, and disputes within Congress that concern legislative matters, must be settled through political processes and at the ballot box rather than in court.

Originally, the Framers of the Constitution modeled the speech or debate clause on the traditional immunity enjoyed by members of the British Parliament and by members of colonial and state legislatures. As cases arose, U.S. courts up to the Supreme Court have interpreted the clause to demarcate its meaning in the evolving work of Congress. In *Kilbourn v. Thompson* (1881), the Supreme Court decided that the immunity protected members of a committee who had voted to arrest a resisting witness; the Court decided that the committee process was part of the whole legislative process and deserving of the speech or debate protection. However, the Court held that the immunity did not protect the House sergeant at arms, who had carried out the actual arrest of the witness. One of the great twentieth-century cases, *Gravel v. United States* (1972), decided that the immunity protected Sen. Mike Gravel from prosecution for reading documents into a committee record that revealed the secret history of decisions leading to the Vietnam War. The immunity was complete, even though by placing those documents in the public record, Senator Gravel disclosed records bearing national security classifications of a high secrecy level.

Potentially, the speech or debate immunity could make it difficult to prosecute members of Congress for corruption, but Congress has acted in ways that ensure policing of its conduct. It has enacted ethics codes with comprehensive financial disclosure requirements to which immunity does not apply. Additionally, both the Senate and the House have created internal ethics committees. Because the clause only prevents members from being "questioned in any other Place" than Congress, it does not protect members in any way from being questioned or disciplined by the House or Senate through their internal ethics process.

Moreover, the Supreme Court held, in *United States v. Brewster* (1972), that the Justice Department could indict and prosecute a senator for taking a bribe. However, immunity requires that the prosecution not offer evidence about whether the member who received a bribe then actually performed particular legislative acts such as voting, which are protected by immunity. Instead, the prosecution offers proof that the member received a bribe and proof of what he said when arranging to receive it.

In general, the Supreme Court has interpreted the immunity expansively to preserve Congress's independence in modern conditions. However, in *Hutchinson v. Proxmire* (1979), the Court decided that speech or debate immunity does not protect members when they talk to the press, even when they are informing their constituents about public affairs. This deters Congress from performing what Woodrow Wilson called its "informing function."

[*See also* Gravel v. United States; Kilbourn v. Thompson.]

BIBLIOGRAPHY

Cella, Alexander J. "The Doctrine of Legislative Privilege of Speech or Debate: The New Interpretation as a Threat to Legislative Coequality." *Suffolk University Law Review* 8 (1974): 1019–1905.

"Evidentiary Implications of the Speech or Debate Clause." *Yale Law Journal* 88 (1979): 1280–1298.

Wittke, Carl. *The History of English Parliamentary Privilege.* 1970.

CHARLES TIEFER

SPONSORSHIP. Members of Congress express their endorsement of legislation by associating their name with it in a formal act known as sponsorship. The member who introduces the bill, resolution, or amendment is known as the measure's sponsor. Only a member of Congress can sponsor legislation. Therefore, when the term *by request* appears along with the sponsor's name, it is an indication that the member introduced the measure as a courtesy on behalf of an individual or organization outside the Congress (e.g., the president). However, such sponsorship by request does not necessarily imply endorsement by the sponsor.

Members who simultaneously or subsequently affiliate themselves with a proposal upon its introduction are known as cosponsors. The primary reason for cosponsorship in both the House and Senate is for members to have a concrete proposal to point to, a proposal that expresses their position on an issue and demonstrates their political support for its concept. Gaining cosponsors is accomplished by personal lobbying and by soliciting them through internal letters known as "Dear Colleagues."

In the House, the original sponsor frequently seeks cosponsors for the legislative initiative prior to introducing it. In a body of 435, one way members have found to distinguish their measure from all the rest, and thus encourage its progress, is to accumulate a large number of cosponsors.

Only those members who agree to become cosponsors prior to a measure's introduction will have their name printed on the face of the legislation. Members may cosponsor the measure subsequent to its introduction but, while their names will be noted in the *Congressional Record,* they will not appear on the face of the bill. There is no limitation on how many cosponsors a measure may have, and in practice the number ranges widely. Amendments, however, are rarely cosponsored by more than one or two individuals.

The House, in 1967, adopted a change to House Rule XXII, which allows members to have up to twenty-five cosponsors per measure. Prior to this change, members frequently introduced hundreds of identical proposals, thus incurring substantial printing costs. A further change was made to Rule XXII in 1979 to permit an unlimited number of members to cosponsor a measure upon its introduction and up until it is reported from committee.

In the Senate, cosponsorship does not play as significant a role as in the House. The smaller size of the Senate decreases the need for large numbers of cosponsors to distinguish one senator's proposal from the next. There has been no limitation on how many senators can cosponsor a measure since at least 1937. Cosponsorship practice in the Senate differs somewhat from the House when it comes to its timing. Rather than signing on to a measure when it is introduced, senators will more frequently ask unanimous consent to cosponsor a measure or an amendment during its floor consideration, often just moments before the vote on final passage.

Cosponsorship can be withdrawn in both chambers, but only by unanimous consent.

BIBLIOGRAPHY

Briscoe, Cynthia. *Co-sponsorship of Bills and Resolutions in the House of Representatives.* Congressional Research Service, Library of Congress. CRS Rept. 76-237G. 1976.

Overby, Peter. "Is There a Co-sponsor in the House?" *Washington Post,* 6 January 1991, p. C4.

U.S. House of Representatives. Committee on Science, Space, and Technology. *Legislative Manual.* 5th ed. 102d Cong., 1st sess., 1991. Committee Print.

ILONA B. NICKELS

JOHN C. SPOONER. In 1902.   LIBRARY OF CONGRESS

SPOONER, JOHN C. (1843–1919), senator from Wisconsin, Republican party leader and policymaker. After a successful career assisting Wisconsin's railroad and lumber interests John Coit Spooner was elected to the state assembly in 1871. An active legislator and lobbyist for these clients, he was first elected to the U.S. Senate in 1885, lost his seat in 1891, and was reelected in 1897 and again in 1903. As part of the Senate leadership known as The Four, Spooner worked with Republicans Nelson W. Aldrich of Rhode Island, William B. Allison of Iowa, and Orville H. Platt of Connecticut to help control the direction of policy in the Republican-dominated Congress during the presidency of William McKinley. Restraining reform impulses related to currency inflation, tariffs, and trusts, he and the others appointed themselves to or controlled membership on all important Senate committees to prevent significant legislative change.

A supporter of the Spanish-American War and territorial acquisition, Spooner helped to draft the laws that governed the colonies the United States gained in the wake of the war. He wrote the bill selecting Panama as the site for the Central American canal, much to the delight of McKinley's successor Theodore Roosevelt. But in general Roosevelt relied less and less on Spooner and his old-guard colleagues.

Reform impulses in Wisconsin led by insurgent Republican Robert M. La Follette politically weakened Spooner, who had generally neglected state politics. Spooner gradually lost political control to

La Follette, whose election to the Senate in 1905 he considered personally offensive. The waning of Spooner's influence at both the national and state levels led to his resignation in 1907 and his subsequent move to New York to practice corporate law until his death in 1919.

BIBLIOGRAPHY

Fowler, Dorothy Ganfield. *John C. Spooner, Defender of Presidents*. 1961.
Parker, James R. "The Business of Politics, the Politics of Business: The Career of John C. Spooner, 1868–1907." *The Maryland Historian* 17 (Fall–Winter 1986): 3–20.
Parker, James R. "Paternalism and Racism: Senator John C. Spooner and American Minorities, 1897–1907." *Wisconsin Magazine of History* 57 (Spring 1974): 195–200.
Parker, James R. "Senator John C. Spooner, Advocate of the American Empire, 1899–1906." *The Maryland Historian* 5 (Fall 1974): 113–129.

JAMES R. PARKER

SPORTS. Aside from a 1912 law that forbade the sending of prizefight films through the U.S. mail, Congress made little response to the rise of organized sports. In *Federal Baseball Club of Baltimore v. National League of Professional Baseball Clubs* (1922), the U.S. Supreme Court held that the business of baseball was neither commerce nor interstate, and thus was not covered by federal antitrust law. This was interpreted by later courts to mean that Congress had not intended to include baseball within its antitrust coverage.

In the 1950s, however, a number of decisions, such as the Court's ruling in *Radovich v. National Football League* (1957), held that other professional sports leagues were engaged in interstate commerce, and that federal antitrust law did apply to their activities. Although the actual antitrust law at the time did not specifically single out sports, these holdings led to congressional involvement in the realm of sports; in particular, the Sports Broadcast Act of 1961 (15 U.S.C., secs. 1291–1295). Prior to the passage of this act, professional teams sold the broadcast rights to their games on an individual basis. The act allowed the pooling of rights and their sale on a league-wide basis. This in turn led to lucrative network contracts that provide much of the economic clout enjoyed today by professional sports in the United States.

The Sports Broadcast Act did impose certain restraints on the professional leagues. For example, it protects college and high school football by in effect prohibiting telecasts within seventy-five miles of any such game on Friday evenings and Saturdays between mid September and mid December. Since it is virtually impossible to arrange telecasts that would avoid the seventy-five-mile criterion, this section of the act effectively precludes the National Football League from playing on Fridays and Saturdays for much of its season.

Major league baseball club owners joined with owners from other sports leagues to lobby intensely for the ability to enter into television contracts on a leaguewide basis. The baseball owners felt that the networks would be hesitant to enter into such contracts without congressional protection, since the networks did not share baseball's antitrust immunity. There is, however, a certain redundancy in the act's specific exemption of baseball, in addition to football, basketball, and hockey, from antitrust restrictions, even though the Supreme Court had already held that baseball was not covered by federal antitrust law. This exemption was specifically for professional sports. The National Collegiate Athletic Association (NCAA) sought unsuccessfully to avail itself of such protection in a lawsuit in the 1980s. The Supreme Court in *National Collegiate Athletic Association v. Board of Regents of the University of Oklahoma and the University of Georgia Athletic Association* (1984) held that colleges pooling their individual broadcast rights in one contract under NCAA aegis violated antitrust law.

Congress in 1966 allowed professional football leagues to merge if "such agreement increases rather than decreases the number of professional football clubs so operating." This permitted the National and American football leagues to become a single powerful league, but the exempting language was specifically restricted to professional football clubs, which became an important point when rival leagues appeared in basketball and hockey. These leagues could not merge, and had to seek alternative legal remedies to make possible later consolidations.

Television sports fans gained a small victory when Congress in September 1973 enacted a law that restricted local blackouts of televised sports events under certain conditions. Although that law expired in December 1975, sports leagues still adhere to its strictures on a voluntary basis in order to avoid future congressional action.

Congress has also become involved with so-called amateur sports, most notably through the Amateur Sports Act of 1978. This was passed in response to the problems created by competing amateur sports associations, and in so doing to reorganize and coordinate amateur athletics in the United States. Another purpose was to encourage and strengthen the participation of American amateurs in international competition. The act addresses two major areas: the relationship between athletes eligible for international amateur competitions and the ruling bodies that govern those competitions, and the relationship among the ruling bodies themselves. The statute empowered the United States Olympic Committee (USOC) to select one national governing body for each Olympic or Pan-American sport, and enumerated their specific responsibilities. It called also for the encouragement of and assistance to other amateur athletic programs, including competition among handicapped persons. To date the USOC has largely confined its role to the Olympics and other international competitions. As the international governing bodies for various sports have broadened their eligibility rules as to who may enter Olympic competition, the amateur emphasis of the act has become archaic. But the basic support of international sports competition is still greatly aided and abetted by the act's provisions.

The most recent enactment by Congress, the Student Athlete Right-to-Know Act, took effect 1 July 1992. This law requires colleges and universities that award athletics-related student aid to make certain disclosures. The first requirement is annual reports to the secretary of Education on the number of students at the institution, the number receiving such aid, and their graduation rates, broken down by sex, race, and sport. This information must also be given to every potential student athlete to whom the institution offers aid, as well as to the athlete's parents, guidance counselor, and coach. The legislation was a response to increased concern about low graduation rates by student athletes at many colleges and universities. It forced disclosure in order to compare athlete graduation rates with those of the general student population.

Sports leagues and associations have also been affected by congressional tax provisions. One example is the limit on the depreciation of player contracts that can be claimed upon the purchase of a professional sports franchise.

Numerous sports-related bills are introduced into Congress each year. Many seek to either expand or restrict antitrust coverage; others would affect the activities of the National Collegiate Athletic Association and universities and colleges in general. Although few of these bills stand much chance of passage, their introduction and the attendant publicity generated by congressional hearings affect the operations of sports at all levels. Owners of sports franchises constantly fear government intrusion into their business and often adjust business practices to avoid additional regulations. A prime example of this is the National Football League's aforementioned adherence to the tenets of Congress's antiblackout legislation of the 1970s to avoid congressional reenactment of the legislation. The NFL has adhered to the legislation for almost twenty years since its expiration. Another example is the expansion of the number of clubs in each league of Major League Baseball when certain members of Congress threatened that baseball might well lose its antitrust immunity if it did not expand.

BIBLIOGRAPHY

Berry, Robert C., and Glenn M. Wong. *Law and Business of the Sports Industries.* 2 vols. 1986. Vol. 2, 2d ed. 1993.
Johnson, Arthur T., and James H. Frey, eds. *Government and Sport: The Public Policy Issues.* 1985.

ROBERT C. BERRY

SPOUSES OF MEMBERS. *See* Members, *article on* Spouses and Families.

ST. *Names beginning with St. are alphabetized as if spelled out.*

STAFFING. The end of the nineteenth century and the beginning of the twentieth brought enduring changes in the type and amount of Congress's work; with this workload expansion came the need to augment staff resources. During most of the nineteenth century, Congress neither needed nor authorized appropriations for staff for itself, with two exceptions. First, under the direction of each chamber's officers was a small cadre of employees who performed security, maintenance, postal, and administrative tasks; as late as 1918, this group numbered fewer than 700 employees (compared with more than 5,000 today). Second, starting in the 1840s, Congress hired a handful of clerks, messengers, and janitors for its committees; these "clerk hires" (the term remains part of congressional lingo to this day) totaled fewer than 150 as late as 1890 and about 400 in 1920 (compared with almost 4,000 today).

Several reasons account for Congress's lack of need for staff assistance during the nineteenth century; they include the limited number and kinds of issues on Congress's agenda; the short duration of congressional sessions; a belief in a relatively short rotation in office—the citizen legislator concept—that largely prevailed until the end of the nineteenth century; a lack of office space; minimal constituent demand on members other than by those seeking patronage appointments to federal jobs; and a commitment to limited government, including a laissez-faire attitude toward economic and social regulation.

Growth of Congressional Staff

It is likely that the large number of Senate committees that existed until their consolidation in 1947 existed in part to provide personal staff for senators. The extent to which individual members of both chambers paid for personal staff from their own pockets between 1789 and 1885 or thereafter remains unrecorded, though debate on legislative appropriations through the first half of the twentieth century was punctuated by claims from members that they had to dip into their private funds to supplement the public funding provided to them for staff. Currently members may use only public funds to pay for their staffs.

Personal Staff. The Senate system for funding personal staff is more complicated than that in the House. Moneys for personal office staffing were appropriated first in the Senate, then in the House. In 1885 the Senate authorized a clerk for each senator not entitled to one "under the rules" as chairman of a committee—a practice that, though later modified, continued in the Senate until 1947 but that the House followed for less than a decade (1893–1902).

Senate. In earlier years, because of the large number of standing and select committees, some senators would chair more than one committee but could use committee staff as personal staff on only one of the committees they chaired. For example, in 1891 there were 88 senators and 55 Senate committees, including 13 select committees, but because of multiple chairmanships, only 49 senators were staffed through their committees, while 39 senators were authorized a clerk for their personal office.

The Senate practice of funding chairmen through one of the committees they chaired while funding nonchairmen through their personal offices lasted with some variation for fifty years, until 1935, when the Senate passed a resolution (S. Res. 144) authorizing an additional clerk for all ninety-six senators. Approximately twenty-five years before, however, the Senate had begun to deviate from the practice of funding chairmen only through the committees they chaired, with anywhere from seven to eleven chairmen in any year being entitled to one or more personal clerks in addition to staff they received through their positions as chairs of Senate committees. The public record does not explain why this occurred.

By 1930, for example, Senate membership and the number of committees had stabilized at 96 and 33, respectively. Yet 70, not just 63, senators were authorized to have personal staff even though all committees were staffed and no senator chaired more than one committee.

Table 1 illustrates the fluctuation in the number of House and Senate committees from 1891 until the modern committee system was established in 1947. On the Senate side, these variable counts affected the number of senators during any session who were not chairmen of a committee and thus entitled to personal staff.

In 1940 the Senate commenced a practice that evolved into the current method for funding personal staff. In the Third Deficiency Appropriation

TABLE 1. *Congressional Committees: 1891, 1914, 1924, 1930, 1946, 1947*

YEAR	HOUSE		SENATE			
	Standing	Select	Standing	Select	JOINT	TOTAL
1891	49	13	42	13	0	117
1914	58	0	73	0	4	135
1924	61	4	34	0	5	104
1930	47	0	33	0	9	89
1946	48	7	33	11	9	108
1947	19	3	15	3	6	46

SOURCE: Author's count from the *Congressional Directory* for the years indicated: 15 January 1891, 2d ed., 51st, 2d; February 1914, 2d ed., 63d, 2d; May 1924, 3d ed., 68th, 1st; 18 January 1930, 2d ed., 71st, 2d; 29 March 1946, 2d ed., 79th, 2d; and 11 January 1947, 2d ed., 80th, 1st.

Act of that year, senators from states with populations of three million or more were authorized to have one more clerk than were senators from states with populations under three million. With the passage of time additional adjustments based on population were made.

Seven years later, because of the Legislative Reorganization Act of 1946 (P.L. 79-601), the Senate stopped distinguishing between chairmen and nonchairmen in the allocation of personal staff. This occurred because section 202 of that law forbade use of committee staff for any purpose other than committee business. In 1946 each senator was authorized to hire an administrative assistant in addition to any other clerks.

In 1947 the Senate eliminated its practice of specifying in legislative-branch appropriation bills the exact number of clerks to be hired by senators—and, for that matter, by committees—as well as the maximum salary each could be paid. Over the next several years, the Senate gradually replaced these specifications with a personal staffing system based on state population categories (at one time there were as many as twenty-nine categories), which prescribed differing annual allotments of money for each population category, putting restrictions on the minimum and maximum salaries payable to personal and committee staff rather than limiting their numbers.

Since 1992 there have been twenty-four such categories, ranging from states with fewer than five million inhabitants to states with a population of twenty-eight million and above. In 1993, seventy-four of the one hundred senators fell into the lowest category and thus were eligible for $1.4 million a year for personal staff through their combined administrative-clerical and legislative assistance allowance. By contrast, senators from California, the most populous state, were entitled to $2.3 million each. In 1990, the size of senators' staffs ranged from twenty-four to seventy-three, with forty-one as the average.

House. The House developed a more straightforward way of funding personal staff. It could do so because, for the most part, representatives have constituencies of roughly the same size, which, of course, is not the case for senators. In 1893, at the outset of House personal staffing, the House copied the Senate by giving fifty-six chairmen authorization for combined personal and committee staff, while the 269 members who were not chairmen were each authorized $100 per month to hire one clerk while the House was in session. Three years

hence the House removed the "in session" limitation and the next year granted chairmen the same clerk-hire privilege as nonchairmen when the House was out of session. Five years later, in 1902, the House abandoned the distinction between chairmen and nonchairmen and granted all representatives the right to a personal staff.

Table 2 indicates the years (beginning in 1893) in which increases were made in the number of staff authorized for representatives. In 1992, each representative was authorized up to $515,760 annually to pay for the eighteen permanent and four temporary personal staff to which each was entitled. Members, however, seldom use all the money available for this purpose.

Table 3 shows that on average the number of personal staff per representative did not reach double-digit figures until around 1970—even though each representative was allowed ten as of 1965. While senators reached an average of ten or more personal staff in the 1950s, the growth in personal staff, for senators did not surge until the 1970s.

Committee Staff. A parallel development occurred with committee staff, as documented in table 4, which shows modest staffing until 1947, the

TABLE 2. *House Personal Staff Authorization Increases: 1893–1992*

YEAR	AUTHORIZED STAFF	STAFF FOR DISTRICTS OVER 500,000
1893	1–2	NA
1919	2	NA
1940	3	NA
1945	6	NA
1949	7	NA
1954	8	NA
1955	9	10 (1956)
1961	10	11
1965	11	12
1966	12	13
1969	13	14
1971	15	16
1972	16	NA
1975	18	NA
1979	22	NA

NOTE: Eighteen permanent and four nonpermanent staff were authorized as of 1979; there have been no increases since that year.
SOURCE: U.S. House of Representatives. Legislative Branch Appropriations Subcommittee. *Legislative Branch Appropriation Bill: Fiscal Year 1992.* 1991. P. 27 (as corrected by author).

TABLE 3. *Senate and House Personal Staff: 1891–1991*

YEAR	HOUSE	SENATE	TOTAL	AVG. PER REP.	AVG. PER SEN.
1891	0	39	39	0	1
1914	435	72	507	1	3
1930	870	280	1,150	2	4
1947	1,440	590	2,030	3	6
1957	2,441	1,115	3,556	6	12
1967	4,055	1,749	5,804	9	17
1977	6,942	3,554	10,496	16	35
1987	7,584	4,075	11,659	17	41
1991	c. 8,000	c. 4,100	12,100	18	41

SOURCES: *Vital Statistics on Congress, 1991–1992*, p. 126, for 1891–1987, based on data through 1967 from Fox and Hammond, *Congressional Staffs*, 1977, p. 171; author's data for House for 1914 and House and Senate for 1991.

year that marks the beginning of the modern committee system in Congress. Numbers of committee staff almost doubled within three years thereafter, nearly tripling by 1970 and more than quintupling by 1980, when they peaked. They have since leveled off. The growth in the number of committee staff since 1947 is only partially attributable to growth in the number of committees and subcommittees (230 in 1947 and 284 in 1991, an increase of roughly 25 percent).

Total Staff, 1918 and 1991. Table 5 reports the approximate number of staff who worked for Congress in 1991; table 6 shows comparable data for 1918. Included in the 1991 totals are not only personal and committee staff but also employees of

TABLE 4. *Standing Committee Staff: 1891–1989*

YEAR	HOUSE	SENATE	TOTAL
1891	65	73	138
1914	120	239	359
1924	129	139	268
1930	122	172	294
1947	246	300	546
1950	440	470	910
1967	589	621	1,210
1970	702	635	1,337
1980	1,917	1,191	3,108
1989	1,986	1,013	2,999

NOTE: To arrive at total committee staffing, the number of staff for joint and House and Senate select and special committees must be factored in. For 1980, for example, add 400 to the "Total" column; for 1989, add 500.
SOURCES: *Vital Statistics on Congress, 1991–1992*, p. 130, 1930–1967 based on data from Fox and Hammond, *Congressional Staffs*, 1977, p. 171; author's count from *U.S. Statutes* for 1891, 1914, and 1924.

party leaders, the several officers of the House and Senate, the Architect of the Capitol, the Capitol police, and employees of the four agencies that provide policy research and information assistance to Congress (the Congressional Budget Office, the Congressional Research Service, a portion of the General Accounting Office, and the Office of Technology Assessment—none of which existed in 1918 as they are known today).

Staff numbered 2,000 in 1918, but more than 24,000 in 1991. For each year, nearly 70 percent were staff for members, leaders, or committees. In 1918 only three buildings were needed to house the entire congressional staff (the Capitol, and the Longworth and Russell buildings), but by 1991 congressional staff were scattered among sixteen buildings on or near Capitol Hill or in one of twelve hundred district and state offices.

The legislature of no other nation comes close to matching the staff available to the U.S. Congress. In part this is because most other democracies are of the parliamentary type, in which the government's leaders come from the legislature and so can draw on ministry staff—that is, the executive bureaucracy—for assistance. By contrast, the U.S. Congress is a coequal and separate branch of government, which has come zealously to guard its independence from the executive, including the independence of its staff and information resources.

Professionalization of Congressional Staff

Congressional staff have become increasingly credentialed and professionalized since the end of World War II. For committee staff, this professionalization was mandated by law; for other offices it

TABLE 5. *Congressional Staff: 1991 (approximate)*

HOUSE		SENATE		SUPPORT AGENCIES		JOINT		CONGRESS	
Leaders	150	Leaders,		CRS	800	Architect	980	All leaders	340
Officers	1,180	incl.		CBO	220	Capitol		All officers	5,040
Committees	2,400	vice pres.	190	GAO (30% of		police	1,350	All committees	3,940
Personal	8,000	Officers	1,500	workforce)	1,530	Attending		All personal	12,100
		Commit-		OTA	150	physician	30	All support	
		tees	1,400			Committees	140	agencies	2,700
		Personal	4,100						
		Total		Total					
Total House	11,730	Senate	7,190	support	2,700	Total joint	2,500	Total Congress	24,120

SOURCES: Compiled by the author from hearings, reports, and prints issued by the House or Senate Legislative Branch Appropriations subcommittees, the *Report of the Clerk,* and the *Report of the Secretary of the Senate.*

has resulted from the increasingly diverse and sophisticated needs of Congress and from ever-expanding reliance on a range of new technologies.

Personal Staff. Until the middle of the twentieth century, personal staff were basically what their generic title implied: clerks. Indeed, not until 1970 did the House authorize variable titles for personal staff, although the Senate had begun doing so piecemeal and in largely informal fashion in 1947.

Before the days of typewriters—let alone computers and modern printing, copying, recording, and communications equipment—everything had to be handwritten. Accordingly, even well into the twentieth century members needed secretarial and stenographic assistance, especially as their correspondence and legislative work loads increased. With the advent of electronic communications technologies, however, the number of secretaries on personal and committee staffs dwindled to insignificance, with secretaries being replaced by computer operators and other technically skilled staff.

Developments in personal staffing since World War II have included the hiring of administrative assistants (now also called chiefs of staff), legislative assistants, press aides, constituent-service staff, and technical and support staff. Because senators

TABLE 6. *Congressional Staffing: 1918*

CATEGORY	SENATE	HOUSE	JOINT	TOTAL
Leaders, incl. vice pres.	4	5	NA	9
Personal	72	870	NA	942
Committees	248	132	3	383
Officers	224	308	134	666
Totals	548	1,315	137	2,000

SOURCE: Author's count from H. Rept. 65-346, Legislative, Executive, and Judicial Appropriation Bill (1918).

average twice the number of staff of representatives, senators' staffs include more of each type of worker.

Neither chamber has yet established detailed hiring, firing, or other employment rules and regulations—although of late both the House and Senate have accorded employees protection against arbitrary and capricious actions by their employers. Nor have they agreed on formal position descriptions or official job titles. (The existing descriptions and titles, while sometimes technically accurate, are something of an art form.) Working within the prescribed limits on numbers of staff persons they can have, the ceilings on the amount of money they can spend on staff, and the minimum (around $1,500) and maximum (more than $100,000) they can pay in individual salaries, members hire, promote, terminate, pay, and assign work to personal staff as they wish with minimal guidance or interference from their respective chambers. Traits that members look for and value in their staffs include intelligence, trustworthiness, loyalty, enterprise, good judgment, political astuteness, and energy.

Types and titles. Personal office staff can be categorized as follows: administrative, executive, and political; technical, clerical, and support; legislative and research; constituent-related; and media.

The first category includes the administrative assistant, usually the most powerful staffperson; office manager; legal counsel; scheduling assistants; personal, executive, or special counsels, advisers, or assistants; state, regional, or local office directors; and appointment and personal secretaries. Technical, clerical, and support employees have titles such as systems administrator; computer or entry operator; mailroom coordinator, supervisor, or clerk; files supervisor or clerk; secretary; typist; receptionist; and just plain clerk.

There are several titular variants for legislative assistants, the most commonly used title among legislative and research staff. These include legislative director, often the senior legislative assistant overseeing the others; legislative aide; legislative correspondent, the lowliest legislative assistant but also the workhorse of office operations; policy-specific assistants, advisers, or counselors (frequently correlated with a member's committee assignments); research director or assistant; special assistant; and staff assistant (a title also used for many state and district office employees).

Constituent-related staff, mostly housed in state or district offices, bear the titles of caseworker, constituent-service or field representative, specialist, liaison, project assistant, state or district assistant, and the ubiquitous staff assistant.

Media staff have titles such as director or coordinator of communications and press secretary. Senators may have two or three media staff; representatives rarely employ more than one, with some members either serving as their own press spokespersons or delegating these responsibilities to, for instance, their administrative assistants.

Duties. Collectively these staff perform the numerous tasks associated with the operation of a member's office, which, despite increasing formalization, is still apt to be run more like a small business than a bureaucracy. Although lines of authority exist, the atmosphere of a congressional office is frequently informal, and teamwork is essential to the routine daily work load. Because Murphy's Law frequently seems at play in congressional life, everyone must be ready to adapt and respond to whatever crises the day may bring. The amount and kind of interplay between a member and the staff is still largely a function of the member's style.

Office management and support services. Besides making sure that an office runs as smoothly as possible, administrative staff, particularly the administrative assistant and the schedulers, see to political business. Political business includes organizing and coordinating the member's busy schedule, which comprises legislative obligations in committee and on the floor, meeting with constituents and others interested in conferring with him or her, and political appearances in Washington and at home.

The administrative assistant is often called on to meet with important constituents, make and take critical calls, orchestrate reelection activity (a continuous task for House members), stand in for the member as needed, and in other ways serve as the member's alter ego. The administrative assistant frequently hires, evaluates, dismisses, and sets the pay of all other staff, subject, of course, to the member's approval.

Increasingly, scheduling staff operate from district and state offices, from which vantage they survey the mood of their members' constituents and of the electorate in general. Caseworkers, who are mostly quartered in district and state offices, have become additional sources of the people's concerns and their problems with government.

Support and technical staff perform the myriad tasks of office operations, including mail intake and outflow, filing and archiving, computer operations, receiving calls and visitors, and secretarial assistance to the member and high-ranking staffpersons.

Mail. One major office enterprise is responding to the mail that floods members' offices. Virtually all staff are to some extent involved in this work, although legislative correspondents are specifically charged with the responsibility of assembling letters of response to inquiries about legislative and political issues.

While there is no exact measure of the amount of mail requiring written response, the total amount of mail coming into the House approaches 300 million pieces a year; the Senate receives more than 40 million pieces. But, as in every American household, a portion of this mail is composed of magazines, newspapers, books, and junk mail and therefore requires no response.

The extent to which the amount of outgoing mail reflects the volume of incoming mail is also unknown, because members send out unsolicited letters and engage in mass mailings—to "postal patron" or specifically targeted audiences—in addition to responding to correspondence.

Generally, members receive greater volumes of mail in election years than in nonelection years. In the House, where all members must stand for reelection every second year, outgoing mail totals around 400 million pieces in a nonelection year and more than 500 million in an election year. Because only one-third of the Senate stands for reelection at a time, the volume of its outgoing mail is not so closely tied to the electoral cycle and in fact has fluctuated considerably from year to year: for example, the Senate's outgoing mail totaled 156 million pieces in 1987, 256 million the next year, 226 million in 1989, but only an estimated 116 million in 1990. It rose sharply in 1991, however, to more than 230 million pieces. Since 1989 steps have been taken to restrict the types and amount of "franked" mail—the mail that senators and representatives can send out at no cost to themselves.

Another factor that makes generalizing about mail a complicated affair is that members vary widely in their mailing practices; some mail a lot, others little, and still others a lot or a little, depending on whether it is an election year. Newer members tend to mail more than senior members, and those in competitive election contests more than incumbents whose seats are relatively safe.

Whatever the numbers, mail operations have grown increasingly sophisticated and efficient in order to keep pace with volume. The days when members could peruse much of their mail and craft individual responses have vanished; now most responses are generated using computerized methods. Nowadays administrative, legislative, and press staff draft position statements on the issues that constituents inquire about most frequently. After review and approval by the member or a key staffer, this boilerplate is stored in computers and retrieved as needed for composing letters.

Constituent assistance. Letters, calls, or visits by constituents seeking a member's assistance with a federal agency or foreign government are handled individually, although standardized letters of acknowledgment and interim responses (progress reports) are customary. Members place a high premium on this kind of work, fervently believing that assisting and intervening on behalf of their constituents is both an important service and sound politics. So important is this service that as late as the 1940s members themselves frequently accompanied constituents to meetings with federal agencies. In the 1990s their busy schedules permit this, or other forms of personal intervention on behalf of constituents, only on rare occasions. Most often it falls to staff to perform the crucial task of acting as liaison for constituents and intervening with agencies and governments.

Constituents seek help from their members of Congress mostly as a last resort, and members know this. Accordingly, when requests for assistance arrive, staff spring into action, learning why a constituent has experienced difficulty—if this is the case—and ascertaining what a constituent must do in order to obtain relief. Constituents seek a variety of kinds of assistance, from claiming benefits they think are due them (casework), to requesting federal funds for businesses or local governmental bodies (project work), to needing fair decisions on matters of special consideration. While member intervention cannot always guarantee an outcome

that will satisfy the supplicant, the assistance is frequently helpful and almost invariably appreciated.

Legislative work. Another nucleus of staff assists members with legislative work. Many members tie most of their legislative work to their committee assignments. Some, however, introduce legislation across a wide range of policy areas.

The number of legislative staff and the amount of work they do varies according to the aims and activities of the member they serve. Their duties include identifying policy options and gathering and analyzing information and views on these alternatives; helping the member to determine a position on pending legislation; and assisting the member in defining the scope and substance of legislative proposals he or she is considering or planning to sponsor. If the member is introducing legislation, staff make sure that policy ideas are transformed into properly worded bills by the expert legal staff of the House or Senate Office of Legislative Counsel. Staff are responsible for devising legislative strategies and guiding legislation through the many wickets that lie between submission and enactment. They assist at committee hearings and meetings and help with committee and floor statements or floor management of a bill if that task falls to their member. Beyond these jobs, legislative staff perform various other tasks related to a member's legislative and representational duties—including assisting in drafting letters to explain the member's policy choices and assisting in obtaining information for or drafting portions of the member's speeches.

This component of personal staffing has swollen in numbers and risen in influence since the 1960s. Over time, members have come to rely on these staffers for legislative intelligence and networking with other members' offices and with committees—in other words, they serve as members' eyes and ears.

Media relations. Press staff assist members in communicating with voters through the media—a task that, in the years before World War II, was almost entirely handled by members themselves.

Gaining media coverage—and thus being able to highlight activities, goals, positions, and proposals—is easier for congressional party leaders and chairs of important committees than it is for new members or members who lack positions of authority. Senators are likely to command more coverage than representatives.

The House and Senate press and radio and television galleries, with more than forty-five hundred accredited print or electronic journalists, are regularly populated by a handful of correspondents of the so-called prestige press, that is, radio and television network reporters and reporters for newspapers such as the *Washington Post* and *New York Times* and wire services such as the Associated Press and United Press International. Of necessity, the prestige press is highly selective about what and whom it covers.

Network television and the wire services—along with syndicated Washington columnists—constitute the major source of news about Congress and its members for most local stations and newspapers. Their coverage focuses on policy actions, leadership announcements, and news about the institution itself—especially scandals and executive-legislative relations and tensions—rather than on the work of individual members of Congress. Accordingly, members must cultivate and promote coverage in home-state and home-district newspapers, television, and radio. They do so by taking reporters' calls, soliciting media coverage through press interviews or comments on presidential initiatives and congressional actions, holding press conferences when warranted, issuing traditional press releases, and appearing on radio or television either in interviews—for instance, on news talk shows—or in prepared audio or video feeds for satellite broadcast to local stations serving their constituency.

Relatedly, the advent and spread of cable television, including the public affairs and news channels C-SPAN and CNN, have led to greater television coverage of committee hearings and thus have expanded members' "electronic visibility." The House authorized gavel-to-gavel television coverage of daily floor proceedings in 1979 and the Senate followed suit in 1986. Both House and Senate proceedings are carried by C-SPAN and available in more than fifty million homes, meaning that members now get a degree of public exposure heretofore unavailable. At the same time, network television news increasingly uses clips from floor and committee telecasting for stories on legislative activity, thus providing additional notice for members.

Credentials, age, tenure, and pay. Most professional and some clerical personal staff have had some higher education. Studies by the Congressional Management Foundation, a Washington-based non-profit educational organization, show that 76 percent of those who work in House offices and almost 80 percent of those in Senate ones have at least a bachelor's degree, as compared with 35 percent of federal civilian employees and 17 percent of the general U.S. adult population. In the House, only 13 percent of personal staff have not gone beyond high school, while in the Senate less than 7 percent fall into this category. Members want bright and informed people working for them.

These same studies show that the average age of Senate and House personal staff is less than thirty-five, which is about two years below the median age of the U.S. labor force and seven years below the average age of federal civilian employees. In large measure this is the result of short tenure and the attendant high turnover. (Among Senate staffers, the average tenure on the Hill is less than six years; in the House, five, with average tenure in a given position running about three and one-half years in the Senate and just under three years in the House.)

Few staff make a career of working for members, in part because, on average, members serve only ten years (five terms) in the House and twelve years (two terms) in the Senate. People also leave congressional staff jobs because of personal ambition and the low pay—salaries average about $30,000 in the House and $33,000 in the Senate, compared with almost $34,000 for all federal workers and $42,000 for Washington-based federal workers. Comparable workers in the private sector earn anywhere from 28 to 35 percent more.

Committee Staff. Congressional committee staff now number about four thousand. Their principal job is to provide information of various sorts to help the committees meet their several responsibilities, which include exploring the need, feasibility, consequences, risks, benefits, and political consensus for policy change and innovation; authorizing and reauthorizing government programs and activities, appropriating money to pay for them, and raising revenue to fund the government; inquiring into foreign policy and foreign governments and evaluating treaties with other nations and international organizations; overseeing federal programs, agencies, and expenditures to ensure they are administered in ways that are economical, effective, equitable, and efficient; investigating wrongdoing, malfeasance, or chicanery; and, in the Senate, conducting inquiries into executive, judicial, and ambassadorial nominees as part of the confirmation process.

These dedicated men and women must be familiar with their committees' jurisdictions and the programs and activities for which they have sole or shared responsibility. They must be highly informed, intelligent, and savvy and possessed of good political judgment and negotiating skills. While data on the education, experience, tenure, and age of committee staff (comparable to those for personal staff) are not available, it is known that in all these characteristics committee staff match or exceed personal staff. Because their work is far more concentrated—that is, program- and agency-specific—and because their relationships with agencies are closer and endure longer than those of personal staff, professional committee staff tend to be better informed, more experienced, and more influential than personal staff. When allegations are made that congressional staff have become overly powerful, critics are usually referring to committee staff. Top committee staffers make more than $100,000 annually.

Administrative and Housekeeping Staff. Congress also has the basic need to keep its physical plant operating. Congressional administrative and housekeeping staff include engineers, architects, maintenance workers, postal clerks, restaurant and dining room workers, police, computer specialists, bill drafters, people who help with the floor operations in each chamber, and employees who see that checks are written and financial and other records are maintained.

Leadership Staff. This small complement of staff, numbering fewer than 350, assists party leaders in each chamber—the Speaker of the House, the vice president, the president pro tempore of the Senate, and the majority and minority leaders and whips of the House and Senate—with the many chores that accompany framing and promoting party policy programs, scheduling and managing floor business, rounding up votes, and maintaining party coordination and communication. Such staff are usually party loyalists who are mentally agile and politically astute.

Support Agency Staff. Finally, each of the four congressional support agencies has its own staff. Together, these staffs number about three thousand and represent a pooled resource for members and committees.

The Congressional Budget Office, established in 1974, principally provides neutral and competent economic, fiscal, and budgetary analysis and information. Its major clients are the budget committees, appropriating committees, and finance committees in each house.

The Office of Technology Assessment, established in 1972, provides a limited number of in-depth studies each year on the impact of technology on society, the economy, and the ecosystem. A major

information resource for congressional committees, these reports evaluate existing or proposed policies and programs across a spectrum of issues—education, health, defense, the environment, energy, foreign policy, and so forth.

The General Accounting Office, established in 1921, assists committees with their oversight activities. It is also the principal agency in the government vested with authority to conduct audits of programs and activities to ascertain whether they are being managed effectively and in accordance with law.

The Congressional Research Service, a separate department in the Library of Congress since 1914, serves all members and committees equally by quickly providing them with information, research, and analysis on virtually any topic or issue of interest to them.

Issues in Staffing. The growth of congressional staff has elicited concerns and criticisms in and outside Congress. Worth noting is that some of these concerns have been voiced since the late nineteenth century, when Congress inaugurated the modern system of staffing. As Fox and Hammond pointed out in *Congressional Staffs*, six themes have recurred in congressional staffing debates: (1) managing increases in work load; (2) improving economy and efficiency in government—including congressional—operations; (3) the cost of increased staffing; (4) members' concerns about adverse public reaction to the growth in Congress's operating costs; (5) minority party concerns that their members be given adequate committee staff and that there be equitable distribution of committee staff resources between minority and majority party members; and (6) the effect of institutional reform on staffing.

Other concerns have arisen as congressional staffs have grown to current levels. These concerns have centered on, among other things, the need to arrive at an appropriate balance between staff allocated to members and staff allocated to committees; members' judgment in hiring the right mix of staff and members' ability to use their staffs with maximum effectiveness; and the Hill's idiosyncratic, highly autonomous employment practices, including the lack of systematic rules regarding hiring and firing and the absence of meaningful job protections for some employees. Concerns have also been expressed about the increasingly rapid turnover of congressional staff, particularly in the House, resulting in staffs that are inexperienced and unseasoned, and about how staff salaries are set. Current practice allows for a host of salary inequities: between House and Senate staff, between committee and personal staff in each house, and between men and women in identical positions. The ease with which members and committees raid one another's staffs and the propensity of congressional staffers to "job hop" are blamed on these inequities. The crowded conditions under which congressional staffers too often work have also been assailed.

Beyond these complaints, there is the reiterated criticism that congressional staff have come to wield too much influence and to exercise powers that should belong to members alone.

The history of congressional staffing suggests that over time these issues and concerns will be addressed and to some extent remedied. Despite repeated calls for substantial cuts in staff, need and work load appear to make unfeasible any significant reduction in the number of congressional staff.

[See also Offices, Congressional; Offices, District.]

BIBLIOGRAPHY

Chaleff, Ira, et al. *Setting Course: A Congressional Management Guide.* 3d ed. 1988.

Congressional Quarterly, Inc. *Congressional Pay and Perquisites: History, Facts, and Controversy.* 1992.

Cooper, Joseph, and G. Calvin Mackenzie, eds. *The House at Work.* 1981.

Fox, Harrison, and Susan Webb Hammond. *Congressional Staffs: The Invisible Force in American Lawmaking.* 1977.

Hammond, Susan Webb. "Legislative Staffs." *Legislative Studies Quarterly* 9 (1984): 271–317.

Heaphey, James J., ed. "Public Administration and Legislatures." *Public Administration Review* 35 (1975).

Johannes, John R. *To Serve the People: Congress and Constituency Service.* 1984.

Kofmehl, Kenneth. *Professional Staff of Congress.* 3d ed. 1977.

Malbin, Michael J. *Unelected Representatives: Congressional Staff and the Future of Representative Government.* 1980.

Pauls, Frederick H. *Clerk Hire Authorizations for Senators and Representatives.* Congressional Research Service, Library of Congress. CRS Rept. 93-595 S. 1993.

Pauls, Frederick H., ed. "Congress and the Bureaucracy." *The Public Manager* (summer 1992). A special issue, with articles on constituency service, congressional office operations, leaders, and congressional oversight.

Rundquist, Paul, Judy Schneider, and Frederick H. Pauls. *Congressional Staff: An Analysis of Their Roles, Functions, and Impacts.* Congressional Research Service, Library of Congress. CRS Rept. 92-905. 1992.

FREDERICK H. PAULS

STALWARTS. *See* History of Congress, *article on* The Age of Machine.

STANDARDS OF OFFICIAL CONDUCT COMMITTEE, HOUSE.

The House Committee on Standards of Official Conduct was established on 13 April 1967 to fulfill the House's responsibility for self-discipline authorized by Article I, section 5 of the Constitution: "Each House may determine the Rules of its Proceedings, punish its Members for disorderly Behaviour, and, with the Concurrence of two thirds, expel a Member."

The committee, often referred to as the House Ethics Committee or House Standards Committee, is authorized to recommend administrative actions to establish or enforce standards of official conduct and to investigate alleged violations by House members, officers, or employees of any law, rule, regulation, or standard of official conduct relating to their official duties. After several stages in an investigative process, the committee may recommend to the House any appropriate sanction, including expulsion of a member.

Members of Congress are reluctant to sit in judgment of their peers, and the Committee on Standards of Official Conduct has operated cautiously in exercising its authority. The committee is careful not to publicize allegations received or those being reviewed before determining their merit or deciding to begin a formal inquiry. In 1970, the writer Robert Sherill (*New York Times Magazine*, 19 July 1970) characterized the congressional ethics committees as "watchdogs without teeth."

The first announced disciplinary case considered by the committee was in 1975. After completing its investigation in 1976, the committee recommended and the House concurred in the reprimand of Rep. Robert L. F. Sikes (D-Fla.). The committee has since publicly acted on cases involving thirty-nine other representatives, including one that resulted in the expulsion of Rep. Michael O. Myers (D-Pa.) by the House on 2 October 1980.

In addition, during the 102d Congress (1989–1991) the committee considered allegations of impropriety involving the House bank and post office. On 3 October 1991 the House directed the committee to review the bank's records for abuses by members who allegedly bounced checks there. Following instructions from the House, the committee released the names of the worst abusers on 1 April 1992 and a few weeks later released information on all members who had had overdrafts on their accounts. On 22 July 1992 the House voted to direct the House Administration Committee to transmit to the Ethics Committee all records obtained during its investigation of the House post office. However, at the request of the Justice Department, the committee has deferred action pending completion of the department's investigation.

In other cases, the committee's final recommendations have encompassed the full range of sanctions: reprimand, censure, expulsion. Typically, the House supports the committee's recommendations, in some instances changing a reprimand to a censure and vice versa. In some cases the accused member has resigned from the House or been defeated for reelection before final disposition of the case, thus ending the proceedings because the House does not have jurisdiction over former members. In other instances the committee has dismissed complaints, recommended no sanctions, or simply issued letters of reproval.

Before the creation of the Ethics Committee, the House had no uniform or consistent mechanism for self-discipline. Some allegations of misconduct were investigated by existing committees or, more often, in an ad hoc manner by special or select committees; others were considered by the House without prior committee action. Creation of the Committee on Standards of Official Conduct responded to a need for systematizing House responses to questions of official misconduct and members' need to have their questions answered about potential conflicts of interest and the other dilemmas inherent to serving in Congress.

A temporary committee was created in October 1966 during the concluding days of the 89th Congress (1965–1967), following the recommendations of the Joint Committee on the Organization of Congress as well as highly publicized allegations of misconduct by former representative and House Education and Labor Committee chairman Adam Clayton Powell, Jr. (D-N.Y.). This committee's jurisdiction, a model for what was ultimately included in that of the later Standards Committee, was limited to recommending additional House rules or regulations necessary to ensure proper standards of conduct by House members, officers, and employees; and reporting violations of any law, by a majority vote, to the proper federal and state authorities. Like the current committee, its membership was equally divided between the majority and minority parties. Its short span prevented the committee from making any recommendations other than one for its continuation in the 90th Congress (1967–1969) as the repository of proposed standards-of-conduct legislation.

On 13 April 1967 the House established the bipartisan, twelve-member Committee on Standards of Official Conduct. Its sole function was to establish and enforce standards of conduct in the House. Rep. Melvin Price (D-Ill.) was appointed chairman.

As a result of the committee's deliberations and recommendations during the next year, the House on 3 April 1968 voted its continuation as a permanent standing committee, redefined its jurisdiction and powers, and adopted for the first time a code of official conduct and a rule providing for limited public financial disclosure by members, officers, and designated employees of the House of Representatives.

Included in the committee's expanded and continuing jurisdiction were the code of official conduct and the financial disclosure rule; recommendations of means for establishing or enforcing standards of conduct in the House; investigations, subject to limitations, of alleged violations of the code of official conduct or of any other law, rule, or other standards of conduct applicable to House members, officers, and employees; reports to appropriate state and federal authorities, subject to House approval, of evidence of violations of law by members, officers, and employees in the performance of official duties; and advisory opinions for the guidance of members, officers, and employees.

Since 1968 several changes have been made in the committee's jurisdiction, composition, and rules of operation. On 8 July 1970, the committee was given jurisdiction over lobbying activities as well as the raising, reporting, and use of campaign contributions. In 1975, the jurisdiction over campaign contributions was transferred to the House Administration Committee. In 1977, the committee was authorized to issue regulations for House compliance with the Foreign Gifts and Decorations Act as well as to establish standards for the acceptance and disclosure of gifts of more than minimal value tendered by foreign governments to members, officers, and employees. That same year jurisdiction over lobbying was placed in the Judiciary Committee, and jurisdiction over the financial disclosure rule went to the Rules Committee.

Also in 1977, the House amended its code of official conduct and added rules of conduct that included the first annual public financial disclosure requirements for members, officers, and designated employees as well as restrictions on outside earned income, gifts, the franking privilege, foreign travel, and unofficial office accounts. As a result, the Standards Committee was authorized to maintain these annual disclosure reports and were given jurisdiction over the added rules of conduct. In 1978 governmentwide public financial disclosure requirements were enacted in the Ethics in Government Act (P.L. 95-521, 92 Stat. 1824–1885), and the committee was assigned review and compliance responsibilities for the House.

The most far-reaching changes in the committee, however, came after the adoption of the Ethics Reform Act of 1989 (P.L. 101-194, 103 Stat. 1716–1783) on 30 November 1989, during the 101st Congress (1989–1991). This act mandated committee reforms that were subsequently incorporated into the House rules at the beginning of the 102d Congress (1991–1993). The reforms included the following:

1. An increase in the committee's size (from twelve to fourteen members) and a time limit on committee service (no more than three out of any five consecutive Congresses).
2. "Bifurcation," that is, separation of the committee's investigative and adjudicative functions into two subcommittees.
3. A requirement that the committee report to the House on any case it votes to investigate, no matter the final disposition, and that any letter of reproval or other administrative action by the committee be issued only as part of a final report to the House.
4. A statute of limitation for investigations of alleged violations.
5. The right of accused members to be accompanied by counsel on the House floor when the House is considering Standards Committee recommendations on their cases.
6. The establishment within the committee of an Office of Advice and Education to provide House members, officers, and employees with guidance on standards of conduct affecting official duties.
7. Responsibility for House enforcement of the act's honoraria ban, outside earned-income limitations, and restrictions on the acceptance of gifts.

[See also Ethics Committee, Senate Select.]

BIBLIOGRAPHY

Congressional Quarterly Inc. *Congressional Ethics.* 1992.
Congressional Quarterly Inc. "House Ethics Committee." *Congressional Quarterly Almanac* 23 (1967): 579–582.
Congressional Quarterly Inc. "Seating and Disciplining" and "Ethics and Criminal Prosecutions." In *Congressional Quarterly's Guide to Congress.* 4th ed. Edited by Mary Cohn. 1991. Pp. 758–783; 785–816.
Mills, Mike. "Ever-Changing Ethics Panel Could Get New Rules." *Congressional Quarterly Weekly Report,* 8 July 1989, pp. 1677–1681.
U.S. House of Representatives. Committee on Standards of Official Conduct. *House Ethics Manual.* 102d Cong., 2d sess., 1992.

MILDRED LEHMANN AMER

STANDING COMMITTEE. *See* Committees, *article on* Standing Committees.

STATE DELEGATIONS. Group consultations and collaboration among members of Congress from the same state have been commonplace since the Congress under the Articles of Confederation. Although each state had only one vote under the Articles, states could send as many delegates to Congress as they wished. Consultations among state delegates were thus frequent, often dealing with vital tactical considerations. Because delegates to the Confederation Congress were limited to serving no more than three years out of any five, turnover was frequent; often a delegation found its membership depleted either because a term had expired, a replacement delegate had not yet arrived, or a sitting delegate decided to take time off to return home. When the Congress was not in session, a committee of the states, containing one delegate from each state, exercised supervisory responsibility over the government.

Under the Constitution of 1787, the role of state delegations in certain circumstances was of paramount importance. In the event that no presidential candidate received a majority of the electoral vote, the election of the president fell to the House of Representatives, with each state casting one vote. In the 1801 and 1825 elections, which were decided by the House, strategic voting was commonplace: a number of representatives cast their votes (or abstained from voting) in order to create ties within their delegation and thus prevent any vote from their states.

In the late eighteenth and early nineteenth centuries, House delegations in the nation's capital often lived together in the same boardinghouses because the short congressional sessions made owning a residence in the capital uneconomical. Representatives frequently traveled to the capital together and sought rooms together as well. The boardinghouse meeting was important to the Pennsylvania delegation in the First Congress, when they met to consider strategy to gain the speakership for Frederick A. C. Muhlenberg, and later when the compromise package on the location of the capital and the assumption of the Revolutionary War debts was put together. Boardinghouse and delegation voting blocs were also crucial to the election of Henry Clay as Speaker in 1811. As sessions lengthened and the living standards in Washington, D.C., improved, boardinghouse life became less attractive, and the influence of delegation and boardinghouse voting blocs declined. Nevertheless, many scholars continue to see major voting linkages and voting cue patterns among House delegations; certainly, similarity of districts and shared economic bases contribute to encouraging representatives from adjacent districts to vote in similar ways.

By the twentieth century, state party delegations came to play a key role in the House committee assignment process. After the revolt against Speaker Joseph G. Cannon in 1910, House Republicans gave their committee assignment power to a new Committee on Committees, comprising representatives from all House state delegations that had Republican representation. On this committee, each state delegation member cast as many votes as his or her state had Republicans in the House. A smaller executive committee consisted of heads of the larger Republican state delegations plus members representing collectively states with four or fewer House Republicans.

It was not until 1974 that House Democrats set up a committee assignment process giving a comparable role to their state party delegations. In that year, Democrats transferred committee nominating power from the Democratic members of the House Ways and Means Committee to an expanded Democratic Steering and Policy Committee. In the 103d Congress, the Steering and Policy Committee consisted of thirty-five members, including twelve elected regional representatives. Four of the regions comprised only one or two states, and typically the dean of a state party delegation was elected to serve on the Steering and Policy Committee.

State delegations were given additional power in Democratic committee assignments through liberalized caucus rules dating from the 1970s. Under these rules, the Steering and Policy Committee was required to consider for assignment to any committee a member whose assignment was recommended by a majority of the Democratic members of a state delegation.

For most of the twentieth century, congressional delegations have operated informally. Typically, delegations met periodically to discuss issues of mutual concern to their states. With the rise of the seniority system, the influence of particular states was enhanced when several members held committee or party leadership positions simultaneously. At times, the California, New York, or Texas state delegations were particularly prominent, not only because of their numerical size, but also because of the number of party and committee leadership positions held by members of the state delegation.

State delegations do not always work well together. For example, in the 1970s, major ideological divisions impeded effective working relationships among House Democrats from California. Historic divisions within states (such as the divergence in policy views between New York City and upstate New York representatives) can also limit delegation operations.

With the rise of informal member organizations and issue caucuses in the 1970s, several state delegations organized themselves to hire shared policy analysis staff, set up office space, and pool other resources to enhance their issue-monitoring capability. In the 103d Congress, such delegations included California, New York, Pennsylvania, and Texas, as well as House and Senate members from Long Island. To some extent, state delegations have been superseded in importance by regional groups of House members. The Congressional Border Caucus, the Northeast-Midwest Coalition, and the Sunbelt Caucus may exert more influence than an individual state delegation could because of their greater voting strength, better representation on all important committees, and greater institutional prominence.

BIBLIOGRAPHY

Arieff, Irwin B. "State Delegations Strive to Protect Their Interests Through Concerted Effort." *Congressional Quarterly Weekly Report*, 2 August 1980, pp. 2185–2189.

Bogue, Allen G., and Mark P. Marlaire. "Of Mess and Men: The Boardinghouse and Congressional Voting, 1821–1842." *American Journal of Political Science* 19 (May 1975): 207–230.

Born, Richard J. "Cue-Taking within State Party Delegations in the U.S. House of Representatives." *Journal of Politics* 38 (February 1976):71–94.

Warren, Sarah. "The New Look of the Congressional Caucuses." *National Journal* 10 (29 April 1978): 677–679.

PAUL S. RUNDQUIST

STATEHOOD. The birth, development, integration, and formation of the United States has been an unprecedented experiment of nation building that has brought together the most dissimilar and diverse groups, races, religions, cultures, and peoples of distinct ethnic origins into one unitary political whole. The fundamental building blocks of this unique experience of integration are the individual states.

The United States is, first, a nation built on a federal constitution, adopted by a citizenry willing to unite under a common government to "promote the general Welfare, and secure the Blessings of Liberty." In many ways, the Union began to form itself long before 1776 and long before the concept of a written American constitution was ever conceived.

In the Albany Congress of 1754, delegates from the original thirteen colonies conceived a "Plan of Union" under which all British colonies of North America would organize under a common government, with equal representation for each. As originally conceived by Benjamin Franklin, this intercolonial union would be gradually expanded by the creation of distinct governments in the new territories formed by the process of settlement and colonization in the West.

This plan established the blueprint for the creation of a broad anti-British front, which culminated in the two Continental Congresses of the mid-1770s, the Declaration of Independence, and the American Revolution. In 1776 the colonies, declared now to be independent associated "states," led the first successful revolt in history against an established empire.

Much more than a mere anticolonial struggle of national liberation, these first steps of American statehood were the beginning of a slow process of political and socioeconomic integration between thirteen different geographic societies, precariously united by land, common democratic ideals, shared political goals, and a war against tyranny. This revolt against concentrated power became the hallmark of negotiations between the first thirteen original states. The founders sought to effect a delicate balance between the local governments and the weak confederation formed out of necessity during the Revolution. A balance of power was sought not only between the central and state governments, but also between large and small states, northerners and southerners, the rich and the poor, eastern merchants and seamen and southern planters, and settlers of English descent and those of eastern European, French, and Spanish stock.

This new order, of a liberated America, indeed represented the institutionalization of compromise and constitutional checks and balances that would ordain for posterity not only the government of the nation but also its pluralistic growth. It is no coincidence that Article XI of the 1781 Articles of Confederation provided for the automatic admission of French-speaking Quebec with its distinct culture. It also provided for the admission of new "states" with the vote of nine states or more.

The 1780 Resolution of the Continental Congress laid the statutory foundations for the state-building process. It vested in Congress the power to establish regulations for the settlement, colonization, and formation of new states. This blueprint was later adopted by the Northwest Ordinances of 1784 and 1787, which resolved the problem of which states were to control the unexplored western lands and upheld the delicate balance of power between diverse states and ethnic groups. In the Constitutional Convention of 1787 this controversy was again addressed with a compromise. Each state would renounce its claims to the western lands and would cede title to Congress, which would in trust carve up, organize, and colonize the new territories until their final admission as states.

Constitutional and Legal Framework. Article IV, sections 3 and 4 of the newly adopted United States Constitution established in 1787 the legal parameters of territorial governance and political integration. In essence, it granted Congress the power to dispose of and regulate all matters respecting the territory and other property of the United States. The power to admit new states into the Union was vested in Congress, provided no new state would be carved out of any other state, nor any state be formed by the junction of two or more states, without the consent of the states concerned.

The Supreme Court in the landmark 1868 case *Texas v. White*, defined *state* as

> a political community of free citizens, occupying a territory of defined boundaries, and organized under a government sanctioned and limited by a written constitution, and established by the consent of the governed. It is the Union of such states under a common constitution which forms . . . the United States.

Thus, under the Constitution, Congress disposes of territories or admits new states into the Union by a simple majority vote in each house. However, the power to create a state and to gain its admission into the Union rests exclusively with its citizens.

This doctrine became known in the twentieth century as the self-determination principle, and it guided the decolonization of former European colonies after World War II.

In addition to the limitations on the power of Congress to admit new states expressly established in Article IV, section 3, other constitutional provisions limit Congress's discretion in this matter. Article IV, section 4 of the Constitution commands that every state must have a republican form of government based upon the principles of representative government and the consent of the governed, a right denied to citizens living in territories that are devoid of full congressional representation and participation in presidential elections.

The Tenth Amendment of the federal Constitution, with its reservation of powers clause, also limits the powers of Congress in admitting new states into the Union, insofar as it cannot impose upon a new state any condition that may invade its state sovereignty or diminish its equality in power, dignity, and authority with the rest of the states. This requirement is the essence of American federalism, as it delineates not only the limits of federal authority, but also protects the sovereignty of the states and the citizens' rights and individual freedoms.

This delicate balance of constitutionally distributed powers between federal government, states, and citizens has given the statehood process its characteristic flexibility and adaptability through its two-hundred-year history. In addition, it has converted the process of national unification into an extraordinary experiment in social, political, economic, and cultural interaction. It is the integration of diversity and the diversity of integration that has allowed America to become what political and social analyst Ben J. Wattenberg has called "the first universal nation."

The equation boils down to what has become known as the equal-footing doctrine. Upon admitting a state, Congress may impose the terms, conditions, and concessions it deems appropriate, as long as these are framed within its general constitutional supremacy. However, any condition that intrudes upon the states' reserved powers or upon the citizens' constitutional rights would be null, void, and unenforceable. Congress thus would have the power to impose restrictions on the state's powers to regulate interstate commerce, tax foreign corporations, or guarantee civil and religious liberties under the Bill of Rights. Congress would not, however, be allowed to impose a particular city as the seat of the state's government, to set rules for eligibility of state judges or, for that matter, to impose cultural patterns, religious mores, or an official language on the population, for all these areas are either reserved to the sovereignty of the state or would invade constitutionally protected individual freedoms.

The Jeffersonian Guidelines of Admission. Since the adoption of the federal Constitution, and commencing with Vermont in 1791, thirty-seven states have been admitted by Congress into the Union, under the most diverse circumstances and conditions. After the Ordinance of 1787, which guided the admission of the northwestern territories, Congress has never passed legislation to regulate the state admission process. Yet, in time, through custom and tradition, Congress has considered three general guidelines for the admission of a state, taken from Thomas Jefferson's standards originally incorporated in the Northwest Ordinances: a majority of eligible voters in the territory must desire statehood; the citizens of the aspiring state must be ingrained with and devoted to the principles of democracy and self-government as exemplified by the federal Constitution; and the new state must have enough population and resources to support a state government.

The Process of Admission. Congress has never refused admission to any territory that has formally requested it; although it has at times delayed the process of admission for partisan and political considerations.

There is no specific or formal path to integration. The original colonies, for example, declared their independence from Britain, organized their own constitutional state governments, established the Continental Congress, and ended up integrating themselves through the Articles of Confederation and the Constitutional Convention in 1787.

Texas (1846), for example, is the only independent republic admitted as a state, ten years after declaring its independence from Mexico. Texas gained admission into the Union in 1846 through the Act of Annexation and Admission. During the Civil War, the state again set a precedent and provided the U.S. Supreme Court with the opportunity to establish the concept of permanent union. In *Texas v. White* (1868), the Supreme Court ruled that no state can withdraw from the Union or nullify its admission through secession.

Four other states—West Virginia (1863), Kentucky (1792), Maine (1820), and Vermont (1791)—were carved out of other states following the procedure established in Article IV, section 3 of the Constitution. There was controversy over the constitutionality of the admission of West Virginia, since it was carved out of the western counties of Virginia during the Civil War without the consent of the legislature of the mother state, which at the time had seceded.

Seven other states, starting with Tennessee in 1796, followed a more assertive road to equality, which some have characterized as "shotgun fashion." The so-called Tennessee Plan represented a bold demand for statehood as a matter of right that entails not only a formal mandate for political integration but also a fully created state that knocks on the door of Congress with a complete and duly elected congressional delegation of senators and representatives. This method was successfully copied by Michigan (1837), Iowa (1846), and California, which gained admission in 1850, eleven months after creating a constitution and electing a congressional delegation, bypassing the usual stage of an organized territory. Oregon followed suit in 1857, Kansas in 1861, and more recently, the District of Columbia, which seeks admission as the state of New Columbia and has sent to Congress its own "shadow" senators and representatives elected with a mandate to request admission.

Alaska and Hawaii. Perhaps the most successful implementation of the Tennessee Plan was that pursued by Alaskans, who were disappointed with repeated congressional delays during the early 1950s, after a 58-percent majority of Alaskans endorsed statehood in 1946. During the next nine years, Alaskan statehood bills died in congressional committees, blocked by a coalition of southern Democratic and western Republican members. Opponents argued that Alaskan statehood would strain the federal budget, destroy the relatively underdeveloped and dependent territorial economy, and dilute other states' voting power. Partisan politics and the territory's inclination toward the Democrats were undercurrents of the debate.

Fed up with the petty politics and procrastination, Alaskans voted overwhelmingly for statehood and in 1956 elected two "senators" and a "representative" and sent them to Washington with a mandate for admission. Two years later, Congress finally capitulated and approved an admission bill that gave Alaska unprecedented land grants with incalculable economic value, extremely generous grants-in-aid, and a favorable economic package that allowed the new state to pull itself up by its bootstraps and out of the long years of territorial neglect and scarcity.

A parallel path was followed by Hawaii. In 1959, it broke new ground in being the first state with a predominantly Polynesian and Asian population. Hawaiians had to overcome enormous racial, cultural, political, and geographical obstacles in their quest for political integration. Although Hawaii never elected a "shadow" congressional delegation, in a 1940 referendum on status 67 percent of its citizens endorsed statehood.

During the next fifteen years, Hawaii's path toward integration was delayed by World War II, the Korean conflict, and the lobbying efforts of the "Big Five" corporations that dominated Hawaii's economy and opposed statehood. Although in the 1950s Hawaii was a relatively prosperous territory, its economy was highly dependent on military expenditures and on its agricultural industry. In spite of this, the territory convinced the 86th Congress to allow its admission with appropriations for the establishment of a state university, the construction of new highways, and a compact providing for the management and disposition of native Hawaiians' homelands. In addition, a Statehood Omnibus Act passed eleven months after Hawaii's admission into the Union gave the state certain exemptions from a federal tax on persons traveling by air between the mainland and the new state.

Hawaii's admission into the Union brought to the new state meteoric economic growth. Between 1960 and 1970, the gross state product tripled from $1.6 to $4.4 billion a year. Per capita personal income rose from $2,103 in 1959 to $4,960 in 1970. The most spectacular jump was reflected in the tourism industry, from 296,517 visitors and 9,502 hotel rooms in 1959 to over 5,607,000 visitors and 66,308 hotel rooms in 1986. Statehood thus produced, in tourism, the chief propellant for the fiftieth state's remarkable growth.

The Terms of Admission. When considering a statehood enabling bill, congressional committees have generally explored the following subjects: delineation of the new state's boundaries; whether a majority of its citizens desire statehood; the population of the state and the need to provide for the apportionment of the new congressional delegation; economic needs of the new state; what type of legal or statutory mechanisms are needed to provide a smooth transition from territorial to state economy; and the appropriations required to enable the new state to stand economically on its own.

With the admission of Ohio in 1803, Congress began the tradition of granting each new state generous economic concessions. This recognized that the process of decolonization necessarily entails more federal aid to the new state, block grants, land grants, and other types of fiscal measures necessary for the transition. The total aid conferred to each state varied depending on the territory's state of underdevelopment, its unemployment and poverty rates, and other factors. No state was ever rejected for economic reasons. Nor was any state ever required to forego a revenue-neutral transition from territory to state, because admission was generally viewed as a civil- and political-rights matter, not subject to nickel-and-dime haggling.

In considering the democratic mandate in favor of statehood, Congress has always required majority rule. The experience of thirty-seven states shows that only seventeen held statehood referendums prior to admission. Congress has never required anything more than a simple majority for statehood. In addition, in all cases the only question presented to the voters was "Statehood, yes or no?"—in other words, whether the citizens accepted the terms in the admission or enabling legislation.

Statehood in the Twenty-first Century. The process of becoming a state of the Union is not only a nation-building process but also the natural denouement of the United States territorial system. Recent historical events suggest that toward the end of the twentieth century Congress may be faced with petitions for admission from the citizens of the District of Columbia and from the Commonwealth of Puerto Rico. The demands for political integration from these two areas present new challenges for Congress and new questions for the nation. The country would be faced with parallel demands of political empowerment from a geographically small and predominantly African American federal district and from a Hispanic, Spanish-speaking commonwealth with 3.6 million citizens living on the island and 2.8 million residing on the mainland. The two issues come precisely at a time when, demographically, America is changing from a predominantly white society to a multiracial and multiethnic nation.

[See also Federalism; States' Rights; and entries on each of the fifty states of the union. See also District of Columbia; Puerto Rico.]

BIBLIOGRAPHY

Anson, Jones. *The Republic of Texas: Its History and Annexation.* 1966.

Dávila-Colón, Luis R. "Equal Citizenship, Self-Determination, and the American Statehood Process: A Constitutional and Historical Analysis." *Case Western Reserve Journal of International Law* 13 (1981): 315.

Dávila-Colón, Luis R. "The American Statehood Process and Its Relevance to Puerto Rico's Colonial Reality." In *Time for Decision: The United States and Puerto Rico.* Edited by Jorge Heine. 1983.

Deutsch, Karl W. *Nationalism and Its Alternatives.* 1969.

Forsyth, Murray. *Unions of States: The Theory and Practice of Confederation.* 1981.

Grupo de Investigadores Puertorriqueños. *Breakthrough from Colonialism: An Interdisciplinary Study of Statehood.* 2 vols. 1984.

Pomeroy, Earl S. *The Territories and the United States, 1861–1890.* 1969.

Wattenberg, Ben J. *The First Universal Nation.* 1991.

LUIS R. DÁVILA-COLÓN

STATE OF THE UNION MESSAGE.

The Constitution says little about the president's legislative role. It does, however, state that the president "shall from time to time give to the Congress Information of the State of the Union, and recommend to their Consideration such Measures as he shall judge necessary and expedient." From this clause developed the tradition of the president's annual message to Congress, or State of the Union address, as it has been known since 1945. Today this message is the most prominent forum in which presidents review their past accomplishments and outline their future goals, but it has not always played so central a role in presidential policy-making.

Although George Washington and John Adams appeared personally before Congress to deliver their annual messages, in 1801 Thomas Jefferson began a century-long practice of presidents sending their State of the Union messages to Congress to be read by the clerk of the House rather than delivering them in person. Jefferson, the leader of the Jeffersonian Republicans, intended to attenuate what he considered to be the monarchical trappings of the Federalists, whose addresses recalled the speeches from the throne that traditionally opened sessions of the British Parliament.

Nineteenth-century presidents continued Jefferson's practice. Their annual messages were usually ritualistic accountings of administrative activities. Consistent with the prevalent view that Congress alone made law, the addresses seldom contained substantive legislative proposals. When Grover Cleveland deviated from tradition and devoted his entire 1887 message to ideas about tariff reform, he sparked a great debate in the press and divided his own Democratic party, contributing to his defeat in 1888.

In 1913 Woodrow Wilson, who believed that the president's role included strong personal appeals to the nation and active leadership of Congress, revived the practice of appearing before Congress. He saw the change as a way to make the addresses more personal and dramatic and used them to announce his annual legislative agenda and priorities and to urge Congress's support. Since Warren G. Harding, every president with the exception of Herbert Hoover has chosen to deliver at least some of his annual messages in person, and these addresses constitute the great majority of presidential appearances before Congress.

Radio and television have fundamentally changed the nature of the address. Presidents still formally address Congress, but the primary audience for their remarks is the American people. Chief executives have used this opportunity to attempt to mobilize the public on behalf of their legislative programs. With its unique capacity to convey powerful visual images, television has also accorded the State of the Union address major national symbolic importance.

The setting for the address reinforces the image of the president as the preeminent leader of the nation. The members of Congress and the cabinet, Supreme Court justices, the Joint Chiefs of Staff, foreign dignitaries, and other special guests assemble in the House of Representatives and await the president's arrival. The president is announced twice, first on entering the House chamber and then after arriving at the podium. Each time the president receives a standing ovation from both sides of the aisle. That it is the president alone who addresses the other branches of government reinforces the notion of presidential preeminence.

In this moment of political pageantry, presidents proclaim successes, express their grand desires for the future, and engage in political drama. John F. Kennedy is often viewed as the first "television president," and he used his State of the Union messages to advocate his principal legislative initiatives, including accelerated space exploration, international trade, and tax cuts.

Ronald Reagan, a master of television speeches, used his State of the Union messages with great skill. He lauded his administration's accomplishments, promoted his current policies, praised heroes seated in the gallery (affirming core values in the process), and projected his vision for the nation. These speeches succeeded in sparking debate on tax reform, aid to the Contra rebels in Nicaragua, the Strategic Defense Initiative, and a host of other controversial proposals.

As a result, the annual televised addresses have become less an enumeration of dull facts and more an opportunity to set the terms of debate on issues of public policy. All eyes are on the president, and reactions to his message are carefully gauged. Even during the speech, television cameras scan the House chamber to capture the responses of members of the audience to various statements and proposals. Media commentators and other political experts routinely judge presidential performance—even counting the number of times the audience applauds. More importantly, many issues raised by the president receive serious attention in the press, at least for a while. The opposition party also takes the president seriously, requesting and receiving broadcast time to respond to the message and to present its own views.

The ultimate question, of course, is whether the State of the Union address is an effective and reliable means of obtaining public support and setting the nation's legislative agenda. The answer is that presidents have enjoyed only modest success. The State of the Union message has evolved into a central component of presidential-congressional relations. Nevertheless, it, like other resources of presidential influence, is at the margins of leadership in a complex and decentralized system of governing.

BIBLIOGRAPHY

Campbell, Karlyn Kohrs, and Kathleen Hall Jamieson. *Deeds Done in Words*. 1990.

Edwards, George C., III. *At the Margins: Presidential Leadership of Congress*. 1989.

Israel, Fred. *The State of the Union Messages of the Presidents, 1790–1966*. 3 vols. 1966.

GEORGE C. EDWARDS III

STATES' RIGHTS. According to the doctrine of states' rights (or "state rights," the prevalent usage before the Civil War), the individual states possess extensive powers, as opposed to those of the federal government. The idea antedates the U.S. Constitution. Jealous of one another, the colonies refused to yield power to an intercolonial union when Benjamin Franklin proposed one in the Albany Plan of 1754. Because they shared grievances against the British government, however, they managed to join together in the Continental Congress and, as states (from 1776 on), to win the Revolutionary War. But they were unable to agree on the Articles of Confederation until 1781, and the second of the Articles affirmed: "Each state retains its sovereignty, freedom and independence, and every power, jurisdiction and right, which is not by this confederation expressly delegated to the United States, in Congress assembled."

The Constitution, as drawn up in 1787, gave the central government much greater, though still qualified, authority. Congress was now to have primacy over broad areas, including taxation and the regulation of interstate and foreign commerce, plus all powers "necessary and proper" for putting its specified authority into effect. Yet the new plan, the result of compromises, was ambivalent. It was, as its "father" James Madison said, "in structure, neither a national nor a federal Constitution, but a composition of both." The first ten amendments increased the ambiguity. They further limited the powers of the central government, and the tenth provided that "the powers not delegated to the United States by the Constitution, nor prohibited by it to the States, are reserved to the States respectively, or to the people."

There was room for conflict between the implied powers of Congress and the reserved powers of the states, conflict that began early and continued long. Alexander Hamilton found ample authorization in the Constitution for his financial program, including a national bank, but Thomas Jefferson discovered none. Madison and Jefferson thought the Alien and Sedition Acts unconstitutional; they argued in the Virginia and Kentucky resolutions of 1788 and 1789 that the state legislatures could and should declare such acts null and void.

States' rights and "strict construction" of the Constitution were usually the arguments of the party out of power (and remained such throughout American history). Once Jefferson and his Democratic-Republican party were in power, his Federalist opponents accused him of violating the Constitution by purchasing Louisiana in 1803 and imposing the embargo of 1807. New England Federalists refused to support the War of 1812 and, at the Hartford Convention in 1814 and 1815, threatened to bring about their states' secession from the Union.

The states' rights center shifted to South Carolina when cotton planters there objected to the protective tariff as unconstitutional. John C. Calhoun invented a system for "nullifying" federal laws, and South Carolina put his theory to the test in 1832, when a state convention declared the tariffs of 1828 and 1832 null and void within the state. President Andrew Jackson denounced nullification as treason, and no other state officially endorsed the South Carolina stand.

"BACK AGAIN (?)" Cartoon published 16 August 1879 depicting aged former Confederate president Jefferson Davis (U.S. Senate: 1847–1851, 1857–1861) knocking on the door of the Senate, with Confederate specters of the Civil War behind him. The illustration comments on the readiness of Mississippi to return Davis—and states' rights issues—to the Senate. Following the war, Davis had refused to ask for a federal pardon, which he needed to reenter Congress.

OFFICE OF THE HISTORIAN OF THE U.S. SENATE

To Calhoun and other southerners, states' rights was a means of protecting slavery. He disapproved when, in the 1840s, several northern states tried their own brand of nullification by adopting "personal liberty" laws that forbade state authorities to assist in the enforcement of the federal Fugitive Slave Act of 1793. After the Wisconsin supreme court declared the federal Fugitive Slave Act of 1850 unconstitutional, the U.S. Supreme Court in *Ableman v. Booth* (1859) rejected the Wisconsin assertion of states' rights.

During the 1850s proslavery advocates maintained that Congress, in legislating for the territories, must give effect to state laws with respect to slavery. According to this argument, Congress could not prohibit slavery in the territories but must protect it there and everywhere else under federal jurisdiction. Thus states' rights became state powers that extended beyond the boundaries of the state.

The most extreme assertion of states' rights occurred with the secession of southern states in 1860 and 1861. They based their action on Calhoun's theory that secession, like nullification, was a perfectly constitutional procedure. They had acceded to the Union by ratifying the U.S. Constitution; they seceded from it by repealing their ordinances of ratification. Each state was "acting in its sovereign and independent character," the Confederate constitution averred, yet this document (like the U.S. Constitution) contained no provision for either nullification or secession. Nevertheless, the issue of states' rights versus central authority reemerged in the Confederacy.

The Civil War decided that no state could withdraw from the Union, but it did not decide exactly what the relationship of the states to the federal government should be. After the war, Democrats in the North as well as the South condemned Congressional Reconstruction as an infringement upon states' rights, and for decades the Democratic party was known as the states' rights party. Under Presidents Woodrow Wilson and Franklin D. Roosevelt, however, the party sponsored federal programs that, according to critics, usurped powers constitutionally reserved to the states. The American Liberty League and self-styled "Jeffersonian Democrats" raised the issue of states' rights against the New Deal.

After World War II the movement for civil rights provoked a strong reassertion of states' rights. When the Democratic convention of 1948 adopted a platform with a civil rights plank, some southern Democrats formed a separate States' Rights, or "Dixiecrat," party whose nominee, Strom Thurmond, carried four southern states in the presidential election of that year. After the Supreme Court's 1954 decision in *Brown v. Board of Education* requiring desegregation of public schools, southern resisters revived Calhoun's theory. Several southern legislatures adopted resolutions calling for "interposition" (Calhoun's synonym for nullification), though none of the states actually attempted to nullify the desegregation decision or any of the federal measures intended to give effect to it.

Southerners also invoked states' rights against congressional legislation to secure civil rights. In 1964 the Republican party and its presidential candidate, Barry Goldwater, adopted the southern position. Goldwater's overwhelming defeat, together with the passage of the Civil Rights Act of 1964 and the Voting Rights Act of 1965, meant the end of the effective use of the states' rights doctrine against such measures.

The states' freedom of action steadily shrank as the powers of the federal government expanded. In 1969 President Richard M. Nixon proposed a "New Federalism," which he described as an effort to "reverse the flow of power and resources from the states and communities to Washington and start power and resources flowing back . . . to the people." Nevertheless, the centralizing trend continued, and states' rights became more and more an empty slogan. Without invoking the states' rights doctrine, however, opponents of a particular use of federal power—the regulation of abortion, for example—proposed that the power be exercised only by the states.

BIBLIOGRAPHY

Current, Richard N. *John C. Calhoun*. 1963.

Hynan, Harold M., and William M. Wiecek. *Equal Justice under Law: Constitutional Development, 1835–1875.* 1982.

Schlesinger, Arthur M. *New Viewpoints in American History.* 1922. Chap. 10, "The State Rights Fetish."

RICHARD N. CURRENT

STENNIS, JOHN C.

STENNIS, JOHN C. (1901–), Democratic senator from Mississippi, chairman of the committees on Appropriations and Armed Services, and first chairman of the Select Committee on Standards and Conduct. A circuit judge for a decade, John Cornelius Stennis won election to the Senate in 1947 and remained more than forty-one years. Though a lifelong civilian, Stennis possessed a parade-ground voice and carried himself with formidable dignity. His legislative influence peaked when he served as chairman of the Armed Services Committee during the prolonged military budget debates of the early 1970s. As floor manager of annual defense procurement bills, Stennis staved off weapons cuts with his memory for technical detail, vote-counting skill, physical stamina, courtesy to opponents, and effective staff.

Stennis benefited from the South's tradition of reelecting seniority-rich Democratic senators who knew how to bring federal money home. As a member and ultimately chairman of the Appropriations Committee, he fostered the Tennessee-Tombigbee Waterway and other Mississippi public works, while backing farm subsidies and textile import quotas. Stennis for years adopted the orthodox

JOHN C. STENNIS.
OFFICE OF THE HISTORIAN OF THE U.S. SENATE

stance of Dixie's politicians on racial matters. Filibustering the 1964 civil rights bill, he and Georgia's Richard B. Russell taunted northern senators by proposing a "Voluntary Racial Relocation Commission" to help southern blacks move to other states. In 1968 he warned "the colored people" of Mississippi to stay away from the Poor People's March on Washington. But as federal law broadened the South's electorate, Stennis recognized the need to attract black votes. As a prelude to his last reelection campaign in 1982, he voted to extend the Voting Rights Act and endorsed Mississippi's first twentieth-century black Democratic nominee for a U.S. House seat.

In 1954 Stennis joined other Senate Democrats in advising President Dwight D. Eisenhower against a unilateral American rescue of France in Vietnam. Although he opposed many of Lyndon B. Johnson's Great Society programs, Stennis regarded himself as a Johnson loyalist in the Senate, and went along with the president when he committed U.S. troops to South Vietnam's defense in 1965. Stennis became one of the Vietnam War's most steadfast hawks.

President Richard M. Nixon gratefully inherited Stennis's support of the war and later, beset by Watergate, tried to shield himself behind the former jurist's reputation for rigid integrity. Ordered in 1973 by a federal appeals court to surrender his Watergate tape recordings, Nixon offered instead a summary of their contents, to be written by the White House. To check the summary's honesty, the tapes themselves would be listened to by "Judge Stennis, now Senator Stennis," Nixon told a televised news conference. The plan found little support.

The Senate itself sought to use the Mississippian's prestige to deflect criticism of members' ethics. Stung by the Robert G. (Bobby) Baker scandal, the Senate in 1964 created a Select Committee on Standards and Conduct and chose Stennis to head it. Under his chairmanship the committee spent the next two years investigating misconduct charges against Sen. Thomas J. Dodd. The "ethics committee" recommended that the Connecticut Democrat be censured for misuse of campaign funds.

Stennis seemed physically indestructible while in office, surviving a robber's bullet, heart surgery, and in 1984, the loss of a leg to cancer. His long career idealized what many Americans seem to want in their senators—a strong ambassador to Washington. Endorsing Stennis for reelection to a seventh term in 1982, the Jackson *Clarion-Ledger* said, "His power is Mississippi's power."

BIBLIOGRAPHY

Batten, James K. "Why the Pentagon Pays Homage to John Cornelius Stennis." *New York Times Magazine*, 23 November 1969.

Stennis, John C., and J. William Fulbright. *The Role of Congress in Foreign Policy*. 1971.

ARLEN J. LARGE

STEPHENS, ALEXANDER H. (1812–1883),

representative from Georgia and Confederate vice president, leading antebellum southern Whig, Independent, Democrat. A product of the middle-Georgia yeomanry, Stephens was a dominant force among southern members of Congress from 1844 until his voluntary retirement in 1859. Reelected in 1872, he served as an elder statesman until 1883. He never forgot his humble beginnings, and although Stephens rose to prominence as a Whig lawyer and planter, the common people always remained the backbone of his support.

ALEXANDER H. STEPHENS.   NATIONAL ARCHIVES

Although a moderate by later standards of historical judgment, Stephens consistently upheld the interests of the slaveholding South. He defied the Whig leadership by supporting the admission of Texas to the Union and contributed substantially to the resolutions that brought that about. An outspoken opponent of President James K. Polk and the Mexican War, Stephens also opposed the Wilmot Proviso, which would have barred slavery from the new territories. A key southern leader for Zachary Taylor during the 1848 campaign, Stephens became embittered when, as president, Taylor ignored southern interests in congressional clashes over several sectional questions.

Stephens left the Whigs and, with fellow Georgia representatives Robert Toombs and Howell Cobb, formed the Constitutional Union party to support the Compromise of 1850. His parliamentary strategy was crucial in passing the Democratic-sponsored Kansas-Nebraska bill in an intensely divided House in May 1854. Soon afterward, he officially became a Democrat.

Thenceforth, Stephens dutifully served the party's interests. As a member of the Committee on the Territories and later as floor leader for the

Buchanan administration, he labored fruitlessly to have Kansas admitted as a slave state. In 1858 he devised the so-called English bill, which saved face for the administration after the House refused to countenance the Lecompton constitution fraud. Worn out and disgusted, Stephens left Congress in 1859. His manifest ability and congressional prominence were key considerations in his election as Confederate vice president in 1861.

BIBLIOGRAPHY

Schott, Thomas E. *Alexander H. Stephens of Georgia: A Biography.* 1988.

THOMAS E. SCHOTT

STEVENS, THADDEUS (1792–1868), representative from Pennsylvania and leader of the Radical Republicans during the Civil War and Reconstruction. Born in Vermont, Stevens graduated from Dartmouth College in 1814, studied law, and commenced practice in Gettysburg, Pennsylvania, in 1816. He later entered the iron manufacturing business, but his success as a lawyer led him into politics, first as an Anti-Mason and then as a Whig. In the state legislature during the 1830s, he championed free public education and opposed a new state constitution because of its whites-only suffrage restriction. An early convert to abolitionism, Stevens frequently offered his legal services to fugitive slaves and free blacks.

Elected to the U.S. House as a Conscience Whig from 1849 to 1853 and then as a Republican beginning in 1859, he quickly established a reputation for his blistering attacks on southern slaveowners and rigid opposition to further concessions to the South. From his powerful position as chair of the Ways and Means Committee, he helped shape all Civil War financial and appropriations legislation. As a member of the Joint Committee on the Conduct of the War, he pushed vigorously for measures not merely to defeat but to destroy the slaveowning aristocracy. A master of parliamentary tactics and debate, Stevens had no match in the use of invective and sarcastic wit, and he often badgered and even intimidated his colleagues to bring them around to his point of view.

Far in advance of President Abraham Lincoln and moderate Republicans on issues of race and reconstruction, Stevens was among the first of the Radicals to advocate emancipation, then black military service, confiscation of slaveowners' property and its redistribution to the freed slaves, and, by the middle of the war, black male suffrage. Believing that the Confederate states should be treated as "conquered provinces" and totally restructured, he found Lincoln's reconstruction proclamations far too lenient and lamented that the more stringent Wade-Davis congressional plan of reconstruction failed to mandate black suffrage. As President Andrew Johnson's plan of reconstruction unfolded when Congress was out of session in 1865, Stevens fumed at Johnson's liberal pardoning policy that allowed ex-Confederates to take political positions and at the South's creation of black codes that restricted the freedpeople.

Reconvening in December 1865, Congress followed Stevens's lead in refusing to seat representatives from the state governments restored under Johnsonian principles and in creating the Joint Committee of Fifteen to consider additional reconstruction legislation. Disdaining moderate and conservative hopes of working with Johnson to offer more protection for the freedpeople, Stevens became the dominant Radical voice on the joint committee and on the floor. As the House floor leader, he dutifully directed the moderate-sponsored Civil Rights and Freedmen's Bureau bills to passage over Johnson's vetoes, although he favored stiffer measures. The Fourteenth Amendment fell "far short" of his hopes for black suffrage and greater restrictions on ex-Confederates, but his sense of what was politically possible led him to "take all I can get in the cause of humanity and leave it to be perfected by better men in better times."

After the South refused to ratify the Fourteenth Amendment and the North rejected Johnson's policy in the fall 1866 elections, Stevens constantly pushed for Radical measures as Congress took control of the reconstruction process. Again, however, moderate Republicans had the votes to defeat most Radical proposals, and Stevens accepted what he could get—sometimes gracefully, sometimes not. The Radicals did secure black male suffrage, but Stevens never came close to achieving confiscation and redistribution or a more punishing proscription of ex-Confederates. Despite failing health, Stevens continued to shepherd to passage all supplementary reconstruction legislation—often over his own reservations and Johnson's vetoes.

Stevens favored removing Johnson as an impediment to congressional reconstruction, but it was not until the president violated the Tenure of Office Act in February 1868 that moderate Republicans joined the Radicals to impeach him. Stevens helped formulate the articles of impeachment, but his deteriorating health prohibited him from playing an active role in managing the prosecution in Johnson's trial before the Senate. Stevens died the following August, less than three months after Johnson's acquittal.

Stevens's commitment to helping freed blacks to achieve a truly equitable position in American society ran far ahead of the dominant racial attitudes of his time. Although his "bright dream" of "a perfect Republic" tolerating no distinction "but what rose from merit and conduct" failed, he hoped to be remembered as one who "had striven to ameliorate the condition of the poor, the lowly, the downtrodden of every race and language and color." Despite some disagreement with his tactics, modern historians have largely echoed that epitaph.

THADDEUS STEVENS. Photograph by Mathew Brady, colored with oil paints to imitate a painting.

LIBRARY OF CONGRESS

BIBLIOGRAPHY

Brodie, Fawn M. *Thaddeus Stevens: Scourge of the South.* 1959.

Foner, Eric. "Thaddeus Stevens, Confiscation, and Reconstruction." In *The Hofstadter Aegis: A Memorial.* Edited by Stanley Elkins and Eric McKitrick. 1974.

TERRY L. SEIP

STRATEGIC ARMS LIMITATION TALKS (SALT).

In November 1969, representatives of the United States and the Soviet Union began meeting to discuss limitations on long-range offensive and defensive nuclear weapons. In May 1972, following two and one-half years of negotiations, President Richard M. Nixon and Communist party chairman Leonid Brezhnev signed two agreements in Moscow: the Antiballistic Missile (ABM) Treaty and the Interim Agreement on Offensive Forces.

In the ABM Treaty, the United States and the U.S.S.R. agreed to deploy antiballistic missiles at just two sites with no more than 100 missiles at each site. (A 1974 protocol limited each side to only one ABM site.) The ABM Treaty was of unlimited duration and was a remarkable agreement because each side agreed, in essence, not to defend itself against a large-scale attack from the other side. Immediately upon his return from Moscow on 1 June 1972, Nixon went directly to Capitol Hill and presented the two agreements to a joint session of Congress. The Senate, acting with unusual speed and a minimum of partisan debate, approved the ABM Treaty on 3 August by a vote of 88 to 2.

The Interim Agreement placed quantitative limits on the allowable number of intercontinental and submarine-launched ballistic missiles (ICBMs and SLBMs) in the two superpowers' respective arsenals. For various reasons, the U.S.S.R. was allowed to retain more weapons than the United States. This concerned some members of Congress, including, most notably, Sen. Henry M. Jackson (D-Wash), who proposed an amendment stipulating that any future arms control agreement should "not limit the U.S. to levels of intercontinental strategic forces inferior to the limits for the Soviet Union." The Senate passed the Jackson Amendment 56 to 35.

The Interim Agreement was an executive agreement designed to remain in effect from 1972 to 1977. Under the terms of the Arms Control and Disarmament Act of 1961, all arms limitation agreements must be submitted to both houses of Congress for their approval. Following the passage of the Jackson Amendment, the amended Interim Agreement was approved 88 to 2 in the Senate and 307 to 4 in the House. Together, the ABM Treaty and the Interim Agreement were referred to as the SALT I agreements.

The second phase of the Strategic Arms Limitation Talks, called SALT II, began in November 1972. After almost seven years of negotiations by three different presidential administrations (those of Nixon, Gerald R. Ford, and Jimmy Carter), President Carter and Brezhnev met in Vienna in June 1979 to sign the SALT II agreement, which consisted of three parts: a treaty, a protocol, and a statement of principles. This complex agreement placed both quantitative and qualitative limitations on American and Soviet ICBMs, SLBMs, and long-range bombers capable of delivering nuclear weapons.

The Senate held hearings on the SALT II agreement during the summer of 1979. On 9 November 1979, the Foreign Relations Committee voted 9 to 6 to recommend that the treaty be ratified. The Senate Select Intelligence Committee found that the SALT II treaty enhanced the ability to monitor Soviet compliance with the treaty. Only the Senate Armed Services Committee was critical of the treaty.

The full Senate never voted on the SALT II treaty. Three international events during the autumn of 1979—the discovery of a Soviet combat brigade in Cuba, the takeover of the U.S. embassy in Tehran, and the Soviet invasion of Afghanistan—caused President Carter to request the Senate to delay indefinitely its consideration of the treaty. Although the SALT II treaty was never ratified, its terms were formally observed by both the United States and the Soviet Union until late 1986.

[*See also* Antiballistic Missile Systems Treaty.]

BIBLIOGRAPHY

Blacker, Coit D., and Gloria Duffy, eds. *International Arms Control: Issues and Agreements.* 1984.

Caldwell, Dan. *The Dynamics of Domestic Politics and Arms Control: The SALT II Treaty Ratification Debate.* 1991.

Platt, Alan. *The U.S. Senate and Strategic Arms Policy, 1969–1977.* 1978.

Talbott, Strobe. *Endgame: The Inside Story of SALT II.* 1980.

DAN CALDWELL

STRATEGIC DEFENSE INITIATIVE (SDI).

On 23 March 1983 President Ronald Reagan announced the Strategic Defense Initiative, a military research and development program that formed part of his administration's effort to progress beyond the traditional strategic doctrine of deterrence through "mutual assured destruction," which had dominated the relationship of the United States and the Soviet Union throughout the Cold War. Under Reagan's original plan, SDI would seek to develop an impermeable shield against incoming ballistic missiles, to render an attacker's warheads "impotent and obsolete."

Opponents in Congress and elsewhere quickly criticized the revolutionary idea as impractical and destabilizing, and they attached the enduring label "Star Wars" to the program. The annual legislative authorizations and appropriations process became a recurrent battlefield, with partisans attempting to restrict or redefine SDI and to ensure its consistency with the 1972 Antiballistic Missile Systems Treaty, which had undergirded the superpowers' détente. When the Reagan administration propounded a "new interpretation" of the ABM treaty, attempting to permit a still more expansive range of SDI development and testing activities, congressional opponents again adamantly resisted.

At congressional insistence, the SDI program—which consumed about $32 billion over a decade—was gradually redirected away from the most exotic types of systems (such as satellite-based, nuclear-powered laser battle stations) toward more familiar technology relying on ground-based interceptor missiles. In 1993, the Clinton administration formally terminated the SDI program, although related antimissile research continues at a lower level.

Although the SDI program never produced deployed military hardware, some observers credit it with generating at least some of the external pressures that ultimately led to the reform and dissolution of the Soviet Union; others continue to see SDI as a wasteful and illegitimate chimera.

[See also Antiballistic Missile Systems Treaty; Nuclear Weapons.]

BIBLIOGRAPHY

Boffey, Philip M., William J. Broad, Leslie Gelb, Charles Mohr, and Holcomb B. Noble. *Claiming the Heavens.* 1988.
U.S. Congress. Office of Technology Assessment. *Ballistic Missile Defense Technologies.* OTA Rept. ISC-254. 1985.

DAVID A. KOPLOW

STUDY OF CONGRESS. *See* Congress, *article on* The Study of Congress.

SUBCOMMITTEES. The smallest, most specialized, and most accessible panels on Capitol Hill are the subcommittees. They are the point of entry for most citizen activists, bureaucrats, and professional lobbyists who track legislation through Congress. Like their parent committees, subcommittees vary in their attractiveness to members, their visibility to constituents, their legislative activity, and their autonomy. Since the 1950s, the number of subcommittees has ranged from 83 to 135 in the House and 85 to 140 in the Senate. Over the past three decades the number of House subcommittees has been fairly stable at around 130, but the Senate number has been more erratic, in the early 1990s hovering in the high eighties. In accordance with a 1993 initiative to reduce the number of subcommittees in Congress, the figure now stands at 115 subcommittees in the House and 86 in the Senate. This represents an average of five panels per parent committee, with a range of zero (Senate Veterans Affairs) to thirteen (House and Senate Appropriations).

Subcommittees are products not of the U.S. Constitution but of procedural rules, individual ambition, and the political temperament of different periods. They emerged in the early 1900s to establish a comprehensible division of labor that would spread the responsibilities as well as the political fortunes associated with policy-making. They burgeoned after the Legislative Reorganization Act of 1946 consolidated the full committees, paradoxically encouraging the formation of new subcommittees—some along the lines of committees that had been eliminated. Another major boost came in 1973 with the "Subcommittee Bill of Rights." This and other reforms of the day diffused power, allowing congressional newcomers to hold positions of authority on subcommittees with definable jurisdictions and staff.

With few exceptions a bill is considered first in subcommittee, where it undergoes a public hearing and preliminary markup. It takes a majority of subcommittee members to report a bill for full committee review. Usually, the full committee bases its assessment on the preliminary evidence established in subcommittee. Because subcommittee members are the first to pass judgment on bills, they and their staffers are the first to be pressured by interested outsiders. For some powerful subcommittee chairmen the job does not end there. Subcommittee sponsors often champion their bills throughout the legislative cycle, amassing supporters along the way in terms of staff and colleagues at the full committee level.

The responsibilities for creating, renewing, and overseeing governmental intervention are dispersed among subcommittees in such a way that some panels have more appeal than others. The most highly sought-after subcommittees are those that pertain to Congress's role in taxing and spending or have jurisdiction over broad public concerns. These are also the subcommittees that afford their chairs media exposure and recognition that translate into campaign support—money and votes. Other subcommittees are consistently avoided either because they have narrow jurisdictions of interest to few citizens or because they arouse conflict and certain vulnerability at the polls. Subcommittee variations can be explained by (1) the political milieu; (2) procedural rules, precedent, and norms; and (3) their members' individual ambitions.

Political Milieu. Unprecedented demands on Congress elevated the prestige and accompanying attractiveness of office in the wake of the Civil War, and for the first time legislators began to view their work as having real career potential. Changed expectations increased the value of committee seats, so new seats were created. The reforms of the 1970s also followed tumultuous change in the country. This time, public cynicism over the protracted war in Vietnam and the dirty-tricks politics of Watergate contributed to an extraordinary number of electoral upsets. The new and aggressive class of first-year members entering Congress in 1975 promised and delivered change, generally weakening the seniority system, democratizing the committee assignment process, and dispersing power. Ninety percent of members from the majority party in the Senate, for example, chair at least one committee or subcommittee. Although the figure is much lower in the House, the increase is dramatic, from 27.2 percent in 1955 to 48.7 percent in 1992.

Structure and Rules. Whereas the House controls proliferation of the number of subcommittees with rules limiting standing committees to six or eight each, depending on their size, the Senate creates de facto ceilings by limiting the number of panels on which any one senator may participate.

Subcommittee staff resources also vary within and across chambers. While all subcommittee positions are funded at the behest of the full committee leadership, staff allocations are more distinct and routine in the House. Note, for example, that seven of the fourteen standing committees in the Senate centralize all staff at the full committee level and dispatch personnel as needed to the subcommittees; only two House committees engage in this practice. Comparing the fortunes of the two political parties in terms of their share of staff resources, House subcommittee members of the controlling party hire from one to seventeen professional aides, with an average of four per panel. The Senate range is from one to twelve aides, with an average of four. Members of the minority party hire roughly one-third this number of assistants.

The increase in the autonomy of House subcommittees relative to their parent committees gives meaning to the phrase "subcommittee government." In the Senate the role of subcommittees is much more ambiguous. The differences are striking. Eighty percent of House bills go to a subcommittee first, and only if they pass this initial screening are they forwarded to a full committee for a vote. Senate subcommittees perform this function only half as often. A larger proportion of House public hearings are held at the subcommittee level as well—95 percent, as compared with 64 percent in the Senate (1990 figures). Furthermore, bills' sponsors typically defend their initiatives from hostile amendments on the floor of the House, with subcommittee leaders fulfilling the role three times as often as full committee chairmen. The majority party leader in the Senate, who does not sit on either full committees or subcommittees, manages nearly 60 percent of the bills that reach the floor for debate in that chamber.

Membership. Because of their widely differing jurisdictions, committees and subcommittees attract members with differing ambitions, and the bidding for subcommittee assignments, while competitive, is highly responsive to members' preferences. Entrepreneurial chairmen, with the consent of their members, can modify a subcommittee's focus to address emerging policy concerns. The varying composition of subcommittees and the varying ambitions of subcommittee leaders help explain the different levels of activity and productivity between panels.

As a result of the increased division of labor created by subcommittees, more individuals share the work and the fortunes of lawmaking. The screening process through which issues pass is more rigorous as more members and staff participate in new levels of review. Democratizing the policy-making process within Congress serves also to expand the institution's accessibility to interested parties outside Congress. Increased opportunities for involvement and representation are not without costs, however. As the number of players expands, so too does the likelihood of indecision and stalemate.

[See also Committees.]

BIBLIOGRAPHY

Davidson, Roger H. *The Postreform Congress.* 1992.

Deering, Christopher J. "Subcommittee Government in the U.S. House: An Analysis of Bill Management." *Legislative Studies Quarterly* 7 (1982): 533–546.

DeGregorio, Christine. "Leadership Approaches in Congressional Committees Hearings." *Western Politics Quarterly* 45 (1992): 971–983.

Evans, Lawrence, and Richard L. Hall. "The Power of Subcommittees." *Journal of Politics* 52 (1990): 335–355.

Smith, Steven S., and Christopher J. Deering. *Committees in Congress.* 1990.

CHRISTINE DEGREGORIO

SUBPOENA POWER. The authority to issue subpoenas—to require the testimony of witnesses or the production of records, documents, and other materials for congressional inquiries—is granted by the House and Senate to all their standing committees and subcommittees. Special or select committees must be specifically delegated this authority when they are established (by a resolution of the House or the Senate). The Legislative Reorganization Act of 1946 granted subpoena power to all Senate standing committees but not to standing committees of the House because of opposition from Speaker Sam Rayburn (D-Tex.) and House minority leader Joseph W. Martin, Jr. (R-Mass.). It was not until 3 January 1975 that all House standing committees were granted subpoena power (H. Res. 988, 93d Cong.).

First issued in 1792, during the House's inquiry into Gen. Arthur St. Clair's military defeat, subpoenas have apparently been issued with increasing frequency in modern times. The subpoena authority is an integral part of Congress's investigative and oversight powers. Nonetheless, subpoenas must be directly connected with the issuing panel's authority and jurisdiction and may be challenged by claims of executive privilege. Because the subpoena is a legal order, a witness who refuses it can be cited for contempt of Congress and prosecuted in federal court.

Although the Constitution does not expressly grant Congress the power to issue subpoenas, the Supreme Court has recognized an implied subpoena power on several notable occasions. In *McGrain v. Daugherty* (1927) the Court held that "the power of inquiry—with process to enforce it—is an essen-

tial and appropriate auxiliary to the legislative function." The Court reaffirmed this principle in *Eastland v. U.S. Servicemen's Fund* (1975), stating, "The issuance of a subpoena pursuant to an authorized investigation is . . . an indispensable ingredient of lawmaking."

[See also McGrain v. Daugherty.]

BIBLIOGRAPHY

Grabow, John C. *Congressional Investigations: Law and Practice.* 1988.

Hamilton, James. *The Power to Probe: A Study of Congressional Investigations.* 1976.

U.S. Congress. Joint Committee on Congressional Operations. *Leading Cases on Congressional Investigatory Power.* 94th Cong., 2d sess., 1976. Committee Print.

FREDERICK M. KAISER

SUBPOENA SERVED ON RICHARD WHITNEY. Whitney, president of the New York Stock Exchange, was subpoenaed to appear before the Senate Committee on Banking and Currency on 13 February 1934, during an investigation of stock market practices. NATIONAL ARCHIVES

SUFFRAGE. *See* Voting and Suffrage.

SULLIVAN, LEONOR KRETZER (1902–1988), Democratic representative from Missouri, chair of the Committee on Merchant Marine and Fisheries (1973–1977), and author of the food stamp program and other legislative initiatives.

Leonor Sullivan represented the 3d District of Missouri from 1953 to 1977 (83d–94th Congresses), the same seat that her husband John B. Sullivan had held at the time of his death in 1951. Skilled and accomplished in her own right, she had been her husband's closest adviser, working in his congressional office and appearing with him at political events.

Sullivan served on the Committee on Merchant Marine and Fisheries and became the committee's chair in 1973. The following year she mounted a vigorous campaign to forestall a reform plan that would have eliminated the committee. She also served on the Committee on Banking and Currency and chaired its subcommittee on consumer affairs. During her twenty-four years in the House, she held several party leadership posts and was the first woman to be appointed to the House Democratic Steering Committee.

Sullivan was a creative and accomplished legislator. She was a primary author of the Food Stamp Act, Truth in Lending Act, Credit Control Act, Fishery and Conservation Management Act, and Poultry Inspection Act. She vigorously defended consumer protection and consumer rights before her House colleagues and publicly.

Sullivan did not officially use her own first name, preferring to be known professionally as Mrs. John B. Sullivan. She was the only woman member of the House to vote against the Equal Rights Amendment, doing so because she believed it would remove protective legislation for women. She did not run for reelection in 1976, and retired to her home in Saint Louis, Missouri.

BIBLIOGRAPHY

U.S. House of Representatives. Committee on Merchant Marine and Fisheries. *Unveiling of a Portrait of the Honorable Leonor K. (Mrs. John B.) Sullivan.* 93d Cong., 2d sess., 1974. H. Doc. 93–412.

U.S. House of Representatives. Office of the Historian. *Women in Congress, 1917–1990.* 101st Cong., 2d sess., 1991. H. Doc. 101–238.

MARY ETTA BOESL

LEONOR KRETZER SULLIVAN.

LIBRARY OF CONGRESS

SUMNER, CHARLES (1811–1874), senator from Massachusetts, chairman of the Foreign Relations Committee, opponent of slavery, and advocate of racial equality. A member of an old Boston family, Sumner graduated from Harvard College and attended the college's law school. He entered private legal practice but found it intellectually and financially unrewarding; he lectured briefly at Harvard Law School on international law and other subjects. Blessed with a handsome physique and a powerful voice, he became a notable public speaker, got caught up in the cause of reform, and eventually entered state politics. He strongly opposed the Mexican War as an unjust, proslavery venture, became a Conscience Whig, helped found the Free-Soil party, and twice ran unsuccessfully for Congress. In the 1850 state election a coalition of Democrats and Free-Soilers ousted the Whig party from its accustomed control of the state. The Free-Soilers demanded the U.S. senatorship and nominated Sumner, who had never held public office before and had little popularity. Nevertheless, in April 1851 the legislature narrowly elected him.

When Sumner assumed his seat in the Senate, he found himself shunted onto minor committees and without influence. His first major speech was on his motion to repeal the Fugitive Slave Act of 1850; only three senators joined him in supporting his motion. Sumner also was an active participant in the debate over the Kansas-Nebraska bill in 1854, but his pomposity, pedantry, and moral posturing brought down a shower of abuse from his opponents. Sumner's ineffective service in the Senate—his failure to shape legislation, his inability to win support for his positions, and his ineffectiveness in debate—greatly disappointed his supporters, and his prominent role in organizing the new Republican party did little to shore up his sagging support at home. He appeared headed for certain retirement.

The primary issue before the new Congress that assembled in December 1855 was the situation in Kansas. Seeking to regain his political standing in Massachusetts, Sumner in May 1856 delivered a major speech on "The Crime against Kansas." In this speech, which he had carefully rehearsed, Sumner went out of his way to include personal attacks on several prominent Democratic senators, including Andrew P. Butler of South Carolina. Several days later, after the Senate had adjourned, Rep. Preston S. Brooks of South Carolina, a distant relative of Butler's, went up to Sumner, who was seated at his desk, and after saying a few words beat the Massachusetts antislavery leader senseless with his cane, which shattered in three places from the force of the blows on Sumner's head. Overnight, Sumner became a northern hero, and more than a million copies of his speech were distributed. The assault ensured Sumner's reelection in 1857 and indeed made him a senator for life.

Sumner's injuries, which do not seem to have been physical in origin, kept him largely away from the Senate for the next three years, which he spent traveling and undergoing various treatments to restore his health. Once he returned to his seat, he renewed his attack on slavery, pronouncing a severe arraignment of the institution in a speech called "The Barbarism of Slavery," much to the hearty applause of the Republicans' staunch antislavery constituency. He participated in the 1860 Republican campaign and, following Abraham Lincoln's election, was an unbending congressional opponent of compromise during the winter of 1860–1861. When

CHARLES SUMNER
HARPER'S PICTORIAL HISTORY OF THE GREAT REBELLION

the Civil War began in April 1861, he promptly advocated making emancipation a Union war aim.

After secession, the resignations of members from the seceded southern states gave Republicans control of the Senate for the first time, and Sumner became chairman of the Foreign Relations Committee. The Massachusetts senator was eminently suited for this position: he was fluent in several languages, had a wide circle of correspondents in Europe, and possessed a good knowledge of international law. He carefully investigated the matters that came before his committee and came to thoroughly dominate it, since its other members, who were less well-informed, generally deferred to his judgment. He was on good personal terms with Lincoln but distrusted Secretary of State William H. Seward, whom he battled throughout the war for control of foreign policy. Sumner rendered vital assistance in the *Trent* crisis, when a U.S. naval officer removed two Confederate diplomats from a British ship. Sumner smoothed ruffled British feathers, helped secure the release of the two envoys, and made sure that provocative resolutions were buried in his committee. His personal diplomacy helped keep Britain from recognizing the Confederacy.

As a prominent Radical Republican, Sumner repeatedly advocated the policy of emancipation during the war and urged a punitive program of reconstruction. He advanced the idea that the Confederate states had committed suicide when they seceded and thus had lost their rights under the Constitution. He took up the cause of black equality and black suffrage and called on Congress to provide land and schools to the former slaves. Secure in his seat, Sumner constantly lectured his colleagues on the need to remove all racial barriers to equality, views that went far beyond those of most Republicans, including many Radicals. As a result, Sumner, despite his seniority, was shut out of decision making in the Senate. Given management for once of an important piece of domestic legislation, he could not persuade Congress to pass the Freedmen's Bureau bill in 1865. He also played no major role in the drafting of the Thirteenth, Fourteenth, or Fifteenth Amendments, was excluded from the Joint Committee on Reconstruction, and exerted little influence on Reconstruction legislation.

Sumner, like many Radicals, initially expressed confidence in Andrew Johnson, but he soon became convinced that the president was squandering the fruits of the Union's victory by restoring the South's former leaders to power. He was vehement in his criticism of the president's Reconstruction program and supported the unsuccessful effort to remove Johnson from office by impeachment, which he argued was a political and not a judicial proceeding.

Sumner expected his relations with the executive branch to improve following the election of Ulysses S. Grant in 1868, but the erudite Harvard professor had little in common with the taciturn general. They soon clashed over patronage and policy, and the administration's calculated deference to Sumner on diplomatic matters did not lessen his distrust. The major confrontation between the two men took place over Grant's attempt to annex Santo Domingo. Convinced that the scheme was tainted with corruption and a prelude to further expansion in the Caribbean, Sumner opposed the treaty. Grant stubbornly persisted in his plan, goading Sumner into delivering a slashing denunciation of the entire project. Sumner's bold opposition killed the treaty in 1870, but when a new Congress assembled in March 1871 the administration, weary of his dicta-torial attitude, retaliated by inducing the Republican caucus to strip him of his coveted committee chairmanship.

Two years earlier, while his influence on foreign policy was at its height, Sumner had delivered a widely publicized speech outlining American claims against Britain for damages incurred by U.S. shipping during the Civil War. He had argued that the United States was entitled to indirect as well as direct damages, including compensation for Britain's having prolonged the war, which he estimated totaled some $2 billion. When the two countries finally established a commission in 1871 to fix the amount owed the United States, the commission's members went out of their way to court Sumner and informally consulted him despite his recent removal as head of the Foreign Relations Committee. He played an important role in the ratification of the subsequent treaty.

Sumner's personal hostility to Grant and his disgust with the administration's record of corruption propelled him into the Liberal Republican movement in 1872. With Grant's reelection, Sumner's influence in Congress was largely at an end. His last major battle was for enactment of a civil rights bill guaranteeing black Americans equal rights on juries, in schools, on transportation, and in public accommodations. His death in 1874, after twenty-four years of service, precipitated a massive outpouring of grief, and Congress, largely in tribute to his memory, passed his civil rights bill after deleting the provision relating to schools.

Despite his national prominence, his diligent attention to his duties, and his boundless energy, Sumner was temperamentally unsuited for a legislative career. Vain and arrogant, he surrounded himself with a group of flatterers and alienated his colleagues by his inflexibility and his impractical ideas. His endless lectures on principles and his assumption of moral superiority infuriated members who knew that when he believed it necessary Sumner was quite capable of compromising. Devoid of humor, he failed to appreciate the sting of his words, and his extravagant language and lack of tolerance for other points of view won him no friends. Even most Radicals disliked him personally. He was oblivious to party discipline and appeals of party necessity and often opposed on minor grounds legislation desired by the Republican leadership. During his long congressional service he did not author a single piece of important legislation that was enacted during his lifetime, and while he tried to master other subjects, such as finance, he wielded little influence outside of foreign affairs.

"The Vacant Chair in the United States Senate." Representation of the nation mourning the death of Charles Sumner. Engraving published 16 March 1874.

His power derived from his public image as a disinterested statesman and the embodiment of moral principle. Sumner spoke for the potent moral element in northern society, and his carefully crafted speeches were directed more at the nation than at Congress. His lasting legacy was his bold championship of antislavery and racial equality rather than any legislative accomplishments.

BIBLIOGRAPHY

Donald, David. *Charles Sumner and the Coming of the Civil War.* 1965.

Donald, David. *Charles Sumner and the Rights of Man.* 1970.

Pierce, Edward L. *Memoir and Letters of Charles Sumner.* 4 vols. 1877–1893.

WILLIAM E. GIENAPP

SUNSET LAWS. In 1976, Colorado enacted the nation's first sunset law, and by 1980 more than thirty states had followed suit. Sunset measures typically consist of two basic components: a framework or guidelines for systematic program review and evaluation, and an action-forcing mechanism, carrying the ultimate threat of termination. The sunset idea was developed by the Colorado chapter of the public interest group Common Cause as a result of its frustration in efforts to reform Colorado's regulatory structure. Following oversight review, agencies subject to the sunset provisions were to "fade into the sunset" unless the legislature took specific action to continue their existence.

Federal legislators have also shown interest in the sunset approach. Some seventy sunset bills were introduced in the 94th Congress (1975–1977), and sunset measures have been pending in each subsequent Congress. Many hearings have been held on sunset legislation, and on 11 October 1978, a comprehensive federal sunset bill (S. 2, 95th Cong., 2d sess.) passed the Senate. Most sunset bills require some sort of comprehensive review of past performance, according to specified guidelines, prior to an agency's reauthorization. As sunset legislation evolved in Congress, attention came to focus on a version that placed almost all federal programs on a ten-year authorization cycle, with 20 percent due to terminate every two years. The timetable for review of programs sought to schedule functionally related programs and agencies together and also took account of the need to distribute the oversight workloads for the various authorizing committees over the ten-year period. Supporters contended that the sunset review process would provide the necessary incentive for Congress to concentrate on its oversight function. Skeptics argued that the sunset review process would either overload the capabilities of Congress and thus become unworkable or would not be taken seriously and thus result in perfunctory reviews.

Meanwhile, state experience with sunset laws proved mixed. In the 1980s, the growing federal budget deficits led to a preoccupation in Congress with appropriations decisions. Consequently, the authorization phase of the budget cycle, central to the sunset framework, received relatively less notice. Interest in sunset laws thus declined but did not disappear.

BIBLIOGRAPHY

U.S. House of Representatives. Committee on Rules. *A Compilation of State Sunset Laws.* 98th Cong., 1st sess., 1983. Subcommittee Print.

U.S. Senate. Committee on Governmental Affairs. *Sunset Act of 1980.* 96th Cong., 2d sess., 1980. S. Rept. 96-865.

VIRGINIA A. McMURTRY

SUNSHINE RULES. *See* Government in the Sunshine Act.

SUPERFUND ACT. *See* Comprehensive Environmental Response, Compensation, and Liability Act of 1980.

SUPREME COURT. [*The following article focuses on the physical presence of the Supreme Court within the Capitol building. For broad discussion of the relation of Congress with the judiciary, see* Constitution; Judiciary and Congress.] The Capitol housed the Supreme Court, with brief exceptions, for 134 years—from February 1801 until June 1935. The original 1791 plan for the new capital city had provided for a Supreme Court building approximately midway between the Capitol and the executive mansion. But when the financially strapped federal government moved to Washington, D.C., in November 1800, no money had been set aside for the Court's building, and no construction was contemplated. Two months passed before Congress, on 23 January 1801, agreed to provide the Court with temporary space in a first-floor committee room located in the southwest corner of the Capitol's Senate (or north) wing. The Court occupied the uncomfortable 24-foot-by-30-foot room from its first Washington session on 2 February 1801 through its 1807 term. Major reconstruction then necessitated a relocation, during the February 1808 term, to

OLD SUPREME COURT CHAMBER.

the second-floor congressional library (now part of the Senate Republican leader's suite), which the House of Representatives had recently vacated. A year later, dissatisfied with the cold and inconvenience of its library quarters, the increasingly peripatetic Court left the Capitol for the greater hospitality of Long's Tavern (on the modern site of the Library of Congress's Thomas Jefferson Building) for the February 1809 term.

The Court returned to the Capitol on 5 February 1810 and settled into a room on the ground floor of the north wing, previously the Senate's chamber. The space, remodeled by the architect Benjamin Latrobe, was the first to be specifically designed for the Court's use. After invading British troops severely damaged the Capitol in August 1814, the Court moved to a rented, four-story brick house (at a location now occupied by the Longworth House Office Building) in February 1815 and remained there until July 1816; the Court returned to an undamaged portion of the Capitol's north wing in 1817.

On 2 February 1819 the Court once again settled into the chamber it had occupied from 1810 to 1814. The newly restored quarters would serve as the Court's home for the next forty-one years. The semicircular room's most dramatic feature was its handsome lobed half-dome ceiling, with a triple arch, supported by Doric columns along the eastern wall. Justices sat at individual mahogany desks on a raised platform behind a balustrade that separated them from members of the bar. Despite the room's attractive appearance, its occupants routinely complained of its cold and damp "cellarlike" environment.

In January 1859 completion of the Capitol's newly constructed Senate wing provided the Court with another abandoned room for its use. Soon after the Senate moved from its chamber—located on the second floor, directly above—to its current quarters, work began to outfit the vacated site for the Court, which moved in on 3 December 1860. The former first-floor courtroom served as the Court's law library until the mid-twentieth century. It was later restored to its 1850s appearance and is now open to the public as the Old Supreme Court Chamber.

The new setting (now restored as the Old Senate Chamber), a semicircular hall 75 feet long and 45 feet at its greatest width, featured a half-domed ceiling with deeply sunken square panels and an eastern gallery supported by columns of variegated Potomac marble. Although Congress provided rooms adjacent to the chamber for the Court's use, the new location proved unsatisfactory. Justices lacked individual chambers, and they disliked having to cross the frequently crowded public corridor to reach the courtroom. In 1912 President William Howard Taft unsuccessfully urged Congress to authorize a separate Supreme Court structure. After he became chief justice in 1921, Taft renewed his campaign, complaining of cramped conditions. In 1929 Congress finally agreed. Construction of the Supreme Court Building began in 1930, and the Court held its final session in the Capitol on 3 June 1935.

BIBLIOGRAPHY

Lavery, Urban A. "The Supreme Court: Its Homes Past and Present." *American Bar Association Journal* 27 (May 1941): 283–289.

U.S. Senate. Commission on Art. *The Supreme Court Chamber, 1810–1860.* 1990.

Warren, Charles. *The Supreme Court in United States History.* 1923.

RICHARD A. BAKER

SUSPENSION OF THE RULES.

Suspension of the rules refers to procedures by which the House of Representatives acts expeditiously on matters enjoying widespread support among its members.

A bill or resolution considered under suspension of the rules is debated by all members for no more than forty minutes, after which a two-thirds vote is required to pass it. The Speaker may postpone the vote until a later time or the following day. Members cast a single vote on suspending the rules and passing the measure. The bill or resolution may not be amended during its consideration, although the member making the motion to pass the measure under suspension of the rules may include amendments to the measure in that motion.

As time pressures on the House have grown, these procedures have become increasingly popular, and the House rules have been amended to permit suspension motions to be made more often. Once in order only on two Mondays of each month, these motions now may be made on Monday and Tuesday of each week and during the closing days of each congressional session. Toward the end of a session, the House may act on ten or more suspension motions in a single day. However, the Speaker has the authority to determine whether a suspension motion may be offered and, therefore, whether a bill or resolution may be considered in this way. In recent Congresses, the House has used these procedures to act on between one-third and one-half of the measures it has passed.

[*See also* Rule, Special.]

BIBLIOGRAPHY

Bach, Stanley. "Suspension of the Rules, the Order of Business, and the Development of Congressional Procedure." *Legislative Studies Quarterly* 15 (1990): 49–63.

U.S. House of Representatives. *Deschler's Precedents of the United States House of Representatives*, by Lewis Deschler. 94th Cong., 2d sess., 1977. H. Doc. 94-661. Vol. 6, pp. 165–265.

STANLEY BACH

T

TABER, JOHN (1880–1965), Republican representative from New York, chairman of the Committee on Appropriations (1947–1949; 1953–1954). During his forty-year House career (1923–1963), this upstate conservative waged unrelenting opposition to big government. His meticulous scrutiny of the federal budget and his penetrating voice were familiar to generations of House members as he fought the creation and funding of virtually every New Deal and Fair Deal program.

Surviving the Democratic sweep of 1932, Taber overnight climbed from tenth to first in Republican seniority on the Appropriations Committee. His seat on the Deficiencies Subcommittee accorded him substantial influence over many important and controversial social programs of the 1930s and 1940s. A founder of the Republican–southern Democratic coalition, which blossomed in the late 1930s, he led fights against lend-lease agreements, wartime bureaucracy, and postwar foreign aid.

With the election of a Republican majority in the 80th Congress (1947–1949), he became Appropriations chairman, vowing war on excessive federal programs and employment. Seizing on the Congressional Reorganization Act of 1946, which allowed the Appropriations Committee unlimited staff, he assembled a record twenty-seven professionals, known as Taber's Bureau of Investigation, to search programs and agencies for waste. He claimed to have pared $6 billion from budget requests totaling $62.9 billion during his first two-year tenure as chairman. Taber served as chairman again in 1953 and 1954, but under a Republican president, his attacks on federal spending were less

JOHN TABER. Shortly before becoming chairman of the House Appropriations Committee, 30 October 1946. Taber's reputation as a tough but fair guardian of the federal treasury earned him the sobriquet "Old Whang Leather."

LIBRARY OF CONGRESS

vociferous than during the previous twenty-eight years of Democratic rule.

BIBLIOGRAPHY

Henderson, Cary Smith. "Congressman John Taber of Auburn: Politics and Federal Appropriations, 1923–1962." Ph.D. diss., Duke University, 1964.

Reynolds, J. Lacey. "Taber: The Third House of Congress." *New York Times Magazine*, 15 January 1948.

DONALD C. BACON

TABLING. The motion to lay a proposition on the table, if successful, is equivalent to final adverse disposition of that matter without debate in both the House and Senate.

In the Senate the motion to table a matter is in order any time a question is pending before the Senate, unless that question is more privileged than the motion to table itself (i.e., a motion to adjourn, recess, or proceed to consideration of executive business). If successful, the motion does not carry with it, or prejudice, the underlying question as well. This means, for example, that tabling an amendment will not cause the underlying bill to be tabled with it. As a result of this convention, and the fact that the motion is decided upon without debate, the Senate has developed the practice of using the motion for a variety of purposes, including to dispose of a matter immediately, as a vote to test support for an amendment, as a means of avoiding a direct yes-or-no vote on a matter, or to counter dilatory tactics. An important exception is that the motion is not applicable during a period of debate specified in a unanimous consent agreement.

In the House, however, the use of the motion is restricted by the fact that when a proposed amendment is laid on the table, the underlying measure goes there also. It is not in order in a number of circumstances, including with regard to motions to adjourn, to suspend the rules, or to recommit; motions relating to the order of business; or generally motions that are neither debatable nor amendable. It is also not applicable to demands for the previous question, or once the previous question has been ordered, or to motions to resolve into Committee of the Whole; in addition, when the House is operating in Committee of the Whole, the motion to table is not in order at all. Therefore, the chief use of tabling is against matters brought up as privileged that the leadership wishes to remove from consideration.

BIBLIOGRAPHY

U.S. House of Representatives. *Deschler's Precedents of the United States House of Representatives*, by Lewis Deschler. 94th Cong., 2d sess., 1977. H. Doc. 94-661. Vol. 7, chap. 23.

U.S. House of Representatives. *Hinds' Precedents of the House of Representatives of the United States*, by Asher C. Hinds. 59th Cong., 2d sess., 1907. Vol. 5, chap. 119.

U.S. Senate. *Senate Procedure, Precedents, and Practices*, by Floyd M. Riddick. 97th Cong., 1st sess., 1981. Doc. 97-2.

U.S. House of Representatives. *Constitution, Jefferson's Manual, and Rules of the House of Representatives, 102d Congress*. Compiled by William Holmes Brown. 101st Cong., 2d sess., 1990. H. Doc. 101-256.

JAMES V. SATURNO

TAFT, ROBERT A. (1889–1953), senator from Ohio, leader of conservative Republicans, and three-time unsuccessful contender for the Republican presidential nomination. Robert Alphonso Taft was a member of one of America's most prominent Republican families. His grandfather Alphonso Taft had been attorney general and secretary of War under President Ulysses S. Grant. His father, William Howard Taft, became president and later served as chief justice of the United States Supreme Court. Reared to excel and to enter public service, Robert Taft finished first in his class at Taft School in Connecticut, at Yale University, and at Harvard Law School, from which he graduated in 1913. Many of his views on foreign and domestic affairs resembled the ideas of his politically conservative father.

After leaving Harvard, Taft returned to his home city of Cincinnati, Ohio, to join the law firm of Maxwell and Ramsey. During World War I he served as an assistant counsel for the U.S. Food Administration in Washington, where he worked under future president Herbert Hoover. Following the war he went with Hoover to Paris as a legal adviser for the American Relief Administration. Like Hoover, who was a major influence in his life, Taft emerged from these experiences opposed to significant governmental regulation of the economy and to extensive U.S. involvement in Europe's political affairs.

Returning to Cincinnati in 1919, Taft cofounded a law firm and built up a substantial practice, mainly in corporate law. He also entered state politics as a Republican state representative for three two-year terms (1921–1926) and a state senator for one

ROBERT A. TAFT.
OFFICE OF THE HISTORIAN OF THE U.S. SENATE

(1931–1932). Like his father, who had battled progressives under Theodore Roosevelt in 1912, Robert Taft was a leader of Cincinnati's regular Republicans in struggles against insurgents (including his brother, Charles). His party loyalty afforded him a solid base for advancement in state politics.

The Great Depression and President Franklin D. Roosevelt's New Deal provided the setting for Taft's entry into national politics. Having lost his race for reelection in the Democratic sweep of 1932, Taft soon emerged as a highly vocal opponent of Roosevelt's social welfare policies, which he considered wasteful and extravagant. He was especially hostile to Roosevelt's regulatory policies. "There is very little the government can do," he said, "to really modify the tremendous economic forces involved in a world-wide business recession." In 1938, when he sought the Republican nomination for the U.S. Senate, he focused his campaign on the purported errors and excesses of New Deal domestic policies.

During this campaign, as in others throughout his career, Taft was decidedly uncharismatic. He was a dry, didactic speaker and a poor mixer. Staring owlishly from behind rimless spectacles, he filled his speeches with facts and figures. To many, he seemed more the professor than the politician. But then, as later, he impressed people with his integrity and command of information. With the support of the state party organization he won a hard-fought primary. A nationwide trend against the New Deal helped elect him to the Senate in November of 1938.

Few politicians in modern American history rose as quickly as Taft did in the Senate. From the start he was a leader of Republicans opposed to the New Deal and to Roosevelt's increasingly internationalist foreign policies. As in 1918 and 1919, he believed in a foreign policy of America first. Aid to England and France, he argued, would lead to involvement in the European war and to socialism in the United States. His growing prominence made him a leading contender for the Republican presidential nomination in 1940, but he lost on the sixth ballot to the more interventionist candidate Wendell Willkie of Indiana.

Many factors assisted Taft's rapid political ascent: the rising tide of conservative opposition to the New Deal, the paucity of Republican politicians of stature, particularly in the Senate, and the senator's own qualities. Though many people, including members of the more liberal eastern wing of his party, considered him reactionary on domestic issues and isolationist in foreign policy, most of his Republican colleagues in Congress admired his apparently limitless capacity for hard work, his attention to legislative detail, and his straightforwardness. Party regulars especially liked his partisan combativeness, which was so pronounced that he became known as "Mr. Republican." On domestic policy issues Taft was the most powerful Republican on Capitol Hill from 1939 until his death in 1953.

During the war and immediate postwar years Taft reconsidered some of his conservative ideas. He supported federal aid to education and public housing, and in 1949 he and liberal allies succeeded in passing the Taft-Wagner-Ellender Housing Act. But he remained highly partisan and conservative on most other domestic issues. As an advocate of a freer market and of smaller government, he consistently called for reductions in federal spending and taxes; in 1948 he led Republicans to passage of a tax cut that was then enacted over President Harry S. Truman's veto. The cut mainly benefited upper-income groups. An angry foe of militant labor unions, he sponsored the Taft-

Hartley Labor-Management Relations Act, which the Republican 80th Congress passed over Truman's veto in 1947. Denounced (excessively) by unions as a "slave labor act," the law identified a number of "unfair" labor practices, outlawed the closed shop, encouraged states to pass anti-union "right-to-work" laws, and authorized injunctions that could delay for eighty days strikes thought to imperil the national welfare. The law was his major legislative achievement.

Though Taft supported U.S. participation in the United Nations, he remained cool to U.S. political commitments in Europe. After the war he opposed a generous loan to Great Britain and voted regularly to curb the size of foreign aid. Like most Americans, he hated communism, and he repeatedly denounced Democratic leaders for their "socialistic" tendencies. But he did not believe that the Soviet Union possessed either the power or the desire to control Western Europe, let alone to threaten the United States. For these reasons he opposed military buildups under the North Atlantic Treaty Organization.

Taft's opposition to interventionist foreign policies earned him the backing of many Republican colleagues in Congress, especially those from the Midwest. But it damaged him with other Republicans, including Sen. Arthur H. Vandenberg of Michigan, who led a bipartisan congressional bloc that supported Truman's strongly anti-Soviet policies. When Taft sought the presidential nomination in 1948, the internationalist wing of his party opposed him, choosing instead Gov. Thomas E. Dewey of New York.

When Truman surprised the pundits by beating Dewey and carrying with him Democratic majorities to Congress, Taft stepped up his partisan assaults on presidential policies, especially in the realm of foreign affairs. Like other Republicans, he blamed the Truman administration for "losing" China to communism. He encouraged Wisconsin senator Joseph R. McCarthy's reckless charges about communism in the State Department. He denounced Truman for failing to secure congressional support for U.S. involvement in the Korean War and, later, for removing Gen. Douglas MacArthur from military command in Asia. In 1951 he pulled together many of these ideas and published his only book, *A Foreign Policy for Americans*.

Truman's troubles after 1949 promoted a Republican resurgence, and Taft won an impressive senatorial victory in 1950. Encouraged, he embarked on his third and last quest for the presidential nomination. As in his earlier attempts, he enjoyed the enthusiastic backing of many Republican regulars, especially conservative midwesterners. But influential party leaders, including Dewey, worried that Taft lacked political charisma and that he was too isolationist. Supporting Gen. Dwight D. Eisenhower, they defeated the Taft forces in the exciting Republican national convention of 1952.

Taft was deeply disappointed after the convention and seemed unwilling to endorse Eisenhower in the campaign. But Eisenhower went out of his way to appease the Taft forces, closed party divisions behind his candidacy, and swept to victory in November. Taft not only campaigned for his rival, but also agreed to serve as Senate majority leader in 1953. Working closely with Eisenhower, Taft enjoyed the experience—the first of his senatorial career—of leading a majority behind a president from his own party. He also came to like the president personally, and he held the party together behind Eisenhower's more moderate policies. His death in July 1953, from cancer that had begun to afflict him in April, struck him down at the peak of his political powers and deprived the Eisenhower administration of an increasingly valued congressional ally.

In the years since Taft's death, various groups of Americans have appropriated him as their model. Some, in the aftermath of Watergate, have extolled him as an admirably forthright and principled political leader. Others (overlooking inconsistencies and partisan excesses) have praised his aversion to globalist foreign policies and his refusal to overreact to the Soviet threat in the 1940s and early 1950s. He is perhaps best remembered, however, as an able, conscientious, and partisan conservative. Fighting against the liberal internationalist tide of the Roosevelt and Truman years, he lost more battles than he won. He was too far to the right on domestic affairs, too colorless on the stump, and too critical of internationalism to achieve his dream of the presidency. But it is wrong to stress his failures. Taft commanded widespread affection from conservatives and amassed unusual power in the Senate.

BIBLIOGRAPHY

Merry, Robert W. "Robert A. Taft." In *First among Equals: Outstanding Senate Leaders of the Twentieth Century.* Edited by Richard A. Baker and Roger H. Davidson. 1991.

Patterson, James T. *Mr. Republican: A Biography of Robert A. Taft.* 1972.

White, William S. *The Taft Story.* 1954.

JAMES T. PATTERSON

TAFT, WILLIAM HOWARD (1857–1930), civil governor of the Philippines, secretary of War, twenty-seventh president (Republican), and chief justice of the Supreme Court. Born into a Cincinnati, Ohio, family of moderate wealth and political power, Taft absorbed the conservative attitudes of his comfortable middle-class milieu. He graduated from Yale University in 1878 and obtained his law degree from the Cincinnati Law School. Almost all of Taft's posts prior to his election as president in 1908—federal judge, governor general of the Philippines, solicitor general, and secretary of War—were appointive.

As president, Taft was out of his element. His predecessor, Theodore Roosevelt, felt constrained only by what was explicitly prohibited by the Constitution, but Taft, who had a highly legal-judicial conception of government, believed he was limited to those powers granted by or implied in that document. His ability to lead was further limited by a group of congressional insurgent Republicans who demanded reforms that he opposed. Taft rejected social welfare legislation and feared the tyranny of the majority, the passion of the mob, and the power over the people by a demagogue. Above all, he sought to protect the rights of the individual and of private property and sought to promote peace and stability—goals that would not be fulfilled.

Rather than make the presidency the most important of the three branches of government, Taft would keep the branches in equilibrium. Believing that capitalists contributed more to society than any other class, he filled his cabinet with corporation lawyers and failed to include reformers whom Roosevelt believed he would retain. By supporting his secretary of the Interior, Richard A. Ballinger, who would permit the private exploitation of natural resources, he greatly angered Roosevelt, Gifford Pinchot, and others who demanded state or federal ownership and regulation. His ability to lead Congress was further limited by several factors.

Instead of getting rid of the conservative old guard in Congress, for his first two years Taft went along with Speaker Joseph G. Cannon, "Czar" of the House, and Nelson W. Aldrich, who dominated the Senate. In 1910, however, an insurgent revolt provided more democracy in the House by having its membership rather than the Speaker determine the members of an enlarged Committee on Rules from which the Speaker was barred. While Taft did not personally support Cannon, who remained as Speaker, during Cannon's fight Taft praised his

WILLIAM HOWARD TAFT. In 1909.

LIBRARY OF CONGRESS

fighting spirit and his continued attacks upon "disloyal" insurgents.

Meanwhile, in an extraordinary gaffe, Taft called the highly protective Payne-Aldrich tariff bill "the best tariff bill the Republican party has ever passed," a mistake sufficient to ensure insurgent and Democratic gains in the elections of 1910 and a Congress that could thwart his demands. Yet he still managed to secure more reform legislation in his four years as president than Roosevelt won in seven. Taft improved government efficiency and court procedures; obtained a parcel post system and postal savings banks, a federal budget system, and a commerce court; and did more trust-busting than Roosevelt. He extended and gave legal form to Roosevelt's conservation measures and urged Congress to submit to the states the Sixteenth Amendment to the Constitution (for the income tax).

After his defeat in the presidential campaign of 1912, Taft taught law at Yale University, held various posts in Washington during World War I, and served as chief justice of the Supreme Court from 1921 to 1930. He was clearly more at home on the Court than he had been in the White House.

BIBLIOGRAPHY

Anderson, Donald F. *William Howard Taft: A Conservative's Conception of the Presidency.* 1973.
Anderson, Judith Icke. *William Howard Taft: An Intimate History.* 1981.
Pringle, Henry F. *The Life and Times of William Howard Taft.* 2 vols. 1939.

PAOLO E. COLETTA

TAFT-HARTLEY LABOR-MANAGEMENT RELATIONS ACT (1947; 61 Stat. 136–162).

The Taft-Hartley Labor-Management Relations Act of 1947 was an omnibus statute amending and supplementing federal labor relations law as established in the 1935 Wagner-Connery National Labor Relations Act (Wagner Act or NLRA) and administered by the National Labor Relations Board (NLRB). Its passage over President Harry S. Truman's veto was assured by the substantial Republican majorities secured in the 1946 elections and by the support of conservative southern Democrats. Chief sponsors were the chairmen of the two congressional labor committees, Ohio senator Robert A. Taft ("Mr. Republican") and Republican representative Fred A. Hartley, Jr., of New Jersey; important supporters were Joseph H. Ball (R-Minn.) and Irving M. Ives (R-N.Y.) in the Senate, and, in the House, Majority Leader Charles A. Halleck (R-Ind.) and Graham A. Barden (D-N.C.). Opponents included James E. Murray (D-Mont.) and Wayne L. Morse (R-Oreg.) in the Senate and John Lesinski (D-Mich.) and Arthur G. Klein (D-N.Y.) in the House. Initial votes cast were 68 to 24 in the Senate and 308 to 107 in the House (where so many southern Democrats were in favor that in fact majorities of both parties voted for the House bill). This overwhelming support was maintained for the conference version (57 to 17 and 320 to 79) and Truman's veto was easily overridden.

Some components of the act were descendants of congressional campaigns to amend the Wagner Act in the waning years of the New Deal. Others were put forward in response to the rapid growth of organized labor during World War II and the postwar strike wave (a major issue in the 1946 elections). The act typified conservative antagonism to the reformist institutions and policies created during the New Deal's spate of administrative state-building. Particular provisions also marked the resurgence of domestic anticommunism attending the collapse of wartime entente with the Soviet Union and the onset of the Cold War.

Taft-Hartley had four sections. Title I amended both the administration and substantive content of the Wagner Act. It expanded NLRB membership and separated the agency's investigative and judicial functions. It restricted the NLRB's autonomy in determining bargaining units, excluded supervisory employees from coverage, underlined employees' "right to refrain" from collective activity, introduced union "decertification" provisions, and allowed employers to petition for representation elections to be held among their employees. It specified unfair union practices, imposed procedural restraints on contract termination or modification, and defined "good faith" in bargaining. It banned closed shops, required majority approval of union preference clauses, and underlined states' rights to impose additional restraints on union activity by passing "right-to-work" laws. It gave the NLRB authority to determine jurisdiction and demarcation disputes and attempted to ban "featherbedding" (payment for services not performed). Finally, it required unions to register with the secretary of Labor, file annual financial reports, and certify that none of their officers was a member of the Communist party.

The remaining titles endorsed federal conciliation, encouraged parties to develop grievance procedures, and established national emergency strike procedures (Title II); they specified categories of unlawful union and employer behavior, decreed labor agreements legally enforceable, and restricted union political expenditures (Title III); and they established a joint committee of Congress to investigate labor relations (Title IV).

The Wagner Act had committed the federal government to protecting a core of workers' rights against the dominant common-law model of employer primacy. Taft-Hartley embodied a return to the formal authority of employers and suspicion of unions as disruptive interlopers. Wildcat strikes, sit-downs, and slow-downs had already been held to be unprotected under the Wagner Act. But these were now explicitly outlawed. During the 1950s further brakes on union organizing were added through court interpretation of the amended NLRA and by the Landrum-Griffin Act of 1959.

[*See also* Employment Act of 1946; Fair Labor Standards Act; National Industrial Recovery Act.]

BIBLIOGRAPHY

Rogers, Joel P. "Divide and Conquer: Further 'Reflections on the Distinctive Character of American Labor Laws.'" *Wisconsin Law Review* (1990): 1–147.

Tomlins, Christopher L. *The State and the Unions: Labor Relations, Law, and the Organized Labor Movement in America, 1880–1960.* 1985.

CHRISTOPHER L. TOMLINS

TALMADGE, HERMAN E. (1913–), influential conservative Democrat from Georgia and the only senator to be denounced by the Senate. Herman Eugene Talmadge, son of colorful and controversial Georgia governor Eugene Talmadge, played a major role in his state's politics for more than three decades. Talmadge received a law degree from the University of Georgia in 1936 and managed several of his father's political campaigns. Following the death of his father, then governor-elect, the legislature elected Talmadge governor in 1947. Talmadge held the governorship for sixty-seven days until the Georgia Supreme Court invalidated his election. The voters elected Talmadge to complete his father's unexpired term in 1948 and to serve a full four-year term in 1950. Talmadge won election to the Senate in 1956 after the state's senior senator, Walter F. George, declined to seek reelection.

Talmadge was reelected three times and became an influential senator, respected by his peers for his intelligence and diligence. He served as chairman of the Agriculture, Nutrition and Forestry Committee from 1971 to 1981. He also served on the Finance and Veterans' Affairs committees as well as on the Senate's Select Committee on Presidential Campaign Activities (the so-called Senate Watergate Committee). Talmadge played a major role in the passage of the Trade Expansion Act of 1962 and the Rural Development Act of 1972 as well as in the expansion of the national school lunch program. A fiscal conservative, he opposed civil rights, social welfare legislation, and foreign aid. His views on many domestic issues, including civil rights, be-

HERMAN E. TALMADGE. During a joint press conference in July 1971.   LIBRARY OF CONGRESS

came more moderate in the late 1960s as more Georgia blacks registered to vote. Talmadge suffered several setbacks in the 1970s, including a bitter divorce and his denunciation by the Senate for financial misconduct—which resulted in his defeat in 1980.

BIBLIOGRAPHY

Mellichamp, Josephine. *Senators from Georgia.* 1976.

Talmadge, Herman Eugene. *Talmadge: A Political Legacy, a Politician's Life, a Memoir.* 1987.

Talmadge, Herman Eugene. *You and Segregation.* 1955.

HAROLD P. HENDERSON

TARIFFS AND TRADE. Since early colonial days, tariff and trade policy has been the focus of conflict: between the legislative and executive branches; among the competing agricultural, manufacturing and commercial interests; and, for much of the history of the United States, between the two major political parties.

Opposition to the trade restrictions imposed by the British government in colonial times was a major source of the discontent that led to the Revolution. During the years of the Articles of Confederation, the national government was prohibited from imposing import duties without the unanimous consent of the thirteen states—something that was never attained. While the states of the Confederation never did consent to a national tariff, individual states did impose import duties against one anothers' imports as well as against foreign commerce. Massachusetts, Rhode Island, Pennsylvania, and New York levied duties against "foreign" products, including those of other states. Indeed, it was the inability of the Confederation to regulate foreign trade, along with the need to raise money to meet the public debt, that was a prime rationale for the move toward the establishment of a stronger central government.

From the Constitution to the Civil War: Revenue versus Protection. Article II, section 2 of the U.S. Constitution, which defines the powers of the president to conduct foreign relations, grants the chief executive the exclusive authority to make treaties "by and with the Advice and Consent of the Senate." Article I, section 8 states that "Congress shall have the Power to lay and collect Taxes, Duties, Imports and Excises" and to "regulate Commerce with foreign Nations." The conflict inherent in these two grants of power was a significant factor in determining the executive-congressional conflict over U.S. tariff and trade policies. This conflict, combined with the extensive and complex concerns of American economic interests (agricultural, industrial, commercial) over tariff rates, ensured that trade would be one of the largest and most persistent topics of congressional attention.

The First Congress convened in New York City on 4 March 1789. On 8 April, the House of Representatives considered James Madison's resolution to establish specific duties on a variety of products, a tonnage duty on U.S. vessels, and a higher duty on foreign vessels. Madison argued for the measure on the ground it was needed to raise revenues and "that the encouragement of manufacturers was an object of the power to regulate trade." Congress hastily passed this first tariff, and President George Washington signed it into law.

The 1789 tariff was of great importance to the new government—and to the country. It was the first assertion of fiscal authority by Congress. While revenue was the major impetus for Madison's proposal, elements of protectionism were evident from the differential duty on foreign and American tonnage and on duties on such items as salt, tobacco, boots, spirits, and woolen and cotton goods. These were clearly protectionist in the effects they had on imports: for example, no tobacco was imported under the 1789 tariff's provisions. In his first annual address in January 1790, President Washington

said, "Safety and interest require that [a free people] should promote such manufactures as tend to render them independent of others for essential, particularly military, supplies." A week later, Congress reiterated Washington's message, ordering the secretary of the Treasury to prepare a report on plans to encourage and promote "such manufactures as will tend to render the United States independent of other nations for essential, particularly for military, supplies."

This led Secretary of the Treasury Alexander Hamilton to issue his famous "Report on Manufactures." Sent to the House on 5 December 1791, Hamilton's report has served as the philosophical basis for protectionism for most of U.S. history. It argued that it was in the national interest to protect domestic manufacturers for economic reasons as well as national security. Hamilton admitted that completely free international trade would be preferable to protection but argued that since other nations practiced protection the United States must do the same. The report had immediate impact; many of its specific recommendations were included in a tariff act in 1792.

Again in 1794, Madison introduced resolutions proposing higher duties to raise revenues. A committee of fourteen members was constituted in the House of Representatives "to inquire whether any . . . other revenues are necessary for the support of public credit." The committee reported on 17 April 1794, recommending excises on a series of items, and the act was approved in June 1794. Numerous additional tariff measures were passed between 1794 and the War of 1812. With few exceptions, they were designed to raise revenues for the Treasury.

The War of 1812 placed heavy revenue demands on the government and demonstrated the need for protecting productive capacity at home on national security grounds. During and after the war, the fear that European nations would dump products at artifically low prices led to more demands for protection.

Postwar tariff policy was marked by a period of increasing rates until 1833 and then by declines until 1842, when duty levels again approximated those established in 1816. The protectionist tariff bill of 1824 passed both the House and Senate with narrow majorities. Two new issues appeared in the debate that accompanied the passage of this measure. A representative from Virginia raised the question of the constitutionality of protective tariffs, arguing that their purposes had shifted away from the defensible objective of collecting revenue. And for the first time the argument was made that tariff protection was essential to protect the U.S. wage scale (higher than those of its European competitors)—a kind of argument that has persisted in trade debates to this day. Sectional divisions were also emerging in the debate over protection versus revenue. The 1824 act was supported by votes from the midwestern and western states. The South opposed the act, and New England was split, with Connecticut and Rhode Island for and the rest of New England opposed.

In the history of trade legislation, the so-called Tariff of Abominations of 1828 has a notable place. This measure was an early example of political horse trading between sectional interests, leading to high tariff rates on a wide variety of agricultural products, such as hemp, coarse wool, flax, and a number of other raw materials. The cotton-exporting South was deeply angered by this measure, one of the early milestones in the developing sectional clash.

President John Quincy Adams and Henry Clay, his secretary of State, were vigorous proponents of protectionist doctrine. Andrew Jackson thus had a dilemma. Jackson had supported the relatively high 1824 act but was courting the free-trade South in his quest for the presidency. Yet protection was popular in much of the North—particularly New York, Pennsylvania, and Ohio. As a presidential candidate in 1828, Jackson tried to placate both sides and was elected without a clear mandate on trade. He waited until the last year of his administration before attempting to correct the excesses of the 1828 measure.

This effort was complicated by the nullification crisis of 1832 and 1833, which stemmed directly from the 1828 tariff. Sen. John C. Calhoun of South Carolina questioned whether the Constitution sanctioned the imposition of taxes for purposes other than raising revenues and argued that states had the right to nullify the enforcement of federal laws within their borders. A convention in South Carolina nullified the tariffs of 1828 and 1832, forcing President Jackson to support a reduction in the tariff in 1833. The 1833 act provided for a gradual but steady reduction of tariffs to 20 percent, which was achieved by 1842.

Meanwhile, the competing goals of revenue and protection provoked a contest for jurisdiction over trade matters between the committees on Ways and Means and on Manufactures. In 1819, House Speaker Henry Clay had appointed a protectionist

SMOOT-HAWLEY TARIFF. Rep. Willis C. Hawley (R-Oreg.), *left,* and Sen. Reed Smoot (R-Utah).

majority to the Committee on Manufactures and on several occasions had referred tariff matters to this body, which reported out the tariffs of 1824, 1827, 1828, and 1830.

In December 1831 a showdown began. The new Speaker, Andrew Stevenson of Virginia, assigned a majority of "liberal traders" to the Ways and Means Committee. John Quincy Adams, an avid Hamiltonian protectionist and now a member of the House, was chairman of the Committee on Manufactures. President Jackson's annual message to Congress, in which he spoke of "relieving people of unnecessary taxation," was referred to the Ways and Means Committee. That portion of the message devoted to "manufactures and modification of the tariff" went to the Committee on Manufactures. Practically speaking, both committees were assigned the same legislative task. Conflicting measures were reported, resulting in the modest duty reductions of the 1832 tariff. The Committee on Manufactures did not report a bill in 1833, and Ways and Means has dominated the handling of trade policy ever since.

A similar development occurred in the Senate, where the Committee on Manufactures and the Committee on Finance attempted to deal jointly with trade matters during the 1850s and 1860s. Ultimately the Committee on Manufactures was abolished, and the Finance Committee has retained to this day the authority to report all revenue bills.

During the period from 1832 to 1861, the trend of congressional tariff policy was toward reduction, reflecting southern Democratic dominance. A notable development was the compromise tariff of 1833. Henry Clay, a staunch protectionist, agreed with Calhoun on a measure to reduce all rates to 20 percent by 1840. This change of heart on Clay's part reflected a shift in the South toward freer trade. (The tariff of 1843 raised a number of duties, reflecting an interlude of Whig supremacy.) Protectionism was also losing its political appeal in the farm states, and even in manufacturing states—except among those who directly benefited—support for protectionism had cooled. The Democrats won the White House and Congress in 1844. Robert Walker, President James K. Polk's secretary of the Treasury, proposed a "scientific" tariff revision for revenue only, which in fact embodied the Democrats' preference for freer trade. The 1857 tariff act reduced rates by 20 percent and stayed in effect for a decade.

From the Civil War to the New Deal: Protectionism Dominates. The Civil War brought a revival of high tariffs that, with minor exceptions, would dominate trade policy until after World War II. While tariffs remained the primary source of federal revenue, protectionist pressures drove the

rates upward on imports that competed against domestically produced items. The dominant position of the protectionist-minded Republicans in the executive and legislative branches allowed them to maintain an unabashedly protectionist policy.

The Morrill Act of 1861 restored the rates imposed by the Walker tariff of 1846, raising $50 million a year and providing additional protection to industry. The Morrill Act, which became law in March 1861, was the last tariff measure enacted before the start of the Civil War. The war's revenue demands produced the tariff acts of 1862 and 1864, both part of the revenue-raising program to finance the conflict.

The division between Republicans and Democrats on the tariff issue became pronounced during the late nineteenth century. The 1864 rates remained the basis of American tariff policy until the Democrats took control of the House in 1883. Sectional divisions made it difficult to obtain Democratic party unity in support of the leadership's effort to revise the tariff structure, as some northern Democrats stayed on the protectionist side. Rep. Samuel J. Randall (D-Pa.) led a group of protection-

The effects of a Tariff exclusively for Revenue as laid down in the Democratic Platform and which the Democratic Congressmen tried to enact last winter at Washington.

Democratic Free-Trade Means low wages, children in rags and ignorance

If you are satisfied with this picture vote for Cleveland and Hendricks.

The effects of Protection to American Industries as guaranteed by the Republican Party and Platform.

Republican Protection Means good wages, happy homes and education for your children

If you prefer this picture vote for Blaine and Logan.

REPUBLICAN VIEWS. Campaign print for the 1884 presidential race between Grover Cleveland and James G. Blaine, claiming that the tariff sponsored by the Democrats would lead to the impoverishment of the American worker, while the protective tariff endorsed by the Republicans would ensure prosperity.

COLLECTION OF DAVID J. AND JANICE L. FRENT

ist Democrats who frustrated efforts to reduce tariff rates. In the House vote on the tariff bill of 1884, forty-one Democrats and a united Republican vote were enough to defeat the measure.

President Grover Cleveland made tariff reduction a major issue in the 1888 campaign. His message to the Congress in December 1887 was devoted almost entirely to a plea for a reduction of rates, especially the removal of duties on raw materials. The focus of the campaign was on the Democrats' opposition to protective tariffs. This polarized the parties on the issue to a degree greater than at any time since the Civil War. Accordingly, the Republicans regarded their victory in the 1888 presidential race as a victory for protective tariffs. The McKinley Act of 1890 returned the country to higher protective tariffs.

The election of 1890 returned a three-to-one Democratic majority to the House. Even protectionist Republican bastions such as Ohio, Illinois, Massachusetts, and Michigan gave Democrats the majority in their House delegations. The tariff question was a key issue in the campaign. While many issues were involved in the election, tariffs continued to divide the parties. Cleveland returned to the White House in the 1892 election, this time with his party in control of both houses.

The Wilson-Gorman Act of 1894 was a moderate step in the direction of tariff reduction. The House bill contained significant tariff reductions, but in the Senate some Democrats and a few Populists bargained for protectionist amendments, which prevailed in conference over President Cleveland's strong opposition. Cleveland let the bill become law without his signature.

After the enactment of the Wilson-Gorman Act, the issues of free silver and the gold standard, the Spanish-American War and imperialism, and business trusts replaced tariffs as dominant political concerns. The Republicans regained a majority in the House in 1896, and William McKinley was elected president. Congress then passed the Dingley Tariff Act in 1897, which in all important respects represented a return to the protectionist policies of 1890. But the war with Spain negated its effect, and no new changes were attempted until 1909. The Dingley tariff thus remained in effect for twelve years, longer than any other until the enactment of the Reciprocal Trade Act of 1934.

The Republicans remained in power, but adopted a new trade doctrine in their 1908 platform. They attempted to establish a "true principle" of tariff rates as "the difference between cost of production at home and abroad together with a reasonable profit to American industries." But the Payne-Aldrich Act of 1909 reflected the fact that members of Congress could come to no universal agreement as to the precise meaning of the "true principle." Payne-Aldrich introduced a system of minimum and maximum rates, authorizing the president to "retaliate" within limits against discriminatory rates established by other countries. A Tariff Board was created to advise the president on this new authority.

Rep. Sereno E. Payne (R-N.Y.), though a protectionist, was a moderate on the issue, but Sen. Nelson W. Aldrich (R-R.I.), who chaired the Senate Finance Committee, was an unflinching protectionist—not to mention a very strong personality. Aldrich's dominance created the danger that unreasonable rates would emerge from the conference committee. Up to this point, President William Howard Taft had refrained from direct intervention, but, having pledged during his campaign to revise rates downward, he now faced the prospect of vetoing a Republican bill. At the last moment he urged a reduction in duties. This effort moderated the product of the conference committee. Although still protectionist, the Payne-Aldrich Act was less so than previous Republican measures had been.

The Republicans were defeated in the congressional elections of 1910, and Democrat Woodrow Wilson was elected president in 1912. Each party reaffirmed its position on trade, and made it a major part of its program; therefore, the results in 1912 were interpreted as a mandate for lower tariffs. The Democrats responded with the Underwood Tariff Act of 1913. President Wilson and Ways and Means Committee chairman Oscar W. Underwood (D-Ala.) provided the leadership that united the Democrats on the tariff issue. This time most Senate amendments were for lowered rates. The key words in the debate were *legitimate* industries and *competitive* rates of duty—which meant tariff rates that would permit both foreign and domestic industries to compete. Sugar and wool ended up on the free list; the rates on woolen and cotton goods were reduced drastically.

World War I intervened before the results of the Underwood tariff could be measured. The demand abroad for American goods was enormous, and the supply of imports from other manufacturing nations all but dried up. The tariff laws were not changed (as had been done during the Civil War), partly because no considerable revenue could be obtained from tariff duties.

During the war years and the decade that followed, American manufacturing grew rapidly. The creation of many new industries reinforced public pressure to establish protective tariffs. At the same time, agricultural commodity prices fell drastically. These two developments made the decade of the 1920s notable for its protectionist policies. Western agriculture became protectionist as the prices of wheat, corn, cotton, and meats fell by half or more in the years following the war.

The first result was the Tariff Act of 1922. Duties went up across the board on agricultural products. Woolen-goods rates were restored. Cotton duties returned with rates that increased for the finer grades. Iron and steel imports were increased; chinaware went up 60 percent. The war-created U.S. toy industry (Germany had been the leading prewar source) benefited from a 70 percent duty rate. Similarly situated, lace window-curtain manufactures were sheltered by a 90 percent tariff. Coal tar and dyestuffs, which had come almost exclusively from Germany before the war, also benefited from high duties.

The Smoot-Hawley Act, signed by President Herbert Hoover in 1930, raised average duties to their highest levels ever: 60 percent of the value of the products imported. Once again, a major tariff bill was the product of congressional horse trading, with little regard for the larger national interest. Smoot-Hawley triggered widespread retaliation from overseas trading partners, and this worldwide protectionism contributed to the Great Depression. To this day, Smoot-Hawley is cited by free-trade advocates as an example of the drastic impact that beggar-thy-neighbor protectionism can have.

Throughout this period the Ways and Means Committee consisted of fifteen majority-party members and ten minority-party members, a ratio that prevailed until the 1970s. In 1930 the Republicans controlled the Congress, and each Republican on the committee was the chairman of a subcommittee that considered a particular schedule: wool, textiles, metals, and so on. Each subcommittee's chairman tended to be from the area identified with its product of concern. This created a natural structure for vote-trading on particular schedules. Such vote-trading characterized the Smoot-Hawley deliberations to a high degree and met little or no resistance from President Hoover.

Smoot-Hawley's provisions were extreme. Duties were raised to 60 percent of the value of all imports—the highest in U.S. history. Hoover was urged by more than a thousand economists and other opinion leaders to veto the bill. But since he had taken no firm stand while the Republican Congress wrote the bill, he had no political grounds for a veto.

New Deal to New Frontier: Reciprocal Trade Reductions. The coming of the New Deal in 1933 marked a turning point in American trade policy. President Franklin D. Roosevelt was initially reluctant to grant Secretary of State Cordell Hull the authority to negotiate reciprocal trade agreements without ex post facto approval by Congress. Roosevelt was sensitive to Congress's prerogatives on tariff legislation and to the fact that protectionist sentiments, in the face of a 25 percent national unemployment rate, were strong. But by December 1933 Roosevelt had changed his mind, and he put forward the Reciprocal Trade Act of 1934. Congress passed this measure by lopsided (though partisan) majorities. The act granted the executive considerably more flexibility in carrying out tariff agreements.

Most Republicans continued to oppose the reciprocal trade program, whose major purpose was to facilitate the lowering of tariffs. They also began to oppose it as oriented too far toward the policies of the internationalists in the State Department. Yet the 1936 Republican platform supported a flexible (and upwardly adjustable) tariff that vested the executive with a good deal of discretion in negotiating agreements.

Between 1934 and 1945 Congress did not significantly alter trade agreement legislation. The president's discretionary authority was extended for three years in 1937 and again in 1940 and 1943. After the end of World War II, international concerns entered more fully into the ongoing tariff debate. The Republicans began to argue for a "genuine" program of reciprocity that would not use trade policy as an instrument of foreign policy.

Early in 1945, the House of Representatives created the special Committee on Post War Economic Policy and Planning (the Colmer Committee). It met at the same time that the House Ways and Means Committee was holding hearings on the renewal of the Reciprocal Trade Agreement Act. The Colmer Committee recommended renewal of the trade agreements program and an increase in the president's authority. Ways and Means agreed and reported a bill granting the president authority to cut rates by 50 percent from their value in force as of 1 January 1945, replacing the previous 1934 base. The Republicans supported a more restricted version of reciprocal trade, but the Democratic version prevailed. The final vote for the first time demonstrated significant Republican support for the concept of reciprocal concessions. Eighteen Republicans voted for, and 14 against, the measure in the Senate; 155 Republicans voted for it and 52 against it in the House.

After the 1945 act, the United States and Great Britain began to develop an international system to reduce tariffs. This led to a State Department proposal for the establishment of an International Trade Organization (ITO). Meetings held in Geneva in 1947 created the General Agreement on Tariffs and Trade (GATT). GATT was never ratified by Congress, but the United States continued to participate under the executive authority of the president.

The 1946 elections resulted in Republican majorities in both houses of Congress. Harold Knudson (R-Minn.), an ardent old-line protectionist, became chairman of the Ways and Means Committee. President Harry S. Truman tried to blunt protectionist pressures by issuing Executive Order 9832, which provided for the inclusion of an "escape clause" in all trade agreements, thus allowing the United States to retract any concessions that injured or threatened injury to domestic manufacturers. The Republican Congress did not, however, significantly alter the basic framework of the Reciprocal Trade Program.

Soon after Congress renewed the program for one year in 1948, national elections returned the legislature to Democratic control, and Truman won reelection to the presidency. Truman now recommended that Congress renew his reciprocal trade authority for three years. The Ways and Means Committee reported a bill embodying Truman's wishes, but an open rule permitting floor amendments was adopted. This resulted in (1) restoration of the "escape clause" and the "peril point" provision (which set a rate below which the president could not negotiate), (2) restrictions on trade with the Soviet Union, and (3) limits on trade concessions for price-supported agricultural products. The Senate followed suit, and both houses passed a two-year extension by lopsided majorities.

Dwight D. Eisenhower's election to the presidency in 1952, along with the majorities that the Republicans gained in both houses, provided the Republicans with their first opportunity since Smoot-Hawley to devise a trade policy under the leadership of a Republican president. The direction of Republican policy was uncertain. Eisenhower had campaigned for trade expansion, and the Republican platforms of 1948 and 1952 offered in-

creasing support for the Reciprocal Trade Program. The Republican position was to favor reciprocal trade, but with more restrictions than the Democrats wanted. At the same time, strong protectionists led by Sen. Eugene Milliken (R-Colo.) and Rep. Daniel A. Reed (R-N.Y.) remained influential on trade policy.

Before he left office, Truman had appointed the all-private Bell Commission, chaired by Daniel Bell, president of the American Securities & Trust Company, to examine U.S. trade policy. This commission reported to President Eisenhower, recommending a wide-ranging liberalization of trade policy in the national interest and opposing efforts aimed at promoting the "interest of particular industries and groups."

Eisenhower cautiously recommended a one year-extension of the Reciprocal Trade Program. The Ways and Means Committee under Chairman Reed reported the protectionist Simpson bill, which would have established quotas on oil and other imports but not have granted any new trade negotiating authority. A deal was struck: Eisenhower agreed to expand the Tariff Commission from six to seven members, making it a more partisan body, and to appoint a prominent protectionist spokesman, Joseph Talbot, to the new slot. He also agreed to the creation of the new Foreign Economic Policy Commission (the Randall Commission). In return, Eisenhower was granted a one-year extension of the executive negotiating authority. These developments reflected the tensions generated by a Republican Congress in transition from the older trade policy of committed protectionism to the support of open trade in the 1960s and 1970s.

The Democrats regained a congressional majority in the 1954 election. The new party leaders, Speaker Sam Rayburn (Tex.) in the House and Majority Leader Lyndon B. Johnson (Tex.) in the Senate, were strong advocates of freer trade and the Reciprocal Trade Program. Rep. Jere Cooper (D-Tenn.), the new Ways and Means chairman, was also a strong free trader, as was Sen. Harry Flood Byrd, Sr. (D-Va.), the new chairman of the Senate Finance Committee.

In striking contrast to the 1953–1954 experience, these new leaders seized the initiative on the first day of the 84th Congress with H.R. 1, a major trade bill. Hearings commenced in January 1955. A bill was reported out of Ways and Means in February by a vote of 20 to 5. The House initially voted against a closed rule prohibiting amendments (which was essential to the bill's passage in its orig-

THE TARIFF QUESTION. Cartoon portraying the belief that government surplus, considered an economic ill at times during the nineteenth century, was a product of high tariffs. The caption reads: "The opening of the congressional session. The Tariff Monster.—Here I am again! What are you going to do with me?" Lithograph by J. Keppler, *Puck,* 7 December 1887.

LIBRARY OF CONGRESS

inal form), but Speaker Rayburn took the floor and saw to it that several members "corrected" their votes. The closed rule was finally adopted by a one-vote margin, in a striking demonstration of Rayburn's legendary leadership ability.

Motions to recommit the bill revealed the breakdown of southern support for freer trade, as textile industry opposition to trade agreements grew. No region was overwhelmingly committed to either position, however. Party divisions, though still strong, also were increasingly blurred. On the Reed motion to recommit, 66 Republicans voted against (and thus in support of the trade bill), while 119 voted for (thus opposing the bill).

In 1958, when the Reciprocal Trade Act expired, President Eisenhower asked for a five-year extension and for increased authority to lower or increase tariffs and to make peril-point Tariff Commission actions mandatory. Significant shifts occurred in the patterns of sectional voting on

House motions to recommit this bill. The South remained evenly divided, but in contrast to 1955, all other regions of the country joined in support of freer trade. Majorities of both parties opposed recommittal (Democrats, 160 to 61; Republicans, 108 to 85). The final result was a four-year extension of the Trade Act with a 20 percent tariff-cutting authority granted to the president.

The emergence of Japan as a major competitor and the creation of the European Economic Community (EEC; later known as the European Community, or EC) began to have an impact on trade policy in the late 1950s. Multinational trade negotiations became even more complex in the 1960s with the emergence of regional trading blocs and growing efforts to harmonize trade policies within them. The Trade Expansion Act of 1962 represented an extension of the basic principles of the Reciprocal Trade Agreement Program. The new law paved the way for the eventual conclusion of the

Kennedy Round of international trade negotiations. But this growing commitment to trade liberalization had to deal with the growing protectionist claim that imports jeopardized the position of established U.S. manufacturers.

In the early 1960s the textile industry, important in most southern and New England states, could claim significant influence over nearly a hundred members of Congress. Soon after President John F. Kennedy took office in 1961, the administration began looking for ways to satisfy the demands of the textile industry through other than legislative channels. On 22 March 1961, textile industry representatives met with sixty House members. They appointed a fifteen-member constituent body to press certain demands on the administration, including the imposition of textile import quotas. Rep. Carl Vinson (D-Ga.) headed this group. Following a meeting with President Kennedy on 27 March, an impressive show of protectionist strength was organized in the House. On 18 April 1961, forty-eight Democrats and twenty-two Republicans rose to speak on the House floor in favor of imposing textile quotas. This concerted effort led to the administration's negotiation of a textile quota arrangement, the Multifiber Agreement, under GATT auspices. The textile bloc split fairly evenly on the key vote of the Trade Expansion Act, but those who supported the administration had threatened not to do so unless textiles were granted concessions.

Labor's support for a new tariff act also was contingent on aid to workers displaced in import-sensitive industries. In consequence, the 1962 trade bill before the Committee on Ways and Means contained a unique mechanism for providing relief to communities, industries, and workers injured by particular trade agreements. The legislation was supported by President Kennedy on broad policy grounds. The considerations weighing on Kennedy were several: (1) the growth of the European Economic Community (or Common Market) and of Japan and the need to open European and Japanese markets to U.S. exporters, (2) the need for new markets for the products of developing nations, (3) the necessity to offset the communist "trade-and-aid" offensive, (4) the growing pressures of the United States' negative balance of payments, and (5) the need to accelerate U.S. economic growth through increased trade.

The trade bill was reported out by the Ways and Means Committee in June 1962. The bill granted the executive authority to cut tariffs across the board rather than on a product-by-product basis. It also advanced adjustment assistance as an alternative to protectionist relief from import competition, and it created a new office, that of special representative for trade negotiations, to coordinate and conduct trade diplomacy. Opposition to the bill came primarily from midwestern representatives, and it passed handily in the fall of 1962 by votes of 298 to 125 in the House and 78 to 8 in the Senate.

The focus of trade policy for the remainder of the 1960s was on negotiating the so-called Kennedy Round of trade talks authorized by the Trade Expansion Act of 1962. At the same time, efforts to achieve statutory (as opposed to negotiated) restrictions on textile imports continued. In 1968, Sen. Ernest F. Hollings (D-S.C.) proposed an amendment to a tax bill to establish mandatory quotas for textile products and apparel. The Senate approved the amendment. It eventually failed to be enacted when Ways and Means Committee chairman Wilbur D. Mills (D-Ark.), in alliance with President Lyndon Johnson, insisted that the Senate action violated the constitutional requirement that such provisions originate in the House.

Trade Policy since the 1970s. The U.S. approach to trade negotiations from the 1970s on was heavily influenced by the nation's trade deficit, which began to mount in the early years of the decade and peaked at $152 billion in 1987. This development led to increased congressional activism on trade policy and to a reassertion of some of the authority that Congress had delegated to the executive under the 1934 Reciprocal Trade Act.

Pressures increased as the result of import competition in automobiles, steel, and textiles. Unfair foreign competition was thought to be a major factor for growing import penetration. While a concern for international economic interdependence still figured in congressional trade debates, the focus shifted from further liberalization of trade under GATT to the need to open foreign markets. At the same time, pressures mounted for the protection of threatened domestic industries under the mantle of some form of a national industrial policy.

Increasing dissatisfaction with GATT's ability to address trade grievances and, in particular, resentment of Japan's industrial practices triggered a host of reciprocity and other restrictionist bills in the 1970s and 1980s. These bills advocated unilateral changes in U.S. policy without negotiations for balanced concessions under GATT procedures. As the United States' dominant position in world trade was increasingly challenged by Japan and the EC countries in high-tech, high-value products, con-

Landmark Tariff Legislation

Title	Year Enacted	Reference Number	Description
Tariff Act of 4 July 1789	1789	1 Stat. 24	First tariff act; primarily a revenue measure.
Tariff Act of 27 April 1816	1816	3 Stat. 310	First primarily protective tariff.
Tariff Act of 22 May 1824	1824	4 Stat. 25	First relatively high protective tariff; raised high wage abroad argument.
Tariff Act of 19 May 1828 (Tariff of Abominations)	1828	4 Stat. 270	Highest protective tariff; example of horse-trading rates upward.
Tariff Act of 14 July 1832	1832	4 Stat. 583	Restored rates of 1824 act; triggered the nullification controversy.
Tariff Act of 2 March 1833 (Compromise Tariff)	1833	4 Stat. 632	Gradual step-by-step reduction of all protective rates.
Tariff Act of 30 August 1842 (Black Tariff)	1842	5 Stat. 548	Restored protective rates of 1831 act.
Tariff Act of 30 July 1846 (Walker Tariff)	1846	9 Stat. 42	Reduced or canceled most high protective tariffs; established an extensive free list.
Tariff Act of 3 March 1857	1857	11 Stat. 192	Further reduced tariffs.
Tariff Act of 2 March 1861 (Morrill Tariff)	1861	12 Stat. 178, sec. 5 et seq.	Imposed protective duties on many commodities; set stage for high revenue tariffs during Civil War.
Tariff Act of 6 June 1872	1872	17 Stat. 230, secs. 1–11	10 percent reduction of post–Civil War tariffs, repealed in 1875.
Tariff Act of 3 March 1883 (Mongrel Tariff)	1883	22 Stat. 488	Some reduction in rates, but preserved basic protective structure.
Tariff Act of 1 October 1890 (McKinley Tariff)	1890	26 Stat. 567	Extended and increased scope of protection.
Tariff Act of 27 August 1894 (Wilson-Gorman Tariff)	1894	28 Stat. 509	Mild downward revision of rates.
Tariff Act of 24 July 1897 (Dingley Tariff)	1897	30 Stat. 151	Set rates at McKinley Tariff levels or higher on most commodities.
Tariff Act of 5 August 1909 (Payne-Aldrich Tariff)	1909	36 Stat. 11	Revision of rates, but no basic change in protection; maximum and minimum schedules introduced.
Tariff Act of 3 October 1913 (Underwood-Simmons Tariff)	1913	38 Stat. 114	First major downward revision of rates since the Civil War.
Act of 8 September 1916	1916	39 Stat. 756	Title VII established U.S. Tariff Commission.
Tariff Act of 21 September 1922 (Fordney-McCumber Tariff)	1922	42 Stat. 858	Restoration of protective rates similar to those of 1897 act; included flexible-tariff provisions. U.S. Tariff Commission assigned duty of investigating flexible-tariff cases, unfair practices, and discrimination.
Tariff Act of 17 June 1930 (Smoot-Hawley Tariff)	1930	46 Stat. 590	Highest protective rates in U.S. history. Reorganized U.S. Tariff Commission, increased scope of flexible-tariff work.
Reciprocal Trade Agreements Act (Act to Amend the Tariff Act of 1930)	1934	48 Stat. 943	Authorized president to negotiate reciprocal trade agreements and reduce rates of Smoot-Hawley schedules by 50 percent.

Landmark Tariff Legislation (Continued)

TITLE	YEAR ENACTED	REFERENCE NUMBER	DESCRIPTION
Resolution of 1 March 1937	1937	50 Stat. 24	Negotiating authority extended for 3 years.
Resolution of 12 April 1940	1940	54 Stat. 107	Negotiating authority extended for 3 years.
Resolution of 7 June 1943	1943	57 Stat. 125	Negotiating authority extended for 2 years.
Trade Agreements Extension Act of 5 July 1945	1945	59 Stat. 410	Negotiating authority extended for 3 years; president could reduce any existing tariff rate by 50 percent.
Trade Agreements Extension Act of 26 June 1948	1948	62 Stat. 1053	Negotiating authority extended for 1 year (U.S. Tariff Commission to designate peril points).
Trade Agreements Extension Act of 26 September 1949	1949	63 Stat. 697	Negotiating authority extended for 2 years (peril-point provision repealed).
Trade Agreements Extension Act of 16 June 1951	1951	65 Stat. 72	Negotiating authority extended for 2 years (peril-point provision restored, U.S. Tariff Commission ordered to investigate escape-clause cases).
Trade Agreements Extension Act of 7 August 1953	1951	67 Stat. 472	Negotiating authority extended for 1 year.
Trade Agreements Extension Act of 1 July 1954	1954	68 Stat. 360	Negotiating authority extended for 1 year.
Trade Agreements Extension Act of 21 June 1955	1955	69 Stat. 162	Negotiating authority extended for 3 years.
Trade Agreements Extension Act of 20 August 1958	1958	P.L. 85-686	Negotiating authority extended for 4 years.
Tariff Classification Act of 24 May 1962	1962	P.L. 87-794	U.S. Tariff Commission ordered to prepare Tariff Schedules of the United States.
Trade Expansion Act of 11 October 1962	1962	P.L. 87-618	Negotiating authority extended for 5 years; adjustment-assistance provisions to protect firms and workers from foreign competition. U.S. Tariff Commission to report on probable economic effects of concessions and to handle adjustment-assistance cases.
Trade Act of 1974	1975	P.L. 93-618	Negotiating authority extended for 5 years. U.S. Tariff Commission renamed U.S. International Trade Commission, given greater independence from executive branch, ordered to issue probable economic effects statements and to handle relief cases under expanded mandate. Broad authority to president to reduce duties and barriers, provide relief for industries injured by imports, retaliate against discriminating foreign countries, and provide duty-free treatment for imports from less developed countries.
Trade Agreement Extension Act of 1979	1979	P.L. 96-39	Incorporated rules from Tokyo Round into U.S. law. Rewrote antidumping and countervailing duty laws.
Trade and Tariff Act of 1984	1984	P.L. 98-573	Strengthened antidumping to countervailing duty laws, established goals for negotiations in services, reduced barriers to foreign investment and high-tech trade.

Landmark Tariff Legislation (Continued)

TITLE	YEAR ENACTED	REFERENCE NUMBER	DESCRIPTION
Omnibus Trade and Competitiveness Act of 1988	1988	P.L. 100-418	Revised president's authority on export controls, expanded enforcement authority of Commerce and Customer Service, decontrolled certain exports and liberalized licensing. Provided authority to negotiate Uruguay Round of GATT.
North American Free Trade Agreement Implementation Act	1993	P.L. 103-182	Implemented the necessary changes in U.S. statutory law to comply with the North American Free Trade Agreement (NAFTA).

gressional opinion in both parties started shifting toward reciprocity on a bilateral basis as opposed to multilateral reciprocal reductions in trade barriers.

The 1974 Trade Act required more consultations with Congress, set precise negotiating objectives—both tariff and nontariff—and reserved to the legislature the power to implement nontariff changes. "Fast-track" procedures involved the Congress in trade negotiations in a more direct fashion. These required executive-legislative cooperation in devising legislation to implement negotiations, and forced a straight yea or nay vote on the overall package presented by the administration within sixty days of its submission to Congress.

The 1974 act was a result of several years of intense debate. The Tariff Commission was renamed the U.S. International Trade Commission, a title that reflected the fact that tariffs were becoming less important in defining U.S. trade policy in negotiations over the growing use of nontariff barriers. The 1974 act also extended for five years the executive branch's authority to conduct the multilateral negotiations that became known as the Tokyo Round.

In the 1984 Trade Act, Congress (under sec. 301) mandated the executive branch to compile an annual inventory of major foreign barriers to U.S. trade, along with an estimate of their costs to the U.S. economy and a plan of action to correct them. Although this provision was designed to put pressure on the administration to act, only eight country- and product-specific cases were brought between 1985 and 1988. Congress reacted in 1988 by passing the so-called Super 301 provision, which mandated the U.S. trade representative to initiate investigations of unfair foreign traders' practices—with a view toward corrective measures.

Congress on its own initiative passed the Omnibus Trade and Competitiveness Act of 1988. This was the result of a series of efforts in 1985 and 1986 to impose restrictions on textile imports sponsored by Senator Hollings and Rep. Ed Jenkins (D-Ga.), an effort frustrated by presidential vetoes. Sen. John Danforth (R-Mo.) also attempted to enhance "reciprocity" on telecommunications products in a bill that was reported out of the Senate Finance Committee but that went no further. More directly, Senator Danforth, supported by a bipartisan group of thirty-three senators, introduced an omnibus trade bill in 1985. On the House side, the Democratic leadership initiated a campaign to make trade a top priority. These actions led the Ways and Means Committee to report out a bill that would have curbed presidential discretion in trade remedy cases and mandated retaliation when other nations failed to open their markets. The House adopted the famous "Gephardt amendment," named for Rep. Richard A. Gephardt (D-Mo.), which mandated establishing quotas for countries running large trade surpluses with the United States.

The bill passed the House by a bipartisan vote of 295 to 115, but it was opposed by the Reagan administration, which viewed it as "pure protectionism" and a step toward unilateralism that would establish standards for fair trade not sanctioned by the GATT rules. Many Senate Republicans, despite President Ronald Reagan's opposition, supported Senator Danforth and joined most Democrats in support of the bill. Because of a crowded Senate schedule and the president's opposition, however, the bill died in the Senate in 1987.

President Reagan needed an extension of fast-track authority in order to proceed with the Uruguay Round of multilateral trade negotiations that had been initiated in September of 1987. But the Democratic House did not proceed with the administration proposals. Instead, it took up H.R. 3, a measure similar to its 1986 effort. The Gephardt amendment was dropped in Ways and Means in an effort to produce a more moderate bill. But Representative Gephardt obtained a rule permitting consideration of his amendment on the floor, and it prevailed by a vote of 218 to 214.

The Senate Finance Committee, chaired by Lloyd Bentsen (D-Tex.), took the lead in reporting the bill, with a 19-to-1 bipartisan vote. In the Senate version the Gephardt amendment was dropped, new procedures were imposed on the fast-track authority for the Uruguay Round, and retaliation against unfair foreign trade practices was mandated. The bill was combined with provisions reported by eight other Senate committees and passed the Senate by a vote of 71 to 27.

An alternative to the Gephardt amendment, mandating the U.S. trade representative to designate countries that maintained patterns of unfair trade restrictions—the so-called Super 301 provision—prevailed. After a series of compromises with the administration, Congress passed the 1988 act by lopsided majorities of 312 to 107 in the House and 63 to 36 in the Senate. President Reagan vetoed the bill, citing a provision requiring notification of plant closings that had been included by the Senate Labor and Education Committee and an obscure provision relating to Alaskan oil. The bill appeared to be dead. But the Democratic-controlled Congress, repassed the bill without the provisions mentioned in the president's veto message, and this version became law as the Omnibus Trade and Competitiveness Act of 1988.

The role of key leaders in Congress was central to trade legislation in the 1970s and 1980s. In a period when labor, some agricultural groups, and specific industrial sectors (automobiles, steel, textiles, semiconductors) were opposed to trade concessions, increasing numbers of Democrats supported unilateral efforts to deal with trade disparities.

As a majority of Democrats moved toward this position, the role of the Democratic chairmen of the House Ways and Means and the Senate Finance committees became critical. In the 1960s and early 1970s, Ways and Means chairman Mills dominated trade policy in the House, playing an essential role in the passage of the 1974 act. In the 1980s, Chairman Dan Rostenkowski (D-Ill.) continued to support trade negotiating authority and opposed protectionist measures in the face of growing opposition in his own caucus. With the support of Rep. Sam M. Gibbons (D-Fla.), chairman of the Trade Subcommittee, Rostenkowski took the lead in the effort to enact the Trade Act of 1984 and the Omnibus Trade Act of 1988. They also led the 1991 fight to extend fast-track authority, permitting congressional approval of trade agreements without extraneous, crippling amendments.

Most of the business community, particularly the manufacturing and service sectors, has favored open trade. Their allies in the Reagan and Bush administrations and the Republicans on Capitol Hill led the way to promote open trade in the 1980s. Many senior Democrats, who were in the old Democratic tradition of free-trade advocacy, joined with the majority of Republicans to offset growing protectionist pressures—particularly among Democrats—that were reviving during this period.

The development of regional trade blocs throughout the world—a more integrated EC, Japanese efforts at regionalism in East Asia, various agreements in South America, and U.S. attempts to negotiate a North American Free Trade Agreement (NAFTA)—had the potential to threaten the fairly effective GATT efforts to open markets globally and to maintain international rules. The increasing focus on nontariff barriers, both real and perceived, led to "reciprocity" measures promoted by many in Congress as means of achieving "fair" trade. These efforts stood the chance of fundamentally reorienting U.S. trade law, away from a system based on reciprocal agreements aiming at trade reductions under international disciplines and toward one of bilateral arrangements aimed at trade restrictions. The principal author of these proposals during the early 1990s, House Majority Leader Gephardt, sought to force a closer balance in U.S. trade accounts with other nations, principally Japan. These measures were supported by the most embattled sectors of U.S. industry (automobiles, steel, textiles), by the labor movement, and by economists who believed that industrial policies were necessary to achieve greater control over U.S. economic policy in an era of increasing global competition. How this debate played out would determine U.S.—and indeed global—economic trade development in the twenty-first century.

Almost from the time that political parties began to function in the United States, party divisions over tariff matters have provided a focal point for the resolution of trade policy questions. The Whigs and their Republican successors were the advocates of protection, whereas Democrats were traditionally "free traders."

These partisan divisions substantially blurred as the influence of the textile industries in the South and oil interests in the Southwest brought many

Figure 1
Percent of Federal Revenue Generated by Customs Duties[1]

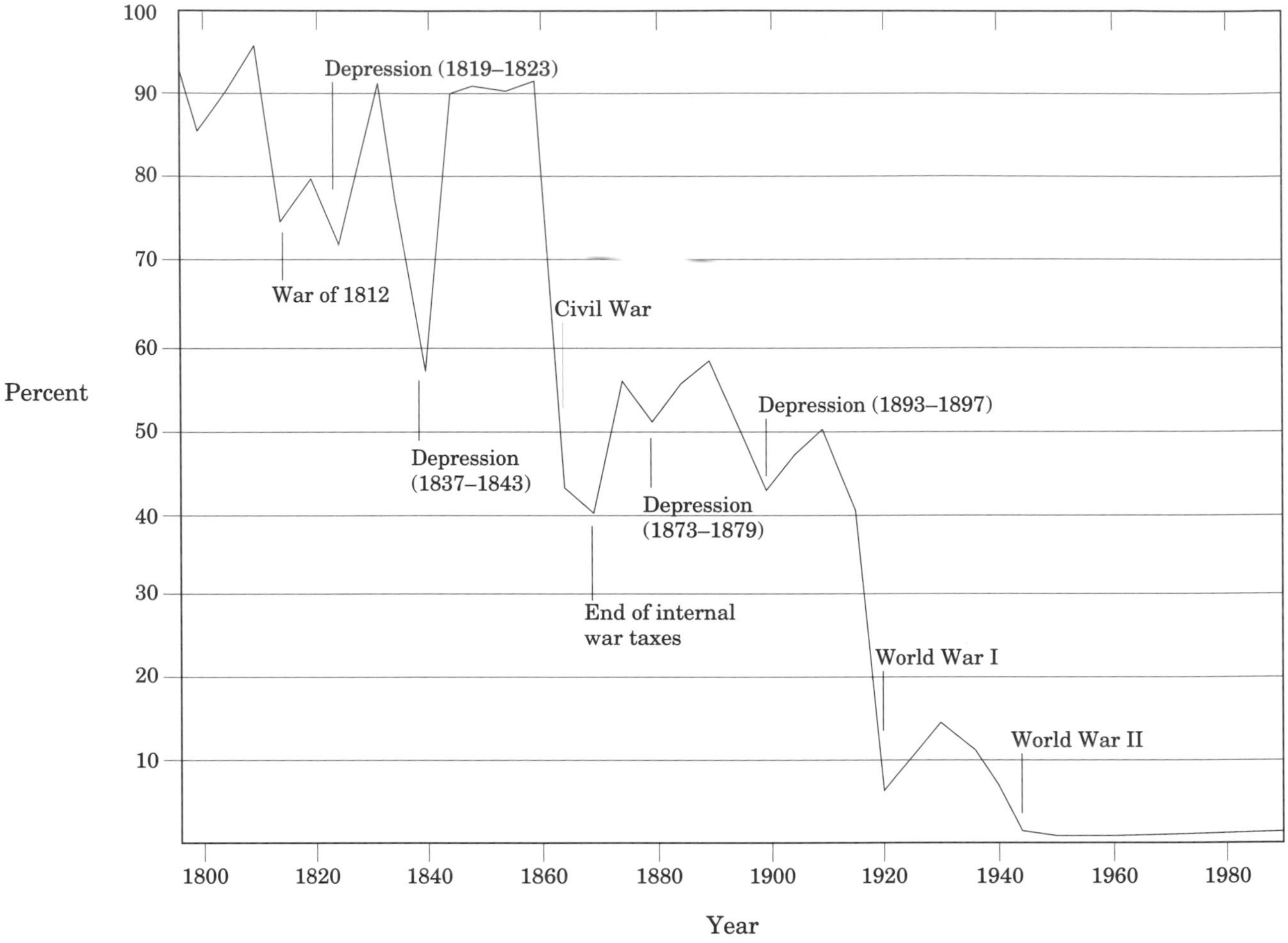

[1]Each break denotes an average of five years preceding that date (e.g., point at 1800 is the average percent for the period 1796–1800).

SOURCE: John M. Dobson, *Two Centuries of Tariff: The Background and Emergence of the United States International Trade Commission*, International Trade Commission, 1976.

Democrats to a more protectionist position. This trend accelerated as large labor unions representing workers in the textile, automobile, and steel industries felt threatened by increased imports from abroad and in consequence adopted protectionist positions. Auto- and steelworker unions supported a major expansionist trade bill as late as 1962; by the 1970s, they had reversed their position. In 1992, the Democrats were split, with most following Majority Leader Gephardt in supporting more restrictive measures.

The protectionist trend of congressional Democrats continued with the NAFTA debate. A wide margin of Democrats (156 to 102) led by Majority Leader Gephardt opposed President Bill Clinton on NAFTA. Clinton, however, followed the tradition of all Democratic presidents since Jackson, and supported the trade opening provisions of NAFTA.

As American business interests shifted to global concerns and manufacturing exports rose in the 1940s and later, the orientation of Republicans also shifted. An "internationalist" wing of the party emerged from 1940 through 1960: presidential candidates Wendell Willkie, Thomas Dewey, Dwight D. Eisenhower, and Richard M. Nixon gradually shifted the Republican party toward a moderate stance that favored more open trade. A preponderance of Republicans now support freer trade.

Sectionalism began to lose its force as a major determinant of American trade policy. From before the Civil War until the New Deal, the South was the center of free-trade sentiment, while the Northeast and the West were the major strongholds of protectionism. The South has shifted toward a protectionist stance since the 1950s. Today, the major regions of the nation are rather evenly divided in their support of and opposition to measures liberalizing trade.

In the 1960s, as barriers other than tariffs began to dominate trade negotiations, the need for a closer relationship between Congress and the executive became apparent. Changes in nontariff barriers involved the need to alter domestic laws, which only Congress could do. Yet the executive had to have reasonable assurance that what it negotiated with other nations could be implemented. The fast-track authority initially passed in the 1974 Trade Act was a procedure designed to permit the executive to negotiate nontariff barriers—that is, government trade restrictions covered by legislation—with some assurance that Congress would enact the needed legislative changes without deal-breaking amendments. All trade agreements since 1974 have been implemented under fast-track authority, including NAFTA and the Uruguay Round.

The future of trade policy will be influenced by its past. But the United States in the early 1990s may be at another turning point, when existing international institutions are no longer able to accommodate new challenges. Whether the United States would sustain the current worldwide effort at negotiations under GATT, or concentrate on regional bloc negotiations, or seek some combination of approaches remained an open question.

[*See also* Finance Committee, Senate; Hawley-Smoot Tariff Act; McKinley Tariff Act; Ways and Means Committee, House.]

BIBLIOGRAPHY

Barrie, Robert W. *Congress and the Executive: The Making of U.S. Foreign Trade Policy, 1789–1986.* 1987.
Destler, I. M. *American Trade Politics.* 2d ed. 1992.
Meier, Gerald. *Problems of Trade Policy.* 1973.
Ratner, Sidney. *The Tariff in American History.* 1972.
Schattschneider, E. E. *Politics, Pressures and the Tariff: A Study of Free Enterprise in Pressure Politics, as Shown in the 1929–1930 Revision of the Tariff.* 1935.
Stanwood, Edward. *American Tariff Controversies in the Nineteenth Century.* 1903.
Taussig, G. W. *The Tariff History of the United States.* 7th ed. 1922.
Terrill, Tom E. *The Tariff, Politics, and American Foreign Policy, 1874–1901.* 1973.

ROBERT W. BARRIE

TAXATION. Taxation was a critical issue in American public policy even before the formal birth of the nation. As the country developed and the government expanded in powers and presence, taxes remained a foremost issue. The key questions have been what taxes should be levied, how much the government should tax, and who should bear the greatest tax burden.

Historical Overview. Pivotal in igniting the American Revolution was the perception held by many colonial Americans that British taxation of the colonies was unfair. The Boston Tea Party, a protest over import duties placed on tea, is the most famous expression of their grievance. During and after the Revolutionary War the absence of a national power to tax became a critical issue. Under the Articles of Confederation, which were replaced by the Constitution in 1789, the national government lacked this power and had to rely on voluntary contributions from the individual states. The accumulated national debt and the continuing threat from foreign powers required a central source of revenue for the new nation.

That source was secured in Article I, section 8 of the Constitution: "The Congress shall have the Power To lay and collect Taxes, Duties, Imposts and Excises, to pay the Debts and provide for the common Defence and general Welfare of the United States; but all Duties, Imposts and Excises shall be uniform throughout the United States." To ensure that taxation would be subject to the broadest representation of interests, the Constitution also specified that all revenue bills must originate in the House of Representatives, not in the Senate or the executive branch.

From the earliest colonial days the sources of tax revenue were relatively few, but some have endured for more than three centuries. The most significant tax levied in the colonies was on property. In most colonies, and later in the states, the tax was levied on land and buildings but also on personal property such as livestock, carriages, and even household goods. Tax collection was local. Most people lived in small communities, and it was relatively easy to assess or simply list such property. Although personal property taxes lasted in some states into the twentieth century, as communities became larger and household goods and property became more complex these taxes were dropped in most states. Property tax, which is still the largest source of local tax revenue, was essentially limited to land and buildings.

The colonies and towns also taxed consumption,

through excise taxes on such products as liquor and tobacco. Poll taxes, levied on those who voted, were also used from the very beginning and only died out in the 1960s when they were held to be unconstitutional barriers to voting rights. Initially, poll taxes were conceived of as proper payment for the right of democratic participation. They were also an easy form of revenue to collect: put your money in the box and get a ballot.

Income taxes also began in a strange form during the colonial period. Several of the colonies had what they termed *faculty taxes*. Although definitions varied from colony to colony, the idea was to tax the potential of people to earn money. One of the original colonies at New Plymouth (Massachusetts) promulgated a tax statute in 1643 that taxed its members "according to their estates or faculties, that is, according to goods lands improoued [improved] faculties and psonall [personal] abilities." The idea of taxing potential earning ability has intrigued tax philosophers ever since, but the difficulty in measuring this value led other colonies, such as the Massachusetts Bay Colony, to define the faculty tax as one levied on "returns and gains" from commerce or trading activity, something of a cross between an individual and a business income tax.

As the country developed and the national government began to use its taxing powers as defined in the Constitution, two types of taxes became critical sources of federal revenue and the focus of more than a century of political battles. The lesser of these were excise taxes on consumption of everything from whiskey to tonics. The greater were customs duties on every conceivable imported good. For the first 140 years of the nation's history these two sources of revenue accounted for approximately 90 percent of all taxes collected at the federal level.

National tax policy debates in the first century of the United States centered on these major revenue sources and were shaped by political and geographic divisions. Industry and manufacturing were located primarily in the North and East, with the New England states and large states such as Pennsylvania, New Jersey, and later Ohio established as commercial centers. Because their major competition was foreign commerce, primarily British, these states favored protective tariffs imposing high customs duties on incoming foreign goods.

Additional customs made all goods, both foreign and American, more expensive for consumers. Thus states that were primarily rural and agricultural and that consumed rather than produced manufactured goods generally were against high customs. They were also against tariffs because increasingly they were exporting their crops to Europe and elsewhere. The high U.S. tariffs encouraged foreign powers to pass similar retaliatory tariffs on U.S. products, thus lowering the profits of exporters. The manufacturing states also favored taxing farmland and, if additional revenues were needed, internal consumption (excise taxes). Again, the agricultural states were in hostile opposition.

Thus the battle lines were drawn, with geography playing a major role. The polarization was most evident in the South, which was exporting large quantities of high-quality cotton. The geographic disagreements over tax policy reinforced the more volatile debate over slavery. For most of the period before the Civil War the federal government was controlled by the northern states, and thus high tariffs were erected. The tax battle reached a peak in 1832, when the South Carolina legislature voted to nullify tariff acts passed by Congress in 1828 and 1832. President Andrew Jackson threatened to send troops to South Carolina to enforce customs collection. A compromise reached in early 1833 averted a military confrontation and postponed the Civil War for a number of years.

Tariff and excise tax legislation dominated congressional tax policy until well into the twentieth century. Appropriately, when the permanent income tax was enacted on 13 October 1913, it was as an 8-page amendment to the 814-page Underwood-Simmons Tariff Act. Congressional involvement in tariffs essentially ended in 1934, following a recommendation and executive order establishing the modern system in which tariffs are negotiated periodically by the executive branch and then approved as a major package by Congress. This arrangement, and the resulting abdication of power, was agreed to by Congress because the high duties established by the 1930 Smoot-Hawley Tariff Act were prominently (and probably erroneously) cited as a major contributor to the worldwide depression. By this time, however, the collection of individual and corporate income taxes had replaced tariffs and excise taxes as the primary source of federal revenue.

The first national use of an income tax was during the Civil War. The war created a financial emergency because excise and tariff revenue had dropped precipitously while expenditures had increased sharply. However, the first income tax legislation, passed in July 1861, was never implemented and generated no income. This legislation was revised in 1862 with a slightly progressive rate structure. A second tax, with progressive rates up to 10 percent, was enacted in 1864. Although the tax was bitterly fought on the House and Senate floors, the case for passage was compelling: borrowing, through the sale of government bonds, had created a then-frightening debt of $1.8 billion. The tax raised considerable revenue until its repeal in 1872. The majority of the revenue (70 percent) was raised in the seven New England states and California. These states led the repeal effort, voting 61 to 14 for repeal in the House of Representatives. The thirteen southern and western states, which had paid 10 percent of the income taxes collected, voted 61 to 5 against repeal.

This geo-economic division, pitting the Northeast against the South and West, also determined the support for and reenactment of an income tax in 1894. The movement for the tax was headed by William Jennings Bryan (D-Nebr.), Benton McMillin (D-Tenn.), and Uriel S. Hall (D-Mo.) in the House and two Populists, William V. Allen (Nebr.) and James H. Kyle (S. Dak.), in the Senate. The most strident opposition came from the New York delegation, headed by Democrats W. Bourke Cockran in the House and David B. Hill in the Senate. Passage of the bill, as an amendment to the Wilson-Gorman tariff bill, was by relatively wide margins in both the House and Senate.

The tax was immediately challenged on constitutional grounds. A 5 to 4 Supreme Court decision *(Pollack v. Farmers' Loan and Trust Co.)* held that the income tax was a form of direct excise tax and that it violated a provision of the Constitution requiring that all direct taxes be equally apportioned among the states. The Court took into account evidence from the Civil War and other economic estimates that demonstrated that individuals in some states (primarily in the Northeast) would bear much more of the burden than residents in other states. If an income tax were to be created, a constitutional amendment overriding the equal apportionment clause was required.

After more than a decade of inaction the Sixteenth Amendment, permitting such an exception for an income tax, was passed by Congress in 1909. Ratification by the required number of states was completed in February 1913. The timing was propitious: in the November 1912 elections Democrats supportive of an income tax had captured the presidency and both houses of Congress. With Woodrow Wilson's support an income tax was passed in October 1913.

The initial income tax was modest in scope. It did have a mildly progressive rate structure that included a "normal" rate of 1 percent and surcharges up to 6 percent on very high incomes. But it also included a $3,000 exemption of income for everyone and an additional exemption of $1,000 for married couples. Because almost all incomes then were below these levels, only 2 percent of the labor force filed tax returns in the first year. Thus when Republican senators such as Henry Cabot Lodge declared the tax "class legislation," they were essentially correct. But its effect on the wealthy few initially was quite modest indeed.

The relatively small revenue derived from the individual income tax and the accompanying corporate income tax increased rapidly with U.S. involvement in World War I. After the war declaration of 5 April 1917 expenditures rose as never before in U.S. history. Customs collections dropped off as revenue needs shot up, and a squeeze even greater than that experienced during the Civil War resulted.

The president and Congress quickly realized that the income tax could be transformed into a major money machine. What was needed was to: (1)

"DEMOCRACY PONDERING INCOME TAX LAW." Political cartoon reflecting early congressional debate over establishing a permanent income tax, which did not become law until 1913. Louis Dalrymple, *Puck*, 7 February 1892.
LIBRARY OF CONGRESS

lower the exemption for individuals and corporations, thus making many more people and businesses subject to the tax, and (2) increase the rates. Both ends were effected in a series of tax bills from 1916 to 1918. By the end of the war individual exemptions had been cut by more than half, and the top individual rate had increased from 7 percent to 77 percent. Corporate exemptions also were dramatically reduced, normal tax rates were increased, and an "excess profits" tax (based on profits in the prewar period) was enacted in addition to the normal corporate tax. The excess profits surcharge had a top rate of 60 percent. In terms of revenue these taxes, which produced less than 2 percent of federal revenues before the war, accounted for almost 60 percent of all revenues by 1920. The United States had discovered the income tax.

With the exception of a brief period between the wars, individual and corporate income levies replaced customs and excise taxes as the primary sources of national revenue. In terms of federal finances, World War II was a replay of World War I, with even more dramatic shortfalls. In a series of tax bills passed in the 1920s, the individual and corporate rates instituted during the previous conflict had been incrementally decreased. With the onset of World War II, a steeply progressive rate structure was implemented, together with a modest personal exemption of $500 per person. The top rate reached 92 percent. In addition, withholding of taxes by employers began in 1942. As a result of these changes, the percentage of the labor force filing returns went from fewer than 15 percent in 1939 to more than 90 percent by 1944. The percentage of taxable returns rose from fewer than 10 percent to more than 70 percent in the same five-year period.

Because the Korean conflict so closely followed the end of the world war, after a brief reduction in taxes in 1947, the wartime tax system was essentially put back in place in 1950. The continuing Cold War with the Soviets and Chinese also delayed post-1945 tax reductions. Major changes in tax rates and exemptions were not enacted until a decade after the end of the Korean War.

Since 1962, income tax laws have changed very frequently, with a major tax bill passed on average every other year. Although those bills varied considerably in what they accomplished, the common trend was to reduce legislated tax rates and increase the number and revenue loss of specialized provisions that are sometimes termed *tax loopholes*. Perhaps the worst example of increasing loopholes

occurred in 1981 in the Economic Recovery Tax Act. That bill, which cut revenues more than $750 billion over five years, thereby producing an enormous deficit, was created through a bipartisan effort, with both sides of the aisle recommending liberal special provisions. The trend in rate reduction reached the lowest point with the passage of the Tax Reform Act of 1986. The top rate was reduced to 31 percent, with most people paying either 28 or 15 percent. That law, however, also reversed the trend in opening up new loopholes. It repealed a number of provisions that aided special groups of taxpayers and cut the revenue loss of many more specialized provisions.

The Social Security Act of 1935 created the final tax in the nation's modern federal tax system. The act included provisions for retirement benefits (Social Security), unemployment compensation, disability income, and aid to families with dependent children. Although revenues went into separate trust funds and programs, the money was collected in one payroll tax, which was matched by employers. Major increases in the system came in 1966 with Medicare, medical insurance for the elderly, and Medicaid, medical insurance for the poor. A steep increase in these tax rates, which had lagged considerably behind benefit payouts, was passed in 1982 and phased in over a number of years. The share of federal revenues accounted for by social insurance taxes has increased considerably since 1970.

Tax Policy in Congress. The institutional base for congressional tax policy is as old as Congress itself. The Ways and Means Committee in the House of Representatives was first created in 1789, but this committee never met and was "discharged" after only two months. The reason was that the Treasury Department had the responsibility for reporting revenue needs and also had been given the "ways and means" to raise taxes. The committee was revived in 1794 in the midst of a heated political battle between Congress and Secretary of the Treasury Alexander Hamilton. Its size was set at fifteen members. Through the Civil War, Ways and Means not only had responsibility for taxes but also carried out the functions now performed by the appropriations committees and the committees overseeing banking and currency matters.

The Senate Finance Committee handles tax matters in its house. It became a standing committee in 1816 and initially dealt with both revenue and appropriations. Because the Constitution specifies that revenue legislation must originate in the

REP. NICHOLAS LONGWORTH (R-OHIO). Cutting "taxes" around 1924.   LIBRARY OF CONGRESS

House, Ways and Means has over the years been the more important committee on tax policy.

Both committees are considered among the most powerful in Congress and are among the most cherished assignments for members. Ways and Means is the most important domestic policy committee in Congress and has attracted some of the most powerful members to its chairmanship. Thaddeus Stevens (R-Pa.) tyrannically controlled the committee and thus all finance and appropriations issues during the Civil War. Ben Perley Poore, a contemporary observer of Congress, recalled, "No Republican was permitted by 'Old Thad' to oppose his imperious will without receiving a tongue-lashing that terrified others if it did not bring the refractory representative back to party harness." Stevens's raw use of power and his penchant for insulting fellow members led to a postwar revolt against his leadership. It also resulted in the stripping of Ways and Means of its appropriations responsibilities and its oversight of banking and currency matters.

In more recent times, Wilbur D. Mills (D-Ark.),

chairman from 1957 to 1975, was perceived as so powerful that a backlash against him was one of the key factors leading to major congressional reforms during the early 1970s. Ways and Means was enlarged, and the committee was forced to create subcommittees for the first time (although not on tax policy). "Sunshine" rules were enacted by Democrats in the House to make it much more difficult to mark up legislation in closed executive sessions.

An unusual instrument of congressional policy-making is the Joint Committee on Taxation, created as the Joint Committee on Internal Revenue Taxation in 1926. It is composed of five members from the House and five from the Senate. Three members on each side are from the majority party, two from the minority party. They are from and chosen by the Ways and Means and Finance committees and usually include the chairs and ranking minority members of Ways and Means and Finance.

The committee was formed and functions as a bipartisan, objective body. It provides expert advice and analysis on tax issues, aid in drafting tax legislation, and oversight of tax administration. From its inception the committee staff has been exceptionally well qualified and selected for its ability to work with both parties and both houses. The Joint Committee and its staff serve as important links between Ways and Means and Finance and provide links to tax experts in Treasury and key interest groups.

The Policy-making Process. Different types of taxes sometimes are combined in one piece of legislation and sometimes are handled individually. Employment tax increases are almost always treated as separate bills, as are changes in customs legislation. The reason for separate treatment of employment taxes is that they are almost always tied to changes in social security legislation, which is always given special treatment because of its massive constituency. Tariff bills are treated separately because they result from executive branch negotiations with many other countries, and Congress merely ratifies those agreements. Excise tax amendments, in contrast, are often included with bills changing income taxes.

Tax legislation must originate in the House of Representatives. But in periods of crisis such as wars, the genesis of tax legislation is likely to be in the executive branch, initiated by the president and then channeled through the Department of the Treasury. Time is short when crises arise, deliberation is costly, and the nation needs money. Although wars are not the normal impetus for tax policy, they

CONGRESSMEN IN INCOME TAX RUSH. Endeavoring to complete their income tax forms with the aid of several experts from the Treasury, 14 March 1930. *Left to right*, tax expert S. Cattrell, Representatives David Hogg (R-Ind.), William W. Larsen (D-Ga.), Carroll L. Beedy (R-Maine), John Nance Garner (D-Tex.), Harry C. Canfield (D-Ind.), tax expert A. H. Smith, and Rep. J. Mitchell Chase (R-Pa.).   LIBRARY OF CONGRESS

have been important in setting the basic structure of tax policy in the twentieth century.

The usual legislative process begins with a series of proposals to change incrementally selected provisions of the tax codes. The most important tax bills are those altering income taxes. Proposals may come from members of Congress, the president, interest groups, or key policy experts in the Treasury Department. The proposals may be compiled in a draft bill before or after public hearings are held. Hearings are usually held first in the House by the Ways and Means Committee and then in the Senate by the Finance Committee. If the chairs and House and Senate leadership agree that the legislation should proceed, a bill is drafted, usually by Ways and Means, with participation by the Joint Committee on Taxation in consultation with the Senate Finance Committee and the Treasury Department (through the Office of the Assistant Secretary for Taxation and the Office of Tax Analysis).

Once a bill has been drafted it goes to a committee markup session, the purpose of which is to alter draft legislation to produce a final bill that members believe will pass a committee and floor vote. Before 1970 these meetings were executive sessions, meaning that they were closed to the public. In addition to committee members, the meetings are attended by staff and select executive-branch officials or staff. Discussion of individual sections of the bill usually begins with the chair's "mark." This means that chairs have the prerogative of stating their positions on specific sections to begin the discussion. Depending on the style and power of the chair, the mark may stand or be altered. After markup the bill is presented to the full Ways and Means Committee. Further changes can be made then, before a vote on the bill. Votes may occur section by section, but a final vote on the entire bill is almost always taken.

An important step before the bill moves to the

floor is that of securing a "rule" that dictates how the bill will be handled on the floor. The legislative rule is determined by the House Rules Committee. From 1943 to 1975 every major income tax bill going through the House was debated under a closed rule. That meant that two votes were taken. The first was a vote to reconsider the bill. If that passed, the bill was sent back to committee, which usually meant that the bill was dead for that session of Congress. If it passed reconsideration, a final vote to enact the bill was taken. Usually, the crucial tally was the vote to reconsider, because tax legislation often is designed to lower taxes and contains so many special tax breaks that most members do not want to go on record against the bill. Reconsideration is not as final, and a negative vote can be defended as a vote to make a bill better.

Since the 1975 ouster of Wilbur Mills as chairman of Ways and Means, a number of tax bills have come to the floor of the House under modified or even open rules. That is the usual practice in the Senate, which has many fewer members and a strong tradition of open debate. Historically, the result has been that Senate bills cut more revenue, because floor amendments are adopted that lower taxes and provide new and more lucrative tax loopholes.

The results of the Senate floor debates often are overturned in conference committee, which decides the final shape of the bill. Conference committee membership is divided between the Senate and House, and its partisan makeup is approximately proportional to that of each chamber. Committee chairs and the ranking minority party members sit on the conference committee and determine who joins them. This assures these leaders considerable power and influences the behavior of other committee members throughout the policy process.

As with other legislation, once a conference committee has acted on a bill it is normal practice for both parties to support the bill when it returns to the floor for a final vote. Presidential vetoes of major tax bills are rare. During wartime the nation desperately needs more revenue, and the president will not stand in the way of bills providing it. In peacetime, tax bills almost always provide tax cuts, and the president is in the same position as Congress, not wishing to register a veto that can then be used by an opponent in a later election.

An exceptional case occurred in 1947, when President Harry S. Truman was upheld on two vetoes of tax legislation that would have reduced wartime taxes. But early in 1948 a new bill even more liberal in its tax reduction provisions was introduced.

When Truman vetoed this time, he was overridden. But because he argued that the bill was irresponsible in the face of huge wartime debt and because it benefited the well-off much more than the average family, Truman was able to capitalize on the issue in his upset victory over Thomas Dewey later in the year.

Tax Policy Issues. Although the academic and the political debates over what constitutes "good" tax policy are argued in somewhat different languages, they often involve the same issues. The difference is that the political debate is often overshadowed by constituency interests.

The most significant tax policy issues concern the effects of taxes on the distribution of income and the overall efficiency of the economy, as well as the simplicity and administrative costs of revenue-gathering. Equity issues are usually posed in terms of "horizontal" and "vertical" equity; there is more agreement on the former than the latter. Horizontal equity refers to the condition in which taxpayers with similar incomes pay similar taxes. In practice and in political debate, even this relatively innocuous principle is not so easily applied. Questions arise, for example, as to whether two families with the same income and family size should pay the same amount in taxes if one family has a spouse working in the home and the other has two full-time wage-earners. Should families with equal income but different numbers of children be treated the same or differently? Should families equal in all respects except that one family has incurred a major uninsured loss (such as the destruction of its home) have the same tax burden? Thus even though most would agree that equally situated individuals or households should pay the same tax, defining "equally situated" is often not easy.

Vertical equity concerns the treatment of taxpayers with different incomes and wealth. Here there is no single principle with overwhelming support. Some favor progressive taxation, taxing higher incomes at higher proportional rates; others support a flat rate, which means higher income groups pay more in taxes but everyone pays the same percentage of their income. Finally, at least for some items (such as licenses and fees), some would support equal payment by all taxpayers.

It is often argued that this country has a tradition of supporting a progressive rate system for its income taxes. To a degree that is true: the United States has never enacted a proportional or flat-rate system, although a number have been proposed. However, a careful analysis of the history of the legislation clearly indicates that the progressive rate system is primarily the product of wartime policies. Nearly every peacetime tax bill since 1913 has reduced progressivity by decreasing top rates and providing tax loopholes that disproportionately benefit higher-income groups. An exception was 1986, which lowered rates but also closed tax loopholes.

The effect of taxes on economic efficiency are manifold and are addressed through a number of broad policy questions, on any one of which there is little general agreement. An overarching concern is the degree to which a tax system distorts market decisions. It is generally agreed that a good tax system produces as little distortion as possible in the work choices of laborers, in the investment decisions of management, or in the mix of economic resources used in any industry. The key question concerning labor is the effect of high marginal rates on how much families work. The theoretical debate cuts in both directions: high tax rates make it less profitable to work because the government takes more of the income derived from work, but high tax rates also leave taxpayers with less after-tax income, which may produce an incentive to work more to make up the loss. Empirical studies of labor hours under different tax regimes have produced clouded results, although most agree the effect tends to be that people work less in the face of higher taxes. There is fierce academic debate over how much less.

The effects of tax policy on investment are even more difficult to determine. For example, there has been ongoing debate over the effects on investment of taxing capital gains ever since the first such levy was enacted in 1926. Some believe that taxing capital gains at lower than the ordinary income rate will stimulate investment; others argue that over the long term investment activity will be unaffected by a special rate. Politicians in both parties and academic experts are split on this issue. Another such subject of unresolved debate is the investment tax credit, which is given to companies when they invest in new plants or equipment. The debate over this tax concerns whether the companies would have invested anyway, without the tax credit.

There is more agreement on other types of special benefits, however. If significant tax advantages are provided to a certain sector of the economy, that sector will receive resources that would flow elsewhere under normal market conditions. This leads to economic inefficiencies. One example is the array of special tax benefits that went to the development of certain forms of real estate prior to the Tax Reform Act of 1986. Before 1986 the poten-

tial occupancy rate was much less important for investment decisions than the tax arrangements and advantages that would accrue to investors for certain types of office buildings, shopping centers, and housing projects. The result was considerable overbuilding and a large number of bankruptcies after the law was changed. Similar distortions occur between financial and other industrial sectors due to special provisions affecting banks, credit unions, and insurance companies.

There is much more agreement concerning administrative simplicity, credit feasibility, and expense. Everyone favors simplicity rather than complexity and lower rather than higher administrative costs per dollar of revenue collected. The problem is that these values cannot be treated in isolation. The simplest tax system would treat each household the same, regardless of number of children, income sources, hardship expenses (such as high medical bills), and so on. It would not allow an income exemption and would tax all income for every family at the same percentage rate. But such a system would clash with any sensible notion of vertical or horizontal equity. The poorest members of society would be taxed on all their income at the same rate as the wealthiest; families with very different expenses (due to illness, numbers of dependents, catastrophic losses, and so on) would be expected to pay the same amount of tax as all other families with the same income, regardless of their ability to pay.

Although legislative debates continue to focus on these perennial problems of taxation, since the early 1980s another major problem—the deficit—has had a significant impact on tax politics. In many ways the political process is geared to deficit financing, because elected officials prefer to provide their constituents with benefits, in the form of government subsidies or lower taxes or both.

Small deficits have been incurred consistently throughout the post–World War II years. But with the passage of the Economic Recovery Tax Act (ERTA) in 1981, which produced a five-year tax reduction of $750 billion, a small deficit problem became a huge one. Subsequent efforts to reduce the deficit, either through tax increases (1982, 1984, and 1990) or through spending and budget controls, have not succeeded. As a result, deficits and the national debt reached historic peaks in almost every year during the 1980s and the early 1990s.

Because of the conflicting needs and values at work in policy debates, and because our knowledge of the effects of taxes on economic behavior is uncertain, there is a great deal of room for political bargaining over tax policy. All too often, policy reflects little more than the effort by legislators to secure tax privileges for economic groups in their districts or states. Although often cloaked in arguments invoking equity or efficiency, tax policy usually means broad-based tax reductions, especially for the middle class, and the creation of or increases in special provisions (loopholes). Ironically, the growing deficit has kept the lid on tax reduction, with peacetime tax increases passed for the first time since 1932. Interest groups, attempting to undo some of the reforms enacted in the 1986 Tax Reform Act, have also been stymied because the deficit provides an excuse for turning down their proposals.

Institutional Problems and Prospects. Until the Tax Reform Act of 1986, which closed or reduced a wide variety of tax loopholes, few experts defended either income tax policy or the policymaking process. Some blame the modern tax problems in part on the congressional reforms of the early 1970s. Those reforms were intended to alter what critics felt was an inordinate concentration of power in committee chairs (with Ways and Means seen as a prime example). The reforms required that chairs be elected in caucus rather than being awarded the positions according to seniority; they forced committees to have a minimum number of subcommittees (including Ways and Means, which had never had any); and they initiated "sunshine" provisions intended to prevent committees from making decisions behind closed doors.

The immediate effect on Ways and Means was a much weaker chairmanship, a larger committee (it was increased from twenty-five to thirty-seven members), less reliance on executive sessions, and denial of closed rules for floor action. The policy result, however, was not what the reformers had in mind. Tax loopholes increased in number and in the amount of revenue lost. The tax base began to shrink and middle-class taxpayers were squeezed. During the same period corporate taxes as a percentage of revenues declined precipitously.

What this implies is that the logic of reform may have been wrong. The theory was that if power were decentralized and decision making forced into the open, legislators would be discouraged from offering special benefits to constituents and would be fiscally more responsible. A larger committee with a weaker chairman would make it more difficult to get special benefits through the committee. Open rules for floor debate would make it easier to remove any specialized or irresponsible policies that did get into committee bills.

But until 1986 the opposite occurred. A larger committee with a less powerful chair allowed more members to present their constituent demands, either to the committee or in floor debate. Open meetings merely increased the chances for members to advertise what they were trying to do for their constituents, whether or not they were ultimately successful. Opposition often failed to materialize on the committees as these actions became accepted as the norm. And the committee chairmen often lacked the power to block these attempts. The problem reached its peak during the passage of the Economic Recovery Tax Act in 1981. The policy process became a bidding war between the two parties—each trying to provide more lucrative benefits for special interest groups.

The 1986 legislation marked a reversal of these tendencies. Ironically, a major element in that successful tax reform effort was that the process took on many of the characteristics of pre-1970 tax legislation. Especially in the Senate, where the reform bill finally took hold, the committee chairman, Sen. Bob Packwood (R-Oreg.), acted forcefully. The bill was put together in closed executive sessions attended by a few key senators. Even on the floor, the Senate adopted a debating rule that was uncharacteristically tight, allowing votes only on several predetermined amendments.

The recent history of congressional tax legislation raises serious issues concerning the institutional capacity of Congress to meet the challenges of tax and budgetary policy. Although the 1986 Tax Reform Act was a hopeful sign, most congressional proposals introduced since its passage will undo one or more sections of the 1986 act. In addition, the institutional practices that in part explain its enactment have not been permanently or formally resurrected. In the 1992 campaign year, despite a projected $400 billion deficit for the year, every contender for the presidency proposed some form of tax cut, most including a host of tax loopholes for specialized groups or purposes.

[See also Finance Committee, Senate; General Welfare Clause; Revenue Sharing; Sixteenth Amendment; Social Security Act; Tariffs and Trade; Taxation Committee, Joint; Tax Reform Act of 1986; Ways and Means Committee, House.]

BIBLIOGRAPHY

Birnbaum, Jeffrey H., and Alan S. Murray. *Showdown at Gucci Gulch.* 1987.

Blakey, Roy G., and Gladys C. Blakey. *The Federal Income Tax.* 1940.

Conlan, Timothy J., Margaret T. Wrightson, and David

R. Beam. *Taxing Choices: The Politics of Tax Reform.* 1990.

Kennon, Donald R., and Rebecca M. Rogers. *The Committee on Ways and Means: A Bicentennial History 1789–1989.* 1989.

Martin, Cathie J. *Shifting the Burden.* 1991.

Paul, Randolph E. *Taxation in the United States.* 1954.

Pechman, Joseph A. *Federal Tax Policy.* 1987.

Pechman, Joseph A. *Who Paid Taxes, 1966–1985?* 1985.

Ratner, Sidney. *American Taxation.* 1942.

Steuerle, Eugene C. *The Tax Decade: How Taxes Came to Dominate the Public Agenda.* 1992.

Strahan, Randall. *New Ways and Means: Reform and Change in a Congressional Committee.* 1990.

Witte, John F. *The Politics and Development of the Federal Income Tax.* 1985.

Witte, John F. "The Tax Reform Act of 1986: A New Era in Tax Policy?" *American Politics Quarterly* 19 (October 1991): 438–457.

JOHN F. WITTE

TAXATION COMMITTEE, JOINT. The Joint Committee on Taxation, one of five joint committees in the 103d Congress, is a permanent committee that continues from one Congress to the next. It does not have legislative authority. The joint committee exists primarily to provide the House Ways and Means and the Senate Finance committees with expert staff to analyze revenue-related public policy issues. (Ways and Means and Finance are the congressional standing committees with legislative authority over taxation and other revenue measures.) The Joint Taxation Committee works in tandem with the Ways and Means and Finance committees, and its members are selected from among senior members of the Ways and Means and Finance committees.

Membership on the committee includes an equal number of legislators from the House and from the Senate. In the 103d Congress (1993–1995) five senators and five representatives serve on the Joint Taxation Committee. Traditionally, the chairs of the two standing committees are also the chairman and vice chairman of the Joint Taxation Committee. The chairmanship of the committee is rotated between the Senate and the House; in even-numbered years the chairman of the Senate Finance Committee also chairs the joint committee, in odd-numbered years the chairman of the House Ways and Means Committee chairs the joint committee. The joint committee also has a vice chairman, who is from the legislative body that does not hold the chairman position that year.

The predecessor to the Joint Committee on Taxation, the Joint Committee on Internal Revenue Taxation, was established by Congress in 1926. The panel's name was changed in 1977.

When the joint committee was first established in 1926, it was designed to be an investigative committee staffed by experts in tax legislation. These responsibilities have not significantly changed. The joint committee's jurisdiction includes: (1) overall supervision of the operation, administration, and simplification of the federal tax laws; and (2) supervision of tax refunds in excess of $200,000.

The committee's characteristics include a highly technical work load, a nonpartisan approach, a significant degree of staff independence, and a public profile that has varied over the years.

One characteristic is the technical nature of the work. Joint committee staff are lawyers, accountants, and economists, all expert in the tax code. Joint committee staff provide members of the Ways and Means and Finance committees with expert technical advice and reliable revenue estimates. Joint committee staff also advise congressional conference committees on whether their proposed decisions will meet the requirements of recent budget laws.

The joint committee's staff is nonpartisan; it works for both the Senate and the House and for both Democrats and Republicans. Consequently, staff members present themselves as teachers rather than advocates. Because the Joint Taxation Committee is viewed as nonpartisan, Congress is more receptive to the committee's analyses of the revenue impact of legislative proposals. On occasions when numbers prepared by analysts from the U.S. Treasury Department and by the staff of the Joint Taxation Committee do not agree, Congress more readily accepts the data of Joint Taxation and discredits that of Treasury as coming from a partisan agency.

Some have characterized the Joint Taxation Committee as unique because its staff has been given an unusual amount of professional independence. Professional staff of the committee serve in an advisory or consultative capacity. For example, when drafting tax legislation or analyzing the impact that proposals would have on revenues, Joint Taxation staff might offer their own ideas, as well as the ideas of committee members.

The Joint Committee on Taxation can also be characterized as a filter for revenue-related ideas. Lobbyists often have their proposals reviewed by the joint committee staff before taking them to members of the Ways and Means and Finance committees. Similarly, members of the Senate and of the House of Representatives frequently ask joint committee staff for revenue estimates.

The ability of the Joint Committee on Taxation to have an impact on congressional decisions has varied over the years. Some chairmen have sought to use the joint committee for political ends, resulting in short-term declines in the prestige of the committee. However, the panel has always regained its nonpartisan stature. During the 1990s the joint committee has enjoyed increasing prominence because the political agenda has placed such an emphasis on revenues, taxes, and budgeting.

[*See also* Finance Committee, Senate; Ways and Means Committee, House.]

BIBLIOGRAPHY

Brockway, David H. "How Tax Reform Happens: An Interview with the Chief of the Joint Committee on Taxation." *Trusts and Estates*, March 1986, pp. 17–20, 22–24, 26, 30, 32, 35.
Haas, Lawrence J. "Protection Squad." *National Journal*, 26 May 1990, pp. 1270–1274.
Malbin, Michael J. *Unelected Representatives: Congressional Staff and the Future of Representative Government.* 1980.

MARY ETTA BOESL

TAX REFORM ACT OF 1986 (100 Stat. 2085).

After a roller-coaster ride through an often balky Congress, the Tax Reform Act of 1986 (P.L. 99-514) was signed into law by President Ronald Reagan, its chief champion, on 22 October 1986. It was one of the decade's most unlikely—and most far-reaching—pieces of legislation.

The final bill stripped existing law of dozens of tax breaks that for years had been jealously protected by powerful interest groups. It also included a massive five-year, $120 billion tax increase on corporations. The increase was used to pay for the centerpiece—and primary political motivator—of the entire exercise: a substantial tax rate reduction for both businesses and individuals. The act was the most substantial overhaul of the federal income tax since its inception in 1913.

By rights, the bill should not have passed, and some of its backers believed its adoption was a fluke. The biggest fiscal problem of the day was the huge budget deficit, which the bill did nothing to reduce—in fact, the measure increased it in the short term. Also, the corporate interests that had to be overcome were so plentiful and potent (because of huge corporate campaign contributions) that passage seemed almost unimaginable.

Still, an odd set of forces conjoined to make the bill law. The fundamental catalyst was that the tax system, with its high rates and many exemptions for high-income earners, was widely perceived to be unfair. Some of the nation's most profitable corporations were paying no federal taxes and, in some cases, even getting refunds. Millionaires were able to hide their incomes from taxation by using wasteful paper transactions known as tax shelters.

Another reason for passage was the emergence of a new breed of Republicans, the supply-siders, whose main objective was the reduction of marginal tax rates. Tax reform act advocates of this creed, such as Rep. Jack Kemp of New York and President Reagan himself, were able to find common ground with traditional tax reformers in the Democratic party, who had for years fought to eliminate tax deductions and exemptions for the privileged few. Sen. Bill Bradley (D-N.J.) masterminded the synthesis of lower tax rates and fewer tax breaks that was the intellectual foundation for the Tax Reform Act of 1986.

Bradley's plan, coauthored with Democratic representative Richard A. Gephardt of Missouri, and Kemp's plan, whose coauthor was Republican senator Robert W. Kasten, Jr., of Wisconsin, were the starting points for President Reagan's own proposal, unveiled in 1985. Treasury Secretary James A. Baker III and his deputy, Richard Darman, two of the decade's most skilled executive branch operatives, led the Reagan administration drive for tax overhaul.

In Congress, the battle was led by a host of unlikely reformers impelled not so much by sympathy for the bill as by fear of the political repercussions of allowing a measure labeled "reform" to die. Top among these was Democratic representative Dan Rostenkowski of Illinois, chairman of the House Ways and Means Committee. Rostenkowski had long used the tax code to help his political allies. But after Reagan made a televised pitch for the overhaul in May 1985, Rostenkowski wanted to make sure that the Democratic party did not lose the mantle of reform that it had worn for so long. Republican senator Bob Packwood of Oregon, chairman of the Senate Finance Committee, who had similarly long been enamored of credits and exemptions, was forced to produce a tax reform bill in the Senate once Rostenkowski managed, after failing once, to get such a bill passed in the House.

The special interests failed to kill the bill because they fought it separately rather than by uniting against it. As a consequence of the reform, many were badly hurt, especially in the real estate industry. Whatever its economic and political consequences, however, the Tax Reform Act of 1986 was a landmark piece of social legislation. It removed more than four million impoverished working people from the income-tax rolls. It also launched a no holds-barred attack on tax shelters and narrowed the enormous inequities that permeated the existing tax system. Although it did not greatly change the distribution of the tax burden among income groups, it did increase the likelihood that individuals and corporations with similar incomes would pay similar taxes. In that way, it made the tax system more fair.

BIBLIOGRAPHY

Birnbaum, Jeffrey H., and Alan S. Murray. "Lawmakers, Lobbyists, and the Unlikely Triumph of Tax Reform." *Congress and the Presidency: A Journal of Capital Studies* 15 (Autumn 1988): 185–190.

Birnbaum, Jeffrey H., and Alan S. Murray. *Showdown at Gucci Gulch: Lawmakers, Lobbyists, and the Unlikely Triumph of Tax Reform.* 1987.

JEFFREY H. BIRNBAUM

ZACHARY TAYLOR.   *PERLEY'S REMINISCENCES*, VOL. 1

TAYLOR, ZACHARY (1784–1850), military hero, twelfth president of the United States (1849–1850). Taylor was born in Virginia but reared in Kentucky; ultimately he became a wealthy planter and slaveowner in Louisiana. In 1807 he joined the army and spent a number of years commanding western forts, where he consistently honored treaties with Indians and conscientiously prevented white settlement on Indian lands. As a Whig, Taylor opposed the annexation of Texas, but during the Mexican War he fought bravely, winning several battles against heavy numerical odds and becoming a national hero—all the while quarreling vigorously with president James K. Polk over the prosecution of the war. His heroism, combined with the informal style of dress and command that had earned him the nickname "Old Rough and Ready," made him a natural candidate for president in 1848. Although he owned some 140 slaves, he carried six northern states, including New York, Massachusetts, and Pennsylvania.

Taylor was the first Whig president to actually serve, and he faced a Democratic majority in both houses of Congress. Both Whigs and Democrats were divided along north-south lines. The northern Whigs were split over patronage between the friends of New York senator William H. Seward and Vice President Millard Fillmore, and the most powerful Whig senator, Henry Clay, was still sulking because he had not been nominated for president. Hoping to prevent Taylor's reelection in 1856, Democratic politicians and newspapers alike did everything possible to foment discord between Taylor and Clay and their respective followers, and southern Whigs bitterly resented Taylor's personal friendship with the antislavery Seward.

Taylor considered the Wilmot Proviso, which would have prohibited slavery in the territories acquired from Mexico, dangerous and useless, because he was convinced that slavery would not expand into these new lands. Since states, unlike territories, had the right to decide for themselves whether they would be slave or free, Taylor hoped to prevent conflict by quickly admitting California and New Mexico into the Union. With Taylor's support, California asked for admission as a free state. Meanwhile, Texas, a slave state, laid claim to most of New Mexico, but Taylor was determined to protect the territory. Clay proposed a number of reasonable compromise solutions, but when southerners in Congress combined these measures into an omnibus bill, Taylor opposed it, seeing it as an effort to delay California's statehood and, through amendments, to secure more of New Mexico for Texas. Months of angry debate ensued, and the invasion of New Mexico by Texas may have been prevented only by Taylor's announced intention to defend New Mexico with the army if necessary.

On 4 July 1850, Taylor developed gastroenteritis after eating green apples, spending three hours in the blazing sun at an Independence Day celebration, and eating cherries and milk. He died five days later, his death undoubtedly hastened by the atrocious medical practices of the day. After his death, the omnibus bill was defeated, but Congress then separately passed its amended parts, which are collectively known as the Compromise of 1850. Taylor would probably have approved of the measures as passed.

BIBLIOGRAPHY

Bauer, K. Jack. *Zachary Taylor.* 1985.
Hamilton, Holman. *Zachary Taylor, Soldier of the Republic.* 1941.
Hamilton, Holman. *Zachary Taylor, Soldier in the White House.* 1951.
Smith, Elbert B. The *Presidencies of Zachary Taylor and Millard Fillmore.* 1988.

ELBERT B. SMITH

TEAPOT DOME. In 1915 the Wilson administration set aside several oil reserves, primarily to assure the navy an adequate supply of fuel in the future. Secretary of the Navy Edwin Denby allowed himself to be persuaded by Secretary of the Interior Albert B. Fall, a New Mexico rancher and a believer in exploiting the nation's natural resources, to transfer the reserves from Navy to Interior in 1921, and a complaisant President Warren G. Harding did so.

One of the reserves, Teapot Dome in Wyoming, was leased to oilman Harry F. Sinclair, who had close ties to Fall. Harry A. Slattery, onetime secretary to conservationist Gifford Pinchot, reported this apparently corrupt arrangement to Sen. Robert M. La Follette (R-Wis.). (Pinchot in 1909 had made strikingly similar charges, regarding Alaskan wetlands, against William H. Taft's secretary of the Interior, Richard A. Ballinger.) La Follette did not want to go to the Naval Affairs Committee, which was full of administration stalwarts, and persuaded the Committee on Public Lands and Surveys to arrange hearings, in the knowledge that although its chairman, Sen. Reed Smoot (R-Utah), was a Harding supporter, it contained several Republican independents, and especially Sen. Thomas J. Walsh (D-Mont.), a constitutional lawyer of sterling integrity. At first Walsh was mildly interested. Then he was alerted by a reporter from Albuquerque that Fall, who meanwhile had left the cabinet, was suddenly displaying financial well-being and making "beautiful" improvements on his ranch at Three Rivers, New Mexico.

Soon Walsh was dominating the hearings, supported by the independents and by Democratic colleagues who permitted the Democratic senator to announce committee findings to reporters. Fall said he had borrowed $100,000 in cash from Edward B. McLean, the publisher of the *Washington Post.* McLean was in Florida and refused to go to Washington; he claimed to have a sinus condition that made travel impossible. Walsh journeyed to Florida only to have McLean deny that he had lent the money. On 24 January 1924, however, oilman Edward L. Doheny, who had leased the Elk Hills naval reserve in California, testified to the Senate committee that he had lent Fall the money and that his son in 1922 had carried it in cash to Fall "in a little black bag."

President Calvin Coolidge moved to control the damage, announcing: "Every law will be enforced. And every right of the people and the government will be protected." He nominated two special counsels; one of them, Woodrow Wilson's attorney general Thomas W. Gregory, turned out to have been in Doheny's employ. In his stead he nominated a former Democratic senator from Ohio, Atlee Pomerene. For a Republican counsel he chose a well-known lawyer, Owen J. Roberts. By that time the presidential campaign of 1924 was shaping up, and the Democrats found themselves in trouble. Information appeared that Wilson's son-in-law William Gibbs McAdoo, the party's leading candidate for the nomination, was involved with Doheny, McAdoo's firm having received a fee of $100,000, with McAdoo on an annual retainer of $25,000. The Senate in February 1924 demanded that Coolidge accept Denby's resignation for agreeing to the transfer of the reserves, and Coolidge indignantly declined, quoting his predecessors James Madison and Grover Cleveland on the sanctity of the separation of the three branches of government. Shortly afterward Denby resigned, ending that problem. Senatorial and public fury turned on Attorney General Harry M. Daugherty, the late Harding's close friend and a friend of McLean, Sinclair, and Doheny. Coolidge delayed pressing Daugherty but finally

EDWARD B. MCLEAN. Publisher of the *Washington Post,* testifying during the Teapot Dome investigation.

accepted his resignation after the president's secretary sent the attorney general a message that "he directs me to notify you that he expects your resignation at once."

The slowness with which Coolidge moved to confront the troubles of Fall and the resignations of Denby and Daugherty, all the while asserting that he would punish malefactors, together with the fact that the criminal action had occurred during the Harding administration, saved the president from embarrassment during the 1924 election. La Follette and Walsh had displayed considerable ability in pushing the investigation, but the Senate dropped in public esteem because Fall had been a senator before he became a cabinet member.

Fall was convicted of accepting a bribe from Doheny, fined $100,000 (which he did not pay because Doheny evicted him from Three Rivers and he had no other resources), and went to prison in 1931.

Sinclair was convicted of contempt of the Senate and of contempt of court for refusing to testify about his lease of Teapot Dome; he was jailed in 1929. Doheny went free under a rule of the criminal code that he was in a different position from Fall, who had accepted the bribe; the giver must be convicted of giving with intent to bribe, and Doheny avowed his intentions had been good.

The significance of the Teapot Dome scandal lay in its exposure of a corrupt cabinet member, the first in American history, the besmirching of the reputation of a president whose death in office had brought national mourning, and confirmation of a public sense that Congress was a fragile reliance for investigating malfeasance by one of its former members. The decade of the 1920s was noted for its cynical outlook upon U.S. participation in the recent world war. Teapot Dome extended this belief to domestic politics.

BIBLIOGRAPHY

Murray, Robert K. *The Harding Era: Warren G. Harding and His Administration.* 1969.

Noggle, Burl. *Teapot Dome: Oil and Politics in the 1920s.* 1962.

ROBERT H. FERRELL

TECHNOLOGY. *For discussion of technology as an area of public policy, see* Science and Technology. *See also* Office of Technology Assessment.

TECHNOLOGY IN CONGRESS. Congress's need to keep pace with the implacable increase in the complexity of its operations as well as with its expanding membership and staff, has motivated a series of initiatives to improve efficiency. During the two hundred years of Congress's existence, in times of peace and strife alike, the desire to function as efficiently as possible has spurred members to embrace technological change. Among the improvements introduced—some of which were initially viewed merely as conveniences rather than necessities—were such basic systems as steam heat, plumbing, and forced-air ventilation (introduced in 1865), elevators (1874), and electric lighting (which replaced gas lighting and was completed in 1900). Air-conditioning installation was completed in 1932. A small subway system was in place prior to World War I, and in an expanded form now links the Capitol with the Senate and House office complexes, facilitating the rapid movement of busy members and staff.

In the 1990s, senior governmental decision makers, both in Congress and in the executive branch, have an acute need for useful information and expeditious ways of handling information flow. Every age, however, has had its political crises, and lawmakers have always sought to utilize technological innovations allowing swifter, more efficient handling of the ever-mounting paperwork that results. The manual typewriter (invented in 1868) and then the electric typewriter in turn gave way to the word processor in the 1980s. Automatic letter-writing technologies such as the auto-pen now help members stay in touch with their constituencies, and high-speed printers produce prodigious mailings.

To meet congressional needs in the so-called Age of Information, an array of new information technologies is being used. These include computers (mainframes as well as workstations, network servers, and personal computers), laser printers, graphics plotters, optical storage systems, microforms, audio and video configurations (filming, storage, and presentation systems), versatile copiers, and fax machines, all linked by a variety of telecommunications pathways (including satellite hookups, fiber-optic systems, coaxial cables, twisted copper wires, and microwave units).

Congress has all along shown an unflagging willingness to use the newest tools and techniques. Urban and rural legislators alike perceived the advantages of the newly invented telegraph (1844), telephone (1876), and wireless (1895) and used them to acquire and transport information of value in legislative affairs. The potential values of radio (1920) and television (1941) were also quickly perceived by members of Congress, as had been that of motion pictures (1894) in an earlier day. True, traditionalism sometimes held sway, delaying the adoption of innovative technologies: for example, an early electromechanical voting system was demonstrated in the House of Representatives in 1922 but never installed, and it was not until 1973 that the House finally used an electronic voting system.

Computers actually first appeared on Capitol Hill in the mid 1960s, and were first utilized in the House for payroll and inventory purposes and in the Senate to assist in addressing and mailing functions. Three congressional computing centers were already in operation—in the Senate, House, and Library of Congress—by the time that the Legislative Reorganization Act of 1970 (P.L. 91-510) modestly encouraged such computer facilities.

Among the applications introduced from 1967 through 1972 were computerization of content and status information on pending legislation, the first computerized daily tracking of committee actions (for the House Banking and Currency Committee), House and Senate campaign expenditure accounting systems, and a bibliographic database for various uses by Congress members, committees, and staff.

As the sophistication of various technologies has been matched by a growing awareness of their potential, the demand for more and better devices and systems has grown apace. Optical character-recognition (scanning) devices, which first appeared in 1952, were more and more widely used, and computer-driven printing capabilities appeared on Capitol Hill, in the Government Printing Office, as early as 1959. The importance of versatile, reliable communications led, after 1980, to the development of an array of networks connecting office

SENATE SUBWAY. *Top,* in 1922, *bottom,* in July 1963.

computer systems and providing access to outside computer services.

In the area of user-friendly personal computers, spectacular growth has taken place. The first such devices with their now-familiar CRT monitors, were introduced into members' offices in 1975. By 1993 the inventory of such computers numbered eleven thousand in the House and sixty-five hundred in the Senate, including equipment in district and state offices. This proliferation of PCs allowed an ever-greater portion of the congressional workload to be shifted away from Capitol Hill.

The videotaping of chamber proceedings for subsequent archiving and TV broadcasting was approved only after prolonged negotiation, with the House achieving operational status in 1979 followed by the Senate in 1987. Other significant congressional uses of new technology include electronic mail tying House members' offices to selected federal agencies (introduced in 1981), the computerization of standing rules and precedents (1982), cellular phones (made available to House members on a rental basis in 1984), microcomputer reconfiguration of certain key functions of the Congressional Budget Office (1986), and revamping of the legislative branch telecommunications system (1987). Extensive technical orientation and training of members and staff is a continuing priority.

[*See also* C-SPAN; Telegraph; Voting in Congress, *article on* Voting Methods.]

BIBLIOGRAPHY

Frantzich, Stephen E. *Computers in Congress: The Politics of Information.* 1982.

U.S. Congress. Joint Committee on the Organization of Congress. *Opportunities for the Use of Information Resources and Advanced Technologies in Congress.* A study by Robert Lee Chartraud and Robert C. Ketcham. 103d Cong., 1st sess., 1993.

ROBERT LEE CHARTRAND

TELECOMMUNICATIONS. *See* Communications.

TELEGRAPH. Believing that telegraphy should be developed as a government service, Samuel F. B. Morse sought a congressional appropriation to launch his new communication technology. In February 1838, Morse demonstrated his system—a sending key connected by wire to a receiver that recorded short and long lines on a paper strip—to

SAMUEL MORSE. With his telegraph, c. 1844.
LIBRARY OF CONGRESS

the House Committee on Commerce. The telegraph impressed many of the legislators and other dignitaries, but some, unable to fathom its workings, labeled it a hoax. After all, only Morse could decipher the messages. The Commerce Committee reported a bill favorable to Morse, but it never reached a second reading in the House. Nonetheless, the Committee's chairman, Francis O. J. Smith of Maine, excited by telegraphy's financial prospects, became Morse's partner.

Smith used his position to continue the lobbying for an appropriation, and in March 1843, Congress granted $30,000 to construct a line. On 24 May 1844, Morse sent the famous message, "What hath God wrought!" from the Supreme Court chambers in the Capitol to his assistant in Baltimore, who retransmitted it to Washington. Although the new technology fascinated the public, the number of paying customers fell short of expectations, partly because the relatively short line offered few advantages to businesses. Smith, who had only lost money so far, turned against Morse.

The Post Office Department assumed control of the Baltimore-Washington line in April 1845. A few months later, the postmaster general conceded that the postal telegraph was a financial burden that hurt the department's resources, but he nonetheless urged lawmakers to keep the technology in government hands. Congress declined, and development of the service shifted to private firms, though bills to establish a postal telegraph were regularly introduced until 1920.

BIBLIOGRAPHY

Mabee, Carleton. *The American Leonardo: A Life of Samuel F. B. Morse*. 1943.

Morse, Edward Lind, ed. *Samuel F. B. Morse: Letters and Journals*. 2 vols. 1914.

RICHARD B. KIELBOWICZ

TEMPORARY NATIONAL ECONOMIC COMMITTEE (TNEC). Created by act of Congress in June 1938, the Temporary National Economic Committee conducted a massive three-year study of the concentration of economic power in the United States and its connection to persisting unemployment and depression. The impetus for the investigation was an ongoing debate among proponents of antitrust action, national economic planning, industrial self-government, and federal compensatory spending, all of whom were offering programs for recovery from the recession of 1937. At the height of this debate, on 29 April 1938, President Franklin D. Roosevelt sent a "monopoly" message to Congress denouncing the "private socialism" that had allegedly developed in the United States and urging, among other things, the appropriation of $500,000 for a "thorough study of the concentration of economic power."

Roosevelt wanted the study to be conducted by the Federal Trade Commission, the Securities and Exchange Commission, and the Department of Justice. But Sen. Joseph C. O'Mahoney (D-Wyo.) insisted on congressional participation and became the chief sponsor of a resolution calling for a twelve-member investigating committee with membership evenly balanced between Congress and the administration. The six congressional members subsequently appointed were Senators O'Mahoney (the chairman), William E. Borah (R-Idaho), and William H. King (D-Utah) and Representatives Hatton W. Sumners (D-Tex.), B. Carroll Reece (R-Tenn.), and Edward C. Eicher (D-Iowa). The administration was represented by Thurman Arnold (Justice Department), Herman Oliphant (Treasury Department), Isador Lubin (Labor Department),

William O. Douglas (Securities and Exchange Commission), Garland Ferguson (Federal Trade Commission), and Richard Patterson (Commerce Department). The economist Leon Henderson, who had been calling for such an inquiry since 1935, became the committee's executive secretary. In both makeup and intent, the TNEC resembled the U.S. Industrial Commission of 1898 to 1902, but in the case of the former inquiry the presidential members came from the private sector rather than from the administration, and the mission was to study labor, agriculture, and immigration as well as industrial concentration.

In December 1938 the TNEC opened the first of fifteen separate hearings, which ran until March 1941. Among the subjects explored in the committee's thirty-seven volumes of testimony and in the forty-three research monographs produced by its staff were business cartels, trade barriers, technology, patents, insurance, savings, investment banking, and the competitive structures in leading industries. By 1941 the accumulation of data and expert opinion rivaled that of the Industrial Commission at the turn of the century. But the early disagreements within the committee persisted, and its final report in April 1941 resolved little and recommended nothing beyond some minor changes in the patent and antitrust laws. The report, moreover, received little legislative attention, partly because Congress and the president had by the time of its completion lost interest in the monopoly problem and were preoccupied with the approach of World War II.

The TNEC is sometimes regarded as a product of the late New Deal's antitrust activism. But its work is probably better seen as a way of avoiding the issue and the policy choices that it posed. As former brainstruster Raymond Moley said at the time, it was "an inquiry that would relieve the President from the nagging of his subordinates, put off the adoption of a definite program, and free his mind for consideration of other matters." These goals it achieved, but hopes that it would lead to policy innovation or policy consensus proved ill founded.

BIBLIOGRAPHY

Hawley, Ellis W. *The New Deal and the Problem of Monopoly: A Study in Economic Ambivalence*. 1966.

Lynch, David. *The Concentration of Economic Power*. 1946.

MacDonald, Dwight. "The Monopoly Committee: A Study in Frustration." *The American Scholar* 8 (Summer 1939): 295–308.

ELLIS W. HAWLEY

TENNESSEE. On 1 June 1796, Tennessee entered the Union as the sixteenth state. Voters promptly elected Andrew Jackson to Congress, and the state legislators chose William Blount and William Cocke for the Senate. Tennessee was claimed by North Carolina until 1790, when Congress accepted jurisdiction over western claims and created the Southwest Territory. Congress soon formed a government based upon the Northwest Ordinance of 1787 and confirmed President George Washington's appointment of William Blount as governor. After five years in a territorial status, Tennessee reached the population level necessary for statehood, which it attained after lengthy debates in both the Senate and House of Representatives.

By the time Tennessee sought admission to the Union, the Republican party of Thomas Jefferson had obtained a majority in the House and a strong minority in the Senate. But 1796 was also a presidential election year, and Federalist vice president John Adams planned to succeed Washington as president. Federalist leaders realized that a new state with strong Jeffersonian Republican sentiment would hurt them in a close presidential race. Therefore, they tried to delay Tennessee's admission until at least after the fall elections. Only after several weeks of intensive debate—with Aaron Burr, Albert Gallatin, and James Madison arguing for admission against Federalists Samuel Sitgreaves, Theodore Sedgwick, and William L. Smith—was statehood achieved in June.

Although Tennessee's House delegation initially consisted only of Andrew Jackson, it increased rapidly as the state's population grew. For three decades, Tennessee's congressional delegation was Republican. However, with the advent of Jackson as a presidential contender in the early 1820s, most Tennesseans became Jacksonian Democrats. Jackson held sway in the state for a decade, but when he sought to dictate his presidential successor in 1836, many Tennesseans rebuffed him and became Whigs. For the next two decades, the Tennessee delegation was about evenly divided between Whigs and Democrats.

During the Civil War, the eastern third of the state fought for the North, while most of the central and western counties—being chiefly agricultural and slaveholding—sided with the Confederacy. These Civil War allegiances were reflected in politics and congressional representation after the war. In practically every election since Reconstruction, eastern Tennesseans have sent Republicans to Congress, while middle and western Tennesseans have

elected Democrats. Tennessee generally is considered to be a Democratic state, yet in most of the presidential elections since Dwight D. Eisenhower's first victory in 1952, Tennesseans have voted Republican.

Three Tennesseans have served as Speaker of the House: James K. Polk and John Bell, active during the first half of the nineteenth century, and Joseph W. Byrns, who served during the 1930s. Other Tennessee members of Congress well-known for their national leadership have included such nineteenth-century figures as Felix Grundy, Hugh Lawson White, and Andrew Johnson and such twentieth-century men as Cordell Hull, Kenneth D. McKellar, Estes Kefauver, and Howard H. Baker, Jr. All were mentioned from time to time for the presidency, and Johnson, of course, actually served.

BIBLIOGRAPHY

Bergeron, Paul. *Paths of the Past.* 1979.
Corlew, Robert E. *A Short History of Tennessee.* 1980.
Corlew, Robert E. *Statehood for Tennessee.* 1976.

ROBERT E. CORLEW

TENNESSEE VALLEY AUTHORITY. On 18 May 1933, when President Franklin D. Roosevelt signed the Tennessee Valley Authority (TVA) Act (48 Stat. 58) into law, he endorsed one of the major accomplishments of that hectic period of the 73d Congress (1933–1935) known as the Hundred Days and brought to a close one of the most protracted and bitterly fought legislative struggles of the preceding generation.

The Tennessee River falls 140 feet in a thirty-mile stretch near Muscle Shoals, Alabama, in the upper northwest corner of the state. This drop resulted in a concentration of rocks, rapids, and rugged shoals that seriously impeded navigation but also created an exceptional site for the hydrogeneration of electricity. As World War I approached, the United States recognized the urgency of freeing itself from dependence on foreign sources of nitrates used in manufacturing munitions. The National Defense Act of 1916 gave President Woodrow Wilson authority to select a site and a method for producing nitrates. He chose Muscle Shoals principally because construction of a high dam in this location would provide ample electric power for nitrate production. In peacetime, the nitrate plants would be used to produce fertilizer.

Progressives such as President Theodore Roosevelt and Senators George W. Norris of Nebraska

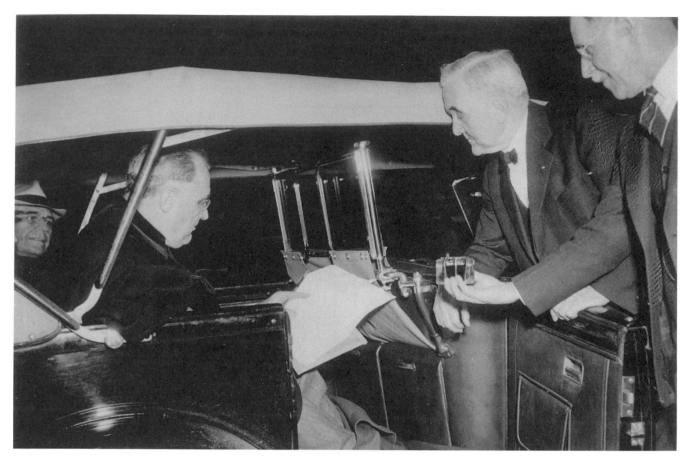

WORKING TO ESTABLISH THE TENNESSEE VALLEY AUTHORITY. President Franklin D. Roosevelt, *second from left*, and Sen. George W. Norris (R-Nebr.), *second from right*.   OFFICE OF THE HISTORIAN OF THE U.S. SENATE

and Robert M. La Follette of Wisconsin fought to preserve the benefits of electric power associated with Muscle Shoals for the general public and to use the facilities there as a "yardstick" against which to measure the performance of private power interests. Senator Norris defeated Henry Ford's popular but extremely self-serving 1921 offer to acquire the Muscle Shoals facilities, including then-unfinished Wilson Dam, for $5 million. The concept of using an independent government corporation for activities normally conducted in the private sector had proved its merit in World War I. Norris, and later, President Franklin Roosevelt, found this to be an appropriate organizational approach for public ownership of the Muscle Shoals facilities.

Meanwhile, the conservation movement developed the philosophy that natural resources and activities related to them were tied together in a seamless web incorporating water, flood control, navigation, waterpower, forests, soil, erosion, fish,

and game. The opportunity to deal with these resources in a unified manner, while at the same time attacking the Tennessee Valley's pervasive poverty, was one motivation for President Franklin Roosevelt's decision to broaden the final TVA Act to encompass the entire Tennessee River watershed, not just Muscle Shoals, thus going beyond Norris's earlier bills.

Norris himself was the indispensable element. A Nebraska Republican, his link to the Muscle Shoals controversy grew out of his chairmanship of the Senate Committee on Agriculture and Forestry, to which was referred all Muscle Shoals legislation. Once involved, Norris totally committed himself to the struggle. From 1921 to 1933, he introduced Muscle Shoals legislation eight times. (In those years, 130 other bills on the subject were introduced by various senators and representatives.) In 1928, President Calvin Coolidge pocket-vetoed legislation Norris had maneuvered through both houses. Three years later, President Herbert Hoover, in a bitter veto message, killed another Norris bill that, he declared, "is not liberalism, it is degeneration."

On 10 April 1933, President Franklin Roosevelt sent a brief message to the 73d Congress suggesting passage of legislation "to create a Tennessee Valley Authority, a corporation clothed with the power of Government but possessed with the flexibility and initiative of a private enterprise." No draft legislation accompanied the message, but none was necessary. Norris quickly adapted his earlier version, vetoed by Hoover, to capture Roosevelt's broader vision. Rep. Lister Hill of Alabama introduced generally similar legislation in the House, although it contained greater restrictions on the corporation's authority to generate and sell electricity. When a deadlock threatened in conference, Roosevelt summoned the Senate and House leaders to the White House. A compromise version that adopted most features of the Norris bill soon emerged, was passed by both houses, and was signed by Roosevelt five weeks after he dispatched his message.

The act created a federally owned corporation governed by a board of three directors, appointed by the president and confirmed by the Senate, serving staggered nine-year terms. The board received broad authority to appoint officials and employees; set salary levels; buy and sell land, materials, and equipment; sue and be sued; and use its revenues from electricity sales in "conducting its business." It was to report directly to the president and was authorized to receive appropriations from Congress. The headquarters of the corporation was to be in the region, not in Washington, D.C.

The act charged the TVA with the unified conservation and development of the Tennessee Valley's natural and human resources. A nine-foot navigation channel was to be built from Knoxville, Tennessee, to Paducah, Kentucky (where the Tennessee flows into the Ohio River). Floods were to be controlled by construction of a system of mainstream and tributary dams. Electric power was to be generated in amounts that did not conflict with navigation and flood control and that was distributed over TVA-owned transmission lines. Electric rates were to be kept as low as possible. Public bodies were to receive preference in purchasing TVA power. Experimental fertilizers were to be produced at Muscle Shoals. Trees were to be planted to combat erosion. Agriculture was to be improved. The board also was authorized to make comprehensive plans for achieving "an orderly and proper physical, economic, and social development" of the region.

Roosevelt envisioned TVA as the first in a net-

work of river-based development authorities, with the Columbia River and Missouri River basins seen as prime future candidates. However, the unique constellation of forces that created TVA was never present in these other locales. Moreover, private power interests vigorously opposed expansion of the TVA concept, as did the mainline federal bureaucracies that regarded TVA's regional development activities as an intrusion on their turf. Consequently, the TVA model was never replicated (although more limited public power entities, such as the Bonneville Power Administration, were established).

In the late twentieth century, the TVA is run under the same organizational arrangement created in 1933. Its broad mission likewise remains unchanged. However, in 1959, Congress amended the 1933 legislation to make the TVA power program self-financing through the sale of revenue bonds. This freed the TVA from dependence on appropriated funds to construct new power facilities and ensured the authority's capability to respond to the region's growing demand for electricity.

In the 1980s and 1990s, TVA again was the focus of controversy in Congress. Costs arising from an extensive but poorly managed nuclear power program drove up electric rates and threatened TVA's congressional support. Deficit-cutting measures also targeted the agency's regional development program supported by appropriations. Even though these forces had not prevailed through the 102d Congress, opposition was likely for the foreseeable future.

BIBLIOGRAPHY

Clapp, Gordon R. *The TVA: An Approach to the Development of a Region.* 1955.

Hubbard, Preston J. *Origins of the TVA: The Muscle Shoals Controversy, 1920–1932.* 1961.

McCraw, Thomas K. *TVA and the Power Fight, 1933–1939.* 1971.

Pritchett, C. Herman. *The Tennessee Valley Authority: A Study in Public Administration.* 1943.

JOHN G. STEWART

TENURE AND TURNOVER. *See* Members, *article on* Tenure and Turnover.

TERM LIMITATION. Restrictions on the number of terms or years an elected official may serve in a specific public office are referred to as "term limitations." Thirty-one states limit gubernatorial terms, and the Constitution's Twenty-second

Figure 1. Federal Term Limitation by State

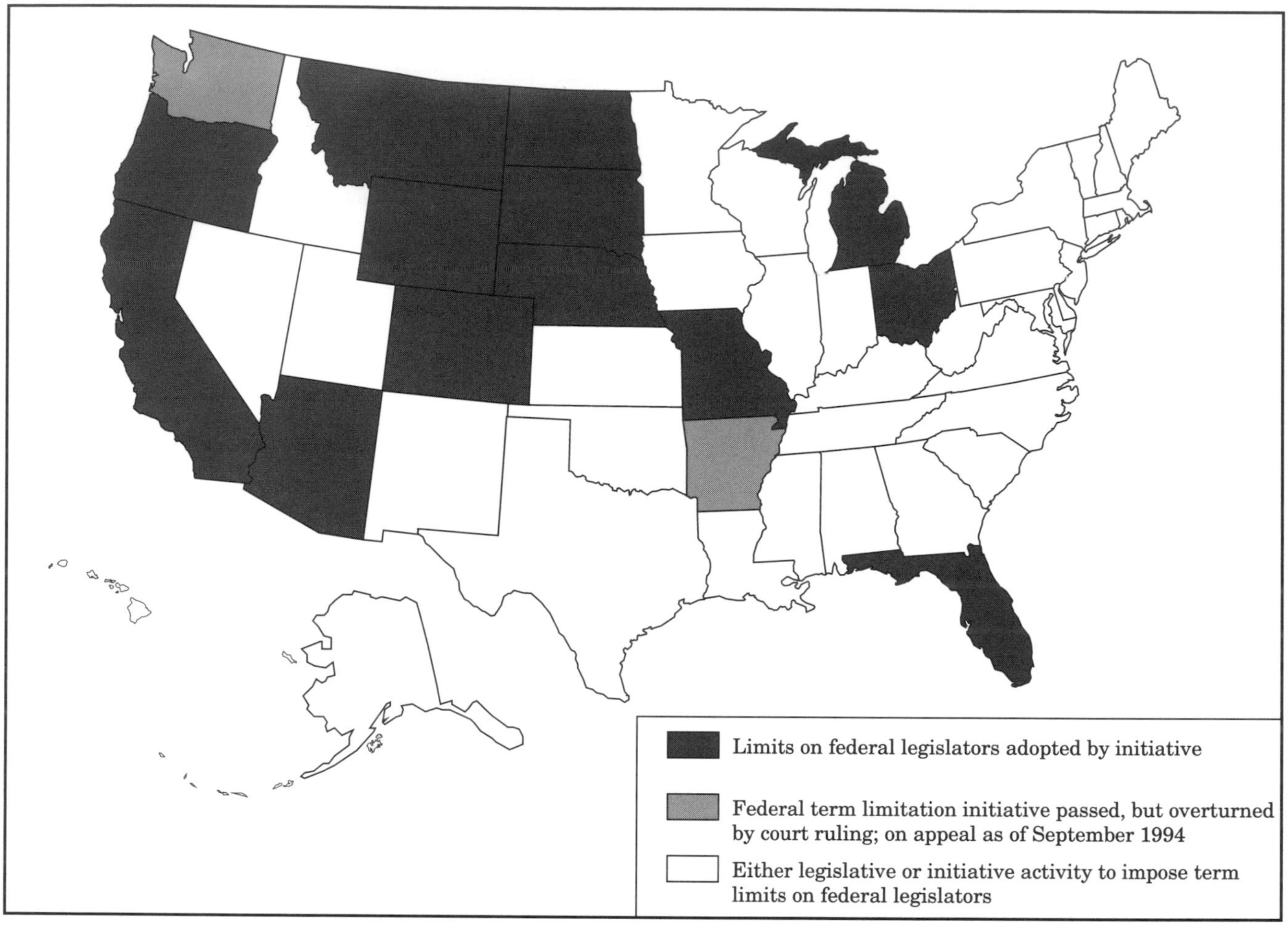

Limits on federal legislators adopted by initiative

Federal term limitation initiative passed, but overturned by court ruling; on appeal as of September 1994

Either legislative or initiative activity to impose term limits on federal legislators

Amendment limits the president to two four-year terms.

The movement to limit legislative terms began in the late 1980s, as voter frustration with the nation's legislatures escalated and as the national media gave increasing coverage to the concept of limitations. To date, citizen initiatives have been the primary vehicle for the adoption of term limits. In 1990 Oklahoma, Colorado, and California adopted initiatives to limit terms for state legislators; Colorado's initiative limited terms for its delegation to the U.S. Congress as well. Forty-five states considered term limit legislation in 1991, though none was enacted. In 1992, however, fourteen states had initiatives on the ballot to limit terms for both state and federal legislators (Arizona, Arkansas, California, Colorado, Florida, Michigan, Missouri, Montana, Nebraska, Ohio, Oregon, South Dakota, Washington, and Wyoming); all were approved. In addition, North Dakota considered and adopted

term limitations for federal legislators only. Efforts to adopt term limits by initiative or legislation are under way in all other states in the Union.

Current term limit initiatives differ as to the length of the legislative limits and in certain respects: whether limits would last a lifetime or only require a break in service; and whether legislative limits would be created by adding qualifications to candidates' eligibility requirements or by restricting access to the ballot.

The idea of elected officials leaving public office after a brief period of service, known as the principle of rotation in office, has long been associated with the development of representative democracy. Praised by Aristotle and Cicero, practiced for a time in Athens and Rome as well as in the Renaissance city-states of Florence and Venice, rotation was also an essential component of classical republicanism for English Commonwealthmen and Oppositionists of the seventeenth and eighteenth centuries, including James Harrington, Walter Moyle, Algernon Sidney, Henry Neville, James Burgh, and John Trenchard.

In eighteenth-century America, required rotation was viewed as a tenet of radical democracy. Practiced by the Dutch in New Amsterdam and in colonial New York, rotation was also found in colonial New England, dating back to the New England Confederation of 1643. The Pennsylvania constitution of 1776 required rotation for all elected state officials. The bills of rights accompanying five other state constitutions adopted between 1776 and 1780 gave citizens the right to expect elected officials to "return to private station" after brief periods of service.

The Articles of Confederation (1781) limited terms for all delegates to three years out of every six and limited the president of the Congress to one year in three. Despite difficulties enforcing rotation in the Continental Congress, the Virginia Plan that was presented to the Constitutional Convention similarly called for restrictions on the re-eligibility of all federal officeholders.

The final draft of the Constitution did not require rotation. Nevertheless, many convention delegates anticipated that voluntary rotation would be the norm—an expectation fulfilled by George Washington's decision not to seek a third term as president and by the high turnover in Congress through the late nineteenth century. The absence of required rotation for the president and the Senate was a major Anti-Federalist argument against ratification of the new constitution.

For Thomas Paine, Benjamin Franklin, John Adams, Thomas Jefferson, George Mason, Melancton Smith, and George Washington, among others, rotation checked the potential abuse of public power, increased the opportunity for citizens to serve in public office, and enhanced the quality of political representation. Conversely, for Alexander Hamilton rotation threatened to reduce incentives for good behavior (inviting "sordid views," "peculation," and "usurpation") and deprived the nation of "the experience and wisdom gained by an incumbent, perhaps just when that experience was needed most."

Rotation became a mainstay of Jacksonian democracy in the 1830s. Endorsing the principle that all persons were capable of holding public office, Andrew Jackson extended rotation to appointed offices, institutionalizing the spoils system. Harsh criticism of the spoils system by the late nineteenth century led to civil service reform and the demise of rotation's popularity.

The contemporary term limitation debate continues to raise fundamental questions about the character and design of representative government. Advocates claim term limits are needed to restore electoral competition, increase legislative turnover, and replace legislative careerists with "citizen-legislators." Term limits would bring fresh ideas to government, enhance political responsiveness, and decrease the influence of special interests. Some advocates contend that term limits would also reduce the size and intrusiveness of government.

Conceding problems with political representation, critics argue that mandatory rotation is an inadequate and potentially destructive reform. The need for greater legislative turnover is vastly overstated, opponents claim. Moreover, term limits would rob voters of their right to vote for the candidate of their choice; increase the power of special interests, legislative staff, and the executive branch; and squander legislative leadership, experience, and expertise. Finally, critics claim that states lack the constitutional authority to impose term limit qualifications on members of Congress, pursuant to Article I, section 2 of the U.S. Constitution. Litigation is under way in Arkansas, Nebraska, and Washington to challenge the constitutionality of state-imposed term limits for federal legislators.

BIBLIOGRAPHY

Benjamin, Gerald, and Michael Malbin, eds. *Limiting Legislative Terms.* 1992.

Coyne, James K., and John H. Fund. *Cleaning House: America's Campaign for Term Limits.* 1992.

Petracca, Mark P. "The Poison of Professional Politics." *Cato Institute Policy Analysis* 151 (10 May 1991): 1–30.

Polsby, Nelson W. "Constitutional Mischief: What's Wrong with Term Limitations." *The American Prospect* 6 (Summer 1991): 40–43.

Will, George F. *Restoration: Congress, Term Limits, and the Recovery of Deliberative Democracy.* 1992.

MARK P. PETRACCA

TERRITORIAL EXPANSION. American territorial expansion was a legacy of the British colonization of North America and of European rivalries over this vast domain. The charters of Virginia, Massachusetts, the Carolinas, Connecticut, and Georgia specified the Pacific Ocean as these colonies' western boundary. Such far-reaching ambitions engendered expansionism and ensured conflict with native peoples as well as with France and Spain and, later, with England and Mexico. Constant border raids and periodic international warfare heightened Americans' commitment to seizing the borderlands. Expansion offered safety and peace, along with speculation, greed, and idealism about the new republic. It also fostered new dangers and, in the years before the Civil War, divided the nation. Nevertheless, expansionism continued, despite repeated scandals, to the end of the nineteenth century.

The origins of the Republic lay in expansion. George Washington's frontier expedition for Virginia land speculators triggered the Seven Years War, which ended in 1763 with France's cessions of Canada to England and Louisiana to Spain. England's Quebec Act of 1774, restricting settlement in the Ohio Valley, threatened speculative interests and fired revolutionary sentiment.

The Revolution and the Confederation Period. During the American Revolution, states without western land claims—such as Maryland and New Jersey—insisted that western lands be ceded to the United States before they would ratify the Articles of Confederation. Speculators, including members of the Continental Congress from these states and from Pennsylvania, owned shares in the Wabash and Indiana companies, which competed with Virginia's Ohio Company in purchasing land from Native American tribes. States without western land claims joined speculators in arguing that all Americans would sacrifice to win the West and that those states with grants should not unfairly obtain the advantages of size and wealth. Fortunately, Virginians such as delegate Richard Henry Lee and Governor Thomas Jefferson believed that the new republic should expand only as a confederation of smaller states. In January 1781 Virginia ceded its territory beyond the Ohio, provided that it be made into new states and that purchases from Native Americans be voided. Speculators caused a wrangle in Congress, but Maryland ratified the Articles of Confederation, allowing the new government to function.

During the war, the Continental Congress, desperate for help and under the influence of French agents, sent commissioners abroad and directed them to be guided by France, America's ally. French minister Charles Vergennes was willing to grant the United States less than full independence and to restrict its size. France's other ally, Spain, wanted to recover the Floridas and push its claims northward to the Great Lakes. Commissioner Benjamin Franklin thought France "intended to coop us up with the Alleghenies." John Jay, abetted by Franklin

and John Adams, therefore risked separation negotiations with England. British prime minister William Petty in October 1782 considered restricting the United States to the area east of the Alleghenies but saw advantages in dealing with the American commissioners and in taking their wishes seriously.

Jay, Adams, and Franklin maneuvered skillfully on territorial issues. The Treaty of Peace of 30 November 1782 established the boundaries of the new nation: in the north, along the St. Croix River to the St. Lawrence watershed and through the Great Lakes to the Lake of the Woods; in the west, the Mississippi River (open to American navigation); in the south, along northern Florida to Georgia. Some in Congress, including James Madison, believed that the commissioners had not been faithful to France, and there were motions to recall them. But others supported their outstanding work, and Congress ratified the treaty after a month of quarrels.

The greatest accomplishments of the Confederation Congress concerned expansion. In 1784 it enacted an ordinance, drafted by Thomas Jefferson, dividing the area west of the Appalachians and north of the Ohio into seven districts, with local self-government and the promise of an ultimate division of the territory into states. A second ordinance in 1785 provided for the survey and sale of lands at no less than a dollar per acre in 640-acre lots. Because the West was filling up with settlers not content to wait for surveys, Congress allowed a new Ohio Company, including corrupt congressmen, to buy one and a half million acres at ten cents per acre. In 1787 it enacted the Northwest Ordinance, which created a conservative structure of government on republican principles: initial governance by officials appointed by Congress, an elected assembly when the territory contained five thousand adult males, and eventual creation of three to five states with rights equivalent to those of the already existing states. The Northwest Ordinance also abolished slavery in the area. The record in the Southwest was not so impressive owing to greedy speculators and an untidy rush of settlers, but this was not Congress's fault. By the 1790s the states of Vermont, Kentucky, and Tennessee had come into being.

Jay's Treaty. After the establishment of the Constitution in 1789, the United States had to clarify its rights as a new nation. England occupied posts in the Northwest, including forts at Niagara and Detroit, and encouraged Indian attacks on American settlements. President Washington sent Jay, now chief justice, as a special agent to England to address the question of the posts and boundary problems as well as more important maritime issues. From the outset, Jay's mission became a catalyst for the emergence of the Democratic-Republican and Federalist parties in Congress. His treaty of 1794 with Lord Grenville, the British foreign secretary, provided for British evacuation of the posts and establishment of an arbitral commission on boundaries. Washington approved the treaty despite Jay's concessions on neutral rights, and the Senate ratified it by the bare margin of 20 to 10, with the vote falling along factional lines. Madison tried to prevent the necessary appropriations but failed narrowly when Washington challenged the House's authority to block a treaty.

Dealings with Spain and France. Similar issues determined American policy toward Spain, which had recovered the Floridas, moved north into Alabama and Georgia, closed the Mississippi to American traffic, and intrigued with dissident frontiersmen. During the Confederation, Jay, then secretary for foreign affairs, had proposed swapping American navigation rights on the Mississippi for rights to trade with Spain's American colonies, but his Jay-Gardoqui treaty failed to be ratified. In 1795, the Senate unanimously ratified Pinckney's treaty, in which Spain acknowledged a boundary between the United States and Spanish Florida at 31° north latitude, as well as the rights of Americans to navigate the Mississippi and to deposit goods at New Orleans for ocean shipment.

President John Adams's most serious problems were with France, which suspended diplomatic relations and attacked American shipping following the adoption of Jay's treaty. The humiliating failure of Adams's bipartisan commission to France led to an undeclared naval war between the two former allies. Rufus King, Adams's minister to England, urged an attack on Spanish Florida and New Orleans. Such expansionism, along with the Alien and Sedition laws, reflected a Federalist desire to embarrass the Democratic-Republicans. Adams, who disagreed with the "high-minded Federalists," dispatched a second commission, which negotiated the Convention of Mortefontaine of 30 September 1800, severing the alliance with France and preserving peace.

On 1 October, French foreign minister Charles Maurice de Talleyrand secured Louisiana for First Consul Napoleon Bonaparte, who feared that the Americans would take New Orleans before he could do so. For the United States, the difference between having Spain or Napoleon (with his powerful armies) as a neighbor was enormous. Jefferson, now president, demonstrated his interest in the West by dispatching the Lewis and Clark expedition, encouraged the purchases of Indian lands for white settlers, and obtained information on Spanish posts. For some months in 1802 Jefferson maintained the fiction that Spain still owned Louisiana. Then he threatened France. The Democratic-Republican–controlled Congress, however, reduced the size of the army. In December 1802, as Napoleon ordered his army in Holland to go to Louisiana, the American minister in Paris, Robert Livingston, encouraged by land speculators, sought to buy Louisiana for the United States. The House of Representatives, by a vote of 50 to 25, expressed "perfect confidence" in the president and appropriated $2 million for expenses. Jefferson authorized spending up to $10 million to buy the Floridas and New Orleans. Pennsylvania Federalist senator James Ross proposed raising an army of fifty thousand men and taking the area by force.

Napoleon then decided to sell for $15 million what he had purchased from Spain because he heard reports of possible American military action. Besides, his army in Santo Domingo was plagued by yellow fever, and his fleet in Holland was frozen in port. Massachusetts senator John Quincy Adams argued that the purchase was unconstitutional, but the Senate ratified the Louisiana Purchase by a vote of 24 to 7, along strict party lines. In one lucky swoop, Jefferson had doubled the size of the United States.

The War of 1812 and After. Historians used to contend that expansionists had brought about the War of 1812 primarily to satisfy land hunger. More recent scholars, however, see the war's origins as lying in the Democratic-Republican defense of national honor against English violations of American maritime rights and view the American attacks on British Canada as a means to that end.

The Treaty of Ghent, signed in 1815, resolved none of the war's causes. But postwar financial considerations halted a potential naval race on the Great Lakes. Old maritime issues faded as the British West Indies declined in importance, and Britain turned toward building a commercial empire. After the Congress of Vienna, the European colonial era in North America effectively ceased. The United States ultimately responded, in 1823, with the Monroe Doctrine, which boldly pronounced the principles of noncolonization, nonintervention, and no-transfer of colonies and sharply

SEN. LEWIS CASS (D-MICH.). An unabashed promoter of territorial expansion, he supported an aggressive U.S. military policy during the Mexican War and supported the U.S. claim to "all of Oregon." Cass was a member of the committee that drafted the territorial legislation that made up the Compromise of 1850.

HARPER'S PICTORIAL HISTORY OF THE GREAT REBELLION

contrasted democratic America with autocratic Europe.

In 1817 President James Monroe dispatched Gen. Andrew Jackson to chastise marauding Seminoles and English renegades in Spanish East Florida. Secretary of State John Quincy Adams negotiated the Adams-Onís treaty of 1819, in which Spain gave up Florida and its tenuous claims to Oregon and established a northern boundary for Mexico in exchange for American abandonment of a claim to Texas as part of the Louisiana Purchase. These territorial agreements involved no financial transactions. The Senate approved the treaty, with four dissenters complaining about the matter of Texas.

Texas and the War with Mexico. The ideology of religion, defense, and patriotism that constituted American manifest destiny became manifest opportunity for American expansion. The young republic entered a brief period of apparent free expansion. In 1821 Mexico granted Moses Austin permission to settle in Texas with three hundred families, who would profess the Catholic faith. Other entrepreneurs received huge grants of Texas land, and thousands of people, including many squatters, flocked into eastern Texas. In 1824 Texas was incorporated into the Mexican state of Coahuila, whose capital was far away, so the settlers set up their own government and courts to settle uncertain titles. By 1830 there were thirty thousand Americans—as opposed to only four thousand Mexicans—in Texas. Both President John Quincy Adams (who offered $1 million) and President Andrew Jackson (who offered $5 million) proposed buying Texas from Mexico.

In 1832, Texans hoped that Gen. Antonio López de Santa Anna would restore the liberal Mexican constitution of 1824 and permit a separate state government. Instead, Santa Anna turned out to be a centralizer, and Mexican forces under his command massacred five hundred Americans at the Alamo and Goliad. But volunteers from as far away as Maine swelled the ranks of the Texan army, which defeated Santa Anna at San Jacinto in 1836 and made Texas independent. Sen. Daniel Webster (W-N.H.) and other Whigs opposed annexation.

South Carolina's John C. Calhoun, who became President John Tyler's secretary of State in 1844, catered to southern sentiment by proposing a treaty annexing Texas. The Senate rejected the treaty by a vote of 35 to 16, as Democrats split badly and all but one Whig voted no. In April 1844, presidential contenders Sen. Henry Clay (W-Ky.) and former Democratic president Martin Van Buren concurred that, to avoid war, the United States should for the time being refrain from annexing Texas. Other Democrats, however, led by Democratic senator Robert J. Walker of Mississippi, insisted on annexation; they nominated James K. Polk for the presidency and offered an enlarged Oregon Territory as compensation to northerners. Clay's statement that he would be glad to see Texas annexed if it could be done without war or dishonor lost him votes in New York and the election of 1844.

The cost of expansion mounted. The House passed a joint resolution to annex Texas, but it appeared that the Senate might refuse to agree. Sen. Thomas Hart Benton (D-Mo.) favored a treaty and a monetary settlement. Mississippi's Walker combined the House resolution with Benton's bill, and the omnibus measure providing for alternative means of annexation passed the Senate by a vote of 27 to 25. Benton and others thought that incoming president Polk would pursue the treaty route. Suddenly, though, Tyler, who was still in office, sent an agent to Texas and annexed Texas under the joint resolution. Whig senators and Bentonians cried treachery. Mexico broke off diplomatic relations.

Polk had little interest in Texas's boundary claims but meant to buy neglected California and the Southwest, which he saw as territory from which new slave states could potentially be carved. He did not want war. But when Mexico refused to negotiate, Polk dispatched troops to California, intending to force Mexico to cede it. Mexico responded by declaring war and attacking American forces north of the Rio Grande.

Polk sent Congress a measure asking for money and volunteers. South Carolinians Calhoun and Democratic representative Robert Barnwell Rhett attempted to delete the bill's preamble declaring that war had been caused by Mexico's action because they believed this argument unproved and opposed Polk's action in dispatching troops to the Rio Grande. A number of Whigs tried to limit American operations to defense. Polk won by large margins in each house. Calhoun warned that war would damage slavery, and Rep. David Wilmot (D-Pa.) introduced a resolution opposing the extension of slavery into any new territories. His proviso was entwined with the Oregon question.

Oregon. Under an 1818 convention, the Canadian-American boundary lay along the forty-ninth parallel, with Oregon jointly occupied. By 1845 the English Hudson's Bay Company had withdrawn to Vancouver Island, and five thousand Americans had settled Oregon. Calhoun favored establishing a border at 49°. Western Democrats, led by Ohio senator William Allen, argued for 54°40′, the southern limit of Russian America. Polk deviously agreed privately to compromise at 49° but publicly insisted on 54°40′. In April 1846 he obtained a resolution to end joint occupation of Oregon. Then, after testing Senate opinion, he submitted a treaty with England fixing the border at 49°.

The Senate ratified the treaty, 41 to 14, but Allen angrily resigned as chairman of the Foreign Relations Committee. In the House the disgruntled 54°40′ faction joined opponents of Polk and slavery by attaching the Wilmot Proviso to Polk's request for $2 million to pay for a boundary "adjustment" with Mexico and other appropriations bills. Calhoun responded with resolutions against the exclusion of slavery from newly acquired territories. The first filibuster in Senate history followed, and Polk's request failed. Congress had become the anvil for hammering out issues that were dividing the na-

tion. Polk feared for the Union. In 1848, the Whigs, who controlled the House, labeled "Polk's war" unnecessary and unconstitutional. Because the country wanted peace, the Senate approved agent Nicholas Trist's treaty expanding Texas to the Rio Grande and acquiring New Mexico and California for $15 million.

Other Antebellum Developments. These acquisitions cost the Democrats the election in 1848. Northern Democrats bolted to form the Free-Soil party, helping Whig Zachary Taylor to defeat his Democratic opponent, Proviso opponent Sen. Lewis Cass of Michigan. Taylor's administration negotiated the Clayton-Bulwer treaty of 1850, which pledged cooperation with England on an Isthmian canal. In the Senate, Clay's Compromise of 1850, following dramatic debate, made California a free state. But Clay could not solve the issue of slavery in the territories, and the Whig party disintegrated.

Southern Democrats continued to push for expansion using new rationales. In 1853 President Franklin Pierce authorized James Gadsden, U.S. minister to Mexico, to purchase a large area south of the Gila River for a railroad right of way to California. (Antislavery senators, however, reduced the size of the Gadsden Purchase and cut its cost to $10 million.) In 1856 Democrats condemned the Clayton-Bulwer treaty and praised the takeover of Nicaragua by Tennessee filibusterer William Walker. In 1860, after controversial efforts by Pierce and President James Buchanan to buy Cuba to create new slave states, the two conventions of the now-divided Democratic party advocated acquiring the island.

Opponents of slavery also looked south. President Abraham Lincoln encouraged William Walker's associate, the idealistic Joseph Fabens, to colonize freedmen in Santo Domingo. (The enterprise failed.) After the Civil War, Fabens interested inveterate expansionist secretary of State William H. Seward in developing a Dominican harbor. Seward also wanted two of Denmark's Virgin Islands for a U.S. naval base, but an untimely hurricane doomed his treaty in the Senate.

Alaska. Seward's only acquisition, besides the unoccupied Midway Islands, was Alaska, which Sen. Robert Walker had long advocated acquiring. Russia agreed to sell Alaska for $7.2 million because of the Russian-American Company's failure and the danger of English attack or American immigration. Sen. Charles Sumner (R-Mass.) hoped that the treaty might lead to the acquisition of Canada and helped win Senate passage. But the ap-

"THE DAILY GRAPHIC INTRODUCES UNCLE SAM TO SOME OF HIS SPANISH-AMERICAN COUSINS." One of the motivations for U.S. territorial expansion was the desire to find markets for U.S. products. This cartoon depicts Uncle Sam, laden with American produce and manufactured goods, being introduced to women identified as Cuba, Mexico, Venezuela, and Central America. Published 28 November 1885.   LIBRARY OF CONGRESS

propriation bill to pay Russia stalled in the House until mid 1868, partly because of impeachment proceedings against President Andrew Johnson. Prior to Ulysses S. Grant's inauguration, a House investigation revealed that Russia had richly rewarded Walker and journalists for lobbying for the bill.

Grant sought to establish a naval base in the Dominican Republic and sent a trusted aide, Orville Babcock, to negotiate for annexation of all or part of that country. The Dominicans were willing. But memories of the Alaska affair lingered, and Sumner accused Grant and Babcock of having a financial interest in the deal. The House investigated, with a minority report castigating Babcock. A special commission cleared Grant, and in March 1871 Sumner was deposed from his chairmanship of the Senate Foreign Relations Committee. All American Dominican ventures were, however, doomed.

Hawaii. Grant's interest in establishing an American harbor in Samoa revived memories of earlier scandals. Special agent A. B. Steinberger quarreled with British officials and was discredited by revelations of his connections with Babcock, recently implicated in the Whiskey Ring scandal. Moralistic president Grover Cleveland objected to later entanglements in Samoa and to the actions of Americans who overthrew the Hawaiian monarchy in 1893. During his second term, Cleveland withdrew his predecessor Benjamin Harrison's annexation treaty and left Hawaii's fate to Congress. Following intense partisan debate, both houses agreed not to undo the revolution and restore the monarchy in Hawaii but would not approve annexation or even the laying of a cable connection between the mainland and the islands. In 1897, President William McKinley revived the annexation treaty, but he could not secure ratification.

Historians have contended that the rise of social Darwinism, missionary impulses, a search for markets, and navalism broke the deadlock on Hawaii. But in actuality intellectuals, missionaries, and navalists (such as Alfred Thayer Mahan) opposed expansion, and trade protectionism prevailed until 1913. A more convincing interpretation is that a purposeful new generation of leaders had come to power. With the outbreak of the Spanish-American War in 1898, McKinley again pursued Hawaiian annexation, using the new argument of wartime necessity. He also concluded that he had no alternative but to take the Philippines as well as Puerto Rico and Guam. Thus, except for minor additions made by Theodore Roosevelt in Panama and Woodrow Wilson in the Virgin Islands, the expansion of the United States was completed by the end of the nineteenth century.

[*For broad discussion of related issues, see* Foreign Affairs Committee, House; Foreign Relations Committee, Senate; Territories and Possessions. *See also* Canada; Jay's Treaty; Louisiana Purchase; Mexican War; Mexico; Monroe Doctrine; Panama; Philippines; Puerto Rico; Spanish American War. *For discussion of territorial administration and the statehood process of each state of the union, see under the name of the particular state.*]

BIBLIOGRAPHY

Beisner, Robert L. *From the Old Diplomacy to the New, 1865–1900.* 1986.

DeConde, Alexander. *This Affair of Louisiana.* 1976.

Holbo, Paul S. *Tarnished Expansion: The Alaska Scandal, the Press, and Congress, 1867–1871.* 1983.

Osborne, Thomas J. *"Empire Can Wait": American Opposition to Hawaiian Annexation, 1893–1898.* 1981.

Sellers, Charles. *James K. Polk: Continentalist, 1843–1846.* 1966.

Stagg, J. C. A. *Mr. Madison's War: Politics, Diplomacy, and Warfare in the Early American Republic, 1783–1830.* 1983.

PAUL S. HOLBO

TERRITORIES AND POSSESSIONS.

Article IV, section 3 of the Constitution vests Congress with the "Power to dispose of and make all needful Rules and Regulations respecting the Territory or other Property belonging to the United States." In the nineteenth century, Congress focused primarily on the organization of territories and their admission as states into the Union. To accomplish these goals, Congress created committees, provided for territorial delegates, and addressed the purchase or disposal of public lands and petitions of territorial residents seeking relief from land problems. For territories acquired after 1898, the dominant concern of Congress in the twentieth century has been administering the territories and granting them greater political autonomy.

The Continental Congress addressed the issue of territorial government as early as 1780, when it resolved that any land ceded to the national government would be organized into distinct republican states with distinct boundaries and would become members of the federal union on an equal footing with the other states. Congress formed a committee in 1783 to devise a temporary plan of organization and government for the territory west of the Appalachian Mountains. The resulting Ordinance of 1784 provided that after the population of a territory reached twenty thousand, it could hold a convention at a time and place set by Congress. Prior to becoming a state, a territory could send a delegate to Congress who had the right to debate, but not to vote. While Congress has provided for territorial representation in the House, it has never done so for the Senate.

Three years later, the Continental Congress modified the procedure for governing territories with the Ordinance for the Government of the Territory of the United States, Northwest of the River Ohio (the Ordinance of 1787). The Ordinance of 1787 provided for the creation of a maximum of five new states, arranged for territorial governments, and established steps by which a territory could become a state.

Over the years, Congress has refined the rules and procedures for the admission of a territory to the Union. Traditionally, once a territory's population reaches the required number, it can petition Congress to become a state. If Congress is so inclined, it passes an enabling act that authorizes the people to write a state constitution. When the populace ratifies the state constitution, it is submitted to Congress for approval. If both the House and the Senate accept it, then Congress passes a joint resolution declaring the area a state. When the president signs the congressional resolution, the statehood process is complete.

Not all territories followed this tradition. To accelerate the statehood process, Tennessee, in 1796, was the first territory to introduce the concept of shadow representation: its territorial legislature elected two "shadow senators" to the Fourth Congress before Congress had granted statehood to the territory. The Senate refused to recognize them as senators on the grounds that Article I, section 2 of the Constitution provides that members of Congress represent states, not territories. Instead Congress received them as spectators and provided chairs for them until Tennessee was admitted into the Union. Since then, other territories have elected shadow representatives, but Congress has never seated any of them.

A number of congressional committees addressed territorial issues. As a result of the Louisiana Purchase, the House in 1805 created the Committee on Public Lands; ten years later the Senate formed its Committee on Public Lands. The House Committee on Public Lands had jurisdiction on matters relating "to the Lands of the United States." The expectation was that a standing committee would accrue more experience and arrive at more uniform decisions on territorial issues than a select committee. The House Committee on the Judiciary and the Senate Judiciary Committee dealt with territorial judicial proceedings and civil and criminal law.

Some members of the House argued that a standing committee to address territorial issues was needed on the grounds that it would facilitate the process of territorial organization and that the territories had no elected representative in the Senate to advance their interests. Consequently, the House in 1825 established the Committee on Territories to oversee the legislative, civil, and criminal proceedings of the territories, and to devise and report on the means by which the rights and privileges of residents and nonresidents could be protected. With the purchase of Alaska in 1867 the committee exercised general jurisdiction over it as well, including such matters as congressional representation, territorial laws, construction and maintenance of roads, and municipal corporations. In 1889, the House gave the Committee on Territories jurisdiction over territorial legislation and the admission of states. This committee assumed oversight of Hawaii, which was annexed in 1898.

Nearly twenty years after the House did so, the Senate on 24 March 1844 created its own standing Committee on Territories to address territorial issues. Shortly after the creation of this committee, the United States acquired new lands (now the states of Arizona, California, New Mexico, Texas, Utah, and western Colorado), which soon were well populated with residents who expected Congress to respond to their many needs. The Senate Committee on Territories aggressively tried to do so but for years was in conflict with other older, more established standing committees on the issue of jurisdiction. Its chairman, Stephen A. Douglas of Illinois, believed that the committee's province included military, judicial, and post office affairs, as well as everything else related to the territories. The fragmentation of territorial issues within the Senate committee structure, coupled with the Senate's reluctance to consider territorial legislation, enhanced Douglas's commitment to the concept of popular sovereignty or territorial self-government. Eventually, differences over jurisdiction were resolved, often through behind-the-scenes accommodations or by redrafting a bill in such a narrow way that it could be referred only to the desired committee.

A foremost concern of Congress in administering territories has been how to exercise its constitutional power to make all laws and regulations regarding territories while still recognizing the constitutional rights of the territorial residents to govern themselves with respect to internal territorial matters. During the antebellum period, maintaining balance between these competing tensions was particularly difficult when Congress considered petitions for statehood, because it had to reconcile the issues of slavery and sectionalism. When deciding if a territory should become a state, Congress has been influenced by political partisanship, the language of territorial residents, the population of a territory (both its size and ethnicity), regional and economic considerations, slavery, and various other issues. Congress considered many of these factors in the debate on the admission of California and New Mexico to the Union. Both were military districts in 1850 when they petitioned for statehood, but because New Mexico's constitution prohibited slavery, congressional representatives of southern states opposed New Mexico's admission. Therefore, Congress granted California statehood and changed New Mexico's status from a conquered military district to a territory. Not until sixty years later, on 6 January 1912, did President William Howard Taft sign into law the measure passed by Congress to make New Mexico a state.

Although, constitutionally, Congress is empowered to make all rules governing territories, that power was tempered to some degree because of the chaotic situation that existed in the territory of Kansas. Slavery played a role in shaping a new congressional policy toward territories, as the major question concerning Kansas was whether it would be admitted as a slave or free state. The Missouri Compromise of 1820 had excluded slavery from that area of the Louisiana Purchase north of 36°30′ latitude, with the exception of Missouri. To stop the sectional controversy over the extension of slavery, Congress passed the Kansas-Nebraska Act of 1854. This act, with the concept of popular sovereignty, allowed territorial residents to assume control over a matter—slavery—that had previously been handled by Congress. It also dropped restrictive provisions on territorial legislation, such as the congressional veto or disallowance, that had characterized earlier acts.

Usually the executive branch of government makes appointments to territorial offices but with considerable input from Congress. Constitutionally, the Senate is empowered to confirm territorial nominations; customarily, the House is consulted concerning such nominations. Congress has exercised its territorial administrative responsibilities in various ways. It has provided territories with detailed legislative standards and adopted resolutions that limit territorial administrative actions by requiring congressional approval or veto of those actions. It has prescribed the form of territorial organization; passed legislation influencing administrative personnel; authorized and appropriated funds for specific uses in the territories; and required submission of periodic and special reports from territorial departments. Also, Congress has investigated the conduct of territorial administrations.

Before 1898, most of the internal growth of the United States consisted of the acquisition of contiguous mainland areas with the expectations that they would become states. But a new era in territorial relations for the United States began in 1898, when Spain, in the Treaty of Paris, ceded the islands of Guam, Puerto Rico, and the Philippines to the United States. Two other noncontiguous territories were added: American Samoa in 1899, when representatives of the United States, Germany, and Great Britain signed a convention to settle claims to the Samoan group of islands; and the Danish West Indies (today's Virgin Islands) in 1917, when the United States, prompted by military security concerns during World War I, purchased the islands from Denmark. While residents of earlier territories acquired by treaties were promised citizenship, the inhabitants of these territories were not; instead, the treaties provided that Congress should determine their civil and political status. A House Committee on Insular Affairs was established on 8 December 1899. It was given jurisdiction over all subjects except for revenues and appropriations regarding the islands acquired as a result of the Treaty of Paris. That jurisdiction was subsumed by the House Committee on Public Lands on 2 January 1947, renamed the Committee on Interior and Insular Affairs four years later.

In a series of cases called the *Insular Cases* (1901–1922), the Supreme Court clarified the administrative powers of Congress over the territories acquired after 1898 and defined their constitutional status. Unlike past incorporated territorial acquisitions, all of these newly annexed territories were declared unincorporated by the Court. That is, they belonged to but were not a part of the United States, and their inhabitants did not enjoy all of the constitutional protections of American citizens. While incorporation of a territory constitutes a commitment (although not a legal requirement) by Congress to eventually admit the territory into the Union as a state, an unincorporated territory cannot have such an expectation. The Court decided that Congress, legislatively, would determine the citizenship status of residents of these areas. Although Congress has provided for the social and economic development of these territories, its primary concern has been with meeting territorial demands for greater political independence.

Although Congress's timetables for allowing more self-government for the post-1898 territories have differed because of their diversity, it has provided for greater local control for each territory in a similar manner. Congressional representation, the establishment of civil government in the territories, and the provision of citizenship for territorial residents have been determined by such factors as the total population of a territory, the extent to which it has become "Americanized," and its natural resources.

In 1900, the Foraker Act ended military rule in Puerto Rico and made it an unincorporated territory. It also provided for congressional representation with the election of a resident commissioner to a two-year term, but the commissioner would not have a vote or voice in congressional deliberations or the privilege of the floor. The House in 1904 amended its rules to give the resident commissioner floor privileges and in 1906 allowed the resident commissioner to participate in debates both in the House and on a committee, but not to vote in either. A resident commissioner for the Philippines was authorized in 1916, and delegates for Guam and the Virgin Islands in 1972. In 1970 the House amended its rules to allow a resident commissioner and a territorial delegate to serve on standing committees with the right to vote in committee, but not on the floor. Its most recent modification of rules, in 1993, allows territorial representatives a floor vote in the Committee of the Whole, but if these votes were to decide a measure, a separate, regular House session vote would be necessary.

While Congress established civil government for Puerto Rico soon after it was acquired, Guam was administered by the U.S. Navy for nearly fifty years before gaining civil government in 1950. In 1900, President William McKinley placed the Samoan Islands under the control of the Department of the Navy until Congress enacted the statutory authority for civil government in 1929. Congress granted citizenship to Puerto Ricans in 1917, and to most Virgin Islanders in 1927, but did not confer citizenship on residents of Guam until 1950. Citizenship was conferred on residents of the Virgin Islands who did not wish to retain their Danish citizenship and on natives of the islands, whether residing in the United States or in Puerto Rico, who were not citizens or subjects of any foreign country on 17 January 1917. In 1932 citizenship was offered to Virgin Islanders residing in the United States or any of its territories or possessions regardless of their place of residence on 17 January 1917. The delay in conferring citizenship on Guamanians occurred because of the island's distance from the United States, national security concerns, and charges that Guamanians were unfamiliar with the democratic system of government. The Philippine Act of 1902 established the temporary administration of civil government in the Philippines, and the Jones Act of 1916 committed the U.S. government to the islands'

Landmark Legislation concerning U.S. Territories and Possessions

Title	Year Enacted	Reference Number	Description
An act for the admission of the state of California into the Union	1850	9 Stat. 452–453	Admitted California to the Union as a free state.
An act for the government of the District of Columbia, and for other purposes	1874	18 Stat. 116–121	Abolished the office of Delegate from the District of Columbia.
Hawaii Annexation	1898	30 Stat. 750–751	Provided for annexation of Hawaii.
Foraker Act	1900	31 Stat. 77–86	Established civil government in Puerto Rico.
Philippine Government Act	1902	32 Stat. 691–712	Provided for temporary administration of civil government in the Philippines.
Jones Act (Organic Act of the Philippine Islands)	1916	39 Stat. 545–556	Authorized a resident commissioner for the Philippines; promised independence "as soon as a stable government can be established."
Convention between the United States and Denmark for Cession of the Danish West Indies	1917	39 Stat. 1706–1717	Provided for the U.S. purchase of the Danish West Indian Islands (the Virgin Islands) from Denmark for $22 million.
An act to provide a civil government for Puerto Rico, and for other purposes	1917	Act of 2 March 1917, chap. 145	Granted U.S. citizenship to Puerto Ricans.
Act of 25 February 1927	1927	P.L. 69-640	Made most Virgin Islanders U.S. citizens.
An act relating to the immigration and naturalization of certain natives of the Virgin Islands	1932	P.L. 72-198	Conferred citizenship on native Virgin Islanders residing in the continental United States or its territories or any of its insular possessions.
Tydings-McDuffie Philippines Independence Act	1934	P.L. 73-127	Provided for eventual complete independence for the Philippines.
An act to provide for the organization of a constitutional government by the people of Puerto Rico	1950	P.L. 81-600	Established the Commonwealth of Puerto Rico.
Organic Act of Guam	1950	P.L. 81-630	Made Guamanians U.S. citizens; provided for civil government in Guam.
An act to establish a commission on the organization of the government by the District of Columbia and to provide a congressional delegate	1970	P.L. 91-405	Provided a delegate to the House of Representatives from the District of Columbia.
An act to provide congressional delegates for Guam and the Virgin Islands	1972	P.L. 92-271	Provided for representation in the House of Representatives for Guam and the Virgin Islands.
District of Columbia Self-Government and Governmental Organization Act (Home Rule Act)	1973	P.L. 93-198	Allowed residents of the District of Columbia greater legislative authority over local matters.

ultimate independence. But these laws did not extend the rights of the Constitution to Filipinos or confer citizenship upon them. Instead, the Philippine Independence Act of 1934 provided for a ten-year commonwealth period for the Philippines, followed by complete independence.

Article I, section 8, clause 17 of the Constitution provided for the establishment of a discrete district, not to exceed one hundred square miles outside the boundaries of any state, to serve as the nation's capital. To create this federal district, the states of Maryland and Virginia ceded parcels of their land on either side of the Potomac River, which were accepted by Congress in 1790. While Congress was granted sole legislative jurisdiction over this area, the Constitution did not address the matter of representation in the Congress for permanent residents of the nation's capital.

In 1871 Congress passed legislation that provided the District of Columbia with a nonvoting delegate in the House of Representatives, an office Congress abolished three years later. In 1970 Congress again provided for a nonvoting delegate from the District. Congress passed an act in 1973 to allow the District more legislative authority over essentially local matters but retained the power to overturn, amend, or repeal acts passed by the city council. In 1978 a proposed constitutional amendment that would have provided for the election of two senators and at least one representative to Congress was passed, but failed to be ratified by the required number of states. With the failure of the constitutional amendment, the movement for statehood for the District of Columbia gained support. In the 103d Congress committee hearings were held on a statehood bill (H.R. 51), but it was defeated in the House by a vote of 153 to 277.

On 14 November 1993 Puerto Rico held a plebiscite to enable voters to choose between three political status options: enhanced commonwealth, statehood, or independence. Of the 1.7 million votes cast (73.5 percent of registered voters) commonwealth status received 826,326 (48.6 percent), statehood received 788,296 (46.3 percent), and independence received 75,620 (4.4 percent). (Blank ballots received 1 percent of the vote.) The results of the plebiscite were to be reviewed by a House committee hearing. On 24 May 1994 the House Subcommittee on Insular and International Affairs held hearings on H.R. 4442, a bill that provides for full self-governance and political empowerment in the United States insular areas.

Both the House and Senate have undergone several committee reorganizations that have affected how territorial issues have been addressed within the congressional committee structure. Standing committees in the 103d Congress with jurisdiction over territorial affairs include the House Natural Resources and the Senate Energy and Natural Resources committees.

During the twentieth century Congress has provided for increased political autonomy for the territories at the local and federal levels. In its commitment to the principle of self-determination, Congress has encouraged residents of insular areas to vote on their relationship with the United States—whether they want the territory to become a part of the United States or prefer some other political arrangement. Through committee hearings, round-table discussions, and conferences, Congress continues to hold dialogue with territorial representatives and leaders in an effort to allow residents of U.S. territories to enjoy the full extension of the U.S. Constitution or to achieve full self-governance and political empowerment consistent with the principles of self-determination.

[*For discussion of past and present organizational units of the United States, see* District of Columbia; Panama; Philippines; Puerto Rico; West Florida; *and entries on each state of the union. See also* Energy and Natural Resources Committee, Senate; Kansas-Nebraska Act; Louisiana Purchase; Mexican War; Missouri Compromise; Monroe Doctrine; Natural Resources Committee, House; Shadow Senators; Spanish American War; Territorial Expansion; Wilmot Proviso.]

BIBLIOGRAPHY

Bloom, John Porter, ed. *The American Territorial System.* 1973.

Journals of the Continental Congress. 13 October 1780. Vol. 3.

Journals of the Continental Congress. 1 October 1783. Vol. 4.

Journals of the Continental Congress. 12 July 1787. Vol. 4.

U.S. Congress. *Annals of the Congress of the United States.* 9th Cong., 1st sess., 1805. Vol. 15.

U.S. Congress. *Congressional Globe.* 31st Cong., 1st sess., 1850. Vol. 19.

U.S. Congress. *Congressional Record.* 56th Cong., 1st sess., 1900. Vol. 69.

U.S. Congress. *Congressional Record.* 103d Cong., 1st sess., 5 January 1993. Vol. 139, pp. H47–H48. Daily Edition.

U.S. House of Representatives. *History of the United States House of Representatives,* by George Barnes Galloway. 87th Cong., 1st sess., 1962. H. Doc. 87–246.

GARRINE P. LANEY

TEST BAN TREATY. *See* Limited Test Ban Treaty.

TEXAS. After three centuries of Spanish and Mexican rule, Texas declared its independence from Mexico on 2 March 1836. It effectively secured this claim seven weeks later, when troops commanded by Sam Houston defeated a Mexican army at the Battle of San Jacinto. That September, Houston was elected president of the new Republic of Texas, and was given an overwhelming mandate to seek annexation to the United States. Mexico, however, had not recognized Texas's independence, and annexation threatened to destroy any chances of recovering debts owed by Mexico to U.S. citizens. Further, the acquisition of Texas would shatter the delicate political balance between slave and free states.

Refusing to take such risks, President Andrew Jackson recognized Texas's independence but refused to back annexation. Texas negotiators again pressed their case during Martin van Buren's administration, only to be rebuffed by Secretary of State John Forsyth's contention that the Constitution did not permit annexation of a foreign country. President John Tyler and Secretary of State John C. Calhoun proved more receptive, however, and a formal treaty of annexation was signed on 12 April 1844. The move would have made Texas a territory and placed its public lands in the hands of the federal government, which had agreed to assume the Republic's debt. But the proposal became an issue in that year's presidential contest between James K. Polk (a Democrat who supported annexation) and Henry Clay (a Whig who opposed annexation because it might lead to war with Mexico); a skittish Senate thus rejected the treaty by a 35 to 16 margin.

Polk's subsequent victory was viewed as a popular mandate for expansion, allowing lame-duck president Tyler to resume negotiations. Now holding the diplomatic advantage, Texas secured major concessions: immediate statehood, the right to divide into as many as five states, and retention of its public lands. In return, Texas kept its debt. With party and sectional rivalries still keen, negotiators bypassed the treaty format and proposed that Texas be annexed by a joint resolution, which the Senate and House approved by 27 to 25 and 120 to 98, respectively. In Texas, a special convention also favored annexation, and on 13 October 1845 voters approved the measure by 4,254 to 257. President Polk signed the act into law on 29 December 1845;

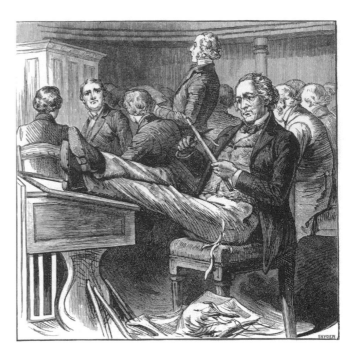

SEN. SAM HOUSTON (D-TEX.). Whittling in the Senate. Known in the Senate for his rough-hewn manner, Houston became governor of Texas in 1859. Always a strong Unionist, he refused to swear allegiance to the Confederacy when Texas seceded, and he was subsequently removed as governor. *PERLEY'S REMINISCENCES*, VOL. 1

in Texas, Republic officials relinquished authority to newly elected state authorities on 19 February 1846.

Texas quickly became a major factor on the national scene, as annexation proved an important cause of the resulting war with Mexico. The state's ambitious western and northern land claims remained unresolved until the Compromise of 1850, when Texas accepted its present northwestern boundary in return for a ten-million-dollar government payment. As one of only four senators to support each part of the compromise proposal, Sen. Sam Houston, a consistent Unionist, played a crucial role in its passage. But on 23 February 1861 Texas voters approved secession from the Union by a 46,129 to 14,697 vote, and shortly thereafter the Lone Star State joined the Confederate States of America. With the collapse of the Confederacy on 17 June 1865, President Andrew Johnson officially began the process of reconstructing the state's civil government. Republicans eventually secured majorities in Texas politics, and by an act of 30 March 1870, Texans were once again admitted to the U.S. Congress. Following Reconstruction, conservative

Democrats quickly regained control. Bolstered by the state's growing population, the Texas delegation increased from four in 1870 to twenty by 1931. Major Texas figures during the late nineteenth century included Roger Q. Mills, chair of the House Ways and Means Committee, and Sen. John H. Reagan, coauthor of the Interstate Commerce Act.

In 1931, John Nance Garner became the first Texan elected Speaker of the House; fellow Texans Sam Rayburn (House Speaker in every Democratic-controlled Congress from 1940 to 1961) and James C. Wright, Jr. (House majority leader from 1977 to 1987 and Speaker from 1987 to 1989), continued Texas's exaggerated influence over House affairs. In the Senate, Lyndon B. Johnson served as majority or minority leader from 1953 to 1961. Other Texas notables included Tom T. Connally, advocate of Franklin D. Roosevelt's policies as chair of the Senate Foreign Relations Committee; Martin Dies, Jr., chair of the House Un-American Activities Committee; and Sen. Morris Sheppard, minority Senate floor leader from 1929 to 1933.

For many years the Texas delegation consisted solely of Democrats who often maximized their power and minimized political risks at home by voting in unison on controversial issues. For instance, after the Supreme Court ruled in the so-called Tidelands cases that oil-rich submerged lands off the Texas, California, and Louisiana coasts belonged to the federal government, not to the states, the delegation fought as a unit to overturn the decision legislatively. Twice Congress passed quit-claim statutes ceding the disputed lands to the states only to have President Harry S.

Truman veto the measures. Victory finally came in 1953 with passage of the Submerged Lands Act (P.L. 83-31), which granted coastal states their claims to submerged lands within their traditional seaward boundaries. (Such distance varied from three and one-half miles to, in Texas's case, ten miles from the shoreline.) President Dwight D. Eisenhower, indebted to Texas for its support in the previous election, signed the legislation. A sister statute, the Continental Shelf Lands Act (P.L. 83–212), retained federal ownership of all submerged land beyond the state boundaries to the edge of the continental shelf.

During the 1960s and 1970s, the traditional white male Democratic dominance over Texas politics was gradually shattered. The first Texan of Hispanic origin in Congress, Democrat Henry B. Gonzalez, was elected in 1961, and by 1989 had become chair of the House Banking, Finance, and Urban Affairs Committee. In 1972, Barbara Jordan became the first black female House member from the South. When Lyndon B. Johnson became vice president in 1961, his vacated Senate seat was won by John Tower, the state's first Republican senator since Reconstruction. By 1993, both Texas senators were Republican, as were nine of the state's thirty House members.

[*See also* Mexican War.]

BIBLIOGRAPHY

Richardson, Rupert N., et al. *Texas: The Lone Star State.* 6th ed. 1993.

Webb, Walter Prescott, et al., eds. *The Handbook of Texas.* 3 vols. 1952, 1976.

Robert Wooster

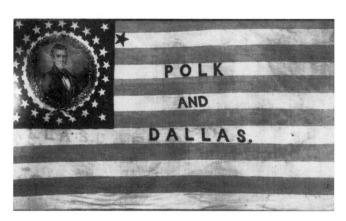

Campaign banner. For the 1844 Democratic ticket of James K. Polk and George M. Dallas. Polk's support of the annexation of Texas is indicated by the extra star on the flag.   Collection of David J. and Janice L. Frent

THINK TANKS. Nonprofit public policy research organizations are informally known as think tanks. Along with executive agencies and Congress's four research arms—the Congressional Research Service, the Congressional Budget Office, the Office of Technology Assessment, and the General Accounting Office—think tanks are an important source of policy expertise and advice for Congress.

Interactions between think tanks and Congress take many forms. Think tank scholars testify frequently before congressional committees, and some think tanks prepare issue briefs on specific pieces of legislation as they come up for votes in Congress. Legislators and congressional staff are frequent participants in think tank symposia and conferences. Informal contacts between think tank scholars and legislative staff are also widespread within specialized Washington issue networks dealing with issues as diverse as health care and defense. There is some interchange of personnel between the legislative branch staff and think tanks: each of the heads of the Congressional Budget Office, for example, has come from a think tank. And think tank staff members serve as interpreters of Congress and legislative policy-making to the public through their own writings and through "punditry" in the print and electronic media.

Locating in and around the nation's capital offers think tanks important advantages both for access to policymakers and visibility in the national media. An estimated one hundred think tanks, most focused on national policy-making, are based in the Washington, D.C., area. The oldest of these is the Brookings Institution, which was formed from a merger of several organizations (the oldest dating back to 1916) in 1927. Other large think tanks in Washington include the American Enterprise Institute for Public Policy Research (founded in 1943), the Carnegie Endowment for International Peace (1910), the Cato Institute (1977), the Center on Budget and Policy Priorities (1981), the Center for Strategic and International Studies (1962), the Heritage Foundation (1973), and the Urban Institute (1968). Prominent think tanks outside the Washington area that focus on national policy-making include the Hoover Institution on War, Revolution, and Peace in Stanford, California (1919); the Hudson Institute in Indianapolis (1961); and the RAND Corporation in Santa Monica, California (1948).

A large number of new think tanks have been established since the 1970s. Given the high start-up costs of such institutions, many of the newer think tanks have chosen to specialize in a few issues. The Institute for International Economics, for example, focuses on the issues implied in its name; the Center on Budget and Policy Priorities focuses on issues relating to low-income Americans; and the Joint Center for Political and Economic Studies concentrates on the concerns of African Americans.

Think tanks vary widely in size: the largest, the RAND Corporation, had an annual operating budget of more than $100 million in 1990–1991. The smallest may have staffs of only one or two people, with most of the research contracted out to university-based scholars. More important, think tanks also differ in their sources of funding, staffing arrangements, and the types of research they produce. Contract research organizations, typified by the RAND Corporation and the Urban Institute, rely for most of their financing on government agencies, and their most common research output is in the form of reports to those agencies, released to the public only if the agencies choose to do so. Other think tanks, such as the Brookings Institution and Russell Sage Foundation, focus on basic social science research, with monographs and other books as their most common research products. Institutions of this type generally take no institutional positions on issues and try to portray themselves as nonideological and nonpartisan. Still others, commonly known as advocacy tanks, do take institutional positions and hew more closely to a particular ideological line. The conservative Heritage Foundation, the libertarian Cato Institute, and the liberal Economic Policy Institute are examples of this type of think tank.

The range of think tank activity in the United States is much broader than in most other Western industrial democracies. The separation of executive and legislative powers is one of the most important reasons for this pattern. The existence of a strong, autonomous national legislature in which individual legislators do not have to vote according to the party line and have opportunities to act as policy entrepreneurs creates a ready audience for independent policy information. The relationship between think tanks and legislators in the American system is a symbiotic one: think tank researchers want to show that they have influence to justify further contributions from the foundations, corporations, and individuals who provide most of the funding for most of these organizations, while legislators want policy ideas that will heighten their reputations with their colleagues and constituents.

While legislators and their staffs value think tank expertise for its independence—especially independence from executive branch control—think tanks do have disadvantages relative to other sources of policy expertise, especially the congressional research agencies. Think tank studies focusing on basic social science research may be too long and technical or may conflict with legislators' needs for results that are timely, unambiguous, and easily translatable into policy prescriptions. Studies by advocacy tanks, on the other hand, may be discounted—especially by legislators with generally opposing views—as too predictable.

Competition among think tanks has been intensified in recent years not only by the growing ranks of these organizations, but also by cutbacks in federal funding for social science research and by the decision of many large foundations to devote more resources to demonstration projects rather than research. Under U.S. tax laws, think tanks as nonprofit organizations are prohibited from directly lobbying for the adoption of their proposals. Competition, however, has led many think tanks to give increased attention to marketing their research, for example by making their analyses briefer and less technical in order to make them more accessible to legislators and other policymakers.

The amount of influence that think tanks, individually and collectively, have on legislative policymaking is inherently difficult to judge, and most of the evidence is anecdotal. Because most congressional policy-making takes place slowly and involves a melding of different proposals, it is difficult to establish with certainty where ideas have come from. Many are eager to claim parentage of successful proposals; unsuccessful proposals are usually orphans. It is even more difficult to try to determine the policy influence of one think tank as opposed to another because the various ways that think tanks attempt to influence the development of public policy are not comparable, either in the kind of impact they have or the time frame in which the effects of think tank analyses could be expected to be visible to observers. The relevance of basic social science research, for example, may not become clear for many years. Program evaluations and brief analyses of particular bills, on the other hand, are likely to be more immediately relevant to policymakers but may become obsolete quickly.

BIBLIOGRAPHY

Smith, James A. *The Idea Brokers: Think Tanks and the Rise of the New Policy Elite*. 1991.
Weaver, R. Kent. "The Changing World of Think Tanks." *PS: Political Science and Politics* 21 (1989): 563–578.
Weiss, Carol. *Organizations for Policy Analysis: Helping Government Think*. 1992.

R. KENT WEAVER

THIRTEENTH AMENDMENT. Abraham Lincoln's Emancipation Proclamation, effective 1 January 1863, added the abolition of slavery to the Union's Civil War aims, but it did not apply to the border slave states or to those areas of the seceded states under Union army control. Concerned that the Proclamation, a war measure based on military authority, might not stand up to judicial scrutiny and that legislation alone could not achieve the complete destruction of the institution of slavery,

Congress moved to write the abolition of slavery into the Constitution. Drawing from the familiar wording of the Northwest Ordinance of 1787, Sen. Lyman Trumbull of Illinois, chairman of the Judiciary Committee, reported a proposed amendment stating, "neither slavery nor involuntary servitude, . . . shall exist within the United States, or any place subject to their jurisdiction." Trumbull turned back a Radical Republican proposal to explicitly guarantee personal equality before the law, but added an important second section that empowered Congress "to enforce this article by appropriate legislation." With Lincoln's endorsement and full Republican support, the amendment passed the Senate by the necessary two-thirds majority (38 to 6) on 8 March 1864. Because of Democratic opposition to the enforcement clause, however, the House could not muster a two-thirds margin and the proposal failed (95 to 65) in mid June.

The National Union (Republican) party endorsed the amendment in the November 1864 presidential campaign, and Lincoln took his reelection as a mandate to pass the amendment. Rather than waiting for the new, more heavily Republican House to come into office in March 1865, Lincoln and congressional Republicans decided to push the amendment through in the lame-duck session of the 38th Congress beginning in December 1864. With heavy lobbying of key House Democrats by Secretary of State William H. Seward, the amendment passed the House on 31 January 1865 by a vote of 119 to 56—a bare two-thirds majority made possible by the yea votes of sixteen Democrats and the absence of eight other Democrats. Abolitionists and blacks celebrated the achievement as a fitting climax to their long crusade against slavery.

In the belief that the seceded states were merely out of their proper relationship with the Union, Lincoln and Seward adhered to the constitutional requirement of ratification by three-quarters of all the states, including those still in rebellion. With the exceptions of Delaware, Kentucky, and New Jersey, the Union states promptly ratified the amendment, as did Arkansas, Louisiana, and Tennessee, all Confederate states with Unionist governments. But it was not until President Andrew Johnson made approval of the Thirteenth Amendment a requirement of his plan of reconstruction that it was formally added to the Constitution on 18 December 1865.

Initially hopeful that the amendment would provide the freed slaves with equality before the law and protection against the "residual effects of bondage," the Republicans were soon disappointed

ABRAHAM LINCOLN'S EMANCIPATION PROCLAMATION. The entire text of the Proclamation is printed inside the oval and dated 22 September 1862. The names of Confederate and Federal states are linked together in a chain surrounding the oval. At the bottom, freed slaves pray under the inscription "Give thanks all ye people, give thanks to the Lord." The proclamation's aim of abolishing slavery, effective 1 January 1863, was later embodied in the Thirteenth Amendment to the U.S. Constitution.

LIBRARY OF CONGRESS

THE ABOLITION OF SLAVERY. The print depicts the U.S. House of Representatives on 31 January 1865, when congres
sional approval of the Thirteenth Amendment was announced.   LIBRARY OF CONGRESS

when the southern states passed "black codes" restricting the liberties of freedpeople. As a consequence, Republican congressmen relied on the
amendment's enforcement clause to pass an act
strengthening the Freedmen's Bureau and a Civil
Rights Act, which included the freedmen in the first
national definition of citizenship and enumerated
specific protected civil rights (those relating to person and property—as distinct from political or social rights in that period). Both were passed in 1866
over Johnson's veto and conservative protests, with
Trumbull arguing that the second section of the
Thirteenth Amendment gave "Congress authority to
see that the first [section] was carried out in good
faith" and that the amendment offered protection
for "every person in the United States in all rights of
person and property belonging to a free citizen." In
this interpretation, the Thirteenth Amendment thus
significantly altered federal-state relations with its

expansion of national responsibility to guarantee
personal liberty and equality before the law against
state or private infringements. Still, in the Republicans' concept of states' rights nationalism, this was
a qualified expansion of federal authority. Although
often not fulfilled in the years to come, the hope
was that the states would assume their constitutional obligation to protect personal liberty with little federal interference.

During the late nineteenth century and well into
the twentieth, the Supreme Court took a narrow
view of the Thirteenth Amendment, holding that it
had little application beyond the prohibition of
chattel bondage by states or individuals. During the
civil rights revolution of the 1960s and beyond,
however, the Court began to rely on the Thirteenth
Amendment and the Civil Rights Act of 1866 to curtail the "badges and incidents" of slavery in decisions involving racial discrimination.

BIBLIOGRAPHY

Belz, Herman. *Emancipation and Equal Rights: Politics and Constitutionalism in the Civil War Era.* 1978.

Hyman, Harold M., and William M. Wiecek. *Equal Justice under Law: Constitutional Development, 1835–1875.* 1982.

TERRY L. SEIP

THURMAN, ALLEN G. (1813–1895), Democratic representative and senator from Ohio, vice presidential candidate (1888). Born in Lynchburg, Virginia, Alan Granberry Thurman moved with his father to Chillicothe, Ohio, in 1819. He became a successful lawyer and was elected as a Democrat to the 29th Congress (1845–1847). After one term, he resumed his legal practice in Ohio and served as an associate justice (1851–1854) and then chief justice (1854–1856) of the state supreme court. Thurman was a Douglas Democrat during the crisis years of the late 1850s and favored a negotiated peace during the Civil War. Wartime passions had sufficiently subsided by 1868 to produce a Democratic majority in the Ohio legislature, which sent Thurman to the U.S. Senate.

During the next dozen years, the "old Roman" became one of his party's leaders in the Senate. His Jeffersonian Democratic beliefs and his commitments to strict construction and states' rights made it easy for him to reknit old alliances with southern Democrats in the wake of the Civil War. A member and sometimes chairman of the Judiciary Committee, he was a prominent opponent of the Civil Rights Act of 1875, a supporter of the resumption of specie payments, and a Democratic member of the 1877 Electoral Commission that settled the Hayes-Tilden presidential contest.

The growing strength of Republicanism in Ohio led to Thurman's rejection for the Senate by the state legislature in 1881. He returned to the practice of law in Columbus. He was the running mate of Grover Cleveland in Cleveland's unsuccessful 1888 bid for reelection as president.

BIBLIOGRAPHY

Flick, Alexander Clarence, and Gustav S. Lobrano. *Samuel Jones Tilden: A Study in Political Sagacity.* 1939.

Merrill, Horace S. *Bourbon Democracy of the Middle West, 1865–1896.* 1953.

Rothman, David J. *Politics and Power: The United States Senate, 1869–1901.* 1966.

PAOLO E. COLETTA

ALLEN G. THURMAN. Caricature of Thurman taking some snuff, which is falling from his thumb. Lithograph by J. Keppler, *Puck*.   LIBRARY OF CONGRESS

TILLMAN, BENJAMIN R. (1847–1918), Democratic senator from South Carolina and self-styled champion of white supremacy and agrarian insurgency. The youngest son of a prosperous Edgefield County planter, Benjamin Ryan Tillman became a successful farmer during the Reconstruction era, but by the mid 1880s he had turned his attention to politics, transforming a state farmers' association into a powerful political organization. In 1890 a coalition of disaffected white farmers elected him governor, displacing the venerable conservative Democrat Wade Hampton. Inspired by his rhetorical pledge to go after President Grover Cleveland "with a pitchfork and prod him in his old fat ribs," the South Carolina legislature elected him to the Senate as a free-silver Democrat in 1894. Henceforth known as "Pitchfork Ben," Tillman was reelected in 1900, 1906, and 1912.

During his time in the Senate, he gained a repu-

SENATOR TILLMAN'S ALLEGORICAL COW.

SENATOR TILLMAN'S ALLEGORICAL COW No. 2.

TILLMAN'S ALLEGORICAL COW. The caption for the top drawing reads: "This cartoon, designed by Senator Tillman, shows his idea of the present American situation. The cow, symbolical of natural resources, is feeding on the produce of the farmers of the West and South, while her golden milk is all drawn away by the 'sharpers,' gamblers, and speculators in Wall Street." The caption for the lower drawing reads: "In this cartoon Senator Tillman shows the result of the attempt of farmers to turn the big cow around, to let her feed on income tax in the East while they should milk her in the West and South. . . . As soon as she tried to feed on income tax the Supreme Court seized her by the throat as a reminder that she must do her eating exclusively in the agricultural regions. The farmers in the West are disappointed and get no income-tax milk." Drawn by Tom Fleming, *New York World*, 1 March 1896. On 3 October 1913 this became the first and only cartoon published in the *Congressional Record*. Congress reacted with a law barring the publication from carrying illustrations in the future.   LIBRARY OF CONGRESS

tation as a fiery orator with a tempestuous personality. In 1902 he was formally censured for assaulting a fellow senator in the Senate chamber. An outspoken critic of the McKinley, Roosevelt, and Taft administrations, he railed against economic protectionism, the annexation of the Philippines, and moderate racial policies that, he warned, threatened white supremacy. Despite his "Popocratic" image, Senator Tillman was a mercurial reformer who opposed the Pure Food and Drug Act, the eight-hour day for federal employees, child labor laws, woman suffrage, and most federal conservation programs. However, to the relief of President Theodore Roosevelt and Senate progressives, he lent strong support to the controversial 1906 Hepburn railroad rate bill.

The election of Democrat Woodrow Wilson to the presidency in 1913 provided new opportunities for senatorial leadership, but fending off challenges to his longstanding political hegemony in South Carolina drew most of Tillman's attention from 1912 on. During his final years in the Senate, Tillman grew increasingly conservative, displaying more interest in patronage than reform. From 1913 to 1918 he chaired the Committee on Naval Affairs, but he never became a major force in the Wilson administration. Tillman and Wilson frequently clashed over patronage matters, but the senator's ardent support of Wilson's war policies brought a presidential endorsement during the 1918 senatorial primary campaign. Only Tillman's death in July 1918 prevented his reelection to a fifth term.

BIBLIOGRAPHY

McGhee, Zach. "Tillman: Smasher of Traditions." *World's Work* 12 (1906): 8013–8020.
Simkins, Francis Butler. *Pitchfork Ben Tillman, South Carolinian.* 1944.

RAYMOND ARSENAULT

TILSON, JOHN Q. (1866–1958), representative from Connecticut and conservative Republican House majority leader (1925–1931). Tilson was born in the Republican hill country of Tennessee in 1866. After migrating to New Haven, Connecticut, to attend Yale University, Tilson settled there and established a law practice. Elected to the Connecticut state house of representatives in 1904, Tilson became speaker of that body in 1906. Tilson's congressional career began with his election as congressman-at-large for Connecticut in 1908, although he was defeated for reelection in 1912.

Tilson returned to the House from the 3d District in Connecticut in 1915 and won appointment to the influential Military Affairs and Ways and Means committees. Tapped for majority leader by Republicans in 1925, Tilson acted as a key legislative strategist for the Coolidge and Hoover administrations and, with Speaker Nicholas Longworth, Rules Committee chairman Bertrand H. Snell, and Longworth's close associate James T. Begg of Ohio, formed the ruling inner circle that dominated the House during that period.

Tilson guided the passage of the landmark Reapportionment Act of 1929. The act, one of the most far-reaching pieces of legislation to affect representation in Congress, broke a stalemate that had lasted through the 1920s. It permanently fixed the size of the House of Representatives at 435 members and provided for the automatic apportionment of the chamber after each decennial census.

Tilson was successfully challenged for the party leadership in 1931 by Snell. Speaker Longworth had died, and the Republican contingent in a closely divided House shrank to minority status with the deaths of fourteen representatives. Some observers saw Tilson's defeat as a repudiation of President Herbert Hoover's leadership, particularly because Tilson was a close friend of the president. Tilson resigned from Congress in 1932 and taught parliamentary law at Yale until his death in 1958.

BIBLIOGRAPHY

Ripley, Randall. *Majority Party Leadership in Congress.* 1969.
Sweeting, Orville J. "John Q. Tilson and the Reapportionment Act of 1929." *Western Political Quarterly* 9 (June 1956): 434–453.

RICHARD C. BURNWEIT

TOBACCO. Congressional activity related to the regulation of tobacco products reflects critical questions about the role of the federal government in making public health policy. Since the development, beginning in the 1950s, of persuasive medical evidence linking cigarette smoking to serious disease, Congress has debated a range of measures intended to control or restrict the use of tobacco. Following release of the report of the Surgeon General's Advisory Committee on Smoking and Health in 1964, Congress passed the Federal Cigarette Labeling and Advertising Act. This law required that all cigarette packages be labeled, "Caution: Cigarette Smoking May Be Hazardous to Your Health."

Landmark Legislation

Title	Year Enacted	Reference Number	Description
Federal Cigarette Labeling and Advertising Act	1965	P.L. 89-92	Required health warning on all cigarette packages: "Caution: Cigarette Smoking May Be Hazardous to Your Health."
Fair Packaging and Labeling Act	1966	P.L. 89-755	Required fair, nondeceptive packaging and labeling. Tobacco and tobacco products are excluded.
Public Health Cigarette Smoking Act of 1969	1970	P.L. 91-222	Banned cigarette advertising on television and radio and required a stronger health warning on cigarette packages: "Warning: The Surgeon General Has Determined that Cigarette Smoking Is Dangerous to Your Health."
Comprehensive Drug Abuse Prevention and Control Act of 1970	1970	84 Stat. 1236–1296	Tobacco and tobacco products excluded from jurisdiction.
Little Cigar Act of 1973	1973	P.L. 93-109	Banned little-cigar ads from television and radio.
Amendment to Consumer Product Safety Act	1976	P.L. 94-284	Amended to exclude tobacco and tobacco products.
Amendment to Federal Hazardous Substances Act	1976	90 Stat. 503–510	Amended to exclude tobacco.
Toxic Substances Control Act	1976	P.L. 94-469	Tobacco and tobacco products excluded from jurisdiction.
Tax Equity and Fiscal Responsibility Act of 1982	1982	P.L. 97-248	Temporarily doubled the federal excise tax on cigarettes to 16 cents per pack, to be in effect 1 January 1983 to 1 October 1985, the first increase since 1951.
No Net Cost Tobacco Program Act of 1982	1982	P.L. 97-218	Reduced taxpayers' costs for the tobacco price support program.
Comprehensive Smoking Education Act	1984	P.L. 98-474	Required rotational health warning on cigarette packages and advertisements.
Cigarette Safety Act of 1984	1984	P.L. 98-567	Required research and a report on "fire-safe" cigarettes.
Comprehensive Smokeless Tobacco Health Education Act of 1986	1986	P.L. 99-252	Required the rotation of three health warnings on smokeless tobacco packages and advertisements and banned smokeless tobacco advertising on broadcast media.
Tobacco Program Improvement Act of 1986 (Title I of the Consolidated Omnibus Budget Reconciliation Act of 1985)	1986	P.L. 99-272	Further revised the price support program.
Tax Equity and Fiscal Responsibility Act Amendments (Title XIII of the Consolidated Omnibus Budget Reconciliation Act of 1985)	1986	P.L. 99-272	Extended permanently the 16-cents-per-pack federal excise tax on cigarettes.
Federal Aviation Act Amendments	1988	P.L. 100-202	Congressionally mandated smoking ban on domestic airline flights scheduled for 2 hours or less. Northwest Airlines voluntarily bans smoking on all flights in North America.
Department of Transportation and Related Agencies Appropriations Act of 1990	1990	P.L. 101-164	Congressionally mandated smoking ban on all domestic airline flights.
Comprehensive Omnibus Reconciliation Act of 1990	1990	P.L. 101-508	Federal excise tax increased from 16 cents to 20 cents; further increased to 24 cents, effective 1993.

Although the tobacco industry initially opposed this legislation, it eventually acquiesced, in part to avoid state labeling initiatives, which were preempted by the federal act.

In 1970, Congress took further action, passing the Public Health Cigarette Smoking Act, banning cigarette advertising on television and radio and mandating stronger warning labels on all packages ("Warning: The Surgeon General Has Determined that Cigarette Smoking Is Hazardous to Your Health"). The broadcast ban released broadcasters from the requirement of airing free antismoking messages. Moreover, it led to great increases in advertising in print media and on billboards and to tobacco industry promotion of sports and cultural events. In 1984, Congress passed the Comprehensive Smoking Education Act, requiring four rotating warning messages on cigarette packages. The Comprehensive Smokeless Tobacco Act of 1986 required similar package warnings on chewing tobacco products and banned broadcast ads for these products.

Efforts to label cigarettes and restrict advertising were bitterly contested in Congress. While representatives of the tobacco industry framed the debate in terms of rights and freedoms, public health advocates saw a compelling health interest in the control of tobacco products. As medical data regarding the harmful effects of smoking accrued in the 1950s, the industry acted in 1958 to form the Tobacco Institute, which conducts lobbying and public relations efforts. The Tobacco Institute has worked aggressively to restrict regulatory legislation, arguing that the evidence of tobacco's harm is inconclusive. Southern congressional delegations, especially from the tobacco-producing states of North Carolina, Kentucky, South Carolina, and Virginia, have long regarded tobacco as a vital economic interest and have worked diligently to oppose any regulations that might depress consumption of tobacco products.

Health activists and consumer groups have formed public interest lobbies, such as Action for Smoking and Health (ASH) and Group Against Smokers' Pollution (GASP), that have contested the tobacco industry's public relations and lobbying campaigns and that have pushed for more regulatory legislation. With increasing medical evidence that cigarette smoke is harmful to nonsmokers as well as smokers, Congress has supported restricting smoking in public places. Although most such regulation has taken place at the local and state level, Congress in 1988 mandated that all domestic airlines ban smoking on all flights within the United States of two hours or less. This ban was then extended to all domestic flights in 1990.

Although federal regulation of tobacco increased from the 1960s through the 1980s, such actions must be viewed in the context of earlier congressional actions that awarded price supports to tobacco producers and consistently excluded the industry from consumer-protection initiatives.

While the still-looming specter of Prohibition's failure probably precludes legislation that would ban the production and sale of cigarettes, the current economic and political environment may well lead to further restrictions on cigarette advertising and smoking in public places as well as to higher excise taxes.

Since the 1960s the percentage of Americans who smoke has declined from approximately 45 percent to 26 percent. Nevertheless, cigarette smoking continues to contribute to more than 400,000 deaths each year.

The growing recognition of the addictive qualities of nicotine has led to new congressional hearings as well as proposals for tobacco to come under the regulatory aegis of the Food and Drug Administration.

BIBLIOGRAPHY

Fritschler, A. Lee. *Smoking and Politics: Policymaking and the Federal Bureaucracy.* 1969.

Sapolsky, Harvey M. "The Political Obstacles to the Control of Cigarette Smoking in the United States." *Journal of Health Politics, Policy, and Law* 5 (1980): 277–290.

U.S. Department of Health, Education, and Welfare. *Smoking and Health: Report of the Advisory Committee to the Surgeon General of the Public Health Service.* 1964.

U.S. Department of Health and Human Services. *Reducing the Health Consequences of Smoking: Twenty-five Years of Progress.* 1989.

ALLAN M. BRANDT

TONKIN GULF RESOLUTION (1964; 78 Stat. 384). On 2 August 1964 the American destroyer *Maddox*, on patrol off the North Vietnamese coast, was attacked by three North Vietnamese torpedo boats. Two days later the *Maddox*, joined by the destroyer *Turner Joy*, reported a second attack. In response President Lyndon B. Johnson ordered air strikes against North Vietnamese targets, which were made on 5 August. He also asked Congress to approve a statement of support for his Southeast Asia policy.

On 7 August the Southeast Asia Resolution, known as the Gulf of Tonkin Resolution, was approved by a unanimous House and in the Senate by a vote of 88 to 2. The resolution declared that the United States regarded the maintenance of international peace and security in Southeast Asia as "vital to its national interest and to world peace," and it approved the determination of the president "to take all necessary steps, including the use of armed force," to repel further attacks and aggression.

Although he had voted to approve the resolution, Sen. J. William Fulbright (D-Ark.) and other members of Congress later charged that the resolution, described as the functional equivalent of a declaration of war, had been extorted from Congress through misrepresentation and deception. Controversy has centered on the location of the American ships and on whether a second attack indeed took place. It appears that while the president did not deliberately fake the news of a second attack, he seized on an ambiguous set of circumstances to obtain congressional backing for his Vietnam policy.

In December 1970, Congress repealed the Tonkin Gulf Resolution. The Nixon administration regarded repeal as irrelevant to the policy of withdrawal then under way, especially since Congress continued to appropriate funds and rejected resolutions for the termination of the war.

BIBLIOGRAPHY

Stockdale, Jim, and Sybil Stockdale. *In Love and War.* 1984.
Windchy, Eugene C. *Tonkin Gulf.* 1971.

GUENTER LEWY

JOHN G. TOWER. During a press conference, 12 August 1970.   LIBRARY OF CONGRESS

TOWER, JOHN G. (1929–1991), Republican senator from Texas, chairman of the Committee on Armed Services, and a leading advocate of a strong defense policy. John G. Tower rose from hardscrabble origins to leave a lasting mark on Texas politics and on U.S. military policies during a quarter century in the Senate. His career ended in humiliation when his nomination to be secretary of Defense was rejected in 1989.

Born in Houston, Tower made political history in 1961 by becoming the first Republican from the former Confederacy to win election to the Senate since Reconstruction. Filling the seat left vacant when Lyndon B. Johnson was elected vice president, the conservative Tower was instrumental in building the Republican party in the formerly one-party state.

A dapper, diminutive man, Tower had an abiding interest in defense. When the Republicans captured control of the Senate in 1980, Tower became chairman of the Armed Services Committee and was a principal architect of the military buildup undertaken by President Ronald Reagan.

He retired from the Senate in 1985 and later became a strategic arms negotiator for the United States. In 1987 he chaired the commission that criticized operations of Reagan's National Security Council in the wake of the Iran-contra scandal.

In December 1988, president-elect George Bush nominated Tower to be secretary of Defense. The nomination set off a bitter, partisan confirmation fight, marked by charges of drinking, womanizing, and conflicts of interest. Tower vigorously defended himself, but after an angry floor debate the nomination was rejected 53 to 47.

Tower was killed in a commuter plane crash on 5 April 1991.

BIBLIOGRAPHY

Knaggs, John R. *Two-Party Texas: The John Tower Era, 1961–1984.* 1986.

Tower, John G. *Consequences: A Personal and Political Memoir.* 1991.

DANIEL J. BALZ

TRADE. *See* Tariffs and Trade.

TRADEMARKS. *See* Copyright, Trademarks, and Patents.

TRANSITIONS, PRESIDENTIAL. *See* Presidential Transitions.

TRANSPORTATION. Efficient and economical transportation has always been a major American policy concern. And from its earliest days, Congress has played a very significant role in the development and evolution of the nation's transportation systems. This discussion of congressional transportation policy consists of three sections. The first presents an overview of the powers of Congress to influence transportation and the legal and social context within which that influence functions. The second provides a historical overview of changes in transportation technology and congressional policy responses. The third discusses likely transportation issues facing Congress in the 1990s and beyond.

Legal Powers of Congress. From 1789 to the present, the history of transportation in the United States has involved the creation of private industries operating within a context of federal, state, and local government subsidies and regulations. Only rarely and in limited circumstances, such as the federal takeover of railroads during World War I or the settling of labor disputes in national emergencies, has the national government exercised total authority over a mode of transportation.

The U.S. Constitution empowers the federal government to regulate commerce between the states and with foreign nations. Article I, section 8 states that "Congress shall have Power . . . to regulate Commerce with foreign Nations and among the several States," "To establish Post Offices and post Roads," and to "provide for the common Defence and general Welfare of the United States." Supporters of congressional involvement in transportation have pointed to those clauses as legal justification for the legislature to provide subsidies—ranging from land grants to loan guarantees—for dredging harbors and building roads, railroads, airports, public transit systems, and more.

The constitutional power to regulate commerce is based upon English common law, the legacy of judicial decisions that the colonists inherited from England. Carriers that provided transportation service to the general public, and were thus known as common carriers, had certain legal obligations. They were to serve the public regularly and at reasonable times, deliver passengers and cargoes safely, charge reasonable rates, and treat all shippers equally. When carriers failed to perform these obligations, government intervened.

Regulation has involved both economic and noneconomic matters. Economic regulation typically has focused on rates charged to shippers, entry into and termination of service, and business practices fostering monopoly. Noneconomic regulation has included standards for fuel efficiency, specifications for safety and noise pollution, requirements for the submission of environmental impact statements, and prohibitions against racial segregation.

Congress has used a variety of means to regulate transportation. Some laws restrict transportation companies directly; others establish and guide regulatory agencies that oversee them. The first and most prominent among the agencies is the Interstate Commerce Commission. Ultimately, congressional committees review the work of independent agencies and the executive branch. Congress as a whole must approve the budgets of the regulators and so has significant influence on their policies.

Era of Development (1789–1870). Initially, Congress focused on developing a transportation system, not regulating it. As the population sought to take advantage of virgin lands and other natural resources, the pressing need was to enable people and goods to move within a national market that by the 1890s extended some three thousand miles from east to west and fifteen hundred miles north and south. To accomplish this, Congress provided subsidies for the creation and improvement of roads, waterways, and railroads.

From 1789 to 1815, commerce moved on waterways, especially along the Atlantic coast. Seaport cities such as Philadelphia, New York, and Boston dominated the national economy. Most roads were little more than broad trails that proved treacherous in wet weather. In 1789, President George Washington sailed from Virginia to New York City to attend his inauguration. In the South, most plantations were within five miles of a waterway. Until the transportation system reached across the Appalachian Mountains, settlers in the West remained isolated from patterns of commerce and economic development in the East.

The transportation issues considered by Congress were as much political as economic. Disagreements centered on the extent of federal authority to assist transportation projects within the states. The Constitution provided federal authority for postal roads but not highways or canals, and while section 8 of Article I empowered Congress to act for the "general Welfare of the United States," Article X declared that all powers not delegated to the government of the United States belonged to the states and the people.

As demands for congressional transportation assistance multiplied, the legislature responded to each request individually without formulating a comprehensive policy. Subsidies for water-borne transportation were relatively noncontroversial. Thus, in 1789 Congress aided American shipping by providing for a 10 percent reduction on duties for imports arriving on American vessels and imposing a tonnage tax on the cargoes of foreign-owned ships. Congress regularly provided money to improve harbor facilities. Shipbuilders and owners benefited greatly when President James Madison signed the Navigation Act of 1817, which excluded ships owned by foreigners from carrying passengers and goods along the coast of the United States.

The years from 1815 to 1860 were prosperous ones for steamboats. However, this new means of transportation was plagued by numerous accidents resulting from overheated boilers. In 1838, Congress improved steamboat safety by establishing a system of inspection and regulation of those engaged in interstate commerce.

Communities clamored for access to waterways that would connect isolated lands in the interior to major rivers and lakes. Thus, in 1822 New York state began the Erie Canal to connect New York City with Lake Erie. The success of that state-financed venture led to similar canal efforts, especially in Pennsylvania and Ohio. Congress contributed financially to the construction of canals, and in 1823 it approved a significant Rivers and Harbors Act that provided federal support for im-

proving the inland waterways system. By 1860, Congress had subscribed to over $1 million of stock in canal companies, the most notable being the Chesapeake and Ohio in 1824, and had donated approximately four million acres of federal land to build canals in Ohio, Michigan, Indiana, Illinois, and Wisconsin.

Congressional road subsidies proved far more controversial. In 1803, as states began chartering private companies to build and operate turnpikes, Congress authorized the use of money from the sale of federal land in Ohio to assist construction of the National Road. This well-engineered road began in Cumberland, Maryland, crossed western Pennsylvania, and eventually reached the new state of Ohio and later Illinois.

However, attempts in Congress to fund highway improvements on a national and massive scale met with opposition. Critics argued that national funding of transportation projects within the boundaries of a single state was unconstitutional and would favor some areas while leaving others underdeveloped. On these grounds, President Madison vetoed the bonus bill of 1817. In 1830, President Andrew Jackson vetoed the Maysville Road bill, an intrastate connection to the National Road in Kentucky. He also returned responsibility for funding of the National Road itself to the states within which it passed. But Congress continued to approve appropriations for "postal" roads as the merits of each case—and the politics of each situation—demanded.

Congress also subsidized the development of railroads. Between 1824 and 1838, Congress authorized land surveys that were invaluable to railroads. In addition, from 1830 to 1843, Congress reduced the tariff on imported iron because the nascent U.S. iron industry could not provide all the rails that the railroads needed. Nevertheless, private investment, foreign and local, and state charters and assistance provided more stimulation for railroad expansion than federal assistance.

During the 1840s and 1850s the war with Mexico and the expansion of slavery into the territories fractured the national political parties. As a result, Congress was stalemated in dealing with national transportation issues. However, in 1850, an unusual set of political circumstances caused Congress to support railroad development in a significant way. Easterners with real-estate investments in Illinois joined forces with westerners and southerners to persuade Congress to support a railroad connecting Illinois, Mississippi, and Alabama. An act of 20

September 1850 gave federal lands in Illinois, Mississippi, and Alabama to those states to help construct the north-south Illinois Central Railroad. In exchange, federal troops and property would travel free on the railroad, and Congress would fix the mail rates. This land grant set off a flurry of similar proposals. Most of them failed, but by 1857 Congress had granted approximately eighteen million acres to support the building of approximately twenty-three railroads.

The Civil War left its mark on transportation in several ways. First, the need to move large quantities of troops and supplies greatly enhanced the importance of the railroads. Second, the secession of the Democratic South ended the partisan and regional stalemates of the prewar period in favor of Republican domination of Congress. Third, the war and postwar Reconstruction substantially increased the power of the federal government over the states. Conscription, the creation of a national currency or greenbacks, and the first national income tax were evidence of the federal government's new power. And in 1862, Congress chartered two railroads, the Union Pacific and the Central Pacific, to build the first transcontinental railroad.

The years following the Civil War were ones in which the national government fostered economic expansion generally and the development of railroads specifically. High tariff policies, endorsed by the dominant Republican party, helped to foster American industries, especially producers of the iron and steel that was needed by railroad builders. Meanwhile, grants of federal land went directly to private railroad companies rather than to states. In 1869, the Union Pacific and the Central Pacific, both of which had received federal land grants, linked up to form the first transcontinental railroad. By the time the land grant program ended in 1871, Congress had awarded a total of 131 million acres of federal land to encourage the construction and extension of railroads. Railroad miles increased by almost sixfold over 1850, reaching a total of 52,922 miles. By 1870, more transportation moved by rail than by water. Railroads, developed by state and private subscription and assisted with federal grants, were the key transportation element in the creation of a national market.

The Railroad Era (1870–1920). By 1870, regulating railroads to protect shippers and investors had become a national concern. Railroads expanded by merging with the lines of competing companies to become interstate systems. By 1886, three-fourths of railroad traffic crossed state lines. Some railroads favored national regulation to protect themselves from other railroads and powerful shippers. Standard Oil, for example, accounted for so much freight that it could dictate favorable rates and even extract rebates from railroads whose solvency depended upon its business.

Beginning in 1872, a series of congressional committees studied the railroad industry and national transportation concerns. In the *Wabash* case (1886), the Supreme Court ruled that railroads passing through states could be regulated only by Congress. Congress quickly passed the Interstate Commerce Act of 1887, sponsored by Sen. Shelby M. Cullom (R-Ill.), who had headed a special committee to investigate railroad practices.

The 1887 law looms large in transportation history for several reasons. For the first time Congress concerned itself with regulating rather than simply promoting transportation. The act forbade railroads from discriminating among shippers, prohibited long haul–short haul rate discrimination, forbade railroad rate pools, and required that all rates be reasonable and maintained as published. Congress created a special commission, the Interstate Commerce Commission (ICC), whose members were appointed by the president and confirmed by the Senate, to hear complaints, decide cases, and develop regulations within the mandate of the act.

Decades of legislation further defined and expanded the powers of the ICC. The Compulsory Testimony Act of 1893 gave witnesses in ICC hearings immunity from prosecution for their testimony, thereby strengthening the commission's ability to extract testimony from reluctant parties. The Elkins Act of 1903 attempted to eliminate rebates to favored shippers by making only published rates lawful. The Hepburn Act of 1906 enabled the ICC to prescribe uniform accounting and reporting rules and prohibited rail carriers from transporting articles in which they had a financial interest. That act also authorized the ICC to set maximum rates after finding an existing rate to be unreasonable and expanded the commission's power to include such related transportation industries and services as railroad cars, terminal services, and pipelines. In 1910, the Mann-Elkins Act brought telegraph, telephones, and cable under the jurisdiction of the ICC. In 1914, the Clayton Antitrust Act authorized the commission to bar railroad corporations from owning stock in another railroad if the effect of that ownership was to reduce competition.

By 1917, the railroad industry that had once dominated national transportation was falling on

THE FIRST TRANSCONTINENTAL RAILROAD. Formed by the joining of the Union Pacific Railroad and Central Pacific Railroad lines. The photograph shows the driving of the last stake at Promontory Point, Utah, 10 May 1869. Photograph by A. J. Russell.   LIBRARY OF CONGRESS

hard times. Many companies had laid rails where the volume of traffic did not justify expansion. Furthermore, their heavy capitalization made it difficult for them to raise the additional funds necessary to modernize their railbeds and rolling stock. As a result, cost cutting and reductions in railroad service became common. So, too, did labor strikes as workers faced reduced wages. When the United States entered World War I in 1917, rail service was so unreliable that the federal government temporarily nationalized the railroads as an emergency measure.

The Regulatory Era (1920–1976). Congress continued to search for a balance between the pressure to keep railroad rates low and the profit-making needs of a network of private railroads. But increasingly, Congress attempted to balance the interests of railroad owners not only with shippers but also with alternative modes of transportation such as trucks, buses, and airplanes. Congress also sought to limit destructive competition among transportation businesses.

The Transportation Act of 1920 marked a new direction for Congress, setting a pattern of regulation and support that would continue for the next half century. Essentially, it returned the railroads to private control after the period of wartime ownership and operation and attempted to strengthen their financial standing in a number of ways. The act charged the ICC to establish a fair rate of return. At first, this rate was set at 6 percent. It also empowered the commission to establish minimum as well as maximum rates so that excessive competition among the railroads would not undermine the industry.

At the same time, the Transportation Act of 1920

encouraged railroads to consolidate their routes and shed unprofitable services. The ICC was given authority over extensions of railroad track and abandonments of service. The act ordered the commission to develop a master plan for a limited number of railroad systems. Finally, it sought to avoid disruptions of rail service during labor disputes by creating a Railroad Labor Board.

In the end, the 1920 legislation failed to revive the declining railroad industry. In 1922, a national railroad strike caused Congress to deal with the labor issue again in the Railway Labor Act of 1926, which replaced the Railroad Labor Board with the prewar mediation system. Nor did plans for pooling and combining railroads proceed as anticipated. Then the Great Depression precipitously reduced the total volume of commerce.

Meanwhile, competition from automobiles and trucks ensured the continuing decline of the railroad industry. The United States quickly became the leading car culture in the world by far, and congressional appropriations assisted states in building more and better roads to accommodate the movement of an ever-increasing number of trucks and automobiles. The Post Office Act of 1912 provided $500,000 for states to improve post roads. In 1916, the Federal Road Act added another $75 million over five years and also required states to create highway departments to inspect road construction as a condition for receiving matching grants. In 1921, the Highway Aid Act attempted to focus federal support on a few major roads. It required each state to designate principal highways, which were not to exceed 7 percent of the state's total mileage. Federal assistance for highway building benefited a new mode of transportation that competed with railroads.

Congress also aided the development of another transportation industry: the airlines. World War I had demonstrated the military value of airplanes. After the war, many planes and trained pilots formed the core of a new transportation industry. In 1925, the Air Mail Act authorized the Post Office to contract with air transportation companies to deliver mail. These contracts sustained air transportation companies at a time when the industry lacked cargo and passengers. The Air Commerce Act of 1926 created the Bureau of Air Commerce in the Department of Commerce and directed it to establish, operate, and maintain all necessary air navigation facilities, except airports. It empowered the bureau to develop air safety regulations and inspect aircraft and pilots.

Congress also continued to assist water carriers. The Rivers and Harbors Act of 1902 established a formal program to review proposed waterway improvements. In 1916, the Shipping Act established the United States Shipping Board, which had regulatory jurisdiction over common carriers operating in international waters and the Great Lakes. The Merchant Marine Act of 1920 affirmed that coastal and intercoastal transport had to be in vessels constructed, owned, and operated by U.S. citizens.

The Great Depression of the 1930s spurred Congress and the federal government to assist transportation in order to revive the national economy. The Emergency Transportation Act of 1933 created a temporary official, the Federal Coordinator of Transportation, who was to work with the railroads to eliminate duplication of service and equipment and reduce ruinous competition. The coordinator studied government involvement in all modes of transportation and made recommendations to Congress, ultimately persuading it that the government could not rescue the railroads without also regulating its competitors.

The Motor Carrier Act of 1935 put most interstate trucks and buses under the jurisdiction of the Interstate Commerce Commission. It required carriers to apply for permission to engage in interstate commerce and to prove that there was a sufficient volume of traffic to sustain a new carrier. After approving a carrier, the ICC then determined the reasonableness and lawfulness of the rates it charged shippers.

Congress also extended its powers over the airline industry. It established the Civil Aeronautics Authority in 1938 (later the Civil Aeronautics Board) with powers similar to those of the ICC. The CAA approved applications to engage in commercial aviation and reviewed rates. In addition, the act removed previous restrictions on federal participation in airport development and improvement.

Meanwhile, Congress continued to support maritime shipping. The Merchant Marine Act of 1936 provided for a federal subsidy to shipbuilders in the United States to enable them to compete with foreign competitors. It also furnished an operating subsidy that reimbursed U.S. ship operators to the extent that their operating costs exceeded those of foreign competitors. The Federal Maritime Administration, a descendant of the Shipping Board of 1916, administered the subsidies as a unit of the Department of Commerce.

The Transportation Act of 1940 put interstate water carriers under ICC control. They, like motor carriers, had to obtain certificates of public convenience and necessity from the ICC. The commission could establish maximum, minimum, or exact rates.

Involved as it was in different and competing modes of transportation, Congress found it necessary to forge a statement of intermodal policy to guide the ICC. The Transportation Act of 1940 required the commission to administer regulations impartially for all modes of transportation, to protect the inherent advantages of each mode of transportation from unfair competition, and to assure the public of access to an efficient system of transportation. It left to the ICC the definition of "inherent advantages." The commission also had to balance the wishes of shippers seeking inexpensive rates with those of transportation enterprises needing adequate earnings to maintain and upgrade equipment and pay employees.

World War II ended the Great Depression and, temporarily, the economic concerns of America's transportation industries. But the wartime burden on the railroads and the rationing of steel accelerated the deterioration of track and rolling stock. Meanwhile, increasing numbers of trucks, buses, and automobiles traversed highways that for lack of money and material were not being properly maintained. The Federal Aid Highway Act of 1944 provided for a maximum of forty thousand miles of high quality roads, but Congress failed to agree on a plan of funding.

During the 1950s, a series of congressional actions dealt with the postwar circumstances of American transportation: an expanding economy; booming motor and air carriers; and a declining railroad industry. In 1954, Congress voted to join with Canada in the Saint Lawrence Seaway project to provide a navigable waterway between Lake Ontario and the Atlantic Ocean. Two years later, Congress turned its attention to highways. The Highway Act of 1956 provided for the creation of 42,500 miles of high-quality and high-speed interstate highways that spanned the nation and enabled people and goods to move rapidly and conveniently from coast to coast. It allowed states to propose the routes that would receive financial assistance and created a highway trust fund to support construction. The funds were to come from highway users in the form of taxes on gas, tires, rubber, vehicles, and more. Eventually, the principle of funding improvements to transportation through user taxes would be extended to airlines and water carriers.

By the late 1950s, airlines had surpassed railroads as the leading long-distance carriers of people. Two major airplane accidents spurred passage of the Federal Aviation Act of 1958. That legislation provided for a Federal Aviation Agency to take over the physical facilities of civil aviation, investigate accidents, and make safety rules for air traffic. The act also perpetuated the economic regulations of the Civil Aeronautics Board (CAB). The CAB approved airline rates, forbade airlines from abandoning routes without approval, reviewed all proposed mergers and consolidations, and continued to require airlines to prove that the transportation market justified new routes of service.

At the same time, Congress attempted to halt the decline of the railroads. The Transportation Act of 1958 provided a loan guarantee program that enabled railroads to borrow money from banks to finance new equipment and maintain their railbeds. The act also gave the ICC jurisdiction over all proposals to discontinue passenger trains, including intrastate routes. To enable railroads to better compete with trucks, it reduced the number of classes of motor carriers exempt from economic regulation. Finally, it instructed the ICC not to use rates to protect one type of carrier over another.

One consequence of the Transportation Act of 1958 was to speed up the pace at which railroads abandoned passenger service to cities. Automobiles and improved roads had already encouraged people to move from cities to suburban areas. With population declining and the urban tax base shrinking, cities' public transportation systems fell into disrepair and bankruptcy. Mayors and city planners protested that transportation policies made in Washington were undermining urban transportation systems. The Housing Act of 1961 addressed the crisis by providing for matching grants to foster demonstration projects in mass transportation, and the Urban Transportation Act of 1964 increased the scale and scope of federal assistance. Finally, in 1973, Congress made urban transportation eligible to receive financial support from the Highway Trust Fund.

As Congress became more involved in subsidizing and regulating competing modes of transportation, the need for a central agency responsible for research and recommendations became apparent. Therefore, the Transportation Act of 1966 created the Department of Transportation in the executive branch. The department brought together the many agencies that had been dealing with individual modes of transportation throughout the federal bureaucracy.

Landmark Transportation Legislation

TITLE	YEAR ENACTED	REFERENCE NUMBER	DESCRIPTION
Navigation Act of 1817	1817	14th Cong., 2d sess., chap. 31	Excluded foreign shipping from trading along U.S. coast, thereby benefiting domestic shipbuilders and operators.
Rivers and Harbors Act of 1823	1823	17th Cong., 2d sess., chap. 56	Provided federal funding for improving inland water system.
Act to Regulate Commerce (ICC Act)	1887	24 Stat. 379	Established the Interstate Commerce Commission
Rivers and Harbors Act of 1902	1902	P.L. 57-154	Established formal review program of proposed improvements to rivers and harbors.
Elkins Act	1903	P.L. 57-103	Declared that only published railroad rates were legal; raised penalty for rebates.
Hepburn Act	1906	P.L. 59-337	Gave ICC power to set maximum rates and extended ICC authority to railroad cars, terminals, and pipelines.
Mann-Elkins Act	1910	P.L. 61-218	Shifted the burden of proof that a railroad rate was reasonable to the railroads.
Federal Aid Road Act	1916	P.L. 64-260	Established program of formula-based grants for federal assistance to states for roads; states, in turn, had to establish highway departments for purposes of planning and safety.
Shipping Act	1916	P.L. 64-260	Established the United States Shipping Board, which had authority over shipping in Great Lakes and in international waters.
Esch-Cummins Transportation Act	1920	P.L. 66-152	Returned nationalized railroads to private ownership and instructed ICC to permit minimum profit of 6 percent, with money deducted from those earning more to go to a fund to support those earning less than 6 percent.
Air Mail Act	1925	P.L. 68-359	Provided for subsidies to commercial airplanes for carrying the U.S. mail.
Air Commerce Act	1926	P.L. 69-254	Created the Bureau of Air Commerce in the Department of Commerce and empowered it to establish, operate, and maintain air navigation facilities.
Railway Labor Act	1926	P.L. 69-257	Established basic pattern of arbitration and mediation in transportation industries.
Emergency Railroad Transportation Act	1933	P.L. 73-68	Temporarily created Office of Transportation Coordinator, which developed recommendations for congressional action in transportation.
Motor Carrier Act	1935	P.L. 74-255	Put trucks under economic and noneconomic regulation of ICC and required applications for new routes.
Civil Aeronautics Act	1938	P.L. 75-706	Provided for economic regulation of airlines and created Civil Aeronautics Board (CAB).
Transportation Act of 1940	1940	P.L. 76-785	Placed inland water transport under the jurisdiction of the ICC; included first statement of national transportation policy.

The Era of Deregulation (1970s and 1980s). The growing federal involvement in transportation created an escalation of criticism in the 1960s and 1970s. Protests arose over the degree to which highway building and airport expansion disrupted the environment. Congress responded with the National Environmental Policy Act of 1969, which required that highway planners file environmental impact statements. The Arab oil embargo of 1973 and the resulting fuel shortages strengthened support for mass transit. The National Mass Transportation Assistance Act of 1974 opened the pros-

Landmark Transportation Legislation (Continued)

TITLE	YEAR ENACTED	REFERENCE NUMBER	DESCRIPTION
Wiley-Dondero Act	1954	P.L. 83-358	Committed United States to cooperate with Canada in the Saint Lawrence Seaway Project, providing a navigable waterway between Lake Ontario and the Atlantic.
Federal-Aid Highway Act of 1956	1956	P.L. 84-627	Provided for an interstate highway system and the creation of a fund from user taxes to support highway development.
Transportation Act of 1958	1958	P.L. 85-625	Provided loans to railroads and gave ICC total power over requests for abandonments of service.
Federal Aviation Act	1958	P.L. 85-726	Created the Federal Aviation Agency and continued economic regulation of airlines.
Housing Act of 1961	1961	P.L. 87-70	First federal assistance to mass transportation.
Urban Mass Transportation Act of 1964	1964	P.L. 88-365	Increased scale and scope of federal assistance to mass transportation.
Department of Transportation Act	1966	P.L. 89-670	Created Department of Transportation.
National Environmental Policy Act	1969	P.L. 91-190	Required environmental impact statements from states that were planning highways.
Airport-Airway Development Act	1970	84 Stat. 219	Provided for user taxes, which would constitute a fund to develop and maintain airports and airways.
Railway Passenger Service Act	1970	P.L. 91-518	Created a semipublic corporation charged with the mission of preserving a basic level of intercity rail passenger service by identifying the most important routes, which would receive government subsidies and loan guarantees; established AMTRAK from railroads that had been privately owned, the shareholders of which received stock in the corporation.
Regional Rail Reorganization Act	1973	P.L. 93-236	Intended to preserve a network of railroads to move freight by creating a semipublic corporation, the Consolidated Rail Corporation (CONRAIL), maintaining it with subsidies and loan guarantees.
National Mass Transportation Assistance Act	1974	P.L. 93-503	Significantly increased federal money available for mass transit and provided for operating subsidies.
Railroad Revitalization and Regulatory Reform Act	1976	P.L. 94-210	Established zones of rate freedom for railroads, enabling them to raise or lower fares without ICC review.
Airline Deregulation Act	1978	P.L. 95-504	Provided for phasing out of CAB and for lifting of economic regulations.
Motor Carrier Act of 1980	1980	P.L. 96-296	Lifted economic regulations from the trucking industry.
Staggers Rail Act	1980	P.L. 96-448	Continued lifting of economic regulations from railroads, further limiting ICC approval of rates and requiring speedier conclusion of railroad abandonment decisions.
Bus Regulatory Reform Act	1982	P.L. 97-261	Extended economic deregulation of motor carriers to interstate buses.

pect of billions of dollars of federal aid to build and operate mass transit in order to lessen the nation's dependence on automobiles.

The continuing decline of the railroads, despite congressional support, necessitated new and costly rescue efforts. In 1970, the Penn Central, the largest American railroad, filed for bankruptcy. Congress responded by enacting the Railway Passenger Service Act of 1970. It created a semipublic corporation, the National Railroad Passenger Corporation (AMTRAK), with the mission of preserving and upgrading rail passenger service by consolidating the lines into a single public corporation. With the help of congressional subsidies and loan guarantees, AMTRAK began functioning in 1971.

Congress next addressed the freight portion of the railroad industry. The Regional Rail Reorganization Act of 1973 created another public corporation, the Consolidated Rail Corporation, to operate the freight services of restructured railroads. Massive loans and subsidies, it was hoped, would maintain the nation's freight service.

However, critics increasingly argued that legislation initiated in the 1930s to protect the transportation industry in a shrinking economy only preserved inefficient companies in the 1970s, thereby wasting financial resources. In the 1970s, a burgeoning consumer movement argued that regulators and regulations served carriers more than consumers.

During the 1970s and 1980s, congressional transportation policy toward airlines, railroads, and motor carriers moved in the direction of reducing economic regulation. The Airline Deregulation Act of 1978 limited the Civil Aeronautics Board's involvement in reviewing rates, permitted more airlines to propose routes without having to prove that market conditions justified the application, and provided for the phasing out of the CAB itself by 1985. Similarly, the Motor Carrier Act of 1980 limited the ICC in restricting new carriers from entering the trucking business. Potential carriers needed only to prove competence, not that the market justified another carrier. In addition, the act established zones of freedom in which carriers could raise or lower rates without ICC review. The Bus Regulatory Reform Act of 1982 extended the same freedom from economic regulation to buses.

To make them more competitive with other modes of transportation, Congress also limited its regulation of railroads. The Railroad Revitalization and Regulatory Reform Act of 1976 forbade the ICC from deeming a rate too low if railroads could prove that it was adequate to recover expenses and generate a profit. It also provided railroads zones of rate freedom in which they could raise or lower fares up to 7 percent annually without ICC approval. The Staggers Rail Act of 1980 further limited ICC review of railroad rates and required the commission to respond more quickly to requests to terminate unprofitable service. Both acts also provided public funding for railroads to improve their tracks and equipment. Congress expected that market circumstances and changes in economic regulation would enable the railroad industry to become sufficiently profitable to take care of itself without further subsidies.

The 1990s and Beyond. Predicting the future is a perilous undertaking. Nevertheless, the problems and actions of the past provide both a setting for the present and landmarks that point to the future. Four issues in transportation policy will likely draw the attention of Congress in years to come. The first is the impact of deregulation. Has the removal of restrictions on transportation rates and entry into the transportation industry increased public access to transportation? Has it reduced the cost to users without undermining the profitability of the industries themselves? Congress will continue to balance the interests of users and of owners.

Second, Congress is likely to continue to wrestle with providing financial support to transportation. Everyone can agree that a healthy system of transportation is critical to the health of the national economy. Public investments in the infrastructure of transportation—roads, harbors, airports, and the like—usually stimulate business activity, which in turn generates revenue for the national treasury. Nevertheless, it is difficult to identify precisely how much the general public benefits from each tax dollar invested in transportation. Does a million dollars in a road in rural Mississippi produce more economic gain than a million dollars invested in improving an airport runway in Chicago? How are nationally funded improvements to transportation determined when the immediate impact is local?

Even more controversial is determining the proportions of the cost of improvements to transportation that should be paid by state and local governments, the transportation user, and the federal government. The Airport-Airways Development Act of 1970 created a fund based on user taxes to maintain and develop air transportation facilities. Similarly, in 1978, Congress sought to pass on some of the costs of public improvements to rivers and harbors by taxing diesel fuel and investing the revenue in a trust fund. How much of the cost of improvements in the transportation infrastructure can private carriers bear before they must raise prices? If state and local governments pay more for improvements to national transportation, should they have greater power in setting the priorities for national funding?

A third concern is the coordination of transportation industries. Historically, each mode of transportation has evolved separately, and in each case, Congress has responded with a mixture of subsidy and regulation. Sometimes, as with highway construction, subsidies advanced one industry—automobiles and trucking—in its competition with another, railroads. Until the era of deregulation, carriers in one industry could not own or invest in carriers of another because of the same fear of transport monopoly that led to the creation of the ICC in 1887. For many years, the trust funds created from the proceeds from one form of transportation could not be used to improve another.

This attention to individual industries has impeded the development and implementation of a national transportation system. As Congress evaluates the effectiveness of its subsidies and economic regulations, it will probably give more attention to fostering coordination and cooperation among modes of transportation. The goal will be to improve efficiency and effective planning without further taxing the national treasury.

Finally, Congress will continue to concern itself with the social costs of transportation. Nonpolluting means of transportation will necessitate balancing the consequences of the marketplace with environmental priorities. Passenger trains, for example, that cannot compete with airlines, cars, and buses may be sustained with public dollars—local, state, and federal—out of concern for the environment and declining supplies of fossil fuels. Similarly, Congress may subsidize transporters using alternative sources of energy, such as propane gas or electricity or nonpolluting coal.

[*For discussion of related public policy issues, see* Automobile Safety; Commerce Power; Internal Improvements; Interstate Highway System; Railroads; Regulation and Deregulation. *See also* Commerce, Science, and Transportation Committee, Senate; Public Works and Transportation Committee, House. *For discussion of related legislation, see* Hepburn Act; Interstate Commerce Act; Pacific Railroad Acts; Rural Post Roads Act; Urban Mass Transportation Act of 1964.]

BIBLIOGRAPHY

Daniels, George H., and Mark H. Rose, eds. *Energy and Transport: Historical Perspectives on Policy Issues.* 1982.

Felton, John Richard, and Dale G. Anderson. *Regulation and Deregulation of the Motor Carrier Industry.* 1989.

Larson, John Laurintz. "Bind the Republic Together: The National Union and the Struggle for a System of Internal Improvements." *Journal of American History* 74 (1987): 363–387.

Rose, Mark H. *Interstate: Express Highway Politics, 1939–89.* 1990.

Scheiber, Harry N., et al. *Transportation and the Early Nation.* 1982.

Smerk, George M. *Urban Mass Transportation: A Dozen Years of Federal Policy.* 1974.

Stover, John V. *Transportation in American History.* 1970.

Taylor, George Rogers. *The Transportation Revolution, 1815–1860.* 1958.

U.S. National Transportation Policy Study Commission. *National Transportation Policies through the Year 2000.* 1979.

RAIMUND E. GOERLER

TRAVEL. Members of Congress and their staffs, whether shuttling between Washington, D.C., and their home states or visiting foreign lands, find that travel is a necessary component of their jobs. Excessive or unjustifiable travel (commonly known as junketing), however, has frequently gotten members into trouble. In 1848, for example, Rep. Horace Greeley, who remained editor of the *New York Tribune* while serving part of a House term, and who had great disdain for his congressional colleagues, spent much of his time exposing their foibles in his newspaper. At one point, he computed the travel reimbursements to which certain members were entitled, compared these amounts to what they actually collected, and published stories about their overbilling. Included in Greeley's exposé was a member of Congress from Illinois named Abraham Lincoln, whom Greeley alleged had submitted $676.80 in excess mileage bills.

Similar articles published cooperatively by *Life* magazine and Knight-Ridder newspapers in 1960, and based on reporters' examinations of some 25,000 travel vouchers submitted by House members between July 1957 and June 1959, alleged that many members inflated the amount of money due them for per diem and other travel expenses.

Another furor arose after an August 1985 trip to Brazil by Rep. Bill Alexander (D-Ark.). Although a large air force plane had been booked to carry several members of Congress, Alexander was the only member to show up for takeoff, along with his daughter and a handful of other nonmembers. His trip ridiculed by the press, Alexander ultimately resigned his position as chief deputy whip.

Usually after attention has been called to a particular problem, Congress has reacted by tightening its standards, in this case standards governing reimbursements for transportation and subsistence expenditures. In 1958, Congress began to gradually institute requirements for the disclosure of taxpayer-funded travel expenditures, and in 1960, in the wake of the expense-account-padding stories, Congress increased the requirements for organized public disclosure. Today, the House provides a much fuller public accounting of its travel expenditures than does the Senate.

Championed by Sen. John J. Williams (R-Del.), the 1960 reforms also ended a practice in which U.S. shipping companies gave members' spouses free or cut-rate passage for voyages undertaken by the members for official business.

House members receive funding for thirty-two round-trips to their districts each year. Senators are reimbursed for about forty trips home, depending on the population of the states they represent. (Campaign activity also takes members home from Washington, but these trips must be paid for by political contributions and not federal funds.)

Travel to other states may come as part of a member's committee work, for hearings or for on-site inspections of existing or proposed projects, for example. Domestic travel taken under the auspices of a committee is paid for out of the panel's budget, except for most use of military aircraft. Per diem allowances for lodging and food vary from city to city based on the cost of living.

Official travel has also led to tragedy. In the early days, members on trips to and from Capitol Hill were sometimes injured or killed in railroad and other vehicular accidents and even in steamboat explosions. The advent of commercial airlines made travel much safer, but some risk remained. In 1978, Rep. Leo J. Ryan (D-Calif.) was ambushed and killed while investigating a religious cult led by Rev. Jim Jones, an American, near Port Kaituma, Guyana. Hours after Ryan's assassination, Jones and some nine hundred of his followers died in a ritual of murder and mass suicide. Rep. Larry McDonald (D-Ga.) was aboard Korean Airlines' Flight 007, which was destroyed by a Soviet air-to-air missile over the Sea of Japan in September 1983 with no survivors. Rep. Mickey Leland (D-Tex.) and three House staffers were killed in August 1989 when the small plane in which they were crossing Africa en route to an Ethiopian refugee camp crashed into a mountain. Less than two years later, Sen. John Heinz (R-Pa.) was killed in a plane crash while flying between meetings in his home state.

Travel Abroad. Much more controversial than domestic travel is travel abroad. Foreign travel is undertaken as part of Congress's responsibility to oversee U.S. interests, including military, diplomatic, and intelligence installations, and the disbursement of billions of dollars per year in foreign aid.

Expenses incurred in official foreign travel are generally paid out of the budget of the State De-

partment. When abroad on government business, members may claim per diem allowances through U.S. embassies. Such allowances often are dispensed from embassy-controlled accounts that contain "counterpart funds—local currency received from the host country in payment for U.S. aid. Congress does not require its members and staff to account for travel expenditures paid for with counterpart funds; any per diem money not spent may be kept, although there is usually little or none left. Indeed, the allowances, based on outdated cost-of-living computations, are relatively modest, and congressional travelers often complain of having to use their own money for meals in some high-cost cities abroad.

Depending on their itineraries, members may travel abroad on either commercial aircraft or one of twenty-two air force planes in the 89th Airlift Wing, which is based at Andrews Air Force Base and maintained for the use of government officials, including the president and vice president, other executive branch officials, and Congress.

Foreign and domestic travel in these aircraft is funded out of the air force budget and is not reimbursed by Congress or other users for trips deemed necessary to check on congressional spending estimates that involve military business or are authorized by the White House. Members of Congress may bring spouses—who receive no per diem—on trips for which military aircraft are used when this is authorized for "protocol" or health reasons, and did so on about 40 percent of members' trips over a one-year period examined recently by the General Accounting Office.

While abroad, members generally have one or more military officers along as an escort and trip coordinator. The officer will often set up a "control room" with telephones and refreshments for members, and has petty cash available for contingencies.

Public Disclosure. Congressional travel is disclosed in documents compiled for public examination by the secretary of the Senate and the clerk of the House. Both officers also include travel disclosures in irregular insertions in the *Congressional Record*—generally long after the travel has taken place. According to the Congressional Research Service, the first disclosure in the *Record* was in 1959, with reports on total amounts of counterpart funds spent by each committee. In 1961, these published reports were expanded to include an itemization of expenditures of appropriated funds, in addition to the counterpart moneys.

In 1973, Congress eliminated the printing of travel expenditures in the *Record*, requiring instead

CONGRESSIONAL DELEGATION. Touring Achaemenid ruins, Persepolis, Iran, 1976.

OFFICE OF THE HISTORIAN OF THE U.S. SENATE

that the State Department inform committee chairmen of counterpart funds spent by the panel's members. These reports were to be available for public inspection. After media reports drew attention to the disclosure cutbacks, Congress in 1976 restored the requirement that foreign travel expenditure reports be published in the *Record*.

House records detail the cities visited by its delegations and the dates the travel took place, as well as the per diem and some transportation expenses. The Senate's far more hazy disclosures reveal only some per diem figures and the names of countries, not the cities, visited by senators and their staff. Nor does the Senate reveal travel dates, only the quarter in which the travel took place. Noting the disparity between House and Senate travel disclosure rules, Speaker of the House Thomas S. Foley said at a May 1991 press conference, "I think the House clearly today reports that more than any other branch, executive, or certainly more than the Senate, on the time, purpose, place, direction, and cost of travel."

Self-styled watchdog groups such as Public Citizen's Congress Watch and the National Taxpayer's Union (NTU) complain most about the difficulty of learning the full cost and nature of congressional travel, a task made difficult because the informa-

tion that is disclosed is scattered among the records of scores of congressional committees and the sporadic disclosures by the House clerk and Senate secretary in the *Congressional Record*. Congress Watch estimated in 1989 that three hundred representatives and eighty senators took about one thousand trips abroad between January 1987 and December 1988 at a total cost of some $13.5 million. The study found that the most common destinations were, respectively, West Germany, France, Britain, Italy, South Korea, and the Soviet Union.

Commonly cited as examples of abuse are the biennial Paris Air Show and winter trips to conferences in the Caribbean and warmer parts of the United States such as Florida, California, and Hawaii. Many members' sensitivity about travel was heightened in 1990 when ABC-TV's "Prime Time Live" followed and videotaped an eight-member delegation from the House Ways and Means Committee on a nine-day visit to Barbados that appeared to involve only one official meeting, which was actually a party-like reception. Also heightening awareness was the 1991 controversy surrounding White House Chief of Staff John Sununu's use of military aircraft for political and personal trips.

Advocacy groups also have criticized the free trips many members accept from interest groups, many of which are seeking to influence legislation that is before Congress. Such groups arrange conferences, convention speeches, plant tours, and other visits for members, often in exotic vacation spots in the United States and abroad. Members and some staffers are required to note such trips on their annual financial disclosure forms. Members who participate insist that the trips help increase their understanding of relevant issues.

Even the harshest critics of Capitol Hill travel habits, however, including Congress Watch and the NTU, concede that some trips are necessary for members to be properly informed on matters under their jurisdiction. Defenders of necessary congressional travel also note that, while Congress is responsible for overseeing a $1.5-trillion budget for the entire U.S. government, Congress's travel budget is much smaller than that of the executive and judicial branches: $6.85 billion for the executive branch and $54 million for the judiciary, according to fiscal 1991 figures.

BIBLIOGRAPHY

Congressional Quarterly Inc. *Congressional Quarterly's Guide to Congress.* 4th ed. Edited by Mary Cohn. 1991.

Dwyer, Paul. *History of Reporting Requirements for Foreign Travel Expenditures by Members and Employees of the House of Representatives.* Congressional Research Service, Library of Congress. 1985.

Lawton, Margaret, and Peter Meryash. *A Study of Congressional Foreign Travel, January 1987–December 1988.* A Report by Public Citizen's Congress Watch. 1989.

Ritchie, Donald A. *Press Gallery: Congress and the Washington Correspondents.* 1991.

U.S. General Accounting Office. *Policies on Government Officials' Use of 89th Military Airlift Wing Aircraft.* 1992.

TIMOTHY J. BURGER

TREASON. Congress is restricted in its authority to define treason. The United States Constitution (Art. III, sec. 3) states that "Treason against the United States, shall consist only in levying War against them, or in adhering to their Enemies, giving them Aid and Comfort"; the essential word is *only.* Congress is thus constitutionally prevented from modifying or altering, enlarging or narrowing, the meaning of treason, or from creating new types. Treason is the only crime defined in the Constitution.

The prosecution of treason is likewise restricted by the same section of the Constitution: "No Person shall be convicted of Treason unless on the Testimony of two Witnesses to the same overt Act, or on Confession in open Court." Neither conspiracy alone nor intention to commit treason are sufficient to convict if there is no enactment of the betrayal. "The concern uppermost in the framers' minds," the Supreme Court said in *Cramer v. United States* (325 U.S. 1, 28 [1945]), is to ensure "that mere mental attitudes or expressions should not be treason."

A further restriction on congressional authority is found in section 4: "The Congress shall have Power to declare the Punishment of Treason, but no Attainder of Treason shall work Corruption of Blood, or Forfeiture except during the Life of the Person attainted." Thus while Congress may set the punishment for treason, it is barred from extending it to future generations. Unlike the practice in English history, in which heirs were made to suffer for treasons of an ancestor, this provision of the Constitution was, according to the Supreme Court, "a declaration that the children should not bear the iniquity of the fathers" (*Wallick v. Van Riswick,* 92 U.S. 202, 210 [1875]).

These constitutional limits on treason reflect the Framers' reaction against historic English abuses in which treason was perverted "by established authority to repress peaceful political opposition" and to convict "the innocent as a result of perjury, passion, or inadequate evidence" (*Cramer v. United States,* 27). According to James Madison, the Framers sought to prevent "new-fangled and artificial treasons," which "have been the great engines by which violent factions, the natural offspring of free government, have usually wreaked their alternate malignity on each other" (*Federalist* 43).

Because its authority over treason is circumscribed, Congress has enacted laws that do not use the label *treason* but punish acts resembling it. During the 1798 fear of an invasion by France, Sen. James Lloyd of Maryland sought to punish "domestic traitors" with bills "to define more particularly the crime of treason, and to define and punish the crime of sedition." His attempt to define treason in peacetime did not carry, but the sedition bill did. The 1798 Sedition Act (1 Stat. 596) made seditious conspiracy and seditious libel crimes. That law expired in 1801, but Congress has since enacted legislation paralleling the 1798 act: in 1917 the Espionage Act (40 Stat. 217); in 1918 the Sedition Act (40 Stat. 553); in 1940 the Alien Registration Act, or Smith Act (54 Stat. 671); in 1950 the Internal Security Act, or McCarran Act (64 Stat. 987); and in 1954 the Communist Control Act (68 Stat. 775).

BIBLIOGRAPHY

Chapin, Bradley. *The American Law of Treason: Revolutionary and Early National Origins.* 1964.

Hurst, James Willard. *The Law of Treason in the United States.* 1971.

RON CHRISTENSON

TREATIES. Under international law, a treaty means any legally binding agreement between nations. In the United States, the term *treaty* is reserved for those international agreements submitted to the Senate for its advice and consent. Other international agreements, often called executive agreements in the United States, are not treaties in U.S. parlance but are considered treaties under international law and are legally binding on the United States.

Treaties submitted to the Senate are the most formal international undertakings and commitments of the United States. Past treaties provide a history of U.S. foreign policy. For example, the Treaty of Ghent with Great Britain of 24 December 1814 provided for settlement of issues after the War of 1812. In the Treaty of Paris of 10 December 1898, Spain ceded Puerto Rico, Guam, and the Philippines to the United States. The Hay-Pauncefote Treaty of 18 November 1901 gave the United States the right to build a canal across the Isthmus of Panama, and the Panama Canal Treaty of 7 September 1977 provided for Panama's assuming total control of the canal after 31 December 1999. The United States did not become a member of the League of Nations because President Woodrow Wilson and the Senate disagreed on reservations to the Versailles Treaty of 1919, while ratification of the United Nations Charter of 1945 and the North Atlantic Treaty in 1949 launched a new period of international involvement and leadership.

Because the treaty power is divided or shared under the Constitution, numerous controversies have arisen between the Senate and the president over the proper roles of each branch.

Constitutional Provisions. The Articles of Confederation, which formed the basis of the relationship among the thirteen states from 1776 to 1789, vested the treaty power in the Congress, the only central organ, and required nine states for assent to a treaty. During the Constitutional Convention, the Virginia and New Jersey plans, representing the views of the large and small states, respectively, did not specify how treaties were to be made, both apparently assuming that Congress would continue to make them. On 18 June 1787, Alexander Hamilton presented a plan under which the chief executive "with the advice and approbation of the Senate" would have the power to make treaties, and similar language was ultimately adopted. Article II, section 2, clause 2 of the Constitution provides that the president "shall have Power, by and with the Advice and Consent of the Senate, to make Treaties, provided two-thirds of the Senators present concur."

Three other provisions of the Constitution complete the framework for U.S. law on treaties. Article I, section 10 restricts the states from entering into any treaty or compact without the consent of Congress, making treaties solely the responsibility of the federal government. Article II, section 2, clause 1 provides that the judicial power extend to all cases arising under the Constitution or U.S. laws and treaties. Article VI, section 2 provides that treaties be the supreme law of the land, along with the Constitution and laws.

The Constitution thus created the dilemma in which treaties are part of the supreme law of the land but are not formed by the regular legislative process. Some Framers of the Constitution objected to having instruments with the status of law concluded without the concurrence of the House of Representatives. The view prevailed, however, that the necessity for secrecy precluded referring treaties to the entire Congress.

Evolution to Modern Practice. The original intention of the Framers was that the Senate and the president share the treaty-making process and that the sharing begin early, with the proposal to enter negotiations and the appointment and instruction of negotiators. The Senate was to serve as a council advising the president. On 22 August 1789, in one of the first treaty actions, President George Washington came into the Senate chamber to present a proposal for a treaty with specific questions; he returned two days later for votes on additional questions related to the treaty. Both the president and the Senate were dissatisfied with that encounter, however, and Washington did not again visit the Senate to consult on a treaty. On occasion he sought advice by written message to the Senate before opening negotiations, but by the end of his administration, Washington was informing the Senate about a proposed treaty for the first time when he sought approval of a negotiator, and was submitting the negotiating instructions with the completed treaty.

By 1816, the practice became established that the

Senate's role was to approve, to approve with reservations or other conditions, or to disapprove treaties after they had been negotiated by the president or his emissary. In the European monarchies prior to that time, it had been considered obligatory for a monarch to ratify a treaty if his emissary had stayed within his instructions and no practice existed of making reservations to parts of a treaty, but gradually the American practice was accepted. After considering Jay's Treaty of 19 November 1794 with Great Britain, the Senate approved it on 24 June 1795, with the condition that the twelfth article be amended, and the amendment was accepted by President Washington and Great Britain. In the Treaty with Tunis of 1797, the Senate gave its advice and consent subject to renegotiation of an article; the article was renegotiated and the Senate subsequently approved the treaty. The King-Hawksbury Convention of 12 May 1803 became the first treaty not to enter into force because the other party, in this case Great Britain, would not accept an amendment by the Senate.

U.S. Treaty Process. The negotiation of a treaty is undertaken solely by the president and executive branch officials, although members of Congress frequently suggest ideas for negotiations and sometimes participate as observers or advisers. The president or his representatives decide whether to sign a treaty and when to submit it to the Senate for advice and consent. Once submitted to the Senate, the treaty is referred to the Foreign Relations Committee. If the committee decides to report the treaty to the Senate, it proposes a resolution of ratification that may contain various conditions. Conditions may include amendments (changes in the text of a treaty), reservations (qualifications that change obligations under the treaty), understandings (an interpretation or elaboration clarifying the treaty), and declarations, provisos, or other statements (statements of policy relating to the subject of a treaty but not necessarily affecting its provisions). The important distinction among various kinds of conditions is the legal effect. Whatever a condition is named, if the president considers that it constitutes an amendment or reservation that changes a treaty obligation, he is obligated to transmit it to the other party for a decision on whether to accept the condition, reject the treaty, or seek renegotiation.

After the treaty is reported from the committee, the leadership determines when it will be considered by the full Senate. The Senate first considers any proposed conditions or amendments to the

REACTION TO JAY'S TREATY. U.S. Chief Justice John Jay burned in effigy. Sent to London by George Washington to address U.S. grievances against Britain, Jay negotiated a treaty that was extremely unpopular with Jeffersonian members of Congress and the general public.

LIBRARY OF CONGRESS

treaty to be placed in the resolution of ratification; in 1868 the Senate changed its rules to permit adoption of such amendments by a simple majority vote. The final resolution of ratification must be adopted by a two-thirds majority. The Senate procedure has been simplified since 1986, when the Senate amended Senate Rule XXX to eliminate a step in which the Senate met "as in Committee of the Whole" to consider amendments to the treaty.

After the Senate adopts the resolution of ratification, if the president wants the treaty to enter into force and accepts any conditions added by the Senate, he signs a document called the instrument of ratification. He then exchanges the instrument of ratification with the other party to a bilateral treaty or deposits it with a depository in the case of a multilateral treaty. When the ratifications are exchanged or the required number of ratifications deposited, the treaty enters into force (becomes legally binding internationally) and the president signs a proclamation publicizing that fact domestically. If the president objects to any of the Senate conditions, he does not sign the ratification, and if the other party objects, it does not exchange ratifications, and the treaty does not enter into force.

Use of the Senate Treaty Power. Normally the Senate gives its advice and consent to treaties without conditions. The Senate has approved approximately 90 percent of the treaties submitted to it, and most of these have been approved without conditions.

The requirement for its advice and consent is a powerful tool for the Senate in foreign affairs because it gives the Senate a veto power over treaties. The requirement for a two-thirds majority enables a minority of one-third plus one, or thirty-four senators, to cast that veto. The Senate veto power over treaties has been recognized as permissible by the Supreme Court. In *Immigration and Naturalization Service v. Chadha* (1983), which held many legislative vetoes unconstitutional, the Court cited the Senate's "unreviewable power to ratify treaties negotiated by the President" as one of only four provisions in the Constitution by which "one House may act alone with the unreviewable force of law, not subject to the President's veto."

Outright rejection of a treaty by Senate vote is rare. Fewer than twenty treaties have been brought to a vote by the full Senate and have subsequently failed to receive the required two-thirds majority. The Treaty with Wabash and Illinois Indians of 27 September 1792 was the first treaty defeated by the Senate. The Treaty with Colombia on Suppression of the Slave Trade, concluded 10 December 1824, was rejected by the Senate on 9 March 1825. The most famous rejection was that of the Treaty of Versailles, signed 28 June 1919, containing the Covenant of the League of Nations. The Senate attached such conditions that, although President Wilson had negotiated the treaty, he requested his supporters in the Senate to vote against the final resolution of ratification because he believed that the reservations nullified rather than ratified the treaty. The treaty finally failed on 19 March 1920 with a vote of 49 in favor to 35 opposed, falling short of the required two-thirds majority.

When the Senate defeats a treaty, it usually employs means other than a direct rejection by vote.

The most frequent of these is lack of action. If the Senate Foreign Relations Committee opposes a treaty or believes that it lacks adequate support, the committee does not report the treaty to the Senate. Alternatively, the Senate may choose not to vote on a treaty that has been reported favorably because the leadership believes that the treaty does not have a two-thirds majority, and the treaty is returned to the Foreign Relations Committee calendar. More than one hundred treaties have failed because the Senate did not act on them. Such treaties may be withdrawn, may be renegotiated and resubmitted, or may remain pending on the Senate Foreign Relations Committee calendar.

Sometimes the president makes known that he does not wish the Senate to act on a treaty. An example was the treaty with the Soviet Union on the limitation of strategic offensive arms, known as the SALT II Treaty, signed 18 June 1979. The Foreign Relations Committee reported the treaty with various conditions on 19 November 1979. After the Soviet invasion of Afghanistan in December 1979, President Jimmy Carter asked the Senate to delay consideration. The treaty was referred back to the Foreign Relations Committee calendar, and President Ronald Reagan did not ask for further action.

Some treaties fail because the Senate approves them with conditions that are subsequently refused by the president or other countries. The Department of State has attributed the failure of at least forty treaties to Senate reservations or amendments not acceptable to the president or the countries party to the treaty. For example, in January 1926 the Senate approved adherence to the Permanent Court of International Justice with five reservations, but other members would not accept the reservation that the court should never entertain a request for an advisory opinion on a dispute affecting the United States without the consent of the United States. (The Senate defeated a revised version on 29 January 1935. The United States became a member of the new International Court of Justice as part of its acceptance of the United Nations Charter, approved by the Senate on 28 July 1945.) A series of arbitration treaties signed in the early 1900s failed because of Senate conditions, as did several income tax treaties after 1965.

Even if the Senate gives its advice and consent unconditionally, it can exert influence on a treaty. Throughout the negotiation of a treaty the president is aware that the completed agreement must obtain the approval of a two-thirds majority, and he is commensurately alert to Senate views. On sever-

WORLD WAR I. A French delegation and members of the Senate posed for a photograph on the Capitol steps in autumn 1918. Within a year, the Senate was embroiled in bitter controversy over the Versailles treaty.

OFFICE OF THE HISTORIAN OF THE U.S. SENATE

al occasions when the Senate has approved a treaty without formal conditions, senators prior to the approval have insisted on assurances about various concerns. In considering the Limited Nuclear Test Ban Treaty in 1963, for instance, the Senate turned down a reservation stating that the treaty did not inhibit the use of nuclear weapons in armed conflict, but it insisted on written assurances on this issue. Subsequently, on 23 September 1963, President John F. Kennedy wrote to Senate leaders that the treaty in no way limited the authority of the commander in chief to use nuclear weapons for defense of the United States or its allies, should such a need arise, and that such a decision would be made in accordance with American constitutional processes.

Treaties in International Law. Under international law an international agreement is considered a treaty—and therefore binding on the parties

under international law—if it meets four criteria: (1) it is intended to be legally binding and subject to international law, (2) it concerns significant matters, (3) it clearly and specifically describes the legal obligations of the parties, and (4) its form indicates an intention to conclude a legally binding agreement. International undertakings not intended to be legally binding, such as joint communiqués and final acts of conferences, are not considered treaties, but other international agreements that are intended to be legally binding, such as executive agreements, are considered treaties under international law.

On 23 May 1969, a United Nations conference of 110 nations adopted the Vienna Convention on the Law of Treaties, codifying international law on treaties. Although the United States signed the Vienna Convention on 24 April 1970, it had not ratified the convention by 1993 and so was not a party for which the treaty was in force. Nevertheless the executive branch considered that the convention reflected customary international law and generally followed its provisions. President Richard M. Nixon submitted the convention to the Senate on 22 November 1971, but the Senate Committee on Foreign Relations had not, by 1993, reported the convention to the Senate. The committee was concerned primarily because of the differing usage of the term *treaty* in the convention and in U.S. parlance. In 1972 the committee sought executive branch agreement on an interpretation and understanding stating that it is a rule of internal U.S. law that no treaty is valid unless the Senate has given its advice and consent or the terms have been approved by law; the Department of State, however, opposed the wording. Twenty years later the convention remained pending on the committee's calendar, reflecting the differing institutional interests of the legislative and executive branches.

Treaties in Domestic Law. Intermittently throughout U.S. history some have expressed concern that the president or Senate might use the treaty power to impose something as the law of the land without going through the legislative process. The treaty power is broad, extending to all matters considered proper for negotiation with foreign countries, but there are limitations. One is that the power does not extend to rights reserved to the states, except the unspecified reserved rights under the Tenth Amendment. Another limitation concerns participation in certain kinds of international judicial tribunals because of the final appellate jurisdiction of the Supreme Court and other constitutional concerns. Still another concerns subjects that lie within congressional delegated powers, such as foreign commerce, in which implementing legislation may be necessary for an agreement to become effective as domestic law. Some treaties expressly call for implementing legislation or clearly require additional congressional action, such as the appropriation of funds or enactment of domestic penal provisions.

Treaties that do not require implementing legislation are called self-executing treaties and become part of domestic law as soon as they enter into force. When a treaty is deemed self-executing, it overrides any conflicting provision of the law of an individual state. Courts try to harmonize domestic and international obligations, but if a treaty conflicts with a federal law, the one enacted later prevails.

During the 1950s some senators became concerned that treaties or executive agreements might be used as instruments of domestic legislation, and Sen. John W. Bricker (R-Ohio) proposed a series of constitutional amendments dealing with treaties and executive agreements. In 1953 he and sixty cosponsors introduced Senate Joint Resolution 1, which would have amended the Constitution to make a treaty effective as internal law only through the enactment of appropriate legislation, and to permit executive agreements only to the extent to be prescribed by law. As amended before being voted on, the resolution stated that any provision of a treaty that conflicted with the Constitution would be of no effect, and an international agreement other than a treaty would become effective as international law only by act of Congress. On 26 February 1954, the vote on the resolution, as amended, was 60 yeas to 31 nays. Since a two-thirds vote was required for a constitutional amendment, the resolution failed by one vote.

Growth in International Agreements. Since the end of World War II, tremendous growth has occurred in international agreements concluded by the United States, reflecting increased U.S. involvement in the world, the growing number of sovereign states, and the interdependence of those states.

In the first fifty years of U.S. history (1789–1839), the United States concluded approximately sixty treaties and twenty-seven executive agreements; in the second fifty years (1839–1889), more than two hundred treaties and a slightly higher number of executive agreements; in the third fifty years (1889–1939), more than five hundred treaties and more than nine hundred executive agreements; and in the fourth fifty years (1939–1989), more than seven hundred treaties and almost eleven thousand executive agreements. The average number of treaties per year has leveled off at about fifteen to twenty, while the average number of executive agreements per year has soared to three or four hundred.

The growth in the number of international agreements has not brought a corresponding growth in the importance of the Senate role primarily because of the ever-increasing proportion of executive agreements—that is, international agreements that are not submitted to the Senate for its advice and consent. Such agreements have the same standing as treaties under international law, although not necessarily in domestic law. Many legal authorities hold that some executive agreements, which might be called congressional-executive agreements because they have been specifically authorized or approved by law, are virtually interchangeable with treaties. The domestic legal effect of executive agreements made pursuant to treaties and especially those concluded solely by the president on his own authority remains controversial.

The greater use of executive agreements reflects the ease of that mode of agreement making compared with the process of ratification, in which a Senate minority of one-third plus one can defeat a treaty. When laws authorize the conclusion of agreements in a field, such as postal services or space cooperation, or the president believes that he has adequate authority from a treaty or his own executive powers, the agreements receive no further congressional action. On some occasions presidents choose the congressional-executive agreement form by submitting an agreement to both houses of Congress rather than to the Senate alone. A president may want to involve the House of Representatives, or he may believe that an agreement can obtain the support of a majority of both houses but not a two-thirds majority of the Senate. This is what happened, for example, with the annexation of Texas. A treaty with the Republic of Texas providing for annexation concluded 12 April 1844 was defeated in the Senate on 8 June 1844. The next year, on 1 March 1845, at the request of the president, Texas was admitted into the Union by joint resolution. Similarly, the St. Lawrence Waterway Treaty with Canada of 18 July 1932 was rejected by a Senate vote of 46 to 42 on 14 March 1934. On 13 May 1954, Congress approved the Saint Lawrence Seaway by public law.

On other occasions, Congress through legislation directs the procedure for making international agreements in certain fields. Legislation has established special procedures for making and approving agreements in trade, nuclear cooperation, international fishery, and social security.

Growth in Multilateral Treaties. Although the United States participated in relatively few multilateral agreements prior to the twentieth century, such agreements have become common since World War II. They have comprised some of the most important U.S. commitments, such as membership in the United Nations and Organization of American States. Because of its importance, the likelihood of a multilateral agreement being submitted to the Senate as a treaty is much higher than in the case of a bilateral agreement. Of the almost one thousand international multilateral agreements the United States entered through

1992, approximately one-third were treaties and two-thirds were executive agreements.

Multilateral treaties pose special problems for the Senate because they are often negotiated by many nations in large international organizations over a long time period. The result frequently constitutes an intricate package that the Senate must accept or reject as a whole. Although amendments to the treaty are discouraged because renegotiation would be so difficult, the Senate, often at the request of the president, sometimes places reservations or other conditions on its approval of a multilateral treaty.

To enhance the prospects of Senate approval of a treaty, especially a multilateral treaty in which renegotiation of a completed treaty is impracticable, presidents have on some occasions appointed senators or representatives as delegates or observers to the negotiations. Of the eight members of the official U.S. delegation to the San Francisco Conference that in 1945 adopted the United Nations Charter, four were members of Congress: Senators Tom T. Connally (D-Tex.) and Arthur H. Vandenberg (R-Mich.) and Representatives Sol Bloom (D-N.Y.) and Charles A. Eaton (R-N.J.). One issue is whether appointment of senators or representatives to serve on a delegation violates the separation of powers or creates a conflict of interest because they will later be called on to pass judgment on the completed treaty. A compromise solution has been to appoint members of Congress as advisers or observers, rather than as members of the delegation.

Other Treaty Issues. The Constitution makes no mention of the interpretation, amendment, or termination of treaties, and each of these processes has from time to time been disputed by the two branches.

While U.S. termination of a treaty ideally occurs through the same procedure as the original treaty was made, in practice a wide variety of methods have been used. The president has terminated treaties pursuant to prior authorization or direction of Congress or of the Senate alone, without prior authorization but with subsequent approval, or without any authorization or approval. On 15 December 1978, without any authorization from the Senate or Congress, President Carter gave notice of termination of the 1954 Mutual Defense Treaty with Taiwan. In *Goldwater v. Carter* (1979) Sen. Barry Goldwater (R-Ariz.) attempted to force a judicial resolution of the issue of whether the president could terminate the treaty without the advice and consent of the Senate or the approval of both houses of Congress. The Supreme Court dismissed the complaint, vitiating any precedent-setting value of earlier court rulings in the cases and leaving the issue unresolved.

Similarly, the general rule holds that an amendment to a prior international agreement should be made, domestically, in the same way as the original agreement. Thus an executive agreement may be modified by another executive agreement, but a modification of a treaty that received the advice and consent of the Senate should also be submitted to the Senate. In this case the president submits the formal amendment, often called a protocol, to the Senate as if it were a new treaty. On occasion, however, treaties have been modified through executive action or interpretation, by tacit understanding, or by legislation.

Treaty reinterpretation became an issue after 1985, when the Reagan administration announced a new interpretation of the 1972 Anti-Ballistic Missile (ABM) Treaty that would have permitted virtually unrestricted research and development of the Strategic Defense Initiative. The reinterpretation raised sharp debate in the Senate in 1987 about whether the president could interpret a treaty differently from the way it had been presented to or understood by the Senate at the time the Senate gave its advice and consent to ratification. State Department legal adviser Abraham Sofaer contended that the president was not bound to the original interpretation because the Senate had not been informed of some relevant aspects of the negotiating record and there was no formal record of the Senate's understanding of the issues. As a result of the controversy, in 1987 Sen. Sam Nunn (D-Ga.) requested the entire negotiating record of the Intermediate Nuclear Force (INF) Treaty with the Soviet Union, and the State Department supplied the documents. When the Senate gave its advice and consent to the INF Treaty on 27 May 1988, it did so with the condition, among others, that the United States would interpret the treaty in accordance with the common understanding shared by the president and the Senate at the time it gave its advice and consent, and that the United States would not adopt a different interpretation except pursuant to Senate advice and consent or the enactment of a statute. In 1993 the Clinton administration made clear it had returned to the traditional interpretation of the ABM Treaty.

[*For discussion of related issues, see* Advice and Consent; Bricker Amendment; Executive Agreement; Foreign Policy; Immigration and Naturalization Service v. Chadha; Veto, *article on* Legislative Veto. *For discussion of particular treaty agreements, see* Antiballistic Missile Systems Treaty; Genocide Convention; Indian Treaties; Jay's Treaty; League of Nations; Limited Test Ban Treaty; North Atlantic Treaty; Nuclear Non-Proliferation Treaty; Panama Canal Treaty; United Nations.]

BIBLIOGRAPHY

American Law Institute. *Restatement of the Law First, Second, and Third. The Foreign Relations Law of the United States.* 1987. Part 3, "International Agreements."

Dangerfield, Royden J. *In Defense of the Senate: A Study in Treaty-Making.* 1933.

Fleming, Denna Frank. *The Treaty Veto of the American Senate.* 1930.

Glennon, Michael J. "The Senate Role in Treaty Ratification." *American Journal of International Law* 77 (1983): 257–280.

Hayden, Ralston. *The Senate and Treaties, 1789–1817.* 1920.

Holt, W. Stull. *Treaties Defeated by the Senate.* 1964.

U.S. Department of State. Office of the Legal Adviser. *Treaties in Force: A List of Treaties and Other International Agreements of the United States in Force on January 1, 1993.* 1993.

U.S. Senate. Committee on Foreign Relations. *Legislative Activities Report; 102d Congress, January 3, 1991–October 8, 1992.* 103d Cong., 1st sess., 1993. S. Rept. 103-35.

U.S. Senate. Committee on Foreign Relations. *Treaties and Other International Agreements: The Role of the United States Senate.* 98th Cong., 2d sess., 1984. S. Rept. 98-205. Includes annotated bibliography.

ELLEN C. COLLIER

TRUMAN, HARRY S. (1884–1972), Democratic senator from Missouri (1935–1945), vice president (1945), and thirty-second president of the United States (1945–1953). Elected to the Senate at the age of fifty, Truman had previously pursued careers as a farmer, small businessman, combat artilleryman and army reservist, and local politician. He had been an effective and respected administrator of Missouri's largest county, Jackson, which contains Kansas City. Truman waged an exhausting personal campaign but owed his election to Kansas City's Democratic machine, run by Tom Pendergast, which turned out an enormous vote for him and influenced the state administration to use its patronage in his behalf.

A shrewd practitioner of coalition politics, Truman had moved easily from a small, homogenous, rural and small-town political base to a large and diverse urban political setting. Consistent with his background as an organization professional, he considered the dispensing of patronage and the satisfaction of interest groups at least as important as principle in day-to-day politics.

Legislative Career. Like most Missouri Democrats, Truman professed a commitment to nineteenth-century Jeffersonianism, but, unlike his Missouri Senate colleague, Joel Bennett Clark, he generally honored it in the breach and was a reliable supporter of President Franklin D. Roosevelt's New Deal. His association with the Pendergast machine left him somewhat tarnished, especially when he opposed the reappointment of Maurice Milligan, the federal prosecutor who was investigating its leaders. He was nonetheless widely popular among his fellow senators, who appreciated his modesty, hard work, and capacity for friendship.

During his first term in the Senate, Truman, who as a local administrator had been known as a road builder, was most prominent for his engagement with transportation issues. Appointed to the Interstate Commerce Committee, he worked closely with its chairman, Burton K. Wheeler, on an investigation of railroad financing, and he advocated a major overhaul of the Interstate Commerce Act.

The investigation, however, proved better at digging out old abuses and engaging in questionable charges of financial misconduct than at addressing existing problems. It blamed the plight of the overextended railroads on the machinations of Wall Street financiers and stock manipulators in the 1920s. The charges contained a grain of truth but overlooked far more fundamental causes—excessive debt that antedated the 1920s, high labor costs, weak federal policy, the rise of motor transportation, and the Great Depression itself. The focus on Wall Street reflected a fundamental aspect of Truman's worldview—a neopopulist distrust of big business and finance that he shared with older "insurgent" progressives such as Wheeler.

The legislative effort became gridlocked in the clash of interests between the rail corporations, the unions, stockholders, and bondholders. Especially supportive of the railway unions, Truman opposed company efforts to cut salaries. The ultimate outcome, the Transportation Act of 1940, gave some assistance to the railroads by subjecting inland-water carriers to federal regulation but did little else to change transportation policy.

Truman also played a role in developing the Civil Aeronautics Act of 1938; he differed with the bill's major sponsor, Sen. Patrick A. McCarran of Neva-

da, on the issue of presidential power to remove members of the regulatory and safety boards that the law created; the eventual result was a compromise. For political reasons Truman wanted to ingratiate himself with the Roosevelt administration, but it was also true that he had long been a believer in strong executive authority. He also took a keen interest in the development of civil aviation, and by the end of the decade he had become known and respected in business circles as one of its more effective promoters in Washington.

By the late 1930s, Senator Truman was taking a greater interest in foreign policy. Unlike his colleague Clark, he was a strong advocate of military preparedness to meet the challenge of German Nazism and Japanese militarism. After the start of World War II in Europe, he publicized his commitment to defense by taking an extensive inspection tour of U.S. military bases from Panama to California; in the process, he polished a reputation as a military expert.

Truman's approach to foreign policy was that of an old Wilsonian idealist who believed in the concept of an international organization as the only feasible way of bringing peace to a disunited world. But, largely as the result of his World War I combat experience, he had a strong appreciation of the role of power in international relations. Writing to a constituent in February 1941, he declared, "We are facing a bunch of thugs, and the only theory a thug understands is a gun and a bayonet." By that time, he had supported the Burke-Wadsworth Selective Service Training Act of 1940 and was preparing to vote for the lend-lease bill that provided Great Britain with necessary war matériel.

Truman was reelected to the Senate in 1940 against all the odds, Boss Pendergast having been sent to prison. His political enemies, conceding his honesty, believed nonetheless that his continued refusal to renounce the machine disqualified him from a return to Washington. His opponents in the primary were former U.S. district attorney Maurice Milligan, who had spearheaded the drive against the machine, and Gov. Lloyd Stark, a onetime friend who had joined the anti-Pendergast movement.

With his machine support weakened and the influence of the governor's office against him, Truman seemed a sure loser. Nevertheless, he waged a hard campaign that capitalized heavily on his incumbency and the record of his first term. The support of the railway unions was especially critical. Blacks seem to have found his public support of civil

HARRY S. TRUMAN. As senator, in his office.　　　　　　　　HARRY S. TRUMAN LIBRARY

rights bills preferable to Stark's lukewarm attitude (although Truman privately doubted the constitutionality of antilynching legislation and publicly denounced social mixing). Joel Bennett Clark, who saw the governor as a rival for leadership of the state Democratic party, made speeches attacking him and quietly organized support for Truman.

After the fall of France in June 1940, Truman's long advocacy of a strong military program and his reputation as a defense expert helped him greatly. His forces also negotiated a coalition with St. Louis political leaders, who needed his support for their candidate for governor. On 6 August, carrying both Kansas City and St. Louis to overcome a solid plurality for Stark elsewhere, he won the primary by fewer than eight thousand votes. In November, with Roosevelt at the head of the ticket, he defeated his Republican opponent with just over 51 percent of the vote.

Back in the Senate, Truman used his enhanced prestige and his good relationship with the administration to get authorization for a select committee to investigate defense production. Starting modestly, the Truman Committee, as it soon became known, emerged as a major force on Capitol Hill. Investigating almost every aspect of the war effort except actual military operations, it exposed waste and extravagance in military construction, faulty equipment choices by military bureaucrats, fraudulent practices by contractors, and abuses by labor unions.

Its allegations were not always well conceived. Sensational accusations that Standard Oil of New Jersey had dealt a setback to the war effort by conspiring with the German cartel I. G. Farben to prevent production of synthetic rubber in the United States amounted to little more than the big-business bashing to which Truman had long been addicted. On the other hand, its charges that a Curtiss-Wright plant had been turning out faulty airplane engines with the connivance of military inspectors appear to have been well founded.

In addition to looking for specific abuses, the committee gave attention to the big picture. It developed recommendations on the rubber shortage that became the basis for administration policy, advocated unified civilian control of the economic war effort, consistently criticized excessive military claims on production, pressed the case of small business for war contracts, and called for an early reconversion to a civilian economy (a recommendation that, if followed, could have saved President Harry Truman a lot of difficulty).

The committee attracted much praise because it established itself as a watchdog over the defense program, guarding the interests of the ordinary American against the military brass, big business, big labor, and the politicians. Truman later liked to boast that it saved the country $15 billion. It surely turned a net profit, but there is no solid basis for Truman's figure, which amounted to about 5 percent of the more than $300 billion spent on defense procurement. In fact, the committee seems to have made little or no difference in the course of the war itself. Its achievement was psychological—it delivered a sense that someone in Washington was representing the needs of "the little people."

The committee made Truman a major figure in the Senate. A *Look* magazine survey of Washington correspondents named him one of the ten most valuable officials in Washington (he was the only member of Congress on the list). By then he had also established himself as an important player in the foreign policy debate, having become an important spokesman for postwar international involvement and a strong United Nations.

Executive Career. In 1944, Truman was a natural compromise choice for the vice presidency. His popularity on Capitol Hill made him acceptable to both liberals and conservatives within the Democratic party and especially attractive to President Roosevelt, who wanted to restore the effective congressional liaison that he had had during the vice presidency of John Nance Garner (1933–1941). Nominated over the incumbent, Henry A. Wallace, Truman was elected with Roosevelt that November and assumed office on 20 January 1945.

His vice presidency lasted less than three months, during which his major achievement was to engineer the confirmation of Wallace as secretary of Commerce over the bitter opposition of Republicans and conservative Democrats. Roosevelt, frequently out of Washington during these months, rarely saw him. On 12 April 1945, he was called to the White House, informed of Roosevelt's death, and given the presidential oath of office.

Over the next seven and three-quarter years, Truman dealt with four Congresses, all of them moderate to conservative, and thus at odds with both his own worldview and his new imperatives as the head of a national Democratic party in which urban, labor, and liberal forces were dominant. Affected by the open and vehement hostility to Roosevelt that existed on Capitol Hill during the war years, he attempted to practice compromise and conciliation with his old colleagues in the 79th Congress (1945–1947) but scored few successes. The Republican victory in the 1946 congressional elections, however, cleared the path for him to open an adversarial relationship with the 80th Congress (1947–1949), which he used as a foil to demonstrate the anti–New Dealism of his opposition and to win reelection in 1948 against Gov. Thomas E. Dewey of New York. His campaign attacks on Congress represented an about-face from his earlier conciliatory attitude and established the tone of his congressional relationships for the remainder of his presidency.

Despite a lack of consensus on domestic issues, however, Truman worked shrewdly and successfully with internationalist Republicans and conservative Democrats to get congressional approval for his major foreign policy initiatives—the Truman Doctrine, the Marshall Plan, and the North Atlantic Treaty. After mid 1949, however, the bipartisan foreign policy consensus began to come apart as a result of the fall of China to the communists, the Soviets' development of an atomic bomb, the rise of McCarthyism, and the Korean War.

The 81st Congress (1949–1951) was more receptive than its immediate predecessors to liberal reform, but it confined itself for the most part to making additions to existing programs and rejected most of Truman's Fair Deal agenda. Truman spent his last two years with the 82d Congress (1951–1953) simply trying to hold his party together and muster enough support to manage the Korean War.

Although Truman had begun his presidency attempting to conciliate Congress, his relationship with it was predominantly adversarial at the end. He used the veto freely, at times impounded appropriated funds, and invoked the doctrine of executive privilege against congressional investigators. Most spectacularly, he won the election of 1948 by running against the 80th Congress.

Declining to run for reelection in 1952, he briefly toyed with the idea of standing for the Senate from Missouri while still president. He subsequently proposed that former presidents should be made nonvoting members of the Senate, where he felt he had spent his happiest days as a public servant.

BIBLIOGRAPHY

Donovan, Robert J. *Conflict and Crisis: The Presidency of Harry S. Truman, 1945–1948.* 1977.

Donovan, Robert J. *Tumultuous Years: The Presidency of Harry S. Truman, 1949–1953.* 1982.

Hamby, Alonzo L. "'The Modest and Capable Western Statesman': Harry S. Truman in the United States Senate, 1935–1940." *Congress and the Presidency* 17 (Autumn 1990): 109–130.

Hamby, Alonzo L. "'Vultures at the Death of an Elephant': Harry S. Truman, the Great Train Robbery, and the Transportation Act of 1940." *Railroad History* 165 (Autumn 1991): 6–36.

McCullough, David. *Truman.* 1992.

Miller, Richard Lawrence. *Truman: The Rise to Power.* 1986.

ALONZO L. HAMBY

TRUMAN COMMITTEE. The Senate Special Committee to Investigate the National Defense Program—popularly known as the Truman Committee—has been characterized as "the most successful congressional investigative effort in United States history." Certainly, the Truman Committee played an important role in the ebb and flow of executive-legislative relations defining America's mobilization during World War II. Created because of a junior senator's pique about allocation of defense contracts, the Truman Committee metamorphosed into the dominant congressional body scrutinizing the production program. While not dealing with all the political, economic, and constitutional issues stemming from wartime mobilization, it established an admirable standard of responsible, restrained investigation.

In times of national crisis, the constitutional demarcations between the legislative and executive branches have shifted dramatically. Prior to World War I, Congress and the president contended for supreme control over the manner of conducting war. On the basis of explicit constitutional authority, Congress appeared to have the upper hand. That the president has come to dominate warmaking is attributable to executive aggrandizement and congressional ineptitude and abdication of responsibility. World War I strengthened the president's hand. As the United States drifted toward war in 1939 and 1940, President Franklin D. Roosevelt could rely on receiving a broad delegation of authority from Congress during wartime.

Not until March 1941, when the Senate Special Committee to Investigate the National Defense Program was created, did a serious challenge to executive preeminence arise. Even then, Harry S. Truman (D-Mo.) and his Senate colleagues did not challenge presidential authority, carefully avoiding the stalemate that had wrecked congressional inquiry during the Civil War.

Though a strong supporter of the Roosevelt administration, Senator Truman was alarmed by the waste and lack of direction in the military construction program. He was determined that Missouri and small business generally receive a fair share of the lucrative defense contracts being

TRUMAN COMMITTEE MEMBERS. Visiting the Ford Motor Company, 13 April 1942. *Left to right,* Sen. Joseph H. Ball (R-Minn.); Hugh S. Fulton, chief counsel of the committee; Sen. Prentiss M. Brown (D-Mich.); Sen. Harry S. Truman (D-Mo.); Paul Brown, *in front of Truman;* Sen. Ralph O. Brewster (R-Maine); Sen. James M. Mead (D-N.Y.); a Ford representative; Sen. Monrad C. Wallgren (D-Wash.); Sen. Harold H. Burton (R-Ohio); and Sen. Harley M. Kilgore (D W.Va.).

COMMITTEE MEETING. In the Senate Caucus Room. *Left to right, foreground,* Sen. James M. Mead (D-N.Y.); Charles Patrick Clark, committee attorney; Senators Harry S. Truman (D-Mo.); Ralph O. Brewster (R-Maine); Joseph H. Ball (R-Minn.); and visiting senator Gerald P. Nye (R-N.Dak.). HARRY S. TRUMAN LIBRARY

awarded. On 10 February 1941, Truman proposed a special committee to investigate the defense program. The White House was initially unhappy about the prospect of congressional snooping into contracts and other sensitive aspects of mobilization, but pressures for a congressional inquiry proved irresistible. On 1 March, the Senate unanimously adopted a resolution creating the committee, setting its membership at seven, designating Truman its chairman, and bestowing a budget of $15,000.

The Truman Committee quickly earned a reputation for responsible conduct and produced a tidal wave of congressional and media support. A principal reason for its effectiveness was the fifty-seven-year-old junior senator from Missouri, who received enormous publicity for his role on the committee. He recruited a politically savvy and efficient staff. The committee's membership, soon enlarged to ten, comprised mostly insiders and proved remarkably stable during Truman's tenure.

Between 1941 and 1948, the Truman Committee held 432 public hearings, convened 300 executive sessions, and released 51 reports. Empowered to study all aspects of the defense program, the committee focused on waste and corruption. It examined such issues as policies for war contracts, training-camp construction, the aluminum shortage, the comparative merits of rayon and cotton tire cord, Sen. Albert B. Chandler's swimming pool, and the Canol Project to build a pipeline across the arctic tundra from Norman Wells to Whitehorse in Canada's Yukon Territory. Estimates of tax dollars saved ranged from $10 billion to $30 billion. Though Truman pushed for central direction of war production and clashed with army and navy leaders, the committee refrained from any denunciation of the administration's conduct of the war. Whenever the White House signaled that an investigation might jeopardize the nation's security (as when the committee questioned the priority of the Manhattan Project), Senator Truman relented.

Truman's resignation on 4 August 1944 to accept the Democratic vice presidential nomination proved a watershed in the committee's history. By then, the Truman Committee had resolved major jurisdictional and procedural questions and had released nearly two-thirds of its projected investigation reports. Headed by James M. Mead, Harley M. Kilgore, and Ralph O. Brewster, the committee existed until April 1948, conducted forty-five public hearings, and issued reports on reconversion, disposal of surplus property, and other important topics. However, it also experienced a large turnover of membership, erosion of prestige, and displays of partisan bickering.

BIBLIOGRAPHY

Riddle, Donald. *The Truman Committee: A Study in Congressional Responsibility.* 1963.
Wilson, Theodore A. "The Truman Committee." In *Congress Investigates, 1792–1974.* Edited by Arthur M. Schlesinger, Jr., and Roger Bruns. 1975.

THEODORE A. WILSON

TRUMBULL, JONATHAN (1740–1809), Revolutionary War patriot and soldier, member of Congress and senator from Connecticut, Speaker of the House, and governor of Connecticut. Trumbull was born to one of Connecticut's most prominent families: his father was governor and his younger brother, John, was the distinguished artist. Trumbull served in the legislature intermittently between 1774 and 1788 and was active in the American Revolution, holding the office of comptroller of the Treasury in 1778 and part of 1779. In 1781 General George Washington chose Trumbull to be military secretary on his staff. Participating in the siege of Yorktown, he wrote Washington's response to Lord Cornwallis's surrender offer. Trumbull, then a colonel, remained at Washington's Newburgh, New York, headquarters until autumn 1783.

With the surge in federal sentiment in 1788 and 1789, Trumbull was appointed to the Connecticut Council, then elected as representative in the First Congress, where he supported Hamilton's financial program and Federalist policies in general. Reelected in 1791, Trumbull was chosen to be the second Speaker of the House, before it was a powerful political position. When Sen. Steven M. Mitchell retired in 1794, Trumbull succeeded him but resigned in June 1796 to accept the more enticing position of deputy governor of Connecticut. He became governor in 1797 and remained in that office, annually reelected by large majorities, until his death in 1809. An efficient and energetic administrator, Trumbull evoked popular support while voicing the views of the state's entrenched Federalist party.

BIBLIOGRAPHY

Grossbart, Stephen Reed. *The Revolutionary Transition: Politics, Religion, and Economy in Eastern Connecticut, 1765–1800.* 1989.
Ifkovic, John W. *Connecticut's Nationalist Revolutionary: John Trumbull, Junior.* 1977.

Shipton, Clifford K., ed. *Sibley's Harvard Graduates.* Vol. 12. 1962.

WINFRED E. A. BERNHARD

TURNOVER. *See* Members, *article on* Tenure and Turnover.

TWELFTH AMENDMENT (1804; 2 Stat. 306). The Twelfth Amendment was adopted because the provisions of the Constitution for the operation of the electoral college (Article II, section 1, clause 3) could not adequately deal with the various complications that arose from the development of political parties during the 1790s. The Constitution provided that each elector was to cast two ballots and that the person with the most electoral votes, provided he had a majority, would become president and the runner-up vice president.

The Framers, however, had not anticipated the emergence of partisan politics. The destabilizing consequences became clear in 1796, the year of the first contested election for the presidency, when John Adams, a Federalist, won the election, and his chief opponent, Thomas Jefferson, a Jeffersonian Republican, became vice president. In 1800 a major constitutional crisis occurred when the Jeffersonian Republicans won the election. Because of disciplined voting within the Republican party, Jefferson and Aaron Burr, the ticket's two candidates, received the same number of electoral votes. According to the Constitution, in case of a tie vote, the matter was to be decided by the House of Representatives, with each state's delegation having one vote. The House balloted in February 1801; the lame duck, Federalist-dominated body, elected in 1798, finally managed to select Jefferson as president and Burr as vice president after thirty-six separate ballots and much political maneuvering.

In order to make sure that in the future the wrong person was not selected president, the Jeffersonian Republicans, secure that they now had the necessary two-thirds majority in both chambers, introduced an amendment to the Constitution in 1803 requiring electors to cast separate ballots for president and vice president. It further provided that if no candidate received a majority of the electoral votes for president, the House of Representatives would choose from among the top three candidates instead of the top five, as the Constitution originally stipulated. If no candidate received a majority of electoral votes for vice president, the Senate would choose between the two with the most votes.

Opposition to the measure came mainly from Federalists and from congressmen from the small states who feared that it would diminish their influence in presidential elections by reducing their options in selecting the vice president. Also, opponents argued that the amendment violated the original intent of the Framers, who had expected most presidential elections ultimately to be decided by Congress. Nevertheless the Twelfth Amendment was quickly adopted by Congress (22 to 10 in the Senate and 83 to 42 in the House) and ratified by the states in time for the 1804 election.

The Twelfth Amendment, in conjunction with the two-party system of politics, has allowed the Electoral College to provide clear-cut resolutions to most presidential contests without the involvement of Congress and has ensured that the president and vice president would be of the same party. Only once since 1804 has the electoral college failed to select a president. That occurred in 1824, when there were four major candidates for the presidency; the House, on the first ballot, selected John Quincy Adams, even though Andrew Jackson had received a plurality of the electoral and popular votes. Some complications also followed the election of 1876, when the electoral returns of several states were disputed. To clarify matters, Congress passed an act in 1887 providing that in order to be counted, a state's electoral returns had to be certified by its governor unless both houses of Congress agreed to accept them.

[*See also* Electoral College.]

BIBLIOGRAPHY

House, Lolabel. *A Study of the 12th Amendment to the Constitution of the United States.* 1901.
McCormick, Richard P. *The Presidential Game: The Origins of American Presidential Politics.* 1982.

RICHARD E. ELLIS

TWENTIETH AMENDMENT (1933; 47 Stat. 745). In January 1923, Sen. Thaddeus H. Caraway of Arkansas presented a resolution on behalf of a farm organization in his state repudiating "lame ducks"—that is, defeated members of Congress who served until the next session convened, usually in December of the year following their defeat. As something of a joke, the resolution was sent to the Committee on Agriculture and Forestry, chaired by Sen. George W. Norris (R-Nebr.), who took it seri-

ously. He drafted a joint two-part resolution that required a constitutional amendment to achieve its purpose. One part pertained to presidential electors; the other called for the convening of the new Congress elected in November on the first Monday in January. In this way, the lame-duck, or short, session of Congress would be eliminated. After the full committee approved, Norris was directed to report the joint resolution to the Senate. Thus, for the only time in the nation's history, a proposed constitutional amendment emanated from outside the Judiciary Committee.

Finding little support for the part pertaining to the Electoral College, in February 1923 Norris agreed to eliminate it. The part attracting serious attention called for the commencement of Congress two weeks prior to the inauguration of the president and

"THE POST-SEASON PARADE." Cartoon published after the end of the lame-duck session of the 63d Congress, portraying the unseated members of Congress as lame ducks limping toward the White House, possibly to receive employment as ambassadors or other appointed officials. Clifford K. Berryman, *Washington Evening Star*, 5 March 1915.

U.S. SENATE COLLECTION, CENTER FOR LEGISLATIVE ARCHIVES

vice president. Thus the new Congress would be organized and the electoral votes canvassed as called for in the Constitution; members of Congress would begin their service two months after their election, thereby eliminating the prevailing delay of more than a year; and the serving president and vice president would serve six weeks less than their full four-year terms. Although the resolution passed the Senate, it never came to a vote in the House owing to the opposition of the Republican leadership during the 67th Congress.

The same situation prevailed during the Coolidge administration. In the 70th Congress, however, after gaining Senate approval, the resolution was reported favorably by the House Judiciary Committee and on 9 March 1928 narrowly failed to win the required two-thirds majority.

Shortly after Herbert Hoover's inauguration, Norris again introduced his resolution. For the fifth time it passed the Senate. Speaker Nicholas Longworth delayed sending the resolution to committee, but he finally acquiesced. He accepted Norris's resolution with a crippling amendment that ensured that the Senate conferees would not accept the version approved by the House on 24 February 1931.

The 1930 election, by giving Democrats control of the House for the first time since 1917, finally broke the alliance between the president and the Speaker in opposing the joint resolution. For the sixth time Norris introduced his resolution, and this time it was quickly approved in both chambers. The House added an amendment requiring that at least one branch of each state legislature be elected after its submission. The version that emerged from the conference committee did not differ substantially from Norris's resolution, and the Senate quickly accepted. In the crux of the amendment, section 1, the date for convening Congress was changed from 2 to 3 January, and inauguration day from 15 to 20 January. Another change accepted by the Senate stated that three-fourths of the state legislatures must ratify the amendment within seven years.

Virginia, on 4 March 1932, was the first state to ratify. When, in January 1933, Missouri became the thirty-sixth state to approve, its adoption as the Twentieth Amendment to the Constitution was secured. Every legislature considering the amendment approved it.

The amendment became operative after 15 October 1933. Members serving in the 74th Congress began their service on 3 January 1935. On 20 January 1936, Franklin D. Roosevelt became the first president inaugurated under the provision replacing 4 March as Inauguration Day.

[*See also* Lame Duck Session.]

BIBLIOGRAPHY

Lief, Alfred. *Democracy's Norris.* 1939.

Lowitt, Richard. *George W. Norris: The Persistence of a Progressive, 1913–1933.* 1971.

Norris, George W. *Fighting Liberal.* 1945.

RICHARD LOWITT

TWENTY-FIRST AMENDMENT (1933; 47
Stat. 1625). The only constitutional amendment ratified by the electorate rather than by state legislators, the Twenty-first Amendment was also the only amendment ever to repeal another. This required an extraordinary shift from endorsement of national prohibition of alcoholic beverages by two-thirds of Congress to opposition by an equally large margin. Not quite fourteen years elapsed between the adoption of the Eighteenth Amendment on 16 January 1919 and the ratification of the Twenty-first Amendment on 5 December 1933.

National prohibition sharply reduced but did not altogether eliminate the use of alcoholic beverages in the United States. Neither state and local law enforcement officials nor the small federal Prohibition Bureau authorized by the Volstead Act (1919) could cope with the variety and volume of prohibition violations. The longer sentences and larger fines imposed by the federal Jones "Five-and-Ten" law (1929) had little effect. Nor did a series of Supreme Court decisions upholding concurrent powers of state and federal enforcement (*United States v. Lanza*, 1922), warrantless automobile searches (*Carroll v. United States*, 1925), restrictions on medicinal liquor prescriptions (*Lambert v. Yellowley*, 1926), and wiretap telephone surveillance (*Olmstead v. United States*, 1928).

Opposition to prohibition came from politically active groups of recent immigrants who saw prohibition as an attack on their cultures and from antiprohibition organizations that argued that the liquor ban encouraged crime and disrespect for all law while simultaneously giving the federal government too much power over people's personal lives. The economic collapse of the early 1930s generated additional arguments that prohibition took away jobs and liquor taxes.

The Democratic platform of 1932 endorsed prohibition repeal, and the party's sweeping November victory over a Republican party that continued to support enforcement of the law brought quick congressional action. On 20 February 1933, the House approved, 289 to 121, an amendment resolution earlier passed by the Senate, 63 to 23, that would repeal the Eighteenth Amendment and, additionally, prohibit transportation of intoxicating beverages into any U. S. state, territory, or possession in violation of its laws. The resolution also called for ratification of the proposed amendment by state conventions rather than by legislatures. Overturning a 1919 Ohio referendum on the Eighteenth Amendment, the Supreme Court in *Hawke v. Smith* (1920) stirred demands that this never-before-employed alternative Article V procedure be used so that delegate elections could express popular opinion on the proposed constitutional change. Congress left the arrangements for ratification conventions to the states.

Between April and November 1933 thirty-eight states held delegate elections; 73 percent of 21 million voters cast ballots for candidates who favored an end to national prohibition, with only South Carolina voters rejecting repeal. Ratification conventions quickly certified the results, and on 5 December 1933, when Pennsylvania, Ohio, and finally Utah acted, national prohibition came to an end. Despite the fact that per capita alcohol consumption rates remained below pre-1920 levels for forty years after national prohibition, the federal effort to forbid adult use of alcohol has been generally perceived as a failure, a futile policy, and a misapplication of constitutional amendment.

[*See also* Eighteenth Amendment; National Prohibition Act; Prohibition.]

BIBLIOGRAPHY

Brown, Everett S., comp. *Ratification of the Twenty-First Amendment to the Constitution of the United States: State Convention Records and Laws.* 1938.

Kyvig, David E. *Repealing National Prohibition.* 1979.

DAVID E. KYVIG

TWENTY-SECOND AMENDMENT (1951; 61 Stat. 959). Breaking with the two-term tradition established by George Washington and Thomas Jefferson, Franklin D. Roosevelt sought and won four terms as president. The belief that he had stayed too long in office, particularly strong within Republican circles, precipitated a spate of term-limitation proposals in Congress after the 1944 election. Not until 1947, however, did these efforts meet with success. Roosevelt's death in 1945, combined with Republican success in recapturing control of Congress in the 1946 elections, ensured that legislators would now give term limitation a more sympathetic hearing.

With the 80th Congress barely a month old, Rep. Earl C. Michener (R-Mich.) introduced House Joint Resolution 27, which proposed that no person be eligible for president if he served "during the whole or any part of each of two separate terms." It further stated that this provision would not apply to the president holding office at the time it was ratified, and that the method of ratification would be by state legislatures. Less than a month after its referral to the House Committee on the Judiciary, five of the committee's twelve Democrats joined all fifteen Republicans in reporting the resolution back to the House with a favorable recommendation. The next day, after only two hours of floor debate, the resolution passed the House by a vote of 285 to 121. Unanimous support within Republican ranks, along with forty-seven Democratic votes, produced the necessary two-thirds majority.

Following two weeks of deliberations, and with only one member dissenting, the Senate Judiciary Committee approved the House resolution, but only after making two changes. It proposed ineligibility only if an individual served a year or more in each of two terms, and substituted state conventions for state legislatures as the mode of ratification. The full Senate rejected the latter change, and in place of the former adopted the Taft-Tydings amendment stipulating that any individual who served more than two years of an unexpired term could be elected to only one term. By a vote of 59 to 23, the Senate approved the final version of the resolution. All Senate Republicans present voted in favor, as did thirteen Democrats. With a surprisingly small number of members present, the House accepted the Senate changes by a vote of 81 to 29.

During floor debates on the amendment, proponents raised the specter of "dictatorship" and "totalitarianism," warning that the president had become far more powerful than the Founders could ever have imagined. With the development of his role as party leader, the president was now able to dominate Congress. Were he to have unlimited tenure, his appointment power would enable him to have inordinate influence over the Supreme Court as well. Thus, they argued, the amendment should be viewed as a further means of protecting separation of powers. Congressional opponents, on the other hand, charged that the amendment was both antidemocratic and imprudent, for it precluded the opportunity to reward effective leadership and retain it during a time of crisis.

So far, at least, the amendment has been notable more for limiting presidents in their second term than for restraining presumably eager presidents from seeking a third. From 1952 to 1992 only Dwight D. Eisenhower and Ronald Reagan completed two terms. Given their age and general health upon leaving office, it seems unlikely that either would have aspired to four more years even had they had the option. On the other hand, presidents and scholars have argued that the lame-duck status of second-term presidents does indeed impede their leverage over Congress.

BIBLIOGRAPHY

Brown, Everett S. "The Term of Office of the President." *American Political Science Review* 41 (1947): 447–452.

Willis, Paul G., and George L. Willis. "The Politics of the Twenty-Second Amendment." *Western Political Quarterly* 5 (1952): 469–482.

ROBERT E. DiCLERICO

TWENTY-THIRD AMENDMENT (1961; 75 Stat. 847–848).

The Twenty-third Amendment, allowing District of Columbia residents to vote for president and vice president, was proposed 16 June 1960 and proclaimed 3 April 1961. It reads:

Section 1. The District constituting the seat of Government of the United States shall appoint in such manner as the Congress may direct:

A number of electors of President and Vice President equal to the whole number of Senators and Representatives in Congress to which the District would be entitled if it were a State, but in no event more than the least populous State; they shall be in addition to those appointed by the States, but they shall be considered, for the purposes of the election of President and Vice President, to be electors appointed by a State; and they shall meet in the District and perform such duties as provided by the twelfth article of amendment.

Section 2. The Congress shall have power to enforce this article by appropriate legislation.

Before the Twenty-third Amendment was adopted, residents of the area within the District of Columbia had not participated in the election of the president and the vice president since 1800, when the national government moved to the federal district. Before Congress assumed jurisdiction over the land ceded by Maryland and Virginia to create the seat of government, residents of the area had been eligible to vote in the respective states.

The ratification of the Twenty-third Amendment represented the culmination of one aspect of a protracted struggle that embraced the general issue of District of Columbia representation at the national level. In the 1880s, Theodore W. Noyes, editor of the *Washington Evening Star,* had been a prime mover in the struggle for the vote in presidential elections. Working closely with the Metropolitan Board of Trade, in 1914 he led in organizing the Citizens' Joint Committee on National Representation for the District of Columbia. In 1929 the committee supported an amendment to the Constitution empowering Congress to grant District citizens voting representation in the Senate and House of Representatives, the right to vote for president and vice president, and access to the federal courts.

While endorsements from African American organizations such as the National Association for the Advancement of Colored People (NAACP) appear to have been missing, the committee enjoyed bipartisan political support as well as support from local fraternal, commercial, trade, and professional organizations. Noyes died in 1946, but his bequest of $50,000 to the committee helped to keep the movement alive and to support the ratification campaign for the amendment in 1960 and 1961.

In the decade leading up to the amendment's adoption, both the racial composition of the District's population and its political party affiliations were more balanced than in the years that followed. In 1956, for example, 23,912 Democrats and 21,670 Republicans voted in the District for their party convention delegates. The 1960 census showed the black population at 54 percent; a much lower percentage of blacks were registered and voting. Congress's proposal of the amendment just before the 1960 presidential nominating conventions brought endorsements from both parties and both presidential candidates, Richard M. Nixon and John F. Kennedy. The perception of partisan balance in the District in 1960 was considered a key factor in the amendment's success.

The joint committee is credited with designing a model strategy for achieving ratification. Because of the District's image as urban, liberal, and black, the committee more or less wrote off the South at the outset, and as it turned out, no southern state ratified the amendment. Ratification of the amendment by the required thirty-eight states was achieved in almost record time (286 days), between 16 June 1960 and 29 March 1961.

In the years since the amendment was ratified the electorate in the district has voted overwhelmingly

Democratic in presidential elections—82.6 percent in 1988, compared to 14.3 percent for the Republicans. In the 1992 presidential election, the Democratic party enjoyed even greater domination in the District than it had in 1988, with 85 percent voting for Bill Clinton, while only 9 percent voted for George Bush.

[See also District of Columbia.]

BIBLIOGRAPHY

Congressional Research Service. "Legislative History of the Twenty-third Amendment and of Related Efforts to Grant Voting Representation for the District of Columbia in the House of Representative During the 86th Congress." Typed report. 1960.

Vose, Clement E. "When District of Columbia Representation Collides with Constitutional Amendment Institution." *Publius* 9 (1979): 105–125.

CHARLES W. HARRIS

TWENTY-FOURTH AMENDMENT (1964; 76 Stat. 1259).

Ratified in 1964, the Twenty-fourth Amendment barred the payment of a poll (or "head") tax as a requirement for voting in federal primary and general elections. It left untouched taxes attached to voting in state and local contests.

By the 1960s the need to abolish the poll tax had become obvious. Such taxes had become useless and disreputable. In the late nineteenth century, southern states had passed poll-tax measures as part of a broader effort to disfranchise the poor, which meant some whites and almost all blacks. But six decades later only five states still imposed such a burden on the franchise, and they did so with only marginal effect. The amounts levied were usually small, and the tax was superfluous because fraudulent literacy tests, intimidation, and outright violence sufficed to keep most southern blacks from the polls. Thus the tax remained important only as an ugly symbol of white opposition to full citizenship for African Americans. As a symbol it was, however, significant.

There was some controversy over whether abolition of the poll tax required a constitutional amendment. States had the constitutional right to set the rules as to who among their citizens could vote—although, after passage of the Fourteenth and Fifteenth Amendments, those rules could no longer be racially discriminatory. The poll tax qualified as racially neutral: it affected blacks and whites equally. Thus, members of Congress who on a variety of grounds were against passing a law to abolish the tax always had a strong constitutional argument. On five occasions between 1942 and 1949 the House approved bills to ban the tax by statute but could not get the Senate to go along.

Of course, not everyone agreed on the wisdom of a constitutional amendment. In 1949 Sen. Spessard L. Holland (D-Fla.) took up the cause, but other southern senators blocked his effort through their control of the all-important Judiciary Committee. Finally, in 1962 a resolution bypassed that committee through a suspension of the rules; the motion went directly to the floor, where passage was inevitable because support was by then overwhelming.

But a number of civil rights groups still expressed qualms. Their concern was with setting precedent; they worried that by implication other civil rights issues would have to be resolved by constitutional change. Not persuaded by that argument, the Senate approved the amendment on 27 March 1962 after a "friendly" ten-day filibuster. The vote was 77 to 16, fifteen more than the necessary two-thirds majority. The opposition included fourteen southern Democrats, one northern Democrat, and one Republican. But eight southern senators were on board, including Democrat Ralph W. Yarborough from the poll-tax state of Texas.

In the House there was also more than enough support. On 13 June 1962, the Judiciary Committee approved the amendment; from there, the bill went not to the Rules Committee but directly to the floor, where the vote was 295 to 86—forty-one more votes than were needed. Fifteen Republicans and seventy-one Democrats voted against the amendment; of the Democrats, all but one (Paul C. Jones of Missouri) were southerners.

The proposed amendment was submitted to the states on 14 September, with a limit of seven years for ratification. On 14 November 1962, Illinois became the first state to approve. South Dakota was the last, on 24 January 1964.

BIBLIOGRAPHY

Graham, Hugh Davis. *The Civil Rights Era: Origins and Development of National Policy, 1960–1972.* 1990.

ABIGAIL THERNSTROM

TWENTY-FIFTH AMENDMENT (1967; Stat. 1327–1328).

The legislative momentum that culminated in the Twenty-Fifth Amendment began in 1881 after the assassination of President James A. Garfield. As Garfield lay in a coma, hovering between life and death, considerable confusion arose over the meaning of the presidential succession provisions of the Constitution. Did the Constitution authorize the vice president to serve as acting president in a case of presidential disability? Or did the vice president become president for the remainder of the term in such a case, based on the precedent of Vice President John Tyler succeeding to the presidency on the death in office of President William Henry Harrison? Who was authorized under the Constitution to declare a president disabled?

After becoming president when Garfield died, Chester A. Arthur urged Congress to answer these questions and thus provide guidance in handling future cases of presidential inability. No action was taken, however, and when President Woodrow Wilson suffered a paralyzing stroke in 1919 affairs of state were practically suspended for the rest of his term. Vice President Thomas R. Marshall hesitated to take any steps toward presidential duties for fear of being labeled a usurper. Secretary of State Robert Lansing's efforts to exercise leadership during the interregnum resulted in his dismissal by Wilson.

Congress once again considered the task of clarifying the meaning of the succession provisions, but interest died as soon as a new administration was installed in the White House.

The subject was again revived during the administration of Dwight D. Eisenhower after the president sustained several disabilities while in office. On each occasion his vice president, cabinet, and staff sought to calm the nation by carrying on the functions of government to the best of their abilities. On recovering from a stroke in 1957, Eisenhower urged Congress to address the matter by means of a constitutional amendment. As debate over his and other proposals went on, he entered into an informal understanding with Vice President Richard M. Nixon concerning procedures to be followed should Eisenhower suffer any further disabilities. According to this ad hoc arrangement, the president would inform the vice president of his inability; if he were unable to do so, the vice president would have the power to declare the president disabled. The arrangement also provided for the vice president to act as president during the period of any inability and for the president to resume his powers on his own declaration of recovery. (Although this understanding never had to be implemented, similar agreements were entered into between President John F. Kennedy and Vice President Lyndon B. Johnson and between Presi-

dent Lyndon Johnson and Vice President Hubert H. Humphrey.)

Many different approaches to a permanent solution were presented to Congress during the balance of Eisenhower's term, but neither house took action. The assassination of President Kennedy in 1963 finally jolted Congress into action because of the realization that, had Kennedy survived but been completely disabled by his injuries, the nation would have been presented with a constitutional crisis, as the informal understanding between him and Johnson did not have the force of law. In 1965 both houses of Congress proposed the Twenty-fifth Amendment to the Constitution. It was quickly ratified, becoming law in 1967. This historic amendment came into being largely because of the leadership in Congress of Sen. Birch Bayh of Indiana.

The amendment filled major gaps in the Constitution. First, it sets forth a procedure for filling a vacancy in the vice presidency, authorizing the president to nominate a successor, who becomes vice president once confirmed by both houses of Congress. Second, the amendment sets forth guidelines for determining presidential inability. It provides for the president to declare his own inability, transfer power to the vice president as acting president, and then resume his powers on his own declaration of recovery. It also empowers the vice president and a majority of the cabinet (or such other body as Congress may substitute for the cabinet) to declare the president disabled in the event the president is unable or unwilling to do so. Their declaration may be challenged by the president, in which case the amendment provides for Congress to resolve the dispute. A two-thirds vote of each house is necessary to prevent the president from continuing to discharge his powers and duties.

The Twenty-fifth Amendment spared the nation a constitutional crisis during the scandals of the early 1970s, when both President Nixon and Vice President Spiro T. Agnew had to resign from office. Gerald R. Ford replaced Agnew and, when Nixon resigned, became president. Ford then took Nelson A. Rockefeller as his vice president under the amendment's vice presidential vacancy procedures. During the administration of Ronald Reagan the presidential inability procedures were implemented for the first time, with Reagan transferring his power to Vice President George Bush for a brief period in July 1985 when he underwent surgery for colon cancer. Although Reagan disclaimed having invoked the Twenty-fifth Amendment at the time, he later admitted to having done so.

The Twenty-fifth Amendment does not, however, deal with every possible contingency, as, for instance, when a vice president suffers an inability to discharge his duties or when simultaneous vacancies occur in the presidency and vice presidency. In the latter case, a succession statute passed by Congress in 1947 would apply. According to that statute, the Speaker of the House of Representatives and then the president pro tempore of the Senate are the next in line, followed by the members of the cabinet in the order that their departments were created. By ensuring that there will always be a vice president, the Twenty-fifth Amendment makes the contingencies of the succession statute less likely.

BIBLIOGRAPHY

Abrams, Herbert L. *The President Has Been Shot.* 1992.
Bayh, Birch. *One Heartbeat Away.* 1968.
Feerick, John. *The Twenty-Fifth Amendment.* 1976.
Hanson, Richard H. *The Year We Had No President.* 1962.
Silva, Ruth E. *Presidential Succession.* 1951.

JOHN D. FEERICK

TWENTY-SIXTH AMENDMENT (1971; 85 Stat. 825–825). The Twenty-sixth Amendment was proposed by Congress early in 1971, approved by the requisite number of states within four months, and certified to have been duly ratified on 5 July 1971. The amendment guarantees "citizens of the United States who are eighteen years of age or older" the right to vote.

Voting age, along with most other qualifications, was regulated by the states at the time the Constitution was adopted and was almost universally set at twenty-one. Proposals to lower the voting age to eighteen began to attract public support during World War II, when large numbers of Americans between eighteen and twenty-one served in the armed forces. The House of Representatives held hearings on the issue in 1943. The first reform, however, was at the state level, when Georgia, in 1943, dropped the voting age to eighteen. By 1959, only Kentucky had followed Georgia's lead, while Alaska and Hawaii set voting ages of nineteen and twenty, respectively.

The eighteen-year-old age requirement was endorsed by Presidents Dwight D. Eisenhower, Lyndon B. Johnson, and Richard M. Nixon, and constitutional amendments were introduced in the 83d and all subsequent Congresses, although there

was no floor action in either chamber after the Senate failed to approve a proposed amendment in 1954.

Throughout the post–World War II period, public support for lowering the voting age grew steadily, particularly during the Vietnam War, in which young Americans once again served in the armed forces in large numbers.

Although amendments to the Constitution had been introduced in the 91st Congress (1969–1971) to lower the voting age, the House and Senate passed, and President Nixon signed, legislation extending the Voting Rights Act (P.L. 91-285) that included an amendment lowering the voting age to eighteen. A number of states, however, challenged the legislation as unconstitutional because it conflicted with their constitutions, and on 21 December 1970, the Supreme Court in *Oregon v. Mitchell* ruled that the voting age provisions were valid only as applied to federal elections, and that voting age in state and local elections could not be changed by statute.

On 7 January 1971, Sen. Jennings Randolph of West Virginia, an early supporter of lowering the voting age, introduced a constitutional amendment to guarantee the right to vote of all citizens aged eighteen or older. The resolution was reported favorably from the Judiciary Committee on 8 March and approved by the Senate on 10 March, by a vote of 94 to 0. A House of Representatives version was introduced by Judiciary Committee Chairman Emanuel Celler on 29 January 1971, was reported from committee on 2 March, and was passed by the House by a vote of 400 to 19 on 23 March. The House then endorsed the Senate version and laid its own resolution on the table. Having passed both houses by the required two-thirds majority, the Twenty-sixth Amendment was submitted to the states, where the ratification process was completed.

Although some observers predicted that a lower voting age would have a profound effect on American electoral politics, in fact younger voters have tended to register and vote at levels significantly lower than those of the general population in the years since ratification of the Twenty-sixth Amendment. Between 1972 and 1988 the gap widened, although participation by all age groups also fell during this period. In the 1992 presidential election, when overall turnout rose, the difference narrowed somewhat as participation by eighteen-to-twenty-year-olds grew at a substantially higher rate than that of the general population.

BIBLIOGRAPHY

U.S. Senate. Committee on the Judiciary. Subcommittee on Constitutional Amendments. *Passage and Ratification of the Twenty-sixth Amendment.* 92d Cong., 1st sess., 1971.

Cohn, Jonathan S. "A Lost Political Generation?" *American Prospect* 9 (1992): 30–38.

THOMAS H. NEALE

TWENTY-SEVENTH AMENDMENT.

As part of the original Bill of Rights, James Madison proposed that any salary increase for members of Congress could not take effect until after the next election. He offered the following addition to Article I: "but no law varying the compensation last ascertained shall operate before the next ensuing election of Representatives." Although Madison did not think that "in the ordinary course of Government" the power of members of Congress to raise their own salaries would be abused, still it seemed to him an "impropriety" to have no restriction on public officials putting "their hand into the public coffers." There was a "seeming indecorum" in such power, he said.

The First Congress established a committee to report a list of amendments to the Constitution. These words were to be added to Article I, section 6: "but no law varying the compensation shall take effect, until an election of representatives shall have intervened." Rep. Theodore Sedgwick of Massachusetts thought "much inconvenience" and "very little good" would result from this amendment. It might, he said, serve "as a tool for designing men." They might reduce legislative salaries below the levels of a living wage "in order to procure popularity at home." Such actions might prevent "men of shining and disinterested abilities, but of indigent circumstances," from serving in Congress.

Rep. John Vining of Delaware, a member of the committee responsible for the proposed amendments, said that there was a "disagreeable sensation occasioned by leaving it in the breast of any man to set a value on his own work." The proposition to delay pay increases until the next Congress passed by a vote of the House 27 to 20. The Senate passed a similar provision. The following language, then, was one of twelve amendments sent to the states for ratification: "No law, varying the compensation for the services of the Senators and Representatives, shall take effect, until an election of Representatives shall have intervened."

From September 1789 to December 1791, six states approved the salary amendment. Only two more states ratified it from 1791 to 1978. Beginning in 1983, however, states began ratifying the amendment at an accelerated rate. The major drive behind this momentum was a staff aide in the Texas legislature, Gregory D. Watson, who assiduously urged state legislatures to approve the amendment. By 7 May 1992, he had achieved the required three-fourths of the states. There was some doubt about whether a 203-year-old amendment could be ratified. Constitutional scholars generally held that ratification should be contemporaneous, reasoning that when too much time elapses there is a lack of contemporary consensus. To eliminate any legal uncertainty, the House and the Senate acted in May 1983 to accept the ratification. Debate in the two chambers emphasized that ratification after 203 years is an exception, not a precedent. For example, in 1789, 1810, 1861, and 1865, Congress had passed constitutional amendments without placing a time limit on ratification, but it is widely agreed that the time for ratifying those amendments has lapsed.

BIBLIOGRAPHY

Miller, Robert S., and Donald O. Dewey. "The Congressional Salary Amendment: 200 Years Later." *Glendale Law Review* 10 (1991): 92–109.

Strictland, Ruth Ann. "The Twenty-Seventh Amendment and Constitutional Change by Stealth." *Political Science and Politics* 26 (1993): 716–722.

LOUIS FISHER

TYLER, JOHN (1790–1862), representative and senator from Virginia, vice president, tenth president of the United States. Born into the Virginia aristocracy, Tyler earned a degree from William and Mary College, studied law, and went to the state legislature. In 1816 he was elected as a Jeffersonian Republican to the U.S. House of Representatives, where he served for five years. His early congressional career illustrated his strict-construction constitutional principles. As a member of a special investigating committee, he favored revoking the charter of the second Bank of the United States. He also opposed federal aid for internal improvements and a protective tariff, and voted against the Missouri Compromise on the grounds that Congress had no power over slavery in the territories. He grew tired of his duties, however, and voluntarily retired.

After twice being selected governor of Virginia,

JOHN TYLER.   LIBRARY OF CONGRESS

he was elected to the U.S. Senate, where in 1828 he opposed the so-called Tariff of Abominations. He backed Andrew Jackson for president that year, although without enthusiasm. While he applauded the Maysville Road veto and Jackson's opposition to the national bank, he broke with the president over the removal of the deposits from the national bank and, especially, over Jackson's vigorous opposition to nullification. Tyler voted for the resolution censuring Jackson's handling of the deposits and was the only senator to vote against the Force Bill in 1833.

An ardent defender of states' rights, Tyler nevertheless cooperated with the new Whig party, which was the proponent of nationalism. He was reelected in 1833 but resigned in protest in 1836 when the legislature instructed him to vote to expunge the resolution censoring Jackson for removing the deposits.

Despite his lack of sympathy with the party's principles, he was selected by the Whigs in 1840 as their vice presidential candidate, and he succeeded to the presidency when William Henry Harrison died a month after assuming office. Tyler retained Harrison's cabinet but soon clashed with Sen.

Henry Clay, who was the real leader of the Whig party. Clay was determined to enact the party's economic program quickly, an objective supported by virtually every Whig member of Congress. Tyler approved the repeal of the subtreasury, which the Democrats had established during Martin Van Buren's administration, but he refused to accept a higher tariff until the distribution of proceeds from land sales to the states was abandoned, and he was generally opposed to federal internal improvement projects.

The major dispute between Tyler and the Whigs in Congress arose out of their attempt to establish a new national bank. After Tyler vetoed two separate bills to charter a bank, the entire cabinet except Secretary of State Daniel Webster resigned, the Whig congressional caucus formally read Tyler out of the party, and resolutions were introduced calling for his impeachment. Disgruntled Whigs began referring to the chief executive as "His Accidency." The Democrats had no intention of taking him back, and, with his support limited to a few southern radicals and federal officeholders, Tyler became a president without a party. His relations with Congress remained chilly for the rest of his term.

Despite his political isolation, Tyler was eager to obtain a second term. He never grasped how politically fatal his rupture with the congressional Whigs had been, and he remained convinced that if he found the right issue he could win reelection as an independent candidate. With this purpose in mind, Tyler pushed for the annexation of Texas, heedless of the sectional dangers it posed. In 1844 he submitted a treaty of annexation to the Senate, but it was decisively rejected by a margin of 16 to 35: twenty-eight of twenty-nine Whigs, joined by seven Democrats, voted against the treaty, testimony to Tyler's lack of influence over Congress. Following James K. Polk's election, however, Tyler urged Congress to accomplish annexation by a joint resolution, which required only a majority vote; the resolution passed both houses, winning approval in the Senate by only the narrowest of margins (27 to 25). On his final day in office, Tyler formally invited Texas to join the Union under the terms of the joint resolution.

Following his retirement, Tyler remained out of public life until 1861, when he presided over the Washington peace conference and served in the Virginia secession convention. He died the following year. Tyler's personal warmth masked his doctrinaire mind, soaring vanity, and political stubbornness. His congressional service was largely negative, expressed primarily in terms of policies he opposed. Inflexible, intellectually pedestrian, and politically unastute, he supported few measures of any consequence other than the annexation of Texas, and his promotion of this policy without regard to sentiment in Congress did much to weaken the party system and ultimately the Union.

BIBLIOGRAPHY

Chitwood, Oliver P. *John Tyler: Champion of the Old South.* 1939.

Morgan, Robert J. *A Whig Embattled: The Presidency under John Tyler.* 1954.

Seager, Robert, II. *And Tyler Too: A Biography of John and Julia Gardner Tyler.* 1963.

WILLIAM E. GIENAPP

U

UDALL, MORRIS K. (1922–), representative from Arizona and a leader of the Democratic party's liberal faction. Born in St. Johns, Arizona, Morris King Udall attended the University of Arizona. His college career was interrupted by four years as a U.S. Army Air Force officer in World War II. Following the war, he returned to the University of Arizona, received a bachelor's degree in law in 1949, and took up a law practice. In 1961, Udall was elected to the House of Representatives in the 87th Congress in a special election. (He succeeded his brother, Stewart L. Udall, who had been appointed secretary of the Interior by President John F. Kennedy.) He then served sixteen consecutive terms until his resignation for reasons of health in May 1991.

Udall had a distinguished career as a representative and party leader. His committee service included the chairmanship of the Committee on Interior and Insular Affairs (1977–1991) and membership on the Committee on Foreign Affairs. In 1976 he was a serious contender through several primaries for the Democratic nomination for president, and four years later he was the keynote speaker at the party's national convention.

Affectionately known as "Mo," Udall was one of the most respected and popular members of the House, known for his wry, engaging sense of humor and his skill as a debater. Prominent in the liberal wing of his party, he fought to protect the environment and reform the congressional seniority system and abuses of the mail-franking privilege. He was an outspoken critic of the Vietnam War. Courage in defense of his principles, even when unpopular, marked his long career in public service.

MORRIS K. UDALL. In his office, July 1967.

BIBLIOGRAPHY

Tacheron, Donald G., and Morris K. Udall. *The Job of the Congressman.* 2d ed. 1970.

2005

Udall, Morris K. *Education of a Congressman: The Newsletters of Morris K. Udall.* Edited by Robert L. Peabody. 1972.

Udall, Morris K. *Too Funny to Be President.* 1988.

PAUL HUBBARD

UN-AMERICAN ACTIVITIES COMMITTEE, HOUSE.

During the 1930s, American concerns over domestic subversion prompted the creation of three special House committees to investigate communist and fascist organizations. The first two, directed by Rep. Hamilton Fish (R-N.Y.) and Rep. John W. McCormack (D-Mass.), respectively, conducted hearings in 1930 and 1934 and quickly passed into obscurity. The third, chaired by Rep. Martin Dies, Jr. (D-Tex.), became a near-permanent fixture in the House. The Dies Committee, known formally as the House Special Committee to Investigate Un-American Activities and later referred to by the acronym HUAC, was created in May 1938 by a House resolution authorizing an eight-month Investigation into "the extent, character, and objects of un-American propaganda activities in the United States." This vague mandate, adopted by a vote of 191 to 41, would serve as the committee's charter for thirty-three years.

The Dies Committee quickly attracted controversy. Its public hearings served as a forum for those who believed that the federal government, the labor movement, and many liberal organizations had been deeply infiltrated by communists. Witnesses branded hundreds of organizations as communist fronts, claiming that several CIO-affiliated unions were communist controlled and blaming liberal politicians and New Dealers for aiding the communist cause. This testimony was accepted into the record with little effort to establish its accuracy; few of the organizations and individuals were given an opportunity to refute the allegations.

Although condemned in the liberal press, the 1938 hearings attracted sufficient public support to ensure a one-year extension of the committee's work. In 1939 the Dies Committee improved its procedures, but its techniques and targets remained the same. Like later HUAC chairs, Dies directed only token interest toward the activities of fascist and right-wing organizations, reserving his primary attention for the radicals of the left. Also like later chairs, he consistently exaggerated the extent of communist infiltration and frequently blurred the distinction between communism and liberalism. As Americans' fears intensified following the Nazi-Soviet pact in August 1939 and the onset of war in Europe, Dies found an increasingly receptive audience and in 1940 and 1941 won further extensions from the House.

The nation's entry into World War II drove the Dies Committee from the headlines, and Soviet-American cooperation diminished the appeal of anticommunism. Yet the House renewed the committee's mandate yearly through 1944. But when Dies announced his intention to retire at the end of that year, it looked as if HUAC would pass quietly from the political scene. House leaders planned to bury any extension proposal in the Rules Committee, but when Congress convened in 1945, Rep. John E. Rankin (D-Miss.) outmaneuvered the leadership. On the opening day, when the resolution to adopt the rules of the preceding Congress was presented, Rankin offered an amendment adding the committee, renamed the Committee on Un-American Activities, to the list of permanent standing committees. Since in any given Congress, committees do not formally exist until the adoption of the resolution, Rankin's proposal could not be avoided. The initial vote was anonymous, with 146 against and 136 in favor, but since Rankin knew that few representatives dared publicly oppose an anticommunist measure, he called for a record vote. The amendment then passed 207 to 186.

During the 79th Congress (1945–1947) the new standing committee was chaired by both Rep. Edward J. Hart (D-N.J.), who resigned in July 1945, and Rep. John S. Wood (D-Ga.). Under Wood's direction, HUAC avoided the controversy that followed Dies by confining the committee's investigations to relatively obscure organizations. But during the Republican-controlled 80th Congress (1947–1949), the committee returned to the headlines with a vengeance, achieving its greatest notoriety under the chairmanship of Rep. J. Parnell Thomas (R-N.J.). In October 1947, the Thomas Committee conducted highly publicized hearings designed to expose communist influence in the motion picture industry. The Hollywood hearings opened with a parade of screen stars and movie moguls who supported the claims of communist infiltration, followed by ten accused writers and directors who were quizzed concerning their membership in subversive organizations. Each of the so-called Hollywood Ten denied the committee's authority to inquire into political beliefs and associations and refused to answer; each was subsequently cited and convicted for contempt of Congress. The spectacle prompted the movie industry to ban performers suspected of communist sympathies, and the resulting blacklist spread to radio, television, and other industries. HUAC's hearings and its ever-expanding files provided many of the names for this blacklist.

The year 1948 brought further headlines. In February, a subcommittee chaired by freshman representative Richard M. Nixon (R-Calif.) held hearings on a bill introduced by Rep. Karl E. Mundt (R-S.Dak.) requiring that all communist organizations register with the Justice Department. The Mundt-Nixon bill was later incorporated into the Internal Security Act of 1950, HUAC's only significant legislative accomplishment. In July the committee launched its most celebrated hearings. They began with confessed spy Elizabeth Bentley, who provided the committee with the names of U.S. officials she claimed had been involved in transferring secret documents to the Soviets during World War II. She was followed by Whittaker Chambers, an editor for *Time* magazine, who described his collaboration with a communist cell in Washington in the 1930s. Nearly all of those named by Bentley and Chambers took refuge in the Fifth Amendment. One of those named, Alger Hiss, a former State Department official, flatly denied Chambers's charges, and the remainder of the hearings focused on determining who was lying, he or Chambers. The session climaxed on 25 August 1948, when the committee grilled Hiss for six hours and Chambers for three, failing, however, to resolve the issue. That fall, Chambers produced secret State Department papers supposedly traceable to Hiss, which resulted in the latter's conviction for perjury.

In the early 1950s, the emergence of Sen. Joseph R. McCarthy (R-Wis.) and the creation of the Internal Security Subcommittee of the Senate Judiciary Committee forced the House Un-American Activities Committee to share the investigating spotlight. But HUAC remained active, with its probes often focusing on a particular region. In 1954 alone, HUAC conducted hearings in Albany, Chicago, Los Angeles, Detroit, Lansing, Seattle, Portland, Philadelphia, and Dayton. As the number of hearings increased, so did the committee's expenses. By 1960, it had a permanent staff of forty-nine and an annual appropriation of more than $300,000.

Under Illinois Republican Harold H. Velde (1953–1954) and Pennsylvania Democrat Francis E. Walter (1955–1963), HUAC's public hearings followed a predictable format. Friendly witnesses, often FBI informants or disenchanted communists, provided testimony on party members and sympathizers. The individuals named were then called to answer the famous question, "Are you now or have you ever been a member of the Communist Party?" Because the committee frequently received information from secret FBI files, its staff knew the past affiliations of witnesses, so the question was designed less to illicit new information than to expose those called to public humiliation. If they answered affirmatively, they were required to provide the names of others who cooperated with the party. To avoid this, many invoked the self-incrimination clause of the Fifth Amendment and refused to answer any questions.

The stigma attached to the label "Fifth Amendment communist" caused a few witnesses to seek legal alternatives. Several agreed to provide testimony on their own activities but refused to inform on others. Others relied on the First Amendment to defend themselves, but invariably the committee cited such witnesses for contempt. These legal strategies prompted the first serious judicial scrutiny of HUAC's functions. In *Watkins v. United States* (1957), Chief Justice Earl Warren criticized HUAC for using its hearings as punishment but would otherwise go no further than to reverse the contempt conviction on a narrow point of law. Two years later, in *Barenblatt v. United States* (1959), the Court did take up the more substantive issues, including the constitutionality of HUAC's vague mandate and its authority to inquire about political associations. This time the Court upheld the conviction and fully endorsed the committee's authority.

HUAC faced little opposition in the House throughout the 1950s. Its appropriation requests and contempt citations were approved with little debate by overwhelming margins. But as the nation's fears of domestic communism abated, the committee's activities drew increasing criticism. In May 1960 the committee's San Francisco hearings led to a violent confrontation between protesters and the police. HUAC sought to label its opponents communists or dupes and even prepared a film, *Operation Abolition*, to support its claims, but the protests continued. The American Civil Liberties Union and the National Committee to Abolish HUAC organized opposition to committee hearings and sought House votes for the committee's abolition. In the more liberal climate of the 1960s such efforts began to attract support.

Under Edwin E. Willis (D-La., chairman, 1963–1968), HUAC sought to win support through investigations of the Ku Klux Klan in 1965 and the antiwar movement in 1966, but these did little to alter the growing perception that the committee had become an expensive anachronism. To shed this image and circumvent new legal challenges, committee members Richard H. Ichord (D-Mo.) and Del M. Clawson (R-Calif.) introduced a resolution to change HUAC's name and its mandate. The measure was adopted by a vote of 305 to 79 on 19 February 1969 and HUAC became the House Committee on Internal Security.

Chaired by Ichord, the new committee was authorized to investigate organizations bent on the overthrow of the government; but to most of its opponents it was still HUAC. The committee's final demise owes much to the Watergate scandal. The revelations concerning domestic spying and political harassment that flowed from the Watergate hearings left many Americans suspicious of all government security agencies. In this climate, the committee's conduct was no longer defendable, and on 14 January 1975 the House voted to terminate it.

[*See also* McCarran Internal Security Act of 1950; Watkins v. United States.]

BIBLIOGRAPHY

Carr, Robert K. *The House Committee on Un-American Activities, 1945–1950.* 1952.
Goodman, Walter. *The Committee: The Extraordinary Career of the House Committee on Un-American Activities.* 1968.
Ogden, August Raymond. *The Dies Committee: A Study of the Special House Committee for the Investigation of Un-American Activities, 1938–1944.* 1945.

JEROLD L. SIMMONS

UNANIMOUS CONSENT. Members of both the House and Senate regularly use unanimous consent to request permission from their colleagues to set aside the normal rules of procedure or to take a procedural action not expressly provided for in the rules. Unanimous consent is used for a wide variety of actions, ranging from adopting legislation, amendments, or motions to more routine matters such as extending debate time.

The use of unanimous consent provides the House and Senate with flexibility to set aside formal procedures in order to facilitate the business at hand. Yet it preserves the standing rules of each chamber by setting them aside only temporarily. Thus any single member can call upon the full protection of the regular order if necessary.

A unanimous consent request must receive the approval of every member present on the floor at the time it is made; a single objection will block its implementation. Agreement to a unanimous consent request does not require a vote. Instead, the presiding officer can ask if there is an objection to the request. Without objection, action proceeds as outlined in the request.

There is a difference between unanimous consent requests and unanimous consent agreements. Requests are routinely offered in both chambers by any member, and normally receive immediate consideration. Agreements are more extensive and cover a broader range of procedural activity (e.g., setting terms for calling up, debating, amending, and voting on a bill). They require extensive negotiations and are usually proposed only by a member of the chamber's leadership.

In the Senate, unanimous consent has been common practice since 1789 and is expressly provided for by Rule V. In the House, regular use began around 1832. Although not specifically authorized by any House rule, unanimous consent is addressed in House precedents and remains unchallenged as standard operating procedure.

[*See also* Unanimous Consent Agreements.]

BIBLIOGRAPHY

Nickels, Ilona B. *Unanimous Consent: A Study of Its Use in House and Senate Practice from 1979–1984.* Congressional Research Service, Library of Congress. CRS Rept. 23 November 1984.
U.S. Senate. *Committees and Senate Procedures: A Compilation of Papers Prepared for the Commission on the Operation of the Senate.* 94th Cong., 2d sess., 1977. Committee Print. See especially Robert Keith, "The Use of Unanimous Consent in the Senate," pp. 140–168.

ILONA B. NICKELS

UNANIMOUS CONSENT AGREEMENTS. Typically a complicated special rule governing procedure on a single legislative matter before the Senate, a unanimous consent agreement is used to limit debate on both the underlying measure and any amendments that may be offered. A unanimous consent agreement states which Senators may control the debate and is designed to avoid nongermane or irrelevant amendments. (In structuring floor debate, a unanimous consent agreement serves roughly the same purpose in the Senate as does a special rule in the House of Representatives.)

Almost every important piece of legislation that passes the Senate is governed at some point by a unanimous consent agreement. The use of such agreements on a regular and systematic basis can be traced to Lyndon B. Johnson (D-Tex.), who served as majority leader from 1955 to 1961 and who was the first leader to regularize Senate proceedings through their use. He was able to obtain such agreements, which often required senators to relinquish significant rights, through his extraordinary powers of persuasion. Building on Johnson's precedents, every majority leader since has sought to achieve a measure of control over Senate proceedings through the prerogative of obtaining unanimous consent agreements.

A typical unanimous consent agreement on a bill contains the following orders: the day and time at which the Senate will proceed to the bill; a list of amendments identified by senators and their subject matter, although usually not the order in which they will be offered; a limitation on what amendments to these amendments will be in order, if any; a requirement that all amendments be germane or relevant to the bill under consideration; a limitation on debate of any debatable motions, appeals, or points of order submitted to the Senate; a proviso giving control over debate to the manager of the bill or the leadership, allowing them to decide which senators will speak and for how long; and a time certain for final action without any further debate of the bill under consideration.

Because any senator can object to a unanimous consent agreement, extensive behind-the-scenes negotiations occur before an agreement is formally proposed on the Senate floor. The negotiations may last for hours, even days, and usually occur in the Republican or Democratic cloakrooms or in the offices of the majority or minority leaders or of the chairperson or ranking members of the committee managing the legislation. Agreements are not formally proposed until all senators have been notified and given at least a brief period to register their objections. Any change to a unanimous consent agreement requires a further unanimous consent agreement, which is negotiated and cleared in much the same way.

Although unanimous consent agreements are not debatable on the Senate floor, it is customary for senators to speak on possible agreements, beginning their discussion with the statement "reserving the right to object," which gives them the floor and the chance to bargain for favorable terms. Then they proceed to debate the terms of the agreement "for the purpose of clarification." Such discussion often can consume twenty minutes to half an hour prior to formalizing a unanimous consent agree-ment. Once they are formalized, unanimous consent agreements are printed on the front of the Senate calendar.

[*See also* Senate, *article on* Daily Sessions of the Senate; Unanimous Consent.]

BIBLIOGRAPHY

Riddick, Floyd M. *Senate Procedure.* 1981.
Smith, Steven S. *Call to Order.* 1989.

ROBERT B. DOVE

UNDERWOOD, OSCAR W. (1862–1929), lawyer, Democratic representative and senator from Alabama, House majority leader, and Senate minority leader. Born in Louisville, Kentucky, Oscar Wilder Underwood was educated at the University of Virginia and practiced law briefly in Saint

OSCAR W. UNDERWOOD. With Bertha, his wife, at the White House, 1920s. LIBRARY OF CONGRESS

Paul, Minnesota, where he had lived as a boy. In 1884 he established a law practice in Birmingham, Alabama, a burgeoning iron and coal center. In 1894, representing Birmingham interests, he wrested the Democratic congressional nomination from the incumbent, who was from Greensboro, in the black belt—a crescent of alluvial soil in central Alabama. He won the general election by espousing a "tariff for revenue only" and free silver, thus accommodating populists as well as Democrats. Although he served most of the first session of the 54th Congress, he was unseated by its Republican majority following a challenge to the election result involving accusations of vote buying in black precincts. He was elected to the 9th Congressional District seat in 1896 and remained a member of the House until he entered the Senate in 1915.

Underwood methodically mastered the rules of the House. In 1900 he was selected as one of the two Democratic party whips. While becoming known as a tariff reformer, despite his marriage in 1904 to the heiress of a Birmingham pig iron fortune, he advanced to House leadership through membership on the Ways and Means Committee. In 1910, following Democratic victories in the House elections, Underwood catapulted to majority leader. He put through schedule by schedule tariff reduction bills that embarrassed the Taft administration, welded the Democrats into an effective force, and prepared the ground for the Democratic victory in the presidential election of 1912. Underwood sought the Democratic nomination, and the selection of Woodrow Wilson was delayed until Alabama's delegates shifted. Underwood's outstanding legislative leadership substantially helped the passage of Wilson's New Freedom legislation, including the Underwood-Simmons Tariff Act of 1913.

Underwood, an antiprohibitionist, defeated Democratic congressman Richmond P. Hobson, a nationally known prohibitionist, for election to the Senate in 1914. Slow to advocate intervention in World War I, he eventually supported war legislation. He endorsed the Treaty of Versailles but, seeing that it would not otherwise pass, suggested dropping the League of Nations from the treaty.

President Warren G. Harding named Underwood to the Washington naval disarmament conference of 1921 and 1922, and Underwood was crucial in securing ratification of the resulting treaties. Harding also offered to consider him for the Supreme Court, but Underwood declined, looking ahead to a 1924 try for the presidency.

Underwood became leader of the Democratic minority in the Senate in 1920. He was never happy in the Senate, maintaining that the lack of cloture prevented the smooth passage of legislation. He resigned from the minority leadership in 1923 and turned his attention to the 1924 presidential nomination. Although a southern candidate, Underwood forthrightly opposed the Ku Klux Klan. He received some northern votes, but of the old Confederacy, only Alabama supported him for the nomination.

Facing a difficult campaign in 1926 and discouraged by the passage of the Eighteenth and Nineteenth Amendments and the failure of his long fight for operation of the Muscle Shoals project by a private corporation, Underwood did not seek reelection to the Senate. He died in 1929. Underwood was a pristine conservative, but his major accomplishment was his legislative craftsmanship in putting through Wilson's New Freedom programs, including the tariff that bears his name.

BIBLIOGRAPHY

Johnson, Evans C. *Oscar W. Underwood: A Political Biography.* 1980.
Underwood, Oscar W. *Drifting Sands of Party Politics.* 1928.

EVANS C. JOHNSON

UNITED NATIONS. On the last night of the San Francisco Conference in April 1945, Secretary of State Edward R. Stettinius stood looking out of his penthouse apartment at the ships moving under the Golden Gate Bridge, pensively reviewing the tensions and challenges he had experienced in helping to draft the United Nations Charter. As he considered the next step in the U.N. story, he could take satisfaction from the likelihood that the U.S. Senate would prove amenable to charter ratification. That was because of the Roosevelt administration's strategy of patiently cultivating Senate leaders throughout World War II, making them and their House colleagues full partners in the process that had led to this stage of success. Franklin D. Roosevelt had been determined to avoid the errors that had cost President Woodrow Wilson crucial support in his fight to win acceptance of the Covenant of the League of Nations after World War I. Under the meticulous guidance of Secretary of State Cordell Hull, frequent consultations with Congress had been an integral part of creating the U.N. Charter. Hull had spearheaded a special committee of key foreign policy leaders of both houses that met on an almost weekly basis during the year before the San Francisco Conference convened.

Cooperation had not been difficult to attain. Senators such as Tom T. Connally (D-Tex.), chairman of the Foreign Relations Committee, and his Republican colleague on the committee, Arthur H. Vandenberg of Michigan, and their House counterparts, chairman Sol Bloom (D-N.Y.) and ranking Republican Charles A. Eaton (N.J.) of the Foreign Affairs Committee, lent their considerable weight to the challenge of persuading skeptical colleagues to support the creation of a new, postwar international organization. These four members of Congress comprised half of the U.S. delegation at the San Francisco Conference. Vandenberg, in particular, and his adviser John Foster Dulles, played a leading role in the discussions at San Francisco, and had an especially prominent part in obtaining acceptance of Articles 51 and 52 on the right of member nations to take measures of collective self-defense prior to advising the Security Council of their actions.

In converting members of Congress to support a United Nations, Hull was helped by four members, led by Sen. Joseph H. Ball (D-Minn.), who in the spring of 1943 introduced a resolution expressing the will of the Senate that the United States should back the creation of a world peacekeeping organization. Hull feared that the measure would draw the wrath of isolationists, but it passed with solid backing and provided the international movement with the focus it had been missing. The House followed suit in the fall by passing a resolution put forward by Sen. J. William Fulbright (D-Ark.). The Fulbright Resolution placed the Senate on record as "favoring the creation of appropriate international machinery with power adequate to establish and maintain a just and lasting peace." Having gained Congress's full support, the administration prepared to move at full speed toward creation of the United Nations.

The administration unleashed an unprecedented educational and public relations blitz to promote public acceptance of the United Nations during the eighteen months leading up to the start of the San Francisco Conference. Virtually any forum was a venue for spreading the U.N. message. Speakers from Washington appeared in churches, at civic organizations, at Boy Scout functions, and so on. Across America people listened and responded with eagerness and naïveté, placing far too much hope in what the unknown organization could accomplish.

Buoyed by signs of solid congressional approval, the State Department pushed forward with a charter draft that vested the United Nations with vast powers. The Security Council would have broad powers to challenge would-be aggressors and might even have an international military force at its disposal. Such universalist principles were written into the terms of the draft charter adopted at the Dumbarton Oaks Conference in the fall of 1944. But by year's end, the beginnings of the discord that ultimately led to the Cold War were creating suspicions among the Allies, and the prospect of a strong, independent United Nations began rapidly to decline. Thus, the charter accepted at San Francisco enshrined the principles of regionalism. The international organization would consist of a General Assembly and an eleven-member Security Council. The council's five permanent members—Britain, France, the Soviet Union, China, and the United States—would each have the power to veto any substantive action of that body. Furthermore, the powers of the Security Council were sharply pruned, with much of the initiative for peacekeeping being charged to countries acting in their collective self-defense. In addition, all thought of a U.N. military arm was abandoned, and the specter of rising nationalism doomed the organization to become but a shadow of its initial conception.

Congress had watched this transformation without a protest except in connection with the veto provision, in regard to which there was broad belief that permanent powers should not vote on matters pertaining to disputes to which they were a party. In truth, most members of Congress were probably just as happy to see what they regarded as reasonable safeguards placed on the U.N. Some lawmakers protested when it appeared that State Department officials wanted to give the U.S. representative on the Security Council some power to commit U.S. forces to action without Congress's approval. The administration, claimed the protestors, was trying to create a "supergovernment" in the U.N. that would supplant Congress's constitutional power to declare war. Such expressions of opposition were enough to make the administration back off from its proposals and to assure Congress that the U.N. would operate strictly within constitutional guidelines.

Thus mollified, and with its representatives having played a vital role in forging the charter at San Francisco, the Senate approved the charter 92 to 2 after a perfunctory debate in the summer of 1945. The only opposing votes were those of Senators William Langer (R-N.Dak.) and Henrik Shipstead (R-Minn.). Another opponent of the charter, Sen.

Hiram W. Johnson (R-Calif.), was unable to vote because of illness.

Matters then shifted to preparations for formal U.N. meetings and to the critical matter of a permanent location for the organization. Although a European site had some adherents, the most logical choice seemed to be an East Coast city in the United States, and after a vigorous campaign by numerous suitors, New York was selected. In the atmosphere of the early Cold War, there was considerable worry both in Congress and at the State Department that the Soviet Union would use the organization as a base for spying against the United States. This in fact proved to be the case, as many nations housed espionage activities at their U.N. missions. Realistically, the United States could do almost nothing to prevent this activity, largely because of the diplomatic immunity accorded persons accredited to mission staffs.

Congress continued to back the United Nations despite such problems, although in the early 1950s, it ordered special hearings to determine the extent of communist recruitment among U.S. civilian employees at the U.N. The hearings uncovered a number of persons who were unwilling to testify about their possible communist connections. Congress seemed to share President Harry S. Truman's hope that the U.N. could be made into a useful instrument for peace. Accordingly, appropriations by Congress for helping the organization meet expenses were generous compared to the support provided by many other members.

In the 1970s and 1980s, however, members of Congress in growing numbers began to voice their dissatisfaction with the U.N., particularly as the General Assembly increasingly came under the domination of economically underdeveloped nations, many of them allied with the so-called Soviet bloc. Other issues centered on charges of wasteful spending and overstaffing at U.N. headquarters and in various U.N.-sponsored international organizations. In a 1977 report, the Senate Committee on Government Operations cited waste, featherbedding, and ideological bias in many U.N. agencies and questioned the wisdom of further U.S. participation in them.

Such criticism peaked in 1985 with Congress's decision to withhold U.S. financial assistance to the U.N. until the organization initiated spending controls and allowed the United States, its chief financial contributor, a greater voice in budget decisions. Three years later, after receiving U.N. officials' assurances of budget and staffing reforms, Congress resumed full U.S. contributions.

BIBLIOGRAPHY

Acheson, Dean. *Present at the Creation: My Years in the State Department.* 1969.

Campbell, Thomas M. *Masquerade Peace: America's U.N. Policy, 1944–1945.* 1973.

Divine, Robert A. *Second Chance: The Triumph of Internationalism in America During World War II.* 1967.

Eichelberger, Clark M. *The U.N.: The First Fifteen Years.* 1960.

Luard, Evan. *A History of the United Nations.* 1982.

Mazuzan, George T. *Warren R. Austin at the United Nations, 1946–1953.* 1977.

Russell, Ruth B. *A History of the United Nations Charter: The Role of the United States, 1940–1945.* 1958.

THOMAS M. CAMPBELL

UNITED STATES V. CURTISS-WRIGHT EXPORT CORP. (299 U.S. 304 [1936]).

In *United States v. Curtiss-Wright Export Corporation,* the Supreme Court concluded that the president's authority to conduct relations with foreign nations derives neither from attributes of the states nor from constitutionally granted power; therefore, the Court ruled, it is not subject to the restrictions on congressional delegation that control in domestic matters. The decision is clouded by subsequent dictum and scholarly criticism, yet it continues to be cited as support for the notion of inherent executive powers.

The Curtiss-Wright Export Corporation was charged in 1936 with conspiring to violate President Franklin D. Roosevelt's embargo of U.S. arms shipments to the warring countries of Bolivia and Paraguay. The indictment alleged violation of the provisions of a presidential proclamation issued pursuant to a joint resolution of Congress. The resolution authorized the president to restrict such sales if this would contribute to the restoration of peace, and it provided for criminal sanctions in the case of violations. In defense, Curtiss-Wright asserted that the joint resolution constituted an invalid delegation of legislative power, an argument which had prevailed in a pair of earlier Supreme Court rulings striking down New Deal legislation and demonstrating Court concern over excessive delegations by Congress.

This time, however, the Court held that considerations governing delegations of the lawmaking power in domestic affairs are fundamentally different from those that apply in the realm of foreign affairs. Writing for a 7 to 1 majority, Justice George Sutherland declared: "The broad statement that the federal government can exercise no powers except those specifically enumerated in the Constitution, and such implied powers as are necessary and proper to carry into effect the enumerated powers, is categorically true only in respect of our internal affairs."

In language now described by some as going beyond the demands of the case, *Curtiss-Wright* asserts that the powers of external sovereignty do not depend upon affirmative constitutional grants: "The powers to declare and wage war, to conclude peace, to make treaties, to maintain diplomatic relations with other sovereignties, if they had never been mentioned in the Constitution, would have vested in the federal government as necessary concomitants of nationality." Citing numerous congressional delegations of broad authority to the president in matters of foreign relations, the Court declared that in "this vast external realm," only the president is empowered "to speak or listen as a representative of the nation."

The president, then, in limiting arms sales abroad, was acting not solely by authority vested in him by the joint resolution, but also from his plenary and exclusive power as the sole organ of the United States in the field of international relations. The need for secrecy, speed, and confidential sources of information in handling foreign affairs were said to require that the president have a degree of discretion and freedom from restraint not appropriate in domestic affairs.

Portions of Sutherland's view of history and his Hamiltonian perspective on presidential powers have since been challenged by scholars and, on occasion, by the Court itself in dicta, leaving the meaning and vitality of the decision somewhat unclear. Critics have questioned his conclusions regarding the Framers' understanding of the source of the foreign-relations power—specifically, the notion that sovereignty in external affairs passed directly from the British Crown to the colonies and therefore derives from an extraconstitutional source. Nevertheless, while Congress clearly plays a major role in the formulation of foreign policy by means of its appropriations and other powers, the Court continues to rely on *Curtiss-Wright* as available precedent when upholding broad exercise of presidential authority in foreign affairs, citing in *Haig v. Agee* (453 U.S. 280, 291 [1981]) "the volatile nature of problems confronting the Executive in foreign policy and national defense."

BIBLIOGRAPHY

Henkin, Louis. *Foreign Affairs and the Constitution.* 1972.

Levitan, David M. "The Foreign Relations Power: An Analysis of Mr. Justice Sutherland's Theory." *Yale Law Journal* 55 (1946): 467–497.

Lofgren, Charles A. *"United States v. Curtiss-Wright Export Corporation*: An Historical Reassessment." *Yale Law Journal* 83(1973):1–32.

U.S. Senate. *The Constitution of the United States of America: Analysis and Interpretation.* 99th Cong., 1st sess., 1987. S. Doc. 99-16.

KENT M. RONHOVDE

URBAN MASS TRANSPORTATION ACT OF 1964

(78 Stat. 302–308). The Urban Mass Transportation Act of 1964 recognized mass transit as a national problem and provided that the federal government support urban mass transportation systems through a program of federal loans and grants. By 1960, many Americans had stopped using public transportation and traveled by private automobile instead. Suffering financially, transit companies raised rates, abandoned routes, and laid off scores of transit workers. Environmental problems also arose, including smog pollution and the use of scarce urban land for highways and parking lots.

Proposals to provide federal moneys to states and localities to build mass transit systems were highly controversial and politically charged. With active support from the new Kennedy administration, Congress funded a one-year experimental aid program in 1961. Based on the results of the experiment, the administration sent a comprehensive urban mass transportation proposal to Congress. That proposal was reported from the House Banking and Currency Committee but was bottled up by the Rules Committee for the remainder of the 87th Congress (1961–1963). Recognizing the standoff, supporters of mass transit won an extension of the experimental program. The proposal was reintroduced in the 88th Congress (1963–1965), where it was enacted.

Mass transportation was a divisive issue, particularly in the House where it pitted urban Democrats and urban Republicans against southern Democrats and suburban Republicans. Speaker John W. McCormack (D-Mass.) achieved several behind-the-scenes compromises before acquiring enough votes to pass the bill, and Senate majority leader Mike Mansfield (D-Mont.) called House passage a "miracle." Supporters of an urban transportation program included House majority leader Carl B. Albert (D-Okla.) and House Banking and Currency Committee chairman Wright Patman (D-Tex.).

In 1991, Congress reauthorized the Urban Mass Transportation Act as part of a comprehensive six-year Intermodal Surface Transportation Infrastructure Act (P.L. 102–240). It consolidated highway and mass transit programs under a Federal Transit Administration and gave states and cities more options in determining how to use federal transportation dollars.

BIBLIOGRAPHY

Smerk, George A. "The Urban Mass Transportation Act at Twenty: A Turning Point?" *Transportation Journal* 24 (Summer 1985): 52–74.

Weinberg, Philip. "Public Transportation and Clean Air: Natural Allies." *Environmental Law* 21 (1991): 1527–1542.

MARY ETTA BOESL

URBAN POLICY. Congress has seldom enacted a major policy devoted exclusively to urban problems. Most programs affecting cities are simply the urban component of policies legislated for the country as a whole. Legislation designed specifically for cities has typically been small in size, experimental in nature, and of short-term duration.

The structure of Congress militates against the passage of programs aimed solely at urban areas. Because Congress includes representatives from all states and all sorts of congressional districts, it is reluctant to exclude more than a very few places from the legislation it approves. In order to build the broad coalition necessary to pass legislation, benefits usually need to be distributed over a wide geographic reach.

In keeping with the less than explicit focus on urban matters in Congress, the responsibilities are widely dispersed among congressional committees. The word *urban* does appear at the end of the title of a committee in each chamber—Banking, Housing, and Urban Affairs in the Senate, and Banking, Finance, and Urban Affairs in the House. These committees are responsible for housing and community development policies. But committees without an explicitly urban focus are at least as influential on urban matters. In the House, the Committee on Education and Labor has been responsible for education, skills training, and poverty programs; Ways and Means is responsible for income maintenance and general revenue sharing. Transportation policies fall into the jurisdiction of the Committee on Public Works. The division of responsibilities in the Senate is comparable.

This political inhibition against urban-focused policy-making was reinforced in the nineteenth century by Supreme Court interpretations of Congress's constitutional powers. The federal and state governments were said to be dual sovereigns, each exclusively responsible for governing within its own domain. Since local governments were considered creatures of the state, policies affecting specific geographic areas within states were considered outside the congressional domain.

Despite these political and constitutional inhibitions, the changes in cities wrought by industrialization and immigration began to place urban problems on the congressional agenda toward the end of the nineteenth century. Spurred by Jacob Riis's *How the Other Half Lives* (1890), Congress in 1892 asked the commissioner of labor to conduct a study of big-city slums. The commissioner's report, submitted two years later by the Cleveland administration, made no recommendations. It simply reported that residents of slums were more likely than other urban residents to be foreign-born, illiterate, crowded into tenement housing, and living in close proximity to a saloon. A Democratic administration sensitive to the rights of states was not about to take responsibility for the social problems of the inner city.

An official investigation of urban problems again took place in 1908, when a presidential commission appointed by Theodore Roosevelt reviewed slum conditions in Washington, D.C. While this commission made numerous recommendations with respect to social conditions in the nation's capital, it studiously avoided mention of urban problems elsewhere. Republicans were no more willing than Democrats to encroach upon state sovereignty.

New Deal Policies. This narrow conception of the appropriate federal role was finally challenged by Franklin D. Roosevelt's New Deal. To stimulate economic recovery, Congress passed numerous laws affecting urban areas: cities received financial aid under the Federal Emergency Relief Act of 1933; home ownership was made more accessible to middle- and working-class families in 1934, when their bank mortgages were reinsured by the Federal Housing Authority (FHA); states and localities received funds for roads and highways under the Interstate Highway Act of 1934; the urban poor received public assistance as part of the Social Security Act of 1935; and the Public Works Administration (PWA), established by the National Industrial Recovery Act of 1933, built roads, dams, and public housing, spending half of its allocation in urban areas. Taken all together, federal aid to local governments increased from $68.3 million in 1934 to $2.6 billion in 1940. (To facilitate comparisons across time, all financial figures in this essay are calculated in 1990 dollars.)

After initially questioning the constitutional basis for New Deal policy, the Supreme Court eventually handed down a series of decisions that expanded congressional prerogatives. The Court enhanced Congress's capacity to regulate commerce by deciding in *National Labor Relations Board v. Jones & Laughlin Steel Corp.* (1937) that Congress could regulate commercial activities occurring within a state if these activities had implications for commerce outside the state. The Court also conceded to Congress the authority to influence state policies under its taxing and spending powers in *Steward Machine Co. v. Davis* (1937) by ruling that moneys contributed to state unemployment funds could be credited against a federal unemployment tax. This congressional power was reaffirmed and extended in 1987, when the Court in *South Dakota v. Dole* approved a law requiring states to raise their minimum legal drinking age to twenty-one in order to receive federal highway funds.

Congress's authority in relation to state and local governments became so complete that the Court virtually obliterated the dual-sovereign theory of federalism. In *Garcia v. San Antonio Metropolitan Transit Authority* (1985), the Court concluded that Congress could set the hours and wages of employees of state and municipal governments as part of its overall regulation of the economy. The Court justified this grant of authority to Congress by observing that the rights of states under the Tenth Amendment were protected by the presence in Congress of senators and representatives from states and districts. Deeming additional court protection to be unnecessary, the Court implied that Congress could pass any law encroaching on state authority that senators and representatives found appropriate.

The Court qualified the *Garcia* doctrine in *County of Cortland, New York v. United States* (1992) by stating that Congress could not directly impose a regulation on a state government unless it was part of a more general law regulating economic activity. Congress had enacted a law requiring that states must either provide sites for the disposal of radioactive waste or else assume direct legal liability for the lethal garbage. This congressional requirement was said to be distinctive in that it was neither part of any federal grant program, as in the case of *Dole*, nor a part of any overall regulation of economic activity, as in the *Garcia* case. Instead, the Court asserted, the law was a direct command to states by the federal government and so a violation of the sovereignty of the state of New York. While it remains to be seen whether *Cortland* is an aberration or the beginning of a rediscovery of dual sovereignty, the federal government's constitutional capacity to formulate policies affecting cities remains essentially intact.

Urban America after World War II. If the 1930s' Depression and the New Deal changed the country's constitutional framework, it was not until after World War II that urban problems provoked widespread policy discussion. Beginning in the 1950s, it became increasingly apparent that the problems that central cities were experiencing were not just by-products of the depression but a consequence of underlying technological changes. As trucks, automobiles, and airplanes replaced railroads, steamships, and river barges, it became less necessary to concentrate industrial production around those few points where land and water transport conjoined. The telegraph and telephone reduced the importance of face-to-face interactions for commercial exchange. The resulting economic decentralization was accompanied by residential deconcentration. As the construction of high-speed highways facilitated movement to and from central business districts, prosperous white Americans moved outward from the core of the metropolitan area toward its periphery, where land was cheaper, lots were bigger, houses newer, and grass "greener." The dirty, congested inner city was left to African Americans and immigrants from Latin America and Asia.

In many metropolitan areas, political and governmental stagnation aggravated the problems created by these economic and social changes. During the nineteenth century, most central cities had extended their political jurisdictions as their populations grew. Outlying areas agreed to incorporation in order to gain access to city-built sewers, roads, and streetcar lines. But as the twentieth century progressed, these outlying areas, now called suburbs, resisted (in state legislatures and local elections) takeover attempts by the central cities they surrounded. Almost all cities in the Northeast and Midwest became locked into fixed political boundaries that usually encompassed less than half the metropolitan area's population. Although cities of the rapidly growing South and West were less constricted, by the 1990s even they rarely incorporated outlying areas.

With their ability to annex inhibited, central cities became increasingly distinct from their suburban hinterlands. Central-city residents, instead of being financially better off, became less well off than the average American. Median family income in big cities with more than 300,000 inhabitants

SENATE HEARING ON THE FEDERAL ROLE IN URBAN DEVELOPMENT, DECEMBER 1966. Floyd McKissick of the Congress of Racial Equality (CORE), speaking before the Senate. *Facing page,* Sen. Robert F. Kennedy (D-N.Y.), *at left,* and Sen. Abraham A. Ribicoff (D-Conn.).   LIBRARY OF CONGRESS

was 15.2 percent higher than the national median in 1950 but 7.8 percent lower by 1990. The poverty rate of these big-city residents was 1.4 percentage points higher than the national rate in 1970 and 5.9 percentage points higher in 1990. The nonwhite percentage of big-city populations was 13.8 percent in 1950, just 3 percentage points above the national average; by 1990 the nonwhite population was 42.5 percent, 22 percentage points above the national average. Politically, central cities became heavily Democratic in their voting propensities, while suburban areas tended to be more Republican.

Central-city governmental structures were also differentiated from those in the suburbs. Central cities established large bureaucracies with uniform policies for large, heterogeneous populations, while suburbia was divided into many small governmental units. Each town, village, or special district was responsible for governing a small and usually quite homogeneous population. Though cities had the advantage of the economies of scale that accrue to large jurisdictions, they had the fiscal disadvantage of being vulnerable to wage demands and strike threats by their large municipal work forces. For all these reasons, cities began turning to the federal government for assistance.

The congressional response to these demands went through three major stages in the postwar era. Congress first tried to revive the economic vitality of central cities by redeveloping areas surrounding central business districts. Congress then turned to the amelioration of the social and fiscal problems of cities. Finally, Congress backed away from urban problems, cutting back much of the assistance it had been providing.

Central Business District Redevelopment. Direct federal grants to all local governments totaled little more than $1.5 billion in 1957. While many

of these grant programs were of marginal significance, one of them, the 1954 urban renewal program, constituted the first major attempt by the federal government to shape the urban future. Significantly, this attempt was never explicitly conceptualized by Congress as an urban policy. Instead, it was tucked away in a series of seemingly minor amendments to the Housing Act of 1949.

Public housing had long been controversial. When the PWA had set aside 30 percent of its public housing units for African Americans, southerners complained that the program was encouraging racial integration. When it had begun buying land and constructing houses, lower federal courts said the PWA had exceeded its constitutional authority. Congress responded to this constitutional attack in 1937 by taking the authority to build public housing away from the PWA and giving it to the U.S. Housing Authority, which, instead of erecting its own housing, gave housing construction loans to local governments. Although this delegation of direct responsibility to local governments placed the program on stronger constitutional footing, it did

not end the criticism that government was unfairly competing with private developers, and as a result not much public housing was constructed until the passage of the 1949 Housing Act.

As originally signed by Harry S. Truman, this act stated as its national goal the provision of a decent home and a suitable living environment for every American family. To facilitate this objective, it offered low-interest grants and loans for the redevelopment of blighted areas within cities. Nearly all expenditure was limited to residential construction for low-to-moderate-income people.

To expand political support for housing legislation, congressional supporters loosened the low-income residence restriction in 1954, 1959, and 1961 with amendments that allowed states and localities to use an ever-increasing share of the moneys appropriated under the act for commercial revitalization and the construction of higher-income housing. Many central-city leaders recognized that these revisions in the legislation provided them with an opportunity to revive their central business districts. From their perspective, big cities needed to provide better access and more ample parking for trucks and automobiles as well as relaxing, mall-like atmospheres for retail shopping. Residential construction was needed for college-educated employees hired to work in the new high-rise offices. Poor minorities could be asked to move to areas more distant from the central business district.

If these plans seemed in theory to give big cities a chance to renew their economic vitality, they were, in practice, a mixed blessing. Some cities combined federal dollars with private development moneys in ways that facilitated their transformation from manufacturing to office-oriented economies. Chicago is the outstanding case. Faced with the loss of millions of manufacturing jobs, Chicago managed to redesign its central-city core so that its position as the heartland's dominant commercial, financial, and administrative center was strengthened and reinforced. Building on Chicago's past architectural triumphs, the city fathers constructed a skyline of unsurpassed variety and monumentality. Capitalizing on the city's magnificent lakefront, they attracted a young, prosperous population to newly constructed and refurbished condominiums. Anticipating the college boom, they used urban renewal moneys to stabilize the racially changing neighborhood near the University of Chicago and to help construct an entirely new Chicago campus for the University of Illinois within a stone's throw of the city center.

In other cities, outcomes were not as favorable. In New Haven, Connecticut, an urban renewal program was expected to revitalize the downtown business district and attract middle-class residents back to areas adjacent to the city center. Despite the infusion of federal funds and private development money, however, New Haven, unlike Chicago, could not make a successful transition from the industrial city it once had been to the commercial city it needed to become. Too close to New York City to become an independent financial and administrative center yet too far to become a satellite office center, New Haven was unable to benefit from the office boom of the 1970s and 1980s. And without the presence of central-city office workers, retailers' efforts to compete effectively with suburban shopping centers failed dismally.

If the benefits of urban renewal varied from city to city, the costs were evident almost everywhere. Residents of blighted neighborhoods were usually the minority poor. When they lost access to housing in areas adjacent to central business districts, they migrated to aging neighborhoods further from the

city center. This migration, reinforced by an influx of African Americans from the South, accentuated the racial tensions that culminated in civil rights demonstrations, racial violence, and, eventually, a white backlash. Urban renewal was criticized by both liberals and conservatives for contributing to—rather than reversing—the process of urban decline. With the 1964 election of President Lyndon B. Johnson, federal urban policy would take a new direction.

Cooperative Federalism. In formulating these new policies, Congress adopted the theory of cooperative, or "marble cake," federalism. As initially propounded by political scientist Morton Grodzins, cooperative federalism criticized as outmoded the dual-sovereign theory, which imagined government to be like a layer cake, with each level independent of and separate from the other. Grodzins pointed out that, in practice, agencies from different levels of government typically worked together to solve problems, combining and intertwining their functions to such an extent that the intergovernmental system resembled a marble cake.

With the onset of cooperative federalism, the institutional design of federal programs became more varied. Since all levels of government could work together, it did not make much difference what combination of governments were active in any particular circumstance. Some federal grants went to states to assist in state-run programs. Other federal grants were given to states to be distributed by each state to its local governments. Still other federal funds were allocated directly to local governments.

The cake was well leavened. Between 1962 and 1977, direct federal grants to local governments increased tenfold, from $3.2 billion to $32.3 billion. They increased from 0.1 percent of the nation's gross national product (GNP) in 1962 to 0.8 percent of GNP in 1977. The federal government also expanded its state grant program from $29.5 billion to $89.7 billion during this same period.

Big cities were among those invited to the dessert table. The value of direct federal grants to cities with populations of 300,000 or more multiplied tenfold between 1962 and 1977, from $0.9 billion to $9.3 billion. In addition, state grants to these cities rose somewhat more than threefold, from $5.1 billion to $17.8 billion. Since this represented the same rate at which federal grants to states were growing, big cities were getting a proportional share of the new federal dollars being passed to the states. The moneys were directed toward ending poverty, financing welfare reform, educating disadvantaged children, subsidizing low-income housing, encouraging mass transit, and providing general fiscal support for cities.

The war on poverty. If any single initiative symbolized the urban policy of Johnson's cooperative federalism, it was the modestly funded but politically explosive "war on poverty." Proposed in the aftermath of John F. Kennedy's assassination and on the eve of Johnson's triumphant campaign to secure the presidency in his own right, the Economic Opportunity Act of 1964, the statutory basis for the war on poverty, directed the bulk of its fiscal resources to cities. Several accomplishments remain evident two decades later. The popular Head Start program for preschoolers anticipated and paved the way for the child-care and nursery school programs that subsequently spread throughout the country. The Job Corps, a residential education and training program, was expensive but paid off in better wages and employment prospects for difficult-to-employ young people. The legal services program changed the standing of poor people in the courts by challenging the constitutionality of a wide variety of local police and administrative practices. And by providing political, administrative, and employment opportunities to emerging African American and other minority activists, the antipoverty program facilitated the incorporation of minority leaders into the fabric of urban political life. From the ranks of the antipoverty warriors of the 1960s came many of the minority mayors, state legislators, and members of Congress elected in the 1970s and 1980s.

Despite these achievements, the war on poverty is better known for the combative criticism it engendered than for its substantive results. Its modest size—an average of $4.9 billion annually over the nine-year life of its existence—belied its ostensibly warlike character. Its efforts to coordinate local social services failed dismally. Most of its job search, worker readiness, summer job, and other short-term worker training programs had few long-term economic benefits.

The main objection to the war on poverty was its emphasis on political action. In many cities, it antagonized local agencies and elected officials by encouraging protests, demonstrations, legal action, and minority electoral mobilization. To some Washington policy analysts, an emphasis on political action made sense. Getting the poor involved in the system could forestall political alienation and, perhaps, even reverse the social apathy that seemed endemic to inner-city life. From a narrow partisan standpoint, an energized African American community, newly enfranchised in the South by civil rights legislation, could give Democrats a massive, enthusiastic bloc of supporters. But if these policy and partisan objectives made sense to some in Washington, local officials wondered why federal moneys should fund their political opposition. Unsurprisingly, the program was blamed for the wave of violence that swept through American cities in the two years immediately after its adoption. Some argued that it had broken up the biracial Democratic coalition that had made a war on poverty possible. Few local tears were shed in 1974 when Richard M. Nixon, who had campaigned against the war on poverty, persuaded Congress to transfer its popular components to other agencies and to shut down the remainder.

Welfare reform. As part of the Social Security Act of 1935, Congress authorized federal grants to states to pay one-third of the cost of a program of income maintenance for needy mothers with dependent children. In 1939, Congress increased the federal share to 50 percent, and in 1959 it further increased the federal government's share of the payment to states whose per capita income was below the national average. The federal role nonetheless remained secondary to that of state and local governments. Benefit levels and most eligibility requirements were determined by state legislatures.

With the coming of cooperative federalism, income maintenance programs changed markedly. In 1962, the name of the program was changed to Aid to Families with Dependent Children (AFDC), with states now being allowed—but not required—to aid two-parent families of low income. The passage of Medicaid in 1965 made AFDC families eligible for free medical services. Aides hired by the poverty program helped poor people obtain better access to AFDC assistance. Lawsuits brought by the war on poverty's legal division challenged state administrative requirements. In response to one of these, the Supreme Court in *Shapiro v. Thompson* (1969) ruled that states could no longer deny AFDC benefits to families until they had been residents of the state for twelve months. With all these changes, the number of people receiving AFDC more than doubled between 1960 and 1970, from 3.1 million to 7.4 million.

Congress continued to make important changes in income maintenance policy after 1970 in response to Nixon's proposed Family Assistance Plan. While not passing the plan's most controversial features, Congress funded a national minimum benefit standard for the blind, aged, and disabled in 1972, expanded the food stamp program to all parts of the country (adding, in the average state, as much as $270 to the monthly budget of the most needy families), and in 1975 approved an earned income tax credit that eliminated federal taxes for and supplemented the income of the working poor.

Education. Before cooperative federalism, Congress had authorized only three small education programs: impact aid (to school districts affected by the presence of federal personnel); vocational education; and a combination of mathematics, science, and library programs. Although cities received some of the moneys distributed through the three programs, no urban policy was implicit in any of them. A larger federal role had been inhibited by conservative opposition to federal control of education, southern opposition to desegregation, and public school opposition to sharing federal funds with nonpublic, sectarian schools.

To overcome these sources of opposition, President Johnson proposed that federal aid to education be designed to help fight the war against poverty. Couching the aid in these terms, Johnson was able to obtain compromises on which public and nonpublic school officials could agree, and the large Democratic majority in Congress quickly passed the legislation. The resulting compensatory education programs had a strong urban emphasis; 37 percent of the pupils participating in compensatory education programs in 1985 lived in central cities (as compared to 25 percent of all pupils). Congress in subsequent years also appropriated moneys for special education for the handicapped, bilingual education, and aid to assist in school desegregation. In 1978 Congress acknowledged the increased federal role in education by transforming the Office of Education into a cabinet-level department.

The compensatory education program, though controversial, continued into the 1990s. Its propensity to pull students out of regular classrooms and teach them in special remedial settings has been criticized for stigmatizing educationally disadvantaged children. But it has also been praised for symbolizing the country's commitment to equal educational opportunity and has been given some of the credit for the gains in educational achievement made by African Americans.

Housing and urban development. Although housing and urban development were, together, given cabinet-level status in 1965, public housing and urban renewal were coming under disrepute. Public housing was symbolized by ugly, dirty, crime-infested, segregated high-rise apartment buildings, while urban renewal became synonymous with black removal. To correct these failings, housing policy under the new cooperative federalism undertook two new initiatives.

The first, the 1966 Demonstration Cities and Metropolitan Development Act, called for a comprehensive, coordinated, carefully planned attack on a wide variety of physical and social problems within designated inner-city neighborhoods. Known as the Model Cities program, it came as close to being a specifically urban policy as any that Congress has ever passed. But the program became bogged down in bureaucratic and intergovernmental conflict and, in the end, mainly demonstrated that the intergovernmental system could not easily plan comprehensive solutions to urban problems.

The second strategy, aggressively pursued after 1968, relied more heavily on the private market to provide low-income housing units. It encouraged developers to build low- and moderate-income housing by subsidizing the interest rates on its construction. More than 1.6 million such units were constructed between 1968 and 1972, a figure larger than the total number of federally subsidized public housing units previously erected. In 1965 Congress also approved an experimental rent-supplement program that paid the portion of the rent for an approved housing unit that exceeded 25 percent of a low-income family's income. By 1970, forty-two thousand new families of low income were being assisted under this program. Congress then expanded it in 1974, so that, at its height, it served an estimated half-million new families.

Transportation. In 1956, Congress passed the Federal Aid Highway Act, which created a highway trust fund into which were directed revenues from a sales tax on gasoline. From this fund, the federal government paid for 90 percent of the cost of the construction and maintenance of the comprehensive system of limited-access highways that revolutionized American transportation. But even while the program was contributing to the growth of the U.S. economy, it was helping to intensify traffic congestion within central cities. As commuters utilized the new interstate highways to get to work, use of buses, trains, and trolleys declined. By 1960, only 26 percent of central-city workers were using public transportation systems.

When central-city officials asked for help in shoring up mass transit systems, Congress in 1961 responded by funding demonstration projects and offering to help cities to plan their mass transportation systems better. In subsequent years, the scope of federal involvement increased. Congress authorized aid for mass transit construction in 1964; two years later, it established the Department of Transportation; in 1973, it antagonized the highway lobby by diverting funds to mass transit that had accumulated in the highway trust account; and in 1974, for the first time, it appropriated funds for transit operations. But despite these efforts to support mass transit, Americans became increasingly dependent on the automobile; by 1980, the percentage of central-city workers commuting by public transport had declined to 14.3 percent.

Block grants and fiscal relief. The shape of cooperative federalism was modified somewhat with the Republican victories in the 1968 and 1972 presidential elections. Local officials had been complaining that federal bureaucrats were burdening local governments with unnecessary regulations. In his campaign for the presidency, Nixon promised relief. Instead of a system of categorical grants, which regulated the way in which state and local governments used federal dollars, he proposed block grants that would distribute federal moneys for locally defined purposes.

Congress responded by enacting three major block-grant programs. The first, the General Revenue Sharing Act of 1972, corresponded most closely to the Nixon administration's conception of an ideal federal system. Local governments needed to submit no more than the most cursory application in order to receive the funds for which they were eligible, and moneys were distributed with only minimal restrictions on their use. The program was expected to marry the federal government's ability to raise large amounts of funds equitably with the ability of local government officials to spend moneys sensibly and efficiently. Although in some ways general revenue sharing was the very antithesis of an urban policy—the program had no substantive or territorial focus at all—many city governments were grateful for the financial relief it offered.

The second block grant, the Community Development Block Grant of 1974 (CDBG), consolidated Model Cities, rent supplements, and five other categorical programs into a single grant that was to be used to provide decent housing, suitable environments, and economic opportunities for community residents, particularly residents of low and moderate income. The legislation represented a compromise between the Nixon administration and the Democratic Congress. On the one side, the Repub-

lican administration succeeded in achieving a substantial amount of deregulation; the number of pages contained in the relevant regulations was reduced from 2,600 to 120, and the average application was cut to 50 from 1,400 pages. On the other side, the Democratic Congress was able to expand rent supplements and other housing programs for low-income families.

Since CDBG distributed its funds widely to communities of all sizes and fiscal capacities, Congress, at the prompting of the Carter administration, added Urban Demonstration Action Grants (UDAGs) to CDBG. A throwback to the days of urban renewal, this short-lived program, passed in 1977, assisted the economic and commercial development of cities with especially disadvantaged populations.

The third block grant, the Comprehensive Employment Training Act of 1974 (CETA), replaced seventeen worker training programs established by the war on poverty and related programs with a block grant that gave local governments considerable flexibility in designing training for jobless community residents. Congressional Democrats supported the legislation because it authorized funds for public-sector employment in any community where the unemployment rate exceeded 6 percent. When Jimmy Carter became president, the public-sector employment component of CETA expanded rapidly, so that by 1978 it accounted for 58 percent of CETA funding. But the discretion that CETA gave to local governments came under criticism when it was discovered that many CETA workers were not particularly disadvantaged and that others were hired to perform traditional municipal functions.

While block grants were the Nixon and Ford administrations' most innovative urban policies, the 1975 New York fiscal crisis had greater long-term impact. It both prompted the most direct federal financial relief ever given to a big city and induced the backlash against big cities that would cause Congress's urban programs to contract. New York's steadily growing civic expenditures on an unusually broad range of public services, including hospitals, welfare, and a tuition-free university, combined with a tax base that was shrinking under the pressure of exceptionally high tax rates, produced a series of budget deficits first evident in the late 1960s. Several years later, when financial markets lost faith in the city's ability to repay its debts, New York lurched toward bankruptcy. The administration of Gerald R. Ford initially rejected New York's request for aid, provoking the famous *New York*

Landmark Urban Policy Legislation

Title	Year Enacted	Reference Number	Description
Housing			
Home Owners Loan Act	1933	P.L. 73-43	Gave Homeowners Loan Corporation power to buy residential mortgages threatened with foreclosure.
National Housing Act of 1934	1934	P.L. 73-479	Created Federal Housing Authority.
Serviceman's Readjustment Act	1944	P.L. 78-346	Made available residential mortgage loans for veterans.
Housing and Rent Act of 1949	1949	P.L. 81-31	Made a home for every family a national goal.
Housing Act of 1954	1954	P.L. 83-560	Urban renewal.
Housing Act of 1959	1959	P.L. 86-372	Made available federal loans to nonprofit sponsors of elderly and handicapped housing.
Housing Act of 1961	1961	P.L. 87-70	Made available below-market interest rates for low-income home buyers.
Housing and Urban Development Act of 1965	1965	P.L. 89-117	Expanded low-income family subsidies.
Demonstration Cities and Metropolitan Development Act	1966	P.L. 89-754	Subsidized model projects in poor neighborhoods.
Housing and Urban Development Act of 1968	1968	P.L. 90-448	Subsidized moderate-income housing.
Housing and Urban Development Act of 1970	1970	P.L. 91-609	Emphasized inner-city development.
Housing and Community Development Act of 1974	1974	P.L. 93-383	Consolidated categorical grants into block grants.
Housing and Community Development Act of 1987	1987	P.L. 100-242	Extended existing programs and increased role of rent subsidies.
National Affordable Housing Act	1990	P.L. 101-625	Created home investment partnerships and sold some public housing to tenants.
Poverty, Welfare, and Health Policy			
Social Security Act	1935	P.L. 74-271	Established national public assistance and unemployment and retirement insurance.
Social Security Amendments	1950	P.L. 81-734	Expanded public assistance program for families with dependent children.
Economic Opportunity Act	1964	P.L. 88-452	War on poverty.
Food Stamp Act of 1964	1964	P.L. 88-525	Established food stamp program.
Social Security Amendments	1965	P.L. 89-97	Established Medicare and Medicaid.
Food Stamp Act of 1970	1970	P.L. 91-671	Established nationwide standard for food stamp program.
Social Security Title III Amendments	1972	P.L. 92-603	Provided national minimum benefit for blind, aged, and disabled.
Tax Reduction Act, Title II	1975	P.L. 94-12	Reduced taxes and supplemented income of working poor.
Family Support Act	1988	P.L. 100-485	Assisted low-income families with two parents; enforced collection of child support payments.
Education and Job Training			
Smith-Hughes Act	1917	P.L. 64-347	Provided aid for vocational education.
National Defense Education Act	1958	P.L. 85-864	Established grants for math and science education and for libraries.

Landmark Urban Policy Legislation (Continued)

TITLE	YEAR ENACTED	REFERENCE NUMBER	DESCRIPTION
EDUCATION AND JOB TRAINING *(Continued)*			
Manpower Development and Training Act	1962	P.L. 87-415	Retrained family heads whose skills were obsolete.
Elementary and Secondary Education Act	1965	P.L. 89-10	Provided aid for education of disadvantaged children.
Comprehensive Employment and Training Act	1973	P.L. 93-203	Consolidated job training and employment programs into block grant.
Education of All Handicapped Children Act	1974	P.L. 94-182	Established right to education for handicapped persons.
Department of Education	1979	P.L. 96-88	Gave education cabinet-level status.
Job Training Partnership Act	1982	P.L. 97-300	Redesigned job training programs; eliminated public-sector employment.
TRANSPORTATION			
Federal Aid Highway Act	1944	P.L. 78-521	Initiated national system of interstate highways.
Federal Aid Highway Act	1956	P.L. 84-627	Expanded interstate highway system and created highway fund.
Urban Mass Transportation Act	1964	P.L. 88-365	Funded planning of mass transit.
Department of Transportation Act	1966	P.L. 89-670	Gave transportation cabinet-level status.
Urban Mass Transportation Assistance Act	1970	P.L. 91-453	Funded mass transit construction.
Federal Aid Highway Act	1973	P.L. 93-87	Permitted states to use moneys in highway funds for mass transit.
National Mass Transportation Assistance Act	1974	P.L. 93-50	Funded mass transit operating expenses.
Surface Transportation Assistance Act	1982	P.L. 97-424	Instituted gasoline tax for highways and mass transit.
Surface Transportation and Uniform Relocation Assistance Act	1987	P.L. 100-17	Provided funding for highways and mass transit.
Surface Transportation Reauthorization Act	1991	P.L. 102-240	Extended local government discretion to use highway trust fund for mass transit.
OTHER URBAN POLICIES			
Omnibus Crime Control and Safe Streets Act	1968	P.L. 90-351	Gave law enforcement grants to states and localities.
Omnibus Crime Control Act of 1970	1970	P.L. 91-644	Authorized appropriations for law enforcement; increased federal share of certain programs.
State and Local Fiscal Assistance Act (General Revenue Sharing)	1972	P.L. 92-512	Made federal aid to local governments easier to obtain.
New York City Seasonal Financing Act	1975	P.L. 94-143	Provided loan guarantees to New York City.
Economic Recovery Act	1981	P.L. 97-34	Instituted cuts in personal and corporate tax rates.
Omnibus Budget Reconciliation Act	1981	P.L. 97-35	Reduced regulation and federal funding of a broad range of intergovernmental programs.

Daily News headline: "Ford to New York: 'Drop Dead.'" Congress nonetheless authorized $2.3 billion in loan guarantees for New York on the condition that the city impose a more disciplined budgeting system on itself. Ford then lost New York State in his failed attempt at reelection, but New York City became a symbol of urban profligacy that would subsequently undermine pro-urban forces in Congress.

Urban Retrenchment. Few realized in 1977 that the dramatic expansion in federal aid to cities would soon be reversed by an almost equally rapid contraction. Yet the marble cake was beginning to crumble under the impact of both intellectual and political change. The intellectual charge against cooperative federalism came from those who studied the implementation of federal programs. They pointed out that when small-scale, experimental, minimally funded programs are justified with grandiose rhetorical flourishes, program outcomes necessarily disappoint constituents. When many different government agencies must agree before action can be taken, delays and confusion are almost inevitable. If success is to occur, it will become evident only years, perhaps decades, later, long after political support has begun to wane. And when liberal congressional subcommittees, responding to narrowly focused interest groups, sponsor innovative programs, local officials may find them politically threatening. Not all of these difficulties bedeviled every urban policy, but these problems of implementation occurred often enough that cooperative federalism proved less enduring than its founders had hoped.

These intellectual challenges to marble-cake federalism were reinforced by conservative political trends. Even before the Reagan administration, urban political muscle was growing flabby. Between 1960 and 1980, the percentage of the U.S. population living in big cities had fallen from 21 to 17 percent; furthermore, President Carter had received little help from big city mayors in his pursuit of the Democratic nomination. As budget deficits grew, Carter's urban and welfare policy initiatives encountered increasing resistance in Congress, and the president himself lost enthusiasm for new intergovernmental programs. His Republican successors, Ronald Reagan and George Bush, who were even less dependent on urban voters, urged deep cuts in social programs. By 1990, Congress's urban policies would be only modestly larger than they had been during the Eisenhower years.

Direct federal assistance to all local governments fell from $32.3 billion in 1977 to $18.4 billion in 1990. When these figures are calculated as percentages of GNP, the sharpness of the decline becomes even more apparent—from 0.8 percent to 0.3 percent. Cuts in benefits to big cities were even steeper than the overall cuts to local governments. Federal direct aid to the big cities fell from $9.2 billion in 1977 to $4.5 billion in 1990. As a percentage of GNP, direct assistance dropped from 0.24 percent to 0.08 percent.

During this same thirteen-year period, federal aid to states rose modestly, from $89.7 to $118.4 billion. But states did not pass on much of this increase to local governments; state aid to big cities increased only from $16.8 to $17.8 billion between 1977 and 1990. For every dollar that states were receiving from the federal government, they were passing on to big cities only fifteen cents in 1990, down from twenty-one cents in 1972.

Two pieces of legislation provided the framework for the urban retrenchment: the 1981 Economic Recovery and Omnibus Budget Reconciliation acts. By cutting taxes more sharply than at any time in the nation's history, the first ushered in a decade or more of deficit politics that tightly constrained domestic spending programs and largely foreclosed the possibility of major urban initiatives. The second act deregulated and cut expenditures for most intergovernmental programs. Between 1980 and 1990, funding for mass transit was cut from $5 billion dollars to $3.7 billion. Moneys for compensatory education were reduced from $5.3 billion to $4.4 billion. Desegregation assistance was eliminated altogether. By 1990, eligibility for welfare benefits had been tightened and public-sector employment abolished, and only 70,000 new families were receiving rent supplements. Only the highway program was still being funded at 1980 levels.

Congress was even less enthusiastic about block grants during the Reagan years. General revenue sharing was eliminated in 1985; urban development action grants were abolished in 1988, and CDBG was cut from $6.1 billion in 1980 to $2.8 billion in 1990. Democrats on Capitol Hill joined the Reagan administration in block-grant bashing, partly because they wanted to save moneys for the categorical grants over which they had greater control. Also, it was easier to cut block grants when local government coffers were swelling with additional revenues generated by the economic growth of the mid 1980s. Even New York City was able to balance its municipal budget.

Some new initiatives consistent with conservative philosophy were signed into law during the Reagan-Bush years. In 1982 the training component of

CETA was replaced by a much smaller Job Training Partnership Act, which required that local governments design training programs in close association with local businesses. The Family Support Act of 1988 stiffened efforts to collect support payments from absent spouses and required states to extend AFDC payments to two-parent families. An experimental sale of public housing to tenants was approved under the National Affordable Housing Act of 1990. The Surface Transportation Act, passed in 1991, in addition to authorizing highway improvements, approved, subject to appropriation, $31.5 billion dollars for mass transit over the next six years. Also included in the authorizing legislation was the option—at the discretion of state and local officials—to spend on mass transit an additional $65 billion from the Highway Trust Fund.

Urban Issues in the 1990s. The debate over renewing the nation's cities continued into the 1990s. Reform proposals went in three quite different directions. The National League of Cities and the U.S. Conference of Mayors proposed block grants to cities to relieve them of renewed fiscal distress caused by the 1991 recession. The Bush administration called for market-based solutions to urban problems. It recommended that enterprise be stimulated through tax cuts and industrial deregulation in specifically designated urban zones. It also proposed the continued sale of public housing to tenants and the distribution of tuition vouchers that would give inner-city families a choice between public and private schools. Several Democratic members of Congress recommended that the federal system be simplified by turning over transportation, education, and other small programs entirely to state and local government while absorbing at the national level such costly social programs as AFDC and Medicaid. As of the early 1990s, no consensus on any of these policy proposals had emerged, and few analysts believed the federal role in urban affairs would soon regain the prominence it had possessed in the mid 1970s.

[*For discussion of two congressional committees with specific responsibility concerning urban policy, see* Banking, Finance, and Urban Affairs Committee, House; Banking, Housing, and Urban Affairs Committee, Senate. *For further discussion of urban policy and related congressional committees, see the following entries on policy issues with significant impact on urban affairs:* Crime and Justice; Education; Health and Medicine; Housing Policy; Public Works; Social Welfare and Poverty; Transportation. *See also* Grant-in-Aid; Urban Mass Transportation Act of 1964.]

BIBLIOGRAPHY

Caraley, Demetrios. "Washington Abandons the Cities." *Political Science Quarterly* 107 (1992): 1–30.
Conlan, Timothy. *New Federalism: Intergovernmental Reform from Nixon to Reagan.* 1988.
Gelfand, Mark I. *A Nation of Cities: The Federal Government and Urban America, 1933–1965.* 1975.
Fuchs, Ester. *Mayors and Money.* 1992.
Grodzins, Morton. *The American System.* 1966.
Kantor, Paul, with Stephen David. *The Dependent City: The Changing Political Economy of Urban America.* 1988.
Peterson, Paul E. *City Limits.* 1981.
Peterson, Paul E., Barry Rabe, and Kenneth Wong. *When Federalism Works.* 1985.
Peterson, Paul E., and Mark C. Rom. *Welfare Magnets: A New Case for a National Standard.* 1991.
Pressman, Jeffrey L., and Aaron Wildavsky. *Implementation: How Great Expectations in Washington Are Dashed in Oakland.* 1973.
Weir, Margaret. *Politics and Jobs: The Boundaries of Employment Policy in the United States.* 1992.
Wilson, James Q., ed. *Urban Renewal: The Record and the Controversy.* 1966.

PAUL E. PETERSON

U.S.-U.S.S.R. ANTIBALLISTIC MISSILE SYSTEMS TREATY. *See* Antiballistic Missile Systems Treaty.

UTAH.

As early as 1849, the Mormon settlers of Utah sought admission to the Union as the state of Deseret. Instead, in an act of 9 September 1850, as part of the Compromise of 1850, Congress made Utah a territory. Not until 4 January 1896 did Utah become a state, the nation's forty-fifth. The long delay in Utah's statehood is primarily attributable to Congress's antipathy to the territory's Mormon inhabitants, who embraced theocratic government and practiced polygamy as sanctioned by their Church of Jesus Christ of Latter-day Saints.

In the interim, through passage of the Anti-Bigamy Act of 1862, the Poland Act of 1874, the Edmunds Act of 1882, and the Edmunds-Tucker Act of 1887, Congress actively worked to end polygamy and to restrict the political strength of the Mormon Church. Tensions between Congress and the citizens of Utah eased in the early 1890s with the church's decision to stop sanctioning plural marriages and with the demise in the territory of both the People's party (backed by the Mormon hierarchy) and the opposition Liberal party. During the 53d Congress (1893–1895), Utah's delegate

Joseph L. Rawlins put together a bipartisan coalition in support of Utah statehood. In the House of Representatives, the enabling act passed with only five dissenting votes.

From 1896 until 1913, Utah had a single statewide congressional district. In 1913 the state House delegation increased to two, and seventy years later it added another representative. Despite the state's considerable size, the majority of the population lives in a narrow, 150-mile-long north-south strip along the western front of the Wasatch Range, with its center in Salt Lake City. Accordingly, in the early 1990s the three-person House delegation represented a population more than 80 percent of whom were classified by the Census as urban dwellers. The only women to serve Utah in either the House or the Senate were Democratic representatives Reva Z. B. Bosone (1949–1952) and Karen Shepherd (1993–).

Of the six men elected to the Senate by the Utah state legislature prior to ratification of the Seventeenth Amendment, five were Republicans. During the period between the two world wars, Utah had two long-serving senators, Republican Reed Smoot (1903–1933) and Democrat William H. King (1917–1941). King's career was cut short when he failed to gain renomination by the Democratic party, in part because of his opposition to Franklin D. Roosevelt's Court-packing proposal.

During the New Deal years, only Democrats represented Utah in the Senate. Republicans held exclusive sway in Utah's Senate delegation from 1951 through 1958 and from 1977 through 1992. Beginning with Reed Smoot's election and continuing through the 102d Congress, every Utah senator but one has served at least two consecutive terms.

Utah's senators have on the whole been relatively low-profile national leaders. One of the best known was Smoot, a conservative businessman and Mormon religious leader, who chaired the Senate Committee on Finance from 1923 to 1933. His stance on protective tariff legislation, culminating with the Hawley-Smoot Tariff Act of 1930, provided benefits to Utah's sugar beet and wool industries. Smoot is also remembered for his impact on western land policy. In the 1930s and 1940s, Democrat Elbert D. Thomas, as a member of the Senate Committee on Military Affairs, helped ensure that Utah would receive its share of federal military installations, including Hill Air Force Base. In the 1940s and 1950s, the Republican senator Arthur V. Watkins strongly influenced reclamation efforts involving the Colorado River Storage Project and the Central Utah Project.

BIBLIOGRAPHY

Lyman, Edward Leo. *Political Deliverance: The Mormon Quest for Utah Statehood.* 1986.

Poll, Richard D., ed. *Utah's History.* 1989.

RODNEY A. ROSS

V

VACANCY. Vacancies in the U.S. Senate or House of Representatives occur when incumbent members die, resign, or are expelled or excluded by the action of either house. Historically, the reasons for exclusion and expulsion have included conviction for a felony, serious misconduct, election fraud or irregularities, and treason. The Constitution makes each house the ultimate judge of the elections, returns, and qualifications of its members and also authorizes both houses to expel an incumbent for any reason by a two-thirds vote of that house's members. Exclusion and expulsion were more common in the nineteenth century than afterward; in the late twentieth century, vacancies almost invariably occurred as the result of the death or resignation of senators or representatives.

The Constitution outlines basic requirements for filling vacancies in Congress but leaves the states considerable leeway in establishing detailed procedures. The Constitution authorizes state governors to call for special elections to fill a Senate vacancy, while also authorizing state legislatures to empower the governor to make temporary appointments to fill the vacancy until an election is scheduled. In practice, forty-nine of the fifty states provide their governors with this appointment power; Arizona is the sole exception, requiring a special election to fill any Senate vacancy. In the event a senator resigns, members of the incumbent's staff continue to be compensated for a period not exceeding ninety days, performing their duties under direction of the secretary of the Senate.

Governors have wide discretion in appointing senators to fill vacancies, although some states require that the appointee be either a registered voter or a member of the same political party of the former incumbent.

Nomination procedures are established by state law and most frequently provide for a primary election or state party action, such as a convention. Scheduling for special elections varies by state, but all require that they be held at the next statewide general election (which can, for example, be for state elected officials for statewide local elections). Senators appointed to fill a vacancy falling between a statewide election and the end of the incumbent's term generally serve the balance of the term. Historically, appointed senators have had a mixed record of electoral success. From 1939 to 1992 there were 101 appointed senators, of whom sixty-five subsequently ran in special elections. Of these, only twenty-six (40 percent) were elected.

Procedures governing the House differ from the Senate primarily in that all House vacancies are filled by special election, with no provision for temporary appointments. The Constitution authorizes state governors to issue writs calling for special elections in such cases. Members of the staff of a deceased or resigned representative are compensated until a successor is elected; in the interim, they perform their duties under the direction of the clerk of the House.

Special election nominations for filling House vacancies vary according to state requirements. Nomination can be by petition, primary election, or party action such as a convention or caucus. Some states do not provide for a primary and require all candidates to compete in the general election, with a majority of the vote in the first round necessary for election. In the event no candidate receives a majority, the two candidates receiving the most votes, regardless of party affiliation, compete in a runoff. This procedure sometimes leads to first-round special elections in which several candidates from each of the major parties compete with minor-party and independent nominees, and such elections frequently require a runoff to determine the winner.

House vacancies that occur during the first session of a Congress are invariably filled by a special election that coincides, if possible, with a regularly scheduled election in the affected district. Procedures differ from state to state for vacancies that occur within six months of the expiration of a previous incumbent's term: in the interest of convenience and economy, many states require special House elections to be held on the date regularly scheduled for elections to the next Congress. In these cases, voters in affected districts simultaneously elect both a representative to fill the seat for the balance of the term and a representative to the next Congress. Often these may be the same person. In other states they simply elect a representative to the new Congress, with the seat remaining vacant until the new Congress convenes.

Winners of special House elections held late in a Congress are frequently not sworn in, Congress having usually adjourned sine die before election day. They are, however, accorded the status of incumbent representatives for the purposes of seniority, office selection, and staff hiring.

The incidence of vacancies during the life of a particular Congress depends largely on circumstance and tends to fluctuate. Since 1971, Senate vacancies have been one or two per Congress, while those in the House have ranged from a low of four (98th Congress, 1983–1985) to a high of ten (92d Congress, 1971–1973, and 101st Congress, 1989–1991), for an average of seven per Congress.

Special elections to fill vacancies in both houses are often observed as indicators of the popularity of an incumbent president and his party. For example, as the Watergate scandal developed in 1973 and 1974, Republican losses in several special elections appeared to indicate declining public support for the administration of Richard M. Nixon. Similarly, a 1991 election held to fill the vacancy created by the death a Pennsylvania Republican senator was widely characterized as a referendum on the presidency of George Bush: the election of an appointed Democratic senator Harris Wofford, over better-known Republican challenger Richard Thornburgh, who had resigned as U.S. attorney general to run for the seat, embarrassed the Bush administration.

General theories concerning the predictive value of special elections are disputed by many observers, however. A wide range of factors, including local economic conditions, comparative candidate name recognition, and the level of party and special interest group efforts, are cited to argue against the validity of determining an incumbent president's popularity through observation of special elections.

[*See also* Discipline of Members.]

BIBLIOGRAPHY

Feigert, Frank B., and Pippa Norris. "Do By-Elections Constitute Referenda?" *Legislative Studies Quarterly* 15 (May 1990): 183–200.

Morris, William D., and Roger H. Marz. "Treadmill to Oblivion: The Fate of Appointed Senators." *Publius* 11 (Winter 1981): 65–80.

Sigelman, Lee. "Special Elections to the U.S. House: Some Descriptive Generalizations." *Legislative Studies Quarterly* 6 (November 1981): 577–588.

Studlar, Donley T., and Lee Sigelman. "Special Elections: A Comparative Perspective." *British Journal of Political Science* 17 (April 1987): 247–256.

THOMAS H. NEALE

VALLANDIGHAM, CLEMENT L.

VALLANDIGHAM, CLEMENT L. (1820–1871), representative from Ohio, critic of the Lincoln administration and the Civil War. Born in New Lisbon, Ohio, the son of a Presbyterian preacher, Clement Laird Vallandigham taught school for two years before taking up law and politics as an advocate of Jeffersonian democracy. After serving a term in the state legislature Vallandigham moved to Dayton, Ohio, to practice law and edit a Democratic newspaper.

In 1856 he lost an election to the U.S. House of Representatives by nineteen votes, contested the returns, and eventually was seated in Lewis D. Campbell's stead. Reelected in 1858 and 1860, Vallandigham was outspokenly hostile to abolition and the Republicans but worked for compromise during the secession crisis. After the Fort Sumter affair, he became President Abraham Lincoln's gadfly and the "apostle of peace" as a result of his well-publicized antiwar speech of 14 January 1863. Vallandigham became the most prominent "Copperhead," or Peace Democrat. He was chiefly responsible for the law that allowed rabbis to serve as army chaplains.

Defeated for reelection in 1862, Vallandigham returned to Dayton to seek the Democratic gubernatorial nomination. For defying a military edict that

CLEMENT L VALLANDIGHAM.

HARPER'S PICTORIAL HISTORY OF THE GREAT REBELLION

curtailed rights listed in the First Amendment, Vallandigham was arrested, tried by a military commission, and exiled to the Confederacy. His so-called martyrdom won him the nomination for governor, but he lost the October 1863 election while in exile in Canada, where he had gone after a short stay in the Confederacy. He returned from exile in June 1864 to practice law and take an active role in the Democratic national convention of August 1864. He accidently shot himself in June 1871, ending one of the most controversial political careers in Congress.

BIBLIOGRAPHY

Klement, Frank L. *The Limits of Dissent: Clement L. Vallandigham and the Civil War.* 1970.

Korn, Bertram W. "Congressman Clement L. Vallandigham's Championship of the Jewish Chaplaincy in the Civil War." *American Jewish Historical Quarterly* 53 (December 1863): 188–191.

Vallandigham, John L. *A Life of Clement L. Vallandigham.* 1972.

FRANK L. KLEMENT

VAN BUREN, MARTIN (1782–1862), Democratic-Republican senator from New York, Democratic vice president (1833–1837) and then eighth president of the United States (1837–1841), and a central figure in the formation of the second party system. Van Buren's humble origins give little indication of his later achievements. Son of a small innkeeper in Kinderhook, New York, he finished school at fourteen, clerked in a local law office, and then began his own practice. Lacking oratorical skills or an imposing presence, he succeeded by a diligent mastery of details. Success at the bar, complemented by sound investments, rendered him financially secure by middle age. Meanwhile, politics became his passion.

A bemused Virginia aristocrat, John Randolph, later observed that Van Buren rowed to his object—political prominence—"with muffled oars." As state senator in the 1810s he forged a disciplined party, nurtured by spoils, bonded by personal loyalties, and skilled in grassroots organization and mass appeal. Sobriquets such as "sly fox," the "little magician," and "giant of artifice" heralded one of the nation's great political managers. Party control of the state legislature in 1821 assured his election and subsequent reelection to the United States Senate.

Van Buren compiled a modest legislative record in Washington. Support for a federal ban on imprisonment for debt reflected his genuine democratic sentiments, as did his success as head of the Judiciary Committee in defeating insolvency bills for failing businesses. Votes for higher tariff duties addressed vital interests in his state; in like fashion, he opposed funds for internal improvements because New York had already launched its own canal system.

Beyond particular measures, Van Buren used his Senate position to promote the larger goal of reviving party competition, which, with the demise of the Federalist party after 1815, had languished in the "era of good feelings." He could see only bad feelings: many Jeffersonian Republicans were embracing Federalist ideas of an active government; without party competition across sectional lines, the debate over admitting Missouri as a slave state grew bitter; finally, the contest among Jeffersonian Republicans for president in 1824 unleashed powerful political passions when, absent a majority in the Electoral College, the House of Representatives chose John Quincy Adams, in Van Buren's eyes a closet Federalist, over the more popular Andrew Jackson.

Emerging as Senate leader by 1825, Van Buren worked to fashion a coalition against the Adams

MARTIN VAN BUREN.   LIBRARY OF CONGRESS

administration and to encourage party activity across the country in behalf of Jackson's election in 1828. He sought to revive the old Jeffersonian party of southern "planters" and northern "plain republicans" on a platform of states' rights and strict construction of the Constitution. He courted southern favor by opposing internal improvements, by backing proposals for reducing the power of the Supreme Court, and with his purely political speech in 1828 on the "history of parties." In this speech he traced the genealogy of his Democratic-Republican party back to the Jeffersonian Republicans of the 1790s and, in parallel fashion, the party behind Adams back to the Federalists. Two other actions looked to the upcoming election. Key provisions of the tariff, which he helped craft in 1828, raised duties on wool, iron, and hemp in order to attract the support of middle and western states. He then ran for governor, calculating that his election might strengthen Jackson's chances in New York.

Van Buren resigned the governor's office in early 1829 to join Jackson's administration, serving successively as secretary of State, minister to England, and vice president during Jackson's second term. Except for the message he wrote in support of Jackson's veto of the Maysville Road bill, however, Van Buren exerted relatively little influence over specific policies. His main achievement was to convert Jackson—otherwise so easily perceived as a hero above party—to the idea of party government, one in which Jackson identified with the people as a leader of party and carried measures through Congress by party votes.

The dramatic struggle over the national bank in 1833–1834 sealed Jackson's conversion. As vice president, Van Buren rallied the administration party in Congress against the opposition, which then called itself the Whig party, and rejoiced to see party conflict revolving around the issue that had originally separated Federalists and Jeffersonian Republicans. Although the battle grew furious at times, one striking incident nicely captured Van Buren's notion of party government. Responding to an emotional plea from Henry Clay that he exercise a restraining influence over Jackson, the vice president rose from his chair as if to confront the Kentucky senator but, upon arriving at Clay's desk, bowed politely and asked for a pinch of snuff. Civility, he supposed, should always govern the relations between political foes. After Clay pushed through resolutions censuring Jackson's presumably unconstitutional behavior, Van Buren managed to tone down the part of Jackson's response that asserted strong executive claims. Here, as with the veto power, he did not favor a powerful executive over Congress; he wanted, instead, to restrain both branches under a Constitution of limited powers, and to have each branch respect the separate sphere of the other. He carried this same view to the White House.

Van Buren won the presidential election in 1836 over three Whig candidates, but the central measure of his administration served to unify the opposition and secure his defeat when he sought reelection. Calling for a special session in response to the panic of 1837, he laid before Congress his proposal for an independent Treasury. Jackson had separated the Treasury from the national bank; party ideology now dictated that the government handle its funds independently of state banks as well and that only specie be used in its transactions. Whigs seized upon the deflationary effect an independent Treasury would have on the currency and, as hard times continued, made it a winning political issue. Some conservative Democrats defected to the Whigs, but their departure gave greater ideological purity and strength to Van Buren's party. On a straight party vote, the measure finally passed in 1840 and lasted, with one brief interval, until the Federal Reserve System was established in the early twentieth century. But the concept of party government, by which the measure passed, constituted a more important legacy of the "sly fox" of Kinderhook.

BIBLIOGRAPHY

Cole, Donald B. *Martin Van Buren and the American Political System.* 1984.

Van Buren, Martin. *Inquiry into the Origin and Course of Political Parties in the United States.* 1867.

Van Buren, Martin. *The Autobiography of Martin Van Buren.* Edited by John C. Fitzpatrick. 1920.

Wilson, Major L. *The Presidency of Martin Van Buren.* 1984.

MAJOR L. WILSON

VANDENBERG, ARTHUR H. (1884–1951),
senator from Michigan whose commitment to bipartisan cooperation with the Truman administration helped shape American foreign policy after World War II. As a Republican leader and chairman of the Foreign Relations Committee, Vandenberg was instrumental in winning congressional support for the United Nations Charter, the Truman Doctrine, the Marshall Plan, and the North Atlantic Treaty Organization (NATO).

Vandenberg was born in Grand Rapids, Michigan. Son of a harness maker, he completed one year at the University of Michigan before joining the *Grand Rapids Herald* as a reporter. He became editor at the age of twenty-two as a protégé of the newspaper's owner, Republican senator William Alden Smith. Vandenberg wrote three books celebrating his hero, Alexander Hamilton, and an American tradition of "nationalism, not internationalism." Influential in Republican affairs as an editor, orator, and member of the state central committee, Vandenberg in 1920 supplied the party's presidential candidate, Sen. Warren G. Harding, with reservationist arguments regarding U.S. membership in the League of Nations.

Vandenberg was appointed to the Senate on 31 March 1928 to fill a vacancy created by the death of Democrat Woodbridge N. Ferris. Elected to his first full term that November, Vandenberg soon rose to

ARTHUR H. VANDENBERG.
OFFICE OF THE HISTORIAN OF THE U.S. SENATE

prominence as a leader of the Young Turks, mainstream Republicans who supported the Hoover administration. Ever an advocate of compromise and coalition, he tried unsuccessfully to reconcile his party's conservative, predominantly eastern, wing with Sen. William E. Borah and other western and midwestern insurgents.

In 1933, Vandenberg was chiefly responsible for creation of the Federal Deposit Insurance Corporation, a proposal that President Franklin D. Roosevelt had initially resisted but that later came to be viewed as one of the New Deal's most valuable measures. Vandenberg's pragmatic support of some New Deal programs helped him buck a Democratic landslide in 1934, when he became the only Republican senator from a large industrial state to win reelection. His carefully researched attacks on Roosevelt's policies made him the Senate's most effective critic of the administration and a contender for the 1936 presidential nomination. He refused to seek the position, however, and later declined the vice presidential nomination because he anticipated a Republican defeat.

In 1934 he cosponsored legislation creating the Nye Committee to investigate munitions profiteering in World War I and emerged as a spokesman for American neutrality. After the outbreak of war in Europe, Vandenberg fought unsuccessfully to prevent repeal of the arms embargo provision of the 1937 Neutrality Act and later opposed the Roosevelt administration's Lend-Lease program with Great Britain. In 1940, his reputation as an isolationist dashed his hopes for the Republican presidential nomination, although he was reelected to the Senate.

The Japanese attack on Pearl Harbor, as well as arguments advanced by his nephew, Air Force officer Hoyt Vandenberg, began the senator's storied conversion from isolationist to internationalist. In 1943, he drafted a compromise declaration for Republican leaders at a foreign policy conference on Michigan's Mackinac Island. The "Mackinac charter" gave Republican support to American participation in an international organization and influenced later efforts at postwar planning. Vandenberg was also named to the Committee of Eight—a senate committee that met with Secretary of State Cordell Hull to discuss plans for the United Nations.

In a Senate speech on 10 January 1945, on the eve of Roosevelt's Yalta conference with Winston Churchill and Joseph Stalin, Vandenberg called for a postwar treaty of cooperation among the Allied powers. The address reflected a departure from his prewar isolationism, rallied Republican support, and helped galvanize public sentiment on behalf of an internationalist policy. Conscious of the enmity between Woodrow Wilson and Sen. Henry Cabot Lodge that had doomed the League of Nations after World War I, Roosevelt made Vandenberg a delegate to the conference that convened in San Francisco in April 1945 to organize the United Nations. Vandenberg took an active role in negotiations over the structure of the U.N., helped draft its charter, and was regarded as de facto leader of the U.S. delegation.

"The things we did at Frisco to remove potential Senate opposition have paid rich dividends," he wrote after the charter was ratified by a vote of 89 to 2 on 28 July 1945. His stature as a delegate to

UN general assemblies in London and New York and to the Council of Foreign Ministers in Paris helped him win reelection in 1946 without making a single speech in his home state.

After Republicans took control of the Senate in 1947, Vandenberg became president pro tempore and chairman of the Foreign Relations Committee. Always wary of Soviet intentions, he gave critical support to President Harry S. Truman's request for military aid to combat communist threats to Greece and Turkey—a measure that gave rise to the Truman Doctrine. After Secretary of State George Marshall proposed massive aid for European reconstruction in June 1947, Vandenberg worked closely with the State Department to shepherd the Marshall Plan and subsequent appropriations through Congress. In 1948, he introduced the Vandenberg Resolution, which allowed for the creation of regional security treaties and set the stage for NATO.

Vandenberg's two years as Foreign Relations Committee chairman (1947–1949) marked a period of unprecedented bipartisan cooperation. Unanimous committee votes on such key issues as the Truman Doctrine and the Marshall Plan testified to his skill and persuasiveness in what he described as "hunting for the middle ground." Because the vice presidency was vacant during that period, Vandenberg, as president pro tempore, also presided over the Senate. In addition, he served on the Joint Committee on Atomic Energy.

Vandenberg was at the height of his prestige in 1948. At the age of sixty-four, however, with his wife ill, he refused to campaign for the Republican presidential nomination. His own health began to decline soon after the Republican convention. In 1949, he postponed cancer surgery until he had secured appropriations for NATO's military assistance program. With his condition deteriorating, he returned to Grand Rapids in 1950 and died there 17 April 1951.

BIBLIOGRAPHY

Tompkins, C. David. *Senator Arthur H. Vandenberg: The Evolution of a Modern Republican, 1884–1945.* 1970.
Vandenberg, Arthur H., Jr., ed. *The Private Papers of Senator Vandenberg.* 1952.

HANK MEIJER

VERMONT. Vermont entered the Union in 1791 after fourteen years as an independent republic, the first state to be added after the admission of the original colonies. Its allotment of House seats was two in the Second Congress (1791–1793) and increased to six after the 1810 census. However, Vermont's legendary long winters and difficult farming conditions led to substantial outmigration, and the state's population began a steady decline relative to the nation. Seats were lost following the 1820, 1840, 1850, and 1880 censuses. Vermont retained two seats from 1883 to 1933, but since 1932 has had only its constitutionally guaranteed single seat.

House. Vermont provided the Jeffersonian Democratic-Republicans of the House with their major congressional breakthroughs in Federalist New England. The Whigs won most of Vermont's House seats in the transitional years between 1824 and 1854. One noteworthy aspect of Vermont's earliest House members was that two had the same name—Heman Allen—and have had to be identified by their towns of residence ever since.

Vermonters chaired House committees in twelve of the fifteen Congresses that convened between 1823 and 1853, including the Select Committee on Rules (Charles Rich, 1823–1825) and the Committee on Manufactures (Rollin C. Mallary, 1825–1831). Vermont natives elected elsewhere, such as U.S. senator Stephen A. Douglas (Ill.) and U.S. representative Thaddeus Stevens (Pa.), played prominent roles in the Civil War years, but Vermont's elected members did not.

Following the war, Republican domination of the small Vermont House delegation enabled Vermonters to chair House committees in most of the Congresses organized by the Republican party between the Civil War and the New Deal. The two most prominent of these were Justin S. Morrill, who chaired the Ways and Means Committee (1865–1867) and was the author of the Morrill Land-Grant College Act (1862), which created state universities and Luke P. Poland, who chaired the House Select Committee (1873–1874) investigating the Crédit Mobilier bribery scandal. Except for the 1958 election, Republicans held Vermont's House seats from 1855 to 1991.

In the 1990 House election, Vermont's voters elected Bernard Sanders, a socialist-leaning independent, to the state's lone seat. Sanders, four-term mayor of Burlington, was the first independent seated in the House since 1954 and the first identified with socialist politics since New York's Vito Marcantonio (American Labor, 1939–1951).

Senate. Like in many small states, the relative ease of gaining election to the Senate led Vermonters with political talent to seek Senate rather than

House seats. Notable among them were Justin Morrill, Frank L. Greene, Porter H. Dale, Robert T. Stafford, and James M. Jeffords. As a result, Vermont's greatest contributions to the Congress have come from its senators. Three served as presidents pro tempore of the Senate—Stephen R. Bradley, Solomon Foot, and George F. Edmunds. In the post–Civil War period, Edmunds (1866–1891) and Morrill (1867–1898) served simultaneously for twenty-four years in the Senate during which they chaired the powerful committees of Judiciary, Foreign Relations, and Appropriations.

In the twentieth century, George D. Aiken (1941–1974) chaired the Agriculture and Forestry Committee and gained prominence through his efforts as ranking minority member on the Foreign Relations Committee to extricate the United States from its military involvement in Vietnam. Warren R. Austin (1931–1946) served as acting minority leader and left the Senate in 1946 to become U.S. ambassador to the United Nations. Austin's successor, Ralph E. Flanders (1946–1959) was a leader of the eastern moderate Republicans in their efforts to limit the reckless anticommunist crusade of Wisconsin's Sen. Joseph R. McCarthy.

Vermonters have managed to send only one Democrat, Patrick J. Leahy, to the U.S. Senate. First elected in 1974, Leahy in 1987 became chairman of the Senate Committee on Agriculture, Forestry and Nutrition, the fifth Vermonter to hold that position.

Vermont's delegation to Congress continues to be a liberal counterweight to the conservatism of neighboring New Hampshire.

BIBLIOGRAPHY

Bryan, Frank M. *Yankee Politics in Rural Vermont.* 1974.

Doyle, William. *The Vermont Political Tradition: And Those Who Helped Make It.* 1992.

Hill, Ralph Nading. *Yankee Kingdom: Vermont and New Hampshire.* 1966.

GARRISON NELSON

VETERANS' AFFAIRS COMMITTEE, HOUSE.

The House Committee on Veterans' Affairs, one of twenty-two standing committees of the House of Representatives, handles legislative issues affecting veterans. As a permanent committee, it continues from Congress to Congress, writing legislation and conducting oversight on most of the veteran-related public-policy issues that come before the House.

From its earliest days, the House has responded

to the needs of America's veterans by creating committees to address veterans' issues. One of the first two standing committees, created in 1794, was the Committee on Claims, whose jurisdiction included Revolutionary War claims and pensions. In 1813 the House moved jurisdiction over veterans' claims and pensions to the newly established Committee on Pensions and Revolutionary Claims.

During the nineteenth and early twentieth centuries, the House continued to organize various panels with jurisdiction over veterans' affairs. It was not unusual for two or more veterans' committees to exist simultaneously, and by the end of World War II, four veterans' committees had evolved: the Committee on War Claims (1873–1946); the Committee on Invalid Pensions (1831–1946); the Committee on Pensions (1880–1946); and the Committee on World War Veterans' Legislation (1924–1946).

In 1946 the Legislative Reorganization Act streamlined what had become a cumbersome and bloated committee system. The four committees with fragmented jurisdiction over veterans' issues were abolished. Jurisdiction over war claims was moved to the House Judiciary Committee. Other veterans' issues were assigned to the new Committee on Veterans' Affairs, effective with the beginning of the 80th Congress in January 1947.

The modern Veterans' Affairs Committee has jurisdiction over veterans' measures in general, as well as veterans' pensions; service-related life insurance; compensation, vocational rehabilitation, and education of veterans; veterans' hospitals, medical care, and treatment; soldiers' and sailors' civil relief; readjustment of servicemen to civilian life; and national cemeteries. The committee's jurisdiction was expanded in 1967 to include the last of these—the only change in the committee's jurisdiction since 1946.

The House Veterans' Affairs Committee can be characterized in several ways. First, the committee has a narrow legislative focus. Its jurisdictional purview seems particularly limited when compared to the wide-ranging national public-policy issues debated by members of many House standing committees, issues such as national health insurance or the environment or reviving the nation's infrastructure.

Second, since issues considered by the House Veterans' Affairs Committee are typically of interest only to veterans, committee members rarely achieve national public recognition for their work. As a result many junior members of the House are

FEDERAL SPENDING CUTS. In this cartoon, a figure representing the House takes aim at spending for government clerks. He leaves untouched political sacred cows such as veterans' benefits. In 1932, under lobbying pressure from more than twenty thousand war veterans encamped near the Capitol, the so-called Bonus Army, the House passed a bill providing immediate payment of bonuses to World War I veterans. The Senate's rejection of immediate payment led to a confrontation between veterans and police, after which the remnants of the Bonus Army were routed by U.S. Army troops. Clifford K. Berryman, *Washington Evening Star*, 27 April 1932.   LIBRARY OF CONGRESS

appointed to the committee and move to standing committees dealing with public-policy matters of broader interest after they have accumulated seniority. Yet the committee does offer representatives an opportunity to provide very direct and specific service to veterans—who may also be voters—in their home districts. In 1991 there were twenty-seven million veterans in the United States, nearly 11 percent of the U.S. population. Consequently, the opportunity to provide service to many constituents through membership on the Veterans' Affairs Committee makes the committee an attractive assignment to some representatives.

Third, the work of the House Veterans' Affairs Committee is generally conducted without significant internal controversy. Members and staff typically operate in a nonpartisan manner. Most legislation is reported unanimously from subcommittee and accepted without debate by the full committee.

A fourth and unique characteristic of the committee is the close relationships that have developed among the committee, veterans' organizations, and government agencies that provide services to veterans. The three are inextricably linked because all share the common purpose of providing benefits to veterans, a narrow purpose that arouses little general interest. Ties between the committee and groups representing veterans are so close that routinely, at the start of each session of Congress, the House Veterans' Affairs Committee holds public hearings at which witnesses representing all of the major veterans' organizations present these groups' legislative agendas for the year. No other House committee so systematically receives the opinions of the interest groups concerned with issues under the committee's jurisdiction.

When the Veterans Administration was elevated to a cabinet-level department in 1988, jurisdiction over veterans issues was further consolidated under the House Veterans' Affairs Committee, and the panel gained increased power to influence decision making on veterans' issues.

A Department of Veterans' Affairs had been a goal of the committee chairman, G. V. (Sonny) Montgomery (D-Miss.), for several years. The measure to establish the department did not progress until it was endorsed by President Ronald Reagan in November 1987. That same month the House overwhelmingly passed the legislation. Senate passage and final enactment occurred in 1988.

The Veterans' Affairs Committee has considered several broad issues in recent years, including programs for homeless veterans; equity of benefits and services for women in the military; employment counseling for military personnel during the downsizing of the military; concerns of Vietnam era veterans; and the effect of the military on minorities and low-income individuals serving in the armed forces.

[See also Veterans' Affairs Committee, Senate.]

BIBLIOGRAPHY

U.S. House of Representatives. Committee on Veterans' Affairs. *History of House Committees Considering Veterans' Legislation.* 101st Cong., 2d sess., 1990. H. Rept. 101-2.

U.S. House of Representatives. Committee on Veterans' Affairs. *Activities Report of the Committee on Veterans' Affairs.* 102d Cong., 2d sess., 1992. H. Rept. 102-1076.

MARY ETTA BOESL

VETERANS' AFFAIRS COMMITTEE, SENATE.

The Senate Committee on Veterans' Affairs, one of sixteen Senate standing committees, has jurisdiction over the following subjects: (1) compensation of veterans; (2) life insurance issued by the government on account of service in the armed forces; (3) national cemeteries; (4) pensions for veterans of all wars of the United States; (5) readjustment of servicemen to civil life; (6) soldiers' and sailors' civil relief; (7) veterans' hospitals, medical care, and treatment; (8) veterans' measures generally; and (9) vocational rehabilitation and education of veterans.

A specific committee to handle veterans' legislation is a relatively new addition to the Senate standing committee system. Veterans' Affairs, created by the Legislative Reorganization Act of 1970, was organized for the first time at the start of the 92d Congress on 3 January 1971.

The committee can be characterized as having a low public profile and a narrow policy scope. The committee's constituency comprises veterans and veterans' organizations; the broader general public is rarely interested in the committee's work. Veterans' Affairs has developed a particularly close link to veterans' groups and routinely begins each session of Congress with public hearings to receive each group's legislative agenda for the year.

The committee has had a tenuous existence. When the modern committee system was formed by the Legislative Reorganization Act of 1946, the House of Representatives established a veterans' affairs committee, but the Senate did not. In the Senate, veterans' legislation was referred to several different committees, including the Finance, Labor and Public Welfare, Interior, and Post Office and Civil Service committees. Between 1946 and 1970, senators sympathetic to veterans' groups that wanted a Senate standing committee for veterans' issues made several unsuccessful efforts to form a veterans' affairs committee.

During a 1970 legislative reorganization, proponents of such a panel succeeded in establishing the Senate Veterans' Affairs Committee. However, a reorganization committee formed in 1976 recommended that the Veterans' Affairs Committee be abolished; it survived only because the Senate Rules Committee chose not to accept the recommendation.

Historically, the Senate and House of Representatives have chosen different committee structures for processing veterans' legislation. The House has provided veterans with a committee they can consider their own, a panel that interacts almost solely with veterans and veterans' organizations. In the Senate, however, broad policy committees have tra-

COMMITTEE HEARING. Members of the Senate Veterans' Affairs Committee hearing testimony in 1977. *Left to right,* Strom Thurmond (R-S.C.), Robert T. Stafford (R-Vt.), committee chairman Alan Cranston (D-Calif.), and Herman E. Talmadge (D-Ga.).   OFFICE OF THE HISTORIAN OF THE U.S. SENATE

ditionally handled legislation within their jurisdiction as it relates to veterans and to nonveterans. For example, the predecessor to the Labor and Human Resources Committee handled education and job training issues for veterans and for the general public. Consequently, veterans and veterans' organizations were just one of a host of public groups with whom these Senate committees interacted.

The need for a Senate veterans' committee has been repeatedly debated. Proponents of a Senate veterans' affairs committee have argued that there should be parallel committees in the House and the Senate; opponents argue there is no need for such parallelism. Those favoring a Senate veterans' com-

mittee believe that veterans' issues should be consolidated into one committee rather than dispersed among several; opponents disapprove of such close links between a committee and its client-constituents. Some support a veterans' committee because they believe the workload of veterans' legislation is a burden on the broad-based policy committees; others disagree, stating that the workload is not that heavy and that having a separate veterans' affairs committee increases the number of committees on which senators have to serve while also increasing staffing needs, space requirements, and expenditures.

Sen. Vance Hartke (D-Ind.), the committee's first chairman, held that position from 1971 to 1976.

Hartke, an outspoken critic of the Vietnam War, proved an effective supporter of America's veterans. He successfully pressed for enactment of several veterans' benefit laws, including the Vietnam Era Veterans Readjustment Assistance Act and the National Cemeteries Act.

BIBLIOGRAPHY

U.S. Senate. Committee on Veterans' Affairs. *Legislative and Oversight Activities during the 101st Congress by the Senate Committee on Veterans' Affairs.* 102d Cong., 1st sess., 1992. S. Rept. 102-34.

Keller, Bill. "How a Unique Lobby Force Protects over $21 Billion in Vast Veterans' Programs." *Congressional Quarterly Weekly Report* 138, no. 24 (14 June 1980): 1627–1639.

MARY ETTA BOESL

VETERANS' BENEFITS. [*This entry includes two separate discussions, the first providing an overview of veterans' benefits, the second focusing on veterans' pensions. See also* Bonus March; GI Bill of Rights; Veterans' Affairs Committee, House; Veterans' Affairs Committee, Senate.]

An Overview

Indicative of Congress's historical concern for the welfare of the nation's military veterans is the fact that nearly 27 million individuals plus their families, which together are nearly one-third the total population of the United States, received veterans' benefits worth some $33 billion in 1994. The total cost of these benefits equaled about 13 percent of all federal domestic spending.

Congressional authority over veterans' policy largely rests with Article I of the Constitution, beginning with section 1, which grants the general legislative power. Section 8 lists the specific powers directly relevant to veterans' benefits: the power to pay the government's debts, "provide for the common Defense," provide and regulate the armed services and militia, and the power to pass legislation "necessary and proper" for the implementation of government policies.

Colonial and Confederation Systems. Veterans policy arose in the United States during the colonial period, when various colonies used the promise of disability pensions and survivor benefits as an incentive for recruitment. Colonial practice was followed by the Continental Congresses when raising the Continental army during the Revolutionary War.

The weaknesses of the national government, however, meant that most of the promises remained unkept.

At war's end the first veterans' organization was formed, the short-lived Society of the Cincinnati. Membership was limited to the officers of the Continental army and the French army and their dependents. Enlisted soldiers and sailors were excluded. The society was criticized for introducing European corruption through its French membership and hereditary aristocracy, criticism that prevented the society from exerting any significant political influence over veterans' policies.

Pension-Based System. The first veterans' benefits established by Congress—disability pensions, death benefits, and grants of public lands—were used as recruitment incentives. Over time benefits were increased during periods of prosperity, culminating with a pension open to veterans based upon length of military service and, initially, upon financial need.

After the ratification of the Constitution in 1788 the benefits passed by the Continental Congresses were adopted by the First Federal Congress in 1789 (1 Stat. 95). Because payment of these benefits had been made in worthless Continental script, the early Congresses spent much time deliberating over the individual claims of poverty-stricken veterans and dependents. Private bills were used in these cases, making up a significant portion of congressional business. In 1818, three decades after the end of the Revolutionary War, Congress established a pension for disabled or destitute veterans (3 Stat. 410). The pension's requirement was reduced to two years of military service in 1832 (4 Stat. 529).

The benefits provided for veterans of the War of 1812 and the Mexican War closely followed the pattern of those of the Revolutionary War veterans. The initial call for troops promised disability pensions, death pensions, and public land grants. Subsequent Congresses raised the level of payments from time to time. Eventually, pensions were granted to all surviving veterans and dependents based only upon military service during the war. Such pensions were passed by Congress for veterans of the War of 1812 in 1871, nearly sixty years after the end of the war, and for Mexican War veterans in 1887, forty years after peace resumed.

Congress responded to the greater demands of the Civil War by establishing the General Law system in 1862 (12 Stat. 566), which promised Union recruits, as well as recruits for all subsequent wars, disability pensions, generous death benefits, and residency preferences under existing homestead legislation. Other benefits shortly followed: veterans' preference for gaining government jobs was adopted in 1865 (although the patronage system of the time prevented its implementation) and domiciliary and medical care facilities for disabled veterans in 1866 (14 Stat. 10). This package of benefits applied, in turn, to the Indian Wars and the Spanish-American War.

Both the Civil War and the Spanish-American War produced veterans' organizations successful in exerting pressure upon Congress to increase their benefits, usually through a permanent lobbying presence on Capitol Hill. The Grand Army of the Republic (GAR) consisted of veterans of the Union army, and it frequently managed to get Congress to respond to its demands. The GAR's success encouraged the organization of Spanish-American War veterans: the United Spanish War Veterans, the Jewish War Veterans of the U.S.A., and several organizations that later merged into the Veterans of Foreign Wars of the United States (VFW). The demands by these groups, combined with general levels of economic prosperity and a close division of electoral support between the Democrats and Republicans, created a climate where the liberalization of benefits degenerated into a bid for election votes.

The process of liberalizing benefits began less than fifteen years after the Civil War's end. An extension of the filing period for claims in 1879 (20 Stat. 265) allowed claimants to receive, in addition to their pension, all benefits they had missed from their first date of eligibility, or arrears, with interest. Twenty-five years after the Civil War, in 1890, Congress passed a dependent pension act that made veterans and their survivors eligible for a pension upon ninety days of military service, financial need, age, and their inability to perform manual labor (26 Stat. 182). Critics noted that the pension rewarded veterans who did not fight, and that white-collar workers were eligible for a pension under the law's provisions. But the legislation was popular, with proponents turning the debate into a celebration of the Union army. Further expansions of the pension were passed in 1907 and 1912.

Spanish-American War veterans received the same basic treatment from Congress as their Civil War counterparts. In 1918, less than two decades after the war, a pension for war widows was passed with eligibility based on financial need and any form of disability, whether service related or not, that had been incurred by the deceased veteran.

Two years later Congress adopted a pension based upon financial need and age. This opened a flood of liberalizing legislation adopted in 1922, 1926, and 1930. Legislation during the Great Depression reduced the pension rolls of these veterans, but Congress reinstated their benefits in 1935.

Private bills continued to supplement the system of veterans' benefits during this period. Veterans' organizations assisted those veterans, war widows, and orphans who were found by the War Department to be ineligible for pensions or compensation by appealing to Congress for special legislation that allowed them to receive the benefits of the General Law system.

Initial Attempts to Replace the Pension. The political character of the General Law system left Congress dissatisfied with the veterans' system. Two factors provided the opportunity for change. The Progressive Movement early in the twentieth century sought to bring efficiency to government policies and to eliminate political influences. In addition, U.S. entry into World War I in 1917 forced the mobilization of the entire national economy toward the war effort.

Following the recommendations of a Treasury Department commission, Congress devised a new system of veterans' benefits in 1917 (P.L. 65-90). Proponents of the legislation, popularly known as the War Risk Insurance Act, shifted the system away from a reward for military service and toward encouraging self-reliance. Disability pensions were replaced by low-cost voluntary government insurance that paralleled the new workmen's compensation laws; disabled veterans were eligible for vocational rehabilitation that would help them reenter the economy; and medical and hospital care for the disabled was authorized.

The World War I system faltered, however, in its execution. Most servicemen upon discharge did not choose to continue their insurance, which left them unprovided for in case of future disability. Vocational rehabilitation was a new task for the government, and the program was ineffective and mismanaged. Veterans' medical care lacked adequate funding by Congress and was neglected by the Public Health Service, which oversaw the program. Veterans were bewildered by the array of agencies that were unable or unwilling to coordinate their efforts to deliver benefits.

A series of administrative reforms tried to improve the flawed system. A Veterans' Bureau was created in 1921 that centralized all World War I agencies (P.L. 67-47). President Herbert Hoover issued Executive Order 5389 in 1930, acting under the Congressional authorization of Public Law 71-536, that created the Veterans Administration (VA) by merging agencies administering benefits for veterans of earlier wars with the Veterans' Bureau. The reorganization's goals were to reduce costs and eliminate duplication.

While World War I veterans' groups such as the American Legion and the Disabled American Veterans (DAV) welcomed the centralization of veterans' policy in the executive, they remained dissatisfied with the system of benefits devised for them. The war had been a boon to civilian workers, while those in the military had been paid much less. The American Legion argued that those who risked their lives in Europe deserved some adjusted compensation, or "bonus," from the government for their efforts.

Throughout the interwar period Congress responded sympathetically to this call over presidential opposition. Bonus legislation was passed over presidential vetoes in 1924 promising payment with interest in 1945 (P.L. 68-120), in 1931 allowing veterans to borrow in anticipation of their bonuses (P.L. 71-743), and in 1936 when Congress authorized the immediate payment of the bonus (P.L. 74-425). The campaign also produced the 1932 "Bonus March" on Washington by veterans and their families to lobby unsuccessfully for legislation and resulted in their expulsion from the capital by the U.S. Army.

Two other significant developments occurred during the Great Depression. Responding to the plight of the veterans, Congress passed in 1930, over another Hoover veto, a pension for disabled and destitute veterans (P.L. 71-522). Less than twenty years after the introduction of a system of veterans' benefits that was meant to eliminate the need for pensions, Congress admitted the failure of the World War I system and returned to them. In 1933, Congress passed the Economy Act (P.L. 73-2), which repealed nearly all existing veterans' benefits and authorized the president to issue new regulations in order to reduce the government's expenditures. All such regulations would automatically become law in 1935, requiring legislation to change or replace them.

The Economy Act represented a dramatic shift in policy-making over veterans' benefits away from Congress and to the presidency. Roosevelt's forty-one executive orders eliminated pensions for non-service disabilities, reduced compensation rates, introduced a means test, dropped nearly 700,000

from the pension rolls, and saved $460 million annually. While these executive orders became the foundation for veterans' benefits during the New Deal, veterans' organizations managed to convince Congress to pass legislation in 1934 over the president's veto that reinstated many benefits for the veterans of earlier wars.

GI Bill of Rights System. On the eve of U.S. entry into World War II, thinking about veterans' benefits began to emphasize the issue of the veterans' readjustment to civilian life. For example, the Selective Training and Service Act of 1940 (P.L. 76-783) mandated reemployment rights for reservists called to temporary military duty. Several presidential commissions and agencies began developing ideas about veterans as they tackled post-war readjustment. The American Legion advocated vocational training for returning veterans by the government.

These diverse threads came together in the GI Bill of Rights passed in 1944 (P.L. 78-346). In addition to the continuation of death benefits, vocational rehabilitation for the disabled, and medical care, the law provided for employment assistance, educational expenses, and VA-guaranteed loans for homes, farms, or businesses. Legislation soon followed that established an effective system of veterans' preference in government hiring (P.L. 78-359) and provided for compensation to the dependents of disabled veterans (P.L. 80-877).

The success of the GI Bill after World War II led to the adoption of similar provisions for veterans of the Korean War in 1952 (P.L. 82-550). Unlike previous veterans' benefits legislation, the Korean GI Bill was less generous than its predecessor, especially in terms of its educational grants and unemployment insurance. This was, in part, due to the smaller scale of the conflict, that it was an undeclared war, and its inconclusive nature.

The scope of the GI Bill system's benefits and the success of previous veterans' groups encouraged the formation of other such groups after World War II. They made up a formidable veterans' lobby, including such groups as the American Veterans of World War II, Korea and Vietnam (AMVETS), and the American Veterans Committee, Inc. The Veterans of World War I of the U.S.A. ("Wonnies") also organized during the 1940s to lobby for better treatment of their increasingly elderly ranks. More specialized groups, such as the Paralyzed Veterans of America and the Blinded Veterans Association, concentrated their efforts on the burgeoning health care benefits for veterans.

Significant Legislation concerning Veterans' Benefits

TITLE	YEAR ENACTED	REFERENCE NUMBER	DESCRIPTION
Act of 29 September 1789	1789	1 Stat. 95	Provided for service disability pensions, death benefits of the widows and orphans of officers, and pensions for officers who served the duration of the Revolutionary War.
Act of 18 March 1818	1818	3 Stat. 410	Established a pension open to Revolutionary War veterans with service-connected disabilities and to those who suffered financial hardship due to their service.
Act of 1 May 1820	1820	3 Stat. 569	First congressional action aimed at reducing the pension rolls. The legislation required a sworn statement of the claimant's estate and income as proof of financial need.
Act of 4 June 1832	1832	4 Stat. 529	"Pure service" pension for Revolutionary War veterans whereby a pension was due to veterans at full pay dependent upon two years of military service.
General Law	1862	12 Stat. 566	Established a benefits program for veterans of the Civil War and all later wars of the United States. Provided for service disability pensions, death benefits for dependents, and preferred treatment under homestead legislation.
Act of 21 March 1866	1866	14 Stat. 10	Established the National Home for Disabled Volunteer Soldiers, providing domiciliary and medical care for Union veterans disabled during the war.
Arrears of Pension Act, 1879	1879	20 Stat. 265	Extended the filing period for Civil War veterans and their dependents for their benefits.
Dependent Pension Act	1890	26 Stat. 182	Provided expanded benefits for Civil War veterans based on financial need, age, and length of service, and for death and disabilities not service connected.
War Risk Insurance Act	1917	P.L. 65-90	Basic package of World War I veterans' benefits. Provided for low-cost voluntary insurance against death or disability, compensation for service-connected disabilities and for dependents of the dead, vocational rehabilitation for the disabled, and medical and hospital care.
Act of 9 August 1921	1921	P.L. 67-47	Consolidated all executive agencies responsible for veterans' benefits of World War I under a new agency, the Veterans' Bureau.

Significant Legislation concerning Veterans' Benefits (Continued)

TITLE	YEAR ENACTED	REFERENCE NUMBER	DESCRIPTION
World War Adjusted Compensation Act	1924	P.L. 68-120	Provided for the payment of a "bonus" with interest aimed to adjust the pay of armed forces members during World War I in compensation for lost wages in the private sector during their service. The payment was to be made in 1945.
World War Veterans Act, 1924	1924	P.L. 68-242	Reorganized the Veterans Bureau and veterans' benefits programs in light of scandals of the administration of President Warren Harding.
World War Veterans Amendments	1930	P.L. 71-522	Granted a pension to needy and disabled veterans of World War I.
Act of 3 July 1930	1930	P.L. 71-536	Authorized the president to create the Veterans Administration through a subsequent executive order.
Economy Act	1933	P.L. 73-2	Repealed all existing legislation on veterans' benefits and authorized the president to replace them by executive order, and provided that after 1935, all such executive orders would become law. The goal of this delegation was government savings through the reduction of veterans' benefits and of the pension rolls.
Act of 27 January 1936	1936	P.L. 74-425	Authorized the immediate payment of the bonus for World War I veterans.
Selective Training and Service Act	1940	P.L. 76-783	Established reemployment rights in their previous civilian jobs for persons called to temporary military duty.
National Service Life Insurance Act	1940	P.L. 76-801	Replaced the U.S. government life insurance system used in World War I with a new system of low-cost life insurance for members of the armed services.
Servicemen's Readjustment Act (GI Bill of Rights)	1944	P.L. 78-346	Established the basic package of veterans' benefits due to members of the military during World War II. Provided for education and training grants; loans for the purchase of homes, businesses, or farms; and readjustment allowances; and established a veterans' employment service.
Veterans' Preference Act	1944	P.L. 78-359	Established the veterans' preference system for civil service employment. It differed from earlier legislation on this subject in its scope and effectiveness.
Servicemen's Indemnity Act and Insurance Act	1951	P.L. 82-23	Replaced the system of low-cost national service life insurance and government life insurance for veterans with a free system of life insurance for new members of the armed services.

Significant Legislation concerning Veterans' Benefits (Continued)

TITLE	YEAR ENACTED	REFERENCE NUMBER	DESCRIPTION
Joint Resolution of 11 May 1951	1951	P.L. 82-28	Extended medical and hospital benefits for veterans of the undeclared war in Korea.
Veterans' Readjustment Assistance Act of 1952 (Korean GI Bill)	1952	P.L. 82-550	Extended the GI Bill package of veterans' benefits for the military participants of the Korean War.
Servicemen's and Veterans' Survivor Benefits Act	1956	P.L. 84-881	Replaced the previous death benefits system with dependency and indemnity compensation that provided for survivor benefits in cases of service-connected deaths, and brought members of the armed services permanently under the jurisdiction of the Social Security Old-Age and Survivors Insurance system.
Ex-Servicemen's Unemployment Compensation Act	1958	P.L. 85-848	Made veterans' unemployment insurance permanent, thus extending this benefit to veterans serving in peacetime.
Veterans' Pension Act	1959	P.L. 86-211	Introduced a sliding scale of benefits for veterans based upon income and the inclusion of the assets of dependents for survivor benefits.
Act of 15 October 1962	1962	P.L. 87-815	Made the provisions on vocational rehabilitation benefits to veterans permanent.
Veterans' Readjustment Benefits Act (Cold War GI Bill)	1966	P.L. 89-358	Made the GI Bill of Rights system permanent with higher benefits provided for veterans serving in particularly dangerous situations or theaters.
Veterans' Pension and Readjustment Assistance Act	1967	P.L. 90-77	Provided for a package of veterans' benefits for military participants in the undeclared Vietnam War. It maintained the basic GI Bill system.
Act of 24 December 1970	1970	P.L. 91-584	Extended educational and home loan provisions of the GI Bill system to the dependents of prisoners of war and of those missing in action.
Veterans' Housing Amendments Act	1976	P.L. 94-324	Made the Veterans Administration's home loan guarantee program permanent.
Veterans' Education and Employment Assistance Act	1976	P.L. 94-502	Ended the educational benefits under the GI Bill system for new veterans after the end of 1976. It was associated with the shift to an all-volunteer military.

Periodically, other versions of the GI Bill were applied to undeclared wars such as Vietnam in 1967 (P.L. 90-77) and the Persian Gulf War in 1991 (P.L. 102-25). In other cases, the GI Bill was mandated for veterans in more ambiguous situations such as the Berlin Crisis in 1962, when its educational benefits were extended to reservists called up for active duty (P.L. 87-815), or the legislation of 1966 (P.L. 89-358), where Congress recognized that the Cold War between the United States and the Soviet Union created a situation where the military served in a state of limbo between that of war and peace (P.L. 89-358).

Another unusual situation arose with the emer-

Significant Legislation concerning Veterans' Benefits (Continued)

TITLE	YEAR ENACTED	REFERENCE NUMBER	DESCRIPTION
Veterans' Health Care Amendments	1979	P.L. 96-22	Established a program for psychological counseling for veterans of the Vietnam War.
Veterans' Health Care, Training, and Small Business Loan Act	1981	P.L. 97-72	Directed the Veterans Administration to treat Vietnam veterans for ailments associated with the wartime use of dioxin (Agent Orange).
Veterans' Educational Assistance Act	1984	P.L. 98-525	Temporary reintroduction of the GI Bill system of educational benefits as an inducement for recruitment to the armed services. The program was changed from a free system of benefits to a contributory one.
Veterans' Health Care Act	1984	P.L. 98-528	Authorized the Veterans Administration to establish treatment programs for post-traumatic stress disorder and for drug and alcohol abuse and dependency.
Veterans' Dioxin and Radiation Exposure Compensation Standards Act	1984	P.L. 98-542	Established a compensation review and payment system for claims stemming from wartime exposure by former members of the armed services to dioxin (Agent Orange) during the Vietnam War.
Consolidated Omnibus Budget Reconciliation Act	1986	P.L. 99-272	Introduced a means test for free medical care for certain classes of veterans.
New GI Bill Continuation Act	1987	P.L. 100-48	Made permanent the temporary educational benefits program established in 1984.
Department of Veterans' Affairs Act	1988	P.L. 100-527	Established the Department of Veterans' Affairs.
Agent Orange Act	1991	P.L. 102-4	Codified decisions by the secretary of Veterans' Affairs to compensate veterans who were victims of diseases linked to dioxin (Agent Orange) and to establish a review process over future diseases linked to dioxin.
Persian Gulf War Veterans' Benefits Act	1991	P.L. 102-25	Liberalized existing veterans' benefits for those members of the armed services serving in combat during the Persian Gulf War.

gence of the issue of prisoners of war and those missing in action during the Vietnam War. Legislation was passed in 1970 that extended educational and home loan benefits to the dependents of members of the armed services who were in captivity or missing in action (P.L. 91-584).

At the same time, interested observers noted that the New Deal had instituted a comprehensive system of social welfare programs that called into question the need to continue some veterans' benefits that were being provided to the general public by other programs. In 1955 the president's Commission on Veterans' Pensions, chaired by Gen. Omar Bradley, directly addressed these issues in order to modernize the benefits system. However, the Bradley Commission's efforts provoked opposition from veterans' groups and evoked little response from Congress. Only with the introduction of the all-volunteer military after the end of the Vietnam War did Congress begin to search seriously for a new purpose for veterans' benefits.

Expanding Benefits to Peacetime Veterans. The Cold War, which lasted from the late 1940s into the 1990s, forced the United States for the first time in its history to maintain a large combat-ready military force during peacetime. Previously veterans' benefits had been limited to veterans of wars, with few provisions for veterans who served in peacetime. By the late 1950s Congress began wrestling with this distinction, gradually making GI Bill benefits permanent. Unemployment benefits were extended to this group in 1958 (P.L. 85-848); in 1962 Congress made peacetime disabled veterans eligible for vocational rehabilitation benefits (P.L. 87-815). VA-guaranteed home loans were made permanent in 1976 (P.L. 94-324).

The extension of GI Bill education benefits was more difficult. Initially, legislation in 1966 extended these benefits to peacetime veterans (P.L. 89-358), but the transition to an all-volunteer military led Congress to end the program in 1976 (P.L. 94-502). In an effort to improve the quality of recruits, a 1984 law established a contributory system of educational benefits for veterans on an experimental basis (P.L. 98-525). The experiment was declared a success in 1987 when the education benefits were made permanent (P.L. 100-48).

Entering the Twenty-first Century. President Ronald Reagan's surprise recommendation in 1987 for a Department of Veterans' Affairs brought veterans' policies directly to the cabinet table. The Department of Veterans' Affairs Act (P.L. 100-527) passed in 1988, with the first secretary appointed the following year. While the legislation did little to change the administration of veterans' benefits, it ensured a major administrative presence in the field of veterans' policy.

Veterans' benefits will undergo a process characterized by continuity and change in the near future. In the history of the United States, veterans' benefits have been cut back only twice, in 1820 and in 1933—both times in response to economic hard times. Most likely, the scope of benefits promised to surviving veterans will remain in place, a process made easier as mortality reduces the number of veterans.

In addition, legislation will continue to share a growing amount of authority over veterans' benefits with administrative rule making and court decisions. The efforts of veterans' groups to allow benefits for a variety of diseases suspected to be linked to the use of the defoliant Agent Orange during the Vietnam War is a useful illustration of the shifting balance between agencies and the courts on one side and Congress on the other. Much of the progress of this issue took place within the Veterans Administration and its successor, the Department of Veterans' Affairs, as well as in the courts. Among veterans' groups the antiwar Vietnam Veterans of America became increasingly involved in trying to get the VA to change its policies.

Congressional involvement was limited to individual members raising the issue and holding hearings. Legislation passed in 1981 (P.L. 97-72) and 1984 (P.L. 98-542) directed the VA to treat Vietnam veterans claiming disability due to Agent Orange, and established a system of compensation and review for Agent Orange claims. Yet, the law did not prevent continued controversy in the executive branch and the courts over the validity of these claims. The Agent Orange Act (P.L. 102-4), passed in 1991, brought the issue to a close, but, significantly, it merely codified decisions made by the secretary of Veterans' Affairs to compensate veterans who were suffering from diseases suspected to be linked to exposure to dioxin.

The areas of change, however, are substantial. The end of the Cold War promises a smaller military force. Whether Congress continues to maintain a generous system of benefits for a shrinking number of veterans seems unlikely, especially under the continuing burden of large deficits. Efforts to reform the health care system of the United States are bound to spill over to the VA health care system, leading to new procedures to cut costs and reduce its size.

BIBLIOGRAPHY

Ross, Davis R. B. *Preparing for Ulysses: Politics and Veterans during World War II.* 1969.

Severo, Richard, and Lewis Milford. *The Wages of War: When America's Soldiers Came Home—From Valley Forge to Vietnam.* 1989.

Skocpol, Theda. *Protecting Soldiers and Mothers: The Political Origins of Social Policy in the United States.* 1992.

U.S. House of Representatives. President's Commission on Veterans Pensions. *The Historical Development of Veterans' Benefits in the United States: A Report on Veterans' Benefits in the United States.* 84th Cong., 2d sess., 1956. Committee Print 244.

U.S. House of Representatives. Committee on Veterans' Affairs. *The Provision of Federal Benefits for Veterans: An Historical Analysis of Major Veterans' Legislation, 1862–1954.* 84th Cong., 2d sess., 1955. Committee Print 171.

KENNETH T. KATO

Veterans' Pensions

From the American Revolution to World War I, Congress responded to a variety of pressures for veterans' pensions. The practical wartime need for inducements to attract and retain soldiers, the moral obligations of the nation to those who fell in battle, a growing congressional responsiveness to constituents and interest groups, and fiscal policies that generated the revenues to fund soldiers' pensions were significant in shaping congressional pension legislation prior to World War I. From initially modest and limited provisions for Revolutionary War soldiers, Congress passed dozens of increasingly liberal pension laws. By the end of the nineteenth century, no nation matched the United States in the extent of coverage or the level of generosity that it bestowed on its veterans and their dependents.

The Continental Congress passed the nation's first pension law for invalids to encourage enlistment in the Revolutionary Army and, at the urging of General George Washington, passed a resolution for a service pension for officers to prevent more resignations. When the states failed to provide the funds for either, the First Congress was beset with petitions from soldiers seeking relief. After passing a series of temporary measures, Congress adopted a general pension law in 1793 that served as the baseline for pension benefits until passage of the Pension Act of 18 March 1818. "Let us show the world that Republics are not ungrateful," exclaimed an enthusiastic sponsor of the bill in the House. The Act of 1818 provided pensions without regard to disabilities directly linked to service to every soldier who had served for nine months or to the conclusion of the fighting and who could demonstrate a need for support.

During the nineteenth century Congress liberalized veterans' pensions in the context of expanding democracy, increasing nationalism, and broadening suffrage rights for all American white males. Successive Congresses' pension provisions for the War of 1812 and the Mexican War resembled those for the Revolutionary War. Initially modest disability pension laws associated with raising troops gave way to laws that liberalized benefits, expanded eligibility, and raised allowances. These disability provisions were eventually superseded by general service pensions that Congress passed in 1871 for veterans of the War of 1812 and in 1887 for veterans of the Mexican War.

The magnitude and scale of the Civil War left a generation of veterans who brought a new intensity and heightened political significance to pension issues in the postwar era. More than 2,213,000 men served in the Union forces, and the North suffered 364,511 mortal casualties and 281,881 wounded. A Republican-dominated Congress passed an 1862 pension law that linked pension benefits directly to disabilities from military duty or from causes traceable to injuries or diseases contracted while in the service. Widows, orphans, and other dependents of soldiers who died in the Union militia were entitled to pensions equivalent to total disability. Those who supported secession were ineligible to receive the benefits of national pension laws.

The number of pensioners increased to 238,411 by 1873, then declined for five consecutive years. By the end of the 1870s, it became apparent that an enormous pool of veterans or their dependents were not claiming the benefits that Congress had established in 1862. With the return of the Democratic party to competitive status nationally in the 1870s, members of Congress from northern states began to grasp the political potential of military pensions. With Republican control of the White House and Senate slipping and their lock on the House broken, large concentrations of veterans' votes could be decisive in the politically competitive states of Indiana, New York, Ohio, and Pennsylvania. Republican support for protective tariffs that generated the revenues required to fund expanded pensions gave them an advantage over northern, low-tariff Democrats in the bid for veterans' votes.

These partisan pressures on Congress were reinforced by the well-organized and skillful lobbying efforts of claims agents, whose business depended upon the volume of pension claims and who were strategically concentrated in a few large firms of pension attorneys in the nation's capital. George E. Lemon, Washington's most powerful pension attorney and lobbyist, founded a soldiers' newspaper, the *National Tribune*, that reached a circulation of 112,000 and rallied public support for more liberal pension legislation.

Northern Democrats could not afford to ignore the veterans and in a bipartisan bid for the "soldier vote" on 19 June 1878, a Democrat-controlled House passed the Arrears of Pension bill with only four nonsouthern Democrats dissenting and with unanimous Republican support. On 16 January 1879 the bill passed the Senate with virtually unanimous support from northern Democrats and Republicans. The Arrears of Pension Act of 1879 provided that all existing and future pensions accrued from date of discharge or death. The first payment under the act was to include all previous payments or "arrears" due the pensioner. The average first payment to army invalids of $953.62 and to widows, children, and dependent relatives of $1,021.51 were huge windfalls at a time when average nonfarm earnings were about $400 annually.

The tidal wave of new pension claims enmeshed Congress in bureaucratic politics and generated a profusion of private pension bills. The U.S. Pension Bureau's average monthly claims jumped from 1,600 to 10,000. As a massive backlog of claims engulfed the bureau, applicants turned to their representatives. In 1882, Rep. Roswell G. Horr of Michigan estimated that a quarter of his mail came from "soldiers asking aid in their pension cases, and each soldier is clear in his own mind that the member can help his case out if he will only make it a special case and give it special attention." Robert M. LaFollette of Wisconsin spent up to one-third of his time in the House between 1885 and 1891 "examining testimony and untangling . . . records" for the "many old soldiers" in his district.

An immense correspondence developed between members of Congress and the Pension Bureau. The agency reported that the 40,000 written and personal inquiries from Congress in 1880 more than doubled to 94,000 in 1888, before peaking at nearly 155,000 in 1891. If an applicant was not satisfied with the ruling of the Pension Bureau, he or she had little difficulty finding a sponsor or support for a "private pension bill" in the Congresses of the 1880s where more than one-third of the northern and border states' representatives were Union veterans. Private pension bills that added individuals to the pension rolls or that increased benefits for existing pensioners became so numerous that Friday evenings were declared "pension night," when large numbers of private bills were passed by general consent without a quorum present.

Congress reflected the nation's distrust of centralized bureaucracy by largely leaving the administration of the pension laws to local constituents. Applicants easily applied for benefits for which they were not strictly eligible by enlisting the support of sympathetic relatives, local physicians, lawyers, and notaries. Pension officials sought legislation that would strengthen their ability to prevent abuse, but Congress preferred decentralized administration and preservation of their own wide discretionary capacities. In 1886, a growing public awareness of rampant pension fraud and abuse found expression when Democratic president Grover Cleveland singled out instances of flagrant dishonesty, vetoed private pension bills, and castigated Congress for acting as a rival pension court when it reversed bureau rulings. "Our pension system," wrote reformer Carl Schurz, "is like a biting satire on democratic government. Never has there been anything like it in point of extravagance and barefaced dishonesty."

The critics were no match for the more powerful partisan and political pressures pushing Congress toward adoption of a general service pension. The Grand Army of the Republic (G.A.R.), the most powerful veterans' organization with a membership of nearly 400,000, became the leading voice for a universal service pension. In the election of 1888, Republicans mobilized the G.A.R., gained control of Congress, and placed Benjamin Harrison, a "soldier president," in the White House. The Republican "Billion Dollar Congress" passed the Dependent Pension Act of 1890 that provided a monthly pension to every Civil War veteran who had served at least ninety days, received an honorable discharge, and was unable to perform manual labor. Republican-sponsored legislation in 1907, 1909, and 1912 extended the service pension to virtually all remaining categories of recipients.

As the United States moved toward involvement in World War I, the Woodrow Wilson administration made plans to replace the piecemeal, improvised, and Congress-centered approach to veterans pensions that had prevailed since the Continental Congress. Wilson's energetic secretary of the Treasury, William G. McAdoo, regarded the existing scheme of soldiers' pensions as "unscientific" and was eager to "make a fresh start on a better plan" based upon the insurance principle embodied in the War Risk Insurance Act of 1914. Under its provisions, the government underwrote insurance for enlistees in the merchant marines against the hazards of submarine warfare.

A new era of veterans' benefits began when Democratic majorities in both houses of Congress unanimously passed the War Insurance Act of 6 October 1917. This law provided low-cost voluntary government insurance to servicemen and vocational rehabilitation and medical and hospital care for disabled veterans. Congress centralized administration of veterans' programs with the creation of the Veterans Bureau in 1921.

BIBLIOGRAPHY

Dearing, Mary R. *Veterans in Politics: The Story of the G.A.R.* 1952.
Glasson, William H. *Federal Military Pensions in the United States.* 1918.
Skocpol, Theda. *Protecting Soldiers and Mothers: The Political Origins of Social Policy in the United States.* 1992.

RICHARD T. MCCULLEY

VETO. [*This entry includes separate discussions of the legislative veto and the presidential veto. See also Item Veto.*]

Legislative Veto

Declared unconstitutional by the Supreme Court in 1983, the legislative veto was a device that effectively stood the presidential veto on its head by requiring the executive branch to submit "legislation" for congressional review and veto. The legislative veto had many variants, but typically it mandated that the executive branch notify Congress of a proposed action and then wait for a specified time, usually from sixty to ninety days, before carrying out the action. During that time, Congress could prevent implementation by a majority vote in both houses (referred to as the *two-house veto*), by majority vote of either house (the *one-house veto*), or by vote of a single committee (the *committee veto*).

Proponents of the legislative veto argue that it provided a mechanism that allowed Congress to respond more quickly than it can through the more protracted legislative process (which requires bicameral passage and presentment to the president, with the potential need for a two-thirds vote in both houses to overcome a presidential veto). They maintain that legislative vetoes focused the attention of Congress on potential problems before they attained the force of law and enabled Congress more effectively to control the actions of executive bureaucrats who inappropriately or inaccurately interpreted the law. Opponents of the legislative veto argue that it unconstitutionally allowed the legislative branch to intrude into the execution of the law, which the Constitution reserves for the executive branch, and into the interpretation of the law, which the Constitution reserves for the judicial branch. Studies of the legislative veto's effect in a variety of policy areas generally show that in practice it was either ineffective, in that Congress rarely used its potential legislative veto power (especially when foreign policy issues were involved), or that it was used (or threatened) not to hold the executive accountable to the law as passed by Congress and signed by the president but rather to enable individual members and their staffs to force executive-branch actors into interpreting the law so as to protect powerful interest groups.

Some scholars trace the origins of the legislative veto to the nineteenth-century British practice that required ministries to lay decisions before Parliament for approval or annulment and to a 1789 U.S. statute that created the office of secretary of the Treasury, wherein Congress directed the secretary to provide information about his office when required to do so by a resolution of either house. Modern roots of the legislative veto are found in the Legislative Appropriations Act for Fiscal Year 1933, which in Title IV (Reorganization of Executive Departments) authorized the president to transfer, consolidate, and redistribute by executive order any executive agencies or functions. An executive order issued under the act was transmitted to Congress, and if either house passed a resolution disapproving the order within sixty days, it became null and void; if neither acted within that time, the order became effective. As applied to executive branch reorganizations, this legislative veto proved to be an ingenious way to enable Congress to transfer a time-consuming and politically sensitive legislative power to the president while retaining the right to negate the president's exercise of it without having to go through the normal lawmaking process. The potential for the legislative veto's use in other policy areas was soon obvious.

Between 1932 and 1983, Congress passed nearly two hundred statutory provisions containing legislative vetoes. Prior to the 1970s, most of the provisions for veto review were in acts dealing with executive branch reorganizations, conduct of foreign affairs and national defense, and administration of public works programs. Later, Congress expanded veto targets to include termination by two-house veto of assistance to foreign nations as well as annulment by committee-level veto of land and property sales by the military and such domestic agencies as the General Services Administration and the departments of Agriculture and Interior.

During the 1970s, the congressional penchant for adding legislative vetoes to delegations of power to the executive dramatically increased. In some cases,

Congress added controls to regain powers it believed to have been usurped by the "imperial presidency" in general and by the excesses of President Richard M. Nixon in particular.

More significant, though, was the surge throughout the 1970s and early 1980s in congressional legislation attaching legislative vetoes to the actions of officials of independent agencies and of subordinate-level officials of executive agencies. To a large extent this new focus for legislative veto control was occasioned by the enormous explosion of regulations pouring forth from these agencies as they attempted to implement the social regulatory and grant legislation passed between 1964 and 1972—the housing, education, and health legislation of the Great Society programs and the environmental, consumer protection, and safety legislation that followed. The Education Amendments of 1972, which included a legislative veto over the Office of Education's proposed family contribution schedules for its program of basic grants for postsecondary education, marked the first such effort. Soon, dozens of programs and agencies were similarly subject to legislative veto controls.

In addition, between 1976 and 1983 dozens of proposals were introduced in an effort to extend legislative veto review to cover the rules and regulations of all executive branch and independent agencies. Though none of these "generic" legislative veto proposals ever passed, several came quite close.

Congressional initiatives for the imposition of the veto control device came from all quarters—from the Senate and the House, from Democrats and Republicans, from committees as well as individual members. Although presidents of both parties typically opposed legislative vetoes, they were often willing to accept them (sometimes even to suggest them) in order to acquire additional authority. While campaigning for the presidency, both Jimmy Carter and Ronald Reagan voiced support for the veto concept, but having to live with the reality of the legislative veto turned them, as presidents, into adamant opponents.

As the numbers of statutes with legislative vetoes attached increased, opposition to their expansion grew. Public interest groups such as Ralph Nader's Public Citizen and the Sierra Club had fought long battles to get protective legislation passed. Most of that legislation set out broad goals, leaving the specific decisions for agencies to implement by issuing regulations or guidelines. Now they feared that those gains would be lost because of the ability of powerful business interests to press members of Congress to veto costly regulations. Fear became reality when several such regulations—including one aimed at protecting the public against the tactics of used-car dealers and another aimed at protecting home owners against natural gas price increases—were overturned by legislative vetoes.

Many legal experts opposed the legislative veto. They believed that it encouraged off-the-record negotiations to avoid vetoes, thereby undercutting the regulation-making process, which at the insistence of the courts and Congress had been made more open and subject to court review. Other scholars worried about the legislative veto's intrusion into executive branch affairs, especially in foreign affairs areas such as arms sales and foreign aid. Ironically, many of those who opposed the legislative veto for this last reason supported the veto's use against excessive regulations, just as many who opposed the veto over regulations found it attractive when applied to the president.

In effect, support and opposition for the legislative veto mirrored its potential effect on policy outcomes and power distribution. This was true both in and out of Congress, and within Congress there was an interesting twist. The generic legislative veto proposals provided for expedited floor procedures to assure that neither the leadership nor the Rules Committee in the House could bottle up a regulation to prevent a vote. Though rank-and-file members of both parties in the House were overwhelmingly supportive of a generic veto, the leadership and the chairman of the Rules Committee, Rep. Richard W. Bolling (D-Mo.), were unalterably opposed to its potential disruption of their powers.

While the two elective branches battled over the wisdom and constitutionality of the legislative veto, opponents turned to the courts for resolution. On 23 June 1983, the Supreme Court in *Immigration and Naturalization Service v. Chadha* weighed in on the side of the opponents in a broad ruling that effectively outlawed most, if not all, existing veto provisions. The Court relied on a strict reading of the lawmaking process as set out in Article I, which requires bicameral passage and presentment to the president for his signature (and a two-thirds majority in both houses to override his veto) for a bill to become a law. The legislative veto, according to the Court, was an unconstitutional device because it was an attempt by Congress to make law that did not follow the full constitutionally specified lawmaking process.

Court action called a halt to the rapid expansion of the legislative veto, but it did not eliminate it

Laws Congress Passed with Legislative Veto Provisions[1]

YEAR	TITLE
1932	Legislative Appropriations Act
1939	Reorganization Act
1942	Emergency Price Control Act
1943	War Labor Dispute Act
1952	Military and Naval Construction Authorization Act
1952	Immigration and Nationality Act
1954	Public Building Purchase Control Act
1961	Foreign Assistance Act
1973	War Powers Resolution
1974	Foreign Assistance Act
1974	Congressional Budget and Impoundment Control Act
1974	Presidential Recording and Materials Preservation Act
1974	Hopi and Navajo Tribe Act
1974	Education Amendments
1974	Employees Retirement Income Security Act
1974	Motor Vehicle and School Bus Safety Amendments
1974	Federal Elections Commission Act Amendments
1975	Energy Policy and Conservation Act
1975	Amtrak Improvement Act
1975	National Aeronautics and Space Administration Authorization Act for Fiscal Year 1976
1976	International Securities Assistance and Arms Control Act
1977	Emergency Unemployment Compensation Act
1978	Natural Gas Policy Act
1978	Airline Deregulation Act
1979	Department of Education Organization Act
1979	National Historic Preservation Act Amendments
1980	International Security Development Authorization
1980	Act to Improve Coastal Management
1980	Extension of Federal Insecticide, Fungicide, and Rodenticide Act
1980	Federal Trade Commission Amendments
1980	Energy Security Act Extension Amendments

[1] A representative selection from the nearly 200 laws that included at least one legislative veto provision from 1932 until it was declared unconstitutional in June 1983.

completely. Congressional scholar Louis Fisher has tracked numerous instances throughout the 1980s and 1990s of congressional applications of power that look and act much like the outlawed legislative veto. Most of these are in spending bills that require the administration to obtain the written approval of the Appropriations committees in each house before reprogramming funds from accounts set out in the law. Other examples are less formal than the old veto provisions, with the executive offering its word that it will check with appropriate committees before acting but not being bound to do so by a statutory provision that presumably would be unenforceable in court. In function, both of these examples are committee vetoes, the most powerful form of the legislative veto. Their existence, post-*Chadha*, is evidence of the value of this sort of arrangement to both branches. That the executive is willing to accept these provisions of questionable constitutionality is perhaps attributable to their limited use. With *Chadha* to fall back upon, the executive need not worry that Congress will expand vastly its use of the legislative veto as it had in the decade preceding the Court's decision. Unless and until the Supreme Court changes its mind about the constitutionality of the legislative veto, it is unlikely that it will reemerge as the potentially powerful device into which it had once evolved.

[See also Immigration and Naturalization Service v. Chadha.]

BIBLIOGRAPHY

Craig, Barbara Hinkson. *The Legislative Veto: Congressional Control of Regulation.* 1983.
Fisher, Louis. "Judicial Misjudgments about the Lawmaking Process: The Legislative Veto Cases." *Public Administration Review* (November 1985): 705–711.

BARBARA HINKSON CRAIG

Presidential Veto

The presidential power to veto legislation is one of the few explicitly granted powers that formally involves the chief executive in legislative affairs. Described in Article I, section 7 of the Constitution, the veto is the final leg of the legislative gauntlet a bill must run before it becomes law.

When presented with a bill passed by Congress, the president faces four possible choices. First, he may approve the bill by signing it into law; second, he may exercise the regular, or return, veto by returning the bill to the house of origin with a statement of objections; third, he may do nothing, in which case the bill automatically becomes law after ten days (Sundays excepted); and fourth, if Congress adjourns within ten days of having presented a bill to the president and the president does nothing, the bill is pocket-vetoed if, according to the Constitution, "Congress by their Adjournment prevent its [the bill's] Return." (The Constitution requires no written statement accompanying pocket vetoes, but traditionally presidents have issued "memorandums of disapproval.") A return veto is subject to override by a two-thirds vote of both houses of Congress. A pocket veto is not.

The veto power is indisputably a presidential power, yet its location in Article I, the article otherwise devoted to the legislative branch, points to an important fact: the power is a legislative one possessed by the executive, and thus it reflects a sharing of powers between the branches of government.

The Framers' Concerns. Fears of the baneful consequences of a strong executive motivated the country's early leaders to create a governing system, under the Articles of Confederation, that had no independent executive branch. But by the time the Constitution's Framers met in 1787, the prevailing sentiment was toward an independent executive. Even though many still remembered the oppressive veto practices of the British king and his appointed colonial governors before the Revolutionary War, there was little disagreement that the new president should have a qualified veto power. The Framers were adamant, however, that the president's veto not be absolute, as was that of the British monarchs.

A central reason for granting the president this power was the Framers' concern that the executive would need it to protect the executive branch against legislative encroachments on executive power, a tendency observed in many state governments during the time the nation was governed by the Articles of Confederation. The Framers expected that the veto would be used to block legislation that was hastily conceived, unjust, or of dubious constitutionality. In addition, the power was not considered purely negative. Often called the "revisionary power," the veto was conceived as a creative, positive device whereby the president could bring a bill back to Congress for a final round of debate and consideration.

Increasing Use. Early presidents used the veto power cautiously and sparingly, giving rise to claims that the Constitution somehow countenanced restrictions on numbers or kinds of bills vetoed. Neither claim is substantiated by the Constitution itself or the debates of the Framers. President George Washington, who had presided over the Constitutional Convention, used the veto twice in his two terms—once for constitutional reasons, and once for policy reasons. President Andrew Jackson aroused deep antipathy by invoking the veto twelve times. His veto of a national bank bill in 1832 infuriated his foes and also served as the pivotal issue for that year's presidential election. Jackson's sweeping reelection victory was viewed at least in part as a referendum on the bank veto. Some of Jackson's vetoes also focused attention on another major issue of the time—government involvement in public works projects and other internal improvements.

Of the early presidents, John Tyler faced the greatest difficulties in connection with his use of the veto. During his almost four years in office, he vetoed a total of ten bills. While Tyler's political problems sprang primarily from his maladroit political leadership, controversy surrounding his use of the veto contributed directly to the effort to impeach him in 1843. Indeed, the two central impeachment charges brought against him focused on his allegedly improper use of the veto. In 1845, Tyler became the first president to have a veto successfully overridden by Congress.

Veto use exploded after the Civil War. From the first veto to 1868, presidents vetoed 88 bills. From that time to 1992, over 2,300 bills were vetoed. Most of these vetoes were attributable to the proliferation of private pension and related private relief bills, by which members of Congress sought to obtain relief for specific individuals seeking pensions or other private benefits that only Congress could authorize. Many such bills involved dubious claims.

Franklin D. Roosevelt holds the record for most vetoes, blocking a total of 635 bills in his four terms. On a per-year basis, Roosevelt falls second, behind Grover Cleveland, who averaged 73 vetoes per year, with a total of 584 vetoes. Most of their vetoes involved private bills.

As use of the veto increased, its importance ironically seemed to recede, as presidents acquired a wide array of political powers that enabled them to influence virtually every aspect of the legislative process. Yet the veto remained a key means whereby presidents inserted themselves into the legislative process. Early in the nineteenth century, many members of Congress considered it improper for presidents to express public opinions about legislation pending before Congress; they feared that such expressions might taint or alter the deliberations of Congress. Yet as veto use increased, Congress openly solicited the opinions of presidents concerning whether they might be planning a veto. These informal inquiries opened the door to more formal requests that the president submit to Congress a statement of his legislative preferences, a process that now takes the form of extensive legislative agendas submitted to Congress annually by the president.

Consequences of Veto Use. Although use of the veto has expanded the power of the presidency, the delicate politics associated with it are demonstrated by the fact that vigorous veto use has usually been politically detrimental to presidents. This is because the veto is viewed as a negative, reactive measure in contrast to the assertive, positive leadership for which Americans have come to reward presidents. Cleveland's prolific veto use certainly contributed to his defeat in his first bid for reelection in 1888. Franklin Roosevelt's presidency might seem an anomaly, given his high veto use, yet his use of the power was symptomatic of a powerful president who felt free to use all of the tools at his disposal. Moreover, most of his vetoes involved bills of little importance.

In more recent times, President Gerald R. Ford found reliance on a true veto strategy to be both necessary and damaging to his presidency. Appointed vice president by President Richard M. Nixon after the resignation of Spiro T. Agnew in 1973, Ford suddenly found himself sitting in the Oval Office when Nixon resigned the following year. The new president had neither won an electoral mandate nor had time to develop a legislative program of his own. As a result, Republican Ford and his aides felt compelled to rely heavily on the veto to try to control the actions of a headstrong post-Watergate Democratic Congress. Thus, in his two and one-half years in office, Ford vetoed sixty-six bills. Taken together, these vetoes helped encourage the attitude that Ford was unable to engage in affirmative governance and the kind of positive leadership the country had come to expect, an attitude that contributed to his defeat in 1976.

President George Bush also suffered some criticism for overreliance on the veto and for an apparent failure to produce more positive policy alternatives. Yet Bush was also careful in his veto use. In his four years in office, he vetoed 45 bills. Only one of those bills, a measure to regulate cable television rates, was enacted into law over the veto (in October 1992).

For presidents, one appealing trait of the veto is its effectiveness. Of the 1,447 regular vetoes applied by presidents from 1789 to 1992, only 7.2 percent were overridden. When that figure is broken down between public and private bills, the record is somewhat less impressive for important legislation: 19.3 percent of public bill vetoes and 0.8 percent of private bill vetoes were overridden. Still, a presidential success rate of greater than 80 percent for public bills poses a daunting challenge for anyone seeking to overturn a veto.

Presidents are more likely to use a veto when the executive and legislative branches are controlled by different parties, when the president lacks congressional experience, when the president's public standing is low, and during the second and fourth years of a presidential term. Congress is more likely to override a veto when party control is split between the two branches, when the president's popular support is low, after a midterm election, and in times of economic crisis. In short, a veto is most potent when it is least needed by presidents—at the beginning of a term.

VETO OVERRIDE. Senators Mark O. Hatfield (R-Oreg.), *left*, and William Proxmire (D-Wis.) displaying a vote tally sheet after the Senate voted 60 to 30 to overturn a veto by President Ronald Reagan, 10 September 1982.

LIBRARY OF CONGRESS

Handling Vetoes. Presidents rarely act alone in making important decisions, and since Washington they have sought advice on whether to veto bills. Washington often solicited opinions from his cabinet members, especially Alexander Hamilton and Thomas Jefferson, and from members of Congress, especially James Madison. As the presidency became institutionalized in the twentieth century, so too did the way veto decisions were handled.

Until the early twentieth century, when an enrolled bill (one passed by Congress but not yet signed into law) reached the White House, a presidential aide would decide which agencies would be affected, have the bill delivered to them, and then wait for their replies. This process yielded a number of inadequate, ill-considered veto decisions in the nineteenth century. But the growing volume of legislation, combined with the constitutionally mandated ten-day period within which the veto decision must be made, spurred a more formal institutionalization of the process.

The effort to deal more systematically with enrolled bills began with the creation of the Bureau of the Budget (known as the Office of Management and Budget, or OMB, after 1970) in 1921. The Budget Bureau was asked to render its views of enrolled appropriations bills as part of the larger effort to enhance executive authority over the budget process. Naturally, this led to occasional veto recommendations from the bureau. The examination of enrolled bills was expanded by Franklin D. Roosevelt in 1934 to include private bills. By 1938, the Budget Bureau was assessing all enrolled bills, a process that included contacting affected departments and compiling views on the bills under scrutiny. Since the 1930s, these procedures have not changed significantly, except that ever more attention has been focused on the president's priorities, as distinct from the independent opinions of affected agencies.

The Pocket Veto. Early concerns about the pocket veto centered on two principles that weighed heavily on the Constitution's Framers. First, it was thought important that presidents have adequate time to consider the legislation sent to them. The pocket veto would come into play at the end of a congressional session, when Congress would likely present the president with a rush of last-minute bills. The pocket veto ensured that presidents would not be forced into signing imprudent legislation. The Framers also wanted to ensure that Congress would have time to consider and, if it chose, to override the president's objections. Obviously, the pocket veto does not allow for any reconsideration or override; thus, the return veto was the preferred option, if circumstances allowed.

Persisting ambiguities have surrounded the pocket veto power. For example, several court cases have addressed the question of when a congressional adjournment prevents a bill's return. In 1972, Sen. Edward M. Kennedy (D-Mass.) filed suit challenging a 1970 pocket veto by President Nixon that occurred during a Christmas recess. The U.S. Court of Appeals ruled that the president had not been prevented from returning the bill to Congress, voiding the pocket veto and ordering the enactment of the law (*Kennedy v. Sampson*, 511 F. 2d 430 [D.C. Cir. 1974]). Further, the ruling cast doubt on any pocket veto during such adjournments as long as Congress designated an agent to receive veto messages, a practice Congress has maintained for several decades. The Nixon administration declined to appeal the case to the Supreme Court. Presidents Gerald Ford and Jimmy Carter followed the practice of using the pocket veto only when Congress adjourned *sine die* at the end of a two-year Congress, using the return veto in all other instances.

President Ronald Reagan argued, however, that pocket vetoes between congressional sessions (that is, between sessions of the same Congress) should be allowed. Reagan applied such a veto to a bill between the first and second sessions of the 98th Congress in November 1983. The pocket veto was challenged in court by members of Congress from both parties. A federal district court upheld the pocket veto, but the Court of Appeals ruled it unconstitutional on appeal. The Supreme Court declared the case moot, dismissing the suit and avoiding a ruling on the issues, in *Burke v. Barnes* (491 U.S. 361 [1987]). President George Bush went even further, arguing that a pocket veto was justified after any congressional recess longer than three days (as long as the bill's tenth day fell during the break). In his four years, however, Bush never attempted such a pocket veto, and the idea garnered little support.

BIBLIOGRAPHY

Jackson, Carleton. *Presidential Vetoes, 1792–1945.* 1967.
Mason, Edward C. *The Veto Power.* 1890.
Spitzer, Robert J. *The Presidential Veto: Touchstone of the American Presidency.* 1988.
U.S. House of Representatives. Rules Committee. Subcommittee on the Legislative Process. *Hearings on H.R. 849: A Bill to Clarify the Law Surrounding the President's Use of the Pocket Veto.* 101st Cong., 1st sess., 1989.

ROBERT J. SPITZER

VICE PRESIDENT OF THE UNITED STATES.

Although Article II of the Constitution designates the vice president a member of the executive branch, Article I assigns the vice president a limited legislative function as president of the Senate. In that capacity the vice president may preside but without a voting privilege unless the Senate "be equally divided," in which case he or she may cast the deciding vote.

The original intent of the Founders was for the vice presidency to be merely an added responsibility of the president of the Senate, not the other way around. Alexander Hamilton proposed that in the event of the president's death or absence from the country, the president of the Senate would temporarily exercise the powers of the presidency until another president was appointed or the absent one returned.

Hamilton's proposal was rejected on the ground that it would give the Senate undue influence in the executive branch. The Founders then decided that the vice presidency would go to the runner-up in the presidential balloting and that the duly elected vice president would become the Senate's presiding officer as a subsidiary task, with limited voting power.

In the first 203 years of the Republic only 228 tiebreaking votes were cast by the vice president, and ten of the forty-four vice presidents in that period never were called on to break a tie. The first, John Adams, broke the most, 29, a number approached only by the seventh, John C. Calhoun, who broke 28. Beyond this function the vice president has no other official legislative responsibility, although many vice presidents have functioned as emissaries to Congress seeking support for the president's legislative proposals and executive branch appointments.

One of the most memorable tiebreakers was cast in 1832 by Calhoun, then feuding with his president, Andrew Jackson, over the issue of nullification of federal laws by the states. In league with Daniel Webster and Henry Clay, also foes of Jackson, Calhoun worked out a scheme whereby the confirmation vote on Martin Van Buren, given a recess appointment as minister to England by Jackson, resulted in a tie. Calhoun gleefully broke it, voting down Van Buren's appointment.

Later that year Jackson chose Van Buren to replace Calhoun as his running mate for a second term. The new team won the election, but a bitter Calhoun continued to serve out his term—and to preside over the Senate. The impotence of the vice president as president of the Senate was chillingly demonstrated when Calhoun, picking up on a critical remark by Sen. John Forsyth of Georgia, asked from the chair: "Does the senator allude to me?" Forsyth, aware that the president of the Senate's only constitutional role was tiebreaking, shot back: "By what right does the chair ask that question?" Shortly afterward, while still vice president, Calhoun returned to South Carolina and again won election to the Senate, then resigned the vice presidency and took his seat in the Senate, with his right to speak restored.

So infrequently was there occasion for the vice president to break a tie vote in the Senate that the custom developed for some other member of the Senate, most often a very junior member, to occupy the chair, merely recognizing various senators as they sought the right to speak. That custom continues to this day.

The tradition that the vice president as the Senate's presiding officer was to be seen but not heard was rudely ignored in 1928 by Charles G. Dawes, while taking his own oath of office at the inauguration of President Calvin Coolidge. Dawes elected to attack the filibuster rules of the Senate over which he was about to preside and to challenge its members to liberalize their debate procedures. His remarks poisoned his relations with the Senate from the start.

Only two months later Dawes committed the most unpardonable gaffe imaginable. As the Senate debated Coolidge's nomination of Charles Warren for attorney general, Dawes decided to slip back to his hotel for a nap, although a close vote was anticipated. Expecting that the debate would last longer than it did, he was asleep when the nomination vote was called, with a junior senator in the chair. Alerted, Dawes dressed hurriedly, hailed a taxi to Capitol Hill, and raced up the Senate steps—too late. After a tie vote, last-minute vote switching against Warren brought about his defeat—and a red-faced Dawes.

In 1961 Lyndon B. Johnson came into the vice presidency directly from service as Senate majority leader and decided that, as president of the Senate, he was going to continue to wield power. He asked his former colleagues for, and was given, the right to preside over the Democratic caucus but with an embarrassing seventeen dissenting votes that reflected their true disapproval. At the next caucus Johnson called the meeting to order, then turned it over to his successor as majority leader, Mike Mansfield of Montana, and never attended another caucus.

In 1969 newly elected Spiro T. Agnew, a former governor of Maryland who was a stranger to official Washington, set out to be a conscientious president of the Senate. For the first two months he gaveled open every Senate session, but he too stubbed his toe on senatorial protocol. Taking to the Senate floor to lobby for a Nixon administration bill, he asked Republican senator Len B. Jordan of Idaho: "Do we have your vote?" Jordan shot back: "You did have, until now." Jordan vowed that henceforth whenever Agnew asked for his vote, he would cast it the other way. Agnew stopped asking.

Television and the office of president of the Senate have given vice presidents some of their most visible moments. Whenever the president addresses a joint session of Congress in the House of Representatives, the vice president occupies the seat next to the Speaker of the House, directly behind and above the president, in direct view of the nation's television audience.

[*See also* President Pro Tempore of the Senate.]

BIBLIOGRAPHY

Young, Donald. *American Roulette: The History and Dilemma of the Vice Presidency.* 1974.

Witcover, Jules. *Crapshoot: Rolling the Dice on the Vice Presidency.* 1992.

JULES WITCOVER

VOL. XIII.   NEW YORK, MONDAY, MARCH 12, 1877.   NO. 124

WILLIAM A. WHEELER. Running mate of Rutherford B. Hayes, taking the vice presidential oath of office in the Senate chamber. Published 12 March 1877.

OFFICE OF THE HISTORIAN OF THE U.S. SENATE

VIETNAM WAR. "The Constitution," the noted scholar Edward S. Corwin has written, "is an invitation to struggle for the privilege of directing foreign policy." The war powers in particular, granted to both Congress and the president, have been the subject of repeated clashes between the political branches of the government. The manner in which Congress discharged its constitutional responsibility during the Vietnam War has given rise to controversy and conflicting interpretations.

From Support to Opposition. During the course of the Vietnam conflict, America's longest war, Congress recorded well in excess of one hundred votes dealing with proposals to limit or end U.S. involvement. But it was not until 1973, after the last U.S. combat forces had left Vietnam, that Congress enacted legislation restricting the war. Attempts to cut off appropriations, emanating especially from the Senate, were undoubtedly among the important factors that impelled the Nixon administration to sign a less-than-promising peace accord in January 1973. But for the most part Congress quite accurately mirrored public opinion on the war and was careful not to incur the charge of acting unpatriotically. While U.S. combat units were still engaged in Vietnam, the vote for antiwar measures in the House never exceeded 175, or about 40 percent of the membership.

During the years 1964 to 1967 Congress firmly backed President Lyndon B. Johnson's policy of using U.S. military forces to defeat the communist-led insurgency in South Vietnam. The so-called Tonkin Gulf Resolution, adopted by a practically unanimous Congress on 7 August 1964, had approved the determination of the president "to take all necessary steps, including the use of armed force," to repel North Vietnamese aggression against South Vietnam. A proposal to repeal the resolution, put forth in February 1966 as an amendment to a bill to finance the expanding war in Vietnam, was voted down in the Senate by a vote of 95 to 5. The measure, appropriating $12 billion for Vietnam, was approved in the House 385 to 11 and in the Senate 77 to 3.

By the end of 1967 close to half a million U.S. military personnel were in Vietnam and casualties were mounting, but victory was not in sight. As the war dragged on without any obvious progress, discontent spread. For the first time a plurality of Americans indicated a belief that the United States had made a mistake in sending troops to fight in Vietnam. And yet disapproval of administration policy did not mean support for withdrawal from Vietnam. A survey performed in 1968 showed that among respondents who viewed the war as a mistake, those who called for a stronger stand—even if it meant an invasion of North Vietnam—outnumbered those advocating complete withdrawal by a 5

to 3 ratio. In Congress the president was attacked by both hawks and doves. The Senate Preparedness Investigating Subcommittee urged an escalation of the air war against North Vietnam while other influential senators, such as J. William Fulbright (D-Ark.) and John Sherman Cooper (R-Ky.), argued for honorable disengagement. Following the devastating Tet offensive mounted by North Vietnam in January 1968, which cast further doubt on the possibility of seeing an end to the war, prominent Republican members of Congress called for the removal of restraints on the air war before sending more troops to Vietnam.

In November 1968 Richard M. Nixon won the presidency by a tiny margin in the popular vote. Confronting a Republican president, the Democrats, who controlled both houses of Congress, increasingly spoke up against the war, and a growing minority of Republicans sided with them. On 25 June 1969, the Senate by a vote of 70 to 16 adopted the so-called National Commitments Resolution, which affirmed that a commitment to assist a foreign country by armed force "results only from affirmative action taken by the executive and legislative branches of the United States government by means of a treaty, statute, or concurrent resolution of both houses of Congress specifically providing for such a commitment." On 18 December 1969, Congress cleared a defense appropriations bill with an amendment prohibiting the introduction of U.S. ground combat forces into Laos and Thailand.

Nixon's policy of Vietnamization, which aimed at gradually turning combat over to the South Vietnamese, and his promise of a phased American disengagement for a time received congressional support. Yet on 29 April 1970, when Nixon ordered U.S. forces to attack North Vietnamese sanctuaries in Cambodia without first consulting Congress, a flurry of bills seeking to curtail the president's war-making powers was introduced. On 30 June the Senate passed an amendment to the foreign military sales bill, introduced by Senators Cooper and Frank Church (D-Idaho), that prohibited future military operations in Cambodia. Forty-two Democrats and sixteen Republicans voted for the Cooper-Church amendment. Although the measure failed in the House, it marked the first time that Congress had sought to limit the president's powers as commander in chief during a war. Sen. Samuel J. Ervin, Jr. (D-N.C.), perhaps the Senate's preeminent constitutional scholar, called the Cooper-Church amendment unconstitutional because it sought to "have Congress usurp and exercise some of the powers to direct the military forces in the theater of operations which belong, under the Constitution, to the President of the United States."

In an attempt to seize the initiative from the Democrats and to demonstrate that the Republicans, too, were opposed to an expansion of the Indochina war, Sen. Bob Dole (R-Kans.) on 22 June introduced a measure to repeal the Tonkin Gulf Resolution. Congress eventually passed it in December 1970. The Nixon administration regarded the repeal as irrelevant as long as Congress continued to fund military operations and rejected resolutions to terminate the war.

By the end of 1970, U.S. troop strength in Vietnam was down to 334,600, but the country's weariness with the seemingly endless war was growing. The antiwar movement's resort to mass protests was highly unpopular, but these increasingly confrontational tactics gradually did create a sense among the media, lawmakers, and other elite groups that the country was coming apart and that the cost of continuing the war was simply too high. On 22 June 1971 the Senate by a vote of 57 to 42 approved the Mansfield amendment to the Selective Service bill, which called for a withdrawal of all U.S. forces from Indochina within nine months in return for a phased release of all American prisoners of war. This was the first time that the Senate had set a deadline for an American withdrawal. Again, the House failed to concur, but the vote indicated the growing disaffection in Congress.

Peace negotiations had been going on in Paris since the end of 1968 without headway. By the end of 1971 most U.S. ground combat forces had been withdrawn from Vietnam, and Hanoi sought to strike a final blow. On 30 March 1972, the North Vietnamese, throwing fourteen divisions and twenty-six independent regiments into battle, invaded South Vietnam. On 6 April, Nixon ordered the resumption of full-scale bombing of North Vietnam; heavy air strikes and naval gunfire helped the beleaguered South Vietnamese. No U.S. ground troops participated in halting the Easter offensive of 1972, but the renewed air and naval engagement rekindled efforts in the Senate to end all U.S. combat activity. On 24 July the Senate by a vote of 50 to 45 approved an amendment to the foreign military aid authorization bill that called for a complete withdrawal of all U.S. forces from Indochina within four months—enforced by a fund cutoff—provided all American prisoners were released. Thirty-nine Democrats and eleven Republicans voted for the measure. Secretary of State Henry Kissinger

VIETNAM VETERANS. At the Capitol, protesting against continued U.S. involvement in the Vietnam War, 19 April 1971.   LIBRARY OF CONGRESS

commented bitterly that the communists had little incentive to make concessions at the negotiating table and merely had to wait until "Congress voted us out of the war."

Public opinion surveys indicated that a majority of Americans opposed a unilateral withdrawal from Vietnam, and sentiment in the House mirrored this view. On 10 August 1972, the House by a vote of 228 to 178 rejected an end-the-war amendment that the Foreign Affairs Committee had attached to the foreign military assistance bill. When Nixon overwhelmingly won reelection in November, his victory over dovish South Dakota senator George McGovern was widely interpreted as a mandate to continue the policy of negotiated withdrawal, one that would not surrender South Vietnam to the North Vietnamese communists. On 27 January 1973, after another twelve days of concentrated bombing of North Vietnam, a peace agreement was signed in Paris. Secret assurances conveyed to President Nguyen Van Thieu of South Vietnam—that the United States would take "swift and severe retaliatory action" in case Hanoi failed to live up to the terms of the agreement—shortly instigated another dispute between the president and Congress.

On 29 March 1973 the last U.S. prisoners held in North Vietnam were released. When the North Vietnamese violated other crucial provisions of the Paris accords, however, Kissinger and Nixon warned of retaliation. At this point the floodgates of the Watergate scandal opened. Realizing that renewed bombing would spur violent criticism, Nixon canceled a planned series of air strikes. Encouraged by the weakness of the president and worried about the continued fighting in Cambodia, Congress on 30 June voted to cut off funds for all U.S. military activity in and over Indochina, effective 15 August. The enactment on 7 November of the War Powers Resolution, which formalized congressional oversight of the president's use of U.S. troops abroad, lent further emphasis to the retreat from Southeast Asia. With all American troops home (except those missing in action) and all known American prisoners of war finally released from captivity, the U.S. stake in the outcome of the Indochina war had decreased drastically. Even the House, made more liberal by the election in 1972 of seventy-five new Democrats, was willing to approve end-the-war legislation.

When President Nixon signed the legislation that barred U.S. combat activities in and over Indochina after 15 August 1973, he thereby acknowledged the right of Congress to end the U.S. involvement in the Southeast Asian conflict. An important transfer of power had taken place. At the same time the ability of the United States to deter a new North Vietnamese offensive against the South, preparations for which were in full swing, was eliminated. A successful strategy of deterrence depended on uncertainty. When Congress openly prohibited the president from using force, Hanoi was assured it could act without fear of retaliation. Nixon's promises to Thieu, to enforce the Paris agreements with appropriate military action, had become nothing more than ink on paper.

Hope remained that continued economic and military aid to South Vietnam would enable it to defend itself against the expected onslaught from North Vietnam. As Kissinger later explained, the Nixon administration believed that those who opposed the war in Vietnam would be satisfied with the American withdrawal, but this expectation too was incorrect. The president underestimated the resentment that had built up in Congress over being left out of important decisions about the war and being misled over military actions such as the bombing of Cambodia. With public opinion also running against further large-scale aid to Vietnam, Congress moved to assert itself. In fiscal year 1973, America had provided $2.27 billion to support the South Vietnamese armed forces. In fiscal year 1974, assistance was less than half that amount, and for fiscal year 1975 Congress made another cut by one third—authorizing a mere $700 million. The North Vietnamese began to reap the fruits of the congressional reductions in assistance. As Gen. Van Tien Dung, North Vietnam's chief of staff, recalled in a series of articles published after the collapse of the Saigon government, "The enemy became passive and utterly weakened. . . . The reduction of U.S. aid made it impossible for the puppet troops to carry out their combat plans and build up their forces. . . . Nguyen Van Thieu was then forced to fight a poor man's war."

Kissinger pleaded in vain for an increase in support. After four years of Vietnamization, he told the Senate Foreign Relations Committee in July 1974, the South Vietnamese had assumed direct responsibility for their defense: "We owe the Vietnamese people the chance to succeed. Failure to sustain our purposes would have a corrosive effect on interests beyond the confines of Indochina." A war-weary Congress was unimpressed, and the resignation of President Nixon on 9 August 1974 did not end the growing pressure for total American disengagement. The congressional election of 1974, which resulted in a major sweep for the Democrats, increased the number of those prepared to end the war once and for all. The House was now more than two-thirds Democratic; its more liberal character was enhanced by a reorganization plan approved late in 1974 that curtailed the power of committee chairs.

By early 1975 a new congressional majority had emerged that for a variety of motives was prepared to end all U.S. involvement in Southeast Asia. Some, concerned about competing domestic demands, wanted to halt the seemingly endless drain of money. Others felt that further assistance to Indochina would merely prolong the human agony and therefore favored an end to the killing no matter the price. Still others had become convinced that the Saigon regime, which they regarded as corrupt and autocratic, did not deserve to survive. For years the American public had been saturated with stories of South Vietnamese ineptitude and gross misconduct. Often emanating from groups with their own political agendas, some of these stories were true, others were exaggerated, and still others were sheer invention. Not surprisingly, many Americans in and out of Congress had concluded that any further aid to South Vietnam was a waste of money.

On 30 March 1975, slightly more than ten years after U.S. Marines had landed on the beaches of Da Nang, that important port city fell to the North Vietnamese army. By 23 April the North Vietnamese had assembled 120,000 well-armed troops in an ever-tightening circle around Saigon. Ill-led, outgunned, and demoralized by shortages of ammunition and supplies, South Vietnamese resistance collapsed. On 30 April North Vietnamese tanks entered Saigon, and the government of South Vietnam announced its unconditional surrender.

The answer to the question of whether more adequate assistance to the South Vietnamese armed forces might have staved off this defeat and the brutal regime of executions and reeducation camps that followed will never be known. Both critics and defenders of U.S. policy in Vietnam probably agree that, as Kissinger put it in June 1975, "Outside assistance can only supplement, but not create, local efforts and local will to resist." The establishment by Congress in 1973 of a deadline for a total U.S. military disengagement undoubtedly undercut enforcement of the Paris accords. But it is also true that Congress had never been officially informed of Nixon's commitments to Thieu. Indeed, the president kept secret his promise to enforce the accords by renewed U.S. military action precisely because he did not think this policy could win the support of Congress. If deterrence failed, it was hoped that the unpopular conduct of the communist enemy would make Congress acquiesce in a drastic military response. And yet, as Kissinger later acknowledged, the acid test of a policy "is its ability to obtain domestic support." Whether because of the Watergate scandal, the country's war weariness, or the administration's high-handedness and just plain ineptitude, the final phase of Nixon's Vietnam policy failed this crucial test.

The Undeclared War. Throughout the years of the U.S. engagement, the question of the legality of fighting a war without a congressional declaration split the community of legal scholars. Some argued that in the absence of a congressional declaration, the prosecution of the war by Presidents Johnson and Nixon violated the Constitution. Others pointed out that since 1798 the United States had undertaken nearly two hundred military engagements without a declaration of war. The practice of obtaining congressional authorization short of a declaration of war, they maintained, had a long history.

More than twenty courts dealt with challenges to the constitutionality of the war. Many challenges never overcame the threshold issue of standing, the requirement that a person advancing constitutional arguments be a person with a personal stake in the outcome. Others foundered on the doctrine of the political question, the view that certain issues are not justiciable because they are political and therefore should be decided by the political branches of government. Thus, in *Orlando v. Laird* (1971), a case involving a serviceman who challenged the right of the government to send him to Vietnam, a federal court of appeals determined that Congress had approved military operations in Southeast Asia in the Tonkin Gulf Resolution, in military appropriations, in extending the draft, and in other supportive actions. The specific form of a congressional authorization of hostilities, the court ruled, was determined "by highly complex considerations of diplomacy, foreign policy and military strategy inappropriate to judicial inquiry." It involved a political question, "committed to the discretion of Congress and outside the power and competency of the judiciary."

A suit by thirteen members of Congress filed in April 1971 fared no better. Responding to the argument in *Mitchell v. Laird* that the continued commitment of ground troops in Southeast Asia without a declaration of war infringed on their rights as members of Congress, a federal court of appeals ruled in March 1973 that a court could not substitute its judgment for that of the president, except where there had been clear abuse amounting to bad faith. To do otherwise, "a court would be ignoring the delicacies of diplomatic negotiation, the inevitable bargaining for the best solution of an international conflict, and the scope which in foreign affairs must be allowed to the President if this country is to play a responsible role in the council of the nations." The issue, the court reasoned, was clearly a political question beyond the jurisdiction of the judiciary.

Only once—in *Holtzman v. Schlesinger* (1973)— did a court issue a substantive ruling. In response to a suit that challenged the president's right to bomb Cambodia without an explicit authorization from Congress, a federal district court in July 1973 ordered the executive to stop all military activities in or over Cambodia; this decision was overturned by a higher court. "While we as men may well agonize and bewail the horrors of war," the court of appeals ruled, "the sharing of Presidential and Congressional responsibility particularly at this juncture is a bluntly political and not a judicial question." The Supreme Court refused to review this case and all other decisions involving the question of the undeclared war.

Many opponents of the Vietnam War voiced their disappointment over the failure of the courts to halt it. Yet the courts were basically correct in their appraisal that the war in Southeast Asia represented a political rather than a legal problem. It was Congress's use of the power of the purse that in 1973 finally ended U.S. involvement in Indochina. Clearly, in using its constitutional prerogative "to raise and support armies" Congress demonstrated the ability to act decisively in matters of war and peace.

[*See also* Tonkin Gulf Resolution.]

BIBLIOGRAPHY

Franck, Thomas M., and Edward Weisband. *Foreign Policy and Congress*. 1979.

Gelb, Leslie H., and Richard K. Betts. *The Irony of Vietnam: The System Worked*. 1979.

Haley, P. Edward. *Congress and the Fall of South Vietnam and Cambodia*. 1982.

Lewy, Guenter. *America in Vietnam*. 1978.

Mueller, John E. *War, Presidents, and Public Opinion*. 1973.

Reveley, W. Taylor, III. *War Powers of the President and Congress: Who Holds the Arrows and Olive Branch?* 1981.

GUENTER LEWY

VINSON, CARL (1883–1981), Democratic representative from Georgia; chairman of the Committee on Naval Affairs and of its successor, the Committee on Armed Services; advocate of a strong national defense. Vinson represented Georgia from 1914 until his retirement in 1965; his career of fifty years, one month, and two days in the House of Representatives established a record that was not surpassed until 1992. He served on the Naval Affairs and then the Armed Services committees for forty-eight years, chairing the former for sixteen and the latter for fourteen years. Vinson obtained membership on the House Naval Affairs Committee because of his belief at the time that the navy was the United States' first line of defense. Throughout his long congressional career, he advocated a strong national defense as the best deterrent to war. His longevity, strong personality, and legislative ability enabled him successfully to pursue his goal

of doing "everything in my power to maintain a strong national defense." Vinson's effectiveness as a legislator received the praise of House Speaker Sam Rayburn, who called him the "best legislative technician" in the House of Representatives. President Lyndon B. Johnson, himself no stranger to the workings of Congress, called Vinson his "tutor." Although he used his legislative skill primarily in formulating defense policy, Vinson played a key role in the passage of domestic legislation during the Kennedy administration and, until his retirement, in the Johnson administration.

Vinson believed that the primary duty of government was self-preservation, which could be guaranteed only by a strong military. During the 1920s and 1930s, Vinson expressed alarm at the inadequacy of the U.S. Navy. The Harding, Coolidge, and Hoover administrations had sought to limit armaments as a means of preventing war. The United States had agreed to the Washington Treaty of 1922 and the London Naval Treaty of 1930, which limit-

CARL VINSON.   LIBRARY OF CONGRESS

ed the size of the naval fleets of the major powers. Vinson protested that the U.S. Navy's fleet fell short even of what was allowed under these treaties. In 1931 he proposed a shipbuilding program to bring the U.S. fleet up to treaty strength.

Vinson's efforts bore fruit during the Roosevelt administration. From 1935 to 1940, as chairman of the Naval Affairs Committee, Vinson authored and guided through Congress four major naval construction bills—legislation that enabled the U.S. Navy to emerge from World War II with the most powerful fleet in the world. Always contending that national security was a nonpartisan issue, Vinson forcefully fought for a strong military throughout his legislative career and frequently clashed with Democratic and Republican presidents over national security issues. He accumulated so much power over defense policy that when asked by reporters in 1952 about a possible appointment as President Dwight D. Eisenhower's secretary of Defense, Vinson replied, "No, I'd rather run the Pentagon from here."

In appreciation for his dedicated service to the country, President Johnson in 1964 awarded Vinson the Presidential Medal of Freedom, the highest award that a president may bestow on a civilian. President Richard M. Nixon honored Vinson in 1973 by naming a nuclear-powered carrier after him.

At Vinson's death, the *Atlanta Constitution* editorialized, "Perhaps no other Georgian ever had a hand in shaping the history of the country over such a long period."

BIBLIOGRAPHY

Enders, Calvin William. "The Vinson Navy." Ph.D. diss., Michigan State University, 1970.

Walter, John C. "Congressman Carl Vinson and Franklin D. Roosevelt: Naval Preparedness and the Coming of World War II, 1932–40." *Georgia Historical Quarterly* 64 (Fall 1980): 294–305.

HAROLD P. HENDERSON

VIOLENCE. [*The following entry discusses violence against and in Congress in two separate articles.*]

Violence against Congress

Congress's traditional openness to the public has long tempted political extremists and others intent on violent expression of their real or imagined grievances against the government or its representatives. Burnings, shootings, bombings, and other hostile strikes against the Capitol and its occupants have occurred with unsettling frequency.

War of 1812. On 24 August 1814, a British force of about seven hundred, led by Maj. Gen. Robert Ross and Rear Adm. Sir George Cockburn, marched into an undefended Washington, D.C., and torched the Capitol, White House, and other public buildings. Congress was in recess, and President James Madison and most of his cabinet had fled to Virginia along with a poorly led militia that the invaders had routed earlier in a battle at Bladensburg, Maryland.

The fire destroyed much of the Capitol and its contents, including records, documents, and all three hundred books in the congressional library. Only a severe rain storm that evening kept the inferno from destroying the building's exterior walls. The British left the city the following night on their trek toward Baltimore, Maryland.

Congress set up temporary operations in the Patent–Post Office Building, the only unburned public structure, and convened on 19 September 1814. At Madison's insistence, it voted to rebuild the Capitol rather than transfer the seat of government to a safer city. House Clerk Patrick Magruder resigned after an inquiry criticized him for failing to remove books and manuscripts before the British arrived.

The Capitol has incurred significant damage from three accidental fires. In 1825, a candle-ignited blaze in the library ruined an unspecified number of books. A second fire in 1851 destroyed some 35,000 of the library's 55,000 books, including much of the Thomas Jefferson collection, which Congress had purchased to replace books burned in 1814.

On 6 November 1898 a gas explosion, caused by leaking service pipes, and the subsequent fire caused some $25,000 in damage. The fire spread upward through an elevator shaft near the Supreme Court Chamber and destroyed, among other things, priceless manuscript copies of Court decisions from 1792 to 1832.

Bombings. A homemade bomb made from three sticks of dynamite exploded in the Senate Reception Room at 11:40 P.M. on 2 July 1915. The bomb caused no injuries but did considerable damage to windows and furnishings. Erich Muenter, a former language instructor opposed to U.S. involvement in the emerging European hostilities, was arrested for the bombing and for the subsequent shooting of fi-

THE CAPITOL. After the fire started by British troops on 24 August 1814.   ARCHITECT OF THE CAPITOL

nancier J. P. Morgan, Jr. Muenter committed suicide before he could be brought to trial.

There were again no injuries on 1 March 1971, when another bomb, with a force equal to twenty pounds of dynamite, rocked the Senate. Placed in a ground-floor rest room, the device destroyed that facility and severely damaged a nearby hearing room, a barber shop, and several senators' hideaways. Although the Weather Underground, a group militantly opposed to U.S. policies in Vietnam, claimed responsibility, as of 1994 the perpetrator or perpetrators were still unidentified.

On 7 November 1983, at around 11:00 P.M., a bomb exploded in a usually busy corridor near the Senate chamber. Remarkably, there were no injuries. The area was deserted, the Senate having adjourned at 7:02 P.M., hours earlier than originally planned. The blast blew out a wall partition and several windows, knocked doors off hinges, and sent rubble flying. Several artworks, including John Neagle's painting of Daniel Webster, were damaged, as was the elegant "Ohio Clock." In 1990, three members of a self-described "Communist politico-military organization" received lengthy jail terms after pleading guilty to the bombing.

Shootings. On 30 January 1835, Richard Lawrence, a deranged house painter, attempted to assassinate Andrew Jackson as the president led a funeral procession through the Capitol Rotunda. Incredibly, both of Lawrence's two pistols misfired. On 28 February 1890, Charles E. Kincaid of the Louisville *Times* shot and killed former representative William P. Taulbee of Kentucky on a House staircase after they quarreled over a Kincaid article. On 12 July 1947, William L. Kaiser, who had recently lost his patronage job as a Capitol policeman, ineffectually fired two shots at Sen. John W. Bricker of Ohio as the senator entered the Senate subway. In each case, the assailant was arrested and brought to justice.

Shortly after 2:30 P.M. on 1 March 1954, as the House was debating a routine immigration bill, two men and a woman—later identified as Puerto Rican nationalists—stood in the gallery left of the Speaker's rostrum and, armed with pistols, fired randomly at the 243 representatives then in the chamber. In the chaos, members scrambled for cover, some ducking under seats, others bolting for exits. Speaker Joseph W. Martin, Jr., declared a recess and leaped behind a marble pillar. Some thir-

ATTEMPT ON THE LIFE OF PRESIDENT ANDREW JACKSON. Journalist Ben Perley Poore described the unsuccessful assassin as "an English house-painter named Lawrence, who had been for some months out of work, and who, having heard that the opposition of General Jackson to the United States Bank had paralyzed the industries of the country, had conceived the project of assassinating him" (p. 172). Both of his pistols misfired.

PERLEY'S REMINISCENCES, VOL. 2

ty shots rang out before the terrorists were subdued.

Five representatives were wounded: Alvin M. Bentley of Michigan, Clifford Davis of Tennessee, George H. Fallon of Maryland, Ben F. Jensen of Iowa, and Kenneth A. Roberts of Alabama. All recovered from their injuries. The two male snipers and a third man arrested later were convicted of assault with a dangerous weapon and assault with intent to kill. The woman was convicted only of the former charge. All received prison terms, which ranged up to seventy-five years.

Two potentially violent incidents ended peacefully. In 1932, a gallery spectator waved a loaded pistol and demanded to address the House. He was approached by Rep. Melvin J. Maas of Minnesota, who persuaded him to relinquish the weapon. Another House visitor was arrested in 1983 after he entered the gallery with a homemade bomb hidden in his clothing.

Not until increased terrorism became a worldwide concern in the early 1980s did Congress agree to restrict public access to the two-hundred-acre,

twenty-building complex that comprises Capitol Hill. Security forces were bolstered, and electronic metal detectors, through which all visitors must pass, and other protective measures were introduced. Still, in one recent year, the Capitol Police seized 148 weapons, including guns, knives, clubs, and blackjacks.

[*See also* Capitol Police.]

BIBLIOGRAPHY

Barton, Wilfred M. *The Road to Washington.* 1919.

Byrd, Robert C. *The Senate 1789–1989: Addresses on the History of the United States Senate.* Vol. 2. Edited by Wendy Wolff. 1991. Pp. 327–345.

Ellis, John B. *Sights and Secrets of the National Capital.* 1869.

Remini, Robert V. *Andrew Jackson and the Course of American Democracy, 1833–1845.* 1984.

Smith, Margaret Bayard. *Forty Years of Washington Society.* 1906.

DONALD C. BACON

Violence in Congress

Though rare in recent decades, violence has periodically erupted when ideas, tempers, or ambitions have clashed in Congress. Members in the heat of debate have been known to assail one another with fists, pistols, knives, canes, even fire tongs. In the pre–Civil War Senate and House, dueling was a popular recourse for settling trivial as well as serious disputes. Several lawmakers were killed or wounded in such encounters.

Congress in the 1800s was no place for the timid. It was for most of the century an unruly arena into which poured men of vastly differing cultures, education, experiences, and temperaments. From frontier states came rugged individualists, some more accustomed to settling disputes with fists or weapons than with gentlemanly compromise. From the South came a number of hot-tempered aristocrats schooled in the manly arts, brave to a fault, and alert to any slur on their honor. From the urban North came a veritable human menagerie, including agitators whose moral zealotry stirred constant turmoil and discontent, particularly on the defining issue of slavery. The slavery question profoundly affected Congress's behavior, fracturing its membership into irreconcilable factions and creating personal hostilities that diminished civility in the institution until well into the twentieth century.

A sign of the tense and unpredictable nature of early congressional life was the fact that many members armed themselves before entering the House and Senate chambers. In the 1850s, a pistol concealed in a House member's desk accidentally discharged. Instantly, "there were fully thirty or forty pistols in the air," recalled Rep. William S. Holman, who was present. During an angry Senate colloquy in 1850, Henry S. Foote of Mississippi whipped out a Colt revolver and threatened to shoot Thomas Hart Benton as the Missourian advanced menacingly toward him.

Fistfights and Beatings. Rep. Abram P. Maury erred in picking a fight with William B. Campbell in 1838. Holding his colleague by the hair with his left hand and striking him blow after blow in the face with his right fist, Campbell beat Maury without mercy behind the Speaker's chair. In separate inci-

dents in 1840, Rep. Jesse A. Bynum attacked colleague Rice Garland with a cane, and Representatives Kenneth Rayner and William Montgomery broke canes over each others' heads.

Laurence M. Keitt started a House free-for-all when he called Galusha A. Grow a "black Republican puppy" in 1857. John F. Potter of Wisconsin and Roger A. Pryor of Virginia brawled in the House chamber in 1860. Challenged to a duel, Potter gained a sort of immortality by demanding that the weapons be bowie knives. Pryor, refusing to fight with such barbaric weapons, called off the duel, leaving his adversary forever with the nickname "Bowie Knife" Potter.

South Carolina senators Benjamin R. Tillman and John L. McLaurin were censured after they en-

"CONGRESSIONAL PUGILISTS." Fight in Congress Hall, Philadelphia, on 15 February 1798 between Representatives Matthew Lyon of Vermont, wielding fire tongs, and Roger Griswold of Connecticut, holding a cane. The caption of the cartoon reads: "He in a trice struck Lyon thrice / Upon his head, enrag'd sir, / Who sciz'd the tongs to ease his wrongs, / And Griswold thus engag'd, sir." Published in Philadelphia, 1798.   LIBRARY OF CONGRESS

THE ASSAULT ON SEN. CHARLES SUMNER (R-MASS.). By Rep. Preston S. Brooks (D-S.C.) in the Senate chamber.

gaged in a lusty fistfight on the Senate floor in 1902. Later that year, Senators Joseph W. Bailey of Texas and Albert J. Beveridge of Indiana enlivened the Senate with their own public set-to.

Rep. Clarence Cannon (D-Mo., 1923–1964) traded punches at various times with colleagues John Taber, Milton A. Romjue, John Phillips, and others. Rep. Edward E. Cox (D-Ga., 1925–1952) was known for his violent rages. In 1949, at age sixty-nine, Cox furiously but ineffectually attacked eighty-three-year-old Adolph J. Sabath, chairman of the Rules Committee, for denying him more time to speak in debate.

No act of congressional violence caused a greater uproar than the brutal caning of Sen. Charles Sum-ner, Republican of Massachusetts, by Rep. Preston S. Brooks on 22 May 1856. Brooks, accompanied by fellow South Carolina Democrat Lawrence M. Keitt, sought to avenge his cousin, Sen. Andrew P. Butler, whom Sumner had ridiculed in a rambling speech entitled "The Crime against Kansas" three days earlier. Finding Sumner seated at his desk during a recess, Brooks attacked him with an inch-thick cane while Keitt stood by. Brooks repeatedly struck at Sumner's head and neck, and when the cane snapped Brooks continued to swing the part that remained in his hand. Covered with blood and barely conscious, Sumner made a mighty effort to stand and in so doing ripped his desk from the floor. He reeled and staggered down the aisle as

Brooks rained on him blow after blow. Although there were several witnesses, no one intervened until the very end of the bludgeoning.

Sumner's injuries kept him from the Senate for three years. Meanwhile, an investigation by an all-Democratic Senate committee concluded that the incident, while regrettable, was beyond Senate jurisdiction. In the House, a motion to expel Brooks fell short of the necessary two-thirds majority. The House did vote to censure Keitt, prompting both men to resign from Congress. South Carolina voters defiantly reelected them a month later.

Duels and Shootings. The bloody code duello, imported from Europe, flourished in Congress, as elsewhere in the United States, until as late as the 1860s. Among southern and western members particularly, "a case of dueling pistols was part of the outfit," as nineteenth-century journalist Ben Perley Poore observed in his *Reminiscences*.

In 1793, Aaron Burr helped negotiate a peaceful resolution to a dispute between Treasury Secretary Alexander Hamilton and Sen. James Monroe, whom Hamilton had accused of slander. Later, as vice president, Burr chose to settle his own dispute with Hamilton on a dueling field in Weehawken, New Jersey. At their encounter on 11 July 1804, challenger Burr, an expert duelist, fatally wounded the novice Hamilton on the first fire. An enraged public viewed the episode as equivalent to murder. Congress reacted by passing the first federal anti-dueling law, which banned duels in the military. Though Burr became a political outcast, he did return to preside over the Senate and complete his term.

Angered by Federalist representative Barent Gardenier's interminable speeches, opposition leader George W. Campbell decided in 1808 to silence the pesky New Yorker by killing him in a duel. Gardenier was seriously wounded but not silenced. He returned to the House, as talkative as ever.

By the time he entered the White House in 1829, Andrew Jackson was said to have survived more than a dozen duels and scores of other hostile encounters, including a vicious brawl with brothers Jesse and Thomas Hart Benton in Nashville on 4 September 1813. A gunshot wound to the left shoulder, inflicted by Jesse, left Jackson with lifetime impairment. Thomas Benton, later a senator from Missouri, suffered only wounded pride as he, retreating from a Jackson accomplice, plummeted down a stairwell. Thomas Benton's violent tendencies had matured by 1817, when he killed attorney Charles Lucas in a duel near St. Louis. When Jack-

"WISTFUL." Cartoon commenting on the occasional outbursts of violence among members of Congress. A bulldog-faced boxer sees Congress as the perfect arena for his next fight. Clifford K. Berryman, *Washington Evening Star*, 21 January 1914.

U.S. SENATE COLLECTION, CENTER FOR LEGISLATIVE ARCHIVES

son reentered the Senate in 1823, he and Benton patched up their quarrel and eventually became staunch allies.

Kentucky's Henry Clay, a prodigious duelist, and Sen. John Randolph of Virginia had a near-tragic encounter on 8 April 1826. After years of verbal skirmishing, the two rivals met with pistols on the Virginia shore of the Potomac, near Washington. Neither seemed eager to inflict harm. After two bloodless exchanges of fire, they agreed to stop.

Rep. Sam Houston of Tennessee seriously wounded William A. White in a duel on 22 September 1826. White was a stand-in for the postmaster of Nashville, whom Houston had offended. In 1832, Houston was brought to the bar of the House and reprimanded for assaulting Rep. William Stanbery with his cane on a Washington street. Stanbery had answered the attack by trying to shoot Houston, but his pistol misfired.

Some encounters were suicidal. Former senator Armistead T. Mason of Virginia blamed his election loss in 1816 on his brother-in-law, John McCarty, and challenged him to a duel. They finally agreed to fight with muskets at four paces. So close that the muzzles of their guns nearly touched, both fired on the command. Mason was killed; McCarty was seriously wounded. Rep. Spencer D. Pettis of Missouri and Maj. Thomas Biddle traded pistol shots at only five feet on Bloody Island, near St. Louis, on 28 August 1831. Both died.

Freshman representative Jonathan Cilley of Maine paid dearly for his brashness in disputing Henry A. Wise of Virginia in a House debate. Wise's friend Rep. William J. Graves of Kentucky challenged Cilley to a duel. They met to duel with rifles at eighty yards on 24 February 1838, at Bladensburg, Maryland. Both were unscathed after two fires. Instead of stopping the contest after the customary two fires, Wise, acting as Graves's second, insisted that it continue. Cilley was killed on the third fire. The affair was the last straw for many Americans. New restrictions on dueling were demanded. Congress, under intense public pressure, enacted the first ban on dueling in the District of Columbia. The House investigated Wise's murderous role but took no action.

Dueling's final congressional victim was Sen. David C. Broderick of California. His challenger was David S. Terry, former chief justice of the California supreme court, whom Broderick had offended in a speech. On 13 September 1859, Broderick, clumsy with firearms, discharged his pistol prematurely, allowing the more experienced Terry to deliver a fatal shot. Tried for murder, Terry was acquitted.

On 28 February 1890, former representative William P. Taulbee of Kentucky was shot and mortally wounded on the southeastern stairway of the House, near the House restaurant, during an altercation with Charles E. Kincaid of the Louisville *Times*. Taulbee, objecting to one of Kincaid's articles, had apparently pulled the reporter's ear. Kincaid, who claimed self-defense, was tried for murder and acquitted. Legend has it that an indelible stain on the marble staircase marks where Taulbee fell.

BIBLIOGRAPHY

Bates, Ernest S. *The Story of Congress, 1789–1935.* 1936.

Brown, George Rothwell. *Washington: A Not Too Serious History.* 1930. Pp. 143–146.

Cochran, Hamilton. *Noted American Duels and Hostile Encounters.* 1963.

Donald, David Herbert. *Charles Sumner and the Coming of the Civil War.* 1960.

Kane, Harnett C. *Gentlemen, Swords, and Pistols.* 1951.

MacNeil, Neil. *Forge of Democracy.* 1963. Pp. 306–309.

DONALD C. BACON

VIRGINIA. Through their advocacy of the Virginia Plan at the Constitutional Convention, the state's delegates profoundly influenced the structure and activities of the U.S. Congress. Devised by James Madison and introduced at the convention by Edmund J. Randolph, the plan called for a strong government to replace the decentralized regime provided by the Articles of Confederation. At the core of the proposed system was a "National Legislature" not only exercising the powers of the old Continental Congress but also authorized to act "in all cases [in which] the separate States are incompetent." In addition, this new Congress was to elect the officials of a "National Executive" and a "National Judiciary." The Congress itself was to consist of two houses in which state representation would be apportioned according to either the value of taxable property or "the number of free inhabitants." Members of the first branch were to be popularly elected; members of the second branch were to be chosen by the members of the first—from slates of candidates submitted by the respective state legislatures. The principle of checks and balances was embodied in a "Council of Revision" (composed of "the Executive" and a "convenient number" of federal judges) that would be empowered to veto congressional acts.

Convention debates resulted in a U.S. Constitution that varied in important ways from this proposal. Nevertheless, the document that emerged from the Philadelphia gathering reflected the broad outlines of the Virginia Plan: a dramatically strengthened central government, a bicameral Congress with a popularly elected House of Representatives, a system of checks and balances, and a separation of legislative, executive, and judicial powers. Randolph also shaped the new fundamental law by calling for a decennial U.S. census, while agitation for a federal bill of rights by George Mason, another Virginia delegate, ultimately led to approval of the first ten amendments in 1791.

Following nine other states, Virginia ratified the Constitution on 25 June 1788, thus marking the onset of thirty-six years of unrivaled influence within the new national government. In addition to supplying four of the country's first five presidents, Virginia benefited from a massive House delegation that rose to twenty-three members after the 1810 census. Congressional floor leadership by James Madison during the 1790s and by John Randolph of Roanoke and William B. Giles in subsequent years further enhanced the Old Dominion's sway over legislative affairs. In the struggles between Federalists and Jeffersonian Republicans, Virginia's U.S. senators and representatives overwhelmingly supported the latter party.

The election of presidents from Massachusetts and Tennessee in 1824 and 1828 signaled the end of the "Virginia Dynasty," and slow population growth reduced the state's House contingent to thirteen by the 1850s. Despite these adverse trends, Virginians continued to play a pivotal role. Indeed, during the antebellum era four Virginians served as Speaker of the House: Philip P. Barbour (1821–1823), Andrew Stevenson (1827–1834), Robert M. T. Hunter (1839–1841), and John W. Jones (1843–1845). Meanwhile, Whigs and Democrats vied for control of the state. Although Democrats won most of the congressional races, Whigs in the general assembly managed to elect several U.S. senators, one of whom, John Tyler, became the nation's president in 1841.

With the outbreak of the Civil War, Virginia reluctantly voted to leave the Union on 17 April 1861. Determined to thwart this move, President Abraham Lincoln recognized antisecessionist leaders in the trans-Allegheny region as the state's legitimate government. Congress followed suit by seating newly elected senators and representatives from that area (along with a few aspirants to House membership from federally occupied locales in eastern Virginia). After creating a separate, loyalist-dominated West Virginia in 1863, however, Congress closed its doors to those who claimed to represent the Old Dominion. Not until 26 January 1870 would Virginia be officially restored to the Union.

For the next two decades, as the state's House membership dwindled to ten, Democrats and Republicans competed in bitter, emotionally charged campaigns. Attracting votes from mountaineers and newly enfranchised blacks, the Republican party enjoyed its greatest influence during the mid 1880s, when it commanded support from both of Virginia's U.S. senators and a majority of the congressional delegation. In 1888 black activist John M. Langston was elected to the House. Playing upon white fears of "Negro rule," Virginia's Democrats subsequently won landslide victories that neutralized Republican strength outside of the mountainous Ninth District (which continued to send Republican candidates to Congress until the 1920s). Elsewhere, the Democrats established a one-party system that endured, virtually unchallenged, until the middle of the twentieth century.

Deriving its power from racism, poll taxes, and courthouse cliques, the entrenched Democratic party regime left much to be desired. Nevertheless, it did produce a number of highly capable U.S. senators and representatives. Among the most prominent were Carter Glass, legislative architect of the Federal Reserve System; William A. Jones, progressive-era champion of self-government for the Philippines; Thomas S. Martin, Senate majority leader from 1916 to 1918; Harry Flood Byrd, Sr., one of the nation's foremost advocates of fiscal conservatism; and Howard W. Smith, an archreactionary whose adept manipulation of House procedures posed a formidable challenge to liberal reformers during the 1950s and early 1960s.

Meanwhile, exploiting widespread disillusionment with national Democratic policies, Virginia's Republicans began to regain the initiative. Substantial inroads in House elections from 1952 to 1980 made the Republican party competitive throughout the state. Providing additional evidence of this trend, Republicans won five of seven U.S. Senate races between 1972 and 1992.

Recent years have brought other changes as well. Indicative of growth in metropolitan areas, the 1990 census added a seat to Virginia's House delegation. In 1992 voters in the tidewater region elected the state's first black congressional representative (Robert C. Scott) in more than one hundred years, while the new Eleventh District chose Leslie L. Byrne, the first female House member in the Old Dominion's history. Traditional barriers were crumbling. Once again—as in 1787—the outlines of a more dynamic, inclusive political system were coming into view.

BIBLIOGRAPHY

Atkinson, Frank B. *The Dynamic Dominion: Realignment and the Rise of Virginia's Republican Party since 1945.* 1992.

Jordan, Daniel P. *Political Leadership in Jefferson's Virginia.* 1983.

Moger, Allen W. *Virginia: Bourbonism to Byrd, 1870–1925.* 1968.

JAMES TICE MOORE

VIRGINIA RESOLUTION. *See* Kentucky and Virginia Resolutions.

VISITORS TO CAPITOL HILL. The U.S. Senate, meeting for the first time in New York City on 6 April 1789, barred the public from attending its sessions. The senators did not regard this as being in contradiction with democratic tenets. Rather, they felt that admitting the public would interfere with the orderly and "expeditious performance" of its business and "would encourage posturing, waste time, and cost money."

Although the House of Representatives had no such prohibition against public attendance, it took the Senate five years to remove its restriction and an additional two years to provide adequate facilities for observers. Once the barriers were removed, however, the Senate never looked back, and the doors to the Capitol have remained opened to the public ever since. In 1992, 1,224,736 people took guided tours through the Capitol. Almost twice as many toured on their own.

When its first wing, known as the north wing, was completed in 1800, the Capitol was probably not the visitors' attraction it is today. The smaller national population, the difficult traveling conditions of the times, and the fact that the building was under construction undoubtedly dampened enthusiasm. On 24 August 1814, during the War of 1812, British forces burned and nearly destroyed the Capitol. By 1819 a revitalized, reconstructed Capitol evoked new interest, and visitors came in greater numbers. By 1826, when the interior of the building was completed, the Capitol had become a social mecca for the citizens of Washington. Wonderful new paintings and sculpture, newly remodeled chambers, and the emergence of great congressional orators brought an increasing number of tourists and visitors.

Tours. During this postreconstruction period, security guards were first assigned to protect the building from the curious. At times, Capitol guards unofficially acted as guides, but as the public's interest grew, outside tour services sprang up. According to testimony of Benjamin Cady, one of the original guides hired by Congress, however, these so-called guides were largely a "band of con-men and pickpockets," many of whom had invaded the Capitol's Statuary Hall, selling souvenirs and persuading tourists to take their tours.

In 1876, in the wake of criticism, Congress authorized the congressional guide service to provide tours through the Capitol. Cady was one of two guides appointed at the time. The initial authorization established a twenty-five-cent fee for adults and a fifteen-cent fee for school children. These funds, plus tips, went to the guides as compensation. By 1924 there were fourteen guides, each earning on average $2,600 annually. On 3 January 1971, Congress made guides salaried legislative employees under the auspices of the Capitol Guide Board. They can no longer accept gratuities.

Today there are thirty-three permanent guides plus an additional ten college students hired for the summer crunch. The increased number of tourists has forced guides to discontinue their tours through the two legislative chambers. Visitors can, however, attend sessions on their own by obtaining gallery passes from their senators or representatives. Foreign visitors can obtain the proper credentials for the Senate from the visitors' desk on the first floor of the Senate wing and for the House from a doorkeeper on the third-floor gallery entrance to the House chamber.

Regular tours are conducted seven days a week from the Great Rotunda, from 9:00 A.M. to 3:45 P.M. During the spring and summer months, tours leave every two to five minutes. In the late fall and winter months, tours are conducted approximately every fifteen minutes. During peak periods, tours can have as many as fifty people. The Capitol is closed on New Year's Day, Thanksgiving Day, and Christmas. Special tours for constituents of members of Congress are conducted at 8:00, 8:15, 8:30, and 8:45 each morning, seven days a week. Members' offices must arrange these tours six weeks in advance. Unlike the ordinary public tours, these tours cover the entire building, including the House and Senate chambers.

Below the Great Rotunda, in an area known as the Crypt, is the Congressional Special Services office, which provides a variety of services to congressional staff and to tourists and visitors. They include special non-tour-related tours and services, such as wheelchair loans, interpreters for the hearing impaired, assistive listening devices, braille maps, brochures, and telecommunication devices for use by the deaf (TDDs). The office is open to the public Monday through Friday, 9:00 A.M. to 4:30 P.M. Disabled visitors who wish to schedule tours or who need further information should call or write their senators or members of Congress. Phone numbers can be obtained by calling the congressional switchboard at (202) 224-3121 (voice) or (202) 224-3091 (TDD).

Restaurants. Finding a place to eat at the Capitol can be difficult when Congress is in session and during the peak tourist season. Recognizing the need for public dining rooms at the Capitol, Con-

VISITORS TO THE SENATE. Senate Reception Room in the 1800s.   *PERLEY'S REMINISCENCES*, VOL. 2

gress has provided restaurants in the House and Senate wings and snack bars in the basements. Because they are small, and in order to accommodate members, their guests, and staff, the House restaurant is closed to the public from 11 A.M. to 1:30 P.M. when the House is in session. The restaurants usually close at 2:30 P.M., except when Congress is working late. These hours and restrictions generally also apply to cafeterias located in adjacent House and Senate office buildings, except that they do not stay open during late sessions.

The Capitol snack bar on the Senate side never restricts public access, but it closes at 4:00 P.M. The snack bar on the House side is not open to the public from 11:45 A.M. to 1:15 P.M. when the House is in session, and it closes at 3:30 P.M. The House and Senate restaurants presently accept major credit cards. They are located on the first floor of the Capitol.

Parking and Dress. Parking at the Capitol is not available to tourists or other visitors. Security requirements forced the Capitol Police Board in the late 1980s to recommend prohibiting visitor parking on the east front plaza and surrounding driveways. Tourists' best options for reaching the Capitol are taxis and the Washington, D.C., subway system.

There are subway stops within a few blocks of either side of the Capitol. There is no official dress code for those visiting the Capitol. Obviously, dignified apparel is always encouraged.

Security. On 1 March 1954, four Puerto Rican nationalists, having easily penetrated a rather unsophisticated security system, fired pistols into the House chamber from a gallery behind the Speaker's dais, wounding five members. None of the five members died from his wounds, and all the assailants were captured and served long prison sentences.

This event and subsequent bombings in the Capitol in 1971 and 1983 were the catalysts for a tightening of security, leading to creation of a professional police force at the Capitol that in the 1990s numbers more than twelve hundred officers. Beginning in the early 1970s, sophisticated electronic security systems were put in place at all entrances to the Capitol and the adjacent office buildings. All entrants must pass through magnetometers. Carrying guns or other weapons in the buildings is strictly illegal. When entering either legislative chamber during a session, visitors are again required to pass through a magnetic security machine. Umbrellas, radios, cameras, packages, and so on can be stored at nearby counters.

The freedom and ease with which visitors are allowed to enter and traverse the corridors of the U.S. Capitol are quite unique among world capitals. This privilege, however, does have restrictions. Public access to the second floor is prohibited in the vicinity of either house chamber when it is in session. When Congress is not in session, the rules are somewhat less restrictive. Tourists are advised to pay attention to signs posted throughout the Capitol's corridors. The first and third floors have fewer restrictions than the second. For those on official business, special-area passes can be acquired from the visitors' desk on the first floor of each wing.

Taking pictures inside the Capitol is permitted with certain important exceptions, the most notable being inside the House and Senate chambers at any time and in the third-floor corridors. Tourists and other visitors are urged to check with a police officer when in doubt. Visitors will have no problem in the Rotunda, Statuary Hall, the first-floor corridors, the Old Senate Chamber, the Old Supreme Court Chamber, and the Crypt. A souvenir stand on the first level sells film, books, and souvenirs.

Attractions. Viewing the building's beautiful and unusual architecture makes any tour of the Capitol worthwhile, but the experience is greatly enriched by attending a congressional session in either the Senate or House chamber. The building also features a wide variety of paintings, sculptures, and artifacts. Visitors are acquainted with the panorama of American history through this art, much of it commissioned by Congress or donated by individual collectors. The Great Rotunda—a spectacular architectural achievement in its own right—is also the backdrop for some of the Capitol's most famous and dramatic works of art, including Constantino Brumidi's 4,664-square-foot fresco *The Apotheosis of Washington* in the canopy of the dome.

Other points of interest include Statuary Hall, which honors prominent figures chosen by each of the fifty states; the Senate's ornate Brumidi Corridors, where Daniel Webster, Henry Clay, and John C. Calhoun debated; and the Old Supreme Court Chamber, which has been restored and decorated largely with original furniture. A ride on the world's shortest underground railroad—the electric cars that transport members of Congress between the Capitol and nearby congressional office buildings—is popular with children and adults alike. (The public is allowed to ride along with senators and representatives except during roll calls, when subway access is restricted.)

A study to build an elaborate visitors' center beneath the east front plaza of the Capitol has been completed. Despite enthusiasm for the project, a lack of funds has delayed its construction. If it is built, it will be the organizing point for all Capitol tours and will disseminate educational material, show movies about the Capitol, exhibit historical photographs, and feature computer displays and a bookstore.

[See also Capitol, The; Capitol Hill; Capitol Historical Society; Capitol Police.]

BIBLIOGRAPHY

Aikman, Lonnelle. *We the People: The Story of the United States Capitol.* 14th ed. 1991.
Michaelson, Mike. *Exploring the Capitol: A Self-Guided Tour through the Halls of Congress.* 1992.
U.S. Senate. *The Capitol: A Pictorial History of the Capitol and of the Congress.* 9th ed. 100th Cong., 1st sess., 1983. S. Doc. 99-17.

MIKE MICHAELSON

VOCATIONAL EDUCATION ACT OF 1963

(77 Stat. 403). The Vocational Education Act of 1963 was the most important vocational education legislation since 1917. The law amended the Smith-Hughes Act of 1917 and the George-Barden Act of 1946 and authorized a new program of permanent federal assistance for vocational education. These funds were in addition to both annual appropriations under previous laws and appropriations for residential schools and work-study programs. The funds under the new act were allocated among the states on the basis of population and per capita income. Each state was required to match federal funds on a fifty-fifty basis.

The 1963 act originated in a report of the Panel of Consultants on Vocational Education appointed by President John F. Kennedy. Two principal recommendations of the panel were reflected in the act: a significant increase in the level of federal funding for vocational education and, by deletion of the categorical limitations of earlier legislation, a more inclusive definition of the kinds of occupations for which vocational education funding could be used. The panel had criticized existing programs for directing their funds into old occupational categories, such as agriculture, and giving insufficient attention to training in more technologically advanced occupations. The new funds were allotted for any program designed to embrace training in all occupations. And while the existing programs focused on assisting rural youth, the 1963 act stressed urban areas.

The act was part of a broad array of education legislation sent to Congress by the Kennedy administration. Coming shortly after Kennedy's assassination, the legislation was passed during a period of bipartisan cooperation.

BIBLIOGRAPHY

Venn, Grant. *Man, Education, and Work: Post-secondary Vocational and Technical Education.* 1964.

GARY MUCCIARONI

VOLSTEAD ACT. See National Prohibition Act.

VOTING AND SUFFRAGE.

In two centuries of government under the Constitution, suffrage in the United States has expanded from a small portion of the adult population (9 percent of adults voted in the presidential election of 1824, the first for which reasonably accurate records are available) to the point where, at the present time, the right to vote of nearly every American citizen eighteen years of age or older is guaranteed by the Constitution and federal law.

This growth was achieved through state legislation prior to the Civil War. It was subsequently further expanded and guaranteed by a series of constitutional amendments and federal laws, so that in the late twentieth century, minimum qualifications to vote in elections on all levels of government are protected and cannot be substantively abridged by the states. At the same time, with a few notable exceptions—mostly as provided by the Voting Rights Act of 1965 as subsequently amended—administration of the election process, including voter registration and management of elections, remains a state responsibility.

Suffrage in the Early Republic. Although the Declaration of Independence states that governments "derive their just powers from the consent of the governed," only a small percentage of the American people possessed the right to vote in the years following the Revolution. Voting qualifications were established by the states in constitutions and legislation adopted during and immediately after the War of Independence.

The most common requirement, almost universally prescribed, limited voting rights to free, white males twenty-one years of age or older. Only New Jersey, through an apparent oversight, extended the right to vote to "inhabitants of this Colony, of full age" rather than applying the more common gender-specific formulations of men, freemen, or male inhabitants in its revolutionary-era constitution. Under these circumstances, some women are believed to have voted regularly in New Jersey until the state constitution was later amended to restrict suffrage to "male citizen[s]."

Ownership of land or property—usually specified as a freehold to distinguish landowners from renters—of a certain value or size was also required in almost every instance. In some states, a minimum acreage—usually twenty-five or fifty acres—was required; in others, the land had to be of an established minimum value, and owners often were required to have paid taxes in order to vote. Unencumbered ownership of other property equal to or exceeding a prescribed amount provided an alternative to the freeholder requirement for men of some means who did not own land.

Although most African Americans were held in slavery at the time of the Revolution, about 8 percent were listed as free persons of color in the census of 1790. Three states (Georgia, South Carolina, and Virginia) specifically barred the members of this small group from voting, while in a fourth, Pennsylvania, the status of their voting rights was unclear.

One of the most important changes in voting requirements made by the revolutionary-era state constitutions was the elimination of restrictions based on religion. By the time of the Constitutional Convention in 1787, Catholics and Jews, who had previously been denied suffrage under colonial charters and laws, had been enfranchised in nearly every state.

It is difficult to arrive at accurate estimates of the number of people or the percentage of population of the United States eligible to vote in the early days of the Republic. Estimates range from 6 percent of the free population (William Miller, *A New History of the United States* [1958]) to about 25 percent (Dudley McGovney, *The American Suffrage Medley* [1949]). The effect of state requirements during this period was to limit suffrage to the middle and upper economic levels and to exclude not only women, African Americans, and American Indians but also most of the rural and urban poor. Although restrictions on suffrage during this period appear to have limited the number of voters, in many parts of the nation, particularly in rural areas, they were not strictly enforced. It has been estimated that as many as half of the white male population may have been able to vote in at least some places.

The Constitutional Convention. The Philadelphia Convention of 1787, despite its many achievements, made no effort to establish a uniform set of voting qualifications for the whole country, preferring to leave these arrangements in the hands of the states. Of the three branches of federal government established by the Constitution, one—the judiciary—was entirely appointive, with all judges nominated by the president and approved by the Senate. Of the three categories of federal elective officers, two, the president and vice president and the Senate, were indirectly elected. The chief executive was, and is, actually chosen by electors, who themselves are appointed by each state "in such manner as the legislature thereof may direct" (Article II, section 1, clause 2). The members of the Senate, allocated two to each state to reflect the principles of both federalism and state equality, were to be elected by state legislatures. Only the House of Representatives, conceived by the Convention as most closely reflecting the democratic principle, was intended to be elected by the largest electorate possible.

The Virginia Plan of Union, offered early in the Convention as a rough draft, specified that members of the larger house of Congress (the House of Representatives) be elected by "the people of the several states." A number of delegates favored election by the state legislatures, but their proposals were rejected in several votes. Later, a national freehold requirement, similar to those used by the states to determine eligibility to vote, was suggested, but this was also rejected by the Convention. The consensus that emerged from the debates indicated that the delegates favored the broadest possible qualifications for voters for the House of Representatives but were unwilling to infringe on existing suffrage arrangements in the states. This compromise view was reflected in the final language of the Constitution, which provides (in Article I, section 2, clause 1) that representatives are to be chosen by "the people" and that "the electors in each state shall have the qualifications requisite for electors of the most numerous branch of the state legislature."

Attaining Universal White Male Suffrage. Even as the delegates to the Philadelphia Convention worked to complete the Constitution in 1787, there was growing popular support for the idea of suffrage as a basic right of white male citizens of a free nation. Over the next half century, this view resulted in the first great expansion of the right to vote. This extension of suffrage was accomplished almost entirely on the state level.

Vermont, which entered the Union in 1791, is generally credited as the first state to guarantee the right to vote to all "freemen" in its constitution. Kentucky was admitted as a state the following year with similarly liberal provisions in its charter. Louisiana, Mississippi, Ohio, and Tennessee (admitted in 1812, 1817, 1803, and 1796, respectively) initially established payment of taxes or ownership of land as a qualification to vote, but no state entering the Union after 1817 required that its voters either own land or other property or be taxpayers.

The expansion of suffrage in the first half of the nineteenth century was influenced by several developments in American society. Among these were the desire of recently settled states and territories to attract population and the eagerness of political parties to increase their share of the vote in elections and thus win power.

Most important, however, were changing public perceptions of democratic government. In the decades following the Revolution, undemocratic colonial institutions, particularly the hierarchical structure of social class, began to evolve in an egalitarian direction. The social and political ferment of the time was perhaps epitomized in Andrew Jackson, who rose from back-country poverty to the White House. His election as chief executive in 1828 brought an end to the succession of aristocratic Virginia planters (and the two Adamses) who had dominated the presidency since 1789, and was widely celebrated as a democratic triumph for "the people." His administrations (1829–1837) in particular, and the period in general, are sometimes characterized as the Age of Jackson, or Jacksonian Democracy. Continuous immigration, the movement of the population to settle lands west of the thirteen original states, the growth of widespread land ownership, and the informality of the frontier environment promoted the view that all Americans, or at least white males, were political and social equals.

During the same period, many of the remaining restrictions on suffrage began to be lifted in the eastern states, often after bitter political struggles and social unrest. (In Rhode Island, an armed rebellion in favor of a liberalized voting requirement was threatened in 1842.) Property qualifications were generally the first to be abandoned, with this restriction persisting in North Carolina until 1856. The repeal of tax payment requirements followed in most cases, and even in the few states where these were retained, they were only a minor deterrent to white males wishing to vote. By the time of the Civil War, effective universal white male suffrage had been attained.

The voting rights of African Americans did not undergo a parallel expansion during this period. In fact, between 1792 and 1828, Delaware, Kentucky, Maryland, Connecticut, New Jersey, Tennessee, North Carolina, and Pennsylvania joined Georgia, South Carolina, and Virginia in excluding free blacks from voting. Of states entering the Union after 1800, only Maine did not specifically prohibit voting by blacks. The other New England states made no attempt to bar black voters, while New York imposed restrictive property ownership and taxpaying qualifications that applied only to blacks.

The growing numbers of Irish and German immigrants led to the imposition by some states of new limitations on suffrage aimed at the recent arrivals, particularly the requirement of literacy in English. Reacting to similar prejudices against aliens, California excluded Asians, largely Chinese, from voting on its entry into the Union in 1850.

While some eastern states erected barriers to voting aimed at immigrants, others, particularly in the Midwest and to a lesser extent in the South, sought to attract settlers by allowing noncitizens the right to vote (usually on the condition of their having made a declaration of intent to seek citizenship). In 1848, Wisconsin became the first state to enter the Union with this provision in its state constitution. A number of other states followed this practice, so that by 1875, at least twenty-two states and territories had adopted some form of voting by noncitizens.

The Civil War and After: Black Voting Deferred. In late 1860 and early 1861, eleven southern states reacted to the election of Abraham Lincoln, an opponent of the expansion of slavery, by passing ordinances of secession from the Union and establishing the Confederate States of America. Following the outbreak of armed conflict in April 1861, President Lincoln, who had previously declared that secession was illegal and unconstitutional, called for volunteers to restore the Union by force while at the same time disclaiming any interest in abolishing slavery where it already existed.

Four years of bitter civil war followed, in which federal forces, after a series of disastrous initial defeats, gradually brought the weight of superior force to bear, eventually destroying the Confederate armies and inflicting widespread devastation on the South. During the course of the struggle, northern war aims were expanded by Lincoln in his 1862 Emancipation Proclamation to include the abolition of slavery in states in rebellion, which meant, effectively, those in the Confederacy. In January 1865, Congress completed the process of emancipation by proposing the Thirteenth Amendment to the Constitution, which banned slavery everywhere in the United States. It was the first of three Civil War amendments that sought, with only limited success, to guarantee freedom and equality to African Americans. Congress followed the Thirteenth Amendment, ratified in 1865, with the Fourteenth Amendment, ratified in 1868, which defined citizens as "all persons born or naturalized in the United States. The Fifteenth Amendment, ratified in 1869, declared that "the right of citizens of the United States to vote shall not be denied or abridged by the United States or by any State on account of race, color, or previous condition of servitude."

Under the protection of federal troops that occupied the states of the former Confederacy during the decade of Reconstruction following the Civil War, African Americans were able to vote in relatively large numbers, and succeeded in electing black governors, senators, representatives, and state and local officials in the South.

As southern states were readmitted to the Union when Reconstruction ended, conservative governments dominated by whites, determined to prevent blacks from voting, came to power. Initially, white southerners relied on election fraud and intimidation to discourage black voting. The former included theft of ballots and ballot boxes, false counting of votes, sudden and unannounced movement of polling places, and other actions. Intimidation consisted of threats and sometimes physical violence, particularly by the Ku Klux Klan.

Encouraged by Supreme Court decisions that weakened the force of the Fifteenth Amendment, southern state governments also relied on a wide range of measures that, since they did not mention race, did not technically violate the amendment. These included more demanding literacy requirements, increased poll taxes, and adoption of the "grandfather clause" and "white primaries." Grandfather clauses limited the right to vote to any person eligible to vote in 1867, prior to ratification of the Fifteenth Amendment, thus excluding all blacks. White primaries, which denied blacks both membership in the Democratic party and the right to vote in Democratic primaries, were justified on the grounds that political parties were private associations of individuals. Because the Republican party had practically ceased to exist in most of the region after Reconstruction, Democratic primaries were often more important in electing public officials than the general elections themselves.

The effect of these measures, known collectively as Jim Crow laws, on black suffrage in the South was devastating; at the same time, a substantial number of poor whites were also effectively disenfranchised. After Louisiana adopted a comprehensive program of Jim Crow legislation at its 1898 constitutional convention, African American registration in that state dropped from 130,344 to 5,320, while white registration was also affected, declining by 40,000 (Neal Peirce, *The People's President*, [1968]).

The Progressive Era: State and Federal Reforms. During the last decades of the nineteenth century, there was growing concern among large segments of the American population over election abuses that had been tolerated almost from the beginning of the Republic. Crusading journalists and their political allies, known as Progressives, began to expose the corruption of political machines that routinely dominated large cities, and often entire states, and that engaged in widespread election fraud, among other abuses. Anxieties over growing immigration, particularly from central and southern Europe, contributed to these fears. Native-born Americans, largely of British stock, feared the influx of non-English-speaking immigrants; they assumed that the newcomers shared few of the then-accepted American cultural values and would be subject to manipulation by the political machines. The Progressive movement thus incorporated both reform and nativist elements. Many of the electoral reforms it championed reduced the most flagrant examples of electoral corruption, but they also tended to control and restrict suffrage by recent immigrants.

Perhaps the most important of these reforms was the adoption of the secret, or Australian, ballot, printed by election authorities, which included the names of all candidates competing for each office. The secret ballot was first instituted by Massachusetts in 1889 and gradually spread until it became a universal practice. Voice voting, commonly used in the early days of the Republic, had been largely replaced by paper ballots during the first half of the nineteenth century. Even so, in many states, voters were required to sign their ballots and ballots were printed by the parties, each with its own paper color, including only the names of the party list of candidates. One of the unintended consequences of secret ballots was the spread of split-ticket voting, in which voters could support candidates of different parties for different offices. Split-ticket voting has been subsequently cited by some observers as a contributing factor in the contemporary decline of political parties in the United States.

Another innovation of the period was the establishment of registration as a prerequisite for voting. Traditionally, particularly in rural areas, voters were generally personally known or recognized by election officials, and this recognition was regarded as sufficient qualification to vote. The emergence of large cities in the late nineteenth century made personal recognition difficult, if not impossible. Moreover, urban political machines of the same period often encouraged multiple voting at different polling places. The establishment of prior registration as a qualification to vote tended to reduce these abuses. Many states also established residency requirements at about the same time, requiring would-be voters to have lived at a certain address for a prescribed period of time, typically one or two years, in order to register to vote. While contributing to the reduction of electoral fraud, residency requirements also tended to disenfranchise recent arrivals, transients, and, in many cases, the poor.

A final element in the evolution of voting administration in the late nineteenth and early twentieth centuries was the adoption of primary elections to nominate party candidates for public office. Traditionally, nominations had remained under the control of party officials and were usually made by caucuses or party conventions. The direct primary, established as early as 1842 in Crawford County, Pennsylvania, transferred the nominating function to party members at large, who selected candidates at an election held between two and eight months prior to the general election. Primaries fall into either of two categories: closed primaries, in which only voters who have previously declared their party affiliation are allowed to vote, and only for the candidates of the party with which they have registered; and open primaries, in which all registered voters may choose among the candidates of whichever party they wish.

All of these procedures have changed and evolved over the past century, yet each continues to be an important part of the electoral structure and process in the United States.

The Seventeenth Amendment: Direct Election of Senators. On the federal level, the reforms of the Progressive era eventually resulted in the adoption of two constitutional amendments: the Seventeenth, which provided for the direct election of U.S. senators, and the Nineteenth, which greatly expanded the franchise by establishing the right of women to vote.

Although the Constitution (Article I, section 3) directed that senators be chosen by the legislatures of the states, by the late nineteenth century this practice was widely criticized on the grounds that it resulted in corruption and deadlock and that it was fundamentally undemocratic. During the last decades of the century, corporate interests and some of the very wealthy were accused of essentially bribing state legislatures in order to secure Senate seats either for their favored candidates or for themselves. Moreover, during the same period there were increasing instances of deadlocked Senate elections within the legislatures, leading to long periods of time in which seats remained vacant and states were without full representation in the Senate. These conditions tended to reinforce the assertions of political reformers that the existing system was not only corrupt but undemocratic in that it denied the voting public the right to elect members of the Senate.

While a proposed amendment providing for direct election passed the House of Representatives by the necessary two-thirds majority as early as 1894, the Senate continued to reject reform proposals for nearly two more decades. During this period, more than half the states, mostly in the West, followed the lead of Oregon to establish direct-preference primaries for Senate candidates. Under the Oregon system, the legislature was urged to elect the candidate receiving the largest number of votes in the primary election.

Throughout the first decade of the twentieth century, the Senate was the subject of persistent criticism by progressive journalists, who helped generate growing public pressure for change. At the same time, due in part to the arrival of quasi-popularly elected "Oregon System" senators, the makeup of the body itself was changing in favor of direct election. However, when the Senate finally gave serious consideration to a direct-election amendment in 1911, the legislative process in both houses of Congress was complicated and prolonged by the ultimately successful struggle to delete a "race rider" to the amendment that would have transferred control over the election process to the states. By transferring control, the race rider would have given constitutional sanction to any subsequent state legislation denying blacks or other classes of voters the right to vote for U.S. senators. The final version, which provided for popular election of senators by electors having "the qualifications requisite for electors of the most numerous branch of the State Legislature" (replicating the original constitutional language as applied to voting qualifications for representatives) was adopted by the Senate in 1911 and by the House in 1912. The ratification process for the Seventeenth Amendment was completed a year later, in 1913.

The Nineteenth Amendment: Votes for Women. The Nineteenth Amendment to the Constitution, ratified in 1920, provided the greatest single expansion of suffrage in American history by guaranteeing the right of women to vote.

With the exception of New Jersey, which between 1776 and 1807 extended suffrage to "all inhabitants worth $250" rather than only to men, women were barred from voting throughout the United States during the nineteenth century. From the earliest days of the Republic, however, some women asserted their equality as citizens and demanded the right to vote. In 1848, a convention of three hundred women's suffrage supporters, meeting in Seneca Falls, New York, adopted a Declaration of Sentiment that demanded, among other reforms, the "inalienable right to the elective franchise" for women.

The years following the Civil War saw growing agitation by women suffragists, led by Lucretia Mott, Elizabeth Cady Stanton, and Susan B. Antho-

WOMEN'S SUFFRAGE BOOKLET. An example of the literature published by organizations lobbying Congress to give women the vote.   LIBRARY OF CONGRESS

ny, among many others, for voting rights for women. In addition to their assertions of the natural equality of men and women, they also founded their arguments on the words of the Fourteenth Amendment, which guaranteed "equal protection of the laws" to all citizens and prohibited the states from passing and enforcing laws "which shall abridge the privileges or immunities of citizens of the United States." The movement organized women and their supporters through writing, lectures, and mass meetings and also engaged in direct action by having women attempt to register and vote in various places around the country. Blocked in an attempt to register in St. Louis, Missouri, Virginia L. Minor carried her case to an unsympathetic Supreme Court, which ruled in 1875 that, although women were guaranteed citizenship by the Fourteenth and Fifteenth Amendments, the amendments did not confer the right to vote without specific state action. The various elements of the suffrage movement, which united in 1890 to form the National American Woman Suffrage Association, worked for state suffrage legislation during the last decades of the century while pressing continuously for a federal constitutional amendment guaranteeing women the right to vote.

Action had already begun on the state level when Wyoming, then still a territory, extended suffrage to women in 1859. Utah followed in 1870 as did Colorado and Idaho in 1893 and 1896, respectively. Although Utah's territorial legislation incorporating women's suffrage was revoked by Congress in 1887, it was restored by the state's new constitution when it entered the Union in 1896. Opposition also grew as the movement was finally perceived by its opponents as making serious progress. Arguments as to the intellectual and emotional inferiority of women were reinforced by fears within political party organizations and among liquor interests that women would push for political reform and prohibition if allowed to vote.

The rise of the reforming spirit of progressivism provided additional impetus for the suffrage movement, which was furthered by increased organizational effectiveness within the movement itself. After a fourteen-year hiatus in favorable state action, Washington gave women the franchise in 1910, and by 1920, an additional twenty-five states had adopted some form of women's suffrage by either legislative enactment or constitutional amendment. Turning increasingly to mass actions such as open-air rallies, pickets, women poll watchers, and suffrage parades, the National Suffrage Association, the Woman's Party, and other groups mobilized growing public support.

Although the first proposed amendment extending the right to vote to women was introduced in Congress as early as 1868, four decades passed before it was brought to a vote in both houses. In 1914 and 1915, respectively, the Senate and House rejected the amendment. The suffrage movement intensified both its lobbying efforts and public demonstrations. In 1917 the 65th Congress convened with a woman, Montana representative Jeannette Rankin, among its members for the first time. In March 1917 the United States entered World War I on the side of the Allies; women began to take jobs outside the home both in unprecedented numbers and in occupations where they had never worked before. Their involvement in the war effort

"VOTES FOR OUR MOTHERS." Poster advocating suffrage for women, c. 1920.

COLLECTION OF DAVID J. AND JANICE L. FRENT

engendered additional support for the suffrage amendment.

In January 1918 the House of Representatives approved the women's suffrage amendment, but the Senate, dominated by suffrage opponents, refused to act, despite a declaration of support by President Woodrow Wilson, who, though sympathetic, had previously declined to declare his support.

The congressional elections of 1918 showed a clear trend toward support for the amendment among newly elected members of both houses, and in May 1919, it again passed the House of Representatives, this time by a comfortable margin. Despite determined opposition, the suffrage amendment passed the Senate by a close vote later that year. State ratifications followed, with the necessary three-quarters being reached in August 1920, when Tennessee became the thirty-sixth state to ratify the Nineteenth Amendment.

Voting Rights for African Americans. Throughout the first half of the twentieth century, African Americans were effectively denied the right to vote in the states of the former Confederacy and were subjected to systematic discrimination throughout much of the nation. Civil rights organizations like the National Association for the Advancement of Colored People, organized in 1910, initially directed their efforts to relieving the most egregious aspects of discrimination, such as segregation and widespread lynching, which persisted in parts of the country throughout the early decades of the century.

Following World War I, in which segregated black units had served with distinction, civil rights groups began to turn their attention to the goal of securing the right to vote. The grandfather clause, the first restriction to be banned, had been ruled unconstitutional by the Supreme Court in 1915. White primaries were the next target, although it took nearly two decades of court challenges before they were outlawed. In 1927 the Supreme Court banned white primaries established by state laws, but in 1935 it ruled that they were legal if established by party rules rather than by the states. Nine years later, the Court reversed itself when it decided that any primary restricting voting by race was unconstitutional. Despite these achievements, the remaining structures of discrimination, including intimidation, poll taxes, literacy tests, and restrictive administrative procedures still served as effective deterrents to voting by African Americans.

In the years after World War II, the civil rights movement, aided by an increasingly sympathetic climate of public opinion in much of the nation, began a successful campaign against discrimination and segregation in all aspects of American life. Following the 1954 Supreme Court decision *Brown v. Board of Education of Topeka, Kansas,* which outlawed segregation in public schools, the pace of efforts to secure both civil and voting rights for African Americans quickened.

One element of this process, the abolition of poll taxes, was incorporated as an amendment to the Constitution. During the first half of the twentieth century, a number of southern states abandoned the poll tax, largely because it restricted voting by poor whites. During the 1940s, the House of Representatives passed legislation outlawing the poll tax on seven different occasions, but the Senate re-fused to act on any of the bills. Only in 1962 did Congress propose the Twenty-fourth Amendment incorporating the prohibition, which was ratified in 1964.

The Civil Rights Acts of 1957 and 1960. In 1957, despite a declaration of "massive resistance" to desegregation by southern members of Congress, the House and Senate passed the Civil Rights Act of 1957, the first federal legislation intended to protect black voting rights since Reconstruction. The act established a Federal Commission on Civil Rights and a Civil Rights Division in the Justice Department and provided special federal district courts empowered to hear cases removed from state court jurisdiction by Justice Department action. Nonetheless, continued resistance and the slow pace of adjudication in such cases restricted the act's effectiveness. Congress responded with the Civil Rights Act of 1960, which authorized federal referees to investigate voting discrimination complaints and empowered them to register qualified voters. It also required the states to preserve voting records and empowered federal district court judges both to order registration and to replace state registrars with federal officers, if necessary.

The Voting Rights Act. The Civil Rights Acts of 1957 and 1960 shared a common characteristic in that they required individual citizens to initiate the process of complaint against voting rights abuses and relied on a time-consuming litigation process to achieve remedies. The Civil Rights Act of 1964 sought to remedy some of these deficiencies, but supporters of voting rights for African Americans successfully urged enactment of more comprehensive legislation providing administrative remedies that applied automatically in jurisdictions in which discrimination could be proved. This law, the Voting Rights Act of 1965, served as the vehicle for profound changes in American voting and suffrage. It committed the federal government to a leading role in both determining the extent of discrimination against African Americans in voting and registration and providing for registration of black voters in many parts of the South by federal registrars. Amended and extended in 1970, 1975, and 1982, it had the effect of increasing black and other minority group registration and voting to levels comparable to those of whites.

Among its many provisions, the act suspended the use of literacy tests for voting, later incorporated as a permanent prohibition by the 1975 amendments. It prohibited laws denying or abridging voting rights by reason of race or color, delayed enforcement of new voting rules or practices until federal authorities determined that their effect was not discriminatory (known as the preclearance requirement), provided federal agents to list qualified registrants and to serve as poll watchers, and empowered the attorney general to enforce the act through civil suits. It also provided a mechanism whereby local jurisdictions could be released from its provisions after satisfying certain criteria indicating that discrimination had been ended. States

Landmark Voting and Suffrage Enactments

Title	Year Enacted	Reference Number	Description

CONSTITUTIONAL AMENDMENTS

Title	Year Enacted	Reference Number	Description
Fifteenth Amendment	1870[1]	15 Stat. 346	Prohibited denial of voting rights to citizens "on account of race, color, or previous . . . servitude."
Seventeenth Amendment	1913[1]	37 Stat. 646	Provided for direct popular election of U.S. senators.
Nineteenth Amendment	1920[1]	41 Stat. 362	Prohibited denial of voting rights to citizens "on account of sex."
Twenty-third Amendment	1961[1]	75 Stat. 847-848	Extended voting rights in presidential elections to residents of the District of Columbia.
Twenty-fourth Amendment	1964[1]	76 Stat. 1259	Prohibited denial of voting rights to citizens for "failure to pay any poll tax or other tax."
Twenty-sixth Amendment	1971[1]	85 Stat. 825	Prohibited denial of voting rights to citizens "who are eighteen years of age or older."

FEDERAL LAWS

Title	Year Enacted	Reference Number	Description
Civil Rights Act of 1957, Part IV	1957	P.L. 85-315	Prohibited intimidation to discourage citizen from registering or voting; established Commission on Civil Rights and Civil Rights Division in the Justice Department; authorized U.S. attorney general to bring civil suits in cases where citizens were denied the right to vote on the basis of race or color.
Civil Rights Act of 1960, Titles III and VI	1960	P.L. 86-449	Authorized federal investigation of voting discrimination complaints and empowered U.S. district courts to order registration in cases where discrimination was evident; ordered state authorities to preserve voting records for twenty-two months and subjected them to federal inspection.
Civil Rights Act of 1964, Title I	1960	P.L. 88-372	Required that the same voter registration standards and qualifications be applied to all voters, and prohibited different standards for different groups of voters.
Voting Rights Act of 1965, as Amended	1965 1970[2] 1975[2] 1982[2]	P.L. 89-110 P.L. 91-285 P.L. 94-73 P.L. 97-205	Protected and extended voting rights of African Americans, and later American Indians, Alaska natives, Asian Americans, and Hispanics. Prohibited literacy tests; provided federal registration of voters, election observers, and federal government approval of all election law changes in covered jurisdictions; limited residence requirements for registration to thirty days or less; required registration and election information assistance to language minorities.
Uniformed and Overseas Citizens Absentee Voting Act	1986	P.L. 99-410	Required states to accept registration and voting by mail for military personnel and dependents and U.S. citizens residing abroad.
National Voter Registration Act	1993	P.L. 103-31	Extended motor voter, postcard, and agency registration for federal elections to all states beginning in 1995 and 1996.

[1]Year of ratification
[2]Year of amendment

or localities originally qualified for coverage under the act if they maintained a test or device as a condition for registration (generally defined as requirements of literacy, educational achievement, or good moral character) on any of the following dates: 1 November of 1964, 1968, or 1972; and less than 50 percent of the eligible population either was registered or had voted in presidential elections in the year cited for the test or device.

The Voting Rights Act Amendments of 1970 extended the law's provisions through 1975, broadened the original geographical coverage to include areas with substantial Hispanic and American Indian populations in which a pattern of discrimination had existed, and sought, unsuccessfully, to extend the right to vote to those eighteen years of age or older. This last provision was ruled by the Supreme Court in *Oregon v. Mitchell* (1970) to be constitutional only as it applied to federal elections, leading to the subsequent proposal and ratification of the Twenty-sixth Amendment in 1971.

Amendments passed by Congress in 1975 further extended the act. They permanently banned literacy tests, extended coverage to include language minorities (Hispanics, American Indians, Alaska natives, and Asian Americans), and required use of bilingual election materials in areas where more than 5 percent of the voting age population was of a single language minority or where the illiteracy rate in English was greater than the national rate. The amendments also provided for Census Bureau compilation of voting registration and participation data for covered areas.

The 1982 Voting Rights Act Amendments further extended preclearance requirements while allowing covered jurisdictions early release if they could demonstrate that they had met certain standards of nondiscrimination and successful promotion of minority participation. It also extended bilingual provisions through 1992 (subsequently further extended) and permitted the separate release of political subdivisions within states covered in their entirety by its provisions. The amendments also overturned a Supreme Court decision in *Mobile v. Bolden* (1980) by ruling that local election rules and practices were covered under the law if they had resulted in discrimination against minorities, whether or not that effect was intended. Finally, the amendments extended coverage through 2007, although the measure committed the Congress to reconsider the act in 1997.

The greatest effect of this legislation was to increase the rate of registration and voting by African Americans to levels more closely approximating those of the white population. In 1964, 59.2 percent of blacks reported voting, compared with a reported rate of 71.3 percent for whites, a disparity of 12.1 percent. By 1992, notwithstanding a general decline in voting participation, the gap had been reduced to 9.6 percent, with 63.6 percent for whites and 54.0 percent for blacks. In the South, the increase in black participation and officeholding was dramatic. Other minority groups showed similar, if less dramatic, growth in registration and voting.

The Twenty-sixth Amendment. Another major expansion of suffrage in the United States was provided by the Twenty-sixth Amendment to the Constitution, which extended the right to vote to citizens eighteen years of age or older. The states had traditionally set the voting age at twenty-one, although a few lowered the threshold (Georgia and Kentucky to eighteen in 1943 and 1955, respectively, Alaska to nineteen and Hawaii to twenty on their admission to the Union in 1959). During and after World War II, public support increased for a lower voting age; rising educational levels of young people, the eligibility of males for the draft at eighteen, and the assumption of legal self-responsibility at the same age were cited as explanations.

Congress considered proposals to lower the voting age as early as 1941, but despite extensive hearings, no amendment was reported from committees prior to 1971. In 1970, as noted previously, Congress attempted to lower the voting age to eighteen by statute, rather than amendment, when it incorporated language to that effect in the Voting Rights Act Amendments passed that year. The Supreme Court subsequently ruled that the legislation applied only to federal elections, and Congress responded in 1971 by approving the proposed amendment, which was ratified by the requisite number of states within four months.

Easing Barriers to Registration and Voting. For twenty years following ratification of the Twenty-sixth Amendment, the major thrust toward expansion of suffrage came in the states, many of which enacted legislation to facilitate both registration and absentee voting. As concern grew over declining rates of voter participation, these efforts drew increased congressional attention, and contributed to the eventual passage of the National Voter Registration Act of 1993, which incorporated several state innovations and applied to all federal elections.

Most common of these state programs was mail or postcard registration. Under this system, the applicant completes a registration form and mails it to the local election authority, rather than presenting himself personally in order to register. In a later variation, a number of states established agency-based, or "motor voter" registration programs, through which citizens are able either to register directly or obtain mail applications at government offices that deal directly with the public, such as motor vehicle bureaus, libraries, and local tax and public assistance agencies.

A few states (Maine, Minnesota, Wisconsin, and Wyoming) went even further, adopting election day registration. Under this program, the citizen is able to register and vote simultaneously upon presentation of some form of identification. In addition, North Dakota completely abolished voter registration: in order to vote in that state, the citizen simply presents identification at the polls. The remaining states have retained residence requirements for registrants, ranging from five to thirty days prior to general election day.

Beginning in the late 1980s, support grew for proposals to incorporate many of these state measures in federal law. Opponents cited both the potential for election fraud and corruption, and federal intervention in what had been historically a state and local responsibility, but after several unsuccessful attempts, Congress passed the National Voter Registration Act of 1993. This legislation effectively extended motor voter, postcard, and agency registration to all states beginning in 1995 or 1996, depending on state requirements. While the act applied only to federal elections, under constitutional authority to provide for the "times, places, and manner" of holding congressional elections, it was anticipated that the states would extend its provisions to all elections in the interests of administrative economy. States that had previously established more lenient voting requirements, such as election day administration, were exempted from the act.

Some aspects of election administration remained under state control: nearly all states provided for absentee voting for citizens who are disabled or temporarily absent from their voting jurisdictions on election day. Generally, an application for an absentee ballot must be filed in advance of the election itself. Early in the 1990s, several states, notably California and Texas, experimented with liberalized absentee provisions, allowing citizens to cast ballots before the general election day for the purposes of individual convenience.

The Uniformed and Overseas Citizens Absentee Voting Act, enacted by Congress in 1986, guaranteed military personnel and their dependents, sailors of the merchant marine, and citizens residing outside the United States the right to register and vote by mail in the state most recently claimed as their residence. It provided a uniform federal postcard application, valid in all the states, for this purpose.

While the National Voter Registration Act of 1993 promised to achieve major reductions in barriers to registration and voting, some support existed after its passage for additional reforms. Among these were further extension of voting rights to resident non-citizens, at least at the local level, or to citizens younger than eighteen years of age. As of 1994, however, such proposals enjoyed little support at either the state or federal level. State or federal liberalization of absentee voting procedures perhaps offered a more likely focus of further legislation to promote increased voting participation.

[See also Baker v. Carr; Civil Rights Act of 1964; Fifteenth Amendment; Nineteenth Amendment; Seventeenth Amendment; Twenty-fifth Amendment; Twenty-sixth Amendment; Voting Rights Act of 1965.]

BIBLIOGRAPHY

Chute, Marchette. The First Liberty: A History of the Right to Vote in America, 1619–1850. 1969.

Corbin, Carole. The Right to Vote. 1985.

deGrazia, Alfred. Public and Republic: Political Representation in America. 1951.

Flexner, Eleanor. Century of Struggle: The Woman's Rights Movement in the United States. 1959.

Foster, Lorn S., ed. The Voting Rights Act: Consequences and Implications. 1985.

McGovney, Dudley O. The American Suffrage Medley: The Need for a Uniform National Suffrage. 1949.

Peirce, Neal R. The People's President. The Electoral College in American History and the Direct Vote Alternative. 1968. Chap. 5, "The Right to Vote in America."

Porter, Kirk. A History of Suffrage in the United States. 1918.

Rogers, Donald W., ed. Voting and the Spirit of American Democracy: Essays on the History of Voting and Voting Rights in America. 1992.

Scott, Anne Firor, and Andrew MacKay Scott. One Half the People: The Fight for Woman Suffrage. 1975.

Williamson, Chilton. American Suffrage: From Property to Democracy, 1760–1860. 1960.

THOMAS H. NEALE

VOTING IN CONGRESS. [This entry includes three separate discussions of voting within the houses of Congress:

For discussion of the election of members to Congress and the election of the president of the United States, see Elections, Congressional; Presidential Elections. *See* Voting and Suffrage *for broad discussion of Congress's role in determining policies concerning the right to vote.*]

Voting Methods

The very essence of Congress is the mechanism by which Congress makes its collective decisions—that is, voting. By voting, Congress registers whether a sufficient number of members favor a proposed law or other matter to win its approval. Not only do the several methods of voting used in Congress have formal significance for such registration of approval, but voting methods have considerable tactical importance for affecting what is done and even whether a measure will be approved. The different procedures used by the House, the Senate, and their committees warrant separate descriptions, particularly with regard to how they affect tactics and outcomes.

House Floor. Once a bill (proposed law) or other matter has made it to the House floor, a vote on the measure may occur by one of three principal methods. The simplest of these methods is the voice vote. The chair tells the House chamber, "All those in favor say 'Aye.'" If none of the members present is in favor, silence may ensue, but more often a chorus of voices—which may range from a whisper to a roar—answers, "Aye." Then the chair instructs, "All those opposed say 'Nay,'" and an opposing chorus answers, "Nay." After hearing both, the chair states his or her opinion of the outcome, first tentatively—"The chair believes the ayes have it"—and then definitively—"The ayes have it, and the bill is adopted." The voice vote is used if no member invokes the procedure for employing either of the other methods.

The second method is the division vote, in which the chair asks those favoring a proposition to stand, counts them, and then, after they have been seated, asks those opposed to stand, and counts them as well. The chair then announces the totals on each side and the outcome. Any member of the House who wishes to have a division vote instead of a voice vote on a proposition need only ask in timely fashion, and the chair will conduct a division vote. It is more exact than a voice vote, since the chair has precise numbers for and against.

The division vote has much the same tactical effect as the voice vote, however, in that the positions of individual representatives are not recorded. Because the chamber has made no record of how each member voted, constituents cannot determine how their member voted in a voice or division vote, and opposing political candidates cannot readily make an issue of a member's decision in a voice or division vote. Usually, voice or division votes are used when a measure is not particularly controversial or important, but merely a minor amendment, or say, the final passage of a completely noncontroversial bill.

The third method, record vote, is used for important and controversial decisions. Since 1972, the House has used an electronic system for recording votes. Once the chair announces that a record vote will occur on a particular proposition, representatives come to the House floor and go to one of the ten electronic voting stations. Each member inserts his or her voting card (it looks like a credit card) and then punches the "yes" or "no" or "present" button on the voting station. Usually the House al-

RECORD VOTE. Electronic voting station in the House chamber.   WARREN LEFFLER, *U.S. NEWS & WORLD REPORT*

lows fifteen minutes for all members to come to the chamber and vote. At the end, there is not only an exact count but also a list showing how each member voted. From this exact count, the chair announces the outcome. The list of votes is publicly displayed in the House chamber and printed in the *Congressional Record*. When votes are newsworthy, they are reported by the national media. Another method for a vote uses counters, or "tellers." Each member indicates to the tellers which way he or she votes, and the tellers produce a record, which may include the names of those voting on each side. This method is rarely used and then only in the House, not the Senate.

Several different procedures are used at different legislative stages so that representatives can require that a particular vote be a record vote rather than a voice or division vote. Sometimes twenty-five members are required to support a request for a record vote. Sometimes only a single member is required. And sometimes the formal support of more than twenty-five (up to a maximum of forty-four) members is required. The Constitution, in Article I, section 5, clause 3, specifies that "the Yeas and Nays of the Members of either House on any question shall, at the Desire of one fifth of those Present, be entered on the Journal." Although the House rules do, in certain situations, allow fewer than one-fifth of the members to obtain a record vote, the House cannot and does not take away the constitutionally protected right of one-fifth to insist on a recorded yea-and-nay vote at any time when a quorum (half the body) is present. The rules concerning precisely how many members are needed for a record vote to be required are complex, but one general rule that has been in effect since the 1970s, when the rules changed, is that only twenty-five members are required to obtain a record vote on most amendments.

One stage in the House's consideration of legislation is consideration in the Committee of the Whole, a committee of all the House's members. It is at this stage that most amendments are accepted or rejected. Until 1970, no record votes could occur in the Committee of the Whole; since the 1970 rule change allowing such votes, record votes in the Committee of the Whole have become very common. In 1993, the House changed its rules to allow delegates—elected by areas outside the states, such as Puerto Rico and the District of Columbia—to vote in the Committee of the Whole. However, the rules also provided that if the delegates' votes were about to affect the outcome (for example, in a vote of 220 to 219 in which 5 of the 220 were delegates'

votes), then the vote would be followed by a vote in the House without delegates.

The ability of a mere twenty-five representatives (about 5 percent of the House membership) to require a record vote has major tactical implications. The House has many more record votes than it did before the 1970s, when obtaining record votes was more difficult. This means that on most propositions, even a small group of extreme conservatives, or extreme liberals, or members from a relatively small region of the country, or any similar bloc can obtain a record vote. Even when a large majority of House members might prefer to avoid being held accountable for their votes, a relatively small number can require a record vote, forcing the others to take stands that may be controversial and may alienate at least some of their constituents.

For example, on controversial—but unavoidable—bills to raise the debt limit by approving legally required government borrowing, a majority of the members of the House might wish not to have their votes appear on the record. They know that, for the government to function, they must approve the bill, and they know that a fraction of their constituents will nevertheless hold it against them that they voted in a way that will be depicted as favoring more borrowing. When debt-limit bills come up, however, it is often the case that a group of members, often considerably short of a majority, will insist on a record vote. Once controversial issues come to the House floor, members can rarely avoid having to register their "yea" or "nay" on their record—there for their constituents to see and their electoral opponents to use.

Senate Floor. The Senate uses nearly the same methods of voice votes and division votes, with the minor difference that the presiding officer of the Senate, after tabulating a division, announces the result without announcing the specific counts. Regarding record votes, the Senate's formal rule is that one-fifth of a quorum (which is fifty-one of the one hundred senators), meaning as few as eleven senators, can require a record vote. As an informal matter, the practice since the 1950s has been that the Senate leadership can signal for a record vote even without having eleven senators to back up the request, and usually, as part of Senate courtesy, the Senate leadership will give that signal for any senator who asks.

Because this could subject senators to record votes on so many controversial propositions, the ease of obtaining a record vote has led since the 1950s to the increased popularity of a particular

Senate procedure: the motion to table. Before a proposition comes to a vote, senators may move to table it, and if a majority votes "aye" on the motion to table, it is tabled, meaning that it is defeated. It never comes to a vote. While the tabling vote is a record vote of sorts, it is a procedural vote, and Senators can—and do—use the explanation that they voted for the motion to table for procedural reasons, such as to avoid spending time on a matter when their party leader said it was urgent to take up something else. How a senator votes on a motion to table is much less clear a record of his or her view on the merits of the underlying proposition and hence much less of a basis for controversy among constituents than a vote squarely for or against a proposition.

Senate voting differs from that in the House in another way that makes a major practical difference. For a significant number of Senate votes, the outcome depends not on whether a majority votes in favor but on whether a "super" majority, such as sixty out of the hundred Senators, votes in favor. For example, since 1975, it has taken sixty votes for the Senate to invoke cloture to stop a filibuster. Pursuant to the successive tightenings of budget procedure in 1985 and 1987, it takes sixty votes for the Senate to waive one of the budget rules. Tactically, this makes an enormous difference. For example, during the many Congresses when the majority party has fewer than sixty senators, it can never invoke cloture to cut off debate on an issue that pits one united party completely against the other united party. House voting rarely requires supermajorities except on those propositions, such as overcoming a president's veto or approving a constitutional amendment, for which the Constitution itself requires such a vote by both chambers. This is one of the differences that guarantees the minority party in the Senate a more potent role than that played by the minority party in the House.

If a tie vote occurs in the Senate, the Constitution provides (in Article I, section 3, clause 4) that the vice president can vote to break the tie. In the House, the Speaker, by custom, usually does not exercise his vote, but one of the occasions when he sometimes does is when his vote will break a tie.

Committees. As on the House and Senate floors, in committees members may take voice votes, division votes, or record votes. On the floor, however, only representatives or senators actually present in the chamber can vote whereas, in committee, members who are absent can nevertheless vote on some matters by proxy. When a committee member wish-

es to vote by proxy, he or she must give written authorization to some member who will be present to vote for him or her as instructed. Most often, the committee chair has proxies from absent members of the majority party, and these guarantee victory on many questions. Both the House and Senate have adopted rules requiring specificity in the subject for which any particular proxy is given and limiting when they can be used.

BIBLIOGRAPHY

Oleszek, Walter J. *Congressional Procedures and the Policy Process.* 1989.

Smith, Steven S. *Call to Order: Floor Politics in the House and Senate.* 1989.

Tiefer, Charles. *Congressional Practice and Procedure.* 1989.

CHARLES TIEFER

Voting Analysis

Congressional members' voting in the two chambers has probably received more attention from scholars and journalists than any other aspect of legislative politics. Committee and floor votes are core "events" reported by the media. Newspapers, especially those with more than a local readership, routinely publish individual legislators' votes on major legislation. In congressional scholarship, the study of voting decisions and patterns dates from Abbot Lawrence Lowell's turn-of-the-century research on the congressional parties' voting to the wide-ranging research agenda of the 1990s.

The sustained attention that voting has generated is a function of several factors. First, voting is fundamental to legislative policy-making. The basic connection between legislative voting and legislative policy-making is strengthened in the Constitution's institutional framework of separation of powers. In contrast to parliamentary systems, where votes in the legislature may be mere confirmation or rubber-stamping of executive-branch policy proposals, the U.S. system's separation of powers means such pro forma confirmation is the exception rather than the rule. The institutional power of Congress is firmly linked to its institutional independence, and this independence is rooted in Congress's ability to propose, transform, and nullify policy, all of which result from the act of collective voting.

Another important factor in focusing attention on voting was the shift in political science during the 1950s away from the discipline's legalistic and normative traditions and toward a behavioral orientation. As in other disciplines, the effect of the behavioral revolution in political science in general and legislative studies in particular was to open whole new sets of research questions and to heighten sensitivity to the value of empirical study. Thus the focus shifted away from questions about how the legislature should operate and toward questions about how the legislature does operate. The study of voting was integral to many of the questions that most intrigued students of legislatures. These questions concerned the nature of representation; the relationship between constituents and their legislators; how legislators arrive at their voting decisions; the sources and extent of presidential influence in Congress; and the strength of congressional parties, factions, and coalitions, among other topics.

Third, the availability of data also helped revolutionize the study of Congress. Unlike many aspects of congressional politics, official voting records are accessible and amenable to empirical and statistical analysis. Certainly, the impact of behavioralism on the study of legislative voting was partly a function of the greater availability of voting records, but the behavioral agenda itself encouraged systematic collection and distribution of these records to the scholarly community. Thus, even in the postbehavioralist era, which began in the mid 1970s, voting records remain a central resource in the examination of unresolved research questions.

Thus the study of voting in Congress can be linked to (1) the centrality of voting in the U.S. legislative process, (2) the stimulus provided by the behavioral revolution and the theoretical and empirical breadth it inspired in research, and (3) the accessibility of voting records. As an object of research, congressional voting is unsurpassed in its connection to numerous compelling issues in legislative studies and in the study of American politics more generally.

Voting and the Legislative Process. If the kinds of voting in Congress were limited to those prescribed by the Constitution, a procedural description of congressional voting would be simple and straightforward. In Article I, the Constitution identifies two basic types of votes. One is the vote of a simple majority, necessary in both chambers before a bill can be presented to the president. The second is the vote of a two-thirds majority, necessary in both chambers for Congress to override a presidential veto of legislation and in the Senate alone to ratify treaties.

The importance of voting in Congress is not, however, limited to these constitutional prescrip-

tions. For example, one of the most publicized types of vote, whose origin lies not in the Constitution but in the rules governing the Senate, is the cloture vote, which ends extended debate (that is, stops a filibuster).

In general, voting on important legislation occurs in both chambers at several main stages in the legislative process. The first stage occurs when legislation is considered in subcommittee and full committee, where approval requires a majority vote. Most legislation introduced in Congress dies before reaching the chamber floor, having failed to generate majority support in committee or subcommittee. Proxy voting, in which legislators may cast a vote for an absent colleague, is permitted in committee and subcommittee sessions (but prohibited on the House or Senate floor). Since the practice of referring legislation to more than one committee in each chamber began in the mid 1970s, voting at the committee stage may occur in multiple committees. Used infrequently in the Senate, multiple referral occurs on virtually all major legislation in the House. For a bill to reach the floor, all committees to which the bill has been referred must report it.

The second stage in which legislation is considered on the floor is governed by a different set of rules in each chamber. The House employs several procedures for bringing legislation to the floor. One is the use of calendars, which differentiates legislation by calendar and enables the House to dispose of private or noncontroversial legislation on designated days. For example, items on the Consent Calendar are considered on the first and third Mondays of the month. A second is suspension of the rules, which requires a two-thirds majority vote; in this case, the vote is tantamount to a vote on the bill or resolution in question. Another is the provision of privileges, which expedites floor access for certain types of legislation, such as revenue-raising bills. A final procedure is the use of special rules issued by the Rules Committee. Such rules specify for a particular piece of legislation the terms of debate and the extent to which the bill can be amended. If granted, the rule is then approved or disapproved by majority vote. If approved, the bill and amendments to it are first considered in Committee of the Whole, which is a reorganization of the House into a forum designed to hasten floor action. Most serious efforts to amend legislation begin in the Committee of the Whole and, usually, only amendments that are approved in this forum can be considered later by the full House. When voting on all amendments is concluded, the Committee of the Whole dissolves and the membership votes on the bill as well as any amendments approved by majority vote in Committee of the Whole.

In the Senate, major legislation is usually considered under unanimous consent agreements, which basically amend the rules that would normally govern consideration of a bill on the floor. As the name implies, a unanimous consent agreement signifies unanimity on the amended rules, even though no formal vote is taken. (Such agreements are negotiated among party leaders and key senators.) Probably the consent agreement's most important role is to exclude nongermane amendments and to restrict debate. In the absence of a unanimous consent agreement, it is more likely that a greater number of amendments will be voted on, and the potential for filibuster is heightened. As in the House, the last important step in the "floor" stage in the Senate is the final vote on the bill by the entire membership.

Unless a bill is passed in identical form in the Senate and the House (which is uncommon), it is referred to a conference committee whose membership is composed of key senators and representatives and whose charge is to reconcile differences between the bills passed by the two chambers. Frequently, reconciliation occurs informally, but most major legislation requires conference committee action. Conferees are limited to considering only the points of dispute between the chambers. Once agreement is reached in conference, a bill must be approved by majority vote in both chambers for it to be considered by the president.

The fact that voting is integral to each stage of the legislative process has several implications for the connection between voting and congressional policy-making. First, it is important to see that congressional policy-making is better characterized as a majorities-building process than a majority-building process. Policy-making is never just a function of simple majority support. Rather, majorities must be constructed at different stages of the legislative process. Another related implication is that legislative procedures, perhaps especially those regarding voting, have an impact on policy. The requirement that the House's Committee of the Whole approve amendments before their consideration by the full House is but one example of this. Yet another implication is that members of Congress have incentives to exploit this necessity of constructing multiple majorities. Because of the majorities-building process, there are multiple opportunities to change or kill legislation; support at one stage is no guarantee of support at another.

Not only are there multiple stages (and multiple votes) in the legislative process, there are different kinds of votes. Both the House and the Senate have voice, standing (or division), and record (or roll-call) votes. Voice votes are decided merely by the volume of the yeas or nays. Members may also request a standing vote, where a head count is taken of yeas and nays. The record vote is a roll call of the membership, where individuals' votes are recorded for public record. Most of the time, final passage of a bill is by record vote. Until 1971, the House also employed teller voting in the Committee of the Whole, a practice in which members indicated to one of two tellers whether they supported or opposed the amendment in question. In 1970, amid a controversy over the secretive nature of teller voting, the House amended its rules to provide for record teller voting in the Committee of the Whole if requested by some of the membership. The amended rule took effect in 1971.

Virtually all research on congressional voting has examined record votes only. Their attractiveness stems mainly from the fact that by connecting individual legislators to their vote, the importance of a variety of other characteristics of the legislator to his or her voting decision can be examined. The voting behavior of parties and coalitions can also be analyzed by looking at record votes.

Individual Decision Making. One of the most important areas of research on congressional voting concerns the question of why members of Congress vote the way they do. During the 1950s, analysts were primarily interested in the relative impact of a member's party and constituency on his or her voting decision. In *Party and Constituency: Pressures on Congress* (1951), Julius Turner showed that members split along party lines more frequently than along constituency lines but that constituency characteristics were related to members' party loyalty. His findings inspired a variety of studies that sought to specify the relationship among individual members' voting decisions, constituency characteristics, electoral margins, and party loyalty. These efforts produced a variety of findings that together suggested that the impact of party and constituency varied between Democrats and Republicans, across issue areas and over time.

Two decades later, researchers began to reexamine the impact of constituency concerns on legislative voting, but this time the orientation of the research was more explicitly tied to assessing the quality of representation rather than party and constituency "pressures" per se. As did the earlier research, these studies primarily examined the influence on voting decisions of factors outside the legislative environment—factors such as constituency opinion, presidential influence, and electoral margins. Most recently, the study of constituency influence has been conducted within the framework of principal-agent relationships. This kind of research explores the degree to which legislators (agents) depart from the instructions of their constituents (principals), a practice researchers call "shirking" and that is motivated by the agent's own policy preferences or ideology.

Complementing this body of research on voting and representation were several new models of individual decision making. These included John Kingdon's "consensus" model, presented in his book *Congressmen's Voting Decisions* (1973), according to which legislators' decisions result from their search for consensus among a variety of actors. Donald Matthews and James Stimson, in *Yeas and Nays* (1975), proposed a "cue-taking" model in which legislators develop hierarchies of cue-givers who inform their decisions. In *Representatives and Roll Calls* (1969), Cleo Cherryholmes and Michael Shapiro put forward a "predisposition-communication" model in which voting decisions are determined by legislators' predispositions combined with their interactions with other legislative actors, and, in *How Congressmen Decide* (1973), Aage Clausen constructed a "policy-dimension" model in which legislators refer to different actors and considerations in different issue areas. In Herbert B. Asher and Herbert F. Weisberg's "voting history" model, members develop voting histories in broad policy areas, and in Morris Fiorina's "electoral incentive" model, presented in *Representatives, Roll Calls, and Constituencies* (1974), the quest for reelection dictates which groups of a member's constituency have an impact on particular votes.

In contrast to studies that examine voting in the context of party or constituency pressure, most of these models make claims about the effect of Congress's internal environment on members' voting decisions. These internal factors identified by researchers include the fact that legislators face too many decisions (that is, that they suffer "decision overload"), that they routinely operate under conditions of inadequate information and uncertainty, and that they independently form ideology or policy preferences that compete with, if they do not actually displace, other factors affecting their votes. The models differ on a number of key points. For example, the importance of constituency opinion is conditional on policy area in the policy dimensional model, whereas in the consensus model constituency opinion's weight depends on whether and how much controversy exists in the legislative arena. Similarly, policy areas make a difference in how much influence different actors have in the policy dimensional model but not in the cue-taking model.

In sum, the study of individual decision making has been a major focus in legislative voting research since the mid-twentieth century. This research has collectively produced a variety of findings and has raised a variety of questions. Among the unresolved issues are whether and under what conditions the extralegislative environment becomes the legislator's primary referent, the degree to which legislators' own policy predispositions overshadow other actors' influence, and whether legislators' decision making rules of thumb are universal.

Party Voting and Coalitions. The second major area of research on legislative voting concerns the analysis of voting cleavages and alignments. Traditionally, interest has focused on party behavior—that is, on assessing the degree of importance that party strength or weakness has on congressional voting. Party strength is measured in terms of the parties' internal cohesion and the incidence of party conflict. The coincidence of high intraparty cohesion and high interparty conflict on votes has been interpreted to signal that the legislative parties are at peak significance; at such times, U.S. congressional parties best approximate their counterparts in parliamentary systems, where party discipline is conventionally much stronger.

Research on the parties' voting behavior over time and across different policy areas has linked party polarization in Congress with the passage of major innovations in public policy. While policy innovation is theoretically possible in Congress even in the absence of united and opposed legislative parties, it is characteristic of periods of political realignment, where, as David Brady has shown in *Critical Elections and Congressional Policy Making* (1988), the electorate sends a united majority party to Congress that is able to pass its program over the united opposition of the minority party.

Political realignments have, however, been relatively infrequent in U.S. political history, and the levels of partisanship with which they are associated hardly typify party voting behavior in Congress. Rather, the congressional parties' voting behavior is more stereotypically associated with dissension and defection from party ranks and with consensus between the parties. Instead of exemplifying intense partisanship, congressional voting cleavages more often show multiple factions and coalitions that cut across party lines.

One of the most widely noted of such coalitions was the conservative coalition, an alliance of Republicans and southern Democrats who for several decades joined to obstruct labor and civil rights legislation in the Senate and, less visibly, the House. Clausen's *How Congressmen Decide* and Barbara Sinclair's *Congressional Realignment* (1982) have illustrated the development and importance of different coalitions in different policy areas in the post–New Deal period and, conversely, the limited degree to which strong partisan conflict characterizes congressional voting.

Later empirical research has expanded the discussion about the relative importance of party strength versus coalition strength in legislative voting. Until the 1980s, partisan conflict in congressional voting had erratically declined since the turn of the century; limited upswings were apparent during the 1930s and again, more briefly and more weakly, during the 1960s. Collie's research suggests that declining partisanship in voting after the New Deal period was associated with increasing factionalism and universalistic voting; as partisan polarization declined, coalitions became ever more fluid and issue-specific at the same time that universalism, or near-unanimous voting, became more commonplace. Research by Keith Poole and Steven R. Daniels, in contrast, has concluded that a single, ideological alignment that transcends party lines and overshadows individual coalitions and factions had by the 1980s predominated for several decades.

In the 1980s, congressional voting defied expectations. Scholars had traditionally explained partisan polarization in Congress in terms of partisan polarization in the electorate, the relationship between the two being at the heart of theories of partisan realignment. During the 1980s, partisan polarization in congressional voting increased to a level that rivaled the first years of the New Deal. But, unlike the 1930s, the connection between partisanship in Congress and partisanship in the electorate appeared loose at best, as the electorate in the 1980s became increasingly detached from parties and from politics as a whole.

When these findings are juxtaposed with earlier research, congressional voting patterns show themselves to be more complex than had been thought. The reasons for cleavages and alignments cannot be adequately or accurately captured by investigations, say, of party voting or crosscutting coalitions. To date, researchers have not attempted to account for congressional voting cleavages and alignments by methods that integrate or reconcile the influence of ideology with growing or waning partisanship, nor have they shown how and why partisanship displaces, or is displaced by, crosscutting coalitions.

BIBLIOGRAPHY

Asher, Herbert B., and Herbert F. Weisberg. "Voting Change in Congress: Some Dynamic Perspectives on an Evolutionary Process." *American Journal of Political Science* 22 (1978): 391–425.

Collie, Melissa P. "Legislative Voting Behavior." In *Handbook of Legislative Research*. Edited by Gerhard Loewenberg, Samuel C. Patterson, and Malcolm E. Jewell. 1985.

Collie, Melissa P. "The Rise of Coalition Politics: Voting in the U.S. House, 1933–1980." *Legislative Studies Quarterly* 13 (1988): 321–342.

Collie, Melissa P. "Universalism and the Parties in the U.S. House of Representatives, 1921–1980." *American Journal of Political Science* 32 (1988): 865–883.

Jewell, Malcolm E. "Legislators and Constituents in the Representatives Process." In *Handbook of Legislative Research*. Edited by Gerhard Loewenberg, Samuel C. Patterson, and Malcolm E. Jewell. 1985.

Oleszek, Walter J. *Congressional Procedures and the Policy Process*. 3d ed. 1989.

Poole, Keith, and Steven R. Daniels. "Ideology, Party, and Voting in the U.S. Congress, 1959–80." *American Political Science Review* 79 (1985): 373–399.

MELISSA P. COLLIE

Ratings by Interest Groups

During the late 1940s, interest groups began the now familiar practice of rating congressional voting records on a yearly basis. For twenty-five years, ratings were the domain of a few principal groups. Today, dozens of interest groups organized around a wide range of issues and interests, from agriculture to zero population growth, select a few votes on issues important to them from the hundreds of roll-call votes that members cast on the floor of the House and Senate each year. These report cards, as they are sometimes called, are compiled by each group on the basis of a few votes (typically 12 to 25) and are widely distributed. A numeric value (from 0 to 100) indicates the percentage on which each member voted in agreement with the group's position. As such, ratings have become important tools in lobbying and political organizing.

Annual ratings began in 1947, when a group of liberal Democrats formed the Americans for Democratic Action (ADA) and issued its gauge of members' "liberal quotient." In 1958, Americans for Constitutional Action (ACA), founded as a conservative counterforce, began its ratings. Another conservative group, the American Conservative Union (ACU), was organized in 1964 and began its annual ratings in 1971. Since then, the ratings produced by these three ideological groups have become tools for measuring the liberal or conservative leanings of members of Congress.

A few other groups, including some organized around agriculture, labor, and business interests, were also pioneers in the ratings movement: the National Farmers Union (NFU), which first issued ratings in 1919 and began issuing annual scores in 1948; the American Federation of Labor and the Congress of Industrial Organizations (AFL-CIO) and its political arm, the Committee on Political Education (COPE), which began issuing ratings in 1956; and the Chamber of Commerce of the United States (CCUS), which began publishing voting reports in 1966 but did not calculate numeric "scores" in its reports until 1971. (Congressional Quarterly has published some of the ratings of these and other groups since 1960.)

Most of the early ratings were calculated and reported by a few multi-issue groups, but the number of groups that rate members has greatly increased, reflecting the number and various types of interest groups with competing constituencies, differing perspectives, and opposing views that have sought to identify their friends and foes in Congress.

Interest groups added a new dimension to their ratings during the 1970s, when Environmental Action launched its "Dirty Dozen" campaign to unseat twelve members of Congress, because of their low ratings in the group's tallies and their perceived electoral vulnerability. The campaign was a prototype for other groups, which launched similar attention-getting campaigns for and against their own high and low scorers.

The 1970s also marked the emergence of public interest groups such as Common Cause and Public Citizen's Congress Watch. The former rates members on government reform, operations, and ethics while the latter concentrates on consumer, environmental, and social issues. Several single-issue interest groups (e.g., antiabortion and gun control groups) and political action committees (PACs) also began rating members' voting records.

By 1980, more than seventy national groups, as well as numerous state and local interest groups, were issuing ratings (Keller, 1981). Ratings had become a familiar facet of interest-group politics, and their proliferation, high visibility, and wide distribution gave rise to a debate on their use and value.

Criticism of ratings frequently focuses on the in-terest group's subjectivity in defining and identifying crucial issues, in selecting votes, and in analyzing both the substance and the context of any given vote. Ratings simply indicate whether a member has voted for or against a bill or resolution without explaining the reasons for a vote, which are sometimes more revealing than the "yea" or "nay" cast. For example, the "correct vote" according to two ideological counterparts—the ADA and ACU—on the budget summit resolution for fiscal year 1991 (H. Con. Res. 130) did not reflect the fact that both groups opposed adoption of the resolution, but for different reasons. ADA's opposition was based on the budget resolution's proposed cuts in Medicare and other programs as well as the burden of additional taxes on low- and middle-income taxpayers; ACU's opposition was based on the measure's reliance on new taxes (Congressional Quarterly Weekly Report, 30 March 1991, p. 788).

Ratings may vary among groups and even within the same group over time, and the results may misrepresent a member's stance on a given issue or set of issues. This can occur because of the different criteria used to select votes, different formulas used to tabulate scores (e.g., weighting all votes equally or not), different methods used to compile scores (e.g., whether to count missed votes), and changes in ideological perceptions and concepts.

Ratings have also been criticized because they serve only as a limited snapshot of a member's congressional performance; they do not reflect members' work on committees and subcommittees, where crucial votes occur; and they may distort a member's overall position on an issue by reflecting only a very small part of the totality of his or her efforts, particularly given the relatively small number of votes that most groups use for their ratings.

Interest groups use ratings to attract attention to the issues of concern to them. Moreover, they use ratings to decide which incumbents to endorse or oppose and how vigorously to do so. Endorsements can result in campaign support (e.g., monetary contributions, campaign workers, mailing lists, publicity). Voters may use ratings to help them judge where members stand on issues and whether members are in tune with voters' philosophical and legislative goals. Political observers may use ratings as shortcuts to analyze ideological, party, and regional voting patterns and trends. Indeed, group ratings have become so prominent a feature in Washington, D.C., that the raters have come to be rated themselves, in terms of the frequency with which their positions prevail in Congress.

Ratings cannot substitute for a thorough review of a member's entire voting record, but they can serve as a convenient shortcut through the myriad of legislative votes, as depicted by admittedly biased sources. Their inherent limitations notwithstanding, ratings have some value if used carefully and with knowledge of the rating group and its philosophy, the criteria for selecting issues and votes, and the methods used to compile scores.

[*See also* Interest Groups; Lobbying.]

BIBLIOGRAPHY

Congressional Quarterly Inc. *Congressional Quarterly's Guide to Congress.* 4th ed. Edited by Mary Cohn. Pp. 577–597.

Fowler, Linda. "How Interest Groups Select Issues for Rating Voting Records of Members of Congress." *Legislative Studies Quarterly* 7 (1982): 401–413.

Hrebenar, Ronald J., and Ruth K. Scott. *Interest Group Politics in America.* 1990. Pp. 147–153.

Keller, Bill. "Congressional Rating Game Is Hard to Win." *Congressional Quarterly Weekly Report,* 21 March 1981, 507–512.

SULA DYSON RICHARDSON

VOTING RIGHTS ACT OF 1965 (79 Stat.
437–446). The 1965 Voting Rights Act fully enfranchised southern blacks, thereby fulfilling the promise of the Fifteenth Amendment. Earlier civil rights statutes, federally initiated litigation, and local marches and registration drives costing money and lives had all failed to have any significant effect. In the mid 1960s fraudulent literacy tests, intimidation, and violence still kept most southern blacks from the polls.

Overt, violent resistance, though, was the white South's fatal error. In March 1965, an outraged nation watched Selma, Alabama, police assault blacks and whites marching to secure the right of citizens to vote. Eight days later President Lyndon Johnson went to Congress and in a nationally televised speech urged new legislation. On 6 August he signed the Voting Rights Act into law.

The act had one simple aim: guaranteeing the right to vote, the most fundamental attribute of citizenship. A simple statistical rule of thumb identified voting rights violations. A state or county that had employed a literacy test in November 1964, and in which less than half the total voting-age population had cast ballots, was assumed to have engaged in electoral discrimination, with the burden on the jurisdiction to prove otherwise.

From the inferred presence of Fifteenth Amendment violations, several consequences followed. In "covered" jurisdictions, literacy tests were suspended. Federal registrars (examiners) and election observers could be dispatched to those areas when necessary. Moreover, those states and counties could institute no new voting practice without approval (preclearance) by the attorney general or the District Court for the District of Columbia. Southern states could not invent new devices that robbed blacks of their basic right to a ballot.

The act was a mixture of permanent and temporary provisions. Those sections that banned literacy tests and conferred extraordinary power on federal authorities to override traditional state prerogatives had an expected life of only five years. Nevertheless, members of Congress on both sides of the aisle objected to their unprecedented stringency. Most Republican members of the House Judiciary Committee complained of an "indiscriminate" statistical test that would engulf counties innocent of discrimination in a "tidal wave of Federal control of the election process." Southern Democrats saw the ghost of Reconstruction. The drastic, temporary provisions of the act applied to six southern states in their entirety, a seventh in substantial part, and only scattered counties elsewhere. This was punitive legislation aimed at the South, Sen. Samuel J. Ervin, Jr. (D-N.C.), and others complained; Virginia representative William M. Tuck called it a "studied insult" to the region's honorable people.

Such charges, however, were not persuasive. The act was indeed a harsh and blunt instrument, but the South, with its hands dirty on questions of race, was in no position to protest its passage. By a margin of 70 to 30 a filibuster was easily beaten in the Senate, which then went on to pass the bill 79 to 18. In the House the vote was 328 to 74.

The emergency temporary provisions of the act were extended and strengthened by amendments in 1970, 1975, and 1982 (when the act's provisions were renewed for twenty-five more years). Blacks had quickly gained access to the polls, yet with black enfranchisement came new congressional efforts to protect against disfranchisement. As the emergency subsided, the emergency powers expanded.

Thus in 1970, with blacks throughout the South registering and voting, Congress renewed the special provisions for five years; imposed a five-year, nationwide ban on literacy tests; and extended the preclearance and other emergency provisions to a wide variety of nonsouthern states and counties in which voter turnout had dropped below 50 percent in 1968. Many of these states and counties had no history of electoral discrimination remotely comparable to that of the South in 1965.

The changes in 1975 permanently banned all literacy tests, redefined such tests to include English-only ballots (where more than 5 percent of the voting-age population were members of a single "language minority" group), further extended the geographical reach of preclearance, and brought under coverage four additional groups: Hispanics, Asian Americans, American Indians, and Alaskan natives. In 1982 the statute was altered to give minority voters greatly increased leverage in challenging districting plans and other electoral arrangements all across the nation. A radically altered provision now allowed plaintiffs to file suits against districting plans, city-wide voting, and other electoral practices, the "results" of which were discriminatory. In theory, the concern was with blocked electoral opportunity; in practice, the level of minority officeholding became the standard against which impact was routinely measured.

In neither 1975 nor 1982 was there serious, sustained congressional opposition to the proposed amendments, in part because civil rights lobbyists skillfully minimized the revolution in southern black politics and painted a picture of ever more subtle disfranchisement. Thus, members of Congress tempted to question the necessity for more voting rights protection were forced to defend themselves against anti–civil rights charges. Given the glare of publicity under which all business was conducted and the power of the highly organized, well-funded civil rights community, few were willing to take that political risk.

The Voting Rights Act and its amendments raise basic issues about the meaning of the right to vote that Congress never tackled. For instance, when do black ballots "count"? Do majority-white districts in which blacks also live disfranchise black voters? To how much protection from white competition are black and Hispanic candidates entitled? Congressional reluctance to debate these issues in effect encouraged further amendment through the process of administrative and judicial enforcement. By 1993 the statute bore little resemblance to the initial and amended legislation Congress had approved in 1965.

BIBLIOGRAPHY

Grofman, Bernard, and Chandler Davidson, eds. *Controversies in Minority Voting: The Voting Rights Act in Perspective.* 1992.

Thernstrom, Abigail M. *Whose Votes Count? Affirmative Action and Minority Voting Rights.* 1987.

ABIGAIL THERNSTROM

W

WADE, BENJAMIN F. (1800–1878), Whig and Republican senator from Ohio, leader of Civil War radicals. Benjamin Franklin Wade was reared in poverty near Springfield, Massachusetts. He moved to Andover, Ohio, in 1821 and worked as a farmer, laborer on the Erie Canal, medical student, and grammar school teacher before being admitted to the Ohio bar in 1828.

Wade was elected to the Ohio senate in 1837 and soon identified himself with the Free-Soil movement. His reelection bid in 1839 was unsuccessful due to his opposition to a stringent Ohio fugitive slave law. Appointed presiding judge for the third judicial circuit in 1847, he gained statewide popularity for his vigorous decisions on the bench. He was elected to the U.S. Senate by the Whig party in 1851. Wade switched his party affiliation to Republican in 1856.

Blunt, tempestuous, frequently intransigent, Senator Wade was nicknamed Bluff because of his predilection to challenge proslavery senators to duels. In 1858, he vowed to defend any abolitionist senator by personally "carry[ing] the quarrel to the coffin." His advocacy of emancipation was not his only concern: He supported measures to help farmers, laborers, and students as well.

When the Civil War began, Bluff Wade pressed the Lincoln administration to defeat the South quickly and decisively. A vituperative antagonist of Gen. George B. McClellan, Wade demanded that the president remove the cautious commander of the Army of the Potomac. He helped to organize the Joint Committee on Conduct of the War, which challenged the patriotism and loyalty of anyone opposed to its methodology or purpose. As chairman of this partisan group, Wade worked diligently with Secretary of War Edwin M. Stanton and often against President Abraham Lincoln. Wade was incensed when Lincoln proposed a lenient policy of postwar reconstruction of the South. To counteract it, he joined with Rep. Henry Winter Davis of Maryland to formulate a harsher congressional alterna-

BENJAMIN F. WADE.   *PERLEY'S REMINISCENCES*, VOL. 2

tive. When Lincoln pocket vetoed the Wade-Davis bill, the two lambasted the president for "executive usurpation" of congressional authority to settle postwar conflicts. This effort to force Lincoln to reconsider his position backfired and aroused widespread disapproval of Wade among his constituency. Ultimately he supported Lincoln's renomination, but continued to characterize the president's formula for reconstruction as "absurd, monarchical, and anti-American."

Lincoln's assassination ushered in the Andrew Johnson administration, and Wade initially hailed the change but soon turned against the new president when it became clear that Johnson had turned to a prowhite reconstruction policy.

On 2 March 1867 Wade became president pro tempore of the Senate. This ploy by the Radical Republicans to place one of their members into the number two position behind Johnson ultimately hurt their chance of ousting the president. After impeaching Johnson for violating the Tenure of Office Act of 1867, the Senate tried the president on 30 March 1868. However, Wade's potential elevation to the presidency was cause for concern among moderate Republicans, and in part assured Johnson's presidential survival. Wade had generated too many enemies and spoken too harshly to be a viable candidate. He retired from the Senate in 1869 and resumed his Ohio law practice.

BIBLIOGRAPHY

Hyman, Harold M. *The Radical Republicans and Reconstruction, 1861–1870.* 1967.

Trefousse, H. L. *Benjamin Franklin Wade: Radical Republican from Ohio.* 1963.

DANIEL PATRICK BROWN

WAGNER, ROBERT F. (1877–1953), Democratic senator from New York, chairman of the Banking and Currency Committee, and champion of liberal social programs. Robert Ferdinand Wagner was born in Germany and emigrated with his parents to the United States in 1885. He graduated from the College of the City of New York and New York Law School. In 1908 he was elected to the New York Senate, where he became floor leader in 1913 and remained until 1918. In 1919 he was elevated to the New York State Supreme Court.

In 1926 Wagner was elected to the U.S. Senate, defeating James W. Wadsworth, Jr., the Republican incumbent. He was reelected in 1932, 1938, and 1944. Rising in seniority in the Senate, he became

ROBERT F. WAGNER. Speaking in favor of the Social Security bill, 1935.   LIBRARY OF CONGRESS

chairman of the Committee on Banking and Currency and the second-ranking member on the Foreign Affairs Committee.

During the administration of Franklin D. Roosevelt, Wagner was assigned the task of drafting the National Industrial Recovery Act (1933), which created the National Recovery Administration and a vast program of public works that constituted an important part of the New Deal's experiment in "government partnership with business." The act included the now historic section 7(a), which for the first time guaranteed by law labor's right to bargain collectively for wages and working conditions. After the Supreme Court held the act unconstitutional in 1935, Congress passed the National Labor Relations Act (known as the Wagner-Connery Act), the most significant of the many labor laws sponsored by Wagner. This act, which put the federal government even more solidly behind labor's right to bargain collectively, established the National Labor Relations Board (NLRB), which Wagner chaired. It remained the basic law covering labor relations in the United States until the passage of the Taft-Hartley Act in 1947.

As one of the sponsors of the Social Security Act of 1935, Wagner continued his push for humanitarian social legislation. He was a pioneer in federal support for housing, repeatedly sponsoring bills designed to promote long-range slum clearance and low-cost housing plans. In 1937 Congress passed the Wagner-Steagall Act, which established the U.S. Housing Authority. With his last major work in the Senate, the Wagner-Ellender-Taft housing bill, Wagner presented legislation that addressed long-range residential building needs by implementing the construction of fifteen million homes over a ten-year period. With this bill, which became the Public Housing Act of 1949, Wagner reached beyond the urban liberal coalition by providing government loans for small builders, slum clearance, and other general incentives to low-cost housing construction. Though his national health program and anti-lynching legislation bills were never enacted, Wagner remained unstinting in his efforts for more comprehensive social welfare legislation.

Forced by ill health to retire in 1949, Wagner died of heart disease on 4 May 1953.

BIBLIOGRAPHY

Bernstein, Barton, ed. "The New Deal: The Conservative Achievements of Liberal Reform." In *Towards a New Past: Dissenting Essays in American History.* 1968.

Huthmacher, J. Joseph. *Senator Robert F. Wagner and the Rise of Urban Liberalism.* 1968.

SHARI L. OSBORN

WAGNER-CONNERY NATIONAL LABOR RELATIONS ACT (1935; 49 Stat. 449–457).

The National Labor Relations Act (NLRA), also known as the Wagner Act, was one of the most controversial New Deal statutes. It made collective bargaining between employers and employees an essential component of federal economic recovery policies, and it committed the government to the principle that workers have a right to organize into unions free from employer interference. Most important, it created a powerful executive agency, the National Labor Relations Board (NLRB), to implement those commitments.

Before the NLRA's passage little existed in the way of substantive law regarding labor organiza-

tion aside from that applying to the railroad industry. Regulation was largely left to the courts, where unions were extremely vulnerable to common-law conspiracy prosecutions and the increasingly frequent use of injunctions in labor disputes.

Attempts to escape the courts' reach through federal legislation were unsuccessful until 1932. Then, the Norris-LaGuardia Act imposed strict procedural limits on federal courts' resort to injunctions. Free association and bargaining for workers was endorsed in section 7(a) of the National Industrial Recovery Act (1933). Facilitating collective bargaining became an ever more prominent element of recovery policy, culminating with the NLRA.

The act's legislative history shows that its radicalism went far beyond the redress of previous legal imbalances. Its earliest incarnation—as the Labor Disputes bill of 1934—sought "to equalize the bargaining power of employers and employees." Drafted by New York senator Robert F. Wagner's principal aide, Leon Keyserling (later chairman of the Council of Economic Advisers during the Truman administration), this bill prohibited obstructive employer practices and provided for enforcement of the section 7(a) self-organization rights, going beyond the simple mediation of disputes that had satisfied the National Recovery Administration (NRA). Implementation was made the responsibility of a new agency, known at this stage as the National Labor Board.

Lacking administration support, the Labor Disputes bill failed to clear Congress, but Wagner directed Keyserling to redraft the bill for resubmission in 1935. The new bill strengthened the independence and enforcement powers of the proposed new agency and more fully defined unfair employer practices. It also underscored the relationship between the enforcement of workers' rights and the general social welfare. After attracting belated support from an administration robbed of its recovery policy by the Supreme Court's anti-NRA *Schechter* decision (1935), the new bill passed virtually as drafted. Recorded votes were 63 to 12 in the Senate and 132 to 42 in the House.

Three circumstances were fundamental to the act's adoption: the Depression, the tendency of the time to ascribe weak consumer demand to maldistribution of income and purchasing power, and the growing political support for policies that linked recovery to more equitable income distribution. But there were two problems: the NLRA's commitment to redistribution was fiercely controversial, and it was not clear whether union organization and collective bargaining were regarded as means to be administratively tailored to economic policy ends or as democratic goods in their own right.

These problems involved the NLRB in major conflicts with employers hostile to federal regulation of their labor practices and with established American Federation of Labor unions seeking to face down rank-and-file challengers largely organized in the rival Congress of Industrial Organizations. By 1938 both were pressing Congress for amendments that would limit the NLRB's capacity to intrude upon their affairs. After the 1938 elections increased the strength of New Deal opponents in Congress, President Franklin D. Roosevelt moved to appease NLRB critics by appointing new members inclined to support existing interests, to link collective bargaining to the "stabilization" of industrial relations, and to downplay the act's macroeconomic redistributive objective. So matters remained until the Taft-Hartley Labor-Management Relations Act (1947) effected a more thoroughgoing revision of policy.

[*See also* Fair Labor Standards Act; New Deal.]

BIBLIOGRAPHY

Casebeer, Kenneth M. "Holder of the Pen: An Interview with Leon Keyserling on Drafting the Wagner Act." *University of Miami Law Review* 42 (1987): 285–363.

Tomlins, Christopher L. *The State and the Unions: Labor Relations, Law, and the Organized Labor Movement in America, 1880–1960.* 1985.

CHRISTOPHER L. TOMLINS

WALL STREET INVESTIGATION. *See* Pecora Wall Street Investigation.

WALSH, THOMAS J. (1859–1933), Democratic senator from Montana, credited with exposing the Teapot Dome scandal in the Harding administration. Thomas James Walsh was the son of Irish Catholic immigrants who settled in Wisconsin, where Walsh attended public schools and took a law degree at the University of Wisconsin. He began his legal practice in Dakota Territory, moved to Montana in 1890, and soon established himself as one of the state's outstanding lawyers.

Twice unsuccessful in bids for national office, he was elected to the U.S. Senate in 1912 and reelected in 1918, 1924, and 1930. Walsh was a progressive Democrat in a state dominated by the Anaconda Copper Company. As a freshman senator he generally supported Woodrow Wilson's domestic

THOMAS J. WALSH. Arriving at the Capitol for a Senate Teapot Dome hearing, 4 March 1924.

LIBRARY OF CONGRESS

policies, helping to write such key legislation as the Clayton Antitrust Act. He voted for war in 1917 and endorsed Wilson's version of the League of Nations until January 1920, when he broke with the president to accept certain of Henry Cabot Lodge's reservations. In the 1920s Walsh sharply criticized the probusiness policies of the Republican majority.

Walsh's career reached its peak in 1924 with his relentless investigation of the Teapot Dome and related oil-leasing deals. Thereafter, he received recognition as one of the Senate's most able members. In 1924 and 1932 Walsh was chosen permanent chairman of the Democratic National Convention. In 1933 Franklin D. Roosevelt selected him as his attorney general, but Walsh died before taking office. Uncharismatic and seldom demonstrative, Walsh won respect for his legal brilliance, political acumen, honesty, courage, and commitment to public service.

BIBLIOGRAPHY

Bates, J. Leonard. "Senator Walsh of Montana, 1918–1924: A Liberal under Pressure." Ph.D. diss., Univ. of North Carolina, 1952.

Bates, J. Leonard. "Thomas J. Walsh: His Genius for Controversy." *Montana: The Magazine of Western History* 19 (1969): 6–15.

RALPH A. STONE

WAR HAWKS. A group of House Republicans in the first session of the 12th Congress (1811–1812), the War Hawks were outspoken proponents of war with England and thus helped bring on the War of 1812. Although scholars differ over who (if anyone) ought to be classified as a War Hawk, the traditional list includes Speaker of the House Henry Clay (the leader of the group); Richard M. Johnson of Kentucky; Felix Grundy of Tennessee; Langdon Cheves, William Lowndes, John C. Calhoun, and David R. Williams of South Carolina; George M. Troup of Georgia; Peter B. Porter of New York; and John A. Harper of New Hampshire. Too young to remember the horrors of the American Revolution, the War Hawks were willing to risk another war with England to vindicate American rights on the high seas.

Although the War Hawks differed over certain key issues, such as the merits of naval expansion and the expediency of new taxes, between December 1811 and April 1812, they closed ranks to secure the adoption of an ambitious program of war preparations. Unceasing in their denunciations of England, the War Hawks made clear their willingness to go to war if the British did not make concessions. When none were forthcoming, President James Madison sent a war message to Congress on 1 June 1812. The War Hawks responded by pushing a declaration of war through the House in only two days. Their role in bringing on the War of 1812 was critical.

[*See also* War of 1812.]

BIBLIOGRAPHY

Fritz, Harry W. "The War Hawks of 1812." *Capitol Studies* 5 (1977): 25–42.

Hickey, Donald R. *The War of 1812: A Forgotten Conflict.* 1989.

DONALD R. HICKEY

WAR OF 1812. Fought between Britain and the United States and lasting from 1812 to 1815, the War of 1812 was one of the worst-managed wars in American history. Although much of the responsibility rests with President James Madison, Congress must share the blame. Throughout the war both houses suffered from deep divisions, and endless debate and hostility to the administration combined to prevent or delay much-needed legislation. As a result, instead of winning any concessions from the British on the maritime issues in dispute, the United States was lucky to escape from the conflict without making major concessions itself.

When the 12th Congress, also known as the War Congress, convened in November 1811, President Madison asked that body to put the nation "into an armor and an attitude demanded by the crisis." Spurred on by Henry Clay (a first-term representative who molded his position as Speaker of the House into one of great power), the War Hawks pushed through a program of war preparations between December 1811 and April 1812.

When Madison sent a war message to Congress on 1 June 1812, both houses responded favorably, though the vote on the war bill (79 to 49 in the House and 19 to 13 in the Senate) was the closest on any declaration of war in the nation's history. Every Federalist in Congress voted against the war, as did a number of Democratic-Republicans (Jeffersonian Republicans). Before passing the bill the Senate, in a tie vote, barely defeated a proposal that would have limited hostilities to the high seas.

Most Democratic-Republicans assumed that the British would quickly cave into American demands. But even after it became clear that the conflict was likely to last, Congress was slow to adopt the measures needed to support the American war effort. The Federalists remained implacable in their opposition, and in both houses they were able to thwart and embarrass the administration and its allies by combining with dissident Democratic-Republicans.

The Senate was particularly obstreperous. The so-called Invisibles, a Democratic-Republican faction that included William B. Giles (Va.) and Samuel Smith (Md.), often sided with the Federalists, not because they opposed the war but because they were hostile to the administration and the way it was managing the war effort. At a special session of the 13th Congress convened in the spring of 1813, the Senate killed an administration proposal for an embargo and blocked two of the president's diplomatic appointments, including that of Secretary of the Treasury Albert Gallatin to the peace commission.

Such was the mood of the Senate that at the end of this session Vice President Elbridge Gerry refused to follow custom and vacate his seat as presiding officer. This prevented the election of a president pro tempore, thus ensuring that Speaker Clay (rather than one of the Senate dissidents) would

RESISTANCE TO THE BRITISH. The citizens of Alexandria, Va., are ridiculed as abjectly submitting to the demands of the invading British force that burned Washington, D.C., *above*, while the citizens of Baltimore are lauded for their repulse of the British troops at Fort McHenry. Etchings by William Charles, 1814.

gain the presidency if both Madison, who was ailing, and Gerry, who was sixty-nine, died.

Congress was slow to adopt an internal tax program, fearing that new duties would make the Democratic-Republican party and the war unpopular. Not until a year and a half into the contest were these taxes finally levied. The delay contributed to the collapse of public credit in the summer of 1814, which compelled the administration to default on public debt payments and to rely increasingly on treasury notes, a form of paper money that rapidly declined in value.

Congress was also reluctant to adopt administration proposals to limit American trade with the enemy, which flourished on the nation's northern border as well as on the Atlantic seaboard. Although Congress ultimately did adopt a number of restrictions, by August 1814, trade with the enemy had reached such scandalous proportions that the governor-general of Canada reported that two-thirds of the British troops in the province were eating American beef.

By the time the 13th Congress met for its third session in September 1814, the nation was on the defensive on every front, and nearly everyone agreed that a crisis was at hand. But Congress was so slow to respond that the Philadelphia *Aurora* claimed that the British could not have been better served if they had bribed its members. Not only was Congress slow to act in this crisis, but it ultimately rejected the administration's two most important proposals: a conscription scheme and a plan for a national bank.

In the end the United States escaped from the war when the British agreed to return to the *status quo ante bellum* in the Treaty of Ghent, which was signed on 24 December 1814. Although the terms fell far short of the Democratic-Republicans' initial war aims, the lopsided American victory in the Battle of New Orleans (fought after the peace treaty was signed in Europe but before news of it reached America) enabled Democratic-Republicans to claim that the entire war had been a success. Both in Congress and out, Democratic-Republicans crowed about how the United States had single-handedly fended off an invasion by the conqueror of Napoleon and mistress of the seas and had decisively defeated Britain's "invincible" troops.

The Senate unanimously approved the peace treaty on 16 February 1815, and when President Madison announced the war's end the following day, he congratulated Americans on their success. The war, he claimed, "has been waged with a success which is the natural result of the wisdom of the Legislative councils, of the patriotism of the people, of the public spirit of the militia, and of the valor of the military and naval forces of the country." Although the president's claims stretched the truth, it served the interests of Democratic-Republicans to remember the war this way.

People quickly forgot how uncooperative Congress had been during the war. But they neither forgot nor forgave the Federalists for opposing the contest, and the rapid disintegration of the party in the postwar era served as a lesson for congressional opponents of future wars. Unlike the Federalists, the Whigs were careful to vote for supplies of men and money even though they opposed the Mexican War, and congressional opponents of other wars have generally followed the same course.

[*See also* Violence, *article on* Violence against Congress; War Hawks.]

BIBLIOGRAPHY

Hickey, Donald R. *The War of 1812: A Forgotten Conflict.* 1989.

Stagg, J. C. A. *Mr. Madison's War: Politics, Diplomacy, and Warfare in the Early American Republic, 1783–1830.* 1983.

DONALD R. HICKEY

WAR POWERS. The Constitution's allocation of war powers has long been a matter of great controversy. While Article I, section 10 of the Constitution grants Congress the power to declare war, Article II, section 2 recognizes the president as commander in chief of the armed forces. These constitutional grants of power create the possibility that Congress and the executive may come into conflict over committing and withdrawing U.S. armed forces from foreign lands.

The executive has never completely dominated Congress in making decisions about troop commitments. Executive power in foreign affairs did become more pronounced, however, as the United States became a world power in the twentieth century. In addition, a congressional-executive consensus over the desirability of containing communism emerged during the Cold War era. This consensus on containment policy occasionally led Congress to endorse broad presidential power to determine when to commit American troops to foreign lands. Most significantly, in 1964 Congress passed the Tonkin Gulf Resolution, which approved virtually unlimited power for President Lyndon B. Johnson, as commander in chief, to commit armed forces to Vietnam.

The War Powers Resolution (sometimes called the War Powers Act, although it was a joint resolution) was a product of the breakdown of the congressional-executive consensus on the containment of communism as well as a reaction to Congress's perception that Presidents Johnson and Richard M. Nixon had abused the unilateral and largely unlimited power that had been granted to the president to further containment goals in the Vietnam War era. With containment an apparent failure and President Nixon ordering secret bombing raids on Cambodia without congressional approval, Congress sought to check unlimited and authorized uses of executive power regarding military commitments. In 1973, Congress adopted the War Powers Resolution. Nixon vetoed it on the grounds that it infringed on the president's ability to fulfill his responsibility to faithfully execute the laws, defend the country from foreign invasion, and uphold the Constitution. Congress then overrode Nixon's veto.

Although the War Powers Resolution states that it does not alter the constitutional authority of the president and Congress regarding the allocation of war powers, its leading sponsors understood themselves to be repudiating a long-standing precedent of executive dominance in foreign affairs. Some sponsors went so far as to contend that the Framers, in writing the Constitution, intended to place war powers under congressional control. However, section 2 of the resolution states that its intent is to promote the collective participation of both Congress and the president in decisions regarding whether and under what conditions U.S. troops should be committed to areas of hostility or imminent hostility.

The War Powers Resolution contains several provisions that attempt to restrict executive power and reintegrate Congress into a cooperative decision-making arrangement with the executive regarding troop commitments. The central provisions of the resolution address the president's responsibility to consult and report to Congress as well as Congress's authority to order troop removals under certain circumstances. Section 3 states that the president, in every possible instance, must consult with Congress before introducing troops into hostilities. Section 4 requires the president to report any troop commitments to Congress within forty-eight hours of their deployment. Finally, section 5 states that the president must terminate the use of military force in sixty days if Congress does not declare war or extend the sixty-day period by law. The president can extend the sixty-day period up to thirty more days, as necessary, to withdraw troops. However, section 5 also states that Congress may at any time pass a concurrent resolution that directs the president to remove U.S. armed forces from foreign lands.

Every president since its passage has resisted the War Powers Resolution. They have claimed that Article II, section 2 of the Constitution—the commander-in-chief clause—grants the president a wider authority than the War Powers Resolution. No president has formally declared the act unconstitutional and nonbinding, however, and various presidential advisers have conceded that it is the law of the land.

Despite general presidential resistance to the authority of the War Powers Resolution, Congress seems to have been largely successful in obtaining presidential compliance with section 4, the act's reporting requirement. Presidents have frequently reported their actions in a manner that seems quite consistent with that provision. But they all have claimed that their reporting stemmed from their constitutional authority as commander in chief rather than from any statutory obligation created by Congress in the resolution. For example, when President Gerald R. Ford committed armed forces to Da Nang to evacuate Vietnamese and American citizens, when he used military forces to evacuate refugees from Saigon and Phnom Penh, and when he used armed forces to liberate the U.S.S. *Mayaguez* from Cambodia in 1975, he reported those troop commitments to Congress. However, after each incident, Ford claimed that his actions were supported by the Constitution. He claimed that the president's constitutional authority as commander in chief and chief executive served as the basis for his actions. Yet although Ford argued that he was reporting because he wanted to keep Congress informed about these matters, he nevertheless expressly noted that his actions were consistent with section 4 of the War Powers Resolution. When President Jimmy Carter sent U.S. military equipment to aid in the evacuation of American citizens from Zaire in 1977 and when he used the military in an attempt to rescue American hostages from Iran in 1980, he also argued that his actions and his subsequent reports to Congress flowed from his constitutional authority as commander in chief.

Exceptions to the general rule of presidential compliance with the reporting provision do exist. For example, in 1981 President Ronald Reagan introduced military advisers into El Salvador without reporting to Congress, and in 1982 he committed armed forces to Lebanon without initially reporting his action.

Congress has been much less successful in obtaining presidential compliance with section 3, the consulting provision of the War Powers Resolution. This failure is due, in part, to the loophole that the wording of section 3 creates for the president; it obligates the president to report only in "every possible instance." Thus, in 1982 President Reagan committed forces to the Sinai without consulting Congress; in 1983 he invaded Grenada and sent troops to Chad without consulting Congress; and in 1987 he sent forces into the Persian Gulf without consulting Congress. Following each incident, Reagan argued that he had acted on the basis of the president's constitutional authority as commander in chief of the armed forces and as chief executive in conducting foreign relations. As of 1993 Congress had failed to compel presidential compliance with the consulting requirement.

In light of Congress's failure to gain full compliance with the War Powers Resolution, several individual members of Congress have asked the judiciary to enforce the resolution. For example, in *Crockett v. Reagan* (558 F. Supp. 893 [1982]), twenty-nine members sought declaratory judgments against President Reagan, Secretary of State Alexander Haig, and Secretary of Defense Caspar Weinberger regarding their support for military assistance to El Salvador and their resistance to the reporting and consultation provisions of the War Powers Resolution. The District of Columbia Court of Appeals, however, refused to compel presidential compliance. Declaring that matters of foreign affairs are nonjusticiable political questions, the court argued that the answers to such questions should be worked out cooperatively between the political branches, Congress and the executive. The court added that it would not allow individual members of Congress to sidestep the political process by asking the court for a declaratory judgment; rather, the conflict would have to come to a head between the executive and Congress—as institutions—before the court would intervene.

Similarly, in *Sanchez-Espinoza v. Reagan* (568 F. Supp. 596 [D.D.C. 1983]) several legislators argued that the executive's actions to subvert the Nicaraguan government abridged the War Powers Resolution. The court dismissed the case using the same political question doctrine as in the *Crockett* ruling. In *Lowry v. Reagan* (676 F. Supp. 333 [D.D.C.1987])

110 members of Congress requested a declaratory judgment that would have obligated the president to comply with the War Powers Act by formally reporting troop movement into the Persian Gulf in 1987. Again, the court used the political question doctrine to reject the request.

In theory, the court's long-standing policy of deferring to the wisdom of the political branches in matters of foreign affairs seems to support the idea that the president and Congress should cooperatively decide such questions. Many scholars have argued that in practice, however, the political question doctrine actually supports executive dominance in these matters. They contend that since the president retains the initiative to act, he may unilaterally commit or withdraw troops as he sees fit, despite congressional pleas for fuller participation. Therefore, when the courts encourage Congress and the executive to settle matters between themselves, they often indirectly support executive preeminence in decision making.

Nevertheless, other scholars contend that it is not clear whether Congress or the executive would prevail in the event of direct conflict on this matter. They argue that that question will remain open until Congress refuses to authorize or support a specific presidential troop commitment. In 1991 Congress came as close as it ever has to refusing to authorize broad presidential power regarding troop commitments. For several days, Congress debated whether President George Bush needed to obtain congressional approval before attacking Iraq or further committing troops to the Persian Gulf. Several members explicitly recalled that Congress had sanctioned broad presidential power in the 1964 Tonkin Gulf Resolution, characterized that decision as mistaken, and argued that the War Powers Resolution was designed to prevent any such broad delegations of power from occurring in the future. A congressional majority defused the potential congressional-executive standoff, however, by authorizing broad presidential discretion in the use of military force in the Persian Gulf. At the same time, Congress asserted that nothing in the Desert Storm Resolution superseded the requirements of the War Powers Resolution.

Disagreement between the executive and Congress about the Constitution's allocation of war powers is likely to continue for some time to come. In lieu of a direct congressional-executive standoff, it remains unclear whether either the executive or Congress retains ultimate authority regarding military commitments, or whether, as other scholars have contended, a more cooperative arrangement is necessary and workable.

[*For broad discussion of relations between the executive and legislative branches concerning war powers, see* President and Congress, *overview article, subsection titled "War." For further discussion of the War Powers Resolution, see* War Powers Resolution.]

BIBLIOGRAPHY

Burgess, Susan. *Contest for Constitutional Authority: The Abortion and War Powers Debates.* 1992.
Fisher, Louis. *Constitutional Conflicts between Congress and the President.* 1985.
Koh, Harold. *The National Security Constitution.* 1990.
Wormuth, Francis, and Edwin Firmage. *To Chain the Dog of War: The War Powers of Congress in History and Law.* 2d ed. 1989.

SUSAN R. BURGESS

WAR POWERS RESOLUTION (1973; 49 Stat. 803–863). Few issues so graphically illustrate the problems of allocating responsibility between Congress and the executive as the power to make war. Few pieces of legislation testify to the difficulties of defining the balance of authority as much as the War Powers Resolution of 1973, which sought to ensure a congressional role in the decision to dispatch the military to combat. The core issues surrounding war powers are still very much alive: the discretion of the president to commit armed forces without congressional participation, when and how Congress should become involved in such decisions, and what the legislature can do if relations with the executive break down.

A growing consensus maintains that the War Powers Resolution has not worked as Congress envisioned. Presidents have refused to invoke the law in ways that could limit their freedom of action; indeed, they have not even conceded its constitutionality. Congress, for its part, has been reluctant to challenge the president.

In more than two hundred cases of the use of armed forces, Congress declared war only four times—the War of 1812, the Spanish-American War, World War I, and World War II—and in a fifth instance—the Mexican War—passed a joint resolution. In short, the executive branch has dominated decisions to send forces abroad.

A combination of forces led to the enactment of the War Powers Resolution. Many in Congress reacted against what was perceived to be the unre-

strained use of executive power in the 1960s and 1970s, exemplified by the Vietnam War. Many who supported American involvement in the Southeast Asia conflict also believed that Congress needed institutional mechanisms to exercise its prerogatives in the future. The diminished power of the presidency in the midst of the Watergate debacle and Democratic control of both legislative chambers facilitated passage of the resolution over President Richard M. Nixon's veto. Only 18 senators and 135 representatives voted to sustain the president's action.

The Sections of the Resolution. The War Powers Resolution has ten sections. Section 2 states that the authority of the president to introduce armed forces "into hostilities, or into situations where imminent involvement in hostilities is clearly indicated by the circumstances," is to be exercised "only pursuant to (1) a declaration of war, (2) specific statutory authorization, or (3) a national emergency created by attack upon the United States, its territories or possessions, or its armed forces." The meat of the resolution, sections 3 to 5, is concerned with consultation, reporting, and congressional action.

Consultation. Under the terms of section 3, the president is required "in every possible instance" to consult with Congress "before introducing United States Armed Forces into hostilities" or "imminent hostilities." Moreover, the chief executive "shall consult regularly with the Congress until United States Armed Forces are no longer engaged in hostilities or have been removed from such situations."

Reporting. Section 4 states that in the absence of a declaration of war the president shall submit a report within forty-eight hours to the Speaker of the House of Representatives and the president pro tempore of the Senate in any case in which armed forces are introduced:

(1) into hostilities or into situations where imminent involvement in hostilities is clearly indicated by the circumstances; (2) into the territory, airspace or waters of a foreign nation, while equipped for combat, except for deployments which relate to supply, replacement, repair, or training of such forces; or (3) in numbers which substantially enlarge United States Armed Forces equipped for combat already located in a foreign nation.

That report, in writing, is to set forth the circumstances of the introduction of forces, the constitutional and legislative authority supporting the president's action, and the estimated scope and duration of the hostilities or involvement. In cases involving hostilities, additional reports are to be made at intervals not less frequent than once every six months for as long as the circumstances continue.

Congressional action. Section 5(a) provides that if the president transmits a report pursuant to section 4(a)(1) during a congressional adjournment, the Speaker of the House and the president pro tempore of the Senate, when they deem it advisable or if they are petitioned by at least 30 percent of the members of their respective houses, "shall jointly request the President to convene Congress in order that it may consider the report and take appropriate action."

The succeeding section, 5(b), at the heart of the congressional mechanism, provides for a sequence of events within sixty calendar days "after a report is submitted or is required to be submitted pursuant to section 4(a)(1)." It requires the president to terminate the use of U.S. armed forces unless Congress has declared war or authorized the action, extended the period by law, or is physically unable to meet as a result of an armed attack on the United States. If the president certifies that "unavoidable military necessity respecting the safety of United States Armed Forces" requires their continued presence in the course of effecting their removal, the sixty days can be extended by thirty days. The language, "after a report is submitted or is required to be submitted pursuant to section 4(a)(1)" is significant, because it means that Congress does not have to rely upon the president to start the sixty-day clock; presumably, the legislative branch could vote that circumstances require the submission of a report, in which case the sixty-day clock would begin to run.

Section 5(c) states that by concurrent resolution Congress can require the president to remove forces at any time. Because of the Supreme Court's 1983 decision outlawing the legislative veto *(Immigration and Naturalization Service v. Chadha)*, and thus possibly section 5(c), Congress later that year adopted a freestanding measure, attached as an amendment to a State Department authorization bill (97 Stat. 1062–1063), which substituted a joint resolution for the concurrent resolution. The procedure provided in the legislation, which did not formally amend the War Powers Resolution, could be invoked if the Supreme Court were to strike down section 5(c).

How the judiciary would interpret section 5(c) has been the subject of debate. Some have argued that section 5(c) is not a legislative veto, where Congress delegates certain powers to the executive but reserves the right to veto the executive exercise of that delegation. According to this view, Congress has not delegated power but has sought "to approximate the accommodation reached by the Constitution's framers, that the President could act militarily in an emergency but was obligated to cease and desist in the event Congress did not approve as soon as it had a reasonable opportunity to do so" (Ely, 1988, p. 1396).

The shift from a concurrent resolution to a joint resolution has important implications for the operation of the War Powers Resolution. A concurrent resolution, unlike the joint resolution, is not subject to a presidential veto; if the president vetoes a joint resolution, Congress must muster a two-thirds majority in each house to overturn it.

Repairing the Resolution. In enacting the War Powers Resolution, Congress sought to claim a role in the decision to commit troops to combat. The measure's very existence provides an outlet for legislators who seek to challenge executive action. Moreover, the resolution has served to create an institutional memory of interbranch debates about the wisdom of various military actions. In the view of some observers, the War Powers Resolution has set the outer boundaries for the presidential commitment of armed forces short of a formal declaration of war. That presidents seek to anticipate congressional reaction as part of their political calculations is undoubtedly true. Even so, it would be hard to make the case that the War Powers Resolution has deterred chief executives bent on engaging troops.

Indeed, a growing sentiment in Congress maintains that the War Powers Resolution needs repair. According to this view, presidents do not adhere to its provisions, largely because of constitutional objections but also because of concern about the law's sixty-day troop withdrawal provisions. Since 1973 chief executives have filed more than a score of reports pursuant to the War Powers Resolution; on only one occasion did a president cite section 4(a)(1)—notification to Congress of imminent involvement in hostilities—and then only when the military action had ended (the *Mayaguez* incident in which President Gerald R. Ford ordered the rescue of the crew and vessel seized by naval patrol boats). One can state with reasonable confidence that chief executives are unlikely to invoke section 4(a)(1), especially if they believe that troops may have to be committed beyond sixty days and if there is a risk that Congress will not vote to approve the action during that period.

For its part, the legislative branch has been unwilling to challenge the president, particularly in those situations in which the chief executive could rally public opinion—as is almost always the case in the early phases of military confrontation. In the one instance in which Congress on its own authority, pursuant to section 5(b), invoked section 4(a)(1)—the Multinational Force in Lebanon Resolution of 1983—the legislature authorized the continued role of the marines in the multinational force for another eighteen months. In authorizing the president to use force against Iraq if that nation did not withdraw from Kuwait, Congress in its 1991 resolution "To authorize the use of United States Armed Forces" did not rely upon the War Powers Resolution, although it declared that nothing in the 1991 resolution supersedes any requirement of the War Powers Resolution. The judiciary quite prudently has steadfastly avoided the attempts of some legislators to trigger the War Powers Resolution's sixty-day cutoff procedure. If Congress will not do what it has the power to do, why should the courts?

Presidents have perceived their interests in terms of maximizing discretion over foreign policy. That has meant a reluctance to involve Congress in warmaking decisions. In reality, the executive will have difficulty sustaining extended military action without popular approval and congressional support. That argues for some legislative involvement in the decision-making process.

There is no single congressional view. A few would grant the president virtually absolute discretion and call for repeal of the resolution. Some argue that the resolution should be basically preserved with some mechanism for judicial enforcement. Still others would call for parity with the executive branch. However, the consensus emerging in 1993 appeared to be that even if the president were to have primacy in the decision to commit troops, Congress should be consulted and involved in the decision-making process in a meaningful way. This perspective cedes the president discretion to commit forces but only after legislative involvement. This position implicitly acknowledges that Congress is generally unwilling to challenge the president; if Congress is to have a role, the law must be changed to make it more likely that the president will comply.

Similarly, the proposal that the courts be given authority to start the sixty-day clock when the president fails to file a section 4(a)(1) report and Congress declines to trigger the withdrawal provision assumes that the legislature lacks the institutional will to participate in the decision to make war. That proposal, moreover, would require the courts to render judgments about military situations that they are not equipped to make.

A compromise approach calls for an amendment that would repeal the automatic requirement for withdrawal of troops sixty days after the president submits a section 4(a)(1) report. Through a joint resolution that would receive expedited attention, Congress could either authorize the military action or require withdrawal. In other words, the presumption would be reversed: troops would be allowed to stay unless Congress voted otherwise. At the core of this approach is consultation. This debate about the War Powers Resolution carries with it the hope of a healthier relationship between the executive and the legislature.

[*See also* Persian Gulf War; Tonkin Gulf Resolution.]

BIBLIOGRAPHY

Cheney, Richard. "Congressional Overreaching in Foreign Policy." In *Foreign Policy and the Constitution.* Edited by Robert A. Goldwin and Robert A. Licht. 1990.

Ely, John Hart. "Suppose Congress Wanted a War Powers Act That Worked?" *Columbia Law Review* 88 (November 1988): 1396.

Glennon, Michael J. *Constitutional Diplomacy.* 1991.

Katzmann, Robert A. "War Powers: Toward a New Accommodation." In *A Question of Balance: The President, the Congress, and Foreign Policy.* Edited by Thomas E. Mann. 1990.

Reveley, W. Taylor, III. *War Powers of the President and Congress: Who Holds the Arrows and Olive Branch?.* 1981.

Rostow, Eugene V. Once More unto the Breach: The War Powers Resolution Revisited. *Valparaiso University Law Review.* 21 (Fall 1986): 1–52.

Smyrl, Marc. *Conflict or Codetermination?* 1988.

ROBERT A. KATZMANN

WASHINGTON, GEORGE (1732–1799), Virginia planter, member of the Continental Congress, commander of the Continental army during the War of Independence, and first president of the United States. Washington emerged from a brief retirement in 1787 to attend and preside over the Constitutional Convention. Two years later, he accepted the public's call to become the first president under the newly ratified Constitution.

Washington entered the presidency with considerable experience in dealing with legislative bodies. Not only had he been a member of Virginia's House of Burgesses for nearly fifteen years, but as commander of the Continental army after 1775, he had dealt with the Continental Congress on a regular basis for more than eight years. General Washington's relations with Congress had been excellent. He had deferred to Congress, and, on occasion, he had expressed displeasure when Congress acted slowly or inadequately, but he had voiced few complaints concerning congressional intrusiveness either with his management of the army or his military strategy. Most members of Congress had responded to Washington by treating him honestly and courteously and with considerable deference. Washington had given Congress what it desired in a commander: someone who acted with dignity, poise, and integrity; who could direct an army on the European model; and who was capable of managing an army composed of citizen-soldiers.

Helped by this store of experience, President Washington was also aided in his earliest relations with the First Congress by James Madison, a fellow Virginian and a trusted adviser and confidant who quickly emerged as a powerful figure in the House of Representatives. Washington also surrounded himself with seasoned and skilled politicians. He relied on the advice of Thomas Jefferson, his choice to head the State Department; Henry Knox, who presided over the War Department; Attorney General Edmund Randolph; and Alexander Hamilton, his secretary of the Treasury. But Washington's greatest asset was his enormous prestige. No subsequent president has assumed the office with the exalted status that Washington enjoyed. Even more striking, perhaps, is that Washington maintained his extraordinary popularity throughout his two terms in office. He was an imposing figure—tall, dignified, graceful, and august. As the triumphant hero of the War of Independence, Washington was seen by contemporaries as the very symbol of America's revolutionary republican ideal—the virtuous and selfless public servant. It was difficult for Congress not to defer to such a man.

During the first months of the new government, President Washington and Congress devoted considerable thought to the nature of the presidential office. Congress saw the presidency as a republican office; it rejected a monarchical title for the chief executive and proposed instead an exquisitely simple denomination, President of the United States. At the same time, Congress fixed the president's salary at $25,000 annually, an enormous amount at the time and an indication that it wished the office to be maintained somewhat regally. Washington was comfortable with Congress's outlook. His philosophical and temperamental inclinations led him to vest the position with an air of royal dignity, but common sense induced him to blend the monarchical trappings with a common touch. Thus, while he endowed the presidency with pomp, ceremony, and solemnity, he opened his office to the public through weekly levees. Ultimately, he fashioned a stately, majestic aura about the presidency that reminded Great Britain's minister to the United States of the royal court of George III.

Hamilton's Economic Program. During his two terms, Washington sought congressional approval for four major administrative programs. His first priority was the enactment of the economic plans of Secretary Hamilton. Between early 1790 and late 1791, the administration introduced four of Hamilton's proposals in Congress. Modeled on Great Britain's financial practices, they included the retirement of the existing foreign, national, and state debts; the creation of a national bank; and federal assistance for the promotion of U.S. manufacturing in order to "render the United States independent of other nations for essential, particularly military supplies." These grand schemes were to be financed largely by a revenue tariff, an excise tax on whiskey, and borrowing. Washington and Hamilton had several motives in introducing the program. They hoped to demonstrate the power of the new national government. They sought to augment the power of the new nation so that it could someday become truly independent of Europe's great powers. Finally, by borrowing—to be accomplished by selling public securities to the one element capable of such investments, the most privileged class of the citizenry—Washington and Hamilton hoped to bond the wealthiest and most powerful Americans to the new government.

Many of these proposals aroused a firestorm of protest, especially in the South and the rural sections of the middle states. Washington was compelled to lobby some members of Congress actively, a practice he found distasteful, and to risk his impeccable reputation, which he contemplated with even more dismay. Most of the Washington-Hamilton program was passed by Congress, principally because of Washington's open and resolute advocacy. But the victories came at a cost. During the bank fight Jefferson and Madison organized the opposition to the centralizing and anglicizing tendencies inherent in the Washington-Hamilton vision. The emergence of the opposition Jeffersonian Republican party was the result.

Frontier Pacification and Strengthening the Army. Washington's second major goal was to pacify the western frontier in Kentucky and Ohio, where Indians were resisting the advance of settlers onto their ancestral lands. The Indians had few friends in Congress, but when Washington advocated doubling the American army—from 694 men to more than 1,200—some protested that this would result in a permanent standing army. Most members of Congress supported the president, however, eventually appropriating funds for three armies—in 1790, 1791, and 1792—until the last, under Gen. Anthony Wayne, accomplished its mission. Before the end of Washington's administration, the first new western states had entered the Union.

Washington's third initiative was realized during this Indian warfare. As some congressional critics suggested, Washington had long sought to create a large regular army. He had hardly assumed command of the Continental army in 1775 before he questioned the efficacy of militia troops and urged establishment of a larger, permanent army. One of his last acts in the War of Independence had been to recommend, in 1783, that the United States maintain a peacetime army of nearly twenty-seven hundred men. He did not have his way. Following the defeat of the armies he sent into the Ohio country in 1790 and 1791, however, Washington persuaded Congress to create a five-thousand-man army comprising five regiments. Congress also passed the Uniform Militia Act of 1792, which directed each state to organize its militia along federal guidelines. The legislature found it difficult to resist Washington, especially when most Americans longed to see the rapid opening of the transmontane West.

Jay's Treaty. Washington's final goal was to secure ratification of Jay's Treaty. Although unhappy with the pact, the president believed it capable of normalizing relations with Great Britain and of helping to avert a ruinous war threatened by British attacks on U.S. shipping to the French West Indies. Washington's stance was the most difficult— and most statesmanlike—act of his presidency, for opposition to the accord was intense in the South and in some northern maritime cities. His advocacy of the unpopular treaty was crucial to its passage. The Senate consented to Jay's Treaty in mid 1795 with the minimum number of votes necessary. The war scare soon abated, but Washington paid a heavy price. His endorsement of the treaty pro-

INAUGURATION OF GEORGE WASHINGTON. Published by Johnson, Fry & Co., 1859, after a painting by Alonzo Chappel.   LIBRARY OF CONGRESS

voked the harshest public attacks ever made on his character, including charges from the opposition press that he was pro-British and a surreptitious Federalist party partisan, not a patriotic leader.

The Jay's Treaty imbroglio brought the president and House of Representatives into an important constitutional conflict. Following Senate ratification, the Jeffersonian Republican majority in the House of Representatives decreed that the House had the right to reconsider treaties and demanded that Washington turn over to it all documents relating to the treaty. Washington not only feared that the House's meddling might destroy the accord and lead to war with Great Britain, but also was angry that the House would seek to encroach on constitutional powers properly belonging to the Senate and the president. Therefore, he refused to turn over the papers on constitutional grounds.

Washington experienced a difficult presidency, one filled with fierce passion and real crisis. Throughout his two terms, however, his relationship with Congress was cordial and based on mutual respect. Congress assented to every enterprise of consequence that Washington advocated. In addition, it approved each of his appointments, agreed that he should have the right to remove his executive officers, and permitted him to select a site for the new federal capital. When he left office in 1797, Washington said that Congress had failed to act on only two of his proposals: it had not created a military academy and had not sufficiently reformed the militia system. None of Washington's successors have enjoyed such protracted cooperation with Congress or experienced such an extended and genuinely amicable and respected response from the members of Congress.

BIBLIOGRAPHY

Ferling, John. *The First of Men: A Life of George Washington.* 1988.
Flexner, James T. *George Washington.* 4 vols. 1965–1972.
Freeman, Douglas S. *George Washington.* 7 vols. 1948–1957.

JOHN FERLING

WASHINGTON. Originally a part of the "Oregon Country" as annexed to the United States in 1846, then of the Oregon Territory beginning in 1848, Washington became a separate territory in 1853. Early settlers wanted to name it Columbia, but Congress decided to honor George Washington instead. The completion of the Northern Pacific Railroad in 1883 provided a transcontinental link that spurred a boom period of rapid growth and development. In 1889 Washington became the forty-second state in the Union. Admitted the same year were the other "omnibus states," Montana, North Dakota, and South Dakota. Idaho and Wyoming won admission in 1890, making six new states created by Congress in less than a year—the most rapid expansion the Union has known.

Since early statehood, Washington in its politics has been characterized by a freewheeling style of voter independence and disregard for party labels. At the climax of the "Populist revolt" in the 1896 election, a fusion slate of candidates won at the polls, subsequently choosing Silver Republican George Turner as a "Fusionist" U.S. senator. During the Progressive era, the state became a stronghold of democratic reform. In 1912, besides giving its presidential electoral votes to Progressive (Bull Moose) Theodore Roosevelt, Washington elected two Progressives out of five representatives and converted Republican senator Miles Poindexter, who enjoyed brief notoriety as the sole Progressive party member in the Senate.

Since the 1920s, minor parties have not done so well. The streak of nonpartisanship continued, however, producing radical economic reform groups during the Great Depression, whose activities drew Democratic National Chairman James A. Farley's often-quoted observation about "the 47 states and the soviet of Washington." Indicative of this maverick quality, the blanket, or "wide-open," primary adopted in 1935 continues as the most distinctive feature of the state's electoral process. With no registration by party, this primary system allows voters to crisscross ballot columns freely in selecting nominees. Even though politics became more staid after World War II, the populist-progressive legacy remained.

Despite the tradition of nonpartisanship, the Evergreen State produced three prominent congressional leaders during the postwar period—all Democrats. Warren G. Magnuson (House, 1937–1945; Senate, 1945–1981) and Henry M. Jackson (House, 1941–1953; Senate, 1953–1983) made a powerful combination in the Senate because of their seniority, effectiveness, and strategic committee assignments. Rep. Thomas S. Foley, first elected in 1964 from the 5th District in agricultural eastern Washington, was chosen Speaker of the House in 1989. The record shows that the state often disregards national trends in electing its congressional delegation and that a compelling personality is frequently more important than party affiliation.

The coastal location of the state, which is known as the "Gateway to the Pacific Rim," its heavy dependence on federal appropriations, the importance of the Columbia River system, and other prominent components of its economy create a local agenda that no Washington representative or senator can ignore. Foreign trade, farm policy, forest programs, water and environmental concerns, military installations and defense contracts, atomic energy and nuclear waste, and aerospace development are all among the priority issues.

BIBLIOGRAPHY

Ficken, Robert E., and Charles P. LeWarne. *Washington: A Centennial History.* 1988.
Nice, David C., et al., eds. *Government and Politics in the Evergreen State.* 1992.
Schwantes, Carlos A. *The Pacific Northwest: An Interpretive History.* 1989.

DAVID H. STRATTON

WASHINGTON, D.C. *See* District of Columbia.

WASHINGTON'S FAREWELL ADDRESS. Upon deciding to retire from the presidency in 1796, George Washington resolved to deliver a valedictory address to the nation. His "Farewell Address," a succinct statement of Federalist doctrine, was published in a Philadelphia newspaper on 17 September 1796. Washington's remarks were directed principally toward the citizenry, not the Congress. Indeed, the word *Congress* appears only once in the address, although he alluded to "your Representatives" and to "the public Councils." Washington sought to convince his countrymen of the benefits of national union and the new Constitution.

Some passages, however, clearly were meant for Congress's consideration. Washington warned of the perils of a large standing army and a vast national debt. He advised Congress not to encroach

GEORGE WASHINGTON'S FAREWELL ADDRESS. The first and last pages of the text of the address.

upon the powers of the executive and judicial branches. He admonished Congress to adequately maintain the nation's military capabilities, saying that it must guard against foreign influences upon public opinion and every attempt to "awe the public Councils." The new nation, Washington added, must cultivate friendship with all nations, but it must shun permanent formal alliances with any country.

Reading the Farewell Address on Washington's birthday became, over time, a tradition in the U.S. Senate. In January 1862, with the nation in the midst of the Civil War, a thousand Philadelphia citizens petitioned Congress to commemorate Washington's birthday with a reading of the Farewell Address before one of the houses of Congress. The Senate passed the resolution on 11 February and the House on 14 February, and on 22 February the Senate was led into a packed House chamber to hear Secretary of the Senate John W. Forney read the Farewell Address.

It was not until 1893 that this form of observing Washington's birthday became regular practice. Since that year, the vice president, as president of the Senate, has selected a senator to read the address in legislative session, the assignment alternating between members of each political party.

BIBLIOGRAPHY

Palsits, Victor H. *Washington's Farewell Address.* 1935.

JOHN FERLING

WATERGATE. Perhaps because the series of governmental offenses popularly known as Watergate occurred during the era of the tape recorder and the ubiquitous television camera, the scandal (1972–1975) had more far-reaching impact—most notably the resignation of a sitting president—than any that had preceded it. For only the second time in history, a committee of the House of Representatives voted articles of impeachment against a president of the United States. Only by resigning was Richard M. Nixon spared a vote by the full House that almost certainly would have sent him to a trial before the Senate. Persuaded by fellow Republicans that a guilty verdict by the Senate was inevitable, Nixon in August 1974 exercised the lone option available to him: he became the only U.S. president ever to resign the office.

Entrusted by the Constitution with the power of impeachment, the House assigned investigation of charges against Nixon to its Judiciary Committee, chaired by Peter W. Rodino, Jr. (D-N.J.). After weighing evidence collected by a grand jury and by its own investigators, the Judiciary Committee in late July 1974 adopted a three-article resolution of impeachment charging Nixon with obstruction of justice, misuse of powers and violation of his oath of office, and failure to comply with a House subpoena for audiotapes made in the president's offices, which came to be known as the White House tapes.

Never before had so many Americans witnessed the interplay and clash of their democratic institutions. Televised hearings of the Senate Watergate Committee attracted millions of viewers, riveted by the dramatic unfolding before their eyes of a scandal that had mushroomed from a minor burglary into the destruction of a presidential administration. The historic House Judiciary Committee impeachment votes, also televised, brought into American living rooms a civics lesson in the workings of a system of checks and balances. An out-of-line executive branch was exposed and stopped in its tracks by the legislature and by an independent special prosecutor and in the end penalized by the judicial branch. Observers are nearly unanimous in their assessment of Watergate as proof that the system as established in the Constitution worked.

The Burglary. At its beginning, no one could have anticipated the final dimensions of the scandal. On 17 June 1972, Washington, D.C., police arrested five men inside the headquarters of the Democratic National Committee in the Watergate hotel-apartment-office complex. Even after the intruders were linked to the White House and the Nixon reelection committee, the press treated the occurrence as a minor burglary. If not for a prolonged and bungled cover-up, it might have remained just that. But, fearing political repercussions because the object of the break-in was to reinstall or repair bugs placed earlier in the telephones of Democratic officials, the Nixon administration orchestrated a policy of denial and concealment. Hush money was paid to the break-in crew, administration officials perjured themselves, and in the end more than seventy presidential aides were convicted or pleaded guilty to criminal violations.

It was not until after Nixon's reelection that Watergate became a national concern. After the burglars were convicted in January 1973, one of them—former Central Intelligence Agency operative James W. McCord—wrote a letter to the trial judge, John J. Sirica, contending that witnesses had committed perjury, that others had been paid to remain silent, that high administration and reelection committee officials were involved, and that other crimes had been committed.

Beginnings of Congressional Investigation. The Senate, disturbed by indications of financial irregularities in the 1972 presidential campaign, then broadened the mandate of its Select Committee on Presidential Campaign Activities, which soon became popularly known as the Senate Watergate Committee. It was chaired by the Senate's foremost authority on the Constitution, Sam J. Ervin, Jr. (D-N.C.). Ervin was a logical choice to direct the committee, not only because of his reputation for fairness and integrity but also because it was clear that the committee's most sensitive judgment would likely be on whether the president had failed the constitutional imperative to "take Care that the Laws be faithfully executed."

By mid April 1973, Congress and the American people made clear they would not tolerate an obviously corrupt administration investigating itself and its campaign organization. The Senate Judiciary Committee refused to recommend confirmation of L. Patrick Gray III as Federal Bureau of Investigation director, regarding him as little more than an administration stooge. Richard Kleindienst resigned as attorney general and two of Nixon's closest personal aides, H. R. (Bob) Haldeman and John Ehrlichman, whose roles in the Nixon-ordered "stonewalling" on Watergate had become known, were forced to quit their posts and hire criminal lawyers. Nixon fired John W. Dean III, the White House counsel, who, sensing his own vulnerability, had begun to talk to the prosecutors in the U.S. attorney's office, hoping to arrange a plea bargain.

On 7 May the Senate Judiciary Committee, agreeing to confirm Elliot Richardson as the new attorney general, insisted that he appoint an independent special prosecutor to conduct the Watergate investigation. Richardson, whose own reputation was beyond reproach but who was nonetheless a Nixon appointee, complied on 21 May, naming Archibald Cox, a Harvard law professor, whose charter specified he could be removed only "for cause."

John Dean's Testimony. Four days before the Cox appointment, the Senate Watergate Committee held its first public hearing. It quickly became clear that the star witness would be John Dean. The committee in late June obtained court orders granting Dean limited immunity from prosecution for his testimony. Cox objected, fearing his prosecu-

tions were being jeopardized, but the Senate held fast to its belief that getting to the truth overrode the importance of criminal convictions. Dean transfixed the committee and the nation in the last week of June by testifying that Nixon had known since at least September 1972 about the break-in and subsequent events and that he, Dean, had warned Nixon of "a cancer on the presidency" the previous April. If Dean's testimony were true, impeachment of a president—not attempted in more than a century—was a genuine possibility.

Dean detailed a litany of "White House horrors." In addition to detailed recollections of "cover-up" meetings he had attended with the president, Haldeman, Ehrlichman, and others, Dean disclosed existence of an extensive "enemies list" of people harrassed by Internal Revenue Service investigations because of their opposition to the Nixon administration.

Most significant in Dean's testimony was a comment all but overlooked at the time by the senators and the news media. In recalling a meeting with Nixon on 14 April 1973, Dean remarked offhandedly that at one point the president had moved to a side of the room and appeared to talk into a bookcase, leading Dean to wonder if the conversation was being taped. After this testimony, Senate staff investigators routinely asked White House aides if that were likely. In early July, they hit pay dirt when a little-known former White House assistant, Alexander Butterfield, uttered these fateful words: "There is tape in the Oval Office." In fact, said Butterfield, there were hidden, voice-activated tape recorders in the president's Executive Office Building office, in the Cabinet Room, in the cabin Nixon stayed in when at Camp David, and in several White House meeting rooms.

Subpoenaing the Tapes. Informed of this bombshell, committee chief counsel Sam Dash passed the information on to Dean. When the former White House counsel could scarcely contain his glee, Dash knew that the tapes would corroborate Dean's sensational testimony—if the committee could obtain them.

The stone wall was crumbling, but Nixon, his lawyers, and his co-conspirators would fight on for another year in an increasingly desperate attempt to salvage his presidency. Both the Senate Committee and the special prosecutor subpoenaed specific White House tapes and dictabelts relevant to Watergate. Later, the House Judiciary Committee won House approval to issue its subpoenas for the materials. Citing executive privilege, Nixon not only ig-

WHITE HOUSE COUNSEL JOHN DEAN. Testifying before the Senate Watergate Committee, June 1973.

OFFICE OF THE HISTORIAN OF THE U.S. SENATE

nored the subpoenas but ordered Special Prosecutor Cox not to resort to litigation to obtain the tapes. When Cox defied the order and rejected suggestions that he resign, Nixon on 20 October 1973 precipitated what became known as the "Saturday Night Massacre" by ordering Attorney General Richardson to fire Cox. Bound by his pledge to the Senate to dismiss Cox only "for cause," Richardson resigned. His deputy, William Ruckelshaus, likewise refused to jettison Cox and was himself fired. The third-ranking official of the Department of Justice, Solicitor General Robert Bork, then fired Cox and ordered the Watergate Special Prosecution Force absorbed into the Justice Department. The offices and files of Cox and his staff were sealed in what was the most frightening episode of the Watergate scandal.

A firestorm of protest swept the country. Not only Congress and the courts were alarmed, but so were the American people, who fully understood that defiance of court orders to produce evidence in a criminal proceeding is unacceptable even by—and perhaps especially by—a president of the United States. When the national outrage showed no sign of abating, Nixon agreed to obey the grand jury subpoena and, three days after the "massacre," ordered Bork to reestablish the Watergate Special Prosecution Force with a new head, Leon Jaworski, a Texas lawyer with a formidable reputation for integrity.

In surrendering the tapes in November, the White House further fueled the firestorm by acknowledging that there was an eighteen-and-one-half-minute gap in a subpoenaed tape of a conversation between Nixon and Haldeman on 20 June 1972, only three days after the break-in. Whatever was said in the gap, which evidence indicates was caused by Nixon himself, remains unknown. But as large numbers of Nixon's aides pleaded guilty to various crimes and went off to prison, the question became, as Solicitor General Bork himself once put it, not whether the president could remain in office but whether he could escape a criminal indictment.

The Move toward Impeachment. While the Watergate grand jury pondered that question, the House Judiciary Committee began consideration of articles of impeachment, its deliberations aided by an order of Judge Sirica's transferring grand jury evidence to the committee.

Chairman Rodino was inundated by forty-four Watergate-related resolutions introduced in late October 1973, half of which focused on impeachment of the president. Others called for the appointment of a special prosecutor with true independence from the White House. Several Republican members of the committee complained that they were not being kept informed and that Rodino, in the words of one, "has been running this inquiry pretty much out of his hat." But the ranking minority member, Rep. Edward Hutchinson of Michigan, worked cooperatively with Rodino. All thirty-eight committee members were lawyers and were therefore expected to act on a basis of the evidence and in accord with the committee's reputation for avoiding partisanship. But politics predictably asserted itself, and Rodino appointed a "supervisory committee" consisting of the seven senior members from each party. Emerging as the most influential in committee deliberations were Democrats Jack Brooks of Texas, Robert W. Kastenmeier of Wisconsin, and William L. Hungate of Missouri. The Republicans most prominent included Robert McClory and Thomas F. Railsback of Illinois, David W. Dennis of Indiana, and Charles E. Wiggins of California. Rodino agreed to share the subpoena power with Hutchinson, thus diluting allegations of partisanship.

Nixon's prolonged resistance to committee subpoenas solidified the committee's will. Its request for specific tapes important to its impeachment investigation passed by a vote of 33 to 3. But subsequent Republican attempts to ease the president's situation were decided along party lines—21 to 17 in favor of the majority Democrats. After months of negotiations, Nixon on 30 April turned over to the committee many heavily edited transcripts of taped White House conversations, and Rodino angrily announced that the subpoena had not been complied with.

On 24 July, the Supreme Court dealt a blow to Nixon when it unanimously upheld Jaworski's subpoena for the White House tapes. This order clearly established the primacy of the law over the authority of the president. Although there had been support in the White House for a refusal to obey the court order, the Court's unanimity and the mood of the Congress and the people rendered such an act impossible. Nixon quickly announced that the court order would be obeyed.

Nixon's Resignation. In the hands of investigators, the tapes quickly supplied "the smoking gun," incontrovertible evidence of the president's leading role in the obstruction of justice. A 23 June 1972 tape of a conversation between Nixon and Haldeman aired their plan to divert an FBI investigation of Watergate by falsely notifying the bureau that it had stumbled on a top secret CIA operation and that it should back off.

On three days in late July 1974, the House Judiciary Committee adopted its impeachment articles. On 9 August 1974, Nixon submitted his resignation to Secretary of State Henry Kissinger and flew off to exile at his estate in San Clemente, California.

Little more than a month after Nixon fled Washington, Gerald R. Ford, who succeeded him, attempted to end what he termed "our national nightmare" by pardoning Nixon, an act that many believed cost Ford the 1976 presidential election. For the rest of his days, Nixon would seek redemption by writing books and speaking to small groups, particularly on foreign policy, an area in which his competence and authority were largely unquestioned. As to Watergate, he never specifically acknowledged being guilty of anything other than poor judgment. Even some of his supporters, however, regarded his acceptance of a pardon that spared him from criminal prosecution as acknowledgment enough.

[*See also* Watergate Committee.]

BIBLIOGRAPHY

Congressional Quarterly Inc. *Watergate: Chronology of a Crisis.* 1975.

Jaworski, Leon. *The Right and the Power.* 1976.

Kutler, Stanley I. *The Wars of Watergate.* 1990.

HAYS GOREY

WATERGATE COMMITTEE. In 1973 the Senate, acting in accord with its own traditions, established the Select Committee on Presidential Campaign Activities, known as the Watergate Committee, to investigate the Watergate scandals of the Nixon administration. Select committees had also been appointed to look into the conduct of Sen. Joseph R. McCarthy in the communist witch-hunting days of the 1950s, into the Teapot Dome scandal of the 1920s, and into numerous other events involving real or suspected malfeasance by high government officials.

Chosen to head the seven-member committee was Samuel J. Ervin, Jr., a widely respected North Carolina Democrat and authority on the Constitution. Through his chairmanship of the most widely televised Senate hearings to that time, the self-described "country lawyer" quickly became a folk hero. Ervin's thick, gyrating eyebrows, heavy jowls, biblical and Shakespearean references, and firm yet courtly conduct of the hearings endeared him to millions of television viewers.

The committee's ranking Republican, Howard H. Baker, Jr., of Tennessee, was far more partisan. Until the hearings made abundantly clear the likelihood of a cover-up managed by top White House advisers, almost certainly with the connivance of the president himself, Baker remained, despite a public posture of neutrality, an administration loyalist behind the scenes. "What did the president know and when did he know it?" Baker asked early in the hearings, and the question became the most memorable and oft-quoted rationale for the committee's investigation, but it also masked Baker's private allegiance to the administration.

An overt Nixon loyalist on the committee was Florida Republican Edward J. Gurney, who belittled the Watergate break-in as signifying no more than "normal" election-year politics. The third Republican, Connecticut's maverick Lowell P. Weicker, Jr., vigorously questioned witnesses and proclaimed his determination to "bring dirty business like the Watergate out in the open."

The three Democrats who joined Ervin to form the committee's majority were Hawaii's Daniel K. Inouye, New Mexico's Joseph M. Montoya, and Georgia's Herman E. Talmadge, none of whom emerged from Ervin's large shadow to make a lasting public impression. Chosen as majority counsel was Samuel Dash, a Georgetown University law professor. Committee Republicans picked Fred V. Thompson, a Nashville lawyer, to be the minority counsel.

The hearings, which began on 7 May 1973, contributed hugely to the search for truth about the scandal, a process that would lead to the only resignation of a president in U.S. history. Speaking in a flat monotone, and under a grant of limited immunity, the committee's star witness, former White House counsel John Dean, told a riveted nation of a White House cover-up in which he, top administration aides, and Nixon himself had participated. Exhibiting a photographic memory for dates and conversations, Dean told the committee he had warned Nixon that Watergate was "a cancer on the presidency" and that the cover-up of involvement of Nixon campaign aides in the Watergate burglary and other crimes amounted to a criminal obstruction of justice.

But how to corroborate Dean's explosive testimony? Dean testified that during one conversation with Nixon, the president had seemed to be making exculpatory comments as if into a tape recorder. When a committee attorney routinely asked Alexander Butterfield, a presidential assistant, if that were possible, Butterfield revealed the extensive White House taping system that Nixon had ordered him to install. "Everything was taped," Butterfield told the startled committee staff. When Dean was informed, his undisguised elation enhanced his credibility with the committee.

The first phase of the hearings, dealing with the Watergate break-in and cover-up, ended on 7 August 1973 after the testimony of sixty-three witnesses. Subsequent hearings, starting in September 1973 and continuing through the winter, focused on alleged political sabotage and finance activities of the president's 1972 reelection campaign. On 12 July 1974, some seventeen months after its creation under Senate Resolution 60, the Watergate Committee issued its final report—a 2,217-page summary of the most intense congressional investigation of its kind in history.

The tape recordings ultimately sealed Nixon's fate. After a clumsy attempt to make public heavily edited transcripts, the president was ordered by the Supreme Court to surrender key tapes to the special prosecutor. Included was a "smoking gun" conversation between Nixon and his top aide, H. R. Haldeman, in which the two discussed diverting Federal Bureau of Investigation agents looking into Watergate funding by warning them they had stumbled across a secret Central Intelligence Agency operation that in fact had never existed. Support for the Nixon presidency, steadily eroding during months of hearings by the Senate Watergate Committee, the House Judiciary Committee, and investigations of the special prosecutor, collapsed. On 10 August 1974 Richard M. Nixon resigned in disgrace.

BIBLIOGRAPHY

Dash, Samuel. *Chief Counsel: Inside the Ervin Committee—The Untold Story.* 1976.
Kutler, Stanley I. *The Wars of Watergate.* 1990.
Congressional Quarterly Inc. *Watergate: Chronology of a Crisis.* 1975.

HAYS GOREY

WATKINS V. UNITED STATES

WATKINS V. UNITED STATES (354 U.S. 178 [1957]). The Supreme Court case of *Watkins v. United States* partly set the pattern for judicial scrutiny of congressional investigations during the red-baiting era of the 1950s. In an investigation of domestic communists generally and sometimes communists from labor unions in particular, the House Committee on Un-American Activities (HUAC) held John T. Watkins, a union officer, in contempt. When questioned loosely about people unrelated to unions, Watkins had refused to identify several as former Communist party members.

The Supreme Court ruled for Watkins, saying that since HUAC's questions wandered from the subject of unions, the committee had failed to establish one of the essential points, the precise subject of its investigation. Also, in its ruling the Court made a number of broad statements, more in the nature of commentary, criticizing HUAC as having violated the First Amendment's binding protections of individual liberty.

Congress responded to the decision by threatening to enact laws to limit the Supreme Court's jurisdiction. Two years later, in *Barenblatt v. United States* (1959), the Court upheld a different HUAC contempt conviction, effectively overruling much of *Watkins's* broad commentary. Thus, *Watkins* and *Barenblatt* together established the pattern for cases during the era of McCarthyism: the courts upheld Congress's investigative power generally while overturning convictions on narrow procedural points. *Watkins* remains memorable for the Court's strong approval of Congress's "broad power" to conduct "probes into departments of the Federal Government to expose corruption, inefficiency or waste."

BIBLIOGRAPHY

Beck, Carl. *Contempt of Congress: A Study of the Prosecutions Initiated by the Committee on Un-American Activities, 1945–57.* 1959.
Grabow, John C. *Congressional Investigations: Law and Practice.* 1988.

CHARLES TIEFER

WAYS AND MEANS COMMITTEE, HOUSE.

The Committee on Ways and Means has long been considered one of the most important and prestigious of the standing committees of the House of Representatives. Although the committee was a principal target of reformers seeking to democratize power in Congress during the 1970s, it has retained an important role in House policy-making due to its broad jurisdiction.

From its inception the jurisdiction of the Ways and Means Committee has involved matters of taxation and finance, to which was added authority over social welfare programs during the twentieth century. The jurisdiction of the committee in the early nineteenth century included revenues and expenditures, the public debt, and oversight of executive departments. Tariffs for protection of domestic manufacturers were referred to other House committees until the 1830s, when the growing revenues produced by protective tariffs allowed the Ways and Means Committee successfully to assert jurisdiction over these measures as revenue matters. The other major change in the committee's jurisdiction during the nineteenth century came in the 1860s, when authority to review spending bills and banking and currency measures was transferred to other House panels. A major expansion of jurisdiction during the twentieth century was set in motion in 1935, when the House assigned responsibility for drafting Social Security legislation to the Ways and Means Committee. All of the programs enacted under the original Social Security legislation were added to the committee's jurisdiction (Old Age and Survivors Insurance, Unemployment Compensation, Aid to Families with Dependent Children), as was the Medicare program, enacted as an amendment to the Social Security Act in 1965. An attempt by House reformers in 1974 to effect a major redistribution of the committee's jurisdiction was only partly successful, resulting in a transfer of authority over some health programs to the Energy and Commerce Committee, but leaving the vast majority of the Ways and Means panel's jurisdiction over tax, trade, and social welfare legislation intact.

Origins. The use of a committee, sometimes called a committee of ways and means, to oversee taxing and spending matters had a long history in both the British House of Commons and in American colonial and state legislatures prior to the creation of the federal Congress. The House of Representatives appointed a committee of ways and means as a temporary (select) committee shortly after the First Congress convened in 1789. However, this panel was quickly superseded by a working arrangement in which the new secretary of the Treasury, Alexander Hamilton, assumed a leading role in economic and budgetary matters. Partly in response to concerns that Hamilton was acting too independently of the House, a new select committee was appointed to review tax and credit measures in 1794. In 1795, a proposal by Pennsylvanian Albert Gallatin to create a standing Committee of Ways and Means was adopted by the House. This early committee reviewed information submitted by the Treasury Department and other executive agencies, made recommendations to the full House, and drafted legislation dealing with financial matters. After having been reappointed in each session of Congress between 1795 and 1801, the Committee of Ways and Means was formally incorporated into the Standing Rules of the House in 1802.

Nineteenth Century. The House rules that conferred standing committee status on the Committee of Ways and Means in 1802 gave the committee jurisdiction over both revenue and spending bills, as well as responsibility for overseeing the expenditures of executive departments. During its early years, the committee was involved in developing legislation to finance the War of 1812 and in initiating the first American protective tariff in 1816. Although jurisdiction over protective tariffs was for a time conceded to the new Committee on Manufactures, during the 1830s the Ways and Means Committee successfully reasserted its authority to review all tariff legislation. By this time the committee had also consolidated jurisdiction over appropriations bills governing expenditures by executive agencies. With responsibility for tax, appropriations, and tariff legislation, the panel was ensured a prominent role in policy-making, and its chairmanship was considered a position of House leadership second only to the speakership during the decades leading up to the Civil War.

The nineteenth-century Ways and Means Committee reached its peak of influence during the Civil War years. Under the chairmanship of Republican Thaddeus Stevens of Pennsylvania, the nine-member panel reviewed revenue and spending measures related to the war effort. Due to the heavy committee work load, legislation first began to be delegated to subcommittees during this period. Measures reported by the committee during the war years established the first national income tax and the first national paper currency. Judging that the Ways and Means Committee had become too overloaded to manage its responsibilities effectively, the House voted in 1865 to transfer jurisdiction over spending measures to the new Committee on Appropriations and to reassign responsibility for measures dealing with the nation's financial system to the new Committee on Banking and Currency.

Although its jurisdiction had been substantially reduced, the Committee of Ways and Means (formally renamed the Committee on Ways and Means during the 1880s) remained a key House unit because of the political prominence of the tax and tariff issues that now constituted its principal areas of jurisdiction. Ways and Means chairs were frequently named floor leaders for the majority party in the House; after 1885, they were regularly appointed to the Rules Committee as well. By the 1890s a Ways and Means Committee numbering fifteen members had become a key part of a system of centralized party leadership directed by the Speaker.

Throughout the late nineteenth century and the early years of the twentieth, the most important issues handled by the committee involved tariffs. The policy of maintaining tariff protection for U.S. industry was advanced primarily by congressional Republicans, although some Democrats from industrialized areas in the East were strong protectionists as well. Support for tariff reductions came primarily from southern and western Democrats until the early 1900s, when tariff reform began to win greater support among Republicans. Tariff politics on the Ways and Means Committee during this period reflected changing revenue needs of the federal government and shifting partisan control of the House. Democratic majorities on Ways and Means recommended but failed to win enactment of major tariff reduction measures in 1884 and 1888. A third attempt at tariff reform initiated by Ways and Means Democrats passed in 1894 (the Wilson-Gorman Tariff), but only after many of the rate reductions voted by the House were rejected by the Senate. Tariff bills enacted by Republican majorities in 1872, 1875, 1890 (the McKinley Tariff), and 1897 (the Dingley Tariff) maintained high tariff rates and reaffirmed the policy of protectionism. The Payne-Aldrich Tariff of 1909 was also drafted by a Republican majority on Ways and Means but reflected a shift among Republicans toward support for a more limited and rationalized system of tariff protection for U.S. goods.

From Party Government to Committee Autonomy. In the aftermath of reforms enacted during 1910 and 1911 to reduce the powers of the Speaker, the Ways and Means Committee was for a brief time at the center of a new system of party government. After 1911 authority to make committee assignments for House Democrats was transferred from the Speaker to the Democratic members of the Ways and Means Committee, and the committee's chairman was also floor leader for the Democratic party. Under the active leadership of Ways and

Means chairman Oscar W. Underwood of Alabama (1911–1915) this new system produced close cooperation among the Democratic caucus and standing committees and resulted in the enactment of major tariff reductions and the reinstatement of the federal income tax in the Underwood Tariff (1913).

After Republicans regained control of the House in 1919, the direct connection between the Ways and Means Committee and the majority party leadership was ended by the adoption of rules that prohibited the majority floor leader from chairing a legislative committee. Following this rules change, selection of Ways and Means chairs began to be governed exclusively by seniority rather than party considerations. Ways and Means Democrats continued to perform the committee assignment function for their party, but no longer was the committee directly linked to the party leadership. In 1919 the committee was also expanded from fifteen to twenty-five members, the size it would remain for more than fifty years.

Although more independent of the majority party organization, the Ways and Means Committee remained at the center of economic policy-making during the Republican-dominated 1920s and in the New Deal era that followed. At the request of Secretary of the Treasury Andrew W. Mellon, three major tax reduction measures were initiated by the Ways and Means Committee and enacted into law during the 1920s, the last of which (Revenue Act of 1926) also established the Joint Committee on Taxation to assist in gathering and analyzing information on tax policy issues. Under the leadership of Chairman Willis C. Hawley of Oregon, in 1929 the committee initiated the disastrous Smoot-Hawley Tariff bill, which provoked similar protectionist responses from countries trading with the United States and contributed to a deepening worldwide economic depression.

After Democrats regained control of Congress and the White House in the 1930s, the Ways and Means Committee participated in the development of major trade policy reforms in 1934, and in passage of the Social Security Act in 1935. The Reciprocal Trade Agreements Act (1934) delegated the task of negotiating tariff rates to the executive branch, shifting the committee's function in the trade area from recommending specific tariff rates to overseeing the broad features of trade policy. The Social Security Act (1935) laid the foundation for the modern welfare state in the United States and led to a major expansion in the committee's legislative and oversight responsibilities as Social Security and other social welfare programs incorporated in the act (including Unemployment Compensation and Aid to Families with Dependent Children) were added to the committee's jurisdiction.

After the late 1930s the Ways and Means Committee began to demonstrate greater independence from House leaders and from presidents of both parties. The committee rejected a number of major tax policy proposals requested by Democratic presidents Franklin D. Roosevelt and Harry S. Truman during the 1940s. Likewise, during 1953 and 1954, when Republicans gained control of both Congress and the White House, the Republican majority on the committee clashed with President Eisenhower over tax and trade measures. The committee did work closely with the Eisenhower administration, however, in drafting the Internal Revenue Code of 1954, a landmark bill that completely revised the existing federal tax system.

Mills Era. Most observers of the modern House agree that the Ways and Means Committee reached the height of its power and autonomy under the leadership of Arkansas Democrat Wilbur D. Mills, chairman from 1958 to 1974. During the Mills era the Ways and Means Committee developed a mode of operation that struck a balance between committee autonomy and responsiveness to majorities in the House. The committee wrote legislation in sessions closed to the public and press, and brought its bills to the House floor under closed rules that prohibited amendments from non–committee members. Members of both parties were carefully recruited to ensure responsiveness to regional interests and to the concerns of the House. House members also viewed the procedural autonomy of the committee as a means to insulate tax legislation from interest group demands, and as a way to protect the institutional power of the House in relation to the executive and the Senate.

An important feature of committee politics during the Mills years was what political scientist John Manley termed *restrained partisanship*. Although Democrats maintained majorities in the House and on the committee throughout this period, members of both parties took part in deliberations through which legislation took form. Party conflict, when it occurred on the committee, was usually limited to splits in voting during the final stages of decision making. Because of Republican participation, bills reported by the committee were often more conservative than the Democratic House leadership would have preferred.

Subcommittees were abolished shortly after Mills became chairman, which placed all of the committee's legislative work under his close direction. For Chairman Mills, effective leadership meant protecting the panel's prestige by ensuring that committee bills were capable of winning support on the House floor. Although members were chosen partly on the basis of party loyalty and were expected to represent their party's positions on issues before the committee, most were also attentive to the goal of protecting the committee's reputation and prestige. Mills paid careful attention to both the substantive and political dimensions of legislation, moving ahead only when he believed approval by the House was assured. Mills was renowned for his influence in the House during the 1960s and early 1970s, but close observers of the Ways and Means Committee argued that the chairman's influence was based more on his mastery of committee issues (especially taxation) and skill at brokering compromises than in use of his formal powers as chairman. Mills's long leadership career ended in 1974 when he resigned from the Ways and Means chair after a period of erratic personal behavior (later attributed by Mills to alcoholism). Among the important bills on which the Mills-era committee left its imprint were trade acts in 1962 and 1974, major tax measures in 1964 and 1969, and the Medicare Act of 1965, which provided health coverage for the elderly and the poor, and expanded the committee's jurisdiction to encompass health care issues.

1970s Reform Era. The Ways and Means Committee was one of the principal targets of the reform movement that swept the House during the 1970s. Partly because of liberal Democrats' frustrations with the cautious approach of the Mills-era committee to new policy initiatives, and partly because of demands for greater openness and participation made by the large numbers of new members elected to the House in the 1970s, reforms were enacted to reduce the autonomy of the committee and increase the control of the majority party over the committee's operation.

The 1970s reforms, the most sweeping since the period from 1910 to 1911, reined in the power of committee chairs, granted greater authority to subcommittees, and reversed the trend toward committee autonomy that had developed over the previous half century. Committee chairs were no longer chosen solely on the basis of seniority. Those who failed to be responsive to the wishes of rank-and-file Democrats risked removal under new rules that required election by a secret ballot of the Democratic caucus.

New rules were also enacted to discourage committees from meeting in closed-door sessions. In addition to these changes, which affected all committees, several reforms were targeted specifically at the Ways and Means Committee. These reforms included transferring the committee assignment function from Ways and Means Democrats to a new Steering and Policy Committee chaired by the Speaker; changes in the "closed rule" procedure to allow amendments to Ways and Means bills to be proposed by a vote of the Democratic caucus; a requirement that subcommittees be reestablished; and expansion of the committee's size from twenty-five to thirty-seven members. A plan to restructure committee jurisdictions—including a transfer of trade legislation and some health and welfare issues from Ways and Means to other panels—was also proposed, but failed to win approval. Finally, budget reforms enacted in 1974 also reduced the autonomy of the Ways and Means Committee by creating new Budget committees in the House and Senate and new procedures for coordinating tax and spending decisions.

New patterns in appointments of members to the committee also began to appear during the 1970s. Whereas Ways and Means Committee appointments had previously gone primarily to senior members from relatively safe districts, recruitment was opened to junior members, including freshmen, and to members from highly competitive constituencies. As during the Mills era, party leaders continued to take an active role in appointments, but different types of members were being attracted to the committee. In earlier years most had sought seats on Ways and Means to enjoy the influence and prestige associated with the committee's broad jurisdiction and committee assignment function; committee members appointed since the 1970s have been more oriented toward advancing policy objectives. Thus as a consequence of reforms and other changes in the 1970s, Ways and Means became a larger, more heterogeneous committee operating in an institutional setting that allowed less autonomy for standing committees and greater influence for the majority party and the parent chamber through the budget process. Along with these organizational changes, the reform-era committee experienced turnover in leadership in 1975 when Al Ullman of Oregon succeeded Wilbur Mills as chairman. Rather than focusing his efforts on protecting the committee's prestige and record of floor success as Mills had, Ullman emphasized open debate and participation by committee members. Chairs of the newly reestablished subcommittees were also allowed wide discretion in hiring staff and granted considerable independence in legislative activity.

Committee decision making during the Ullman years became more partisan and less predictable, and committee recommendations frequently encountered amendments on the House floor. Some expressed appreciation for Ullman's efforts to democratize the committee during his chairmanship (1975–1980), but others expressed frustration over the volatile committee politics that resulted and the impression that Ways and Means had lost influence to its counterpart, the Senate Finance Committee. Operating in a turbulent political environment, the Ullman-era committee was influential in the enactment of tax reform legislation in 1976 and in redirecting tax policy toward concerns with economic growth in the Revenue Act of 1978. The committee also played a major role in reviewing President Jimmy Carter's 1977 energy plan, major Social Security legislation in 1978, and the Trade Agreements Act of 1979.

Postreform Committee. Committee politics in the 1980s and 1990s have taken place in an institutional setting that has been described as the "postreform House." The main features of this new environment include increased partisanship and a more active majority party leadership, an agenda dominated by budget deficits, a more restrictive budget process, and a reversal of some of the decentralizing tendencies of the 1970s' reforms.

New patterns in Ways and Means Committee politics during the 1980s and 1990s reflect both the postreform political environment and new committee leadership. After Al Ullman's electoral defeat in 1980, Dan Rostenkowski of Illinois assumed the chairmanship. An old-school Chicago machine politician, Rostenkowski developed an activist leadership style that centralized authority in the chair. The main elements of Rostenkowski's approach to leadership included: active involvement in committee recruitment; encouragement of group solidarity; consultation and negotiation with committee members to win firm commitments of support for committee bills; threats of punishment for those who failed to support the committee majority; and active monitoring of subcommittee activity and centralized control over staff. To enhance the committee's chances for success in passing bills on the House floor, Rostenkowski preferred to build bipartisan coalitions; however, the highly partisan nature of many of the issues in the committee's jurisdic-

tion and the expectation that committee Democrats will represent the views of the Democratic caucus on major issues limit possibilities for bipartisanship on the postreform committee.

With Rostenkowski's indictment on federal charges of financial misconduct in 1994, the next most senior Democrat, Sam M. Gibbons of Florida, became chairman. New leadership on Ways and Means will be important in shaping relations between majority and minority party members on the committee, in assigning authority over committee staff, and in determining the degree of independence of subcommittees.

Partisan conflict on the postreform Ways and Means Committee varies across issues but is an ever-present factor because of the long-established pattern in both parties of appointing primarily members who have established records of party loyalty. Both before and after the 1970s reform era, Democrats tended to select committee members who were somewhat more liberal, and Republicans chose members who were somewhat more conservative, than the average for their respective parties in the House. By the 1990s, the older pattern of restrained partisanship was little in evidence on Ways and Means. The most common pattern in the committee's politics had become one in which major committee bills took form primarily through deliberations within the Democratic majority. Social welfare issues—health, welfare, and Social Security—tended to produce the most consistent partisan alignments in committee voting; tax and trade issues were somewhat less partisan.

During the 1980s and 1990s, the legislative agenda of the Ways and Means Committee was constrained by the problem of large budget deficits. After competing unsuccessfully with the Reagan administration to control tax reduction legislation in 1981, the committee was involved in developing a succession of deficit reduction packages involving both tax increases and spending controls in the social entitlement programs within its jurisdiction. These efforts have been structured by a succession of budgetary mechanisms including the Gramm-Rudman-Hollings bill, the Budget Enforcement Act of 1990, and further procedural changes incorporated in the Clinton administration budget adopted in 1993. The committee played an important role in the enactment of reforms in the Social Security program in 1983 and in a historic tax reform measure adopted in 1986. The panel remained active in trade policy, reporting out major trade bills in 1984 and 1988 and successfully recommending approval of the North American Free Trade Agreement in 1993. The Ways and Means Committee was also one of the most important congressional panels involved in developing health care reform legislation in 1994 in response to proposals from the Clinton administration.

The House Ways and Means Committee, because of its jurisdiction over finance and economic policy, has remained an important body in national policy-making since its origins in the early nineteenth century. As Congress begins its third century, high membership turnover and new leadership hold out the possibility that the Ways and Means Committee may be on the verge of a new era in its long history as one of the most important standing committees in Congress. Still, for the foreseeable future the Ways and Means Committee will remain at the center of national policy debates involving economic policy, international trade, welfare, and health care policy because of its responsibility for reviewing legislation for the House in these areas.

[*See also* Finance Committee, Senate; Tariffs and Trade; Taxation; Taxation Committee, Joint.]

BIBLIOGRAPHY

Fenno, Richard F., Jr. *Congressmen in Committees.* 1973.

Manley, John F. "Wilbur D. Mills: A Study in Congressional Influence." *American Political Science Review* 63 (1969): 442–464.

Manley, John F. *The Politics of Finance: The House Committee on Ways and Means.* 1970.

Strahan, Randall. *New Ways and Means: Reform and Change in a Congressional Committee.* 1990.

Strahan, Randall. "Dan Rostenkowski: A Study in Congressional Power." In *Congress Reconsidered,* 5th ed. Edited by Bruce I. Oppenheimer and Lawrence C. Dodd. 1993.

U.S. House of Representatives. Committee on Ways and Means. *The Committee on Ways and Means: A Bicentennial History, 1789–1989,* by Donald R. Kennon and Rebecca M. Rogers. 101st Cong., 1st sess., 1989. H. Doc. 100-244.

RANDALL STRAHAN

WEBSTER, DANIEL (1782–1852), representative from New Hampshire and representative and senator from Massachusetts, exponent of constitutional nationalism and defender of the Union. Webster's career in public affairs spanned forty years, from the War of 1812 until his death in 1852. He served in Congress for more than a quarter of a century, first as a representative from New Hampshire (1813–1817), then as a representative (1823–1827) and senator (1827–1841 and 1845–1850) from Massachusetts. The hiatus in the senatorial years is explained by a term as secretary of State (1841–1843), a post he assumed again at the end of his Senate career. Along with John C. Calhoun and Henry Clay, Webster stood out as one of the most important public figures in the second generation of U.S. congressional leadership. In contrast to Clay's legacy, however, Webster's record was not strong in fashioning specific legislation. His importance lay, rather, in his advocacy of certain principles and in the central role he played in the great debates of his time. His historical significance can best be understood and charted through an assessment of his major speeches.

Supported by Portsmouth merchants outraged by Thomas Jefferson's 1807 embargo and James Madison's war, Webster began his political career as an ardent Federalist. As a freshman congressman, he unrelentingly criticized the Madison administration's conduct of the war and championed states' rights. In a speech of 9 December 1814, Webster came close to endorsing nullification when he opposed a conscription bill as tyrannical and unconstitutional. "It will be," he stated, "the solemn

DANIEL WEBSTER. Engraving by J. A. J. Wilcox.

duty of the State Governments to protect their own authority over their own militia, and to interpose between their citizens and arbitrary power." An ironic beginning to a career that came to center on promoting federal authority and national unity, the positions taken by Webster as a New Hampshire Federalist haunted him for the rest of his life and may have prevented him from ever receiving a presidential nomination by a major political party.

In 1822, a committee led by the prominent merchant shipper Thomas H. Perkins persuaded Webster to leave his Boston legal practice and reenter politics. With the core support of Boston's leading bankers, merchants, and manufacturers, Webster did not have to seek political office actively. Public office, as Richard N. Current has observed, "quite literally, sought him" (in Shewmaker, 1990, p. 7).

From 1823 to 1827, as a Federalist and then a National Republican, Webster faithfully represented the interests of his constituents. For example, in the early 1820s he advocated free trade but switched to protectionism as Massachusetts entrepreneurs increasingly turned to manufacturing. In fact, Webster had criticized protectionist theory so effectively that he found himself hard-pressed to refute his own arguments. By the late 1820s, however, he had become a consistent supporter of Clay's so-called American system of a high protective tariff, a national bank, and internal improvements. Along with Clay, he played a key role in securing the election of John Quincy Adams to the presidency in 1824 and 1825. Webster persuaded the Maryland delegation to vote for the New Englander in the House of Representatives. He then functioned as a spokesman for the Adams administration in the House, where he served as chairman of the Judiciary Committee.

In foreign policy, Webster championed the cause of Greek independence and the principles of the Monroe Doctrine. His 1823 resolution calling for the appointment of a commissioner to Greece was defeated. But he won national and international acclaim for his moving appeal of 1824 in which he urged freedom-loving Americans to manifest their moral sympathy "with a long oppressed" people struggling valiantly against "barbaric" Ottoman masters. Regarding the Monroe Doctrine, Webster in a speech of 14 April 1826 called James Monroe's foreign policy principles a "bright page in our history" and a national treasure that he intended to guard.

In 1827 Webster entered the Senate as a National Republican and soon adhered to the emerging Whig coalition that coalesced in opposition to the policies of President Andrew Jackson. It was during his senatorial years that Webster made his greatest mark on American history. His famous Second Reply to Sen. Robert Y. Hayne of South Carolina, a two-day speech delivered on 26 and 27 January 1830, was the pivotal event of Webster's congressional career. In that address, which is still regarded as one of the greatest speeches ever delivered in the Senate, Webster countered Calhoun's thesis that the United States was a loose compact of sovereign states with the argument that the Constitution provided for the perpetual union of one people. In his stirring peroration, he called for "Liberty *and* Union, now and for ever, one and inseparable!" Webster never wavered in his commitment to this view. As a contemporary eulogist wrote, when it came to the great questions involving national unity and constitutional liberty, you could calculate Webster's course "like a planet."

In matters of partisan politics, Webster was less predictable. As a onetime Federalist, Webster adhered to the ideal of government by disinterested gentlemen and never fully accepted the discipline and voter-oriented assumptions of both the Jacksonian Democrats and the Whigs. He scathingly denounced Jackson's 1832 message explaining his veto of a bill rechartering the Bank of the United States. Webster faulted Jackson for gross constitutional fallacies, for inciting class warfare, and for raising the cry that "liberty is in danger" in order to impose an executive despotism on the American people. He sided with Jackson, however, in the nullification crisis with South Carolina. In 1833, Webster took the lead in securing Senate passage of the Force Bill, and he staunchly opposed Clay's compromise tariff as an unprincipled concession to nullifiers. According to Webster, "The principle was bad, the measure was bad, the consequences were bad." Webster even tried unsuccessfully to induce Jackson into joining him in creating a new Constitution and Union party in order to end two-party partisanship. But in 1834, he rejoined the Whig fold when he voted for a resolution censuring the president for unconstitutionally removing federal deposits from the national bank. He became chairman of the Committee on Finance in 1836. Throughout the 1830s, Webster opposed the laissez-faire philosophy of the Democratic majority, advocating instead a Hamiltonian state that would stimulate the economy through means such as federal revenue sharing and easy credit policies. The "very end of government," he stated in 1838, is to "do that for individuals which individuals cannot do for themselves."

After serving as secretary of State under William Henry Harrison and John Tyler, Webster returned to the Senate in 1845. As befitted a former secretary of State, he was appointed to the Committee on Foreign Relations and served on that body until 1850. In 1846, however, Democratic representative Charles J. Ingersoll of Pennsylvania, chairman of the House Committee on Foreign Affairs, attempted to impeach Webster retroactively for alleged high misdemeanors committed while serving as secretary of State. Ingersoll and Webster had been bitter personal and political enemies since the War of 1812. Webster's blistering characterization of Ingersoll as a person possessing a "grotesque—bizarre" mind with screws "loose all over" ensured an investigation of Webster's record from 1841 to 1843 by a House select committee. Primarily because of the decisive testimony of ex-president Tyler, the committee exonerated him.

Two related issues, territorial expansion and slavery, dominated the national agenda from 1845 to 1850. Webster felt that both threatened to undermine the integrity of the Union, and he played a central role in the great debates over each. Webster had resigned from the Tyler cabinet in part because of the president's move to annex Texas, and he became one of the harshest critics of the expansionist policies of President James K. Polk. In 1846, Webster opposed the war with Mexico as unconstitutional, unnecessary, and unjust; voted for the Wilmot Proviso; and supported the Oregon partition treaty. At the same time, when Charles Sumner and other Conscience Whigs asked him to lead them in a crusade to rid the country of slavery, Webster declined. He chose to stand, in his own words, by the Constitution "as it is"; it would have been out of character for him to have done otherwise. To Webster, upholding the Constitution and the Union was no less a matter of moral principle than was opposition to slavery.

Like Abraham Lincoln, Webster took the position that, although slavery was wrong, it was constitutional and legal. He also believed, as did Lincoln, that slavery should not be allowed to spread into the territories. These convictions undergirded his opposition to the Treaty of Guadalupe Hidalgo of 1848, which ended the Mexican War. In a major speech of 23 March, Webster explained why he joined thirteen other senators in voting against that agreement. He denounced the accord as an immoral product of land hunger and advocated an

honorable peace "without territory." Convinced that the annexation of California and New Mexico would jeopardize national unity, he categorically rejected "to-day, and for ever, and to the end, any proposition to add any foreign territory, south or west, north or east, to the States of this Union." There must, he concluded, "be some limit to the extent of our territories, and . . . I wished this country should exhibit to the world the example of a powerful republic, without greediness and hunger of empire."

Webster played a prominent role in the historic crisis of the Union in 1850, and his controversial speech of 7 March marked the last great oration of his long congressional career. Instead of accepting the advice of friends not to alienate northerners by taking too strong a position, he unequivocally supported Clay's compromise proposals. Webster spoke, in his own words, "not as a Massachusetts man, nor as a Northern man, but as an American . . . for the preservation of the Union." He denounced both abolitionists and secessionists, the former as fanatics and perfectionists who dealt "with morals as with mathematics" and ignored the dictum of Saint Paul "that we are not to 'do evil that good may come'" and the latter as irresponsible reactionaries advocating "an utter impossibility." "Never did there devolve on any generation of men higher trusts than now devolve upon us," he concluded, "for the preservation of this Constitution and the harmony and peace of all who are destined to live under it."

Webster's advocacy of a stringent fugitive slave law, a part of the Compromise of 1850, earned him an avalanche of criticism by antislavery New Englanders, who likened him to a god that had failed. William Lloyd Garrison called him "the great apostate," while Horace Mann compared him with the devil, Theodore Parker with Benedict Arnold, and John Greenleaf Whittier with a "fallen angel." In his final address as a senator, on 17 July 1850, Webster proclaimed his determination, whatever the personal consequences, to "stand by the Union, and by all who stand by it." He honored that commitment by making implementation of the Compromise of 1850 the main goal of his two years (1850–1852) as secretary of State under President Millard Fillmore.

Daniel Webster was no ordinary politician. The positions he took often reflected his close ties with the commercial and financial elites of the northeast on whom he was dependent for the monetary subsidies necessary to sustain an extravagant life style.

A compulsive spender, Webster lived most of his life on the brink of financial disaster and was approximately $200,000 in debt when he died. But he also was an unusually gifted person who often took bold and independent positions, and he was capable of such astonishing performances in debate that contemporaries thought of him in superhuman terms as "godlike." "Webster is very dear to Yankees," Ralph Waldo Emerson recorded in his celebrated journal in 1843, "because he is a person of very commanding understanding with every talent for its adequate expression." He stands among the first rank of those who have served in Congress, having made his greatest impact on history as an eloquent expounder and defender of the Constitution. Rep. William Plumer, Jr., of New Hampshire observed in 1853 that Webster left for posterity "speeches and discourses of the very highest and rarest merit."

BIBLIOGRAPHY

Bartlett, Irving H. *Daniel Webster.* 1978.

Baxter, Maurice G. *One and Inseparable: Daniel Webster and the Union.* 1984.

Current, Richard N. *Daniel Webster and the Rise of National Conservatism.* 1955.

Peterson, Merrill D. *The Great Triumvirate: Webster, Clay, and Calhoun.* 1987.

Shewmaker, Kenneth E., ed. *Daniel Webster: "The Completest Man."* 1990.

KENNETH E. SHEWMAKER

WEBSTER-HAYNE DEBATE. The Webster-Hayne debate of January 1830 grew out of a Senate discussion of the public lands, which was touched off when Samuel A. Foote of Connecticut introduced a resolution for the suspension of surveys and sales. Objecting to the Foote resolution, Thomas Hart Benton of Missouri accused New Englanders of conspiring against the West, and Robert Y. Hayne of South Carolina offered westerners the support of the South. Hayne hoped that westerners, in return, would join southerners in both upholding states' rights and opposing the protective tariff.

Replying to Hayne, Daniel Webster of Massachusetts transformed the issues of the tariff and the public lands to the issue of disunionism, which he said was rife in South Carolina. That state's legislature had published in a document (without so identifying it) the nullification theory of John C. Cal-

SEN. DANIEL WEBSTER OF MASSACHUSETTS. Delivering his reply to Hayne.

houn, who now, as vice president of the United States, presided over the Senate. Hayne retorted with a flashing defense of the Calhoun doctrine of state sovereignty. Webster then argued at length that this doctrine contravened the Constitution. "It is, Sir, the people's Constitution, the people's government, made for the people, made by the people, and answerable to the people," he insisted—and he meant *one* people, the whole nation. He concluded with the ringing appeal: "Liberty *and* Union, now and for ever, one and inseparable!"

Far more widely reprinted and read than any previous speech in Congress, Webster's second reply to Hayne headed off a rapprochement of South and West and contributed to the growth of nationalism throughout the North.

BIBLIOGRAPHY

Bartlett, Irving H. *Daniel Webster.* 1978.
Peterson, Merrill D. *The Great Triumvirate: Webster, Clay, and Calhoun.* 1987.

RICHARD N. CURRENT

WELFARE. *See* Social Welfare and Poverty.

WESBERRY V. SANDERS (376 U.S. 1

[1964]). Preceding *Reynolds v. Sims,* in which the Supreme Court held population equality in state legislative districting to be required by the equal protection clause, this case was brought by an Atlanta resident, a state senator, complaining of the enormous population disparities between Georgia's urban areas and its rural territory. After it had found congressional and legislative districting issues justiciable, the Court in an apparent temporizing move in *Wesberry* derived the requirement of population equality in congressional districting from the language of Article I, section 2 mandating that representatives be chosen "by the people of the several States." For the Court, Justice Hugo L. Black reviewed the debates of the Constitutional Convention and found compelling the conclusion that the Framers meant this language to command that districts be equally populated when compared on an intrastate basis. Justice John M. Harlan, dissenting, argued that the statements relied on by the Court all occurred in the context of the Great Compromise—equal representation of the states in the Senate and representation of the states by population in the House of Representatives.

Whoever may have won the argument in 1964, it is evident that the results of *Wesberry* have been wholly successful. The "fundamental goal" of the Constitution, Justice Black wrote, was "equal representation for equal numbers of people." Thus, total population, minus those clearly transient, was the measure by which to compare districts. Subsequent cases established that exact mathematical equality was to be required and that all other standards—local population boundaries, geographic compactness, and the like—must yield to that goal. Indeed, with the advent of computers, precise population equality is achievable. After the 1990 census, a federal court ordered into effect a plan for Illinois's twenty districts; eighteen had 571,530 people each, and the other two each had 571,531.

Wesberry did not speak to such other questions as gerrymandering, but invidious racial line drawing was early held to be impermissible, and an as-yet-tentative restraint on partisan gerrymandering was set forth.

BIBLIOGRAPHY

Mayhew, David. "Congressional Representation: Theory and Practice in Drawing the Districts." In *Reapportionment in the 1970s.* Edited by Nelson Polsby. 1971.

JOHNNY H. KILLIAN

WEST FLORIDA. With the end of the American Revolution, Britain withdrew from its two Florida colonies, and the Spanish flag flew again over St. Augustine and Pensacola. There was no argument over the eastern boundary of West Florida—the Apalachicola River—but there was conflict over the western and northern boundaries. Both the United States and Spain claimed title to a large part of what is today Alabama and Mississippi. The Treaty of San Ildefonson in 1795 settled at least part of the controversy; Spain grudgingly accepted the 31st parallel as the northern boundary of West Florida and agreed to open the Mississippi River to navigation. This was the beginning of Spain's retrenchment in West Florida.

The Louisiana Purchase (1803) stirred up more controversy with Spain when the United States claimed that it included all of the territory west of the Perdido River. A plan to purchase both East and West Florida was discussed in Congress and by administration officials, but when Jefferson left the presidency in March 1809, the matter was still unresolved. Spain still claimed Mobile and Pensacola.

Jefferson's successor, James Madison, although not willing to go to war with Spain, was determined to acquire West Florida for several reasons. Thousands of Americans were moving into West Florida and the lower Mississippi Valley seeking cheap land, and hostile Indians, whom Spain could not or would not control, threatened the settlers. Major rivers—Apalachicola, Mobile, Pascagoula, and Pearl—flowed south through West Florida to the Gulf, and there was some fear that England might try to retake the lost colonies by attacking along the southern frontier.

The time for aggressive action in Florida arrived when some sixty "War Hawks" were elected to Congress in 1810. David Holmes, governor of the Mississippi territory, outlined to Congress the precarious situation in the area, and noted the ardent desire of the settlers, mostly Americans, to be annexed to the United States.

On 25 July 1810 sixteen "delegates," representing the four districts west of the Pearl River, met at St. John's Plain near Baton Rouge planning to establish a government with Tennessee representative John Rhea as chairman of the legislature. Carlos de Lassus, the senior Spanish official in the area, at first worked in harmony with the group, but the accord did not last. In the early morning of 23 September, some eighty men, shouting "Hurrah, Washington," captured the Spanish fort at Baton Rouge, killing one officer and one soldier. The Republic of West Florida was proclaimed free and independent, and it petitioned to be annexed to the United States. Rhea and his coconspirators hoped to acquire large land grants for themselves, but they were soon disappointed.

President Madison refused to recognize the revolutionists or their declaration of an independent West Florida. In a proclamation issued 27 October 1810 he reiterated the United States claim to all the area from the Mississippi to the Perdido as part of the Louisiana Purchase. The territory became part of the Orleans Territory governed by William Claiborne.

On 12 February 1813 Congress approved the occupation of the remaining Spanish territory west of the Perdido, and on 15 April U.S. forces moved into Mobile. Florida west of the Perdido was American. The region between the Iberville River (the eastern boundary of the recently admitted [1812] state of Louisiana) and the Perdido River was organized as a county of the Mississippi Territory. Pensacola remained the capital of Spanish West Florida, but the colony's northern and western boundaries had been reduced to the limits of present-day Florida.

Spain retained Florida east of the Perdido, but lacking the financial resources or the manpower to hold the territory, it was a foregone conclusion that it would become part of the United States. The Adams-Onís treaty negotiated the transfer in 1819, and it became a fact two years later.

[*See also* Florida.]

BIBLIOGRAPHY

Patrick, Rembert W. *Florida Fiasco*. 1954.

Smith, Joseph B. *The Plot to Steal Florida, James Madison's Phony War.* 1983.

Cox, Isaac J. *The West Florida Controversy, 1798–1813.* 1918.

SAMUEL PROCTOR

WEST VIRGINIA. During the congressional debate on West Virginia's application for statehood in 1861, spokesman Waitman T. Willey, later a U.S. senator, argued that the breakaway western portion of Virginia should be admitted because "its coal fields are sufficient to supply the consumption of the entire Union for a thousand years." Statehood, he maintained, was "indispensable to the development of the great natural resources of West Virginia."

Since formation of the Union, the eastern and western sections of Virginia had developed along divergent economic, social, and political paths. It was these sectional differences, most scholars agree, that led to the division of the Old Dominion into two separate states. When Virginia withdrew from the Union at the beginning of the Civil War, a western, mountain economic-political elite seeking to develop the western region seized the opportunity to separate from the mother state.

On 11 June 1861 delegates from Virginia's western region assembled in Wheeling, where they repudiated their state's ordinance of secession, established a "restored government" of Virginia, and chose two U.S. "senators"—Willey and John S. Carlile—whose subsequent request for admission to the Senate floor was granted. The Senate thus acknowledged the validity of the "restored government," although western Virginia's bid to become a separate state would have to be debated.

In both houses of Congress, the admission of West Virginia into the Union encountered fierce opposition. Congressional Democrats charged that the statehood movement was nothing more than a ploy to give the Republican party two more senators and the Republican president more electoral votes. Most of the opposition centered on the con-

WHEELER, BURTON K.   2123

stitutional stipulation that one state cannot be created out of another state without the permission of the parent state.

Rep. Thaddeus Stevens (R-Pa.) countered by pointing out that West Virginia was being admitted "not by virtue of any provision of the Constitution, but under an absolute power which the laws of war give us." Supporters also asserted the right of a loyal minority to govern a state in the presence of a disloyal and rebellious state government.

On 14 July 1862 the application passed the Senate by a vote of 23 to 17. On 10 December 1862 the House approved 96 to 55. The act stipulated that the West Virginia state constitution be amended to provide for the abolition of slavery, and on 23 March 1863 the required amendment was adopted by the state's constitutional convention. President Lincoln gave his approval, and on 20 June 1863 West Virginia became the thirty-fifth state.

As Senator Willey predicted, statehood opened West Virginia for development. Within two decades, railroads and coal mines had been developed and a powerful coal establishment controlled the state's political system.

From 1880 to the 1930s, the state's representatives in Congress were generally either coal operators or were affiliated with the coal establishment. Senators included men like Clarence Watson, president of the state's largest coal company, and Howard Sutherland, a coal operator. In the House were Edward Cooper, a coal operator, and Wells Goodykoontz, a coal company attorney. These congressional representatives were more interested in promoting profits for the state's coal companies than in the general welfare of the state. Thus, the period was characterized by federal neglect of the state's economic and social welfare, and exploitation of its natural resources.

About the only interest Congress showed in the state was occasional investigations into the state's turbulent coal fields. In 1913, the protracted and bloody Paint Creek coal strike prompted a Senate investigation. In 1921, the Armed March on Logan, the largest labor uprising in U.S. history, resulted in violence that inspired a congressional inquiry. In the 1920s, as destitution swept the Appalachian coal fields, Congress studied the hunger and poverty in the region, but it was not until the 1930s, with the establishment of the New Deal, that the people of West Virginia broke the power of the coal establishment.

Since then, West Virginia congressional representatives have been mostly Democrats, and populist in their approach to both politics and economics. They have sought to balance the rights of labor with the interests of business and the general welfare of the state.

House members have included crusaders such as Bob Wise and Nick Joe Rahall. Foremost was Ken Hechler, who was actively involved in grassroots efforts of the 1960s that included the struggle for black lung compensation and the Miners for Democracy.

Senate notables have included the controversial Rush Dew Holt; Harley Kilgore, chairman of the Committee on the Judiciary; and Jennings Randolph, chairman of the Committee on Environment and Public Works. Foremost among them is Robert C. Byrd, who, during his thirty-five years in the Senate, has served as the Democratic party secretary, whip, minority leader, majority leader, president pro tempore, and chairman of the Appropriations Committee.

BIBLIOGRAPHY

Dávila-Colón, Luis R., ed. *Breakthrough from Colonialism: An Interdisciplinary Study of Statehood.* Vol. 1. 1984.
Woodward, Isaiah A. *West Virginia and Its Struggle for Statehood: 1861–1863.* 1954.

DAVID A. CORBIN

WHEELER, BURTON K. (1882–1975), senator from Montana, insurgent Democrat, leading isolationist. Born in Hudson, Massachusetts, Wheeler studied law at the University of Michigan and opened a practice in Butte, Montana, in 1905. Vigorous and combative, he was soon a success, especially in his cases against railroads and mining companies. After a term in the state legislature he became U.S. District Attorney (1913–1918), serving until his insistence upon protecting civil liberties during the hysteria of World War I was seen as a danger to the reelection of his mentor, Sen. Thomas J. Walsh. Supported by labor and farmer movements, he won the Democratic nomination for governor in 1920, but lost badly when his bipartisan opponents called him "Bolshevik Burt" and argued that his victory would ruin Montana's economy.

Wheeler won election to the Senate in 1922 and served four terms. He attracted national attention with his sensational corruption charges against Attorney General Harry M. Daugherty. These led to a Senate investigation with Wheeler as prosecutor, which in turn resulted in Daugherty's forced resignation. Wheeler's exposé of Daugherty dovetailed with Senator Walsh's own committee investigation of the Teapot Dome oil scandals.

In 1924 Wheeler, as the running mate of Sen. Robert M. La Follette on the Progressive party ticket, excoriated the conservative policies of the Coolidge administration. Although the ticket carried only Wisconsin, it fared very well in most of the West. Wheeler did not stop being a Democrat, but he relished being one of "the sons of the wild jackass"—independent, uncontrollable western senators, of generally radical views.

Wheeler became the first national figure to endorse Franklin D. Roosevelt for president, playing an important part in the preconvention election campaigns. Wheeler favored most of the early New Deal, sponsoring two important measures: the Indian Reorganization Act of 1934 and the Wheeler-Rayburn Public Utility Holding Company Act of 1935. In 1935, he became chairman of the Committee on Interstate Commerce.

His break with Roosevelt came in 1937, when Wheeler led the successful bipartisan opposition to the president's judicial reform bill. He saw this Court-packing proposal as a threat to judicial independence. It was his greatest legislative victory and Roosevelt's greatest defeat.

Wheeler did not make foreign policy his chief interest until 1939. He opposed the repeal of the arms embargo as "a step toward getting this country into war." This was to remain his position on each of Roosevelt's major diplomatic and military proposals between 1939 and 1941. He led the opposition to the Lend-Lease Act of 1941 and spoke frequently for the America First Committee.

After Pearl Harbor, Wheeler maintained his critical stance toward Roosevelt's foreign policy, becoming vehement in his anticommunism. Who now remembered "Bolshevik Burt"?

In 1946 Wheeler was defeated in the Democratic primary, losing labor and farmer votes. He had been endorsed by President Harry S. Truman, whose mentor he had been and who had worked closely with him on his last major success, the Transportation Act of 1940. Wheeler practiced law in Washington until his death.

BIBLIOGRAPHY

Howard, Joseph Kinsey. "The Decline and Fall of Burton K. Wheeler." *Harper's* 194 (March 1947): 226–236.
Neuberger, Richard L. "Wheeler of Montana." *Harper's* 180 (May 1940): 609–618.
Tucker, Ray, and Frederick R. Barkley. *Sons of the Wild Jackass*. 1932.
Wheeler, Burton K., and Paul F. Healy. *Yankee from the West*. 1962.

ROBERT E. BURKE

WHEELER-RAYBURN PUBLIC UTILITY HOLDING COMPANY ACT (1935; 49 Stat. 803–863).

The Wheeler-Rayburn Public Utility Holding Company (PUHC) Act was passed by Congress in August 1935, during the period of reformist legislation known as the Second Hundred Days of the New Deal. The purpose of the act was to reform the electrical utility industry, which was dominated by a relatively few large holding companies. Through a pyramiding technique, hundreds of operating utilities were controlled by a handful of corporations. Critics had long contended against this system, arguing that it put control of the industry in the hands of speculative and manipulative financiers and resulted in inflated costs, inefficient operation, and high prices.

Many observers have depicted the PUHC Act, together with the other reform legislation of 1935, as a Second New Deal—a turning from the policy of cooperation with business that characterized the First New Deal of 1933 to a policy of disciplining business and conferring benefits on workers and the unemployed. While this interpretation has some merit overall, it appears President Franklin D. Roosevelt and Democratic leaders in Congress for a long time had been prepared to adopt strong measures against the utility magnates. While governor of New York, Roosevelt championed the development of public power. Congressional pressure, much of it generated by Democrats, induced the Federal Trade Commission to conduct an investigation of the industry in 1928, and the House Interstate and Foreign Commerce Committee initiated an inquiry in 1930.

Reform legislation was inevitable after the Democrats secured control of both Congress and the presidency in the election of 1932. The bill—drafted by two key Roosevelt lieutenants, New Deal lawyers Benjamin Cohen and Thomas Corcoran, and introduced in the Senate by Burton K. Wheeler of Montana—provided for regulation of public utility holding companies by the Securities and Exchange Commission (SEC). The aim was to break up the holding companies and create a network of smaller, efficient, autonomous operating systems. In a famous "death sentence" clause, the SEC was empowered to force this outcome if holding companies refused to cooperate. The bill passed in the Senate by a narrow margin in June

1935 after attempts, supported by many conservatively inclined Democrats, to substitute the concept of regulation in place of forced dissolution of holding companies.

In the House, the Interstate and Foreign Commerce Committee, over the objections of its chairman, Sam Rayburn of Texas, reported a somewhat different version of the measure, which weakened the force of the "death sentence" provision and which Roosevelt strongly opposed. Rayburn attempted to rescue the administration's position by securing a roll-call vote on the House floor on an amendment restoring the "death sentence," a maneuver that would have forced congressmen openly to defy the president. The opposition of House Rules Committee chairman John J. O'Connor defeated this tactic, however, and Roosevelt eventually was compelled to compromise. The difference between the bill ultimately passed and the original Senate bill was actually quite limited, but the controversy reflected a split within the congressional Democrats that gradually became worse and eventually produced the conservative coalition, a voting bloc of Republicans and conservative Democrats.

Initial opposition and delaying tactics by the utilities impeded but did not prevent SEC implementation of the act. The result was a reorganization of the nation's electric utilities that most authorities agree has proved beneficial not only to consumers but to the industry itself.

BIBLIOGRAPHY

Parrish, Michael E. *Securities Regulation and the New Deal.* 1970.
Patterson, James T. *Congressional Conservatism and the New Deal.* 1967.

ROBERT F. HIMMELBERG

WHIG PARTY. The Whigs constituted one of the two major parties, along with the Democrats, in what historians call the second party system, which lasted from the 1830s to the 1850s. The Whig party, an outgrowth of the National Republican party, originated in resistance to the Andrew Jackson administration, incorporating not only National Republicans and Anti-Masons but also disgruntled followers of Jackson. It won only two presidential elections, both of them with military heroes, William Henry Harrison (1840) and Zachary Taylor (1848). Whigs did almost as well as Democrats in local, state, and congressional elections, however, and gained a majority in the U.S. House of Representatives in the elections of 1840, 1846, and 1848.

To show its aversion to the allegedly royal pretensions of "King Andrew I," the party took its name from the English Whigs, who traditionally stood for limiting the powers of the king. The American Whigs favored the supremacy of Congress over the president. They advocated a program of federal intervention to stimulate economic growth, a program consisting mainly of a national bank, protective tariffs, and expenditures on "internal improvements," that is, on highways, railroads, rivers, and canals. Whigs generally opposed territorial expansion.

Their voters were found in all parts of the country and at all levels of society. They were most nu-

WHIG SENATOR HENRY CLAY. Depicted entering the House to observe debate on the seating of two Whigs from Mississippi, whose election had been challenged. The text alludes to Clay's alleged moral and ethical weaknesses and accuses him of ill-tempered remarks aimed at Speaker James K. Polk, whose tie-breaking vote denied seats to the two Whigs. The illustration mentions James Watson Webb, editor of the *Morning Courier and New York Enquirer,* who is credited with popularizing the term *Whig* as a name for the anti-Jackson party. Lithograph on wove paper by W. Charles, published in 1838.

LIBRARY OF CONGRESS

merous, however, in southern New England and in other areas, such as eastern Tennessee, where people hoped to benefit from the party's economic program. The Whig party was said to be the party of the rich, and it certainly appealed to most industrialists, but it also attracted many planters and farmers, especially those producing for a commercial market, as well as workers employed in protected industries. Men of whatever class who voted Whig were mostly Protestants of British stock; non-British and especially Catholic immigrants were inclined to shun the party as nativistic. Blacks, in the few states where they had suffrage, consistently cast their ballots for Whig candidates.

In the Senate the outstanding Whig leaders were Henry Clay of Kentucky and Daniel Webster of Massachusetts. The third member of the "Great Triumvirate" of the Senate, John C. Calhoun of South Carolina, cooperated with the Whigs from time to time. Among the more notable Whigs in the House were Alexander H. Stephens of Georgia and, briefly, Abraham Lincoln of Illinois. Horace Greeley, editor of the *New York Tribune*, was the most influential Whig journalist.

Whig congressmen, as roll-call analyses have shown, were nearly unanimous in voting for Whig measures during most of the party's existence. Slavery was a divisive issue, however, and there were always North-South strains within the party. Finally, in the crisis of 1850, sectionalism overwhelmed partisanship.

The Whig party never quite recovered, though it succeeded in polling 44 percent of the popular vote when it ran another military hero, Winfield Scott, for the presidency in 1852. It could boast twenty-five congressmen (all but two of them from the South), or 10 percent of the House membership, as late as 1860. Meanwhile many Whigs, both northern and southern, temporarily supported the American, or Know-Nothing, party. Most northern Whigs eventually joined the modern Republican party, as did Lincoln.

BIBLIOGRAPHY

Alexander, Thomas B. *Sectional Stress and Party Strength: A Study of Roll-Call Voting Patterns in the United States House of Representatives, 1836–1860*. 1967.

Howe, Daniel W. *The Political Culture of the American Whigs*. 1979.

Silbey, Joel H. *The Shrine of Party: Congressional Voting Behavior, 1841–1852*. 1967.

RICHARD N. CURRENT

WHIPS. In both the House and Senate, the Democratic and Republican whips are the elected party leaders responsible for encouraging party discipline. In the House, the majority whip is the third-ranking party leader, behind the majority leader and the Speaker; the minority whip is his or her party's second in command, behind the minority leader. In the Senate, the majority and minority whips function as either assistant Democratic leader or assistant Republican leader.

As with many things in the U.S. Congress, the position of whip is of British origin. In fact, virtually all parliaments worldwide that model their legislative system on that of Great Britain have party whips. During a May 1769 debate in the House of Commons, Edmund Burke is believed to have first used the term *whip* to denote a party leader. He referred to the "whipper-in," which in ordinary usage meant a huntsman assigned the task of keeping the yelping hounds from straying during a fox hunt, whipping them back into line if necessary. According to one modern member of Parliament, "Since that time the Members responsible for this marshalling of the forces and for giving out information have been called whips, and occupy an important position in both the government and opposition parties."

Neither major party in the U.S. House or Senate officially named lawmakers as whips until the late nineteenth century. Some lawmakers occasionally served unofficially in this capacity. A probable explanation for the lack of whips in early Congresses is that strong political parties evolved only after several decades. For example, James S. Young concluded that from 1800 to 1825 "parties on [Capitol Hill] were largely unorganized groups. They were without an openly recorded membership, much less with differentiated leadership roles" (*The Washington Community, 1800–1828*, 1966, p. 147). That had changed by the end of the century, however.

In 1897, Speaker Thomas B. Reed (R-Maine) named Rep. James A. Tawney (R-Minn.) the first House whip. (The Republican whip is now elected by the Republican conference.) Democrats followed suit three years later, when the Democratic floor leader named Oscar W. Underwood (D-Ala.) that party's whip. (In 1987 Democrats began to elect their whip rather than having the whip appointed by the floor leader in consultation with the Speaker). In the Senate, J. Hamilton Lewis (D-Ill.) became that chamber's first whip in 1913. Election by partisan colleagues continues as the method of selection to this day. In 1915, Senate Republicans

J. HAMILTON LEWIS (D-ILL.). Chosen in 1913 by Senate Democrats as the party's first whip.

OFFICE OF THE HISTORIAN OF THE U.S. SENATE

elected James W. Wadsworth, Jr., of New York as their first whip; Senate Republican whips are still chosen by election. An important reason for creating whips was to assist their party's leadership in handling Congress's growing agenda.

As demands on Congress and on the majority and minority whips increased, the number of assistant whips for each party expanded in both chambers. For example, in the contemporary House nearly one third of Democratic lawmakers are whips of some sort. They are called chief deputy whips, deputy whips, at-large whips, zone whips, and so on. Naming more lawmakers as whips produces more balance in seniority, ideology, and geography in the leadership ranks and gives the whips greater incentive to back their top elective leaders.

Whips have several traditional functions. One of their main responsibilities is to canvass party members on a pending issue and give their floor leaders an accurate assessment of the support or opposition expected. These "whip counts" are important for identifying uncommitted or wavering members who might be persuaded to back the party's position. Whips are also expected to know the whereabouts of their colleagues and to make sure that they are on hand to vote. House whips frequently stand by the doors to the chamber and signal their arriving colleagues to vote yea (thumbs up) or nay (thumbs down). Among other whip functions are gathering political intelligence and conveying the leadership's views to colleagues (and vice versa). The whip's job, in short, is to promote party unity. In the modern Congress this is primarily accomplished by persuasion; these leaders can do little to "whip" independent-minded members into line.

Additionally, whips have an informational duty that can be traced to the British Parliament: the preparation of "whip notices." These written programs identify the weekly schedule of legislative floor business. Each party's whip prepares and distributes these notices to members. Party whips also distribute a variety of other materials and reports to their colleagues. Whips get additional office space and staff assistance to help them function as conduits of information.

The informal responsibilities of whips have broadened to accommodate changing circumstances and needs. They are still vote counters, but now they may also establish ad hoc groups of members, or task forces, to mobilize winning legislative coalitions. To woo lawmakers' votes they may suggest substantive changes in legislation to committee and party leaders. The whip may also be the heir apparent to the position of floor leader.

BIBLIOGRAPHY

Brown, Lynne P., and Robert L. Peabody. "Dilemmas of Party Leadership: Majority Whips in the U.S. House of

Representatives, 1962–1982." *Congress and the Presidency* 11 (Autumn 1984): 179–196.

Ripley, Randall B. "The Party Whip Organizations in the United States House of Representatives." *The American Political Science Review* 58 (December 1964): 561–576.

U.S. Senate. *Majority and Minority Whips of the Senate*, by Walter J. Oleszek. 98th Cong., 2d Sess., 1985. S. Doc. 98-45.

WALTER J. OLESZEK

WHITE SLAVE-TRADE ACT (1910; 36 Stat.
825–827). On 25 June 1910, the 61st Congress (1909–1911) passed the White Slave-Trade Act (known as the Mann Act, after its sponsor, Rep. James R. Mann [R-Ill.]) Its stated purpose was "to regulate and prevent the transportation in interstate and foreign commerce of alien women and girls for immoral purposes, and for other purposes." It was part of an effort in the early twentieth century to control prostitution, which some identified as stemming from lax immigration restrictions allowing prostitutes, their procurers, and employers into the United States. Indeed, the act was Congress's response to a 1909 Supreme Court decision (*United States v. Keller*) that struck down a 1907 law banning the importation of alien prostitutes.

Although the Mann Act was intended to cover only international procurers and employers of prostitutes, it proved more powerful than previous congressional attempts to regulate prostitution through provisions of the immigration acts of 1903, 1907, and 1910. The Supreme Court upheld its constitutionality in *Hoke and Economides v. United States* (1913).

In retrospect, although prostitution was a significant social problem in the Progressive era, passage of the Mann Act was more reflective of the xenophobia characterizing this period than a successful problem-solving effort. It reinforced the popular view of prostitution as originating outside the United States and imported by immigration, rather than as an indigenous problem stemming from women's social and economic deprivation. As a result, it contributed to deflecting attention from such major problems as the discrepancy between women's wages and men's, which others argued contributed to the practice of prostitution. Prosecution under the Mann Act waned after World War I.

BIBLIOGRAPHY

Connelly, Mark Thomas. *The Response to Prostitution in the Progressive Era*. 1980.

Rosen, Ruth. *The Lost Sisterhood: Prostitution in America, 1900–1918*. 1982.

EILEEN L. MCDONAGH

WILMOT PROVISO. Rejuvenating the slavery-extension issue in national politics, the Wilmot Proviso of 1846 was a response to President James K. Polk's pro-southern policies, particularly the war with Mexico, which opponents claimed was being waged to acquire territory and extend slavery.

In August 1846 Polk requested a special appropriation of $2 million that he vaguely indicated would be used to promote peace with Mexico. Critics immediately charged that its real purpose was to bribe the Mexican government to cede additional territory to the United States. In the ensuing debate, Rep. David Wilmot of Pennsylvania introduced an amendment drafted by a small knot of dissident northern Democratic representatives. Known as the Wilmot Proviso, the amendment declared: "That as an express and fundamental condition to the acquisition of any territory from the Republic of Mexico, neither slavery nor involuntary servitude shall exist in any part of said territory, except for crime, whereof the party shall first be duly convicted." The amendment was a slap at Polk and southern Democrats for ignoring northern interests.

Wilmot's amendment passed the House, where it received strong bipartisan northern support, but it died in the Senate without a vote. Reintroduced during the following session, the Proviso carried the House in several forms but failed to get through the southern-dominated Senate. When both parties in the 1848 presidential contest rejected the Proviso, its supporters organized the Free-Soil party, which opposed the expansion of slavery. The party was unable to mount a serious challenge to the major parties, however, and in the early 1850s it disbanded. While it never became law, the Wilmot Proviso documented the growing conflict over the expansion of slavery.

BIBLIOGRAPHY

Foner, Eric. "The Wilmot Proviso Revisited." *Journal of American History* 56 (1969): 262–279.

Morrison, Chaplain W. *Democratic Politics and Sectionalism: The Wilmot Proviso Controversy*. 1967.

WILLIAM E. GIENAPP

WILSON, WOODROW (1856–1924), generally counted as one of the half-dozen "great" presidents, a leader for progressive reform at home, and the vi-

sionary proponent of world peace and the League of Nations. Wilson proved to be a brilliant party leader on domestic issues, but was unable to bring about a party realignment or to win the bipartisan congressional support necessary for U.S. participation in the League.

Thomas Woodrow Wilson was born in Virginia in 1856, the son of a Scots-Irish Presbyterian minister. The young Wilson dreamed of a career in politics, especially one in which he might lead opinion by his oratory in the fashion of the British Parliament of that period. He graduated from Princeton in 1879 and studied law at the University of Virginia but had little aptitude for legal practice. He turned to the then new graduate program at Johns Hopkins University, where he wrote a dissertation looking at the actual workings rather than the ancient origins of U.S. government. This became Wilson's first and most famous book, *Congressional Government* (1885).

Wilson was strongly convinced of the superiority of British parliamentary government, with its clear party responsibility, to the American separation-of-powers system. In *Congressional Government,* he presents a powerful critique of a government dominated by Congress, with Congress in turn dominated by its various standing committees. Wilson's tendency to underestimate the importance of the president and to overemphasize the role of Congress probably reflects both his southern background and his hope that a parliamentary system might evolve in the American case without extensive constitutional amendment. Wilson's more mature but more conventional views are expressed in his *Constitutional Government in the United States* (1908). In it, he emphasizes the central role of the president as national leader, especially in foreign affairs.

Wilson pursued a distinguished academic career from 1885 to 1910, culminating in his selection as president of Princeton University. There, he pushed curricular reform, hired distinguished new faculty, and established a preceptor system to supplement traditional teaching methods. He was convinced that learning was an around-the-clock experience, much of it occurring in informal settings. But increasingly, the sons of the wealthy segregated themselves in expensive housing or exclusive dining clubs. Wilson wanted to introduce a more democratic and more scholarly environment, a quadrangle within which all students would live, dine, and study together. This, however, would be expensive, and the proposal alienated some faculty and wealthy alumni. The dispute over Wilson's quad plan became entangled in the question of where to locate a new building for the graduate program. The graduate dean insisted on a location apart from the main campus; Wilson insisted that it be on the main campus. But when an elderly alumnus died and left his estate in the control of the graduate dean, it became clear that Wilson had lost the struggle and the support of the trustees.

Most publicity about the Princeton fight portrayed Wilson as something of an academic "radical," aligned against the forces of entrenched wealth. This was in marked contrast to his views on most national issues, which were those of a typical conservative, sound-money, northeastern Democrat. With the Progressive movement in full swing, the Democratic bosses in New Jersey saw an opportunity to upset the usually dominant Republicans. For the 1910 election, they turned to Wilson as their candidate for governor. He ran a strong progressive-oriented campaign and with the support of the Democratic organization won the election by an almost two-to-one margin.

In the course of two one-year terms, Wilson established a national reputation as a highly effective reform-oriented governor. He established his independence by fighting the bosses over the issue of legislative choice of a U.S. senator. From there, he went on to push through a revision of the election laws, a corrupt practices act, a workers' compensation bill, and a commission to regulate public utilities. In dealing with the legislature, he refrained from formal messages but worked effectively with individual members. He surprised legislators by personally attending a Democratic legislative caucus to argue for his election reform measure.

In 1911 Wilson was ready to launch a lengthy, almost modern, campaign for the 1912 presidential nomination. As his earlier conservative supporters dropped away, he picked up Progressive and reform support. When the Democratic convention finally met in Baltimore it appeared that Speaker of the House James Beauchamp (Champ) Clark had the most delegates, followed by Oscar W. Underwood (House Ways and Means chairman), and then Wilson. Yet, on the 46th ballot Wilson became the presidential nominee. Underwood declined the vice presidential nomination, preferring to lead the Democrats in the House.

Wilson coasted to an easy Electoral College victory in November 1912, although his popular vote in the four-way presidential race total fell substantially short of the combined vote for William Howard Taft (Republican incumbent candidate), Theodore

INAUGURATION OF WOODROW WILSON. On 4 March 1913.   LIBRARY OF CONGRESS

Roosevelt (Progressive party candidate), and Eugene V. Debs (Socialist party candidate). Wilson had campaigned primarily on domestic reform issues, and he summoned Congress into special session to deal with tariff reduction, antitrust legislation, and monetary reform. To dramatize the issues, he announced that he would address the special session of Congress in person rather than by sending a written message, thereby reversing a tradition that went back to Thomas Jefferson. He followed this up with personal visits to the Capitol and by inaugurating twice-weekly press conferences (a schedule that was later cut back and eventually eliminated). By holding Congress in continuous session for a year and a half, he was able to win passage of most of his New Freedom economic issues. In the House he was aided by effective use of

the Democratic caucus, which in 1911 had sharply curtailed the powers of the Speaker. The most important power, to determine the makeup of committees, went to the Democratic members of the Ways and Means Committee. In the Senate Wilson was fortunate to have as spokesman John Worth Kern of Indiana. Kern's work on behalf of Wilson's agenda was so successful that the period 1913 to 1917 is usually regarded as establishing the modern role of a Senate majority floor leader.

Foreign policy issues were to play an increasingly important role in Wilson's administration. The Mexican Revolution of 1913 was troublesome, but the outbreak of war in Europe a year later posed far more serious problems. The most difficult issue for Wilson was Germany's increasing use of surprise submarine attacks on merchant vessels bound for the British isles. This violated the traditional rules of "cruiser warfare" (developed for surface ships) and threatened American lives, as in the 1915 sinking of the *Lusitania*. As public support for the Allies grew, William Jennings Bryan resigned as secretary of State, voicing his alarm that the country was risking involvement in the conflict.

The 1916 elections saw a return to the traditional two-party contest, which posed a more severe challenge to Wilson than the four-way race of 1912. The Republican nominee was Charles Evans Hughes, a former reform governor of New York. Wilson won by narrowly carrying California and scoring an upset victory in Ohio, previously a Republican stronghold. Democratic strength on Capitol Hill was substantially reduced.

Early in 1917 Germany moved to unrestricted submarine warfare, assuming this would bring about the collapse of the Allies before the United States could intervene effectively. Wilson asked for a declaration of war, which Congress voted, with some dissent. The move split the Democratic party and seriously divided progressive reform forces that had been especially strong among Scandanavian-American, German-American, and Socialist voters, all groups strongly opposed to war.

In most respects, mobilization for World War I provided a pattern for the even greater efforts of World War II (Franklin D. Roosevelt was Wilson's assistant secretary of the Navy). In Congress, the Democrats had narrow majorities in both chambers, and Republicans mounted strong criticism of the mobilization process and of Wilson's increasing aloofness. Businessmen held leading positions of power, such as the seats on the War Industries Board. Wilson had previously emphasized the need for restraint and a "peace without victory" (one of his many memorable phrases). But this attitude was hard to maintain as the war effort moved into high gear and public attitudes hardened. Even to his admirers, Wilson's record had two grave blemishes. One was his acceptance of espionage laws that were used against even mild critics of the administration. The other was his typical southerner's acceptance and reinforcement of racial segregation, admittedly a difficult issue for a Democratic admin-

PRESIDENT WOODROW WILSON. Addressing Congress, 2 December 1918.　　LIBRARY OF CONGRESS

istration dependent on southern support in Congress.

Wilson's greatest claim to fame is his contribution to a new international order. As with his domestic reform program he was a relatively late convert to this cause, but he embraced the progressive internationalist view that traditional power politics led to new sources of conflict. To be worthy of enforcement, the terms of peace must be based on a just and flexible order: national self-determination rather than empire, democratic self-government rather than autocracies, the phasing out of colonialism, and an end to privately owned munitions industries. These measures would both reduce conflict and legitimize collective action against aggressors and constituted the orientation behind Wilson's famous Fourteen Points address to Congress in January 1918 and his role in the struggles over the Versailles treaty.

Unfortunately for Wilson, the November 1918 congressional elections, in which he called for popular support of the Democrats, came days before the joyous announcement of the armistice. An effective Republican campaign and widespread resentment of wartime shortages and controls produced Republican control of House and Senate. Thus, Senate consideration of the peace treaty would be managed by Wilson's bitter opponent, Henry Cabot Lodge of Massachusetts, the new chairman of the Senate Foreign Relations Committee.

Wilson's problems multiplied as he traveled to Europe (another presidential innovation) to participate in drafting the treaty and provisions for the League of Nations. He appointed no leading Republican to the peace commission. In Europe he found the other Allied leaders eager to impose punitive terms on Germany. And Wilson's health was giving him increasing problems, including what probably was a series of strokes. Psychologically, he became less flexible and increasingly dogmatic.

The Senate fight over the treaty and its League of Nations provisions was not just a matter of simple isolationism versus internationalism. It was more a matter of conservative internationalists versus Wilson's progressive internationalist coalition, but Wilson had done little to popularize his views. Senator Lodge skillfully extended the committee hearings, and Wilson stubbornly opposed all reservations that would require renegotiation with the Allies. In this fight, there was little chance of a two-thirds majority, either for the treaty as proposed or for the treaty with reservations (which Wilson opposed). In the fall of 1919, he set out on an extensive speaking tour in support of the League but suffered another stroke. His doctor, First Lady Edith Wilson, and aide Joe Tumulty protected both Wilson and the public from full knowledge of the seriousness of his condition. With inflation and unemployment on the rise, the administration drifted to a tragic end. The Republicans nominated a safe nonentity, Warren G. Harding, and coasted to a landslide victory in 1920. After a turbulent eight years, Republican-business hegemony was restored. Wilson died in 1924.

He left a complex legacy. By moving the Democrats firmly in a progressive direction, Wilson confirmed the Republicans as the conservative party of the business community. He developed important new tools of executive leadership of Congress, such as the personally delivered State of the Union message, direct face-to-face meetings on Capitol Hill, and a generally recognized Senate floor leader. But coherent government lost ground in the House, where the Democratic organization (and later the Republicans) drifted into the practice of reconfirming all previous committee appointments and chairmanships, thereby imposing a strict seniority system, which was in place by about 1920. Wilson also pioneered a strategy of publicly appealing for grassroots support against a reluctant Congress, successfully in the case of war preparedness in 1916 but unsuccessfully in the case of the League in 1919. Finally, the post–World War II United Nations owes much to Wilson, although it blends Wilsonian idealism with the hard-headed concerns of the conservative internationalists. Even in his defeats, Wilson provided useful lessons for the next Democratic president, Franklin D. Roosevelt, who was to face even graver challenges.

BIBLIOGRAPHY

Baker, Ray Stannard. *Woodrow Wilson, Life and Letters.* 8 vols. 1927–1939.

Clements, Kendrick A. *The Presidency of Woodrow Wilson.* 1992.

Heckscher, August. *Woodrow Wilson: A Biography.* 1991.

Knock, Thomas J. *To End All Wars: Woodrow Wilson and the Quest for a New World Order.* 1992.

Link, Arthur S. *Wilson.* 5 vols. 1947–1965.

Link, Arthur S., ed. *The Papers of Woodrow Wilson.* 69 vols. 1966–1994.

Sarasohn, David. *The Party of Reform: Democrats in the Progressive Era.* 1989.

Thorsen, Niels Aage. *The Political Thought of Woodrow Wilson, 1875–1910.* 1988.

Weinstein, Edwin A. *Woodrow Wilson: A Medical and Psychological Biography*. 1981.

Wilson, Woodrow. *Congressional Government*. 1885.

Wilson, Woodrow. *Constitutional Government in the United States*. 1908.

DOUGLAS PRICE

WISCONSIN. Achieving territorial status under its own name in 1836 and within roughly its present boundaries in 1838, Wisconsin entered the Union in 1848 as the last of five states to emerge from the Northwest Territory. Statehood had become possible two years earlier, when the population in the territory was sufficient and when the opportunity for the creation of two new free states had appeared with the admission of Texas and Florida as slave states in 1845. Iowa was admitted in 1846, but Wisconsin was delayed principally because its electorate rejected the first state constitution submitted to it and did not accept a revised constitution until 1848.

During its first century, Wisconsin's elected senators and representatives were mostly Republicans. Only from the late 1950s were there consecutive decades in which Democrats often outnumbered Republicans. Altogether, between 1847 and 1992, about two-thirds of the state's representation in the House and Senate was Republican. The dominance was marked from 1857 to 1933, and especially from 1895 to 1933, during which period the House delegation was almost entirely Republican except during the first years of Woodrow Wilson's presidency. In the early decades of the twentieth century, Wisconsin Republicans in both the Senate and the House were often progressive and therefore maverick Republicans by national standards. Best known were Robert M. La Follette, who served as a progressive Republican senator from 1906 to 1925, and his son, Robert M. La Follette, Jr., who served similarly from 1925 to 1935 and then for twelve more years as a third-party Progressive. That separate label, on the Wisconsin ballot from 1934 through 1944, was used by as many as seven of the state's ten representatives in 1934 and 1936. These Progressives were Wisconsin's most substantial deviation from two-party congressional politics, but also noteworthy was the election of a Milwaukee Socialist, Victor L. Berger, to five House terms (for one of which he was not seated), between 1910 and 1926.

While Republicans dominated Wisconsin's congressional delegation (and Congress itself) during the late nineteenth and early twentieth centuries, several of the state's senators and representatives chaired committees and played other leadership roles. Chief among them was Sen. John C. Spooner, whose legal and parliamentary skills earned him a place among the four most influential Republican senators just before and after the turn of the century. No later Republican from Wisconsin was so prominently a majority party leader, although both of the La Follettes and a few others became consequential figures in other ways. Most notoriously, Sen. Joseph R. McCarthy secured attention and influence by reckless anticommunist charges, particularly when he chaired a Senate investigation committee during the brief period of Republican control of the Senate, from 1953 to 1955. In those same two years, Sen. Alexander Wiley chaired the Foreign Relations Committee.

During the long period of mostly Democratic congressional majorities that began in 1931, Wisconsin contributed little to the leadership of those majorities until the mid 1970s. The Democrats that Wisconsin elected in the early 1930s had soon been defeated by Progressives or Republicans. Only among those first elected in 1948 and afterward were there enough successive terms to provide opportunities to chair standing committees. Rep. Henry S. Reuss became chairman of the House Banking, Finance, and Urban Affairs Committee in 1975; Sen. William Proxmire of the Senate's Banking, Housing, and Urban Affairs Committee in 1975; Rep. Clement J. Zablocki of the House International Relations (later Foreign Affairs) Committee in 1977; and Rep. Les Aspin of the House Armed Services Committee in 1985. Both Reuss and Aspin, though hardly newcomers, secured their chairs because of revolts against aging predecessors rather than by strict seniority rules. Aspin was appointed secretary of Defense by President Bill Clinton in 1993.

Despite the state's large manufacturing enterprises and substantial urban centers, its dairying and other agricultural interests have often been most prominently promoted by Wisconsin senators and representatives. In recent decades, the state's conservationist tradition has also been vigorously represented.

BIBLIOGRAPHY

Nesbit, Robert C., *Wisconsin: A History*. Updated and revised by William F. Thompson. 1989.

Thompson, William F., ed. *The History of Wisconsin*. Vols. 1–3, 5, 6. 1973–1990. Vol. 4, forthcoming.

LEON D. EPSTEIN

WISE, HENRY A.

WISE, HENRY A. (1806–1876), representative from Virginia whose fiery oratory and touchy sense of honor kept him at the center of political controversy. A native of the Eastern Shore, Wise offered himself as an advocate for the interests of the plain people rather than the aristocracy of his state, but he was an avid defender of slavery. Self-consciously intellectual, Wise prided himself on his independence, and he seemed to thrive on conflict. He often was at odds with the powerful faction of the Democratic party of Virginia known as "the chivalry."

Although Wise was first elected to Congress as a Jacksonian Democrat in 1833, he quickly broke with the administration over the issue of withholding government deposits from the Bank of the United States. By 1835, he had joined the Whig opposition. As chairman of the Naval Affairs Committee (1841–1844), he effectively represented his coastal constituency. He made his reputation, however, as a sectional spokesman during the protracted congressional debate over the House gag rule on antislavery petitions. A longtime friend of John Tyler, he was a leader in the small "corporal's guard" of the president's congressional supporters after Tyler's break with the Whig party. By 1843, Wise had again become a Democrat and he remained one, albeit a dissident, until the end of his career. He served as minister to Brazil from 1844 to 1847 and was governor of Virginia from 1856 to 1859.

Wise had presidential ambitions for 1860, but they were thwarted by the disruption of the Democratic party and then the nation. He supported Virginia's secession and served as a Confederate general during the Civil War.

BIBLIOGRAPHY

Simpson, Craig. *A Good Southerner: The Life of Henry A. Wise of Virginia.* 1985.
Wise, Henry A. *Seven Decades of the Union.* 1876.

JOHANNA NICOL SHIELDS

HENRY A. WISE.   *PERLEY'S REMINISCENCES,* VOL. 1

WITNESSES, RIGHTS OF.

WITNESSES, RIGHTS OF. Congressional investigations offer the most vivid and vital dramas in which high officials appear before the people's representatives to account for their conduct in office or their role in scandals. Such investigations serve national democracy as its laboratory for finding truth, its arena for combat, and its theater. Yet congressional investigations pose the potential danger, as during the McCarthy era, of injuring the reputations of witnesses through unfair tactics and accusations. This dichotomy has led to the evolution of witnesses' rights as a way of ensuring that Congress has the power to obtain the evidence it needs while minimizing abuses to the witnesses it calls.

Committees and witnesses often have sharp legal disputes, such as when President Richard M. Nixon withheld tape recordings from the Senate Select Committee on Presidential Campaign Activities (Senate Watergate Committee) in 1973, claiming executive privilege, or when Assistant Secretary of State Elliott Abrams made false statements to committees about the Iran-contra affair. Abrams later pleaded guilty to lying to Congress but was pardoned by President George Bush. Because of the "speech or debate" clause of the Constitution, witnesses cannot initiate lawsuits against a congressional committee to block its questions or to dispute its procedures. Witnesses can have a court decide whether their rights were violated only if they block an investigation and are prosecuted for contempt, or, in the case of some fundamental rights, if they lie and are prosecuted for making false statements. Then, as part of defending the contempt or false statement prosecution, the witness can raise issues challenging the validity of the committee's procedures. Hence, such trials as

Oliver North's in 1989—on charges (among others) that he lied to Congress—turn into unusual occasions for courts to resolve issues about witnesses' rights.

In general, a witness's rights include being accompanied by a lawyer who may provide advice, which sometimes produces exciting confrontations between skilled courtroom-style lawyers and dogged members of Congress. Witnesses usually can read an opening statement that tells their story the way they see it but then have to respond to whatever questions the members or the committee counsel ask them. The committee determines whether to hear a witness in public or in a closed ("executive") session, although the witness may voice a preference. Witnesses have few grounds for general refusal to answer questions, except a claim under the Fifth Amendment that by answering they would incriminate themselves. However, they may require the committee to state the pertinency of the question to the subject of the inquiry. Individual House and Senate committees have rules that may provide further rights, such as defining the minimum number of members—the quorum—that must attend the hearing.

There has always been controversy over televising witnesses. In a famous 1951 incident, the Kefauver Committee (the Senate Special Committee to Investigate Organized Crime in Interstate Commerce) summoned New York City racketeer Frank Costello. Costello objected to being televised and, to the agitation of the watching public, the live television coverage of the hearings showed only his hands, which twisted and clenched as he was subjected to tough questioning. The House has a rule that witnesses who appear pursuant to a compulsory subpoena can require that their testimony not be broadcast at all.

Important congressional investigations may raise questions about a witness's claims of the right to withhold particular information. For example, a lawyer who had handled transactions on behalf of Philippines ruler Ferdinand Marcos attempted to assert attorney-client privilege. Congressional committees have broad discretion whether to accept or reject such an assertion of privilege. The committee rejected that particular assertion, noting that the lawyer had acted as a realtor locating investment properties for Marcos rather than as an adviser on pure legal questions. A witness employed in a business such as pharmaceutical manufacture may ask not to be required to reveal trade secrets to an inquiry about profits. While congressional committees have the power to overrule such claims, they typically weigh them carefully, both to decide well and to visibly provide fair procedures in the inquiry.

[*See also* Investigations.]

BIBLIOGRAPHY

Grabow, John C. *Congressional Investigations: Law and Practice*. 1988.
Hamilton, James. *The Power to Probe: A Study of Congressional Investigations*. 1976.

CHARLES TIEFER

WOMEN IN CONGRESS. The number of women members of Congress has increased slowly over the years, but has not kept pace with women's progress in politics at the state and local levels, in the professions, or in society generally. By 1992, in the 102d Congress, thirty-one women were serving in Congress: twenty-nine representatives (including Eleanor Holmes Norton, the nonvoting House delegate from the District of Columbia) and two senators—the same size as the delegation that had served the previous term. Considering that women make up more than half of the general population and more than half of the voting population, their 5.9-percent share of the total congressional delegation was particularly baffling, especially as it represented such negligible improvement from 1974, when the figure stood at 4 percent, with the same number of senators. This contrasts with women's success on the state level, where they make up 18 percent of legislators.

The 1992 elections brought a significant upturn in women's representation in Congress. The 102d Congress had only two women senators: Nancy Landon Kassebaum (R-Kans.), elected in 1978, and Barbara A. Mikulski (D-Md.), elected in 1986. In the 103d Congress they were joined by four new women senators, all Democrats: Barbara Boxer and Dianne Feinstein of California, Carol Moseley Braun of Illinois, and Patty Murray of Washington. A fifth, Republican Kay Bailey Hutchison of Texas, was elected in 1993 to fill a vacancy. Women also took a great leap forward in the House, where twenty-four new members joined an equal number of returning women representatives (including the District of Columbia delegate) for a total of forty-eight. The 103d Congress thus had fifty-five women members, raising their portion of the total membership to more than 10 percent.

Women Members of Congress, 1917–1994

SENATORS	CONGRESS	REPRESENTATIVES	CONGRESS
Rebecca L. Felton[1] (D-Ga.)	67th	Caroline O'Day (D-N.Y.)	74th–77th
Hattie W. Caraway[2] (D-Ark.)	72d–78th	Elizabeth H. Gasque[3] (D-S.C.)	75th
Rose McConnell Long[1] (D-La.)	74th	Nan W. Honeyman (D-Oreg.)	75th
Dixie Bibb Graves[1] (D-Ala.)	75th	Frances P. Bolton[4] (R-Ohio)	76th–90th
Gladys Pyle[3] (R-S. Dak.)	75th	Florence R. Gibbs[3] (D-Ga.)	76th
Vera C. Bushfield[1] (R-S. Dak.)	80th	Clara G. McMillan[3] (D-S.C.)	76th
Margaret Chase Smith (R-Maine)	81st–92d	Margaret Chase Smith[4] (R-Maine)	76th–80th
Hazel H. Abel[3] (R-Nebr.)	83d	Jessie Sumner (R-Ill.)	76th–79th
Eva K. Bowring[1] (R-Nebr.)	83d	Veronica G. Boland[3] (D-Pa.)	77th
Maurine B. Neuberger[2] (D-Oreg.)	86th–89th	Katharine E. Byron[3] (D-Md.)	77th
Elaine S. Edwards[1] (D-La.)	92d	Willa E. Fulmer[3] (D-S.C.)	78th
Maryon Allen[1] (D-Ala.)	95th	Clare Boothe Luce (R-Conn.)	78th–79th
Muriel Humphrey[1] (D-Minn.)	95th	Winifred C. Stanley (R-N.Y.)	78th
Nancy L. Kassebaum (R-Kans.)	96th–	Emily Taft Douglas (D-Ill.)	79th
Paula Hawkins (R-Fla.)	97th–99th	Helen Gahagan Douglas (D-Calif.)	79th–81st
Barbara A. Mikulski (D-Md.)	100th–	Helen Douglas Mankin[3] (D-Ga.)	79th
Jocelyn Burdick[1] (D-N. Dak.)	102d	Eliza Jane Pratt[3] (D-N.C.)	79th
Barbara Boxer (D-Calif.)	103d–	Chase Going Woodhouse (D-Conn.)	79th, 81st
Dianne Feinstein (D-Calif.)	103d–	Georgia L. Lusk (D-N.Mex.)	80th
Kay Bailey Hutchison[3] (R-Tex.)	103d–	Katharine St. George (R-N.Y.)	80th–88th
Carol Moseley Braun (D-Ill.)	103d–	Reva Z. B. Bosone (D-Utah)	81st–82d
Patty Murray (D-Wash.)	103d–	Cecil M. Harden (R-Ind.)	81st–85th
		Edna F. Kelly[4] (D-N.Y.)	81st–90th
		Vera D. Buchanan[4] (D-Pa.)	82d–84th

REPRESENTATIVES	CONGRESS
Jeannette Rankin (R-Mont.)	65th, 77th
Winnifred S. M. Huck[3] (R-Ill.)	67th
Mae E. Nolan[4] (R.-Calif.)	67th–68th
Alice M. Robertson (R-Okla.)	67th
Florence P. Kahn[4] (R-Calif.)	69th–74th
Mary T. Norton (D-N.J.)	69th–81st
Edith Nourse Rogers[4] (R-Mass.)	69th–86th
Katherine Langley (R-Ky.)	70th–71st
Pearl Peden Oldfield[4] (D-Ark.)	70th–71st
Ruth Hanna McCormick (R-Ill.)	71st
Ruth Bryan Owen (D-Fla.)	71st–72d
Ruth S. B. Pratt (R-N.Y.)	71st–72d
Effiegene (Locke) Wingo (D-Ark.)	71st–72d
Willa M. B. Eslick[3] (D-Tenn.)	72d
Marian W. Clarke[3] (R-N.Y.)	73d
Isabella S. Greenway[4] (D-Ariz.)	73d–74th
Virginia E. Jenckes (D-Ind.)	73d–75th
Kathryn E. O'Loughlin (D-Kans.)	73d

(continued)

REPRESENTATIVES	CONGRESS
Marguerite Stitt Church (R-Ill.)	82d–87th
Maude Elizabeth Kee[4] (D-W.Va.)	82d–88th
Ruth Thompson (R-Mich.)	82d–84th
Mary Elizabeth Pruett Farrington[4] (R-Hawaii)	83d–84th
Gracie B. Pfost (D-Idaho)	83d–87th
Leonor Kretzer Sullivan (D-Mo.)	83d–94th
Iris F. Blitch (D-Ga.)	84th–87th
Kathryn E. Granahan[4] (D-Pa.)	84th–87th
Edith S. Green (D-Oreg.)	84th–93d
Martha W. Griffiths (D-Mich.)	84th–93d
Coya G. Knutson (D-Minn.)	84th–85th
Florence P. Dwyer (R-N.J.)	85th–92d
Julia Butler Hansen[4] (D-Wash.)	86th–93d
Catherine D. May (R-Wash.)	86th–91st
Edna Oakes Simpson (R-Ill.)	86th
Jessica McC. Weis (R-N.Y.)	86th–87th
Catherine D. Norrell[3] (D-Ark.)	87th
Louise G. Reece[3] (R-Tenn.)	87th

[1] Appointed to fill a vacancy.
[2] Appointed to fill a vacancy and then elected for next session.
[3] Elected to fill a vacancy.
[4] Elected to fill a vacancy and then reelected for next session.

Women Members of Congress, 1917–1994 (Continued)

REPRESENTATIVES	CONGRESS	REPRESENTATIVES	CONGRESS
Corrine B. Riley[3] (D-S.C.)	87th	Helen Delich Bentley (R-Md.)	99th–
Irene Bailey Baker[3] (R-Tenn.)	88th	Cathy (Mrs. Gillis) Long[3] (D-La.)	99th
Charlotte T. Reid (R-Ill.)	88th–92d	Jan Meyers (R-Kans.)	99th–
Patsy T. Mink[5] (D-Hawaii)	89th–94th, 101st–	Constance A. Morella (R-Md.)	100th–
Lera Thomas[3] (D-Tex.)	89th	Liz J. Patterson (D-S.C.)	100th–102d
Margaret M. Heckler (R-Mass.)	90th–97th	Nancy Pelosi[4] (D-Calif.)	100th–
Shirley A. Chisholm (D-N.Y.)	91st–97th	Patricia F. Saiki (R-Hawaii)	100th–101st
Bella S. Abzug (D-N.Y.)	92d–94th	Louise McIntosh Slaughter (D-N.Y.)	100th–
Elizabeth B. Andrews[3] (D-Ala.)	92d	Jill L. Long[4] (D-Ind.)	101st–
Ella T. Grasso (D-Conn.)	92d–93d	Nita M. Lowey (D-N.Y.)	101st–
Louise Day Hicks (D-Mass.)	92d	Susan Molinari[4] (R-N.Y.)	101st–
Corinne C. Boggs[4] (D-La.)	93d–101st	Ileana Ros-Lehtinen[4] (R-Fla.)	101st–
Yvonne B. Burke (D-Calif.)	93d–95th	Jolene Unsoeld (D-Wash.)	101st–
Cardiss Collins[4] (D-Ill.)	93d–	Eva Clayton (D-N.C.)	102d–
Marjorie S. Holt (R-Md.)	93d–99th	Barbara-Rose Collins (D-Mich.)	102d–
Elizabeth Holtzman (D-N.Y.)	93d–96th	Rosa DeLauro (D-Conn.)	102d–
Barbara Jordan (D-Tex.)	93d–95th	Joan Kelly Horn (D-Miss.)	102d
Patricia Schroeder (D-Colo.)	93d–	Eleanor Holmes Norton (D-D.C.)	102d–
Millicent Fenwick (R-N.J.)	94th–97th	Maxine Waters (D-Calif.)	102d–
Martha Keys (D-Kans.)	94th–95th	Corrine Brown (D-Fla.)	103d–
Marilyn Lloyd (D-Tenn.)	94th	Leslie L. Byrne (D-Va.)	103d–
Helen S. Meyner (D-N.J.)	94th–95th	Maria Cantwell (D-Wash.)	103d–
Shirley N. Pettis[4] (R-Calif.)	94th–95th	Pat Danner (D-Mo.)	103d–
Virginia Smith (R-Nebr.)	94th–101st	Jennifer Dunn (R-Wash.)	103d–
Gladys Noon Spellman[6] (D-Md.)	94th–97th	Karan English (D-Ariz.)	103d–
Barbara A. Mikulski (D-Md.)	95th–99th	Anna G. Eshoo (D-Calif.)	103d–
Mary Rose Oakar (D-Ohio)	95th–102d	Tillie Fowler (R-Fla.)	103d–
Beverly B. Byron [4] (D-Md.)	96th–102d	Elizabeth Furse (D-Oreg.)	103d–
Geraldine Anne Ferraro (D-N.Y.)	96th–98th	Jane Harman (D-Calif.)	103d–
Olympia J. Snowe (R-Maine)	96th	Eddie Bernice Johnson (D-Tex.)	103d–
Jean Ashbrook[3] (R-Ohio)	97th	Blanche Lambert (D-Ark.)	103d–
Bobbi Fiedler (R-Calif.)	97th–99th	Cynthia McKinney (D-Ga.)	103d–
Katie Hall[4] (D-Ind.)	97th–98th	Carolyn B. Maloney (D-N.Y.)	103d–
Barbara B. Kennelly[4] (D-Conn.)	97th	Marjorie Margolies-Mezvinsky (D-Pa.)	103d–
Lynn Martin (R-Ill.)	97th–101st	Carrie Meek (D-Fla.)	103d–
Marge Roukema (R-N.J.)	97th–	Deborah Pryce (R-Ohio)	103d–
Claudine Schneider (R-R.I.)	97th–101st	Lucille Roybal-Allard (D-Calif.)	103d–
Barbara Boxer (D-Calif.)	98th–102d	Lynn Schenk (D-Calif.)	103d–
Sala Burton[4,7] (D-Calif.)	98th–100th	Karen Shepherd (D-Utah)	103d–
Nancy L. Johnson (R-Conn.)	98th–	Karen L. Thurman (D-Fla.)	103d–
Marcy Kaptur (D-Ohio)	98th–	Nydia Velázquez (D-N.Y.)	103d–
Barbara F. Vucanovich (R-Nev.)	98th–	Lynn Woolsey (D-Calif.)	103d–

[5] Elected to the 101st Congress to fill a vacancy.
[6] Removed from Congress on 24 February 1981 (one month after the beginning of the 97th Congress) due to an incapacitating illness.
[7] Died on 1 February 1987.

SEN. REBECCA L. FELTON (D-GA.). The first woman to serve in the Senate. Appointed at age eighty-seven to fill a vacancy, she occupied a seat from 21 November to 22 November 1922.   LIBRARY OF CONGRESS

The professional backgrounds of women in Congress vary greatly, unlike those of their male counterparts, which tend to be in business and law. Their ethnic backgrounds, too, have been more various. According to Rutgers University's Center for the American Woman and Politics, by 1992 eight black women, one Hispanic woman, and two identified in the report as Asian/Pacific Islander women had served in the House of Representatives.

By the early 1990s, 131 women had served in Congress. The first elected was Jeannette Rankin (R-Mont.). Rankin won her seat in 1916, before the Constitution was amended to give women the vote.

Originally, women were frequently appointed to fill vacancies created by the death of their husbands, a practice known as the "widows' mandate." In some cases, widows led illustrious political careers of their own, at times outshining the husbands who had preceded them. Edith Nourse Rogers (R-Mass.) became a representative as a result of her husband's death in 1925 and remained a distinguished member of Congress until her death in 1960. Margaret Chase Smith, who also succeeded her husband in the House, rose to win election to the Senate, where she became one of the nation's most famous senators. She was the first senator to denounce Sen. Joseph R. McCarthy, which she did in what she called a "declaration of conscience." As these women gained greater political clout, more were elected on the basis of their own credentials and policy platforms.

Several factors account for the gender gap in Congress: latent voter resistance to women candidates, lack of incumbency and previous political experience, absence of party support, and the relative lack of financial resources. The difficulty of financing elections is seen today as women's greatest obstacle: women are less able to raise the amounts of money necessary to win national election, and they are also more conservative about money—less likely than their male counterparts to mortgage the family farm or homestead to further their political careers. Groups like EMILY's (Early Money is Like Yeast) List and the Women's Campaign Fund have somewhat offset this obstacle, and they apparently had a significant effect on the elections of 1992.

Surveys of voter attitudes also show that women are often characterized as having nurturing personalities well suited to issues of education and child care. These attitudes may be reflected in the higher percentage of women in state legislatures, where these issues enjoy a higher priority. In contrast, voters express less confidence in women in relation to national issues such as the economy and defense. By 1992, however, voters were losing confidence in male politicians in these areas as well.

Biological obstacles have also kept women from seeking and winning congressional office: women tend to run later in life, after they have already had children or after their children have left the nest, leaving them with a shorter career span in which to reach congressional office. Rep. Patricia Schroeder (D-Colo.) has sought to overcome both this problem and the problem of stereotypical attitudes. She won her congressional seat while her children were very young, responding to critics with the quip:

"Yes, I have a uterus and a brain and they both work." Schroeder also developed an expertise in defense issues; she has remained a vocal member of the House Armed Services Committee for nearly two decades.

Another issue for female candidates has been lack of party support. Political parties have often discouraged female candidates from running for top positions. This makes campaigning especially difficult, since parties provide the necessary financial and human resources to mount national campaigns. All of these hindrances are beginning to recede, but it will probably be a long time before women achieve truly representative numbers in Congress.

Leadership positions within Congress have also been difficult for women to attain. In the House, only six women have chaired full standing committees: Mae E. Nolan, Committee on Expenditures in the Post Office Department (67th–68th Congress); Mary T. Norton, Committee on the District of Columbia (72d–74th Congress), Committee on Labor (75th–79th Congress), and Committee on House Administration (81st Congress); Caroline O'Day, Committee on Election of President, Vice President, and Representatives in Congress (75th–77th Congress); Edith Nourse Rogers, Committee on Veterans' Affairs (80th and 83d Congresses); and Leonor K. Sullivan, Committee on Merchant Marine and Fisheries (93d–94th Congress). The only woman ever to chair a standing committee in the Senate was Hattie W. Caraway, chair of the Committee on Enrolled Bills (73d–78th Congress).

In the 103d Congress, Rep. Barbara B. Kennelly (D-Conn.) was the House's chief deputy majority whip; Representative Schroeder also served as a deputy whip. While several women in the 103d Congress chaired subcommittees, none chaired full standing committees. Senator Mikulski chaired subcommittees of the Senate Appropriations and the Labor and Human Resources committees. On the House side, Representative Schroeder chaired a subcommittee of Armed Services, while Delegate Norton and Rep. Barbara-Rose Collins (D-Mich.) chaired subcommittees of the Committee on Post Office and Civil Service. Norton also chaired a subcommittee of the Committee on the District of Columbia, and Rep. Cardiss Collins (D-Ill.) chaired a subcommittee of the Energy and Commerce Committee. In early 1991, Schroeder was named chairman of the Select Committee on Children, Youth and Families; this committee was disbanded in the 103d Congress. (A select committee is one step below a full committee, since it cannot originate legislation.)

The bipartisan Congressional Caucus for Women's Issues includes men and women who are involved in issues of concern to women and their families. Only women can serve on the executive committee. Founded in 1977, the caucus in 1993 was chaired by Representatives Patricia Schroeder and Olympia J. Snowe (R-Maine). Membership has risen to 170 members. One caucus effort has been to push for enactment of the Family and Medical Leave Act. That statute, enacted in 1993, provides individuals who work for companies with over fifty employees with up to twelve weeks of unpaid leave during any twelve-month period to tend to a child, a sick relative, or their own illness.

CLARE BOOTHE LUCE (R-CONN.), *LEFT,* AND WINIFRED C. STANLEY (R-N.Y.). On the steps of the Capitol the day before taking their seats in the House of Representatives, 5 January 1943.   LIBRARY OF CONGRESS

Another priority item, the Women's Health Equity Act, would provide for research, services, and prevention on specific health issues that affect women. Since 1981, the caucus has also been working on different aspects of the Economic Equity Act, including equal pay, retirement equity, employment opportunity, and other issues facing women in the workplace, as well as for legislation involving violence against women.

As a result of events of the early 1990s, such as the Supreme Court confirmation hearings of Clarence Thomas and the perceived judicial erosion of reproductive rights assured by *Roe v. Wade* (1973), the issue of increasing the number of women in national office has assumed greater importance than it had in the two preceding decades. One hundred forty women ran for the House and seventeen for the Senate in 1992. A number of pollsters correctly predicted 1992 to be the year of the female candidate because of the anti-incumbent mood, a shift toward domestic issues in which women are often considered stronger, and massive redistricting as a result of the 1990 census, which led to the creation of more open seats. The candidacy of Carol Moseley Braun proved to be the first successful campaign of a black woman for the U.S. Senate, signaling a new era for women in political life.

[*See also biographies of figures mentioned herein.*]

BIBLIOGRAPHY

Rix, Sara E., ed. *The American Woman 1990–1991: A Status Report.* 1990.

Theilmann, John, and Al Wilhite. *Discrimination and Congressional Campaign Contributions.* 1991.

Tolchin, Susan J., and Martin Tolchin. *Clout: Womanpower and Politics.* 1974.

Tolchin, Susan J. *Women in Congress.* 1976.

Witt, Linda, Karen M. Paget, and Glenna Matthews. *Running as a Woman: Gender and Power in American Politics.* 1993.

SUSAN J. TOLCHIN and LINDA FEINSTEIN

WOMEN'S ISSUES AND RIGHTS. From the adoption of the Constitution in 1789 to the Civil War, Congress rarely addressed "women's issues." Most of the legal and social matters that bore directly on women's lives came under the jurisdiction of state governments. These matters included, for example, the rights of married women to control their earnings, to convey their property, to conduct business, and to obtain divorce decrees and guardianship of their children. During the nineteenth century, many states took action to ameliorate some of the disadvantages that affected women, but discriminatory treatment in education and employment went unchecked by legislation. Throughout the century, most states denied women the right to vote.

After the Civil War, women activists hoped that Congress would include them in measures enfranchising former slaves, but they were quickly disappointed. In 1866, during discussion of a voting rights bill for African Americans in the District of Columbia, the Senate defeated a woman suffrage provision by a vote of 37 to 9; the House followed suit, by a vote of 74 to 48 (with 68 abstentions). Congress compounded the injury by explicitly associating suffrage with men in the Fourteenth Amendment to the Constitution. Although a woman suffrage amendment was introduced initially in 1868, Congress remained hostile and in 1889 even attempted to prevent Wyoming from entry into the Union because it included a woman suffrage provision in its state constitution. Although in this instance Congress relented, it did not approve a woman suffrage amendment until 1919.

Until women became voters, only a handful of measures revealed any congressional interest in their well-being. Three laws reflected nineteenth-century concern with sexual exploitation. In 1862, Congress banned polygamy, the first of several such acts aimed at Mormons settling the western territories. The Comstock Act, passed in 1873, prohibited sending obscene material through the mail; its specific target, however, was birth control devices, viewed by many reformers as a tool that would permit men to exploit women sexually by eliminating the possibility of pregnancy. The third law, the Mann Act, was passed in 1910. It prohibited the transport of women across state lines for immoral purposes, thereby protecting them from "white slavers" who sought to force them into prostitution. Two other measures emerged to address women's special role as protector of the home: Congress created the Children's Bureau in 1912 (with the anticipated appointment of a woman, Julia Lathrop, to head it), and in 1917, after decades of agitation by women temperance activists, it proposed ratification of the Eighteenth Amendment to the Constitution, which prohibited the manufacture, sale, or transportation of liquor.

Congress first took notice of women as workers in 1864, when, in the midst of the Civil War, it explicitly authorized hiring women federal clerks—at

WOMEN SUFFRAGISTS. Assembled on the steps of the Capitol, 1918.   OFFICE OF THE HISTORIAN OF THE U.S. SENATE

half the lowest rate of pay offered to male clerks. In 1870, Congress permitted department heads to appoint "competent and worthy" women to any federal job and at the pay rate designated for the position. Women's war work during World War I called further attention to the need to assist women laborers and led Congress, in 1920, to create the Women's Bureau, empowered to conduct research on the conditions under which women worked in private industry.

After the suffrage amendment was added to the Constitution in 1920, Congress assumed that women would vote as a bloc, and members made hasty attempts to court women voters. The first legislation passed with the new voters in mind, the Sheppard-Towner Maternity Act (1921), authorized an appropriation to the states for "promoting the welfare and hygiene" of mothers and infants. In 1922 Congress passed the Married Women's Independent Citizenship Act. Known as the Cable Act, it revised the laws that defined a wife's citizenship

as that of her husband. In 1923 Congress barred discrimination based on sex in pay rates for federal workers. As the 1920s wore on and it became clear that women were neither flooding the polls nor voting as a block, the urge to cater to this segment of the electorate abated. In 1928, when Sheppard-Towner came up for renewal, Congress rejected it.

Two New Deal measures not usually thought of as "women's bills" had tremendous implications for women. The Social Security Act, passed in 1935 and amended in 1939, provided federal aid for the relief of needy children and granted an old age pension to homemakers, based upon their husbands' income. In 1938, Congress stepped out in front of the states with the Fair Labor Standards Act (FLSA), guaranteeing workers employed by covered businesses a federal minimum wage rate with time-and-a-half pay for more than forty hours of work in a week. The legislation and its validation by the Supreme Court in 1941 established the principle that labor laws could apply equally to workers of both sexes.

Women figured only marginally in World War II legislation. The Lanham Act allocated a small amount of money to the states for child care facilities near factories producing war matériel, but the funding ended with the war. Congress also established a wartime women's corps in the military, and in 1948 the Women's Armed Services Integration Act made women's units a permanent part of the military. Women's military roles, however, remained limited for decades to come.

Women's contributions to the war effort led to a renewed interest in the Equal Rights Amendment (ERA) to the Constitution, introduced initially in 1923. In 1946 the Senate held a floor debate on the measure for the first time and then endorsed it by a 38 to 35 vote, not enough to send the amendment to the states. In 1950 Sen. Carl Hayden devised a rider to the amendment that would preserve laws that pertained only to women. Although ERA supporters introduced the amendment in almost every Congress, the Hayden rider effectively nullified it and the battle for the measure was thus stalled for twenty years.

World War II also inspired a more focused, if less comprehensive, attempt to help women: an equal pay bill, introduced in 1945 by Senators Claude Pepper (D-Fla.) and Wayne L. Morse (R-Oreg.). The work of the National Committee for Equal Pay, a group of progressive anti-ERA women, the measure would have offered both recognition and modest protection to the millions of women who had entered the labor force during World War II and who were now being urged to leave. Although introduced in each subsequent Congress, for fifteen years the bill languished. Meanwhile, the GI Bill of Rights (the Servicemen's Readjustment Act of 1944) subsidized the education of veterans (who were overwhelmingly male) and created a dramatic educational advantage for men over women in the 1950s. The resulting disparity in educational opportunity and the preference for veterans seeking civil service jobs posed barriers to women throughout their careers. The postwar "baby boom" did inspire Congress in 1954 for the first time to permit an in-

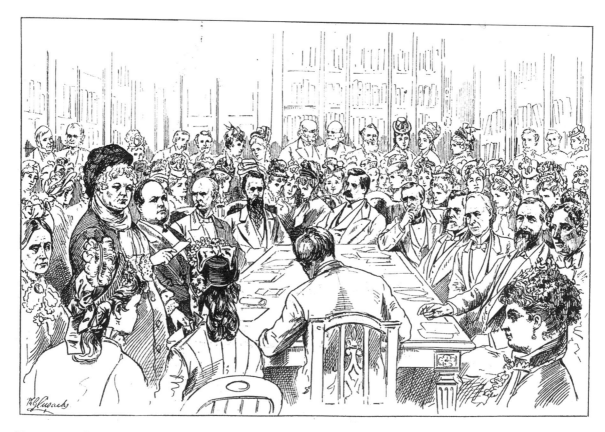

ELIZABETH CADY STANTON. Addressing the Senate Committee on Privileges and Elections, 16 January 1878.

come tax deduction for child care, if the care was necessary in order to permit the parent to work.

During the 1950s, Congress discussed but took no dispositive action on either the ERA or equal pay. A provision added to the 1957 Civil Rights Act in effect barred states from excluding women from federal juries. But the legislation did not require equal treatment for women as jurors, which emerged in later decades from court rulings.

A shift in public opinion toward a more active role for government, signaled by the election of John F. Kennedy in 1960, generated a spate of legislative measures on behalf of women. In 1963 Congress finally passed the Equal Pay Act, requiring employers engaged in interstate commerce to pay men and women the same wage for the same job. The enactment of the omnibus Civil Rights Act of 1964 dwarfed the Equal Pay Act in its effect on working women. Initiated by Kennedy but signed by Lyndon B. Johnson, the act was designed chiefly to prohibit discrimination based on race. However, a coalition consisting of opponents of the bill and ERA supporters succeeded in adding a prohibition against sex discrimination in Title VII, the employment section. The new law created an independent agency, the Equal Employment Opportunity Commission (EEOC), to draw up regulations and to mediate disputes. The EEOC's hostility to women's rights served as one impetus for the creation of a new activist organization—the National Organization for Women (NOW)—to bring pressure to bear upon it. Administration of Title VII continued to be the focus of political conflict through ensuing decades.

The Johnson administration's War on Poverty also produced measures to help women and their families. In 1965 an amendment to the Social Security Act established the Medicaid program, which made medical care available to recipients of public assistance—for the most part women and children. And in 1966 Congress authorized the Head Start program, which brought preschool children into a supervised educational setting, thereby also freeing their parents to find paid employment.

With activist women increasingly well-organized and in substantial agreement about goals, and with a handful of new female representatives elected on specifically feminist platforms, Congress was increasingly responsive to women's issues. Most dramatically, by a vote of 354 to 24 in the House and 84 to 8 in the Senate, it sent the Equal Rights Amendment to the states for ratification in 1972. But the amendment continued to provoke contro-versy. Although in 1978 Congress extended its ratification deadline by thirty-nine months, when the time limit expired on 30 June 1982 the amendment was still three states shy of the necessary three-fourths majority.

Additional congressional action had, however, made the ERA less necessary. The 92d Congress (1971–1973) passed a host of new laws on behalf of women. In addition to strengthening the EEOC and expanding protection against employment discrimination, Congress required, through Title IX of the Education Amendments of 1972, that schools receiving federal aid provide equal treatment to women. Two years later, Congress further encouraged equal educational opportunities for women through a model program law, the Women's Educational Equity Act. In 1978 Congress doubled its funding.

Throughout the 1970s, Congress continued to respond to an apparent consensus that women should be protected against discrimination. In 1974, the legislature prohibited discrimination against women in consumer credit, an initiative with substantial conservative support. (The protection of this law was extended to commercial credit in 1988.) When the Supreme Court ruled in December 1976 that Title VII of the Civil Rights Act of 1964 did not bar discrimination against pregnant women, Congress quickly amended the law to provide that protection. Many initiatives came from a strategy devised by Rep. Bella S. Abzug (D-N.Y.), who served from 1971 to January 1977. By routinely introducing a provision against sex discrimination, she succeeded in ensuring equal treatment for women in a variety of arenas including public works, revenue sharing, and environmental protection. Congressional and agency oversight hearings on women's issues became a regular part of the Washington agenda in these years. In 1975, Congress went so far as to fund a national women's conference to set goals for eliminating sex discrimination.

Although Congress most readily supported legislative initiatives that raised equity rather than class issues, activists made some headway in protecting the poorest and most vulnerable women. In 1974, led by Rep. Shirley A. Chisholm (D-N.Y.), Congress expanded coverage of the Fair Labor Standards Act to include domestic workers, overriding a presidential veto. Two years later, Chisholm and Sen. Walter F. Mondale (D-Minn.) championed equity in Vocational Education through Title II of the Education Amendments of 1976,

Enactments Important to Women's Rights

Title	Date Enacted	Reference Number	Description
Deficiency Act	1870	41st Cong., 2d sess., Chap. 251	Authorized federal department heads to appoint "competent and worthy" female clerks to all government positions.
Comstock Act	1873	43d Cong., 3d sess., Chap. 258	Provided penalties for "circulating" obscene literature and articles, including birth control and abortifacients.
Nineteenth Amendment	1919[1]	H. J. Res. 1	Constitutional amendment guaranteeing women the right to vote.
Women's Bureau Act	1920	P.L. 66-259	Created Women's Bureau to do research about working women.
Fair Labor Standards Act	1938	P.L. 75-718	Established minimum wages and premium pay for work over forty hours for both male and female workers.
Women's Armed Services Integration Act	1948	P.L. 80-625	Temporary women's corps made permanent.
Equal Pay Act of 1963	1963	P.L. 88-38	Prohibited sex-based discrimination by private employers in pay rates.
Civil Rights Act of 1964	1964	P.L. 88-352	Title VII prohibited race and gender-based discrimination by private employers in all terms and conditions of employment.
Economic Opportunity Amendments of 1966	1966	P.L. 89-794	Authorized Head Start (preschool day care); required that 23 percent of Job Corps places go to women.
Equal Rights Amendment	1972[2]	H. J. Res. 208	Constitutional guarantee of equal treatment for women (not ratified).
Equal Employment Opportunity Act of 1972	1972	P.L. 92-261	Extended coverage of Title VII to employees of state and local governments; gave Equal Employment Opportunity Commission power to sue.
Education Amendments of 1972	1972	P.L. 92-318	Title IX prohibited sex discrimination in federally funded education programs.
Equal Credit Opportunity Act	1974	P.L. 93-495	Prohibited sex discrimination in consumer credit.
Department of Defense Appropriation Authorization Act of 1976	1975	P.L. 94-106	Sec. 803 provided for appointment of women to the military academies.
National Women's Conference Act	1975	P.L. 94-167	Authorized $5 million for a national women's conference to set goals for eliminating discrimination based on gender.

[1]Deposited with secretary of State   [2]Recorded in the Federal Register

which provided for a sex-equity coordinator for every state vocational education program and made federal funding dependent on demonstrable equal treatment. Other victories included modest funding for battered women's programs and improved access to retirement benefits for divorced women. In 1978 Congress included displaced homemakers in the Comprehensive Employment and Training Act, and in 1980 Patricia Schroeder (D-Colo.) sponsored a successful bill to give divorced wives of foreign service officers rights to part of their husbands' pensions. That same year, Congress also authorized

$5 million for demonstration programs to help displaced homemakers.

One area where activists had early congressional but not presidential support was day care. Congress in 1971 passed the Comprehensive Child Development Act, legislation that would have provided two billion dollars the first year for a network of day care centers. President Richard M. Nixon vetoed the measure, however, as interference with the family, and Congress was unable to override. President Gerald R. Ford vetoed another child care bill in 1975. Some additional funding for day care came

Enactments Important to Women's Rights (Continued)

TITLE	DATE ENACTED	REFERENCE NUMBER	DESCRIPTION
Departments of Labor and Health, Education, and Welfare Appropriations Act of 1977	1976	P.L. 94-439	First Hyde Amendment: barred federal funds for abortion unless life of the mother was in danger.
Extension of Deadline for Ratification of the Equal Rights Amendment	1978	H. J. Res. 638	Extended ratification deadline for ERA for thirty-nine months.
Pregnancy, Sex Discrimination Prohibition Act of 1978	1978	P.L. 95-555	Amended Title VII to prohibit employment discrimination based on pregnancy or childbirth; no employer would be forced to include abortion in health insurance.
Civil Rights Restoration Act of 1987	1988	P.L. 100-259	Overturned a 1984 Supreme Court decision and required educational institutions receiving federal funds to eliminate discrimination institution-wide.
Family Support Act of 1988	1988	P.L. 100-485	Reformed Aid to Families with Dependent Children (AFDC); strengthened child support laws; provided for child care and health benefits for transition to work.
Women's Business Ownership Act of 1988	1988	P.L. 100-533	Amended Equal Credit Opportunity Act to eliminate discrimination in commercial credit; established National Women's Business Council.
Child Care (Omnibus Budget Reconciliation Act of 1990, Title V, Chapter 6)	1990	P.L. 101-508	Provided grants to states for child care and tax benefits to families.
Civil Rights Act of 1991	1991	P.L. 102-166	Overturned several Supreme Court interpretations of the Civil Rights Act of 1964; established rights for women to punitive and compensatory damages; established "Glass Ceiling Commission."
Family and Medical Leave Act	1993	P.L. 103-3	Provided 12 weeks leave to employees (of companies with more than 50 employees) for illness or to care for children or ill family members.

SOURCE: *Selected Women's Issues Legislation Enacted between 1832 and 1988.* Congressional Research Service, Library of Congress. CRS Rept. 89–514 GOV. 1987. Rev. 1989.

in the 1976 Social Security amendments, and Congress also transformed a tax deduction for child care into a tax credit.

In the area of abortion rights, Congress displayed ambivalence to the feminist agenda. It did not, in the wake of the 1973 *Roe v. Wade* decision invalidating abortion laws, support a constitutional amendment to recriminalize the procedure. But Congress did agree to limit public funding, putting poor women at a disadvantage in securing abortion services. A 1973 Foreign Assistance Act included a ban on the use of these moneys for abortion, and in

1976 Congress amended the Medicaid program to prohibit paying for abortion unless the life of the mother were in danger. Further laws prohibited public funding for abortion on military bases and the use of public money for abortions by the District of Columbia.

A second issue on which Congress diverged from the women's rights agenda was the role of women in the military. Although in 1975 Congress admitted women to the service academies and in 1977 provided veterans' benefits to women pilots who had served in World War II, it drew the line at the draft.

In 1980, at the behest of the Carter administration, Congress passed a draft registration law but refused, despite the administration's request, to include women in the call. The Supreme Court sustained the law.

In 1978 anti-abortionists began to target prochoice legislators (who supported a woman's right to choose abortion), defeating a number of them, and a new conservative impulse led to a 1980 Republican platform that rejected both the Equal Rights Amendment and abortion rights. In order to strengthen its position, the Congresswomen's Caucus, founded in 1977, reorganized in 1981 as the Congressional Caucus on Women's Issues and added more than a hundred male representatives to its roster. With many antidiscrimination provisions now encoded in the nation's laws, and social issues fraught with conflict, sympathetic Congress members began to concentrate more heavily on economic issues.

The first Women's Economic Equity Act was introduced in the 97th Congress (1981–1983) to address the disproportionate presence of women and children among the poor. Designed as a legislative package to be enacted piece by piece, it focused on pensions, insurance, and economic responsibility for children. Its precise configuration changed with each Congress as sections were enacted or dropped. In 1984, the Child Support Enforcement Amendments intensified the effort to have fathers contribute to the financial needs of their children, and the Retirement Equity Act made it easier for divorced or widowed women to gain access to their husband's pensions. In 1986, Congress mandated access to temporary health insurance coverage for newly divorced and widowed women. The continuing entry of women into the labor force and the conservative desire to limit welfare spending finally resulted in a federal child care law enacted in 1990, which President George Bush signed. The measure provided both tax credits and grant money, although the funding was modest.

Throughout the 1980s and into the early 1990s, Congress remained more sympathetic to the activist agenda than did the executive branch. In 1984, the Supreme Court ruled that the legislative ban on discrimination by educational institutions receiving federal funds applied only to the specific program that accepted the funding. The 1988 Civil Rights Restoration Act made it explicit that acceptance of federal funding required educational institutions to eliminate discrimination from all programs. President Reagan vetoed the law, but Congress overrode the veto by a vote of 315 to 98 in the House and 75 to 14 in the Senate.

Similarly, in 1990 Congress passed family and medical leave legislation, proposed initially in 1984. The bill required companies with more than fifty employees to offer twelve weeks of unpaid leave during any twelve-month period to permanent employees who were ill or who needed to take care of infirm elderly dependents or newborn, adopted, or ill children. President Bush vetoed the bill initially and again when it was repassed in 1992. President Bush also vetoed legislation to increase funding for women's health research through the National Institutes of Health, part of an initiative spearheaded by women members to correct a long-standing neglect of women's health concerns in medical research.

Although Congress did not make public funding available for abortion, even in this area it demonstrated more sympathy with women's rights supporters than the executive branch. In 1988 the Reagan administration tried further to limit women's access to abortion services by issuing a regulation—the "gag rule"—forbidding family planning clinics that accepted federal funds from mentioning abortion as an available option to pregnant women or from making referrals to abortion clinics. In 1992, after an initial court challenge failed, Congress passed legislation rescinding the rule, although it was unable to override President Bush's veto.

As the nation turned its attention to the 1992 campaign, women's issues, including abortion rights, family leave, women's health research, economic equity, and employment opportunities, were prominent on the agenda. The results of the 1992 election were impressive for women candidates: four women were elected to the U.S. Senate, raising the number from three to six, and forty-nine women won seats as members of the House of Representatives, up from twenty-nine. Democratic contender Bill Clinton, who had run as a pro-choice candidate, became president.

Keeping promises he had made during the campaign, President Clinton overturned the "gag rule" by executive action on his second day in office and signed the Family and Medical Leave Act on 5 February 1993. In addition, during the first session of the 103d Congress, the legislature passed and President Clinton signed the National Institutes of Health Revitalization Act, which authorized funding for research on women's health issues. Congress, with the president's assent, also liberalized abortion funding through several statutes.

For 1994, Congress considered legislation protecting access to abortion clinics, punishing violence against women, and improving gender equity in education. However, the issues of health insurance reform and welfare reform promised to dominate the congressional agenda. Both members of Congress and women's organizations monitoring congressional activity demonstrated full appreciation of the potential impact of both measures on women's lives.

[*See also* Children, Youth, and Families Committee, House Select; Equal Rights Amendment; Family Policies; Nineteenth Amendment; Women in Congress.]

BIBLIOGRAPHY

Davis, Flora. *Moving the Mountain: The Women's Movement in America since 1960.* 1991.
Freeman, Jo. *The Politics of Women's Liberation.* 1975.
Gelb, Joyce, and Marian Lief Palley. *Women and Public Policies.* 1982.
Harrison, Cynthia. *On Account of Sex: The Politics of Women's Issues, 1945–1968.* 1988.
Hartmann, Susan M. *From Margin to Mainstream: American Women and Politics since 1960.* 1989.
McGlen, Nancy E., and Karen O'Connor. *Women's Rights: The Struggle for Equality in the Nineteenth and Twentieth Centuries.* 1983.

CYNTHIA HARRISON

WORKLOAD. *See* Congress, *article on* Congressional Workload.

WORLD WAR I. The United States entered World War I on 6 April 1917, when President Woodrow Wilson signed a joint congressional resolution declaring war. The president had called Congress into special session and on 2 April addressed the two houses in what was the most eloquent speech of his life, one of the great speeches of the twentieth century. To ask Congress for war, he said, was a distressing and oppressive duty. "But the right," he added, "is more precious than peace. . . ." The nation, he told Congress, had no choice. The war resolution, a declaration of a state of war with Germany, passed the Senate on 4 April by a vote of 82 to 6 and the House, 373 to 50, in the early morning of 6 April.

With two notable exceptions, Congress in subsequent months followed the lead of the administration in passing legislation to support the war. Important measures included the Liberty Loan Act of 24 April 1917, which authorized bonds and loans to finance U.S. and Allied war needs; the Lever Food and Fuel Control Act of 10 August 1917, which empowered the president to regulate production and distribution of essential supplies for the duration of the war; the War Revenue Act of 3 October 1917, which made income tax the chief source of revenue during the war; and the Railroad Control Act of 21 March 1918, which placed the railways under federal control. The Espionage Act of 15 June 1917, aimed at treasonable activities, was followed by the Sedition Act of 16 May 1918, which established severe penalties for persons interfering with furtherance of the war.

This impressive legislative output was not accomplished without some conflict between Congress and the Wilson administration. The first difference had occurred over the draft bill, which the administration had been preparing even before the war declaration. The very notion of instituting a draft brought echoes of the strife that had erupted over a similar bill during the Civil War. It also sparked the first sign of the partisanship that, after victory, would overwhelm the president's proposals for organizing the peace. When the administration went to Congress for draft legislation, key Democratic members of the House—the Speaker, the floor leader, and the chairman of the military affairs committee—refused support. Speaker James Beauchamp (Champ) Clark (D-Mo.) said he had always classed together the conscript and the convict. To introduce a conscription bill, it was necessary to turn to a Republican representative, Julius Kahn of California. In the Senate, Henry Cabot Lodge, Republican of Massachusetts, together with other senators, stalled for time; they hoped to authorize volunteer divisions of troops as in the Spanish-American War, which would allow former president Theodore Roosevelt, Lodge's close friend, to raise a division. Finally, after bitter debate, both houses approved the Selective Service Act by large majorities; the president signed it on 18 May.

A second wartime conflict between the president and Congress, much more serious than the first, occurred during a crisis in the management of the war in the winter of 1917–1918. By that time mobilization, economic and military, was facing serious problems. The crisis first became apparent with a massive tie-up of railroad cars filled with goods and equipment that were headed toward East Coast ports. Cars were backed up as far as Pittsburgh because of lack of cooperation among railroads, which refused to share cars and lines, but most of

PACIFISTS. Opponents of U.S. entry into World War I on the steps of the Capitol.

all, because of lack of warehouse space in the coastal ports. Moreover, a worsening coal shortage was holding ships in port awaiting fuel. The shortage occurred because the government fixed coal prices at too low a figure, which kept marginal mines out of production. The height of the crisis came with a downturn in weather; mid December 1917 saw the beginning of the coldest winter in fifty years, and in January 1918 there were two massive snowstorms. With all these problems, the war economy was verging on collapse. Meanwhile, only four U.S. Army divisions had arrived in France; the army seemingly could not organize itself sufficiently to move troops overseas.

The crisis over economic and military mobilization led to a political crisis, with Congress challenging the president's control of the war. The grand question was who should run things. Sen. George E. Chamberlain (D-Oreg.), chairman of the Military Affairs Committee, scheduled hearings on the crisis. Witnesses paraded before the committee, each describing a different strand of what seemed to be a vast tapestry of incompetence. Chamberlain called for a new cabinet department—a department of munitions—which, he suggested, should perhaps be headed by a Republican. Sensing that such an appointee would be outnumbered in the cabinet, he dropped this idea in favor of a war cabinet of "three distinguished citizens of demonstrated ability." On

the surface, this seemed an effort to demolish the War Department, headed by Newton D. Baker, Wilson's friend and a former student of Wilson's at Johns Hopkins University. In reality Chamberlain's idea was an effort to remove Wilson's war power.

The president refused to accept congressional demands but took measures to resolve the crisis over mobilization, which included bringing in a powerful new head of the War Industries Board, Bernard M. Baruch, and an efficient chief of staff for the army, Gen. Peyton C. March. In May 1918, Congress passed the Overman Act, giving the president authority to override previous legislation and reorganize any government department at will. Baruch and March, both excellent executives, were given authority denied their predecessors. By the summer of 1918, mobilization of the economy and army was on course, and America and its allies were surefootedly headed toward the great victory in France that autumn.

Despite this resolution of the crisis over mobilization, the president unfortunately still failed to understand the need to keep in touch with Congress. Thus, the way was prepared for what proved the most important conflict between the president and Congress (in this instance the Senate) in American history. It is extraordinary that Wilson, a student of relations between Congress and the president, made such an egregious error. His miscalculation could have had some relation to his cardiovascular disease, which was advancing and would lead to his massive stroke of 2 October 1919. Or he may have been looking back to the triumph of the New Freedom legislation during his first term, choosing to believe that, despite the draft bill and mobilization crisis, his relations with Congress were essentially satisfactory. He also believed, as have other twentieth-century presidents, that the conduct of foreign policy was an executive rather than legislative prerogative.

For whatever reason, when, at the beginning of the war, Wilson began to consider how the peace would be organized, he refused to share his ideas with the Senate and did not try to incorporate the ideas of senators into his scheme. He consulted no senators about his basic idea for the boundaries of Europe, or his idea for a powerful League of Nations. He simply announced both ideas, together with other peacemaking details, in a speech to Congress on 8 January 1918. The speech was fairly specific in detailing territorial arrangements, which may not have been wise. The League proposal, fortunately, was less clear, limited as it was to "a general association of nations." In both instances, he would have done better to consult with senators, since the Senate would have to approve any treaty the president negotiated.

Over many years, the Senate had considered that American participation in ensuring world peace could come only through assisting the growth of international law and through bilateral arbitration treaties (but not in the case of American "domestic jurisdiction"—that is, anything Americans deemed their own business). Any pledge involving a League decision to use American military force would interfere, many senators felt, with the chamber's constitutional right to participate in a declaration of war.

Until the summer of 1918, Wilson had gone along with this interpretation. In March 1918, he had told Harvard president A. Lawrence Lowell and former U.S. president William Howard Taft that he opposed a forceful League of Nations because he did not think the Senate would allow the United States to enter into an agreement in which a majority of member nations could tell the country to go to war. But in the summer he changed his mind. He advised the British government not to publish the so-called Phillimore Constitution, a draft of a League

STUCK ON THE JOB. Surrounded by not enacted yet vital emergency wartime measures shortly after the declaration of war on 6 April 1917, "old man Congress," learning of President Woodrow Wilson's decision to remain in Washington during the vacation season, wonders if he too will have to stay on to work. Clifford K. Berryman, *Washington Evening Star,* May 1917.

U.S. SENATE COLLECTION, CENTER FOR LEGISLATIVE ARCHIVES

charter, on the grounds that it had no teeth. Wilson asked his friend and adviser, Edward M. House, to draw up a draft of a League, and Wilson expanded it to include economic and military sanctions. These inclusions were the substance of the great clash he would have with the Senate when the Treaty of Versailles, which in its first twenty-six articles contained the Covenant of the League of Nations, came before the Senate.

As if to guarantee the harsh test of wills that was to come, Wilson in the autumn of 1918 challenged his Republican opponents by asking voters to return a Democratic Congress. He said a Republican majority would "certainly be interpreted on the other side of the water as a repudiation of my leadership." He thereby insulted the patriotism of Republicans throughout the country, who had supported the war as much as had Democrats.

In the congressional elections of 1918, the Republicans triumphed. They won for many reasons, not all of them associated with Wilson's appeal. But whatever the reasons, this meant that the Republicans organized the Senate and controlled the chairmanships of committees. With Senator Lodge serving as chairman of the Foreign Relations Committee, the president's defeat over the Versailles treaty and the League of Nations was under way.

[*See also* Espionage Act; Irreconcilables; Isolationism; League of Nations; Neutrality Debates.]

BIBLIOGRAPHY

Ferrell, Robert H. *Woodrow Wilson and World War I, 1917–1921.* 1985.

Kennedy, David M. *Over Here: The First World War and American Society.* 1980.

Livermore, Seward W. *Politics Is Adjourned: Woodrow Wilson and the War Congress, 1916–1918.* 1966.

ROBERT H. FERRELL

WORLD WAR II. From 1939 to 1945, two issues dominated congressional deliberations: U.S. participation in World War II and the continuing struggle over the New Deal. During the 1930s, the legislative branch had closely monitored foreign policy. After the outbreak of war in Europe in September 1939, Congress gradually relinquished control of foreign and military policies to the executive while exerting greater influence over domestic policy-making and implementation.

During the war years, the Democratic party maintained control of Congress. Influential Democrats included Speaker of the House Sam Rayburn and Senate majority leader Alben W. Barkley. Harry S. Truman, a relative unknown when World War II began, rose to national prominence as chairman of a special Senate committee to investigate the national defense program. In 1944 Truman received the Democratic vice presidential nomination.

Congressional Republicans, led by Joseph W. Martin in the House and by Wallace H. White in the Senate, remained the minority party. However, a conservative coalition of Republicans and anti-administration Democrats offered strong opposition to the president. On domestic issues, Senator Robert A. Taft emerged as the dominant Republican voice, while Senator Arthur H. Vandenberg became the party's principal spokesman on foreign policy.

The Coming of the War, 1939–1941. As fear of war mounted between 1935 and 1938, pacifists and isolationists demanded legislation to prevent U.S. involvement in a future conflict. In 1935, Congress adopted the First Neutrality Act, which prohibited U.S. export or transportation of armaments to belligerent nations. The Neutrality Act of 1935 and additional neutrality legislation passed in 1936 and 1937 embodied the conviction that American entry into World War I had been a blunder and the belief that restrictions on presidential authority were necessary to prevent repetition of the same mistake.

WINSTON CHURCHILL. Addressing the Senate, 1941.   LIBRARY OF CONGRESS

President Franklin D. Roosevelt signed the neutrality laws, but by 1939 he believed that continued isolation in the face of the Nazi menace would endanger national security. Congressional isolationists vehemently disagreed, and the president's attempt in July 1939 to revise the Neutrality Act of 1937 died in the Senate Foreign Relations Committee.

Following the outbreak of the European war, Roosevelt in November 1939 persuaded Congress to amend the neutrality law. The resulting Neutrality Act of 1939 allowed Britain and France to purchase munitions on a cash-and-carry basis. Even so, congressional opposition to Roosevelt's foreign policy remained strong. Isolationists insisted that the president was needlessly intruding into European quarrels, and early in 1940, Congress refused to approve modest increases in military spending.

German victories during the spring of 1940 shocked Congress into action. The defeat of France led the House and Senate to appropriate large sums for national defense. By 15 October 1940, Congress, which began the year squabbling over a total federal budget of $8.4 billion, had appropriated or authorized more than $10 billion for military preparedness. Congress also adopted the Selective Service Act of 1940, which established unprecedented peacetime military conscription. Despite broad support for preparedness, isolationists continued to accuse Roosevelt of seeking war. However, they found it difficult to oppose the president's destroyers-for-bases deal with Britain in September 1940, since the agreement strengthened the defense of the Western Hemisphere.

Congressional debate over aid to Britain intensified in January 1941 with the introduction of the Lend-Lease Act. In an outburst of isolationist fury, Senator Burton K. Wheeler of Montana denounced Lend-Lease as a plan to "plow under every fourth American boy," and isolationists worked frantically to delay or defeat the bill. After adopting amendments restricting the president's authority, on 8 February 1941 the House approved the bill by a vote of 260 to 165, and on 9 March 1941, the Senate voted 60 to 31 in favor of Lend-Lease. Two days later, Roosevelt signed the Lend-Lease Act, thereby assuring a flow of U.S. assistance to Britain.

The passage of Lend-Lease suggested that Congress was now committed to a policy of resisting Nazi Germany. A vote on the future of selective service called that commitment into question. The War Department wanted a term of service for draftees longer than the one year provided by the original conscription law. The draft was unpopular,

and a bill to extend military service elicited little enthusiasm on Capitol Hill. Although the Senate passed a measure lengthening service to a total of thirty months, its fate in the House was uncertain. Only vigorous lobbying by Speaker Sam Rayburn and Gen. George Marshall averted defeat, and on 12 August 1941, the House passed the extension of service bill, 203 to 202. That one-vote victory—less than four months before Pearl Harbor—was a sobering reminder of persisting disagreements over U.S. involvement in the war.

Given those disagreements, a declaration of war seemed impossible. Controversy over lend-lease aid to the Soviet Union, suspicions of secret deals with Britain, debate concerning the undeclared naval war in the North Atlantic, and a close House vote in November 1941 on modifying the Neutrality Act of 1939 revealed a Congress sharply divided over the nation's foreign policy. Then came 7 December 1941 and the Japanese air raid on Pearl Harbor. The next day, the House by a vote of 388 to 1 and the Senate by vote of 82 to 0 declared war against Japan. The only negative vote came from Montana representative Jeannette Rankin, who had also voted against war in April 1917. On 11 December 1941, Germany and Italy declared war on the United States, and Congress responded with war resolutions against Germany and Italy. Dismayed by the sudden turn of events, isolationists and Roosevelt-haters argued that the president had either plotted or permitted the attack on Pearl Harbor, an allegation that eight separate Pearl Harbor investigations (including one unfriendly to Roosevelt carried out by Congress in 1945–1946) failed to verify.

Conduct of the War, 1941–1945. After Pearl Harbor, the president and his advisers directed grand strategy and diplomacy, while the armed forces planned the defeat of Germany and Japan. Congress, meanwhile, exerted indirect influence on the conduct of the war. With fighting under way across two oceans, the House and Senate debated the relative merits of a "Europe-first" versus an "Asia-first" strategy. Congressional Republicans complained that Roosevelt's "Europe-first" orientation was preventing American forces from avenging Pearl Harbor. According to one public opinion poll of February 1942, 62 percent of Americans wanted to concentrate all or most of the nation's war effort against Japan.

Criticism of the administration's Europe-first strategy resulted partly from feelings of rage and powerlessness toward Japan and frustration over humiliating setbacks suffered by U.S. forces during the first six months of the Pacific war. Those emotions caused one of the worst moral errors of World War II—the internment of Japanese Americans living on the west coast.

Early in 1942, the congressional delegations of California, Oregon, and Washington joined a chorus of public officials, pressure groups, and newspapers clamoring that the West was vulnerable to Japanese attack and demanding that Japanese aliens and Japanese Americans be removed from the coast. The War Department urged their evacuation, and in February and March 1942, the president signed executive orders authorizing the relocation of over 110,000 persons of Japanese ancestry to detention camps. On 19 March 1942, the House and Senate endorsed the policy by passing unanimously and virtually without debate a law making it a crime to violate military orders in restricted military zones. Congress thus became an accomplice in this massive violation of civil liberties. (As victims of racial prejudice and wartime emotions, Japanese Americans received partial compensation for their property losses when Congress in 1948 passed the Japanese-American Claims Act. Forty years later, in the Civil Liberties Act of 1988, Congress apologized for the relocation policy and offered restitution in the form of a $20,000 payment to each survivor of wartime incarceration.)

Congress's most significant contributions to the conduct of the war were raising armies and providing money. As troop requirements increased, the House and Senate in 1942 lowered the draft age from twenty to eighteen and in 1943 reluctantly allowed the conscription of fathers, who had previously been deferred. Thereafter, legislators resisted expanding the scope of the draft, a development that in 1944 and 1945 limited the number of U.S. divisions that could be deployed in Europe and the Pacific.

While somewhat grudging about draft calls in the latter stages of the war, Congress proved to be generous with military appropriations. Financing the secret Manhattan Project to build the atomic bomb posed an awkward problem that was solved by special arrangements with a handful of representatives and senators. Secretary of War Henry L. Stimson and General Marshall informed key members of the House and Senate, including Speaker Sam Rayburn, House majority leader John W. McCormack, House minority leader Joseph W. Martin, Jr., Senate majority leader Alben W. Barkley, and Senate minority leader Wallace H. White, about the purpose of moneys hidden in several appropriations bills. In this way, more than $2 billion dollars was diverted to the atomic bomb project.

Atomic weapons ended World War II, but well before the bombs fell on Hiroshima and Nagasaki, Congress debated the postwar international role of the United States. In 1943, the House and Senate passed resolutions pledging U.S. membership in a future international organization. On 28 July 1945, the Senate ratified the United Nations charter, 89 to 2. The lopsidedness of that vote was misleading, however: foreign policy remained controversial. Congressional critics were already attacking the Yalta accords of February 1945 and charging Roosevelt with appeasement of Soviet leader Joseph Stalin. Such accusations would become a staple of Republican campaign oratory for years to come.

The Home Front, 1941–1945. Waging war is primarily an executive function, but Congress played a vital role in economic mobilization needed to fight World War II. Not long after Pearl Harbor, the House and Senate passed the First and Second War Powers Acts, which augmented the president's authority to reorganize the executive branch and to control supply priorities. Many on Capitol Hill were unhappy with the pace of weapons production and wanted a drastic overhaul of defense organization. On 15 January 1942, the Special Committee Investigating the National Defense Program, chaired by Sen. Harry S. Truman, registered its disapproval of the mobilization machinery. Congress seemed ready to create its own defense agency, but the president quickly established the War Production Board and forestalled congressional action. The Truman Committee continued to scrutinize war production for the duration of the conflict and became well-known for uncovering waste and mismanagement in national defense.

Economic mobilization measures frequently provoked controversy because they became entangled in domestic political considerations, especially the continuing struggle over the New Deal. Congressional opponents had halted the president's reform program in 1939, and by 1940 were endeavoring to roll it back. Republicans, led by Sen. Robert A. Taft, and dissident Democrats, led by Sen. Harry Flood Byrd, Sr., and Rep. Edward E. Cox, claimed that reform was crippling national defense and had to be ended.

Tax policy furnished an opportunity for anti–New Dealers to act on their argument that reform interfered with mobilization. The Roosevelt administration wanted to capture excessive profits arising from defense expenditures. Congressional opponents condemned that approach and demanded concessions that would enrich private enterprise. In a defeat for the administration, the First and Second revenue acts of 1940 contained only a disappointingly ineffective excess profits tax.

The prevailing view on Capitol Hill was that business deserved large profits. However, the need for higher taxes could not be denied, and in 1941 and 1942 Congress adopted revenue measures that generated additional money, although not as much as the Treasury Department had requested. The Current Tax Payment Act of 1943 initiated withholding of federal income taxes from wages and salaries but also provided substantial tax forgiveness. In February 1944, the House and Senate passed a tax bill that raised only a fraction of the additional revenue requested by the Treasury and granted several loopholes for business interests. The president vetoed the measure, which he labeled a relief bill for the greedy. Congress speedily overrode Roosevelt's veto, the first time in American history that a veto of a revenue act had failed to stand.

The president's stinging defeat on taxes resulted from disaffection among congressional Democrats and growing Republican strength. In the elections of 1942, Republicans had gained a large number of House and Senate seats as wartime conditions lowered voter turnout. Although the Democratic party retained nominal control of both houses of Congress, a conservative coalition of Republicans and anti-administration Democrats (mostly southern) dominated the House and exerted substantial influence in the Senate. From 1942 through 1944, this coalition carried out a retroactive revenge against the New Deal and tried to prevent a postwar revival of reform.

JAPANESE SUBMARINE CAPTURED AT PEARL HARBOR. Displayed at the Capitol as part of a war bond drive, 3 April 1943.

LIBRARY OF CONGRESS

FRANKLIN D. ROOSEVELT. Signing the declaration of war against Japan, 8 December 1941. DONALD C. BACON

Arguing that huge expenditures for war dictated deep cuts in nonmilitary spending, Republicans and dissident Democrats targeted several New Deal agencies for abolition. The first was the Civilian Conservation Corps, a jobs and conservation program that Congress terminated on 30 June 1942. The Work Progress Administration, the principal relief agency of the 1930s, was next to go, followed by the National Youth Administration, eliminated in July 1943. Another agency, the Farm Security Administration, survived but suffered crippling budget cuts.

The backlash against the New Deal also affected several war agencies. Critics complained that the Office of Civilian Defense, the Office of War Information, and the Office of Price Administration were havens for New Dealers who wanted to pursue social and economic reform. All three agencies became targets of hostile congressional investigations and efforts to reduce their appropriations.

With Congress in a truculent mood, agricultural price control generated a series of bitter confrontations. To restrain inflationary pressures, the Roosevelt administration favored extensive price regulation. In January 1942, a congressional majority thwarted effective price control by adopting a law that permitted steep increases in farm prices. Warning that runaway inflation would wreck the war economy, the president demanded that Congress take action on farm prices by 1 October 1942. Following a rancorous debate, Congress grudgingly passed the Stabilization Act of 1942, which finally granted authority to regulate agricultural prices.

Acrimony over farm prices contributed to passage of legislation eroding the Wagner-Connery National Labor Relations Act of 1935. Angry farm bloc legislators blamed the Roosevelt administration for coddling urban workers and began to push legislation to punish labor unions. A series of coal strikes inflamed antilabor sentiment, and in June 1943

Congress approved the Smith-Connally Anti-Strike Act, which was designed to curb organized labor. The president vetoed the measure, but the House and Senate immediately overrode Roosevelt's veto, thereby foreshadowing a postwar labor policy less favorable to unions.

Congress focused increasingly on postwar policy, as indicated by the controversy over the National Resources Planning Board (NRPB). In its role as chief planning arm of the executive branch, the board was developing programs for the postwar period. Two NRPB reports released in March 1943 recommended completion of the welfare state begun during the 1930s. Republicans and anti–New Deal Democrats exploded with indignation, demanding that the NRPB be abolished. In June 1943 Congress voted to terminate the board. The House and Senate then created special committees on Post-War Economic Policy and Planning, whose recommendations were limited and conservative in character.

The fate of the NRPB demonstrated congressional determination to prevent extensions of the welfare state during or after World War II. Only in the area of veterans' benefits was Congress prepared to consider welfare-state measures. In June 1944, the House and Senate passed the Servicemen's Readjustment Act, popularly known as the GI Bill of Rights, which provided educational assistance, readjustment allowances, and low-interest housing loans for returning veterans. The program turned out to be a rousing success. By 1955, over one-half of all World War II veterans had taken advantage of the benefits furnished by the GI Bill.

Servicemen and servicewomen also attracted congressional attention in connection with the elections of 1944. Public opinion polls suggested that a majority of the troops would vote Democratic, and the president and his advisers wanted as many soldiers as possible to cast ballots. Republicans, on the other hand, feared that a large soldier vote would jeopardize their chance of defeating Roosevelt. They formed an alliance with southern Democrats, who opposed any plan that might enfranchise black soldiers. After a protracted struggle, the coalition of Republicans and southern Democrats, led by Sen. Robert A. Taft, Republican of Ohio, and Sen. James O. Eastland, Democrat of Mississippi, killed the administration's absentee-voting bill and substituted a cumbersome state-controlled plan that would lessen participation and prevent southern black soldiers from voting.

The fight over the soldier-vote bill cemented the already formidable conservative coalition of Republicans and southern Democrats. To be sure,

Roosevelt won reelection in November 1944 (with Harry S. Truman as his new vice president), and the Democratic party increased its majority in the House while losing one Senate seat. But the conservative coalition continued to dominate Capitol Hill. The fate of two presidential appointments in early 1945 revealed the persisting strength of the anti-administration coalition. On 1 March 1945 the Senate confirmed former vice president Henry A. Wallace as secretary of Commerce, but only after Congress had drained most of the power from that office. Three weeks later, the Senate rejected Aubrey Williams, Roosevelt's choice to head the Rural Electrification Administration. The president faced the same degree of opposition in the new Congress as in the earlier war years.

After Roosevelt's death on 12 April 1945, President Truman was preoccupied with pressing military and diplomatic concerns and devoted little attention to the home front. When Japan surrendered on 14 August 1945, he had no clear policy on demobilization. Republicans and anti-administration Democrats insisted on an immediate end to government controls, while administration officials favored gradual reconversion. Squabbling over demobilization policy soon clogged the channels of the legislative branch and reinforced the stalemate that Truman had inherited. The politics of the postwar era had arrived.

[See also Alien Registration Act; GI Bill of Rights; Isolationism; Lend-Lease Act; Marshall Plan; Neutrality Debates; Pearl Harbor Investigation; Truman Committee; Wagner-Connery National Labor Relations Act.]

BIBLIOGRAPHY

Chapman, Richard N. *Contours of Public Policy, 1939–1945.* 1981.

Dallek, Robert. *Franklin D. Roosevelt and American Foreign Policy, 1932–1945.* 1979.

Daniels, Roger, Sandra C. Taylor, and Harry H. L. Kitano. *Japanese Americans: From Relocation to Redress.* 1991.

Polenberg, Richard. *War and Society: The United States, 1941–1945.* 1972.

Young, Roland. *Congressional Politics in the Second World War.* 1956.

Richard N. Chapman

WRIGHT, JAMES C., JR. (1922–), representative from Texas, House majority leader (1977–1986), Speaker of the House (1987–1989), and first Speaker to be forced from office. When Texas Democrat Jim Wright succeeded Thomas P.

(Tip) O'Neill, Jr., as Speaker of the House on 6 January 1987, he intended to transform the speakership into an office only a notch below the presidency in power. As a result, his term as Speaker was marked by increasingly bitter confrontations with congressional Republicans and President Ronald Reagan. Playing out an almost archetypal drama of hubris and nemesis, Wright won almost every battle but destroyed himself in the process.

To transform the speakership, Wright moved on three paths—domestic policy, foreign policy, and parliamentary procedure. Power lay in the control of procedure, and he exploited procedure mercilessly. Wright worked closely with Senate majority leader Robert C. Byrd (D-W.Va.), who, like himself, represented the last of the political generation molded by the Depression and the New Deal. Together they pressed Democrats to pass bill after bill addressing civil rights, the infrastructure, the homeless, foreign trade, and fiscal policy. Routinely, they overrode Reagan's vetoes. Commentators such as the *Washington Post*'s David Broder called the 100th Congress (1987–1989) "significant" and "the most productive since 1965."

A year before Wright became the Speaker, a Harris poll stated that Republicans inspired more overall confidence than Democrats by 52 percent to 38 percent. After the bulk of Wright's legislative program had passed, Democrats led by 52 percent to 36 percent. After the 1988 election, the Harris organization concluded that, based on surprising voter-approval ratings of Congress and Wright, the "country might be entering a Congress-led era."

But Wright's very successes were leading to disaster, and his destruction was already under way. It had begun in July 1987, when the White House asked him to join Reagan in a bipartisan peace initiative in Nicaragua, where Reagan-backed Contras were waging a civil war against a Marxist government. Wright agreed. The plan sparked a peace agreement signed by five Central American presidents, but the White House, fearing the agreement would leave the Marxists in power, withdrew its support. Wright intervened forcefully to move the peace process forward, and in November 1987, against the wishes of the administration, met with Nicaragua's president, Daniel Ortega. Outraged conservatives accused Wright of violating the Constitution, which, they argued, reserved the conduct of foreign policy to the executive branch. (The peace agreement Wright helped implement did ultimately lead to free elections which ousted the Marxists.)

Meanwhile, Wright was ruthlessly manipulating House rules to advance his legislative agenda. In October 1987, when he used parliamentary procedure to turn a crushing defeat on a major tax bill into a one-vote victory, he generated intense personal animosity among House Republicans. Rep. Richard B. Cheney (R-Wyo.) called the vote "the most arrogant, heavy-handed abuse of power I've ever seen. . . ." By driving hard, Wright had made enemies within his own party as well, for example, when he threatened to strip Rep. Dan Rostenkowski (D-Ill.) of his Ways and Means Committee chairmanship if he continued to oppose him. The combination was explosive.

Rep. Newt Gingrich (R-Ga.), who would soon become the House Republican whip, observed, "As a technician of power Wright deserves an A-plus." But precisely because of Wright's use of power, Gingrich had already launched a media-based campaign to undermine him by impugning Wright's personal ethics. Gingrich added, "He's a loner. Being a loner eliminates a safety net of both information and goodwill."

After a year of sowing doubts about Wright's ethics through newspaper stories, Gingrich finally filed a formal complaint with the House Committee on Standards of Official Conduct (the ethics committee) on 26 May 1988. Seventy-one Republican colleagues, including all but one member of the party leadership, signed a letter of support. Common Cause, the public interest group, joined the call for an investigation of Wright, and Democrats could no longer dismiss the complaint as simply partisan politics.

Nor could Democrats control the ethics committee; alone among House committees, it had equal numbers of Democrats and Republicans. Maneuvering on the panel quickly began, and Republicans pushed hard and successfully for the hiring of Chicago lawyer Richard Phelan—a Democrat—to run the investigation. His approach to the case was that of an ambitious prosecutor, and he used it to launch his own political career.

Just as the committee began deliberations, Wright came under attack over an unrelated matter. The public had erupted in outrage over House members' attempt to raise their pay by 42 percent, or $37,500 a year, without a vote. The House seethed and roiled after the public's condemnation and the failure to get the raise, with many members blaming Wright for the fiasco.

Republicans used Phelan's presentation and, ironically, procedural rules to destroy Wright, while Democrats on the committee did nothing to support him. On 17 April 1989, the committee released "a statement of alleged violations" charging that Wright may have violated House gift and income rules in sixty-nine instances.

Most of the allegations related to his wife's job with a wealthy friend of Wright. The committee alleged that she had done no real work and that therefore her seven years' worth of salary and benefits, totaling $145,000, constituted an illegal gift. Transcripts of the executive sessions of the committee indicate little or no evidence to support any charges. But if Wright had not violated any House ethics rules, he clearly had exploited loopholes in them. His most grievous offense was authoring a book, *Reflections of a Public Man* (1984), which paid him 50-percent royalties, and selling it to lobbyists in bulk, often in lots of one thousand copies.

Wright pushed for the trial-like proceeding called for in ethics committee rules so that he could defend himself, but the committee refused to schedule it. Instead its members told reporters that they might expand their investigation into new areas, which would take months. Wright's support within the House disintegrated. On 31 May 1989, under intense media pressure, Wright dramatically announced to the House and a national television audience his decision "to give back this job you gave me as a propitiation for all the season of bad will that has grown up among us."

His relinquishing of the office marked the first forced abdication of a Speaker. On 30 June, Wright completed his severance from Congress by resigning as representative of Texas's 12th Congressional District, a seat he had held since 1955. The investigation was dropped. In reality, Wright was destroyed not by unethical behavior but by the enemies he had created through his precedent-setting involvement in foreign policy and his blunt, autocratic use of power.

BIBLIOGRAPHY

Barry, John M. *The Ambition and the Power: A True Story of Washington.* 1989.

Felton, John. "After Contra Battle, a New Set of Policy Issues." *Congressional Quarterly Weekly Report* 46, no. 14 (2 April 1988): 835–841.

Hook, Janet. "Passion, Defiance, Tears: Jim Wright Bows Out." *Congressional Quarterly Weekly Report* 47, no. 22 (3 June 1989): 1289–1295.

JOHN M. BARRY

WYOMING. Originally part of the Louisiana Purchase, the Wyoming Territory was carved out of the Dakota Territory (at the insistence of the Dakotans) and established by the Organic Act of 25 July 1868. Before 1867, Indian tribes inhabited much of the area. The few white settlements included Fort Laramie (established as a fur-trading post in 1834), where army units were stationed to protect settlers traveling along the trails to California and Oregon.

Construction of the nation's first transcontinental railroad brought the first significant population. The Union Pacific Railroad gained generous land grants from Congress, and as a result of these holdings the company shared political power with the Wyoming Stockgrowers Association throughout the territorial period and into the twentieth century.

Wyoming gained national attention as the first government to give women the franchise. Passage of the suffrage act in the first session of the territorial legislature in 1869 gave Wyoming the nickname the Equality State. In 1889, the act became part of the state's constitution and, despite considerable congressional opposition to such an article, the state was admitted to the Union on 10 July 1890 with full voting rights for women.

Congress established the first national park in the United States, Yellowstone, in northwest Wyoming in 1872. With the combination of national parks, national forests, and grazing lands administered by the Bureau of Land Management, the federal government today owns nearly 50 percent of Wyoming's land. Environmental issues have included disputes over the expansion of Grand Teton National Park and the illegal fencing of federal lands. Water issues have always been important in the arid state.

Wyoming has been reliably Republican in congressional elections since 1976, but throughout most of the state's history, party has been less a determinant of political success than has personality. Wyoming is the smallest state in terms of population, and voters tend to know their elected officials personally.

From Wyoming's admission until 1976, the state's Senate seats were split almost consistently between the two parties. The long tenure of Republican Francis E. Warren (thirty-seven years) was more than offset by a continuous string of Democratic senators—from Texas-born John B. Kendrick (seventeen years) to New Dealer Joseph C. O'Mahoney (twenty-six years) and former history professor Gale W. McGee (eighteen years). Warren served as chairman of the Military Affairs Committee and of the Appropriations Committee from 1921 until his death eight years later.

Wyoming has never had more than one representative. The hardship of having to pursue state-wide reelection every two years has led most of Wyoming's representatives eventually to seek Senate seats, but these bids have usually failed. The longest tenure of any Wyoming representative belonged to Frank W. Mondell, whose thirteen-term stay in Congress ended when he ran unsuccessfully against incumbent senator Kendrick in 1922. The best known Wyoming congressman in recent years was Richard B. Cheney (House, 1979–1989).

BIBLIOGRAPHY

Cawley, Gregg, et al. *The Equality State: Government and Politics.* 1991.

Gould, Lewis L. *Wyoming: A Political History, 1868–1896.* 1968.

Larson, T. A. *History of Wyoming.* 1978.

Miller, Tim R. *State Government and Politics in Wyoming.* 1985.

Trenholm, Virginia Cole, ed. *Wyoming Blue Book.* 1974.

PHIL ROBERTS

X, Y

X Y Z AFFAIR. The X Y Z Affair of 1797 and 1798, like the controversy over Jay's Treaty in 1795, had its origins in the war between Great Britain and France. That ongoing conflict raised serious dangers for the new United States, and the issues that it generated served as a major battleground for the emerging Federalist-Republican party system of the nation's first decade.

Federalists John Marshall and Charles Pinckney, along with the pro-Jeffersonian Elbridge Gerry, were sent by President John Adams to negotiate with the French government over that nation's seizures of American shipping. Foreign Minister Charles Maurice de Talleyrand refused to deal officially with the Americans. Instead, four unofficial representatives, whom Adams identified to Congress only as W, X, Y, and Z, demanded a loan to France and about $250,000 in bribes for French officials.

Adams reported these affronts to American honor in March 1798 messages to Congress. There was an explosion of public indignation, and a frenzy of political maneuvering between the Federalists, who were anxious to capitalize on anti-French feeling, and the Jeffersonian Republicans, who were more sympathetic to the French Revolution and tried to minimize the significance of the incident. Jefferson sought to thwart any congressional response by urging his House and Senate supporters to press for an early adjournment; Adams, initially ready to ask for war with France, contented himself with a call for increased naval and military expenditures.

The X Y Z Affair contributed to the fevered nationalism that led the Federalists in the Fifth Congress to pass the Alien and Sedition Acts later in the year, but most of all, it fed the growing party division that was an increasingly conspicuous feature of American politics.

BIBLIOGRAPHY

DeConde, Alexander. *The Quasi-War: The Politics and Diplomacy of the Undeclared War with France, 1797–1801.* 1966.

Sharp, James Roger. *American Politics in the Early Republic.* 1993.

MORTON KELLER

YOUNGSTOWN SHEET AND TUBE CO. V. SAWYER (343 U.S. 579 [1952]).

At the height of the Korean War, steel workers went on strike, posing, in the view of President Truman, a grave threat to the war effort. Refusing to use the strike provisions of the Taft-Hartley Act, which he had opposed, the president instead seized the steel mills in order to continue operations. A divided Supreme Court held that Truman had exceeded his authority.

Important as the result was, the doctrine of *Youngstown* is far more significant. But it is difficult to divine accurately just what the doctrine is. The opinion does disparage the principle of "inherent" presidential powers, but the context of the case reduces the import of that. The opinion of the Court purported to say that the decision to authorize a seizure was a legislative prerogative that the president was not empowered to exercise; however, the dissent and several concurrences reject what would be a major limitation on presidential powers. What emerges as the common rationale of a majority of justices is that Congress, in considering

Taft-Hartley, had debated and rejected a seizure alternative and had provided an avenue of settlement that remained open. The president could not, therefore, use a method of settlement that Congress in effect had expressly denied him, but he must have recourse to the statutory mechanism Congress did confer.

In the years since, *Youngstown* has been much celebrated but seldom used by the courts. Many have cited the discussions in the individual opinions of the justices. Doctrinally, however, the case has spawned no progeny.

BIBLIOGRAPHY

Corwin, Edward S. "The Steel Seizure Case: A Judicial Brick without Straw." *Columbia Law Review* 53 (1953): 53.

Roche, John P. "Executive Power and Domestic Emergency: The Quest for Prerogative." *Western Political Quarterly* 5 (1952): 592.

JOHNNY H. KILLIAN

The Constitution of the United States

Spelling, capitalization, and punctuation conform to the text of the engrossed copy.

WE THE PEOPLE of the United States, in Order to form a more perfect Union, establish Justice, insure domestic Tranquility, provide for the common defence, promote the general Welfare, and secure the Blessings of Liberty to ourselves and our Posterity, do ordain and establish this Constitution of the United States of America.

ARTICLE. I.

SECTION. 1. All legislative Powers herein granted shall be vested in a Congress of the United States, which shall consist of a Senate and House of Representatives.

SECTION. 2. The House of Representatives shall be composed of Members chosen every second Year by the People of the several States, and the Electors in each State shall have the Qualifications requisite for Electors of the most numerous Branch of the State Legislature.

No Person shall be a Representative who shall not have attained to the Age of twenty five Years, and been seven Years a Citizen of the United States, and who shall not, when elected, be an Inhabitant of that State in which he shall be chosen.

Representatives and direct Taxes shall be apportioned among the several States which may be included within this Union, according to their respective Numbers, which shall be determined by adding to the whole Number of free Persons, including those bound to Service for a Term of Years, and excluding Indians not taxed, three fifths of all other Persons. The actual Enumeration shall be made within three Years after the first Meeting of the Congress of the United States, and within every subsequent Term of ten Years, in such Manner as they shall by Law direct. The Number of Representatives shall not exceed one for every thirty Thousand, but each State shall have at Least one Representative; and until such enumeration shall be made, the State of New Hampshire shall be entitled to chuse three, Massachusetts eight, Rhode-Island and Providence Plantations one, Connecticut five, New-York six, New Jersey four, Pennsylvania eight, Delaware one, Maryland six, Virginia ten, North Carolina five, South Carolina five, and Georgia three.

When vacancies happen in the Representation from any State, the Executive Authority thereof shall issue Writs of Election to fill such Vacancies.

The House of Representatives shall chuse their Speaker and other Officers; and shall have the sole Power of Impeachment.

SECTION. 3. The Senate of the United States shall be composed of two Senators from each State, chosen by the Legislature thereof, for six Years; and each Senator shall have one Vote.

Immediately after they shall be assembled in Consequence of the first Election, they shall be divided as equally as may be into three Classes. The Seats of the Senators of the first Class shall be vacated at the Expiration of the second Year, of the second Class at the Expiration of the fourth Year, and of the third Class at the Expiration of the sixth Year, so that one third may be chosen every second Year; and if Vacancies happen by Resignation, or otherwise, during the Recess of the Legislature of any State, the Executive thereof may make temporary Appointments until the next Meeting of the Legislature, which shall then fill such Vacancies.

No Person shall be a Senator who shall not have attained to the Age of thirty Years, and been nine Years a Citizen of the United States, and who shall not, when elected, be an Inhabitant of that State for which he shall be chosen.

The Vice President of the United States shall be President of the Senate, but shall have no Vote, unless they be equally divided.

The Senate shall chuse their other Officers, and also a President pro tempore, in the Absence of the Vice President, or when he shall exercise the Office of President of the United States.

The Senate shall have the sole Power to try all Impeachments. When sitting for that Purpose, they shall be on Oath or Affirmation. When the President of the United States is tried, the Chief Justice shall preside: And no Person shall be convicted without the Concurrence of two thirds of the Members present.

Judgment in Cases of Impeachment shall not extend further than to removal from Office, and disqualification to hold and enjoy any Office of honor, Trust or Profit under the United States: but the Party convicted shall nevertheless be liable and subject to Indictment, Trial, Judgment and Punishment, according to Law.

SECTION. 4. The Times, Places and Manner of holding Elections for Senators and Representatives, shall be prescribed in each State by the Legislature thereof; but the Congress may at any time by Law make or alter such Regulations, except as to the Places of chusing Senators.

The Congress shall assemble at least once in every Year, and such Meeting shall be on the first Monday in December, unless they shall by Law appoint a different Day.

SECTION. 5. Each House shall be the Judge of the Elections, Returns and Qualifications of its own Members, and a Majority of each shall constitute a Quorum to do Business; but a smaller Number may adjourn from day to day, and may be authorized to compel the Attendance of absent Members, in such Manner, and under such Penalties as each House may provide.

Each House may determine the Rules of its Proceedings, punish its Members for disorderly Behaviour, and, with the Concurrence of two thirds, expel a Member.

Each House shall keep a Journal of its Proceedings, and from time to time publish the same, excepting such Parts as may in their Judgment require Secrecy; and the Yeas and Nays of the Members of either House on any question shall, at the Desire of one fifth of those Present, be entered on the Journal.

Neither House, during the Session of Congress, shall, without the Consent of the other, adjourn for more than three days, nor to any other Place than that in which the two Houses shall be sitting.

SECTION. 6. The Senators and Representatives shall receive a Compensation for their Services, to be ascertained by Law, and paid out of the Treasury of the United States. They shall in all Cases, except Treason, Felony and Breach of the Peace, be privileged from Arrest during their Attendance at the Session of their respective Houses, and in going to and returning from the same; and for any Speech or Debate in either House, they shall not be questioned in any other Place.

No Senator or Representative shall, during the Time for which he was elected, be appointed to any civil Office under the Authority of the United States, which shall have been created, or the Emoluments whereof shall have been encreased during such time; and no Person holding any Office under the United States, shall be a Member of either House during his Continuance in Office.

SECTION. 7. All Bills for raising Revenue shall originate in the House of Representatives; but the Senate may propose or concur with Amendments as on other Bills.

Every Bill which shall have passed the House of Representatives and the Senate, shall, before it become a Law, be presented to the President of the United States; If he approve he shall sign it, but if not he shall return it, with his Objections to that House in which it shall have originated, who shall enter the Objections at large on their Journal, and proceed to reconsider it. If after such Reconsideration two thirds of that House shall agree to pass the Bill, it shall be sent, together with the Objections, to the other House, by which it shall likewise be reconsidered, and if approved by two thirds of that House, it shall become a Law. But in all such Cases the Votes of both Houses shall be determined by yeas and Nays, and the Names of the Persons voting for and against the Bill shall be entered on the Journal of each House respectively. If any Bill shall not be returned by the President within ten Days (Sundays excepted) after it shall have been presented to him, the Same shall be a Law, in like Manner as if he had signed it, unless the Congress by their Adjournment prevent its Return, in which Case it shall not be a Law.

Every Order, Resolution, or Vote to which the Concurrence of the Senate and House of Representatives may be necessary (except on a question of Adjournment) shall be presented to the President of the United States; and before the Same shall take Effect, shall be approved by him, or being disapproved by him, shall be repassed by two thirds of the Senate and House of Representatives, according to the Rules and Limitations prescribed in the Case of a Bill.

SECTION. 8. The Congress shall have Power To lay and collect Taxes, Duties, Imposts and Excises, to pay the Debts and provide for the common Defence and general Welfare of the United States; but all Duties, Imposts and Excises shall be uniform throughout the United States;

To borrow Money on the credit of the United States;

To regulate Commerce with foreign Nations, and among the several States, and with the Indian tribes;

To establish an uniform Rule of Naturalization, and uniform Laws on the subject of Bankruptcies throughout the United States;

To coin Money, regulate the Value thereof, and of foreign Coin, and fix the Standard of Weights and Measures;

To provide for the Punishment of counterfeiting the Securities and current Coin of the United States;

To establish Post Offices and post Roads;

To promote the Progress of Science and useful Arts, by securing for limited Times to Authors and Inventors the exclusive Right to their respective Writings and Discoveries;

To constitute Tribunals inferior to the supreme Court;

To define and punish Piracies and Felonies committed on the high Seas, and Offences against the Law of Nations;

To declare War, grant Letters of Marque and Reprisal, and make Rules concerning Captures on Land and Water;

To raise and support Armies, but no Appropriation of Money to that Use shall be for a longer Term than two Years;

To provide and maintain a Navy;

To make Rules for the Government and Regulation of the land and naval Forces;

To provide for calling forth the Militia to execute the Laws of the Union, suppress Insurrections and repel Invasions;

To provide for organizing, arming, and disciplining, the Militia, and for governing such Part of them as may be employed in the Service of the United States, reserving to the States respectively, the Appointment of the Officers, and the Authority of training the Militia according to the discipline prescribed by Congress;

To exercise exclusive Legislation in all Cases whatsoever, over such District (not exceeding ten Miles square) as may, by Cession of particular States, and the Acceptance of Congress, become the Seat of the Government of the United States, and to exercise like Authority over all Places purchased by the Consent of the Legislature of the State in which the Same shall be, for the Erection of Forts, Magazines, Arsenals, dock-Yards, and other needful Buildings;—And

To make all Laws which shall be necessary and proper for carrying into Execution the foregoing Powers, and all other Powers vested by this Constitution in the Government of the United States, or in any Department or Officer thereof.

SECTION. 9. The Migration or Importation of such Persons as any of the States now existing shall think proper to admit, shall not be prohibited by the Congress prior to the Year one thousand eight hundred and eight, but a Tax or duty may be imposed on such Importation, not exceeding ten dollars for each Person.

The Privilege of the Writ of Habeas Corpus shall not be suspended, unless when in Cases of Rebellion or Invasion the public Safety may require it.

No Bill of Attainder or ex post facto Law shall be passed.

No Capitation, or other direct, Tax shall be laid, unless in Proportion to the Census or Enumeration herein before directed to be taken.

No Tax or Duty shall be laid on Articles exported from any State.

No Preference shall be given by any Regulation of Commerce or Revenue to the Ports of one State over those of another: nor shall Vessels bound to, or from, one State, be obliged to enter, clear, or pay Duties in another.

No Money shall be drawn from the Treasury, but in Consequence of Appropriations made by Law; and a regular Statement and Account of the Receipts and Expenditures of all public Money shall be published from time to time.

No Title of Nobility shall be granted by the United States: And no Person holding any Office of Profit or Trust under them, shall, without the Consent of the Congress, accept of any present, Emolument, Office, or Title, of any kind whatever, from any King, Prince, or foreign State.

SECTION. 10. No State shall enter into any Treaty, Alliance, or Confederation; grant Letters of Marque and Reprisal; coin Money; emit Bills of Credit; make any Thing but gold and silver Coin a Tender in Payment of Debts; pass any Bill of Attainder, ex post facto Law, or Law impairing the Obligation of Contracts, or grant any Title of Nobility.

No State shall, without the Consent of the Congress, lay any Imposts or Duties on Imports or Exports, except what may be absolutely necessary for executing it's inspection Laws: and the net Produce of all Duties and Imposts, laid by any State on Imports or Exports, shall be for the Use of the Treasury of the United States; and all such Laws shall be subject to the Revision and Controul of the Congress.

No State shall, without the consent of Congress, lay any Duty of Tonnage, keep Troops, or Ships of War in time of Peace, enter into any Agreement or Compact with another State, or with a foreign Power, or engage in War, unless actually invaded, or in such imminent Danger as will not admit of delay.

ARTICLE. II.

Section. 1. The executive Power shall be vested in a President of the United States of America. He shall hold his Office during the Term of four Years, and, together with the Vice President, chosen for the same Term, be elected, as follows

Each State shall appoint, in such Manner as the Legislature thereof may direct, a Number of Electors, equal to the whole Number of Senators and Representatives to which the State may be entitled in the Congress; but no Senator or Representative, or Person holding an Office of Trust or Profit under the United States, shall be appointed an Elector.

The Electors shall meet in their respective States, and vote by Ballot for two Persons, of whom one at least shall not be an inhabitant of the same State with themselves. And they shall make a List of all the Persons voted for, and of the Number of Votes for each; which List they shall sign and certify, and transmit sealed to the Seat of the Government of the United States, directed to the President of the Senate. The President of the Senate shall, in the Presence of the Senate and House of Representatives, open all the Certificates, and the Votes shall then be counted. The Person having the greatest Number of Votes shall be the President, if such Number be a Majority of the whole Number of Electors appointed; and if there be more than one who have such Majority, and have an equal Number of Votes, then the House of Representatives shall immediately chuse by Ballot one of them for President; and if no Person have a Majority, then from the five highest on the List the said House shall in like Manner chuse the President. But in chusing the President, the Votes shall be taken by States, the Representation from each State having one Vote; A quorum for this purpose shall consist of a Member or Members from two thirds of the States, and a Majority of all the States shall be necessary to a Choice. In every Case, after the Choice of the President, the Person having the greatest Number of Votes of the Electors shall be the Vice President. But if there should remain two or more who have equal Votes, the Senate shall chuse from them by Ballot the Vice President.

The Congress may determine the Time of chusing the Electors, and the Day on which they shall give their Votes; which Day shall be the same throughout the United States.

No Person except a natural born Citizen, or a Citizen of the United States, at the time of the Adoption of this Constitution, shall be eligible to the Office of President; neither shall any Person be eligible to that Office who shall not have attained to the Age of thirty five Years, and been fourteen Years a Resident within the United States.

In Case of the Removal of the President from Office, or of his Death, Resignation, or Inability to discharge the Powers and Duties of the said Office, the Same shall devolve on the Vice President, and the Congress may by Law provide for the Case of Removal, Death, Resignation or Inability, both of the President and the Vice President, declaring what Officer shall then act as President, and such Officer shall act accordingly, until the Disability be removed, or a President shall be elected.

The President shall, at stated Times, receive for his Services, a Compensation, which shall neither be increased nor diminished during the Period for which he shall have been elected, and he shall not receive within that Period any other Emolument from the United States, or any of them.

Before he enter on the Execution of his Office, he shall take the following Oath of Affirmation:—"I do solemnly swear (or affirm) that I will faithfully execute the Office of President of the United States, and will to the best of my Ability, preserve, protect and defend the Constitution of the United States."

SECTION. 2. The President shall be Commander in Chief of the Army and Navy of the United States, and of the Militia of the several States, when called into the actual Service of the United States; he may require the Opinion, in writing, of the principal Officer in each of the executive Departments, upon any Subject relating to the Duties of their respective Offices, and he shall have Power to grant Reprieves and Pardons for Offences against the United States, except in Cases of Impeachment.

He shall have Power, by and with the Advice and Consent of the Senate, to make Treaties, provided two thirds of the Senators present concur; and he shall nominate, and by and with the Advice and Consent of the Senate, shall appoint Ambassadors, other public Ministers and Consuls, Judges of the supreme Court, and all other Officers of the United States, whose Appointments are not herein otherwise provided for, and which shall be established by Law: but the Congress may by Law vest the Appointment of such inferior Officers, as they think proper, in the President alone, in the Courts of Law, or in the Heads of Departments.

The President shall have Power to fill up all Vacancies that may happen during the Recess of the Senate, by granting Commissions which shall expire at the End of their next Session.

SECTION. 3. He shall from time to time give to the Congress Information of the State of the Union, and recommend to their Consideration such Measures as he shall judge necessary and expedient; he may, on extraordinary Occasions, convene both Houses, or either of them, and in Case of Disagreement between them, with Respect to the Time of Adjournment, he may adjourn them to such Time as he shall think proper; he shall receive Ambassadors and other public Ministers; he shall take Care that the Laws be faithfully executed, and shall Commission all the Officers of the United States.

SECTION. 4. The President, Vice President and all civil Officers of the United States, shall be removed from Office on Impeachment for, and Conviction of, Treason, Bribery, or other high Crimes and Misdemeanors.

ARTICLE. III.

SECTION. 1. The judicial Power of the United States, shall be vested in one supreme Court, and in such inferior Courts as the Congress may from time to time ordain and establish. The Judges, both of the supreme and inferior Courts, shall hold their Offices during good Behaviour, and shall, at stated Times, receive for their Services, a Compensation, which shall not be diminished during their Continuance in Office.

SECTION. 2. The judicial Power shall extend to all Cases, in Law and Equity, arising under this Constitution, the Laws of the United States, and Treaties made, or which shall be made, under their Authority;—to all cases affecting Ambassadors, other public Ministers and Consuls;—to all Cases of admiralty and maritime Jurisdiction;—to Controversies to which the United States shall be a Party;—to Controversies between two or more States;—between a State and Citizens of another State;—between Citizens of different States;—between Citizens of the same State claiming Lands under Grants of different States, and between a State, or the Citizens thereof, and foreign States, Citizens or Subjects.

In all Cases affecting Ambassadors, other public Ministers and Consuls, and those in which a State shall be Party, the supreme Court shall have original Jurisdiction. In all the other Cases before mentioned, the supreme Court shall have appellate Jurisdiction, both as to Law and Fact, with such Exceptions, and under such Regulations as the Congress shall make.

The Trial of all Crimes, except in Cases of Impeachment, shall be by Jury; and such Trial shall be held in the State where the said Crimes shall have been committed; but when not committed within any State, the Trial shall be at such Place or Places as the Congress may by Law have directed.

SECTION. 3. Treason against the United States, shall consist only in levying War against them, or in adhering to their Enemies, giving them Aid and Comfort. No Person shall be convicted of Treason unless on the Testimony of two Witnesses to the same overt Act, or on Confession in open Court.

The Congress shall have Power to declare the Punishment of Treason, but no Attainder of Treason shall work Corruption of Blood, or Forfeiture except during the Life of the Person attainted.

ARTICLE. IV.

SECTION. 1. Full Faith and Credit shall be given in each State to the public Acts, Records, and judicial Proceedings of every other State. And the Congress may by general Laws prescribe the Manner in which such Acts, Records and Proceedings shall be proved, and the Effect thereof.

SECTION. 2. The Citizens of each State shall be entitled to all Privileges and Immunities of Citizens in the several States.

A Person charged in any State with Treason, Felony, or other Crime, who shall flee from Justice, and be found in another State, shall on Demand of the executive Authority of the State from which he fled, be delivered up, to be removed to the State having Jurisdiction of the Crime.

No Person held to Service or Labour in one State, under the Laws thereof, escaping into another, shall, in Consequence of any Law or Regulation therein, be discharged from such Service or Labour, but shall be delivered up on Claim of the Party to whom such Service or Labour may be due.

SECTION. 3. New States may be admitted by the Congress into this Union; but no new State shall be formed or erected within the Jurisdiction of any other State; nor any State be formed by the Junction of two or more States, or Parts of States, without the Consent of the Legislatures of the States concerned as well as of the Congress.

The Congress shall have Power to dispose of and make all needful Rules and Regulations respecting the Territory or other Property belonging to the United States; and nothing in this Constitution shall be so construed as to Prejudice any Claims of the United States, or of any particular State.

SECTION. 4. The United States shall guarantee to every State in this Union a Republican Form of Government, and shall protect each of them against Invasion; and on Application of the Legislature, or of the Executive (when the Legislature cannot be convened) against domestic Violence.

ARTICLE. V.

The Congress, whenever two thirds of both Houses shall deem it necessary, shall propose Amendments to this Constitution, or, on the Application of the Legislatures of two thirds of the several States, shall call a Convention for proposing Amendments, which, in either Case, shall be valid to all Intents and Purposes, as Part of this Constitution, when ratified by the legislatures of three fourths of the several States, or by Conventions in three fourths thereof, as the one or the other Mode of Ratification may be proposed by the Congress; Provided that no Amendment which may be made prior to the Year One thousand eight hundred and eight shall in any Manner affect the first and fourth Clauses in the Ninth Section of the first Article; and that no State, without its Consent, shall be deprived of it's equal Suffrage in the Senate.

ARTICLE. VI.

All Debts contracted and Engagements entered into, before the Adoption of this Constitution, shall be as valid against the United States under this Constitution, as under the Confederation.

This Constitution, and the Laws of the United States which shall be made in Pursuance thereof; and all Treaties made, or which shall be made, under the Authority of the United States, shall be the supreme Law of the Land; and the Judges in every State shall be bound thereby, any Thing in the Constitution or Laws of any State to the Contrary notwithstanding.

The Senators and Representatives before mentioned, and the Members of the several State Legislatures, and all executive and judicial Officers, both of the United States and of the several States, shall be bound by Oath or Affirmation, to support this Constitution; but no religious Test shall ever be required as a Qualification to any Office or public Trust under the United States.

ARTICLE. VII.

The Ratification of the Conventions of nine States, shall be sufficient for the Establishment of this Constitution between the States so ratifying the Same.

The Word "the", being interlined between the seventh and eighth Lines of the first Page, the Word "Thirty" being partly written on an Erazure in the fiftienth Line of the first Page, The Words "is tried" being interlined between the thirty second and thirty third Lines of the first Page and the Word "the" being interlined between the forty third and forty fourth Lines of the second Page.

Attest William Jackson Secretary

Done in Convention by the Unanimous Consent of the States present the Seventeenth Day of September in the Year of our Lord one thousand seven hundred and Eighty seven and of the Independance of the United States of America the Twelfth. In Witness whereof We have hereunto subscribed our Names.

G° WASHINGTON
Presid^t and deputy from Virginia

DELAWARE	GEO: READ GUNNING BEDFORD jun JOHN DICKINSON RICHARD BASSETT JACO: BROOM	NEW HAMPSHIRE	JOHN LANGDON NICHOLAS GILMAN
MARYLAND	JAMES MCHENRY DAN OF ST. THOS. JENIFER DANL. CARROLL	MASSACHUSETTS	NATHANIEL GORHAM RUFUS KING
VIRGINIA	JOHN BLAIR— JAMES MADISON JR.	CONNECTICUT	WM. SAML. JOHNSON ROGER SHERMAN
		NEW YORK	ALEXANDER HAMILTON
NORTH CAROLINA	WM. BLOUNT RICHD. DOBBS SPAIGHT HU WILLIAMSON	NEW JERSEY	WIL: LIVINGSTON DAVID BREARLEY WM. PATERSON JONA: DAYTON
SOUTH CAROLINA	J. RUTLEDGE CHARLES COTESWORTH PINCKNEY CHARLES PINCKNEY PIERCE BUTLER	PENNSYLVANIA	B. FRANKLIN THOMAS MIFFLIN ROBT. MORRIS GEO. CLYMER THOS. FITZSIMONS JARED INGERSOLL JAMES WILSON GOUV MORRIS
GEORGIA	WILLIAM FEW ABR BALDWIN		

AMENDMENT I [1791]

Congress shall make no law respecting an establishment of religion, or prohibiting the free exercise thereof; or abridging the freedom of speech, or of the press; or the right of the people peaceably to assemble, and to petition the Government for a redress of grievances.

AMENDMENT II [1791]

A well regulated Militia, being necessary to the security of a free State, the right of the people to keep and bear Arms, shall not be infringed.

AMENDMENT III [1791]

No Soldier shall, in time of peace be quartered in any house, without the consent of the Owner, nor in time of war, but in a manner to be prescribed by law.

AMENDMENT IV [1791]

The right of the people to be secure in their persons, houses, papers, and effects, against unreasonable searches and seizures, shall not be violated, and no Warrants shall issue, but upon probable cause, supported by Oath or affirmation, and particularly describing the place to be searched, and the persons or things to be seized.

AMENDMENT V [1791]

No person shall be held to answer for a capital, or otherwise infamous crime, unless on a presentment or indictment of a Grand Jury, except in cases arising in the land or naval forces, or in the Militia, when in actual service in time of War or public danger; nor shall any person be subject for the same offence to be twice put in jeopardy of life or limb; nor shall be compelled in any criminal case to be a witness against himself, nor be deprived of life, liberty or property, without due process of law; nor shall private property be taken for public use, without just compensation.

AMENDMENT VI [1791]

In all criminal prosecutions, the accused shall enjoy the right to a speedy and public trial, by an impartial jury of the State and district wherein the crime shall have been committed, which district shall have been previously ascertained by law, and to be informed of the nature and cause of the accusation; to be confronted with the witnesses against him; to have compulsory process for obtaining Witnesses in his favor, and to have the assistance of counsel for his defence.

AMENDMENT VII [1791]

In Suits at Common law, where the value in controversy shall exceed twenty dollars, the right of trial by jury shall be preserved, and no fact tried by a jury, shall be otherwise re-examined in any Court of the United States, than according to the rules of the common law.

AMENDMENT VIII [1791]

Excessive bail shall not be required, nor excessive fines imposed, nor cruel and unusual punishments inflicted.

AMENDMENT IX [1791]

The enumeration in the Constitution, of certain rights, shall not be construed to deny or disparage others retained by the people.

AMENDMENT X [1791]

The powers not delegated to the United States by the Constitution, nor prohibited by it to the States, are reserved to the States respectively, or to the people.

AMENDMENT XI [1798]

The Judicial power of the United States shall not be construed to extend to any suit in law or equity, commenced or prosecuted against one of the United States by Citizens of another State, or by Citizens or Subjects of any Foreign State.

AMENDMENT XII [1804]

The Electors shall meet in their respective states, and vote by ballot for President and Vice-President, one of whom, at least, shall not be an inhabitant of the same state with themselves; they shall name in their ballots the person voted for as President, and in distinct ballots the person voted for as Vice-President, and they shall make distinct lists of all persons voted for as President, and of all persons voted for as Vice-President, and of the number of votes for each, which lists they shall sign and certify, and transmit sealed to the seat of the government of the United States, directed to the President of the Senate;—The President of the Senate shall, in the presence of the Senate and House of Representatives, open all the certificates and the votes shall then be counted;—The Person having the greatest number of votes for President, shall be the President, if such number be a majority of the whole number of Electors appointed; and if no person have such majority, then from the persons having the highest numbers not exceeding three on the list of those voted for as President, the House of Representatives shall choose immediately, by ballot, the President. But in choosing the President, the votes shall be taken by states, the representation from each state having one vote; a quorum for this purpose shall consist of a member or members from two-thirds of the states, and a majority of all the states shall be necessary to a choice. And if the House of Representatives shall not choose a President whenever the right of choice shall devolve upon them, before the fourth day of March next following, then the Vice-President shall act as President, as in the case of the death or other constitutional disability of the President.—The person having the greatest number of votes as Vice-President, shall be the Vice-President, if such number be a majority of the whole number of Electors appointed, and if no person have a majority, then from the two highest numbers on the list, the Senate shall choose the Vice-President; a quorum for the purpose shall consist of two-thirds of the whole number of Senators, and a majority of the whole number shall be necessary to a choice. But no person constitutionally ineligible to the office of President shall be eligible to that of Vice-President of the United States.

AMENDMENT XIII [1865]

SECTION 1. Neither slavery nor involuntary servitude, except as a punishment for crime whereof the party shall have been duly convicted, shall exist within the United States, or any place subject to their jurisdiction.

SECTION 2. Congress shall have power to enforce this article by appropriate legislation.

AMENDMENT XIV [1868]

SECTION 1. All persons born or naturalized in the United States, and subject to the jurisdiction thereof, are citizens of the United States and of the State wherein they reside. No State shall make or enforce any law which shall abridge the privileges or immunities of citizens of the United States; nor shall any State deprive any person of life, liberty, or property, without due process of law; nor deny to any person within its jurisdiction the equal protection of the laws.

SECTION 2. Representatives shall be apportioned among the several States according to their respective numbers, counting the whole number of persons in each State, excluding Indians not taxed. But when the right to vote at any election for the choice of electors for President and Vice President of the United States, Representatives in Congress, the Executive and Judicial officers of a State, or the members of the Legislature thereof, is denied to any of the male inhabitants of such State, being twenty-one years of age, and citizens of the United States, or in any way abridged, except for participation in rebellion, or other crime, the basis of representation therein shall be reduced in the proportion which the number of such male citizens shall bear to the whole number of male citizens twenty-one years of age in such State.

SECTION 3. No person shall be a Senator or Representative in Congress, or elector of President and Vice President, or hold any office, civil or military, under the United States, or under any State, who, having previously taken an oath, as a member of Congress, or as an officer of the United States, or as a member of any State legislature, or as an executive or judicial officer of any State, to support the Constitution of the United States, shall have engaged in insurrection or rebellion against the same, or given aid or comfort to the enemies thereof. But Congress may by a vote of two-thirds of each House, remove such disability.

SECTION 4. The validity of the public debt of the United States, authorized by law, including debts incurred for payment of pensions and bounties for services in suppressing insurrection or rebellion, shall not be questioned. But neither the United States nor any State shall assume or pay any debt or obligation incurred in aid of insurrection or rebellion against the United States, or any claim for the loss or emancipation of any slave; but all such debts, obligations and claims shall be held illegal and void.

SECTION 5. The Congress shall have power to enforce, by appropriate legislation, the provisions of this article.

AMENDMENT XV [1870]

SECTION 1. The right of citizens of the United States to vote shall not be denied or abridged by the United States or by any State on account of race, color, or previous condition of servitude.

SECTION 2. The Congress shall have power to enforce this article by appropriate legislation.

AMENDMENT XVI [1913]

The Congress shall have power to lay and collect taxes on incomes, from whatever source derived, without apportionment among the several States, and without regard to any census or enumeration.

AMENDMENT XVII [1913]

The Senate of the United States shall be composed of two Senators from each State, elected by the people thereof, for six years; and each Senator shall have one vote. The electors in each State shall have the qualifications requisite for electors of the most numerous branch of the State legislatures.

When vacancies happen in the representation of any State in the Senate, the executive authority of such State shall issue writs of election to fill such vacancies: *Provided,*

That the legislature of any State may empower the executive thereof to make temporary appointments until the people fill the vacancies by election as the legislature may direct.

This amendment shall not be so construed as to affect the election or term of any Senator chosen before it becomes valid as part of the Constitution.

AMENDMENT XVIII [1919]

SECTION 1. After one year from the ratification of this article the manufacture, sale, or transportation of intoxicating liquors within, the importation thereof into, or the exportation thereof from the United States and all territory subject to the jurisdiction thereof for beverage purposes is hereby prohibited.

SECTION 2. The Congress and the several States shall have concurrent power to enforce this article by appropriate legislation.

SECTION 3. This article shall be inoperative unless it shall have been ratified as an amendment to the Constitution by the legislatures of the several States, as provided in the Constitution, within seven years from the date of the submission hereof to the States by the Congress.

AMENDMENT XIX [1920]

The right of citizens of the United States to vote shall not be denied or abridged by the United States or by any State on account of sex.

Congress shall have power to enforce this article by appropriate legislation.

AMENDMENT XX [1933]

SECTION 1. The terms of the President and Vice President shall end at noon on the 20th day of January, and the terms of Senators and Representatives at noon on the 3d day of January, of the years in which such terms would have ended if this article had not been ratified; and the terms of their successors shall then begin.

SECTION 2. The Congress shall assemble at least once in every year, and such meeting shall begin at noon on the 3d day of January, unless they shall by law appoint a different day.

SECTION 3. If, at the time fixed for the beginning of the term of the President, the President elect shall have died, the Vice President elect shall become President. If a President shall not have been chosen before the time fixed for the beginning of his term, or if the President elect shall have failed to qualify, then the Vice President elect shall act as President until a President shall have qualified; and the Congress may by law provide for the case wherein neither a President elect nor a Vice President elect shall have qualified, declaring who shall then act as President, or the manner in which one who is to act shall be selected, and such person shall act accordingly until a President or Vice President shall have qualified.

SECTION 4. The Congress may by law provide for the case of the death of any of the persons from whom the House of Representatives may choose a President whenever the right of choice shall have devolved upon them, and for the case of the death of any of the persons from whom the Senate may choose a Vice President whenever the right of choice shall have devolved upon them.

SECTION 5. Sections 1 and 2 shall take effect on the 15th day of October following the ratification of this article.

SECTION 6. This article shall be inoperative unless it shall have been ratified as an amendment to the Constitution by the legislatures of three-fourths of the several States within seven years from the date of its submission.

AMENDMENT XXI [1933]

SECTION 1. The eighteenth article of amendment to the Constitution of the United States is hereby repealed.

SECTION 2. The transportation or importation into any State, Territory, or possession of the United States for delivery or use therein of intoxicating liquors, in violation of the laws thereof, is hereby prohibited.

SECTION 3. This article shall be inoperative unless it shall have been ratified as an amendment to the Constitution by conventions in the several States, as provided in the Constitution, within seven years from the date of the submission hereof to the States by the Congress.

AMENDMENT XXII [1951]

SECTION 1. No person shall be elected to the office of the President more than twice, and no person who has held the office of President, or acted as President, for more than two years of a term to which some other person was elected President shall be elected to the office of the president more than once. But this Article shall not apply to any person holding the office of President when this Article was proposed by the Congress, and shall not prevent any person who may be holding the office of President, or acting as President, during the term within which this Article becomes operative from holding the office of President or acting as president during the remainder of such term.

SECTION 2. This article shall be inoperative unless it shall have been ratified as an amendment to the Constitution by the legislatures of three-fourths of the several States within seven years from the date of its submission to the States by the Congress.

AMENDMENT XXIII [1961]

SECTION 1. The District constituting the seat of Government of the United States shall appoint in such manner as the Congress may direct:

A number of electors of President and Vice President equal to the whole number of Senators and Representatives in Congress to which the District would be entitled if it were a State, but in no event more than the least populous State; they shall be in addition to those appointed by the States, but they shall be considered, for the purposes of the election of President and Vice President, to be electors appointed by a State; and they shall meet in the District and perform such duties as provided by the twelfth article of amendment.

SECTION 2. The Congress shall have power to enforce this article by appropriate legislation.

AMENDMENT XXIV [1964]

SECTION 1. The right of citizens of the United States to vote in any primary or other election for President or Vice President, for electors for President or Vice President, or for Senator or Representatives in Congress, shall not be denied or abridged by the United States or any State by reason of failure to pay any poll tax or other tax.

SECTION 2. The Congress shall have power to enforce this article by appropriate legislation.

AMENDMENT XXV [1967]

SECTION 1. In case of the removal of the President from office or of his death or resignation, the Vice President shall become President.

SECTION 2. Whenever there is a vacancy in the office of the Vice President, the President shall nominate a Vice President who shall take office upon confirmation by a majority vote of both Houses of Congress.

SECTION 3. Whenever the President transmits to the President pro tempore of the Senate and the Speaker of the House of Representatives his written declaration that he is unable to discharge the powers and duties of his office, and until he transmits to them a written declaration to the contrary, such powers and duties shall be discharged by the Vice President as Acting President.

SECTION 4. Whenever the Vice President and a majority of either the principal officers of the executive departments or of such other body as Congress may by law provide, transmit to the President pro tempore of the Senate and the Speaker of the House of Representatives their written declaration that the President is unable to discharge the powers and duties of his office, the Vice President shall immediately assume the powers and duties of the office as Acting President.

Thereafter, when the President transmits to the President pro tempore of the Senate and the Speaker of the House of Representatives his written declaration that no inability exists, he shall resume the powers and duties of his office unless the Vice President and a majority of either the principal officers of the executive department or of such other body as Congress may by law provide, transmit within four days to the President pro tempore of the Senate and the Speaker of the House of Representatives their written declaration that the President is unable to discharge the powers and duties of his office. Thereupon Congress shall decide the issue, assembling within forty-eight hours for that purpose if not in session. If the Congress, within twenty-one days after receipt of the latter written declaration, or, if Congress is not in session, within twenty-one days after Congress is required to assemble, determines by two-thirds vote of both Houses that the President is unable to discharge the powers and duties of his office, the Vice President shall continue to discharge the same as Acting President; otherwise, the President shall resume the powers and duties of his office.

AMENDMENT XXVI [1971]

SECTION 1. The right of citizens of the United States, who are eighteen years of age or older, to vote shall not be denied or abridged by the United States or by any State on account of age.

SECTION 2. The Congress shall have power to enforce this article by appropriate legislation.

AMENDMENT XXVII [1992]

No law, varying the compensation for the services of the Senators and Representatives, shall take effect, until an election of Representatives shall have intervened.

Glossary

This glossary includes terms critical to an understanding of the legislative process. Many of these terms are explained when they occur in particular articles in the encyclopedia, but referring to the brief definitions here will enhance understanding of discussions throughout this work. Other terms not included in the glossary but similar in importance to those given below are the subjects of articles in the encyclopedia. These articles explore their subjects in greater detail than that given for terms included in the glossary. To find them, users should refer to the list of entries at the front of volume 1 as well as to the comprehensive index and the synoptic outline of contents in the back of this volume. See the table of Abbreviations and Acronyms Used in This Work, located in the front of each volume, for explanation of other terms.

Act
Legislation that has been passed by both houses of Congress, has received presidential review, and has become public law. Also used to describe a bill once it has passed at least one chamber.

Adhere, Motion to
The motion used by one house to inform the other that it will not shift from its previous position on a specified provision of a bill. The motion to adhere is one of a series of motions used in the amendments between the houses procedure as an alternative to going to conference.

Ad Hoc Committee
A temporary committee created to deal with a specific subject in a brief time period. Some select committees fall into this category, as do joint House-Senate conference committees. A rarely used House rule, adopted in 1975, empowers the Speaker, with House approval, to appoint ad hoc committees to consider legislation that overlaps the jurisdictions of two or more standing committees.

Adjournment Sine Die
A motion to adjourn finally and thus end a two-year Congress. The Latin phrase, *sine die* means "without a day" (i.e., for reconvening).

Adjournment to a Day Certain
A motion to adjourn, but with a day established for reconvening. If adopted, the motion ends the session or meeting but does not end the Congress.

Administrative Assistant
The top aide to a member of Congress. Usually shortened to AA, the title is gradually being replaced by "chief of staff."

Adverse Report
A report from a House or Senate committee that accompanies a reported bill to the floor and that recommends that the chamber not adopt the measure.

Aisle
The space that divides the majority side from the minority side on the House or Senate floor. It runs from the rear of the chamber to the presiding officer's rostrum. Members of Congress often refer to their party as their "side of the aisle," Republicans on the right side (facing the rostrum), Democrats on the left.

Allocation
A distribution of the budget authority and outlays contained in a congressional budget resolution to the appropriate House and Senate committees. Allocations are in turn subdivided among each committee's programs or subcommittees.

Amendment in the Nature of a Substitute
A complete alternative to the pending bill, offered in the form of a single amendment. Such replacements for an entire bill are normally offered only by the party leadership or by a committee chairman.

Amendments between the Houses
A procedure used by the House and Senate to reconcile the differences between their two versions of a bill, as an alternative to going to conference. The two chambers exchange amendments to a bill until a final agreement on the language is reached.

Amendments in Disagreement
The provisions of a bill not reconciled by House and Senate conferees. They accompany a conference report to the House and Senate floors and are considered separately after the conference report is adopted. Often the disagreements are technical (and not substantive) in nature.

Amendment Tree
A diagram, resembling a tree with branches, used to monitor the number and order of amendments pending to a bill and their relationship to one another. In the House, up to four amendments may be pending at once. In the Senate, an amendment tree may have as many as eleven branches.

Annual Authorization
An authorization of an agency or program for a single fiscal year, usually for a specified amount of money. Such authorizations are supposed to be in place prior to an appropriation; however, Congress sometimes provides appropriations even if they are not.

Appeal from the Ruling of the Chair
An action taken by a House or Senate member on the floor challenging a ruling just made by the presiding officer in response to a point of order. The chamber votes either to overturn or to sustain the chair's judgment. Appeals are considered routine in the Senate but are rare, and thus dramatic, in the House.

At-Large Representative
A legislator elected to represent an entire state. "At-large" refers to senators and to representatives from states entitled to only one House seat. Before a 1967 law forbidding the practice, states with multiple House seats occasionally elected some part or all of their delegations at large.

Bar (of the House or Senate)
The space on the House and Senate floors between the members' seats and the rostrum. Usually referred to as the "well," it is called the "bar" during a quasi-legal or ethical proceeding conducted in the chamber, for example, an impeachment trial, disciplinary rebuke, or administration of the oath of office.

Bicameral Legislature
A legislative body comprising two chambers or houses.

Biennial Budget
A proposal for budgeting over a two-year period instead of the federal government's traditional annual budget.

Bigger Bite Amendment

In parliamentary procedure, an amendment that embraces previously amended language. Once amended, language cannot normally be amended again. But an exception is made for a later amendment that changes a larger portion of the measure and contains both amended and unamended language—thus amending a "bigger bite" of the text—is in order. The biggest possible "bite" alters the entire text of a measure and is called "an amendment in the nature of a substitute."

Billion-Dollar Congress

A description first applied to the Republican-dominated 51st Congress (1889–1891), which reached this unprecedented level of appropriations largely by increasing Civil War pensions. Also used in 1976, when the operating costs of the 94th Congress itself passed a billion dollars.

Bill Time

A Senate term for general debate on a bill. When a voluntary agreement to restrict debate is in place, senators will ask for time to speak "off of the bill." Without a time agreement, debate on a bill is unlimited and not timed.

Bipartisan

The term used to describe a policy measure or organization that is supported by members of both major political parties. A bipartisan committee has an equal number of members from each party.

Blue Slip

The House message to the Senate, printed on blue paper, when it returns a bill or amendment to the Senate without taking any action on it. Used by the House when it refuses to accept Senate provisions that contravene the constitutional requirement that revenue proposals originate in the House of Representatives.

Boll Weevils

A nickname for conservative Democrats who are willing to vote with Republicans, primarily on economic issues. The name, derived from the insect that once ravaged southern cotton plantations, alludes to the fact that most of the Democrats in this category have come from the South.

Borrowing Authority

Statutory authority that permits a federal agency to spend money for particular purposes with funds borrowed from the Treasury or the public.

Budget Authority

The right granted to federal agencies by Congress to obligate a specified amount of federal funds for a specified purpose and period of time. Budget authority may be expressed as an appropriation or as borrowing or contract authority.

Budget Resolution

A concurrent resolution adopted by both the House and Senate establishing an overall spending cap and containing other budgetary guidelines for congressional committees to follow in the next fiscal year.

Budget Waiver

A formal exception from congressional budget restrictions granted a bill or an amendment by vote of the House or Senate. In the House, this is most often accomplished through a special rule granting a waiver. In the Senate, it usually takes the form of a motion to waive the Budget Act, requiring 60 votes.

Bullet Symbol

The large black dot used in the Senate portion of the *Congressional Record* to indicate material that was inserted and not spoken. To avoid bullets at the start and at the end of their statements, senators will often read the first few lines and ask that the remainder be inserted as if it had been read. The House uses a distinctive type style, rather than the bullet symbol, to indicate unspoken material inserted in the *Record*.

Bundling
In campaign finance, the practice whereby interest groups gather donations from many individuals or political action committees (PACs) and present them as a package to a candidate. This magnifies the influence of both the group and the individual donors, often enabling them collectively to circumvent legal limits on contributions.

Burkean Trustee
From the example of the eighteenth-century English statesman Edmund Burke, a legislator who uses independent judgment concerning the welfare of the whole nation rather than following the wishes of a given constituency; the opposite of an instructed delegate.

By-Election
A special election held to fill a House or Senate seat that becomes vacant (through death or resignation) between scheduled elections.

Byrd Rule
Named after Sen. Robert C. Byrd (D-W.Va.), who sponsored the requirement that no provision may be added to a budget reconciliation bill in the Senate unless it meets the goal of reducing the federal deficit.

By Request
The words that appear after the sponsor's name on the face of a bill when the measure is being introduced on behalf of anyone outside of Congress, most frequently the president or a member of the cabinet. Introduction of a measure for another does not imply endorsement but is considered a necessary courtesy since only members of Congress can introduce bills.

Calendar Day
A reference to a day in the usual manner, as opposed to a legislative day. In the House, legislative days are defined as days on which a session is held. In the Senate, they are defined as the period of time from one adjournment until the next. Because the Senate often recesses at the end of a calendar day, a single legislative day in the Senate may continue over several calendar days.

Call of Committees (House)
A calling by name on the House floor of each committee in alphabetical order, permitting the committee named to call up a bill for immediate consideration. Known as the Calendar Wednesday procedure, the practice is largely obsolete, although still authorized in House rules.

Call of the Calendar (Senate)
A largely obsolete practice whereby the bills listed on the Senate's legislative calendar are called up for consideration in the order in which they appear. Although the Call of the Calendar is still authorized under Senate Rule VIII, the Senate's normal practice is to negotiate unanimous consent agreements to call up bills for floor consideration, not in calendar order but rather as the consensus to do so is reached. [*See also* Clearance.]

Call of the House
A motion used to obtain the presence of a majority on the House floor. A call of the House has the same purpose as a quorum call and also results in a roll call. However, while quorum calls are ordered pursuant to a ruling of the chair on a point of order, calls of the House are ordered upon adoption of a motion.

Call Up
To bring an item of business (a measure, report, or nomination) to the floor for immediate consideration.

Carpetbagger
A scornful term for impoverished Northerners who moved South after the Civil War (carrying their worldly goods in carpetbags) to seek public office and enrich themselves. The term is now used to decry any candidate who runs for office in a state or district to which he or she has only recently moved.

Casework

Efforts by members' offices to answer constituents' appeals for assistance ("cases"). These include requests for information or government publications, help in finding government jobs, aid in dealing with such government services as Social Security, veterans' benefits, unemployment compensation, or immigration regulations. Casework is a major activity in both senators' and representatives' offices.

Censure

A resolution adopted by the House or Senate formally to condemn one of its members for misconduct. Censure is the strongest form of discipline short of expulsion from the chamber and may result in the member's losing any chairmanship held.

Central Clearance

The role of the Office of Management and Budget (OMB) in examining proposed legislation and recommending whether it should be supported by the president, that is, "cleared" as an administration-backed measure.

Certificate of Election

The official form required of newly elected members of Congress prior to their taking the oath of office. Signed by the governor of the member-elect's state, it attests that the person has been chosen by qualified electors of the state.

Chairman, Chair

Interchangeable terms used for the presiding officer of a House or Senate committee or floor session. On the House floor, the member presiding may be referred to as "the chair." During the proceedings of the House in the Committee of the Whole the chair is formally addressed as "Mr. [or Madam] Chairman." In the Senate, members presiding over the chamber may also be referred to as "the chair," but are formally addressed as "Mr. [or Madam] President."

Chairman's Mark

The draft text used by a committee for the purposes of discussion and amendment. So named because it is offered by the committee's chairman as the foundation for a markup.

Christmas Tree Bill

A vital bill that becomes a vehicle for amendments that contain special favors for specific districts or states. Because the passage of vital bills (such as continuing appropriations for the entire federal government) is virtually guaranteed, they are popular choices for such amendments.

Citations, Cites

A standardized system for referencing specific acts of Congress, codified statutes, constitutional provisions, or other legal documents.

Claims Bills (Private Bills)

Legislation introduced on behalf of an individual or single legal entity, for example, a small business. If enacted, these measures become private rather than public law. Most private bills concern immigration and naturalization cases, property disputes, or financial claims against the federal government. The enactment rate for private bills is very low. Also called relief bills because the title of each begins with "For the relief of [name of individual or business]."

Class Caucuses, Class Clubs

Informal organizations of House members elected for the first time in a given Congress—for example, the Democratic Freshman Club of the 101st Congress, the Republican Class of '85 (99th Congress).

Classes of Congress

At the start of each Congress, the newly entering members are known as the freshman class, while those starting their second term are known as sophomores. Some members develop an attachment to colleagues who entered Congress at the same time and create class caucuses that meet periodically.

Classes of Senators

Three classes of senators, each comprising that one-third of the body (now thirty-three or thirty-four senators) elected to six-year terms in the same general election. From the First Congress, senators have had staggered terms (initially designated by lot), so that every Senate seat conforms to one of three six-year cycles.

Clean Bill

A bill drafted in a House committee and then introduced by its chairman as a new bill. Also used when an existing bill is extensively marked up with multiple amendments in committee. The revised "messy" text may be introduced as a new, neater bill. Clean bills help avoid confusion on the floor and have some procedural advantages. Although the term is sometimes used in the Senate, "original bill" is the preferred Senate label.

Clearance (Senate)

The assurance that no senator will object to the consideration of a bill or to the implementation of a proposed procedural agreement. The discussions and negotiations undertaken to achieve clearance are led by the majority and minority floor leaders.

Cleaves' Manual

A historical treatise on the logic and guiding philosophy behind conference procedures, prepared in 1900 by Thomas P. Cleaves, a clerk of the Senate Committee on Appropriations. Cleaves' Manual is still published as part of the Senate's Rules Manual, but now inoperative and rarely referenced.

Closed Doors

The expression used to describe a committee or party caucus meeting that is closed to the public and press.

Closed Rule

A resolution reported by the House Committee on Rules governing the consideration of a bill and permitting no amendments to be offered from the floor. Sometimes closed rules do permit amendments reported by the committee of jurisdiction.

Closed Session

A meeting of the entire House or Senate or of a committee that is closed to the public and press (and sometimes staff), usually to consider international or national security issues or legally sensitive ethical matters.

Cluster Voting (House)

Votes on matters debated at an earlier time on the House floor that are taken separately, one immediately after another. The presiding officer has the authority to postpone a vote until a later time when more members are in attendance. Often these postponed votes are grouped together in a cluster.

Coattail Effect

The ability of popular candidates (for example, presidents, governors, senators) to attract votes for candidates of their party up and down the ticket. Presidential coattails were historically strong, but in recent elections citizens tend to vote for individual candidates, often splitting their votes between the parties.

COLA

An acronym for cost-of-living adjustment. In Congress, the term refers to statutory provisions for automatic increases in salaries, wages, and other payments to offset the effect of inflation on Social Security beneficiaries, government workers and retirees, and welfare recipients.

College of Cardinals

A collective nickname for the chairmen of the thirteen subcommittees forming the House Committee on Appropriations. Each subcommittee enjoys wide latitude and considerable independence in formulating the spending bill within its jurisdiction.

Colloquy

A prearranged floor dialogue among members on a specified topic. Also used to describe a pre-scripted exchange between committee members during floor debate to clarify specific provisions of a bill and to create legislative history. Federal agencies and courts examine these exchanges for guidance in interpreting the congressional intent behind a law.

Committee Print

1. A document, printed by a committee for distribution, that does not necessarily relate to a specific piece of legislation, for example, the committee's rules of procedure, a compilation of existing programs under its jurisdiction, a research study commissioned by the committee, a report on an investigation conducted by the committee, or a compilation of evidentiary material used in an investigation. 2. An internal committee draft not publicly distributed but used for the informational purposes of its members, for example, a draft version of a bill not yet introduced. 3. A nickname for the committee-reported version of a bill.

Committee Rises, The

The House term for the act of transforming the Committee of the Whole back into the House itself. The process begins with a "motion to rise." The House normally debates and amends legislation in the Committee of the Whole but votes on final passage in the House proper.

Committee Tables

Two long tables on the House floor, one on the majority side and the other on the minority side of the aisle. During floor consideration of a bill, they are reserved for the use of the members of the committee that reported the bill. The majority and minority floor managers of the bill use the microphones attached to their tables during debate, permitting them to remain near their staff members and background papers. The majority and minority floor leaders often speak from these tables when making announcements or unanimous consent requests or when engaging in colloquies with the chair or other members.

Committee Veto

Congress before 1983 sometimes directed federal agencies to submit plans to a specified committee for approval before implementing them. The practice became constitutionally untenable after the Supreme Court's 1983 *Immigration and Naturalization Service v. Chadha* decision. Although such provisions are no longer legally enforceable, agencies continue to consult on policy changes with their oversight committees in Congress in order to maintain cordial working relationships.

Companion Bill

An identical or similar bill introduced in one chamber as a counterpart to a bill introduced in the other. Companion bills are meant to expedite the process by allowing for simultaneous rather than sequential consideration in each chamber.

Concur, Motion to

Used by one chamber to agree to an amendment offered to a bill by the other chamber. The motion to concur is one of a series of motions used in the amendments between the houses procedure as an alternative to going to conference.

Concurrent Majority

South Carolina senator John C. Calhoun's doctrine, designed to protect the interests of slave states, that important issues dividing the North and South should be settled only if a majority of the states in each section approved.

Conferees

Members of the House and Senate chosen by their respective chambers to represent each house's version of a bill in conference committee negotiations to resolve the differences between them. Technically, conferees are known as managers on the part of the House and Senate.

Conference
A meeting or series of meetings between House and Senate members designated to negotiate a compromise when the two chambers produce differing versions of a bill. The members form a temporary joint committee, called a conference committee.

Conference Report
The compromise version of a bill negotiated by House and Senate conferees. Each chamber must formally adopt the conference version of a measure before it can be enacted. A conference report has two parts: the legislative text and the "statement of managers," explaining conferees' decisions.

Conflict of Interest
A situation in which a member of Congress or a close relative of a member could benefit or could appear to benefit, financially or otherwise, from the outcome of a legislative issue. Members are expected to abstain from voting on matters in which their own personal interest could affect or could be perceived as affecting their ability to act impartially in the public interest.

Continuous Body
A description of the Senate as a legislative body with continuing membership. In every congressional election, only one–third of the Senate's one hundred members are elected for six-year terms. Two-thirds remain in office; therefore, the Senate remains in continual existence. This is in contrast to the House, all of whose 435 members must stand for election every two years.

Contract Authority
Statutory authority that permits a federal agency to incur obligations in advance of appropriations.

Controllable Expenditures
Discretionary spending that presumably can be adjusted upward or downward annually in appropriations bills. In the federal budget, costs that can be raised or lowered at Congress's discretion without changing underlying substantive statutes.

Cordon Rule (Senate)
The name given the requirement, initiated by Sen. Guy Cordon (R-Oreg.) in 1949, that all committee reports contain a side-by-side comparison of the proposed bill's text with the language of current law. The parallel House requirement is termed the Ramseyer Rule.

Cosponsor
The title given a member of Congress who associates with a legislative measure by allowing the bill's primary sponsor to list his or her name as a supporter on the face of the bill. Cosponsorship is given more importance in the House than in the Senate. House members attempt to collect as many cosponsors as possible on their bills before introducing them.

Counterpart Funds
Foreign currencies derived from repayments of U.S. aid and retained by law within the borders of the aid-recipient country. Funds accumulated in large amounts at U.S. embassies in Europe after World War II and became available, with minimal accounting, to members of Congress traveling abroad. Abuses by some lawmakers resulted in widespread criticism and, ultimately, tighter accounting procedures.

Credentials
Proof of election or appointment that incoming members of Congress present to their respective houses before taking the oath of office. A governor's certificate of election or appointment is usually adequate. For members elected or appointed to fill vacancies caused by resignation, a letter of resignation is also required.

Credit Authority
Statutory authority to incur direct loan obligations or to make loan guarantee commitments.

Credit-Claiming
A lawmaker's behavior that conveys the impression that he or she is personally responsible for producing a result (e.g., passing a law or influencing a regulation) desired by constituents or other supporters.

Crosswalk
Conversion of budget amounts from one classification framework to another, for example, from budget resolution categories to committee jurisdictions.

Cue-Taking
Legislators' tendency to seek out and follow the judgments of colleagues with greater expertise on a given matter, expecting that those colleagues will likewise follow the cue-taker's judgment on issues in which they specialize.

Current Services Estimates
Presidential estimates, transmitted to Congress in the president's budget, of the levels of budget authority and outlays that will be required in the next and future fiscal years to maintain existing services.

Custody of the Papers
A description of the requirement that the House or Senate be in possession of the actual paper copy of a piece of legislation before a vote on the matter is in order. The House and Senate must therefore exchange the papers to allow each to cast a vote.

Dean
An honorary title the House informally bestows on the member with the longest continuous service. It conveys no special privileges, except for the honor of swearing in the Speaker at the start of a new Congress. The title replaced that of Father of the House, used for a century and a half. The most senior member of a state's delegation in the House is referred to as the Dean of the Delegation and is often looked to as a mentor for the more junior members from that state.

"Dear Colleague" Letter
The term given the many mass-addressed letters circulated among members of Congress in which they urge one another to cosponsor legislation or to vote a certain way on a specified issue. Each letter begins "Dear Colleague," hence the name.

Decorum
The orderly atmosphere that must exist in the chamber in order for legislative proceedings to be conducted properly. Decorum is enforced by the presiding officer and includes deference to the member speaking, silence in the galleries, and the use only of appropriate and respectful vocabulary during debate.

Deficit
The amount by which the government's outlays exceed its revenues in a given fiscal year.

Degree (of Amendment)
Proposals to change the text of a bill, offered as motions, are termed first-degree amendments. Proposals to change the text of a pending amendment are termed second-degree amendments. Proposals to change the text of an amendment to an amendment, known as third-degree amendments, are not permitted in the House or Senate.

Democratic-Republicans
One of the designations of the Jeffersonian Republican party of the 1790s and the early 1800s. Jeffersonian Republicans were also called Anti-Federalists, Republicans, and (by their opponents) Democrats or Jacobins. Used in more recent times to distinguish the Jeffersonians from the later Republican party.

Desk
The term used to describe the rostrum in both the House and Senate. Senators will often say, "I send an amendment to the desk," when offering it on the floor for consideration. In the House, certain papers received from the president or the Senate are said to be "held at the desk" for future consideration.

Direct Legislation
A term for the various devices that allow citizens a direct voice in the legislative process. They include the initiative, by which citizens propose legislation through petitions, and the referendum, by which citizens can veto legislative enactments before they become effective. Although none apply to the national government, these devices are authorized in some twenty states.

Distributive Policies
Government programs that convey tangible benefits to private individuals, groups, or firms—usually involving subsidies to selected individuals or groups. Some forms are dubbed "pork"—special-interest spending for projects in members' states or districts.

District Work Periods
In the House, periodic scheduled recesses that enable members to visit their districts and tend to constituency business. The Senate terms these breaks nonlegislative work periods.

Division of the Question
A demand from a member on the House or Senate floor that a pending legislative matter be broken into components for separate votes. For example, if an amendment contains several segments that can be separated, both substantively and grammatically, a vote will be held on each segment individually rather than on the entire text as one concept.

Division Vote
The technical term for a standing vote. The chair puts the question by asking all members in favor of the pending proposition to stand and be counted. Then, after the "ayes" are seated, the "nays" are asked to stand and be counted. In the Senate, the presiding officer announces the outcome but does not state the number standing on either side. In the House, the actual count is announced.

Drop-by
A term used by congressional schedulers to let a member know that he or she may simply stop in at an event to shake hands and greet people but that his or her presence is not required for the duration.

Dugout
The Senate term, borrowed from baseball, for the improvisational press conference held by the majority leader on the Senate floor just prior to the Senate's convening. Reporters are permitted to cluster around the leader's desk and ask questions concerning that day's agenda. They must leave the floor as soon as the bells ring to signal the start of the session.

Early Organization
The practice whereby members meet early in December following each congressional election to elect their leaders and consider organizational changes. Adopted by the House in 1974, early organizational meetings are now routinely held by Democrats and Republicans of both chambers.

Earmarks
Provisions that set aside funds for specific purposes or projects. Most appropriations are earmarked, as are some revenue sources, for example, those collected into trust funds.

Elastic Clause
The Constitution's provision (Art. I, sec. 8, cl. 18) empowering Congress "to make all laws which shall be necessary and proper" to carry out its powers as enumerated in the Constitution. The clause is so named because it expands upon Congress's enumerated powers.

Electronic Vote

A term given a roll-call vote held in the House using electronic machinery. Members vote by inserting plastic identification cards in any of several voting stations located on the House floor. Their votes are instantly recorded on a digital wall display located above the speaker's rostrum. The electronic tally links with computers located in each party's cloakroom. Instant read-outs of the vote in progress permit the leadership to identify and make last-minute appeals to those who are undecided or who have voted against the party's position. Members may change their votes up until the announcement of the final result.

Enabling Act

1. A mechanism, first used in preparing Ohio for statehood in 1803, by which Congress oversees and regulates the development of a territory prior to its admission as a state. 2. Legislation granting local officials, entities, or corporations authority to participate directly in particular government programs.

Enactment

The term used to describe the stage of a bill's becoming a law, after receiving presidential approval. Also used to refer to the passage of a bill by one or both houses of Congress.

En Bloc Amendment

The phrase used to describe several amendments packaged together and subjected to a single vote. Under the rules of both houses, an amendment may propose a change to only one portion of a bill. Those that encompass changes to more than one section must either be offered individually or receive unanimous consent to be offered en bloc, as a unit.

Engrossed Bill

A bill that has passed one house. The House or Senate bill clerk is authorized to engross, or prepare a clean copy of, the bill, reflecting the changes made by floor amendments. Once certified by the Clerk of the House or the secretary of the Senate, the engrossed version is sent to the other body for its consideration.

Enrolled Bill

A bill that has passed both the House and the Senate. Once it has been certified by the Speaker of the House and the president of the Senate, the enrolling clerk of the chamber that originated the bill has the responsibility of preparing the final version for presentation to the president.

Equal Proportions, Method of

The mathematical formula for allocating House seats among the states following each decennial census. The first fifty seats are fixed because the Constitution guarantees each state at least one representative. Beyond that, the formula is used to minimize the proportional differences in the number of persons per representative for any pair of states.

Exclusive Committee

Any of the important House committees whose members are prohibited from simultaneously serving on any other committees. Reserved for the most powerful committees, this rule recognizes that assignment to these committees will leave little time for other committee work. The House Ways and Means, Appropriations, and Rules Committees are exclusive assignments. While some restrictions on assignments do apply in the Senate, no Senator is limited to serving only one committee. With fewer members than the House, the Senate has found that assignments to more than one committee are necessary to distribute the workload evenly.

Executive Business

The Senate term for nominations and treaties sent by the chief executive (the president) to the Senate for confirmation or ratification. Because the Constitution limits the role of advice and consent to the Senate, the House does not consider executive business.

Executive Document

A treaty or other document submitted by the president for Senate consideration or approval. Formerly, an executive branch document that the House or Senate had ordered to be printed. Such documents were designated "H.Ex.Doc." or "S.Ex.Doc.," followed by a number and the number and session of the particular Congress. In 1895 Congress ceased identifying executive documents separately from other printed documents.

Executive Session

The Senate term for the consideration of nominations, treaties, or other executive business either in committee or on the floor. Since legislation may not be considered in executive session, the Senate switches over to legislative session when it turns to legislative matters. The change is routine and rarely requires a vote. In the House, the term executive session is akin to a closed session—a meeting of a committee or a floor session from which the public and press are excluded.

Expenditure

The actual money spent by executive-branch disbursing officers, in accord with appropriations made by Congress and signed by the president. Often, expenditures for particular programs do not occur until years after Congress has appropriated the funds to finance those programs.

Expulsion

The severest form of discipline the House or Senate can impose on a member. Expulsion is a response to misconduct while in office and strips a member of office. Less severe forms of discipline—censure resolutions or reprimands—are more frequently used, with the question of removal from office more often left to the voters to decide.

Extraction Power (House)

The authority given the House Committee on Rules to report a special rule removing a bill from another committee that has not yet reported it and granting the bill floor consideration. The special rule must be adopted by a majority vote of the entire House before the extraction can take place.

Fast-Track Procedures

The term for provisions of various public laws, called rule-making statutes, that make rules for committee and floor consideration in both the House and Senate but do so for specified types of measures only. The best-known examples of rule-making statutes are the Congressional Budget Act of 1974, which governs how budget resolutions and reconciliation bills are considered, and the Trade Acts of 1974 and 1988, which govern the consideration of implementing bills for trade agreements, for example, the North American Free Trade Agreement.

Father of the House

See Dean of the House.

Fencing

The term for the legislative practice of placing prerequisites—fences—on the use of appropriated funds. Only if the conditions specified by Congress are met can the money be utilized.

Filed at the Desk

The term for the submission of amendments, committee reported bills, or other legislation to the chamber for its consideration. Legislative papers are held at the presiding officer's rostrum, or "at the desk," until arrangements are made for their further consideration.

Firewalls

The ceilings for discretionary spending in three categories: defense, international programs, and domestic programs. The Budget Enforcement Act of 1990 barred shifts from one category to another, for example, the use of savings in one category to raise spending elsewhere. The three categories were thus said to be protected by firewalls.

First-Degree Amendment

Any proposal to change the text of a bill or resolution. Amendments are expressed as motions to strike out language from a bill, to insert language, or to strike out existing language and replace it with new text. [*See also* Second-Degree Amendments.]

First Reading

See Readings (of a Bill).

Fiscal Policy

Federal government policies regarding taxes, spending, and debt management aimed at promoting the nation's economic goals—for example, high employment, economic growth, low inflation, and a favorable balance of payments.

Five-Minute Rule

The House term for consideration of amendments to a bill while the House is sitting as the Committee of the Whole. A five-minute limitation is imposed on each side during debate on an amendment.

Floor

The meeting place, or chamber, where all members of the House or Senate convene for debate. Members participating in legislative debate are said to be "on the floor."

Floor Manager

The person designated by the majority or minority party to manage the time allotted their side during debate on a bill. The majority floor manager (usually the chairman of the committee that reported the bill) acts in a defensive capacity, protecting a bill's provisions, while the minority floor manager (usually the ranking minority member of the same committee), if opposed to the measure, serves as the head of the offensive team, seeking to change or annul it.

Folding Room

The traditional name for the separate House and Senate service operations that fold newsletters and stuff envelopes for members of Congress in preparation for mass mailings. The operations also, among other things, distribute publications to members' offices. The Senate folding room acquired broader responsibilities and a new name, the Senate Service Organization, in 1954. The House folding room became the House Publications Distribution Service in 1965.

Full Funding

Appropriating the full amount of budget authority specified in authorizing legislation.

Free Conference

A conference called to resolve differences between the House and Senate versions of a bill in which conferees are not restricted by motions from either chamber to adhere to or to abandon a specific provision. The term has become strictly technical in nature because, in contemporary practice, motions to instruct are not considered binding but only advisory. While instructions may at times have political influence, they are not procedurally enforceable.

Gavel

In the House, a wooden mallet, and in the Senate, a solid ivory pestle, used by the presiding officer to pound the podium to achieve order in the chamber. The sound of the gavel also connotes final disposition of a matter when a vote is announced. The gavel is also used to proclaim the convening and adjourning of each day's session.

General Debate

The time set aside for debate on the House floor on the merits of a bill. The time is allotted and monitored separately from that utilized to debate and vote on amendments to the measure. In the Senate, *bill time* is the preferred term.

Gentleman's Agreement

A commitment made by one member to another, most often to vote a certain way. Such informal, private agreements are unenforceable. Gentlemen's agreements are more frequent in the Senate, which is more dependent on negotiated consensus than the House. Breaking one's word, however, is considered quite a serious breach in both chambers and may contribute to a member's losing colleagues' respect.

Gephardt Rule

A provision in House rules named after Rep. Richard A. Gephardt (D-Mo.), who originated the concept of triggering an increase in the public debt without the need for a separate House vote. Any increase to the public debt must be enacted by Congress and is considered a politically risky vote. Under the Gephardt Rule, final House passage of the annual congressional budget resolution simultaneously causes the engrossment of a separate resolution increasing the public debt to a commensurate level. The public debt resolution is deemed to have received House passage, although no separate vote occurs. The Senate has no parallel procedure but has made use of multiyear increases to the public debt as well as the budget reconciliation process to avoid annual or separate votes on increases to the public debt level.

Ghost Voting

A violation of House rules that occurs when someone other than the House member uses that member's electronic voting card to cast the member's vote or record the member as present.

Grassroots Lobbying

The practice whereby interest groups mobilize their supporters or the general public to put pressure on senators and representatives.

Gypsy Moths

Nickname for Republican liberals or moderates, often from urban or northeastern constituencies, who stray from their party's more conservative positions to vote with Democrats. They are analogous to the southern Democratic conservatives known as Boll Weevils, who often vote with Republicans.

Half-Breeds

See Stalwarts and Half-Breeds.

Hereby Rules

Special rules from the House Committee on Rules that provide for the automatic triggering of another action. Language in such rules states that, if the House adopts the rule, passage will have the effect of simultaneously enacting another resolution or amendment without the need for a separate vote. So-called because the phrase utilized in the special rule states that, if it is adopted, the separate matter is deemed to be "hereby" enacted.

Hideaways

Private offices granted senior senators in out-of-the-way areas of the Capitol's Senate wing. Unmarked, they afford a private retreat for meetings or for rest. These offices are much sought after because they are closer to the Senate chamber than the public offices provided each senator in one of the Senate's three office buildings, which are from one to three blocks away from the Capitol.

Hold-Harmless Clause

A provision protecting current recipients of federal funds from receiving less in the future under new federal fund-allocation formulas created in particular pieces of legislation.

Holds (Senate)

An informal practice whereby an individual senator informs his party's floor leader that further action on a specified bill or nomination will meet with his or her objections. The underlying purpose of a hold varies from a desire to participate in negotiations on a bill to outright opposition and a willingness to use every procedural tactic to keep a bill or nomination from moving forward. Although not required to do so, Senate leaders often comply with any senator's request for a hold. To do otherwise risks that senator tying up the Senate by objecting to unanimous consent requests under which much of the institution's business is transacted. However, when an issue is politically imperative or timely, majority leaders have confronted holds by proceeding anyway.

Home Styles

The characteristic ways in which legislators project themselves and explain their records to constituents back home (from political scientist Richard F. Fenno's 1978 book of that title).

Hopper

A mahogany box on the Speaker's rostrum on the House floor in which members drop the text of legislation they wish to introduce. In the Senate, members simply hand the proposed bill to a clerk.

Hot-Line (Senate)

A recorded telephone message automatically transmitted to all Senate offices by their respective party cloakrooms informing senators of votes underway, of leadership negotiations taking place on bringing a bill to the floor, and of other matters with urgent time restraints. Members are usually given a minimal amount of time to inform the cloakroom of their objections, if any, to proceeding with the issue at hand.

Hour Rule

The basic rule of debate in the House of Representatives, providing one hour of debate for each measure, matter, or motion raised in the House. The hour is equally divided between the majority and minority parties.

Incumbent Advantage

Political scientists' catch-all term for the factors that favor incumbent officeholders over nonincumbent challengers in reelection contests. Since World War II, on average, 92 percent of all incumbent representatives and 77 percent of incumbent senators running for reelection have been returned to office.

Independent Expenditures

Spending by individual citizens to influence the outcome of a campaign for federal office. Such spending must be reported, but there are no limits on it as long as the individual can prove that the money was not spent in collusion with the candidate.

Indexing (of Taxes)

A means of offsetting inflation-caused tax increases by automatically adjusting tax rates to reflect changes in the price level.

Inflationary Impact Statement

House committees' reports on proposed legislation are required (by a House rule) to include an economic estimate of the measure's "inflationary impact upon prices and costs."

Informal Rising (in Committee of the Whole)

A transformation of the Committee of the Whole back into the House proper without the need for a formal motion. Unanimous consent is needed for this brief suspension in a bill's consideration. Most often it occurs in order to receive a message delivered by an emissary from the president or the Senate.

Initiative and Referendum

Ways of extending direct democracy. In an initiative procedure, new legislation can be proposed by popular vote or petition; in a popular referendum, voters may approve or reject state constitutional amendments or legislation passed or proposed. Instituted by a number of U.S. states and localities during the nineteenth and early twentieth centuries. Initiatives and referenda do not apply to federal legislation.

Inner Club
A small circle of influential members, many of them southerners who led the chamber's conservative coalition, that was said to dominate the Senate in the post–World War II era. The term gained currency with William S. White's 1956 book, *Citadel: The Story of the U.S. Senate.*

Instruct, Motion to
The means by which the House or Senate gives formal direction to its conferees. Instructions vary but usually ask the conferees either to adhere to their chamber's version or to accept the other body's language on a specified provision. While not without some political influence, instructions are not binding on conferees and are considered only advisory.

Instructed Delegate
A legislator who follows the desires of his constituents rather than exercising independent judgment for the general welfare; the opposite of a Burkean Trustee.

Insurgents
A group of western Republican senators and representatives who challenged their party's conservative leadership on the Payne-Aldrich tariff of 1909 and on House Speaker Joseph G. Cannon's autocratic control over legislation.

Investigatory Staff
In the House, committee staff authorized annually rather than permanently by rule or law. Despite the term, such staff do not necessarily perform investigative duties. Permanent or statutory staff, by contrast, are automatically allocated to each standing committee.

Johnson Rule
A practice, devised in 1953 by Majority Leader Lyndon B. Johnson (D-Tex.) and followed ever since, ensuring that all Senate Democrats are assigned one major committee before any receives a second major assignment. Senate Republicans also follow this practice.

Joint Referral
The simultaneous referral of an entire bill, after its introduction, to more than one committee. The bill may not receive floor consideration until all the committees have reported their versions of it. Joint referrals are only one type of multiple referral, with sequential and split referrals also possible. Because of conflicting schedules and political agendas, any form of multiple referral usually diminishes a bill's prospects for enactment.

Joint Rules
Rules agreed on and honored by both houses of Congress. Early Congresses often established joint rules for internal matters such as operating the Capitol. House and Senate differences over the enforcement of policies such as serving alcoholic beverages in the Capitol led to permanent abrogation of all joint rules in 1876.

Junket
A derogatory description of official travel by a member or delegation of Congress. Described as fact-finding or diplomatic missions by members themselves, such trips are perceived by critics as vacations funded by the taxpayers or by foreign governments.

Killer Amendment
A politically distasteful amendment offered to a bill in order to diminish its chances for final passage or in order to attract a presidential veto.

King Caucus
A disparaging reference to the control over legislation and presidential candidates exercised by the major parties' congressional caucuses before the 1830s.

King-of-the-Hill Rule
A special rule, drafted by the House Committee on Rules, that, as in the children's game, guarantees that only the last victorious amendment in a series of amendments offered to a bill will prevail. Any amendment in the series that was adopted is superseded by the final amendment to be approved.

Lay Aside
The parliamentary act of temporarily suspending consideration of a matter in order to take up other business. A motion to lay a matter aside is not generally in order except by unanimous consent. Senate rules do allow a motion to take up other business while another matter is pending, which, if passed, has the effect of a motion to lay aside. The House, operating as the Committee of the Whole, has procedures for achieving the same result.

Leadership Tables
Tables on the House floor, one on each side of the main aisle, reserved for the use of the majority and minority floor managers of a bill during the measure's floor consideration, and for the majority and minority leaders of the chamber at any time. Also called committee tables.

Leader Time
The time reserved for the use of the majority and minority leaders of the Senate at the beginning of each day's session. Limited to ten minutes each, the leaders usually use the time to discuss that day's legislative schedule or their party's perspective on policy issues of the day.

Leave to Print
Permission granted to a member to insert into the *Congressional Record* remarks not actually spoken on the floor, or to insert material extraneous to the remarks, such as a newspaper article.

Leave to Sit (Committees)
Senate committees must obtain the permission or leave of their chamber to schedule meetings for afternoons when a floor session is scheduled. The prohibition against afternoon meetings is meant to encourage members to participate in the floor session without having also to attend a committee meeting. The House repealed a similar provision in its standing rules in 1993.

Legislative Amendments
Amendments to appropriations bills that forbid spending for certain purposes. Legislative amendments limit federal programs by specifying that none of the funds provided by the legislation shall be used for a given activity. Also called limitation amendments or riders.

Legislative Assistant
A staff aide to a member of Congress responsible for monitoring legislative activity on specific policy issues, maintaining contacts for information on those issues, drafting floor statements and speeches, and assisting in the member's committee work.

Legislative Correspondent
A staff aide to a member of Congress responsible for drafting answers to correspondence received from constituents. The mail volume in most congressional offices is so high that computers and other automated equipment are used to manage the mail.

Legislative Director
The staff aide to a member of Congress responsible for supervising the work of legislative assistants and correspondents, advising the member on policy positions, and representing the member in meetings with constituents and lobbyists.

Legislative History
A compilation of the stages through which a measure has passed, including significant actions, votes cast, and identification of committee reports, floor statements, conference reports, and any other legislative documents that pertain to the measure. Courts and executive agencies consult this history to help them ascertain legislators' intentions and to interpret the statute's provisions.

Legislative Session
A meeting of the Senate for the purpose of transacting legislative business, as opposed to executive business. When transacting executive business, such as approving a treaty or a presidential nomination, the Senate is said to be in executive session.

Letters of Marque and Reprisal
Government commissions issued by Congress, authorizing private shipowners to seize enemy ships and other property. Such commissions to so-called privateers flourished in the Revolutionary War and War of 1812 but declined sharply after the practice was condemned in the Declaration of Paris (1856) as contrary to the law of nations. Although privateers operated for the Confederacy during the Civil War, Congress barred commissions for the Union and has never again allowed them.

Lie on the Table
A measure or amendment that has been "ordered to lie on the table" may have been killed through the adoption of a motion to table. In the Senate, however, the term also describes the practice of holding a matter at the presiding officer's rostrum ("at the desk") while it awaits floor consideration.

Line Item
In budgeting or appropriations, an individual account, program, or item of expenditure. The term is imprecise since "items" range widely in breadth and dollar amounts.

Locality Rule
A loosely enforced requirement that House members keep a residence in the districts they represent. The presumption is that they thus will be more closely attuned to the desires of their constituencies. The British have a different philosophy: members of the British Parliament need not reside in their districts, freeing them, it is argued, to vote in the national interest rather than having to follow the ephemeral passions of their electorates.

Long Session
Prior to the adoption of the Twentieth Amendment in 1933, a term to distinguish between sessions of Congress convening in even-numbered years (the short session) and odd-numbered years (the long session). A long session usually convened in December of an odd-numbered year and adjourned the following June. Short sessions tended to begin later and to end by 3 March, when, under the law then applying, terms of members expired.

Lower House
See Upper House.

Loan Guarantee, Federal
A commitment by the federal government to pay all or part of a loan to a lender in the event of default by the borrower.

Maiden Speech
A term used to describe the first speech given on the floor by a newly elected member of the House or Senate. In contemporary practice, the tradition of deferring to senior members while serving an informal apprenticeship has waned, and new members of Congress no longer hesitate to speak on the floor whenever they choose.

Marginal District

A constituency whose member of Congress has won narrowly, that is, with no more than 55 or 60 percent of the vote. For potential challengers, such constituencies present attractive targets; for incumbents, they signal that intensive efforts will be required to hold the seat.

Micromanagement of the Executive

The practice of drafting legislation so detailed that the executive branch is left with little flexibility in interpreting and administering the law. (Also used critically to describe committees that encroach with a heavy hand into executive areas of responsibility.)

Modified Rule

A special rule drafted by the House Committee on Rules that permits only certain amendments to be offered to a bill during floor consideration. A *modified open* rule permits all amendments except those to a portion of the bill that is declared closed to amendment. A *modified closed* rule permits no amendments to the bill except those amendments expressly allowed by that rule.

Morning Business

In the Senate, an hour reserved for the introduction of bills, filing of committee reports, short speeches on legislative measures, and referral to committee of messages received from the president, federal agencies, or the House. In practice, the Senate does not always have the morning business period in the morning but permits pockets of time to be used for routine business as needed throughout a day's session.

Morning Hour

In the Senate, a two-hour period held only after an adjournment of the previous day's session (as opposed to a recess). The first hour is reserved for morning business and the second hour is used for various procedural motions. Because the Senate recesses rather than adjourns at the end of most of its daily sessions, few Morning Hours are held. In the House, the term refers to a still-experimental period held twice a week, before the regular daily convening time of the House. During Morning Hour in the House, five-minute speeches on any topic may be delivered by members who have reserved time in advance.

Motion to Commit

A motion to refer a bill or resolution or presidential message to a congressional committee rather than schedule it for immediate floor consideration.

Motion to Disagree

The motion used by one house to express disagreement with the language of an amendment that has been passed by the other house. It is used during the procedure known as amendments between the houses. Passage of a motion to disagree paves the way for going to conference, the alternative procedure for resolving differences between the houses.

Motion to Proceed

A motion used in the Senate to call up a bill for floor consideration. Adoption requires a majority vote. The motion to proceed is used sparingly because it is fully debatable and often subject to a filibuster.

Mugwump

A word, possibly of American Indian origin, referring to a self-important leader. It gained political currency when applied by party regulars to Republicans who supported Democrat Grover Cleveland instead of James G. Blaine (R-Maine) in the 1884 presidential election. It came to be a derogatory label for reformers with little party loyalty. Sen. Mike Mansfield (D-Mont.) once provided his own definition: a mugwump is "someone who sits on a fence with his mug on one side and his 'wump' on the other."

Must-Pass Bill

A bill whose passage is needed to keep the government open for business, pay its obligations, or protect its credit. Bills in this category include annual appropriations bills, continuing resolutions, and bills raising the federal debt ceiling. Because the bills' urgency virtually assures that presidents will sign them, lawmakers often try to attach amendments known as *riders* that might otherwise be vetoed.

Negative Campaigning

A campaign practice, magnified by the effectiveness of television advertising, of emphasizing a political opponent's deficiencies rather than one's own platform and personal attributes.

Nongermane Amendment

An amendment on subject matter different from the bill to which it is being offered. Nongermane amendments are sometimes referred to as *riders*. Nongermane amendments are permitted in the Senate but not in the House, which has strict rules prohibiting them.

Not Voting

Members of the House or Senate absent from their chamber and not recorded during a roll-call vote are described as "not voting." Members who do not wish to participate in the vote, but who are present in the chamber, vote "present."

Objection

The words "I object" block any floor action that requires the unanimous consent of all members of the House or Senate. The right to object is particularly important in the Senate, which conducts most of its business by unanimous consent.

Off-Budget Expenditures

Outlays for certain federal programs that have been excluded by law from budget totals. Examples include Social Security and the Postal Service.

Omnibus Bill

A bill comprised of several separate pieces of legislation packaged together into one measure.

Open Rule

A special rule issued by the House Committee on Rules that allows unrestricted amendments to a bill cleared for floor consideration.

Open Seats

Senate or House seats for which no incumbent is running. Such contests involve newly created constituencies (following House redistricting) or those in which incumbents have died or retired. They are targets of opportunity both for political parties and for ambitious politicians.

Organic Act

An act of Congress creating a territory, conferring powers to its government, and establishing the rights of its citizens. Passage of an organic act is the initial step toward statehood.

Original Bill

The term used for bills that are drafted in a legislative committee rather than first introduced by an individual member and then referred to the appropriate committee. Original bills are common practice in the Senate, less so in the House.

Outlays

Government payment of previously incurred obligations. Liquidation of obligations may be made by cash disbursement or by written check.

Override

The successful repassage of a bill by both the House and Senate after the president has vetoed it. Two-thirds of both chambers must vote to override the president's objections for the measure to become law.

Oversight Committee

Each committee of Congress is required to exercise oversight, or supervision, over the implementation by federal agencies of programs that fall within the committee's jurisdiction. Some committees have designated subcommittees to conduct a regular schedule of oversight, while others perform oversight only through the normal course of reviewing programs for reauthorization or appropriation.

Oxford-style Debate

A style of debate modeled after Britain's popular Oxford Debates and adopted by the House of Representatives on a trial basis in 1994. It consists of two teams of members on opposite sides of an issue who debate a specific proposition by cross-examining one another. This formal, structured, and restricted style of debate occurs only sporadically during a special televised evening session set aside for that purpose.

Parliamentary Inquiry

A question posed by a member from the floor to the presiding officer asking for procedural clarification of the pending floor activity.

Party Conference

The name given to the organization of all the Republicans in the House, all the Republicans in the Senate, and all the Democrats in the Senate. The organization of all the Democrats in the House is referred to as a *party caucus*.

Pastore Rule

A Senate rule, seldom enforced, that mandates that all debate be relevant to the pending bill for the first three hours of each new day of session. Named after its author, Sen. John Pastore (D-R.I.), and adopted in 1964.

PAYGO Process

Acronym for Pay-As-You-Go, a procedure established by the Budget Enforcement Act of 1990 that requires that any direct spending or revenue provisions that enlarge the deficit must be accompanied by offsetting savings. Otherwise, a portion of spending is subject to a sequester (removal). The goal is to avoid enlarging the federal deficit.

Perfecting Amendment

An amendment that seeks to refine, or perfect, the underlying legislative text. Whether major or minor in impact, perfecting amendments must stop short of changing the entire text. Full-text alternatives are known as substitute amendments.

Permanent Staff

In the House, staff assured by statute to standing committees without annual reauthorization. Since 1975, each standing committee is entitled to thirty permanent staff members, two thirds appointed by the majority party and one third by the minority. Also called *statutory staff*.

Pigeonholing

The practice of putting aside bills that the majority of a committee, or sometimes the chairman alone, does not want to send forward for debate by the full House or Senate.

Pocket Veto

A form of presidential veto valid during periods of congressional adjournment. Ordinarily, a bill not signed or vetoed by the president within ten days (excluding Sundays) of his having received it automatically becomes law. If Congress adjourns sine die during that period, however, the president must sign the bill for it to become law. By withholding his signature—"pocketing" the bill—the president can effectively kill the measure. Presidents have generally accepted Congress's view that the pocket veto does not apply during recesses or between sessions of the same Congress.

Point of Personal Privilege

A parliamentary device that allows members to speak when they feel that their character has been maligned or rights as a member of Congress have been impeded. The presiding officer must concur that the matter raised is one of personal privilege. In the House, the member is given one hour to discuss the grievance. Senators may rise to a point of personal privilege at any time, and without time limitation, but rarely invoke this procedure.

Policy Entrepreneurs

Legislators who specialize in a given policy area and are viewed as experts (or, so-called cue-givers) in that area by their colleagues.

Political Cover

A legitimate or contrived excuse that allows a public official to deny responsibility for or to give a plausible defense for an unpopular political action.

Popular Name (of a Law)

A descriptive title by which an act of Congress is known. Some names are provided in the legislation itself; others, such as the Fulbright Scholars Act (1946), derive from popular usage. Some statutes have more than one name: the Securities Act of 1933, for instance, is also called the Truth-In-Securities Act. (For a comprehensive list of popular names for acts of Congress see the United States Code Annotated, published by West Publishing Co.)

Position-Taking

Taking a public stand for or against something—a bill, policy, viewpoint, cause, or value—as a way of sending a signal to others, especially constituents and potential supporters. Lawmakers reveal their positions by their votes, speeches, appearances, letters, or bill sponsorships.

Post-Cloture Period

The thirty hours of debate time allowed in the Senate after a successful cloture vote has ended a filibuster and before the vote on final passage of the matter that has been clotured. The Senate rarely uses the thirty hours available for post-cloture debate.

Power of the Purse

Arguably the ultimate power of government: control over the raising and spending of public money. That control begins with the U.S. House of Representatives, which under Article I, section 7 of the Constitution is empowered to originate "all bills for raising revenue." The House has traditionally claimed the right, despite occasional challenge by the Senate, to originate all appropriations bills as well as revenue bills.

Preamble

An introduction setting forth the reasons for and the intent of a measure.

Precedence

The order in which motions and amendments may be offered and considered in committee or chamber deliberations.

Preferential Motion

Motions given priority over other motions by the standing rules of the chamber. For example, the motion to adjourn is granted the highest privilege in both the House and Senate and may interrupt the pending business.

Press Secretary

The staff aide of a representative or senator chiefly responsible for publicizing the member and the member's achievements. The press secretary's duties include maintaining relationships with members of the press corps, acting as the press's first point of contact for information, preparing and distributing press releases, arranging television appearances, and monitoring press coverage of and keeping clippings of articles about the member.

Pressure Group

A term for a lobbying group or association that promotes a viewpoint by educating members of Congress and their staffs about issues of special interest to them and by attempting to persuade (or pressure) members to vote a certain way.

Previous Order

The authority, granted by the House or Senate at an earlier date, to undertake a specific parliamentary action. For example, the Speaker of the House recognizes a member to give a special order speech reserved in advance, by saying: "By previous order of the House, the gentleman [or lady] is recognized for one hour."

Privatization

The process of turning over government functions to private entities by such means as withdrawing federal regulations, contracting with private firms, or creating government-sponsored enterprises.

Privileged Matter

Certain categories of legislation that are granted priority for floor consideration by the standing rules of the chamber. Privileged matter (e.g., conference reports) may be called up at any time and may not be delayed.

Pro Forma Amendment or Motion

A parliamentary device for gaining the floor to make a statement, engage in a colloquy with another member, or obtain additional time for debate on a pending matter. In the House, such motions are valid only during the amending process in the Committee of the Whole. Typically a member moves to "strike the last word" of the section or amendment under consideration and is granted five minutes to speak, ostensibly in behalf of the motion, after which the motion to strike is considered as withdrawn without the need for a vote.

Pro Forma Session

A session of the House or Senate during which no legislative business is conducted. Few members attend such sessions because it is known that no record votes will be held. Business is limited to routine matters and speeches reserved in advance. Pro forma sessions are sometimes held to avoid the necessity of passing an adjournment resolution, which is required if either house does not meet for more than three days.

Proxy Voting

Voting by one member in the name and under the authority of another. Proxy voting is permitted only in committee and never on the floor of either chamber. Most committees require that members casting votes by proxy have written authorization from the absent member.

Public Interest Groups

1. Organized citizens' groups committed to broad, self-defined objectives of social, economic, or political betterment. Some have large memberships and seek to influence Congress primarily by providing information and mounting grassroots lobbying campaigns. Examples include Common Cause, the Sierra Club, and Public Citizen. 2. Washington-based associations that, among other things, conduct research and lobby for state and local governments. Examples include the Council of State Governments, the National Association of Counties, and the National League of Cities.

Purge

A term applied to President Franklin D. Roosevelt's attempt to defeat a number of anti–New Deal congressmen in 1938. Borrowed from the description of the brutal decimation of opponents by Soviet premier Joseph Stalin during the same period. Roosevelt's "purge" resulted in the defeat of only one House member.

Question of Privilege

An assertion in the House that the integrity of the body has been collectively maligned or its responsibility to legislate has been impeded. Valid questions of privilege receive up to one hour of debate. A question of the privileges of the House must be drafted in resolution form and is either voted on or referred to committee. [*See also* Point of Personal Privilege.]

Question Period

In parliaments, a time set aside for members to question government ministers who are members of the body, including the prime minister. Some reformers propose transporting this practice to the U.S. Congress, although cabinet and subcabinet officials repeatedly submit to questioning in congressional committee hearings.

Quids (Tertium Quids)

The label adopted by John Randolph of Virginia and a small number of his southern congressional allies, who regarded the Jefferson administration as having been lured from the purity of its states' rights, small-government Republican principles by the corruption of power. They set themselves apart from both the Jeffersonians and the Federalists: hence their designation as Tertium Quids, or "third somethings."

Ramseyer Rule (House)

A provision, inserted in the rules of the House in 1929 and named after Rep. Christian Ramseyer (R-Iowa), requiring that every committee report contain a comparison of the text of the reported bill with current law. The Senate counterpart is the Cordon Rule.

Randolph Rule

The requirement that senators vote from their desks, named after Sen. Jennings Randolph (D–W.Va.), and adopted in 1984. The rule is usually only enforced on ceremonial occasions. During a routine session, senators vote by approaching the rostrum and giving a hand signal or shouting out their position to the tally clerk.

Ranking Member

The majority-party member with the highest rank on a committee, after the chairman. The ranking member, usually the member with the next longest service on the committee, sits to the chairman's right and presides over the committee in the chairman's absence.

Ranking Minority Member

The minority party member with the highest rank on a committee, usually the minority member with the longest service on the committee. He or she sits to the chairman's left. The ranking minority member usually manages committee bills on the floor for the minority and appoints and supervises the committee staff designated to serve the minority.

Readings (of a Bill)

House and Senate rules require three readings of a bill—at the time of introduction, the beginning of consideration, and preceding a vote on final passage. In daily practice, however, full readings of an entire measure no longer occur. The readings are limited to an oral designation of the short title of the bill. The practice stems from a centuries-old English parliamentary practice established when many legislators were illiterate.

Recall, Motion to

In both houses, a privileged motion calling for the return of bills or papers that have been sent to the other body or the president and that have subsequently become the object of a motion to reconsider.

Recapitulation

A review of the yeas and nays following a roll-call vote to ascertain that votes have been recorded correctly. The procedure became obsolete in the House with the advent of electronic voting, in which votes are displayed on a screen. In the Senate, the presiding officer or any senator may request a recapitulation, but in practice such requests are rare.

Recede

A motion by one house to withdraw (recede) from a previous position in order to reach agreement with the other body on a measure the two chambers have passed in differing forms. Before a measure can be approved and sent to the president, both chambers may have to recede on one or several points of disagreement. Alternatively, either house may decide to insist on, or reiterate, its position.

Recess

A temporary break in the legislative session lasting anywhere from a few minutes to several weeks. The Senate normally recesses for two hours each Tuesday to allow both parties to hold party caucuses. The House sometimes recesses for short breaks within a day's session while awaiting the expected arrival of the next piece of legislation. Congress schedules longer recesses of a week or more around federal holidays and for most of the month of August in non-election years.

Recorded Vote

Any vote in which members are recorded by name for or against a measure. Other terms for a recorded vote include *record vote, roll-call vote,* and *yeas and nays.*

Redistributive Policies

Government policies or programs that shift resources, for example, wealth or preferment, from one group or class of citizens to another.

Regular Order

To follow the procedural order provided for in the standing rules of the chamber, without modification or change. When a member calls out "regular order," he or she is asserting that the floor action is irregular and is demanding that the presiding officer enforce the prescribed order of procedure.

Regulations

Rules and interpretations issued by an executive agency in fulfilling its responsibility to carry out provisions of a statute.

Regulatory Policies

Government policies or programs that set standards governing the activities of individuals or firms. Such policies are usually enacted to protect the public against harm or abuse that might result from unbridled private activity. Another effect of regulation is to grant firms or groups a favored place in the market and protect that place by discouraging the entry of new competitors.

Re-Referral

The reassignment of a bill from one committee to another committee or committees. Most re-referrals are due to an error in the first referral or in response to a political dispute over jurisdiction.

Rescind

To annul an earlier parliamentary action. Also expressed as a request to vacate or vitiate the earlier action.

Reservation of Objection

Members reserve the right to object when a unanimous consent request is pending in order to debate the request or gain more information about its implications before deciding whether or not to object. Members may debate the question under a reservation of objection only for as long as the chair or other members permit. A call for the regular order will force the member either to object and thus block the pending request or withdraw the reservation and allow the requested action to take effect.

Reserved Powers

The powers given to the states or to the people, as stated in the Tenth Amendment. Generally, all powers not delegated to the federal government or prohibited to the states by the Constitution.

Resolution of Inquiry

A form of simple resolution of the House or Senate seeking information from the president or the head of an executive department or agency. By custom the House uses the word "request" in such resolutions addressed to the president and the word "direct" in those addressed to other executive officials. The Senate has shown less uniformity in its handling of such resolutions. The House, especially, views its right to interrogate the executive as an important prerogative, obviating the need for cabinet members to answer questions in person before the House, as British cabinet members must do before the House of Commons.

Resolving Clause

The binding clause of a joint resolution. The clause must appear in the opening section and in the following form: "Resolved by the Senate and House of Representatives of the United States of America in Congress assembled." It is the equivalent of the enacting clause of a bill.

Restrictive Rule

A type of special rule reported from the House Committee on Rules that restricts the ability of House members to offer amendments to a bill. Restrictive rules curtail the amending process to varying degrees. Some completely close off all opportunity to amend while others permit some amendments and prohibit others.

Revise and Extend

Members must ask the unanimous consent of the chamber, which is freely given, to "revise and extend" their remarks in the *Congressional Record* when they desire to edit or expand on the words they actually spoke during floor proceedings. As a result, the *Congressional Record* is not an absolutely verbatim record of floor proceedings.

Revised Statutes

A compilation of general and permanent statutes of the United States, revised, arranged in order, and recodified as a whole. They are collected in volumes entitled Revised Statutes of the United States, which are usually cited as "Rev. Stat." Also used in reference to revised and reenacted statutes of a state.

Revolving Door

Tendency of officeholders, especially in the executive branch, to move into related private-sector posts where their government expertise and contacts can be exploited for profit, and then often later to return to public service. Some repeat the cycle several times in a career.

Rise, Motion to

The motion offered to transform the Committee of the Whole (formally the Committee of the Whole House on the State of the Union) back into the House of Representatives. The *motion to rise* indicates that the committee will return to complete consideration of the bill at a later time, while the *motion to rise and report* indicates an end to consideration and the reporting of the bill to the House for the question of final passage.

Roll-Call Vote

The only type of vote that records the name of the member with the position taken. In the Senate, there is only one type of roll-call vote, the *yeas and nays*. In the House, roll-call votes come in three varieties: the *yeas and nays*, a *recorded vote*, or an *automatic roll-call*. All three types result in a roll-call vote but each is achieved through a different method.

Rolling Quorum
The practice of allowing a quorum for conducting business or casting a vote to be established over a specific period of time rather than requiring the quorum to be physically present all at once.

Rule-Making Statutes
Statutes that set forth certain rules of House and Senate procedure for specific categories of legislation only. The Congressional Budget and Impoundment Control Act of 1974, for instance, requires both houses to follow certain rules and procedures when debating or amending budget resolutions. The Trade Act of 1974 does the same for bills implementing trade agreements.

Ruling of the Chair
The response of the chair to a point of order. If the chairman considers the point of order valid, it is sustained. If deemed invalid, it is overruled. In the Senate, rulings are routinely appealed, the outcome being decided by a vote of the members. Appeals from the ruling of the chair, or Speaker, are rare in the House and considered quite dramatic when they occur.

Safe District
An electoral constituency that almost always heavily favors a given party or candidate and where winning candidates generally capture 60 percent or more of the vote. No matter how wide their most recent victory margin, however, elected officials rarely consider themselves entirely safe from challenge or defeat.

Saving Amendment
An amendment that attracts enough additional support for a bill to ensure its passage. The opposite of a killer amendment.

Scheduler
The staff assistant to a member of Congress responsible for planning and making adjustments to his or her daily schedule, responding to requests for meetings or appearances, and keeping a record of past events attended.

Scorekeeping
Tracking and reporting the status of congressional budgetary actions affecting budget authority, receipts, outlays, surplus or deficit, and public debt limit.

Second-Degree Amendment
A motion proposing to alter the text of a pending amendment, called a first-degree amendment, that seeks to alter the text of a bill. In other words, an amendment to an amendment. Third-degree amendments—amendments to an amendment to an amendment—are not in order in either house.

Second Reading
See Readings (of a Bill).

Self-executing Rule
See Hereby Rule.

Senate Establishment
An amorphous circle of senior, mostly conservative senators who were said to have controlled the Senate agenda prior to the 1970s and to have served as self-appointed guardians of the body's standards and traditions. Changes in Senate procedures and membership led to the disintegration of this so-called *inner club* by the end of the 1960s.

Sense of Congress Resolution
Legislative language expressing the opinion of Congress, without the force of law behind it. *Sense of* provisions are often passed as amendments to other bills, or as free-standing resolutions. Such provisions are

sometimes passed to encourage the president to take a specific action, with the inference that if he does not, Congress may enact a law mandating the action. Similarly, such resolutions may be passed by either house to express the opinion of that house only.

Sequential Referral

The referral of a bill to more than one committee in a stated sequence. If the first committee chooses not to report the measure, the subsequent committee or committees never receive it. In the House, the Speaker can require the first committee to report by a certain date or be discharged. This guarantees the second committee a chance to review the measure. In the daily practice of the Senate, sequential referrals occur only by unanimous consent.

Seven-Day Rules

1. In both houses, time limits intended to prod reluctant committee chairmen to respond to requests from committee members for special meetings or for reports to be filed on measures that the committee has approved. 2. In the House, provisions intended to thwart opponents of a measure that has cleared the Committee on Rules but has not been called up for debate within seven days by those responsible for doing so. In such cases, certain other members may be recognized for the purpose of calling up the special rule or, if the rule has already been debated and approved, the measure itself.

Severability Clause

The language in a statute providing that, if any provisions of the measure are invalidated by the courts, the remaining provisions will remain in effect.

Short Session

See Long Session.

Side-by-Side

A written comparison of two legislative measures or amendments to them displayed in parallel or side-by-side columns of text. For example, side-by-sides of House and Senate bills in conference are prepared by staff for the use of conferees as they negotiate a compromise between the two versions.

Silent Filibuster

In the Senate, a label for various unseen maneuvers that can have the effect of a filibuster; that is, to kill, delay, or force the alteration of a proposal. The mere threat of a filibuster, for instance, can cause proponents to revise or pull back a bill. Since much of the Senate's business is conducted by unanimous consent, a lone senator can exact a price for agreeing to routine matters such as the scheduling of debate or the removal of a hold on an executive nomination.

Silent Gerrymander

Malapportionment caused by failure to redraw electoral district lines to reflect population shifts, for example from rural to urban areas. Although commonplace in state legislatures and even the U.S. House before the mid 1960s, this form of malapportionment has been severely curtailed by court mandates for periodic redistricting according to population.

Single-Interest Group

Groups that concentrate on a single issue and urge their members to judge candidates solely on that issue.

Single-Member District

An electoral constituency in which one and only one representative is elected at a given time. Most U.S. officeholders are chosen from such constituencies—even same-state senators, who are elected in separate contests.

Slip Law

The first official publication, in single-sheet or pamphlet form, of a statute following its enactment.

Social Lobbying

Personal lobbying of members in social settings—at dinner parties, receptions, meetings, sporting events, and the like.

Soft Money

The funds contributed to national parties and redistributed to state and local groups for voter-registration drives, generic political advertising, and similar campaign uses. Such funds are said to be "soft" because they are not subject to the ceiling and accounting requirements that apply to contributions to individual candidates.

Speaker's Lobby

A long corridor just outside the doors to the House chamber, furnished with sofas and chairs arranged to permit private conversations between members. News service machines and daily newspapers from around the country are also available for members' use. Only House members and credentialed reporters interviewing them may use the Speaker's Lobby.

Speaker's Table

The rostrum in the House chamber, where the presiding officer and clerks of the chamber sit during a session. For example, matters are called up for floor consideration by motion to "take from the Speaker's table."

Special Interests

In politics, a pejorative term implying wealthy and powerful forces, generally in industry and finance, whose private agendas are inferred to run counter to the public interest. First popularized by Theodore Roosevelt, the term has become a political cliché.

Special Order (Senate)

A provision for a future parliamentary action that deviates from the regular order. It must be agreed to by unanimous consent. Also used to describe a speech reserved in advance and longer than five minutes given at the beginning of a day of session in the Senate before legislative business commences.

Special Order Speech

A speech given at the end of a daily session in the House, after all legislative business for that day has been completed and members have left the floor. Such speeches require the permission of the chamber, must be reserved in advance, may be up to one hour in length, and may address any subject the member wishes.

Splinter Parties

Minor political parties, often composed of previous adherents of one of the major parties. Examples include the States' Rights and Progressive parties of 1948 and George Wallace's American Independent Party of 1968.

Split Referral

A bill split into component parts for referral to different committees. This type of referral is used most frequently when one committee has jurisdiction over the predominant portion of a bill, with the exception of perhaps one title. Split referrals require unanimous consent in the Senate but may be implemented by the Speaker alone in the House.

Sponsor

1. The member of Congress who introduces a bill and is its primary proponent. 2. The principal advocate of a particular program or proposal. 3. A member of Congress who supports an individual for employment in a patronage job. Once employed, the patronage recipient is expected to remain loyal to the sponsor in order to remain employed.

Stacking

A form of sequential voting, one vote immediately after another, on a cluster of bills. It is an efficient way to dispose of bills that may have been debated days or hours earlier but on which votes were postponed to allow time for assembling the required quorum for final passage.

Stalwarts and Half-Breeds

The terms applied to Republican supporters (Stalwarts) and opponents (Half–Breeds) of President Ulysses S. Grant's quest for a third term in 1880. The Stalwarts were an older generation of party leaders; the Half-Breeds were younger challengers.

Standing Order

A unanimous consent request agreed to by the chamber and put into effect for a period of time extending beyond that day. While a standing order is not made a permanent part of the rules of procedure, it has the same governing force as a rule for as long as it is effective. In the Senate, standing orders stay in effect until rescinded, unless otherwise stated. In the House, they are always given a specified duration, never longer than for one Congress.

Standing Rule

A permanent rule of the House or Senate. The Senate is a continuing body and its rules remain in effect until revoked or modified. The House readopts its rules at the start of each new Congress, at which time any changes are made.

Standing Vote

Another term for a division vote. Members stand and are counted when a division vote is ordered. First those voting "yea" are asked to stand and are counted. After they are seated, those voting "nay" stand and are counted. In the House, the specific count is stated aloud; in the Senate it is not. Standing votes are sometimes used to verify the chair's judgment on a voice vote. In order to force a standing vote, members need only "demand a division."

Standpatters

Republican members of Congress of a conservative bent who resisted the reform demands of Insurgents and Progressive colleagues during the early twentieth century.

Star Print

A reprint of a bill or an amendment with a small black star on its cover, indicating that either technical corrections or substantive changes have been made since the previous printing.

Statutes-at-Large

A chronologically arranged compilation of all public and private laws and resolutions passed by Congress, published by the Office of the Federal Register of the National Archives and Records Administration. Since 1937, a volume has been published for each session of Congress; before that, for each Congress.

Strategic Politicians

A political-science term for serious contenders in congressional races—people who rationally weigh the pros and cons of launching their campaign and take systematic steps to win.

Strike, Motion to

An amendment to delete text from a bill. It can be major or minor in its scope and is in order only during the amending process in both the House and Senate. The most serious of such motions is a motion to strike the enacting clause, which, if adopted, kills the bill.

Strike from the Record

The parliamentary term for the act of removing disorderly remarks from the official record of debate. When House members are disciplined by their chamber for using inappropriate words or unparliamentary speech during the course of floor debate, they are expected voluntarily to edit those words out of the *Congressional Record*. If necessary, the chamber may vote on a motion to strike or expunge the offending words.

Strike the Last Word
See Pro Forma Amendment or Motion.

Substitute
An amendment that offers an alternative for the existing text. Offered as a "motion to strike and insert," it may propose to substitute for an extensive portion of a bill or for just a small part. Proposed substitutes for an entire bill are called amendments in the nature of a substitute in the House and complete substitutes in the Senate.

Sunshine Rule
The mandate in both House and Senate rules that requires committee meetings, hearings, and floor sessions to be open to the public and press, unless members take a roll-call vote in open session on the question of whether or not to meet behind closed doors.

Super–Majority Vote
A vote requirement that exceeds a simple majority needed for adoption. In both the House and Senate, a two-thirds vote is required for adoption of a motion to suspend the rules, to override a presidential veto, to amend the Constitution, or to expel a member. In the Senate, convicting an impeached official and ratifying a treaty also require a two-thirds vote, while invoking cloture requires a three-fifths vote.

Supplemental Appropriation
An appropriation measure passed for a given fiscal year in addition to the regular appropriations bills.

Sweetener
A provision inserted in a bill by its proponents to attract support: often, last-minute amendments allocating funds for members' pet projects, congressional perquisites, and the like.

Swing Ratio
A measure of the relationship between a party's votes in an election and the number of congressional seats it captures; specifically, the change in the proportion of seats won by a party caused by a given change (e.g., 1 percent) in that party's votes.

Table a Bill
In both the House and Senate, a motion to table a bill (or an amendment or motion), if approved, defeats the matter finally. The bill or amendment may not be brought up again.

Tax Expenditures
Tax provisions that confer an exception or preference of some kind, thus forfeiting revenue that would otherwise be collected. Such provisions encourage or subsidize certain activities, and so may be praised as incentives or denounced as loopholes.

Tellers
House members appointed by the presiding officer to serve as tally clerks to count votes as members pass down the main aisle. If the vote is to be recorded, members hand in signed green cards for a "yea" vote and red cards for a "nay" vote. Teller voting is used only on the rare occasions when the electronic voting machinery breaks down.

Tennessee Plan
A strategy first used in 1796 by the government of the Southwest Territory, later to become Tennessee, in which territorial citizens declare, without congressional authorization, their own statehood. The real purpose is to force Congress to act on a pending statehood bill. Variations of the Tennessee plan, which includ-

ed sending two shadow senators to lobby Congress, subsequently have been used in several statehood campaigns, most recently by the District of Columbia.

Third House of Congress
An ambiguous reference to the hidden influence of any one of several forces inside and outside of Congress. The label has been applied at various times to the press, lobbies, the House Committee on Rules, and House-Senate conference committees.

Third Reading
See Readings (of a Bill).

Three-Day Layover Rule
A requirement in the House that committee reports and conference reports be available for three days after they are filed at the desk before the bill they accompany can receive floor consideration. The layover requirement is meant to give members time to study the committee's report on the measure prior to voting.

Ticket-Splitting
Voters' tendency to cast their votes for candidates of different parties in a given election, for example, to support a Republican president and a Democratic representative.

Time Agreement
A voluntary agreement in the Senate, negotiated by the two party leaders with all interested senators, to restrict debate on a specified bill or amendment. It sets aside the rights of senators to unlimited debate under the regular order and therefore requires unanimous consent.

Title (of a Bill)
A brief description of a bill, intended primarily for identification purposes. Both houses technically require three readings of a bill prior to final passage, but normally, to save time, only the title is read.

Track System
In the Senate, the practice of considering several different measures simultaneously during different periods of the day (tracks). The system expedites business, especially when a filibuster in one track can be offset by progress in other tracks.

Trust Funds
Money collected as taxes or fees by the federal government and earmarked for specific purposes, such as highway construction. In theory, though not always in practice, the funds are kept in separate trust accounts and may not be used for general government obligations.

Tuesday-Thursday Club
The slightly derogatory label applied to members of Congress who are in Washington during the middle of the week and in their home states or districts the rest of the time. Because of this pattern, debates and votes on major legislation often are set for midweek.

Twenty-One-Day Rule
A House rule adopted in 1949 that allowed committee chairmen to call to the floor any reported bill that the Rules Committee had not cleared for debate within three weeks. The reform, an effort to break conservatives' power to block civil rights and other liberal measures, caused considerable animosity and was repealed in 1951. A modified version was tried in 1965, but it too was repealed two years later. Efforts to reinstate the rule a third time ended after other reforms somewhat reduced the Rules Committee's power and independence.

Two Congresses

Refers to the dual nature of Congress as an institution that works collegially to enact laws and make public policy and as a collectivity of representatives who act individually to sustain support in disparate constituencies.

Two-Day Rule

A requirement in the Senate that committee reports be filed at the desk and available to the full membership for two days before the reported bill can receive floor consideration. The layover requirement is meant to give senators time to study the committee's report prior to beginning debate.

Two-Speech Rule (Senate)

The requirement in Senate rules, seldom enforced, that senators not speak more than twice on the same question within the same legislative day. What constitutes the same question has been so broadly interpreted that the restriction has lost force in daily practice.

Uncontrollable Expenditures

Federal spending mandated by existing law and thus insulated against adjustments in annual appropriations bills. Examples include entitlement programs such as those concerning social security benefits and fixed-cost items such as interest on the public debt. Changing the existing law to exercise greater control over such spending may be politically or legally risky.

United States Code

A compilation of all general and permanent laws passed by Congress, organized according to subject matter and divided into fifty titles. The code dates from 1926 and is updated annually by the Law Revision Council, a congressional office; a new edition is prepared every six years.

Upper House

The branch of a bicameral legislature, primarily British, that represents the aristocracy or upper class. Inappropriately used in reference to the U.S. Senate, which, like the House of Representatives, represents the general population. Likewise, the term *lower house*, implying inferior status to the other branch, either in power or class representation, does not apply to the U.S. House. Congressional legend has it that, as applied to Congress, the terms have a unique meaning dating back to 1789, when the Senate met on the upper floor of Federal Hall, and the House on the lower floor.

User Fees

Fees charged to users of goods or services provided by the federal government.

Vacate

See Rescind.

Vinton Method

A procedure, attributed to Rep. Samuel F. Vinton (W-Ohio), for automatic reapportionment of the House following each decennial census, enacted in 1850 and abandoned in 1870. The concept of automatic reapportionment was revived in the Apportionment Act of 1941.

Vitiate

See Rescind.

Votes-Seats Gap

A political-science term for the disparity between a party's votes and the seats it captures. Because members of Congress are chosen in winner-take-all contests, the majority party's share of seats normally exceeds that proportion of the vote its candidates receive.

Waiver Rule

A type of special rule reported by the House Committee on Rules that prohibits, or waives, certain points of order from being raised against a bill or an amendment.

Watchdog Function
A colloquialism for the duty of legislative committees to maintain continuous watchfulness over the executive to see that Congress's enactments are properly interpreted and administered.

Watchdog of the Treasury
An informal title that members of Congress accord to colleagues who are particularly adept at uncovering and blocking potentially wasteful spending programs. Starting with Rep. Elisha Whittlesey (W-Ohio) in the 1830s, a handful of lawmakers have shared the title.

Watergate Babies (Watergate Class)
The large group of ninety-two members, many of them reform-minded, who were elected to the House in 1974 as a response to the Watergate crisis surrounding the Nixon presidency. Their votes provided the margin necessary to depose three committee chairmen and make far-reaching changes to House rules.

Well of the House
The space between the Speaker's rostrum and the first row of chairs occupied by members on the House floor. Two lecterns with microphones, one each on the majority and minority sides of the main aisle, are placed in the well. Most members use those lecterns when they deliver a speech or address their colleagues during a floor session.

Winner-Take-All Elections
Elections in which the candidate who captures a majority or even a plurality of votes wins the contest, no matter how close the outcome. Most U.S. elections are of this type. Proportional representation systems, in contrast, award seats to the minority party or parties according to their share of the popular vote.

Without Objection
The phrase used by the presiding officer in both the House and Senate to indicate passage of a measure or approval of an action by unanimous consent. The presiding officer usually pauses after saying "without objection," followed by "hearing none, so ordered." Any member can force the issue to a vote by responding, "I object."

Words Taken Down
In both houses, a procedure used when a member is called to order for disorderly words spoken in debate. The objectionable words are taken down by the clerk and read back to the members. In the House, if the chair rules the words are out of order, the offending member may withdraw them, modify them, retract them and have them stricken from the record, or stand by them and face punishment ranging from a prohibition against speaking on the floor for the remainder of the day to possible censure. Senate rules prohibit a senator only from impugning another senator or making derogatory comments about a particular state, while House rules prohibit maligning any member of Congress, the president, or the Senate.

Wrap-up
A Senate term for the litany of unanimous consent requests exchanged and agreed to at the end of a day of session. The list contains the passage of noncontroversial bills, requests for committees to meet, and other routine matters. The two party leaders or their designees are usually the only senators remaining on the floor and conduct the exchange pursuant to prearranged agreement.

Yielding, Yield the Floor
In both chambers, members who are given a specified amount of time under their control during the course of floor debate may yield part of that time to colleagues for questions or comments without losing their control of the floor. Loss of the floor occurs pursuant to yielding the floor. In the Senate, senators often conclude their remarks by stating "Mr. [or Madam] President, I yield the floor."

Zone Whip
Especially in the House, member assigned by his or her party to canvass members from a particular geographical area and persuade them to vote in accord with the party's position.

Synoptic Outline of Contents

This outline provides a general overview of the conceptual scheme of this encyclopedia, listing the entry term of each article. The outline is divided into eleven major parts. Some of these parts are divided into various subsections, listing principal articles first, followed by supporting articles. Because the section headings are not mutually exclusive, certain entries are listed in more than one section.

1 Powers of Congress
2 Congress and the Executive
3 Congress and the Judiciary
4 History of Congress
5 Congressional Organization, Institutions, and Traditions
6 Public Policy and Legislation
7 International Relations and National Defense
8 Congressional Campaigns and Elections
9 Congress and the People
10 Members of Congress
11 The Study of Congress

1 POWERS OF CONGRESS

Principal Articles

Congress
   Powers of Congress
Constitution
   Congress in the Constitution
   Congressional Interpretation of
     the Constitution

Powers of Congress

Advice and Consent
Bicameralism
Bills of Attainder
Bowsher v. Synar
Checks and Balances
Concurrent Powers
Contempt of Congress
Delegation of Powers
Emergency Powers
Enumerated Powers
Ex Post Facto Laws
General Welfare Clause

*Immigration and Naturalization
   Service v. Chadha*
Impeachment
Implied Powers
Investigative Power
Kilbourn v. Thompson
Legislative Branch
McCulloch v. Maryland
McGrain v. Daugherty
Morrison v. Olson
Oversight
Removal Power
Separation of Powers
Speech or Debate Clause
Subpoena Power
War Powers
Watkins v. United States
Witnesses, Rights of

Amendments to the Constitution

Bill of Rights
Eleventh Amendment

Twelfth Amendment
Thirteenth Amendment
Fourteenth Amendment
Fifteenth Amendment
Sixteenth Amendment
Seventeenth Amendment
Eighteenth Amendment
Nineteenth Amendment
Twentieth Amendment
Twenty-first Amendment
Twenty-second Amendment
Twenty-third Amendment
Twenty-fourth Amendment
Twenty-fifth Amendment
Twenty-sixth Amendment
Twenty-seventh Amendment

Other Supporting Articles

Anti-Federalists
Articles of Confederation
Constitutional Convention of 1787
Federalist Papers

2 CONGRESS AND THE EXECUTIVE

3 CONGRESS AND THE JUDICIARY

4 HISTORY OF CONGRESS

*Other parts of this outline include numerous additional entries on historical subjects.
See in particular Part 5 for entries on political groups and parties, Part 6 on public policy
and acts of legislation, and Part 7 on international relations and wars.*

Bicentennial of Congress
Boardinghouses
Bonus March
Cannon Revolt
Capitals of the United States
Compromise of 1850
Conduct of the War Committee, Joint
Congress of the Confederacy
Court-Packing Fight
Covode Committee
Coxey's Army
Crédit Mobilier
Farm Bloc
Federalists
First Congress
Iran-Contra Committees
Jeffersonian Republicans

Kefauver Crime Committee
Kentucky and Virginia Resolutions
Lincoln-Douglas Debates
Manhattan Project
Missouri Compromise
Nullification
Nye Committee
Pearl Harbor Investigation
Pecora Wall Street Investigation
Progressive Movement
Prohibition
Pujo Investigation
Radical Republicans
Reconstruction
Reconstruction Committee, Joint
Reed's Rules
St. Clair Investigation

Secession
Sectionalism
Silver Issue (Bimetallism)
Slavery
Southern Manifesto
Teapot Dome
Telegraph
Temporary National Economic
  Committee (TNEC)
Truman Committee
Un-American Activities Committee,
  House
War Hawks
Watergate
Watergate Committee
Webster-Hayne Debate
Whig Party

5 CONGRESSIONAL ORGANIZATION, INSTITUTIONS, AND TRADITIONS

Principal Articles

Congress
  Congressional Workload
  Politics and Influence in Congress
House of Representatives
  An Overview
  Daily Sessions of the House
Lawmaking (How A Bill Becomes A
  Law)
Leadership
  House Leadership
  Senate Leadership
Political Parties
Reorganization of Congress
Senate
  An Overview
  Daily Sessions of the Senate
Staffing

Political Parties, Informal Groups, and Party Organization

Parties

Anti-Federalists
Democratic Party
Federalists
Jeffersonian Republicans
Republican Party
Whig Party

Informal Groups and Party Organization

Anti-Saloon League
Blocs and Coalitions
Campaign Committees
Caucus
  Party Caucus
Clubs
Conservatism
Conservative Coalition
Democratic Study Group
Farm Bloc
Floor Leader
  In the House
  In the Senate
Independents
Liberalism
Majority and Minority
Minority Rights
Party Committees
Populism
Progressive Movement
Radical Republicans
Sectionalism
Socialism
Southern Bloc
Southern Manifesto
State Delegations
Whips

Committees of Congress

Principal Articles

Committees
  An Overview
  Assignment of Members
  Committee Hearings
  Committee Jurisdictions
  Markups
  Committee Reports
  Standing Committees
  Select and Special Committees
  Joint Committees
Conference Committees
Contempt of Congress
Seniority
Subcommittees
Witnesses, Rights of

House Committees

Aging Committee, House Select
Agriculture Committee, House
Appropriations Committee, House
Armed Services Committee, House
Banking, Finance, and Urban Affairs
  Committee, House
Budget Committee, House
Children, Youth, and Families
  Committee, House Select
District of Columbia Committee,
  House

Supporting Articles

District of Columbia
Louisiana Purchase
Mexican War
Nullification
Puerto Rico
Spanish American War
West Florida

Alabama
Alaska
Arizona
Arkansas
California
Colorado
Connecticut
Delaware
Florida
Georgia
Hawaii
Idaho
Illinois
Indiana
Iowa
Kansas

Kentucky
Louisiana
Maine
Maryland
Massachusetts
Michigan
Minnesota
Mississippi
Missouri
Montana
Nebraska
Nevada
New Hampshire
New Jersey
New Mexico
New York
North Carolina
North Dakota
Ohio
Oklahoma
Oregon
Pennsylvania
Rhode Island
South Carolina
South Dakota

Tennessee
Texas
Utah
Vermont
Virginia
Washington
West Virginia
Wisconsin
Wyoming

Other Supporting Articles

Awards and Prizes
Blue Ribbon Commissions
Congressional Directory
Congressional Medal of Honor
Delegates, Nonvoting
Government Printing Office
Joint Sessions and Meetings
Libraries of the House and Senate
Library of Congress
Oath of Office
Seals
Technology in Congress
Vacancy

6 PUBLIC POLICY AND LEGISLATION

**Overviews of Major Areas
of Public Policy**

Agriculture
Art and Culture
Banking
Civil Liberties
Civil Rights
Commerce Power
Communications
Crime and Justice
Currency and Finance
Defense
Economic Policy
　Nineteenth Century
　Twentieth Century
Education
Energy and Natural Resources
Environment and Conservation
Family Policies
Federalism
Foreign Policy
Health and Medicine

Housing Policy
Immigration Policy
Indian Policy
Intelligence Policy
Labor
Public Lands
Public Works
Regulation and Deregulation
Religion
Science and Technology
Slavery
Social Welfare and Poverty
Statehood
Tariffs and Trade
Taxation
Territorial Expansion
Transportation
Urban Policy
Veterans' Benefits
　An Overview
　Veterans' Pensions
Voting and Suffrage

Other Policy Articles

Abortion
Aerospace
Alcohol Policy
Arms Control
Automobile Safety
Bankruptcy
Child Labor
Chinese Exclusion Policy
Citizenship
Civil Service
Communism and Anticommunism
Conscription
Copyright, Trademarks, and Patents
Exploration
Foreign Aid
Great Society
Gun Control
Internal Improvements
Internal Security
Interstate Compacts
Medicare

7   INTERNATIONAL RELATIONS AND NATIONAL DEFENSE

8   CONGRESSIONAL CAMPAIGNS AND ELECTIONS

9   CONGRESS AND THE PEOPLE

Constituencies, Lobbying, and Interest Groups

Principal Articles

Constituency Outreach
Constituency Service
Interest Groups
Lobbying

Supporting Articles

Bonus March
Caucus
    Special Interest Caucus
Circular Letters
Common Cause
Congress Watch
Coxey's Army
Crédit Mobilier

Franking
Instruction
Iron Triangle
Legislative Service Organizations
Offices, District
Patronage
Petitions and Memorials
Pork Barrel
Representation
Voting
    Ratings by Interest Groups

Media and Public Opinion

Principal Articles

Broadcasting of Congressional
    Proceedings

Congress
    Public Perceptions of Congress
Press

Supporting Articles

C-SPAN
Congressional Quarterly
Correspondence to Congress
Literature on Congress
Movies on Congress
Muckraking
Press Galleries
Roll Call

10   MEMBERS OF CONGRESS

Names in italics indicate biographical entries on presidents of the United States.

Topical Articles

Members
    Daily Life and Routine in the
        House
    Daily Life and Routine in the
        Senate
    Qualifications
    Demographic Profile
    Congressional Careers
    Spouses and Families
    Retirement
    Tenure and Turnover

Asian American Members
Black Members
    Nineteenth Century
    Twentieth Century
Delegates, Nonvoting
Former Members of Congress
Freshmen
Hispanic Members
Mavericks
Offices, Congressional
Political Dynasties
Representative
Senator
Shadow Senators
Women in Congress

Members of Congress

Adams, John
Adams, John Quincy
Albert, Carl B.
Aldrich, Nelson W.
Allison, William B.
Ames, Fisher
Anderson, Clinton P.
Aspinall, Wayne N.
Baker, Howard H., Jr.
Bankhead, William B.
Barkley, Alben W.
Bayard, James A., Sr.
Bell, John
Benton, Thomas Hart
Berger, Victor L.
Beveridge, Albert J.
Bilbo, Theodore G.
Bingham, John A.
Black, Hugo L.
Blaine, James G.
Boggs, Corinne C. (Lindy)
Boggs, Hale
Bolling, Richard W.
Bolton, Frances P.
Borah, William E.
Boutwell, George S.
Breckinridge, John C.

Bridges, H. Styles
Brooke, Edward W.
Brooks, Preston S.
Bryan, William Jennings
Buchanan, James
Burr, Aaron
Burton, Phillip
Bush, George H. W.
Byrd, Harry Flood, Sr.
Byrnes, James F.
Calhoun, John C.
Cameron, Simon
Cannon, Clarence
Cannon, Joseph G.
Capper, Arthur
Carlisle, John G.
Cass, Lewis
Celler, Emanuel
Chase, Salmon P.
Chavez, Dennis
Chisholm, Shirley A.
Church, Frank
Clark, James Beauchamp (Champ)
Clay, Henry
Cobb, Howell
Colfax, Schuyler
Conkling, Roscoe
Connally, Tom T.

11 THE STUDY OF CONGRESS

Index

Numbers in boldface refer to the main entry on the subject. Numbers in italic refer to illustrations, including charts and graphs. Numbers in regular type frequently refer to the contents of tables.

A

AAA. *See* Agricultural Adjustment Acts
AAAs. *See* Area Agencies on Aging
AARP. *See* American Association of Retired Persons
ABC systems (interstate highways), 1646
Abdnor, James, 1333
Abdul Enterprises, Ltd. *See* Abscam
Abel, Hazel H., 2136
Aberbach, Joel, 413, 1511
Ableman v. Booth (1859), 892, 1887
ABMC. *See* American Battle Monuments Commission
ABM Treaty (1972). *See* Antiballistic Missile Systems Treaty
Abolitionist movement, 248, 249, 377, 1821–1822
  antislavery petitions, 164, 990, 992, 997
  Fugitive Slave Act reaction, 892–893
  Radical Republicans, 1659–1660
  religious influence, 1705–1706
  Stevens (Thaddeus) role, 1890–1891
  see also Wilmot Proviso
Abortion, **1–2**, 166, 960
  Catholic Church position, 1136
  clinic harassment suits, 587
  congressional curbs, 353
  family planning legislation, 807
  Hyde Amendments, **1088**, 1190, 1709, 1710
  religious undercurrents, 1709–1710
  as women's rights issue, 2145, 2146
Abourezk, James, 1111, 1112, 1119, 1128
Abramowitz, Alan I., 719
Abrams, Charles, 1069
Abrams, Elliott, 2134
Abrams v. United States (1919), 774
Abridgment of the Debates in Congress (Benton), 153
Abscam, 2, 642, 644, 776, 780–781, 1370, 1627

Absentee balloting, 2078, 2080
Absenteeism. *See* Voting, voting analysis
Abuse, drug. *See* Narcotics Abuse and Control Committee, House Select; Narcotics and other dangerous drugs
Abzug, Bella S., 2137, 2143
ACA. *See* Americans for Constitutional Action
Accountability, **2–4**, 985, 986
  cabinet and Congress, 242
  civil service, 366
  Common Cause lobby, 434
  constituency displeasure, 1717
Accountability for Intelligence Activities Act of 1980, 1124, 1125, 1128, 1129–1130
Accounting Act of 1920. *See* Budget and Accounting Act of 1921
Accounts Subcommittee, House, 985, 1052
Accounts Subcommittee, Senate, 988
ACDA. *See* Arms Control and Disarmament Agency
Achenbaum, W. Andrew, *as contributor*, 1501–1503
Acheson, Dean, 391, 1221, 1327, 1355
Acid rain, 264, 379, 769, 771
ACLU. *See* American Civil Liberties Union
Acorns (club), 387
Acreage Reserve Program, 25
Act, glossary definition, 2175
Act concerning Aliens of 1798. *See* Alien and Sedition Acts of 1798
Act for Establishing the Temporary and Permanent Seat of Government of the United States of 1790, 271
Act for the Punishment of Certain Crimes of 1798. *See* Alien and Sedition Acts of 1798
Act for the Relief of Sick and Disabled Seamen of 1798, 952
ACTION (agency), 1531
Action for Smoking and Health, 1966

Activism, congressional and presidential, 1580
Act Making Appropriations for the Support of Government of 11 February 1791, 572
Act of Annexation and Admission of 1846, 1883
Act of 2 March 1895, 587
Act Respecting Alien Enemies of 1798, 350
Act to Amend "An Act to Amend the Judiciary Act" of 1868, 350
Act to Eliminate the Gold Reserve of 1968, 601
Act to Establish and Protect National Cemeteries of 1867, 1440
Act to Improve Coastal Management of 1980, 2049
Act to Improve the Administration of Justice of 1988, 1186, 1189
Act to Regulate Commerce of 1887, 674, 1974
ACU. *See* American Conservative Union
ADA. *See* Americans for Democratic Action
Adair, John, 376
ADAMHA. *See* Alcohol, Drug Abuse, and Mental Health Administration
Adams, Abigail, 6
Adams, Brock, 216
Adams, Brooks, 1300
Adams, Charles W., 660
Adams, Henry, 1299, 1300
Adams, John, **4–5**, 6, 50, 150, 1078
  American independence, 973, 976
  colonial-era representation, 973
  on composition of legislature, 1371
  congressional majority and minority, *656*
  extraordinary session, 1804
  Federalist party, 827, 1941
  First Congress, 1359
  foreign policy, 1946, 1947
  Library of Congress legislation, 1289

Annual authorization. *See* Authorization
Annunzio, Frank, 1091, 1798
Antarctica, 798, 799
Anthony, Beryl, 258
Anthony, Daniel R., Jr., 771
Anthony, Henry B., *59*, 1607, 1608
Anthony, Susan B., 291, 771, 1467, 1540, 2075
Anthony Rule, **59**
Antiballistic Missile Systems Treaty (1972), **59–60**, 97, 98, 99, 621, 1892, 1983, 1987
   see also Limited Test Ban Treaty; Nuclear Non-Proliferation Treaty; Strategic Arms Limitation Talks; Strategic Defense Initiative
Anti-Bigamy Act of 1862, 2025
Anticipated reactions, law of, 1152
Anticommunism. *See* Communism and anticommunism
Antideficiency Act of 1906, 625
Anti-Drug Abuse Acts of 1986 and 1988, 47, 588, 1436; *see also* Narcotics Abuse and Control Committee, House Select; Narcotics and other dangerous drugs
Antietam Cemetery, 1440
Anti-Federalists, **60**, *525*, 826, 844, 1174
   argument against navy, 89
   bill of rights advocacy, 161, 162
   Burr (Aaron) role, 233
   caucus, 308–309
   religion and First Congress, 1703
   see also Jeffersonian Republicans
Antilynching laws, 355
Anti-Masons, 7, 1556, 1562, 1811, 1890
Anti-Nebraska party, 1813
Anti-Peonage Act of 1867, 1226
Antipoverty programs. *See* Economic Opportunity Act of 1964; Social welfare and poverty; Urban policy
Anti-Saloon League, 46–47, **60–61**, 694, 1020, 1449, 1631, 1707
Antislavery petitions, 164, 990, 992, 997
Anti-Terrorism Act of 1988, 351, 353
Antitrust and Monopoly Subcommittee, Senate, 956, 1209
Antitrust legislation, 1201, 1202
   broad regulation, 1694
   organized sports, 1868
   Roosevelt, Theodore, 1739
   see also Clayton Antitrust Act of 1914; Sherman Antitrust Act of 1890
AoA. *See* Administration on Aging
AP. *See* Associated Press
Apollo project, 14, 799, *1765*
Apotheosis of George Washington, The (fresco), 289, 298, 2070
Appendix. *See* Extensions of remarks
Appointment powers. *See* Advice and consent; Bureaucracy; Presidential appointments

Appointments, recess. *See* Recess appointments
Apportionment Act of 1842, 651, 652, 653, 911
Apportionment Act of 1872, 653
Apportionment Act of 1901, 653
Apportionment Act of 1929, 653
Apportionment and redistricting, **61–69**
   Arizona, 86–87
   Arkansas, 87
   Baker v. Carr (1962), 62, **127–128**
   black representation, 1378, 1379
   California, 234, 1364
   census, 318–320
   Continental Congress, 973
   Davis et al. v. Bandemer et al. (1986), 63, 68, **605–606**
   districts, 651, 652, 653
   equal population doctrine, 62, 64, 547, 548
   evolution of equity concept, 62–64
   Federal Convention of 1787 plan, 547, 980–981
   governor's veto, 67
   guides to changes, 500
   Hispanic congressional representation, 966
   inexperienced candidates and, 1381
   method, 61–62, 698
   national expansion and, 989, 1016, 1055
   redistricting criteria, 64–66, 359
   redistricting process, 66–68
   single member, simple plurality (SMSP) rules, 64, 65
   urban and suburban, 1034
   see also Gerrymandering
Apprenticeships, 1382
Appropriations, **69–73**
   annual, types of, 70
   arts and culture endowments, 110
   authorization, 71–72, 75, 81, **118–120**
   automatic spending cuts, 129, 130
   backdoor spending, **125**, 264–265
   bill deadlines, 219
   calendar, 243, 244
   as check on civil liberties, 353
   as check on executive branch, 69, 72–73, 78, 225, 394, 461, 560, 561, 1011, 3393
   civil service, 366
   committee power, 70–71
   committees' work and influence, 70–71, 995; *see also* Appropriations Committee, House; Appropriations Committee, Senate; Budget Committee, House; Budget Committee, Senate
   Congressional Budget Committee scorekeeping, 506
   contingent fund, **572**
   continuing resolution, 70, **572–573**
   defense. *See under* Defense

   deferral, 215–216, **624–625**
   deficiency bills, **625**
   for elderly, 1502–1503
   enacting clause, 1639
   entitlements, 69, 77, **755**
   as enumerated congressional power, 755, 756
   farm legislation, 37
   foreign policy role of, 5
   form of, 69–70
   franking, 884, 886, 887
   health-related, 956, 959–960
   House origination, 265, 553, 1055
   House Ways and Means Committee, **2112–2117**
   Library of Congress, 1292–1293
   limitation amendments, 72
   line-item veto, **1162–1163**
   Manhattan Project, 1347–1348, 2152
   nonstatutory controls, 1474–1475
   oversight hearings, 1511
   points of order, 1068
   pork barrel. *See* Pork barrel
   presidential impoundment. *See* Impoundment
   process parameters, 208–209, 504; *see also* Congressional Budget and Impoundment Control Act of 1974
   public works, 1639, 1642, 1647, 1647–1648
   recentralization, 1762
   rescission, 216
   riders, 949, 1729
   scientific projects, 1767
   secret (black budget), **169–170**, 321
   social programs, 678, *1845*
   supplemental, 70, 625, 2205
   World War II, 2151
   see also Budget process
Appropriations Act of 1976. *See* Hyde Amendments
Appropriations Act of 1984, 353
Appropriations Committee, House, 69, **73–78**, 636, 837, 861
   Agriculture Committee relationship, 34, 37
   armed forces bills, 89, 99
   arts projects investigation, 107
   Budget Committee membership, 209, 215
   chairs, 74, 78, 264, 265, 266, 268, 1033, 1525
   District of Columbia subcommittee, 649–650
   early history (1865–1919), 74–75, 78, 1001
   "Guardian of the Treasury" role, 75–76
   health subcommittees, 952, 955–956
   jurisdiction, 428
   Mahon (George H.) role, 1343–1344
   Manhattan Project, 1347–1348
   membership, 410, 413

Base Closure and Realignment Act of 1988, 797
Basic Educational Opportunity Grants, 690, 963
Basset, Isaac, 594
Bassett, Richard, 149
Bateman, Ephraim, 992
Bates, Joshua, 332
Battlefields. *See* National cemeteries, monuments, and battlefields
Baucus, Max, 771, 1414
Baudin, Edmond, *286*, 289
Baum, Lawrence, 1194
Bayard, James A., Jr. (1797–1880), 372, 1552
Bayard, James A., Sr. (1767–1815), **149–150**, 626, 1552, 1836
Bayard, Richard H., 1552
Bayard, Thomas F., 1552, 1608
Bayard family political dynasty, 1552
Bayh, Birch, 773, 1111, 1999
Bayly, Mountjoy, 1802
Bayly, Thomas H., 995
Bay of Pigs (1961), 321, 1212
BCCI. *See* Bank of Commerce and Credit International
BEA. *See* Budget Enforcement Act of 1990
Beale, Robert, 1802
Beaman, Middleton, 150, 1272, 1783
Bean soup (congressional favorite dish), 594
Beard, Charles, 1337
Bear Flag Revolt (1846), 250
Bearss, Edwin C., *as contributor*, 1439–1441
Beautification projects, 1147
Becerra, Xavier, 965
Bechill, William, 1502
Beckley, John, **150–151**, 379, 380, 1293
Bedford-Stuyvesant, 1214
Beedy, Carroll L., *1928*
Beer, Samuel, 488
Beers, Paul, 1770
Begg, James T., 1964
Begich, Nicholas J., 187, 508
Begin, Menachem, 306
Behavioralist scholarship, 492, 1371, 2084
Belarus, arms control, 98, 99
Belford, James B., 397
Belgium, NATO membership, 1479
Belknap, William W., 242, 554, 776, 929, 1102, 1104
Bell, Alexander Graham, 436
Bell, C. Jasper, 1543
Bell, Daniel, 1915
Bell, John, **151–152**, 935, 1862, 1941
Bell, John C., 1569
Bell Commission, 1915
Bell family political dynasty, 1552
Bellino, Carmine, *918*

Bellmon, Henry L., 211, 216, 1413
Bell system, Capitol, 252–252
Bell Trade Act. *See* Philippine Trade Act of 1946
Benedict, Michael Les, *as contributor*, 994–1003
Benefits, members'. *See* Perquisites
Bennett, A. LeRoy, *as contributor*, 1143–1144
Bennett, Charles E., 1798
Bennett, Charles G., 1778
Bennett, Wallace F., 787, 959
Benoit, Robert (Larry), 1802
Bensel, Richard Franklin, *as contributor*, 1778–1782
Benson, Ezra Taft, 1332
Bentley, Alvin M., 2062
Bentley, Arthur F., 424, 1134
Bentley, Elizabeth, 2007
Bentley, Helen Delich, 2137
Benton, Jesse, 152, 2065
Benton, Thomas Hart, **152–153**, 475, 985, 2120
    eulogy for Adams (John Quincy), 788
    expansion advocacy, 798
    Jacksonian democracy, 1284, 1407
    oratory, 609, 611
    Texas annexation, 1948–1949
    violence incidents, 856, 2063, 2065
Benton, William, 1323
Bentsen, Lloyd, 235, 1921
Berger, Victor L., **153–154**, 1838–1839, 2133
Berkman, Alexander, *1839*
Berkowitz, Edward D., *as contributor*, 637–639
Berlin Crisis (1961), 1212
Berlin Wall, 1212
Berman, Daniel, 1456
Berne Convention, 577
Berne Implementation Act of 1988, 105
Bernhard, Winfred E. A., *as contributor*, 607, 914, 941–942, 1169–1170, 1215–1216, 1339–1340, 1427–1428, 1783–1784, 1993
Berry, Jeffrey, 1311
Berry, Robert C., *as contributor*, 1868–1869
Berryman, Clifford K.
    cartoons by, *115, 214, 218, 267, 268, 319, 386, 391, 452, 526, 579, 863, 945, 947, 962, 1053, 1194, 1270, 1280, 1283, 1317, 1326, 1339, 1453, 1459, 1462, 1468, 1479, 1536, 1570, 1589, 1630, 1804, 1860, 1994, 2034, 2065, 2149*
Berryman, Jim, cartoon by, *1445*
Best Man, The (film), 1422, 1425
Bestor, Arthur, 1441
Beth, Richard S., *as contributor*, 243–246, 381, 639–641, 1548, 1626–1627, 1638–1639

Beveridge, Albert J., **154–155**, 180, 613, 1465, 1630, 2064
    child labor laws, 154, 339
Bibby, John F.
    as contributor, 1553–1567
    On Capitol Hill, 141
Bicameralism, **155–157**
    British Parliament, 651
    bureaucracy relationship, 228
    as check and balance, 460, 1055
    colonial assemblies, 651, 970
    conference committees, **452–455**
    Congress of the Confederacy, 520
    Federal Convention of 1787 plan. *See* Great Compromise
    goals, 156, 720
    party caucus differences, 312
    partyless politics, 1554
    separation of powers, 1799
    Sherman (Roger) proposal, 524
    small states' advocacy, 625
    state legislatures, 1784
    tenure equality, 1388–1389
    Upper and Lower House, 2207
    see also House of Representatives; Senate
Bicameral legislature, glossary definition, 2176
Bicentennial of Bill of Rights, 165–166
Bicentennial of Congress, **157–158**, 285, 385
    House Historian Office, 966–967
Bicentennial of the Constitution, 271, 325
Bicentennial of the United States, 285
Bickel, Alexander M., 565, 1192, 1197
Bickford, Charlene Bangs, *as contributor*, 843–845, 1218
Biddle, Nicholas, 132, 144–145, 377, 597, 775, 1303
Biddle, Thomas, 2066
Biden, Joseph R., Jr., 1202, 1203
Bidwell, Barnabas, 983
Biennial budget, 2176
Bierstadt, Albert, 289, 328
Biffle, Les, 158, *1777*, 1778
Big Four of the Senate, 49, 53, 180, 1013, *1014*, 1547, 1867
    Philosophers Club, 387
    see also Aldrich, Nelson W.; Allison, William B.; Platt, Orville H.; Spooner, John C.
Bigger bite amendment, 2177
"Big government" issues. *See* Economic policy; Federalism; New Deal
Big Jim McClain (film), 1425
Bilateral foreign assistance, 863–864
Bilbo, Theodore G., **158–159**, 1406
Bilingual Education Act of 1968, 965
Bilingualism policies, 359, 688, 693
Bill Digest, 502
Billington, James H., 1292, 1293

Bureaucracy, *continued*
deficiency bills, **615**
desegregation, 355
employee political activity ban, **944–945**
executive branch employees, 791–792
funding, 242, 741
General Accounting Office role, 901–904
growth, *1804*
historical development, 224–225, 791
legislative vetoes, 564–565
oversight, 901 904, **1510–1513**
structural change, 226–227
tenure of bureaucrats, 793
see also Agencies, federal; Civil service; Executive branch; Federalism
Bureau of Agricultural Economics, 1763
Bureau of Air Commerce, 1972
Bureau of Alcohol, Tobacco, and Firearms, 48
Bureau of Corporations, 675
Bureau of Education (1870–1939), 684; *see also* Education, Department of
"Bureau of Education" (Longworth-Garner Capitol hideaway), 45, 387, 901, 1022; *see also* "Board of Education"
Bureau of Indian Affairs, 953, 1115, 1116, 1118
Bureau of Investigation. *See* Federal Bureau of Investigation
Bureau of Labor, 1227
Bureau of Land Management, 1638, 2157
Bureau of Mines, 1762
Bureau of Reclamation, 28, 759, 760, 1637, 1762
Bureau of the Budget, 208, 209, 789, 796, 941, 1493, 1644, 1762; *see also* Office of Management and Budget
Bureau of the Census, *227*
Burford, Anne, 767
Burger, Timothy J., *as contributor,* 1528–1530, 1977–1980
Burger, Warren, 1092, 1473
Burges, Tristam, 1078
Burgess, John W., 1018
Burgess, Susan R., *as contributor,* 2097–2100
Burgh, James, 1945
Burk, Francis L., Jr., 1272
Burke, Edmund, 1553, 1717, 2126
Burke, Edward R., 182
Burke, James A., 638
Burke, Robert E., *as contributor,* 2123–2124
Burke, Thomas, 978
Burke, Yvonne Brathwaite, 173, 175, 2137
Burkean trustee, 2178
Burke v. Barnes (1987), 2053

Burke-Wadsworth Selective Service Training Act of 1940. *See* Selective Training and Service Act of 1940
Burleson, Albert S., 310, 774
Burlesque. *See* Humor and satire
Burlingame treaty of 1868, 342
Burlington Railroad, 1227
Burnett, Henry C., 644
Burnham, Walter Dean, 1555
Burns, Arthur, 601, 634
Burns, James MacGregor, 56, 1033
Burns, John A. (Jack), 946
Burns, Ken, 158
Burns v. Richardson (1966), 63
Burnweit, Richard C., *as contributor,* 233–234, 1418–1419, 1687, 1838, 1964
Burr, Aaron, 149, 232–233, 593, 942, 982, 989, 1342
duel with Hamilton (Alexander), 233, 2065
presidential election of 1800, 1466, 1602–1603, 1783, 1836, 1993
Tennessee statehood, 1941
Burr (Vidal), 1301
Burrell, Barbara C., *as contributor,* 802–807
Burr-Wilkinson conspiracy of 1804–1805, 607
Burton, Harold H. *593*, 632, 955, 963, *1287*, *1991*; *see also* Hospital Survey Act of 1946
Burton, Joseph R., 602, 758, 759, 1427
Burton, Phillip, 189, **233–234**, 633
Burton, Sala, 2137
Burton, Theodore E., 758, *1570*
BUS. *See* Bank of the United States
Busbey, L. White, 267
Bush, George H. W., **234–236**, 654, 1366, 1558, 2028
abortion policy, 1088, 1710
arms control, 99
budget policy, 213, 221, 235–236, 601, 679, 1494
cabinet, 1967
civil rights policy, 361, 362
congressional majority and minority, *658*, 723
defense policy, 89–90, 235, 236, 624
disability legislation, 638
drug abuse policy, 588, 1431
economic policy, 383
education policy, 690
energy policy, 743, 748, 753
environmental policy, 379, 768, 1447
executive order use, 1585–1586
family policy, 2146
flag desecration issue, 848
foreign policy, 1158, 1169
health policy, 951, 960
Iran-contra affair, 2134
legislative success, 1587
line-item veto request, 1162

nominee confirmation problems, 456
Panama invasion, 1520
Persian Gulf War, 872, 873–874, **1538–1539**, 1584
pocket veto use, 2053
popularity decline, 236
presidential appointments, 241, 477
presidential campaigns, 383, 395, 719, 728
presidential programs, 235–236, 395
regulatory policy, 1700
as representative, 234–235
rescission authority, 1724
roll-call vote successes, 235, *1035*
savings and loan crisis, 1758, 1759
trade policy, 1921
urban policy, 236, 2024–2025
vetoes, 236, 261, 362, 443, 564, 803, 945, 1160, 1346
vice presidency, 235, 1999
war powers, 461, 622, 2099
Bush, Neil, 1759
Bush, Vannevar, 1347, 1441, 1763
Bushfield, Vera C., 2136
Business
corporate income tax, 1926
federal controls, 672, 674
federal preemption statutes, *405*
health and safety regulation, 1492, 1694–1695
influence on Congress, 1815
interest group role, 1131–1132, 1137, 1303, 1311
New Deal legislation, 1445–1446
political action committees, 1549, 1551
price regulation, 809–810, 1692, 1730
regulation and deregulation, **1692–1703**, 1695
Republican party alliance, 1720, 1721
see also Antitrust legislation; Banking; Commerce power; Currency and finance; Economic policy; Government corporations; Interstate commerce; Tariffs and trade
Business district redevelopment, 2016–2018
Business Roundtable, 1132
Busing, 361–362
Bus Regulatory Reform Act of 1982, 1975, 1976
Bustamante, Albert, 965
Butler, Andrew P., 204, 1897, 2064
Butler, Benjamin, 1359
Butler, C. M., 334
Butler, John G., 333, 335
Butler, Marion, 1569
Butler, Paul, 1671
Butler, Roderick R., 643
Butler, Walter H., 1443
Butterfield, Alexander, 2108, 2111
By-election, 2178

Center for Legislative Archives, 86
Center for Responsive Politics, 63
Center for Strategic and International
    Studies, 1958
Center for the Book, The, 1289, 1292
Center on Budget and Policy Priorities,
    1958
Central Arizona Project, 114
Central cities. *See* Urban policy
Central clearance, 2179
Central Intelligence Agency, **320–321**,
    868, 1449
    black budget, 169, 321, 392, 394
    Boland Amendment, 188, 394
    Bush (George) directorship, 235
    Cold War excesses, 394
    congressional investigations, 1149,
        1150
    covert actions, 1128–1129
    creation of, 93, 95, 320
    domestic operations, 1129
    oversight of, 229, 321, 345, 394, 618,
        1122, 1124, 1126, 1127, 1325
    Reagan (Ronald) policy, 394
Central Intelligence Agency Act of 1949,
    169, 1128
Central Intelligence Group, 1126
Central Pacific Railroad, 672, 1139,
    1663, 1720, 1970
CEQ. *See* Council on Environmental
    Quality
Ceracci, Giuseppe, 283
Ceremonial activities, **321–325**
    Bicentennial of Congress, 157–158,
        285
    commemorations, 325
    funerals and lying-in-state, 298, *299*,
        325
    inaugurations, 323–324
Certificate of election, 2179
CETA. *See* Comprehensive Employment
    and Training Act of 1973
CFE Treaty (1991). *See* Conventional
    Armed Forces in Europe (CFE)
    Treaty
CFTC. *See* Commodity Futures Trading
    Commission
Chad, 2099
Chadha, Jagdish, 1092; *see also*
    *Immigration and Naturalization
    Service v. Chadha*
Chafe, William Henry, 802
Chafee, John H., 770, 1527, 1728
Chain stores. *See* Retail stores
Chairman, chair, 2179
Chairman's mark, 2179
Challenger (space shuttle), 1769
Chalmers, David, *as contributor*,
    1426–1427
Chalmette Monument, 1440
Chamberlain, George E., 2148
Chamberlain, Joseph, 423
Chamberlain, Lawrence H., 1023, 1275

Chamber of Commerce, U.S., 693, 956,
    1131, 1135, 1142, 1305
    congressional voting ratings, 2088
Chambers, John Whiteclay, II, 526–528
Chambers, Whittaker, 1470, 2007
Chambers, **325–331**
    cloakrooms, **385**
    galleries, **897–899**
    House of Representatives, *272*, 276,
        281, 282, 289, *322*, **325–328**, *372*,
        730, *731*, *1055*
    Senate, 281, 282, 289, 323, **328–331**,
        998
Chamber seniority, 1795
Chamizal controversy, 1395
Champagne, Anthony, *as contributor*,
    523–524, 591–592, 900–901, 1076,
    1343–1344, 1528
Champion v. Ames (1903), 583
Chandler, Albert B. (Happy), 1215, 1992
Chandler, William E., 1008
Chandler, Zachariah, 180, 308, 451, 928,
    1204, 1397, 1659, 1720
Chandler Act of 1938, 145, 146
Chanler, John W., 643
Channing, W. H., 333
Chaplains, **331–336**
    table of, 332–335
Chaplin, Charlie, 1425
Chapman, John G., 289
Chapman, Richard N., *as contributor*,
    2149–2155
Charitable donations, 105, 106
Charles I, king of England, 159–160, 968
Charles II, king of England, 160, 969
Chartrand, Robert Lee, *as contributor*,
    1937–1939
Chase, J. Mitchell, *1928*
Chase Manhattan Bank, 1532
Chase, Salmon P., **336–337**, *597*, 831,
    1193, 1439, 1500, 1659
    antislavery, 336–337, 348, 998
    bank charters, 133
    Civil War financing, 598
    Johnson (Andrew) impeachment
        proceedings, 1003
Chase, Samuel, 233, 554, 593, 607, 1357
    impeachment proceedings, 914, 1102,
        1103, 1104, 1172, 1667
Chautauqua movement, 1048
Chavez, Dennis, **337–338**, 964–965, 966,
    1465
CHC. *See* Congressional Hispanic
    Caucus
Cheatham, Henry P., 172
"Checkers speech" (Nixon), 1470
Checks and balances, **338–339**,
    1578–1579, 1712
    accountability, **2–4**
    appropriations power, 69, 72–73, 78
    bicameralism, 156, 157, 460
    congressional powers, 460–461,
        553–556

statutory reversal, 561–562, 562–565
    see also Separation of powers
Cheney, Richard B., 623, 880, 2156,
    2158
Cherokee Indians, 1113, 1114, 1500,
    1705
Cherryholmes, Cleo, 2086
Chesapeake (ship), 6, 1544, 1836
Chesapeake and Delaware Act of 1825,
    1139
Chesapeake and Delaware Canal, 1138
Chesapeake and Ohio Canal Company,
    1969
Chestnut, James, Jr., 645
Cheves, Langdon, 144, 2095
*Chevron v. Natural Resources Defense
    Council, Inc.* (1984), 1277
Cheyenne Indians, *1113*
Chicago, Illinois, Democratic party,
    1091
Chicago-Mobile railroad, 1636
Chicano members. *See* Hispanic
    members
Chickamauga and Chattanooga
    National Military Park Act of 1890,
    1448
Chickasaw Indians, 1500–1501
Child abuse, legislation, 804, 805, 806,
    807; *see also* Child labor
Child Abuse Amendments of 1984, 805,
    806, 807
Child Abuse Prevention and Treatment
    Act of 1973, 804
Child care
    church-state debate, 1710
    legislation, 803, 805, 1709, 2142,
        2143, 2145
Child-Care Programs Act of 1990, 1709
Child labor, 154, **339–341**, 561–562,
    659, 675
    legislation, 801, 1226, 1227, 1229,
        1243
    see also Twentieth Amendment
Child Nutrition Act of 1966, 804, 806
Children, Family, Drugs, and Alcoholism
    Subcommittee, Senate, 48
Children's Bureau, 802, 954, 2140
Children's Caucus, 182, 803
Children's Defense Fund, 1850
Children, Youth, and Families
    Committee, House Select,
    341–341, 433, 802–803, 1850
Child Support Enforcement
    Amendments of 1984, 803, 805,
    2146
Child welfare. *See* Child abuse; Child
    labor; Family policies; Social
    welfare and poverty
Chile, 393, 394
China
    Cold War policies, 392, 447
    Eisenhower (Dwight D.) policies,
        1223

Cooperative Research and Development Act of 1984, 1769
COPE. *See* Committee on Political Education
Copeland, Royal S., 182
Copland, Aaron, 110
Copper Caucus, 182
Copperheads, 1140, 2028
Coppola, Francis Ford, 1425
Copyright Act of 1790, 575, 576
Copyright Act of 1831, 575
Copyright Act of 1870, 283, 575
Copyright Act of 1909, 105, 575
Copyright Revision Act of 1976, 105, 575
Copyright, trademarks, and patents, **574–577**
  bankruptcy law, 146
  copyright registration, 1272, 1288, 1290
  as enumerated congressional power, 551, 576
  intellectual property, 104–105
  landmark legislation, 576–576
  private bills, 1627
  telephone, 436
Corbin, David A., *as contributor,* 2122–2123
Corcoran, Thomas G., 1670, 1783
Cordon, Guy, 431, 2182
Cordon Rule (Senate), 431, 2182
Corlew, Robert E., *as contributor,* 1333–1334, 1941
Cornelius, Edgar Livingstone, 1802
Cornell, Ezra, 1636
Corn-for-porn swap (1991), 147
Corporations. *See* Antitrust legislation; Business; Economic policy; Government corporations
Corps of Engineers. *See* Army Corps of Engineers
Corps of Topographical Engineers, 283, 798, 1761
Correspondence to Congress, 577–578
Corruption. *See* Ethics and corruption in Congress
Corrupt Practices Act. See Federal Corrupt Practices Act of 1925
Corwin, Edward S., 867, 2054
Corwin, Thomas, 578–579, 611, 1077, 1079, 1500, 1823
"Cosa Nostra," 586
Cosmopolitan magazine, 1426, 1427, 1615, 1810
Cosponsor, 2182; *see also* Sponsorship
Costaggini, Filippo, 289
Costello, Frank, 2135
Costello, George A., 167
  as contributor, 799
Costigan-Wagner Act of 1935, 355
Cotton, Norris, *403,* 1084
Cotton farming, 23, 31, 32, 35, 36
Couden, Henry N., 333, *336*

Council of Economic Advisers, 212, 668, 677, 681, 736, 791, 1234
Council of Scholars, 1292
Council of State Governments, 1145
Council on Competitiveness, 1702
Council on Environmental Quality, 1442
Counterintelligence, 1126
Counterpart funds, 2182
Country party, 1727
County of Cortland, New York v. United States, 2015
Courtesies and conventions, congressional, 475–477
Court of Claims. *See* Claims Court, U.S.
Court of Military Review, 1399
Court-packing fight, 407, **579–580**, 1736
  congressional response, 565–566, 1022
  conservative coalition role, 182, 523, 579, 631, 1025
  constitutional issues, 565
  Democratic split over, 148, 182, 1460
  impact of, 817, 1230, 1737
  opponents, 1187, 1201, 1322, 1338, 1413–1414, 1478, 1722, 1838, 2124
  Rayburn (Sam) role, 1670
  Robinson (Joseph T.) role, 1731–1732
  supporters, 131, 148, 168
Courts. *See* Judicial review; Judiciary and Congress; Supreme Court *headings; specific courts*
Courts-martial, 1398, 1399
Courts Subcommittee, Senate, 1196
Covenant Chain, 1120
Covert operations. *See* Black budget; Central Intelligence Agency; Intelligence policy
Covode, John, 451, *580,* 581
Covode committtee, **580–581**
Cowan, Edgar, 371, 1467
Cox, Allyn, 289, 291
Cox, Archibald, 434, 1473, 2108, 2109
Cox, Edward E., 2064, 2152
Cox, James M., *869*
Cox, Samuel S. (Sunset), **581**, 1005, 1077, 1078
Cox, William R., 1778
Coxey, Jacob Sechler, 582
Coxey's Army, 582
Coyne, William J., 1366
Cozy triangle. *See* Iron triangle
CPSC. *See* Consumer Product Safety Commission
CQ. *See* Congressional Quarterly
CQ Almanac, 514
CQ's Guide to 1990 Congressional Redistricting, 500
CQ's WASHINGTON ALERT (data base), 497
CQ Weekly Report, 501
Crabb, Cecil V., Jr., *as contributor,* 867–875
Craft, Edward O., 1272

Craig, Barbara Hinkson, *as contributor,* 1092–1093, 2047–2050
Cramer, William C., 855
Cramer v. United States (1945), 1980
Cranch, John, 282
Crane, Daniel B., 643, 781
Crane, Stephen, 1301
Crane, Winthrop, 1427
Cranford, John R., *as contributor,* 1757–1759
Cranston, Alan, 140, 141–142, 260, *871,* 1759, *2036*
  disability legislation, 638
  Keating Five scandal, 141–142, 543, 644, 646, 783
  reprimand, 644, 646, 783
Cranston-Gonzalez National Affordable Housing Act of 1990, 1071, 1073
Crary, Isaac E., 1397
Crawford, Coe I., 180, 1854
Crawford, Samuel J., 1741
Crawford, Thomas, *286,* 289, 297, 323, 377
Crawford, William H., 6, 179, 180, 247, 309, 907, 989, 1174, 1342, 1411, 1554, 1603, 1605
Crawford County, Pennsylvania, direct primary, 2074
Crawford Fitting Co. v. J. T. Gibbons, Inc. (1987), 1196
Credentials, 2182
Credit. *See* Banking; Debt; Mortgage financing
Credit authority, 2183
Credit-claiming, 2183
Crédit Mobilier, 396, **582**, 775, 899, 929, 1359, 1500, 1613, 1664, 2033
  censures, 643, 775
Creek Indians, 1120, 1406, 1500
"Crime against Kansas" speech (Sumner), 611, 612, 1897
Crime and justice, **582–588**
  Clinton (Bill) crime bill, 384
  commerce clause application, 407, 583–588
  congressional investigations, 1154
  defendants' rights, 159, 160, 162, 351, 352–353, 556, 583
  executive privilege application, 795
  ex post facto laws, 556, **797**
  landmark legislation, 351, 2023
  maritime industry, 1225–1226, 1392
  Military Justice, Uniform Code of, **1398–1400**
  postal service issues, 583, 587
  presidential assailants, 1599
  Senate investigations, 585–586, **1207–1208**, 1211, 1213–1214, 1328
  violence against Congress. *See* Violence against Congress
  see also Juvenile delinquency; Organized crime
Crime Committee, House Select, 1431

New Deal coalition, 1559, 1562, 1778, 1780–1781
Oklahoma politics, 1501
party committees, **1524–1525**
political action committee support, 1551
presidential elections, 1721, 1722
racial segregation acceptance, 1781
sectionalism, 628, 997, 999, 1003, 1015
slavery issue, 1719, 1822
South Carolina politics, 1853
southern bloc, 1008, 1722, 1844, 1854, 1855; *see also* Conservative coalition
strength, 1720
tariff and trade issue, 1912–1913, 1914–1915, 1921–1922
tax issues, 1818, 1819
Tennessee politics, 1941
Texas politics, 1957
Virginia politics, 2067, 2134
World War II, 2149–2150
see also Democratic Study Group; Fair Deal; Great Society; New Deal; New Freedom; New Frontier
Democratic Policy Committee, Senate, 1217
Democratic-Republicans, definition of, 2183; *see also* Jeffersonian Republicans
Democratic Steering and Policy Committee, 1346, 1565, 1797, 1864, 1881
Democratic Study Group, 182, 312, 313, **633–634**, 1030, 1031, 1033, 1038, 1040, 1282, 1325, 1527, 1713, 1845, 1864
chairs, 234, 317
Civil Rights Act of 1964, 363–364
creation and purpose, 632, 633
House rules reform recommendations, 1798–1799
major reforms, 633–634
Demographic information. *See* Census
Demographics of Congress. *See* Congress, demographic profile
Demonstration Cities and Metropolitan Development Act of 1966. *See* Model Cities program
Demonstrations. *See* Protests
Denby, Edwin, 1935, 1935–1936, 1936
Denfeld, Louis E., 39
DeNiro, Robert, 1425
Denmark, 1479, 1949, 1953, 1954
Dennis, David W., 2110
Dennis v. United States (1951), 51
Denunciation, Senate, 1909
Department of. . . . *See* key word, e.g., State, Department of
Department of Defense Appropriation Authorization Act of 1976, 2144

Department of Defense Reorganization Acts. *See* Defense Reorganization Act of 1958; Defense Reorganization Act of 1986
Department of Education Act of 1867, 683
Department of Education Organization Act of 1979, 2023, 2049
Department of Energy Organization Act of 1977, 747, 750
Department of Housing and Urban Development Act of 1965, 1072
Department of Transportation Act of 1966, 13, 2023
Department of Veterans' Affairs Act of 1988, 2043
Departments and agencies. *See* Agencies, federal; Bureaucracy; Executive branch; *specific names*
Departments of Labor and Health, Education, and Welfare Appropriations Act of 1977, 2145
Dependent Pension Act of 1890, 1690, 1842, 2040, 2046
Depew, Chauncey, 1426, 1427
Deportation, 50, 351, 352
Deposit insurance, 135, 136, 137, 142, 600, 634, 676, 680, 735
Depository Institutions Act of 1982, 142
Depository Institutions Deregulation and Monetary Control Act of 1980, 136, 140, **634**, 1073, 1757–1758
Depression, economic
agricultural, 21–22, 27, 675, 941, 947
budget balancing, *218*
congressional response to, 631, 1022, 1023–1024
Coxey's Army, 582
embargo of 1807–1809 effects, 734
Hawley-Smoot Tariff Act effects, 947
Hoover (Herbert) policies, 676, 1050
Long (Huey P.) policies, 1315–1316
protective tariff effects, 671
Roosevelt (Franklin D.) policies. *See* New Deal
see also Panic *headings*; Recession
De Priest, Jesse, 635
De Priest, Oscar, 172, 173, 174, 175, **635**, 1535
Deregulation. *See* Regulation and deregulation
Derthick, Martha
as contributor, 929–931, 1840–1841
on price and entry regulation, 1700
Derwinski, Edward J., 880, 1090
Deschler, Lewis, **635–636**, 850–851, 880, 1016, 1062–1063, 1350, 1522, 1523
Deschler's Precedents of the United States House of Representatives, 1062, 1523, 1577
Deschler's Rules of Order, 636
Descriptive representation, 66
Desegregation. *See* Civil rights

Desert Land Act of 1877, 1451, 1635
Desert Shield (operation), 1538
Desert Storm (operation), 1539, 2099
Desert Storm Resolution, 2099
Desk, 2184
De Sola, Abraham, *1705*
Détente. *See* Arms control; Cold War
Detention Review Board, 352
Detzer, Dorothy, 1488
Development Loan Fund, 878
D'Ewart, Wesley A., 1414
Deweese, John T., censure, 643
Dewey, George, 298, 324, 1857
Dewey, Melvil, 517
Dewey, Thomas E., 632, 636, 939, 1723, 1906, 1922, 1929, 1990
DFL party. *See* Democratic-Farmer-Labor party
DIA. *See* Defense Intelligence Agency
Diagnosis-related groups, 1362
Diary (John Adams), 973
Diary in America, A (Marryat), 43
Diaz-Balart, Lincoln, 965
Dick Acts. *See* Militia Acts of 1903 and 1908
Dickey-Lincoln School public electricity-generating project, 748
Dickins, Asbury, 1778
Dickinson, John, 112, 968, 974, 976
Dickinson, Lester J., 21, 808
Dickstein, Samuel, *1131*
DiClerico, Robert E., as contributor, 1600–1603, 1996–1997
Dictionaries on Congress, 494
Dictionary of American Politics, 1303
DIDMCA. *See* Depository Institutions Deregulation and Monetary Control Act of 1980
Dien Bien Phu (1954), 696
Dies, Martin, Jr., 447, 1141, 1957, 2006
Dies Committee, House. *See* Un-American Activities Committee, House
Diggs, Charles C., Jr., *174*, 175, 643, 650
Dilatory motions, **636**
Dilger, Robert Jay, as contributor, 814–825
Dill, Clarence C., 440; *see also* Communications Act of 1934
Dill-Connery bill (1934), 1840
Dillinger, John, 584
Dillingham, William P., 1094
Dillingham Commission, 1094–1095
Dingell, John D., 738, 739, 953, 1699–1700
Dingley, Nelson, Jr., 43, 1690
Dingley Act of 1884, 1226
Dingley Tariff Act of 1897, 49, 53, 671, 1011, 1335, 1547, 1690, 1913, 1918
Dining rooms. *See* Cuisine of Congress
Dinsmore, Robert, 1364
Dioxin exposure legislation, 2043, 2044
Diplomacy. *See* Foreign policy

Dyer, Rolla E., 955
Dymally, Mervyn M., 175
Dynasties, political. *See* Political
    dynasties

E

Eagleton, Thomas F., 1121, 1332, 1408
Early organization, 2184
Earmarks (budget), 1767, 2184
Earned Income Tax Credit Act of 1975,
    1849, 1850
Eastland, James O., 355, **667–668**, 858,
    1033, 1203, 1406, 1609, 2155
*Eastland v. United States Serviceman's
    Fund* (1975), 425, 551, 1156, 1895
Eaton, Charles A., 1986, 2011
Eaton, John (educator), 684
Eaton, John H. (senator), 935
EC. *See* European Community
ECIA. *See* Education Consolidation and
    Improvement Act of 1981
Eckert, Ralph Lowell, *as contributor*,
    588–589
Economic Committee, Joint, **668**
    chairs, 662
    creation of, 677, 681, 736
    purpose, 668, 677
    staff, 434
Economic Cooperation Act of 1948,
    1470
Economic Equity Act, 803, 2140
Economic Growth and Credit
    Formation Subcommittee, House,
    137–138
Economic Opportunity Act of 1964, 350,
    668–669, 677, 681, 693, 932, 957,
    1238, 1472, 1846, 2019, 2022
Economic Opportunity Amendments of
    1966, 806, 2144
Economic policy, **669–681**
    child labor laws, **339–341**
    commerce power, **404–408**
    conservative position, 529, 531
    Democratic party, 629–630
    executive powers issues, 623–624
    Fair Deal, 631–632
    federal responsibilities, 668
    Great Society, 677–678
    House Ways and Means Committee,
        2112–2117
    inflation, 678
    Joint Economic Committee, **668**
    landmark legislation, *378*, 680–681,
        736
    New Deal, 631, 676–677, 764,
        1023–1024, **1458–1461**, 1734–1736
    1920s, 675
    nineteenth century, **669–674**, 1001
    Radical Republicans, 194
    railroads, 1660–1666

Reagan (Ronald) program, **223–224**,
    655, 678–679, 1674–1675
Roosevelt (Franklin D.) program. *See
    subhead* New Deal *above*
social welfare and poverty,
    1841–1852
Temporary National Economic
    Committee, **1940**
twentieth century, **674–681**
World War I, 675
World War II, 677, 2154–2155
see also Agriculture; Appropriations;
    Banking; Bank of the United
    States; Budget process; Currency
    and finance; Internal
    improvements; Public lands;
    Railroads; Regulation and
    deregulation; Silver issue; Tariffs
    and trade; Taxation; Transportation
Economic Policy Institute, 1958
Economic Recovery Tax Act of 1981,
    106, 218, 679, 681, 1926, 1930,
    1931, 2023, 2024
Economic Report of the President, 668,
    736
Economic Stabilization Agency, 624
Economic Stabilization and Rural
    Development Subcommittee,
    Senate, 140, 141
Economic Support Fund, 864
Economy Act of 1932, 796
Economy Act of 1933, 2039, 2041
Edgar, Walter B., *as contributor*,
    1852–1853
Edgerton, Henry W., 565
Edmunds, George F., **681–682**, 1007,
    1608, 1815, *1816*, 2033
Edmunds Anti-Polygamy Act of 1882,
    682, 1707, 2025
Edmunds-Tucker Act of 1882, 682,
    2025
Education, **682–691**
    academic exchange programs, 107
    agricultural, 20, 21, 28, 689, 1415,
        1416, 1636
    bilingual, 688, 693
    congressional committees. *See*
        Education and Labor Committee,
        House; Labor and Human
        Resources Committee, Senate
    congressional staff, 1876
    contemporary issues, 690–691
    desegregation, 1835, 1855, 1858,
        1888, 2077
    District of Columbia, 648, 650
    elementary and secondary assistance,
        686–688
    equal opportunity, 165, 355, 682, 683,
        686–688, 689, 690, 2143–2144
    federal role in, 683–690, 956, 1419,
        2020, 2024
    Fulbright Scholars Act of 1946, 893,
        894–895

grants-in-aid, 929–930
Green, Edith S., 933, 1507
handicapped provisions, 688
higher. *See* Colleges and universities
integration, 165, 355, 361–362, 365,
    563, 687, 695, 950
integration opposition, 237
intern and fellowship programs,
    1142–1143
landmark legislation, 689, 2022–2023;
    see also Elementary and Secondary
    Education Act of 1965; National
    Defense Education Act of 1958;
    Student aid; Vocational Education
    Act of 1963
medical, 956, 957
military. *See* Service academies
national system proposal, 684
Native American, 1118
nineteenth century, 683–684
pages, 1517–1518
parochial school aid, 1706–1707
preschool, 669, 693, 2019
public land grants. *See subhead*
    agricultural *above*
school lunch program, 26, 29
Senate Labor and Human Resources
    Committee, 1237, 1238
sex discrimination, 564, 688, 689,
    2143–2144
Student Athlete Right-to-Know Act of
    1992, 1869
universities and government research,
    1767
veterans, 677, 685–686, 689, 912, 962,
    2036, 2042, 2044, 2142
vocational, 684–685, 689, 1842, **2070**
war on poverty programs, 669, 689,
    2019
women's rights, 2143–2144; *see also
    subhead* equal opportunity *above*;
    subhead sex discrimination *above*
see also Science and technology;
    Smithsonian Institution
Education, Department of, 2020, 2023
    creation of, 307, 1035
    educational discrimination policy, 687
    forerunner, 683–684
    House Education and Labor
        Committee, 693
Educational vouchers, 1710
Education Amendments of 1956,
    684–685
Education Amendments of 1972, 564,
    688, 689, 962–963, 1196, 2048,
    2143, 2144
Education Amendments of 1974, 564,
    688, 689, 2049
Education Amendments of 1976, 2143
Education and Labor Committee,
    House, **691–694**, 1441, 1492, 2014
    Burton, Philip, 233–234
    chairs, 692–693, 778

EPA. *See* Environmental Protection Agency
Episcopal Church, 1372, 1373
Eppes, John W., 1171
Epstein, Leon D., 1553, 1561
  as contributor, 1240–1242, 2133
Equal Access Act of 1984, 1709
Equal Credit Opportunity Act of 1974, 2144
Equal Employment Opportunity Act of 1972, 1235, 2144
Equal Employment Opportunity Commission, 354, 357, 362, 365, 368, 1181
  hostility to women's rights, 2143
Equal Employment Opportunity Commission v. Arabian American Oil (1991), 1196–1197
Equal-footing doctrine, 1883
Equal opportunity. *See* Civil rights; Education, equal opportunity; Employment, discrimination and equal opportunity
Equal pay, 2141, 2142
Equal Pay Act of 1963, 933, 1234, 1236, 2143, 2144
Equal population doctrine, 62, 64, 653
Equal proportions, method of, 2185
Equal protection clause. *See under* Fourteenth Amendment
Equal Rights Amendment, **771–773**, 774, 1035, 1036, 2142, 2143, 2144
  deadline extension, 2145
  opposiiton, 1896
  religious right opposition, 1710
  state ratification, *772*
ERA. *See* Equal Rights Amendment
Era of Good Feelings, 1171, 1411, 2030
ERDA. *See* Energy Research and Development Administration
Erdman Act of 1898, 1227, 1228, 1232
Erie Canal, 1969
Erikson, Robert S., *as contributor*, 1108–1110
ERTA. *See* Economic Recovery Tax Act of 1981
Ervin, Samuel J., Jr., 198, 360, **773–774**, 880, *918*, 1037, 1118, 1623, 2089
  on Constitution, 2055–2056
  Equal Rights Amendment opposition, 773
  Senate Watergate Committee, 1148, 1473, 1480, 1621, 2108, 2111
Ervin Committee. *See* Watergate Committee, Senate
Esch-Cummins Act of 1920. *See* Transportation Act of 1920
Escobar, Marisol, 291
ESEA. *See* Elementary and Secondary Education Act of 1965
ESF. *See* Economic Support Fund
Eshoo, Anna G., 2137
Eslick, Willa M. B., 2136

Espionage Act of 1917, 164, 349, **774–775**, 1141, 1839, 1980, 2147
  description, 350
  opponents, 192
Espy, Mike, 175
Establishment of the Office of National Parks, Buildings, and Reservations Act of 1916. *See* National Park Service Act
Estes, Billy Sol, 920
Etheridge, Emerson, 380
Ethical Standards Subcommittee, Senate, 1048
Ethics and corruption in Congress, **775–785**, 1810, 1866
  Abscam, **2**, 642, 644, 776, 780–781
  alcohol consumption, 43, 44–45
  Baker (Robert G.) scandal, 126, 127, 778, 787, 1040
  Bilbo (Theodore G.) dealings, 159
  Blaine (James G.) Mulligan letters, 178
  bribery, 1810, 1866
  cause for retirements, 1381
  Common Cause whistle-blowing, 434
  constituency casework, 543–544
  Covode committee, **580–581**
  Crédit Mobilier case. *See* Crédit Mobilier
  discipline measures, 480, **641–646**, 776–778; *see also* Censure; Expulsion
  ethics committees; *See* Ethics Committee, Senate Select; Standards of Official Conduct Committee, House
  fictional depictions, 1081, 1084, 1301
  financial disclosure, **840–843**
  franking, 886–887, 888
  Gilded Age, 1005–1006
  Hays (Wayne L.) case, 778, 951, 1041, 1051
  honoraria, 782, **1048–1049**
  House Administration Committee, 951, 1051
  House bank scandal, 713, 720, 780, 1044–1045, **1053–1054**, 1109, 1121, 1538, 1715, 1716, 1734, 1860, 1878
  House post office scandals, 1121, 1528, 1716, 1860, **1878–1879**
  House Standards of Official Conduct Committee, 1878–1880
  Illinois members, 1091
  impact on public confidence, 482
  Inspector General of the House, 1121
  jokes about, 1082, 1083–1084
  Keating Five bank regulation scandal, 141–142, 543, 644, 646, 776, 781–782, 783, 1045
  lobbying, 1303, 1613
  maritime industry, 1392
  1940s–1960s developments, 786–787

1970s reforms, 779–780, 1040–1041, 1716
1980s developments, 780–782
1990s scandals, 1044–1045
Non-Legislative and Financial Services director, 1473–1474
perquisites abuse, 1538
Powell (Adam Clayton, Jr.) case, 642, 644, 778, 1040, 1575, 1879
public land policy, 673
Rostenkowski (Dan) case, 2116
savings and loan scandal, 1715, 1716, 1758–1759
Senate Banking Committee, 142
Senate Rules and Administration Committee, 1743
speech or debate immunity, 1866
standards, evolution of, 778–780, 781–782
territorial expansion issues, 1950
as Twain (Mark) satirical theme, 1081, 1084
Wright (James C., Jr.) financial dealings, 781, 2156–2157
see also Campaign financing; Ethics in government; Interest groups; Lobbying; Political action committees; Sex scandals; Teapot Dome
Ethics Committee, House. *See* Standards of Official Conduct Committee, House
Ethics Committee, Senate Select, 432, **785–788**, 840, 841, 886
  bipartisanship, 778
  classified information leaks, 1125
  creation of, 778, 1040
  discipline of members, 641, 646, 784
  franking rules, 887
  Keating Five bank regulation hearings, 141–142, 543, 783, 784
  members, 480, 787
  predecessor, 127, 777, 778, 785, 786
  savings and loan crisis, 1759
  see also Financial disclosure; Rules and Administration Committee, Senate; Standards of Official Conduct Committee, House
Ethics in government
  accountability, 3
  air force procurement, 39, 1213
  Harding administration. *See* Teapot Dome
  labor unions, 695
  major scandals, 775–776
  Medicaid and Medicare, 18
  see also Ethics and corruption in Congress
Ethics in Government (Douglas), 662
Ethics in Government Act of 1978, 456, 779–780, 781, 840, 841, 842, 920, 1041, 1417, 1880

Extensions of remarks, 515, **800**
Extraction power (House), 2186

F

FAA. *See* Federal Aviation Agency;
    Federal Aviation Administration
Fabens, Joseph, 1949
Factions
    defined, 179
    intraparty, 1554, 1590–1591
    Madison (James) view of, 1130, 1131,
        1132, 1134, 1302, 1309, 1311
    see also Blocs and coalitions
Faculty taxes, 1924
Fail Safe (film), 1425
Fairbanks, Charles W., 1111, 1427
Fair Credit Reporting Act of 1970, 1623,
    1624
Fair Deal, 631–632, 1581, 1990
Fair Employment Practice Committee,
    Senate Wartime, 159
Fair-employment-practices bill (1940s),
    338, 631–632, 677
Fair Employment Practices
    Commission, 355, 1585
Fair Housing Act of 1968, 359–361, 563
Fair Housing Amendments Act of 1974,
    361
Fair Housing Amendments Act of 1988,
    361, 1073, 1074
Fair Labor Standards Act of 1938, 168,
    693, **801–802**, 963, 1026, 1229,
    1230, 1233, 1238, 1482, 2141, 2144
    Amendments of 1974, 408, 1235
    child labor provision, 340–341, 561
    Supreme Court upholding, 407
Fair Packaging and Labeling Act of
    1966, 1965
Fair Trade Commission, 675
Falk, I. S., 955, 956, 1051
Fall, Albert B., 741–742, 764, 784, 941,
    1150, 1161, 1465, 1935
Fallon, George H., 1146, 1650, 2062
*Fame and Peace Crowning George
    Washington* (frieze), 289
Families of members. *See under*
    Members
Family and Medical Leave Act of 1993,
    803, 805, 2139, 2145, 2146
Family Assistance Plan, 806, 1848, 1850,
    2019
Family Educational Rights and Privacy
    Act of 1974, 1624
Family Planning Services and
    Population Research, 804
Family policies, **802–807**
    dysfunctional families, 802, 806–807
    family and medical leave, 803, 805,
        2139, 2145, 2146
    Ford (Gerald) policy, 2144

House Select Committee on Children,
    Youth, and Families, **341–342**
    housing, 1074
    Hyde Amendments, **1088**
    Johnson (Lyndon B.) policy, 932, 2143
    landmark legislation, 804–805
    Nixon (Richard M.) policy, 2144
    welfare aid, 2019, 2022, 2025
    women's rights, 2141, 2142
    see also Abortion; Child labor; Social
        welfare and poverty
Family Preservation Act, 1365
Family Support Act of 1988, 805, 806,
    1849, 1850, 2022, 2025, 2145
Fannie Mae. *See* Federal National
    Mortgage Association
Fannin, Paul J., 1084
Far East policy. *See* Asia; *specific
    countries and wars*
Farewell address, Washington. *See*
    Washington's Farewell Address
Farley, James A., 1179, 1478, 2105
Farm bills. *See* Agriculture; Agriculture
    Committee, House
Farm bloc, 19, 179, **807–809**, 2154
    agrarian third-party movements, 180,
        181
    bipartisanship, 21, 181
    Capper, Arthur, 304
    decline, 181
    Harding (Warren G.) policies, 946
    House Agriculture Committee and,
        31–33, 34
    influence in Congress, 181, 675,
        1020–1021
    interests shared with southern bloc,
        1854
    interwar period, 1780
    Iowa, 1159
    legislative interests, 181
    McNary, Charles L., 1338, 1339
    Senate Agriculture Committee, 35, 36,
        37, 38
Farm Bureau. *See* American Farm
    Bureau Federation
Farm Credit Act of 1933, 23
Farm Credit Administration, 338
Farm Credit banks, 23–24
Farmer-Labor party, 1402, 1563
Farmers' Alliance, 1817
Farmer's Daughter, The (film), 1421, 1425
Farmers Home Administration, 24, 29,
    813, 1074
Farmers Home Administration Act of
    1946, 29
Farmers' National Council, 1020
Farmers Union, 24, 181
Farm Loan Act of 1916, 23
Farm Product Credit Associations, 23
Farm programs. *See* Agriculture; Farm
    bloc
Farm Security Administration, 24, 29,
    1179, 2154

Farnham, Wallace D., 672
    as contributor, 1660–1666
Farnsworth, David L., 466
Farnsworth, Philo T., 291
Farrington, Mary Elizabeth Pruett,
    2136
Fascelli, Dante B., 855, 860
Fast-track procedures, 2186
Father of the House. *See* Dean of the
    House
Faubus, Orval, 950
Fauntroy, Walter E., 648
Fauquier, Francis, 972
Fausold, Martin L., *as contributor*,
    1049–1050
Fazio, Vic, 1365
FBI. *See* Federal Bureau of
    Investigation
FCC. *See* Federal Communications
    Commission
FCEA. *See* Federal Contested Election
    Act of 1969
FDA. *See* Food and Drug Administration
FDIC. *See* Federal Deposit Insurance
    Corporation
Featherbedding, 1908
FEC. *See* Federal Election Commission
FECA. *See* Federal Election Campaign
    Act *headings*
Federal agencies. *See* Agencies, federal;
    Bureaucracy; *specific agencies*
Federal aid
    abortion prohibitions, 1088
    block-grant programs, 755,
        2021–2022
    education policy, 678, 683, 684–690,
        733
    entitlements, 755
    federal standards contingency, 458
    health care, 956, 957, 958, 959–960
    higher education, 962–963
    internal improvements, 671–672
    local and state law enforcement, 586,
        587
    local governments, 678, 2014,
        2016–2024
    mass transit, **2013–2014**, 2020–2021
    mental health, 954
    transportation (nineteenth century),
        672, 757
    urban policy, 236, **2014–2025**
    vocational education, 684–685
    see also Revenue sharing
Federal Aid Highway Act of 1944, 1146,
    1973, 2023
Federal Aid Highway Act of 1956, 1069,
    1973, 1975, 2020, 2023
Federal Aid Highway Act of 1973, 1147,
    2023
Federal Aid Road Act. *See* Rural Post
    Roads Act of 1916
Federal Alcohol Administration Act of
    1935, 46, 48

Twelfth Amendment, 1993, 1994
view of federal power, 1138
War of 1812 opposition, 1887, 2095, 2097
Webster (Daniel) views, 2118
X Y Z affair, 5, **2159**
Federal Labor Relations Authority, 367–368, 369
Federal land bank system, 23
Federal Land Policy and Management Act of 1976, 743, 1638
Federal Maritime Administration, 1972
Federal Maritime Commission, 1693, 1698, 1701
Federal National Mortgage Association (Fannie Mae), 813, 921, 1071, 1072, 1073
Federal Pay Comparability Act of 1971, 1235–1236
Federal Power Commission, 743, 744, 747; see also Federal Energy Regulatory Commission
Federal Property and Administrative Services Act of 1949, 919
Federal Radio Commission, 439, 440, 444
Federal Register, **828**
Federal Register Act of 1935, 828
Federal Regulation of Lobbying Act of 1946, 782, 1305
Federal Relations Act of 1948, 1651, 1652
Federal Reserve Bank Act of 1913, 137, 140, 375, 599, 670, 675, 680, **828–829**, 914, 1019, 1216, 1462, 1629, 1652, 1696
overview, 134
Federal Reserve Notes, 601
Federal Reserve System, 829, 1155, 1528, 1734, 1757, 1779, 1783
creation of, 134, 599, 631, 675, 680
executive power over, 676
Glass (Carter) role, 914, 915
interest rate ceilings, 136, 601
member bank insurance, 137
regulatory powers, 600, 634
Federal Road Act of 1916, 1972
Federal Safety Appliance Act of 1893, 406
Federal Savings and Loan Insurance Corporation, 135, 136, 1069, 1758
Federal Securities Act of 1933. See Securities acts
Federal Security Agency, 684, 954, 955; see also Health, Education, and Welfare, Department of
Federal Trade Commission, 809, 1698
creation of, 680, **829–830**
public utilities investigation, 438, 2124
removal power, 1711
securities oversight, 1782, 1783

Federal Trade Commission Act of 1914, 375, 680, **829–830**, 1462, 1629, 1694, 1696
Federal Trade Commission Amendments of 1980, 2049
Federal Transit Administration, 2014
Federal Travel Act of 1970, 407
Federal Vocational Education Act of 1917. See Smith-Hughes Act of 1917
Federal Water Pollution Control Act Amendments of 1972, 744–745, 759, 761, 768, 769, 1695, 1697
Federal Water Pollution Control Administration, 760
Federal Water Power Act of 1920, 746
Federation of Atomic Scientists, 115
Feerick, John D., as contributor, 1998–2000
Feingold, Russell D., *712*
Feinstein, Dianne, *1743*, 2135, 2136
Feinstein, Estelle F., as contributor, 524–525
Feinstein, Linda, as contributor, 2135–2140
Feldman, Paul, 538
Fellowship programs. See Intern and Fellowship programs
Felton, Rebecca L., 907, 2136, 2138
Feminism. See Equal Rights Amendment; Women's issues and rights
Fencing, 2186
Fenn, Dan H., Jr., 1596
Fenno, Richard F., Jr., 56, 71, 75–76, 114, 138, 532, 535, 859, 1033, 1198, 1260, 1266–1267, 2189
as contributor, 1784–1789
Fenwick, Millicent, 2137
FERC. See Federal Energy Regulatory Commission
Ferejohn, John, 538, 545
Ferguson, Garland, 1940
Ferguson, Homer, 1323
Ferguson, W. T., *1661*
Ferling, John, as contributor, 2102–2105, 2106–2107
Fernald, Bert M., 1161
Fernandez, Antonio M., 965
Fernandez, Joachim O., 965
Fernow, Bernard E., 758
Ferraro, Geraldine A., 830, 1378, 1383, 1467, 2137
Ferrell, Robert H., as contributor, 573–574, 1935–1937, 2147–2149
Ferris, Woodbridge N., 2031
Ferry, Thomas W., *730*, 1608
FERS. See Federal Employees' Retirement System
Fersh, Seymour H., 1183
Fess, Lehr, 635, 1522, 1523
Fessenden, William Pitt, **830–831**, *1344*
floor leadership, 1001

Reconstruction, 882, 1680, 1681, 1684
Senate Finance Committee, 1515
Fetal rights, 1
Fetal tissue medical research, 1710
Fever in the Blood, A (film), 1422, 1425
Few, William, 906, 1794
FFB. See Federal Financing Bank
FHA. See Federal Housing Administration
Fictional portrayals of Congress. See Literature on Congress; Movies on Congress
Fiedler, Bobbi, 2137
Field, Charles W., 660
Field, David Dudley, *731*
Field hearings, 1248
Fields, Cleo, 175
Fifteenth Amendment, 354, **831–833**, 1196, 1210, 2073, 2078
black male suffrage, 349, 350, 561, 698
coauthor, 193, 194
congressional enforcement, 754–755, 857
Radical Republicans, 1660, 1683
text of, 2171
Voting Rights Act of 1965, 2089
Fifth Amendment
communist probes, 349, 448, 2007
due process clause, 348, 557
fetal due process rights, 1
property protection, 250
text of, 2169
Fifth Congress anti-civil libertarian statute, 348
Fighting Liberal (Norris), 1478
Fiji Islands, 798
Filed at the desk, 2186
Filibuster, **833–835**, 1246, 1261, 2054, 2083
absence of unanimous consent, 1262, 2085
anti-civil rights bills, 159, 182, 355, 356, 357, 359, 361, 362, 1086
Bilbo (Theodore G.) use of, 159
campaign financing reform, 260–261
curb measures, 1029, 1208; see also Cloture
first Senate, 1949
La Follette, Robert M., 1241
legislation obstacle, 818, 1253, 1786
Long, Huey P., 1316
Long, Russell B., 1317
minority rights, 1345–1346, 1714, 1791
Morse, Wayne L., 1418, 1419
motion to proceed, 1252, 1508
Mr. Smith Goes to Washington (film), 1422
Nixon (Richard M.) modification, 1470
in other legislative systems, 487
Republican use, 260–261, 384

Heckler, Margaret M., 32, 2137
Heckscher, August, 1443
Heclo, Hugh, 231, 792, 1161
Heflin, Howell, 36, 1203
Heflin, J. Thomas, 963
Heinz, John, 17, 1534, 1978
Helms, Jesse, 36, 37, 479, 519, 878, 1480, 1798
Helms, Richard, 1150
Helper, Hinton, 1813
Helvering, Welch, and Edison Electric Illuminating Company v. Davis (1937), 817, 1841
Hemphill, John, 645
Henderson, Archibald, 1353
Henderson, David B., 266, 964, 1158, 1863
Henderson, Harold P., *as contributor*, 906, 1909, 2059–2060
Henderson, John B., 372
Henderson, Leon, 1536, 1940
Hendrick, Burton, 1427
Hendricks, Thomas A., 1110, 1111
Henig, Gerald S., *as contributor*, 603–604
Henry, Joseph, 1761, 1837
Henry, Patrick, 88, 162, 375, 1341, 1667–1668
Henshaw, Edmund L., Jr., 380
Hepburn, William P., 759, 961, 1653
Hepburn Act of 1906, 49, 64, 659, 674, **961–962**, 1017, 1145, 1427, 1629, 1664, 1739, 1741, 1964, 1970, 1974
Herberg, John C., 1272
Herdman, Roger C., 1495
Hereby rules, 2188
Heritage Foundaiton, 1958
Hernandez, Benigno (B.C.), 964, 965
Hernandez, Joseph M., 964
Herndon, William H., 1295, 1296
Herrnson, Paul S., *as contributor*, 253–255
Hershey, Lewis B., 528
Herter, Christian A., 1470
Hertzke, Allen D., *as contributor*, 1703–1711
Hesburgh, Theodore M., 1091, 1098, 1100
Hess, Stephen
  as contributor, 1551–1553
  media analyis, 1621
Hester, Douglas B., 1272
HEW. *See* Health, Education, and Welfare, Department of
Heyburn, Weldon B., 1653
HI. *See* Hospitalization Insurance program
Hibbing, John R., *as contributor*, 1386–1390
Hickel, Walter J., 42
Hickenlooper, Bourke B., 116, *117*, 879, 1294, 1486

Hickey, Donald R., *as contributor*, 734, 1455, 2095–2097
Hicks, Louise Day, 2137
Hideaways. *See* Clubs
Hiester family political dynasty, 1552
Higbee, Edward Y., 334
Higgins, Charles P., 1802
Higgins, Daniel Paul, 511
Higher education. *See* Colleges and universities
Higher Education Act of 1965, 688–689, 690, 932, 933, **962–963**, 1238, 1507
Higher Education Act of 1972, 690
Higher Education Facilities Act of 1963, 689
High Noon (film), 1425
Highway safety. *See* Automobile safety
Highway Safety Act of 1966, 120, 121
Highway system. *See* Interstate highway system
Highway Trust Fund, 1146, 1147, 1401, 1646, 2025
Hildenbrand, William F., 1778
Hill, Anita, 201
Hill, Benjamin H., 521
Hill, David B., 1011, 1466, 1925
Hill, Dilys M., *as contributor*, 234–236
Hill, John Philip, *1631*
Hill, Joseph Lister, 963
Hill, Lister, 41, 182, **963**, 1764, 1780, 1858, 1943
  disability legislation, 638
  health policy, 952, 955–956, 963, 1050, 1051
Hill, Robert P., 1413
Hill, Stephen P., 335
Hill & Knowlton, 1136
Hill-Burton Act. *See* Hospital Survey Act of 1946
Hillhouse, James, 1605
Hilliard, Earl F., 175
Hillman, Sidney, 1736
Himmelberg, Robert F., *as contributor*, 1445–1446, 2124–2125
Hinckley, Barbara, 179
Hinds, Asher C., **964**, 1015, 1577
Hinds' Precedents of the House of Representatives of the United States, 298, 1062, 1065, 1577
Hirabayashi v. United States (1943), 352
Hirshhorn, Joseph, 109
Hirshorn Museum, 109
HIS. *See* House Information Systems
Hispanic Caucus. *See* Congressional Hispanic Caucus
Hispanic members, **964–966**, 1371
  Chavez, Dennis, 336–337
  underrepresentation, 1378
  women, 2138
Hispanics
  bilingual education, 688
  New Mexico, 1465

poverty, 1394
voting rights, 2090
Hispanic Society of America, 1292
Hiss, Alger, 447, 1326, 1470, 2007
Historians of the House and Senate, **964–965**, 1776
Historical Almanac of the United States Senate (Dole), 157, 966
Historical Survey (WPA), 106, 107
Historic landmarks and monuments, 760, 762, 1447, 105
Historic Preservation Act of 1966, 105
Historic Sites and Buildings Act of 1935, 1447
History of Congress, **967–1045**
  origins, **967–983**; *see also* Continental Congress
  1774–1802, 161–162, 547, 628, **975–983**
  1801–1840, 628, **983–994**
  1840–1872, 370–374, 628–630, **994–1004**
  1872–1900, 630–631, **1004–1012**
  1900–1933, 631, **1012–1023**
  1933–1964, 631–632, **1023–1032**
  1965 to current times, 632–633, **1032–1046**, 1058–1059
  Articles of Confederation, **111–112**, 161
  bicentennial commmeration, **157–158**
  bill introduction, 462–464
  blocs and coalitions, 179–181
  calendars, 244–245
  Capitol building, **272–285**
  ceremonial activities, **321–325**
  circular letters, **345**
  Civil War, **370–374**
  clerk of the House, **379–380**
  clubs, **387–388**
  commerce power, **404–408**, **404–409**
  Congressional Directory, **509**
  congressional publications, 501–502, 516, 608
  conservative voices, 528–529
  constitutional interpretation during, **557–567**
  criminal justice role, 583–588
  customs and mores, **467–472**
  debate and oratory, 608–613
  debate reporting, **607–608**
  districts, **651–654**
  divided government, **654–659**, 723, 724–725
  executive reorganization, **795–796**
  First Congress, **843–845**, *1466*
  first office buildings, 510
  franking privilege, 884–886
  House chamber, 326–328
  House Rules Committee, 1745
  party caucus, 308–312
  petitions introduced, 164, 463–464, 990, 992, 997

I

K

Members of Congress for Peace through Law, 182

Memorial Day, 811, 812, 1314

Memorials. *See* Petitions and memorials

Mencken, H. L., 1081

Menendez, Robert, 965

Mennonites, 1707

Mental illness
    alcohol and drug abuse programs, 47, 48
    federal programs and funding, 954, 956, 957

Mental Retardation and Community Mental Health Centers Construction Act of 1962, 956

Mental Retardation Facilities Construction Act of 1963, 1238

Merchant marine, **1390–1391**, 1392
    academy, 1803–1804
    federal subsidies, 1972

Merchant Marine Acts of 1920, 1928, 1936, and 1970, 1229, 1390, 1972

Merchant Marine and Fisheries Committee, House, **1391–1392**
    Coast Guard, 389
    jurisdiction, 428
    legislative counsel, 150
    membership, 410
    membership motivation and desirability, 414, 422
    subcommittee orientation, 418
    Sullivan, Leonor Kretzer, 1896

Merck, Carolyn L., *as contributor,* 1384–1386

Meredith, James, 1213

Merit Systems Protection Board, 3–4, 367, 369

Metcalf, Lee, 633, 1033, 1414

Metcalfe, Ralph H., 175

Methods of Business of the Executive Department Committee, Senate Select, 795

Metropolitan Airports Authority v. Citizens for the Abatement of Aircraft Noise (1991), 461

Metropolitan Area Caucus, 182

Metropolitan areas. *See* Urban policy; Suburbs

Metzenbaum, Howard M., 142, 1203, 1500

Mexican American Legal Defense Fund, 359

Mexican War, **1392–1394**, 1952
    Adams (John Quincy) opposition, 8
    army, 100
    Benton (Thomas Hart) participation, 153
    Calhoun (John C.) opposition, 248
    California revolt, 250
    Clay (Henry) opposition, 378
    congressional formal declaration of, 552
    congressional medal, 122

Corwin (Thomas) opposition, 578–579, 611

Crittenden (John J.) opposition, 590

Davis (Jefferson) war heroship, 604–605

declaration of war, 1583, 1949

Democratic party, 628

Douglas (Stephen A.) support, 664

land bounty, 1636

Lincoln (Abraham) views on, 1294–1295, 1297

New Mexico, 1465

Pierce, Franklin, 1545

Polk (James K.) policies, 1568, 1948–1949

slavery issue, 248–249, 997

Taylor, Zachary, 1934

territorial expansion from, 206, 248, 378, 449, 615, 996, 1392–1393; *see also* Compromise of 1850

Texas, 1948

treaty, 87, 249, 250, 378, 1394, 1465, 1617, 2119

veterans' benefits, 2037, 2045

Mexico, **1394–1396**
    free trade agreement. *See* North American Free Trade Agreement

Mexican War, **1392–1394**

migrant workers, 1095, 1097, 1098, 1100, 1395

Texas independence, 1956

Wilmot Proviso, **2128**

Mexico City, Mexico, American cemetery, 1440

Mexico–United States Interparliamentary Group, 1144

Meyers, Jan, 2137

Meyers, Marvin, *as contributor,* 825–826

Meyers, William Starr, 1022

Meyner, Helen S., 2137

Mezey, Michael L.
    Comparative Legislatures, 485, 488, 489
    as contributor, 155–157

Mfume, Kweisi, 175

Michaelis, Patricia A., *as contributor,* 1207–1208

Michaelson, Mike, *as contributor,* 2068–2070

Michel, Robert H. (Bob), 849, 850, 1090, **1396**, 1508, 1525, 1723

Michel-Solarz resolution, 1396

Michener, Earl C., 1996

Michigan, **1396–1398**
    canal construction, 1969
    Cass, Lewis, 307–308
    economic policies, 1913
    first free banking law, 597
    Ford, Gerald R., Jr., 857–859
    Griffiths, Martha W., 933–934
    land-grant colleges, 683
    primary system, 707
    school desegregation, 361–362

shadow senators, 1812

statehood, 1884

statues in Capitol, 292

term limitations, 1944

Vandenberg, Arthur H., 2031–2032

woman suffrage, 1469

Micromanagement of the executive, 2193

Middle Ages, assembly representation, 651

Middle East
    Anti-Terrorism Act of 1988, 351, 353
    Carter (Jimmy) presidency, 306, 307
    foreign aid, 864, 866, 874
    see also Israel; Lebanon; Persian Gulf war

Migrant workers, 1095, 1097, 1098, 1100, 1395

Mikulski, Barbara A., 960, 2135, 2136, 2137, 2139

Mikva, Abner, 633, 880

Milburn, William H., 332, 333, 335

Military. *See* Armed forces; Defense; *specific branches of service*

Military Academy, U.S. (West Point), 100, 604, 605, 1760
    engineering school, 1641
    founding of, 682, 1803

Military Affairs Committee, House, 90, 91, 99
    air force organization, 39
    Atomic Energy Act, 115
    creation of, 985
    Luce, Clare Boothe, 1320

Military Affairs Committee, Senate, 93–94, 1167, 2026
    Atomic Energy Act, 115
    chairs, 605
    creation of, 988
    Proctor, Redfield, 1628
    World War I, 2148

Military and Naval Construction Authorization Act of 1952, 2049

Military-industrial complex, 92, 324, 392, 697

Military Justice Act of 1983, 1398

Military Justice, Uniform Code of, **1398–1400**

Military Reorganization Act of 1986, 916

Military Selective Service Act of 1971, 527, 528

Militia Act of 1792, 100, 619

Militia Act of 1795, 619

Militia Act of 1861, 619

Militia Act of 1862, 1828

Militia Acts of 1903 and 1908 (Dick Acts), 100, 619

Militia Committee, House, 90

Militia Committee, Senate, 988

Milkis, Sidney M., *as contributor,* 728–730, 1734–1738

Milledge, John, 1605

Miller, Cynthia Pease, *as contributor,* 301–302, 1331, 1800–1803
Miller, George (California representative), 802, 1453
Miller, George P. (House Parliamentarian), 1522
Miller, G. William, 634
Miller, James C., III, 1475
Miller, Mark C., *as contributor,* 1198–1200
Miller, Sally M., *as contributor,* 153–154, 1838–1840
Miller, Thomas E., 172
Miller, William M. (Fishbait), 660, 661
Millett, Allan R., *as contributor,* 99–103, 1353–1355
Milligan, Maurice, 1988
Milliken, Eugene, 1915
Mills, C. Wright, 1379
Mills, Elijah, 987
Mills, Robert, 277, 508
Mills, Roger Q., 305, **1400,** 1957
Mills, Wilbur D., **1400–1402,** 1848
    alcohol-related incidents, 45
    health care policy, 638, 952, 956, 957
    House Ways and Means Committee, 45, 87, 1033, 1260, 1317, 1917, 1921, 1927, 1929, 2114–2115
    influence as representative, 87
Mills Bill (1888), 1335, 1400
Mineral Leasing Act of 1920, 741, 742, 745, 746; *see also* Teapot Dome
Minerals. *See* Energy and natural resources
Miners for Democracy, 2123
Mineta, Norman Y., 114, 1650
Minimum wage. *See* Wages and hours
Minimum Wage Act of 1955, 662
Mining Act of 1877, 1635
Mining resources
    House Interior Committee jurisdiction, 1450, 1452
    West Virginia, 2123
Mink, Patsy T., 113, 114, 2137
Minnesota, 1319, **1402**
    Humphrey, Hubert H., 1085–1087
    McCarthy, Eugene J., 1325
    primary system, 707
    railroad legislation, 1515
    shadow senators, 1812
    statues in Capitol, 292
    voter registration, 2080
Minor, Virginia L., 2075
Minorities
    congressional composition, **1371–1372**
    see also African Americans; Asian American members; Black members; Civil rights; Disability legislation; Hispanic members; Hispanics; Women in Congress; Women's issues and rights

Minority rights (in Congress), **1403–1406**
    apportionment and redistricting, 63–64, 65–67
    census accuracy and, 66–67
    disappearing quorum, 1688
    importance of precedent, 1577
    legislative efficiency versus, 1508
    majority and minority, **1345–1346**
    recommital motion, 1677
    Reed's Rules, 1689–1690
    Senate, 1261, 1791
    special rule resolutions, 1742
    table of significant, 1403, 1405
Minor v. Happersett (1875), 570, 1188
Minton, Sherman, 1195
Miranda v. Arizona (1966), 353, 1190
MIRV (multiple warheads) missiles, 621
Missiles. *See* Antiballistic Missile Systems Treaty; Arms control; Defense
Mississippi, **1406**
    Alabama Territory and, 40
    at-large representation, 652
    Bilbo, Theodore G., 158–159
    black senator, 171
    Davis, Jefferson, 604–605
    Eastland, James O., 667–668
    Foote, Henry S., 856
    George, James Z., 905–906
    Lamar, Lucius Q. C., 1243–1244
    primary system, 707
    public lands, 1634
    redistricting, 68, 911
    secession, 605, *1000,* 1774
    statehood, 40
    statues in Capitol, 292
    Stennis, John C., 1886–1888
    voter qualifications, 2072
Mississippi River, 979, 1947
Mississippi Valley, 1417
Missouri, 1319, **1406–1408,** 1987–1991
    Benton, Thomas Hart, 152–153
    Bolling, Richard W., 188–189
    Cannon, Clarence, 264–265
    Clark, James Beauchamp (Champ), 374–375
    Mormons, 1707
    primary system, 707
    railroad legislation, 1515
    river basin study, 904
    statehood, 1820, 1821
    statues in Capitol, 292
    Sullivan, Leonor Kretzer, 1896
    term limitations, 1944
Missouri Compromise of 1820, 1407, **1408–1409,** 1771, 1821, 1829, 1952
    Arkansas Compromise as forerunner, 87
    Clay (Henry) role, 376, 1408, 1409, 1821
    Kansas-Nebraska Act repeal of, 153, 196, 665, **1208,** 1455, 1545

Maine statehood, 1344, 1358
    petitions of Congress and, 990
    Senate Judiciary Committee jurisdiction, 1201
    unconstitutionality, 1194, 1352, 1772, 1826
Missouri Territory, 1453, 1820–1821
Mr. Smith Goes to Washington (film), 1422, 1424
Mistretta v. United States (1989), 627
MIT. *See* Massachusetts Institute of Technology
Mitchel, Charles B., 645
Mitchell, Arthur W., 173, 175
Mitchell, Charles E., 1532
Mitchell, Clarence M., Jr., 361
Mitchell, George J., **1409–1410**
    campaign finance legislation, 260
    Equal Rights Amendment, 771
    floor leadership, 632, 853, 1261, 1264, 1267, 1268, 1269, 1345, 1405, 1508, 1525, 1526
Mitchell, John, 774, 1156
Mitchell, Parren J., 175
Mitchell v. Laird (1971), 2058
Mitchill, Samuel L., 987, 1618
Moakley, John Joseph, 1508, 1747
Mobile & Ohio Railroad, 1662, 1665
Mobile v. Bolden (1980), 359, 2079
Mobsters. *See* Organized crime
Model Cities program, 1071, 1072, 1073, 1074, 1846, 2020, 2021, 2022
Modern Democracies (Bryce), 485
Modified open rule, 1252
Modified rule, 2193
Moe, Ronald C., 791
    as contributor, 445, 1162–1163
Moe, Terry M., 1698
Moley, Raymond, 1783, 1940
Molinari, Susan, 2137
Moline Plow Company, 21, 1339
Molloy, James T., 659, 660, 661
Mondale, Walter F., *306,* 361, 802, 2143
    Democratic-Farmer-Labor party, 1402
    presidential campaign, 830, 1675
Monday Holiday Law of 1968, 811–812
Mondell, Frank W., 759, 849, 1524, 2158
Monetary powers. *See* Appropriations
Monetary system. *See* Currency and finance
Money market funds, 1757
Money Trust investigation, 134
Mongrel Tariff of 1883, 1335, 1918
Monopolies
    cable television, 443
    Celler (Emanuel) investigations, 317
    communications, 435–436
    Kefauver investigations, 1208, 1209
    oil, 741
    see also Clayton Antitrust Act of 1914; Sherman Antitrust Act of 1890

National Committee for Civilian Control of Atomic Energy, 115
National Committee for Equal Pay, 2142
National Committee on Atomic Information, 115
National Committee to Abolish HUAC, 2007
National Committee to Keep America Out of War, 846
National Committee to Preserve Medicare and Social Security, 1133, 1137
National Conference of State Legislatures, 824
National Congress of American Indians, 1117
National Council of Churches, 363, 1708
National Council on the Arts, 109, 110
National Cultural Center. See John F. Kennedy Center for the Performing Arts
National defense. See Defense
National Defense Act of 1916, 100, 1941
National Defense Act of 1920, 100, 101
National Defense Act of 1940, 12, 14
National Defense Education Act of 1958, 618, 689, 693, 733, 956, 963, 1030, 1169, 1237, 1238, **1441–1442**, 1766, 2022
    Cold War motivation, 686
    extension, 678
National Defense Program Investigating Committee, Senate Special, 159
National Defense Research Committee, 1763
National Economic Commission (1988–1989), 183
National Economic Committee, Temporary. See Temporary National Economic Committee
National Emergencies Act of 1976. See National Emergency Powers Act of 1976
National Emergencies and Delegated Emergency Powers Committee, Senate Special, 735
National emergency. See Emergency powers; War powers
National Emergency Powers Act of 1976, 345, 735
National Endowment for the Arts, 109, 110, 147, 230–231, **1443–1445**
    religious right objections, 1710
National Endowment for the Humanities, 109, **1443–1445**
National Energy Conservation Policy Act of 1978, 743
National Energy Extension Service Act of 1975, 749
National Environmental Policy Act of 1960, 1168
National Environmental Policy Act of 1969, 743, 744–745, 746, 748, 752,

761, 767–768, 1035–1036, **1442–1443**, 1472, 1484, 1695, 1696, 1974, 1975
National Farmers Union, 34
    congressional voting ratings, 2088
National Federation of Independent Business, 1132
National Film Preservation Board, 1292
National Film Registry, 1292
National Firearms Act of 1934, 936
National Fish and Wildlife Foundation Establishment Act, 1392
National floral emblem, **1443**
National Football League, antitrust coverage, 1868
National Forests Multiple Use-Sustained Yield Act of 1960, 758
National Foundation on the Arts and the Humanities, 109, 110, 1443
National Foundation on the Arts and the Humanities Act of 1965, 104, 109, **1443–1445**
National Gallery of Art, 109
National Governors' Association, 824, 1850
National Grange. See Grange
National Guard, 88, 89, 99, 100, 619
National Health Council, 953
National health insurance. See Health and medicine
National Health Service Corps, 957, 960
National highway system, 1646
National Highway Traffic Safety Administration, 121, 1694, 1698
National Historic Preservation Act Amendments of 1979, 2049
National holidays. See Federal holidays
National Home for Disabled Volunteer Soldiers, 2040
National Homeownership Trust, 1073, 1074
National Housing Act of 1968, 1846
National Housing Acts (1930s). See Federal Housing Acts; Housing Act of 1934
National Industrial Recovery Act of 1933, 192, 676, 680, 1024, 1232, **1445–1446**, 1843, 2014
    child labor provisions, 340
    oil policy, 742
    passage, 816, 1228–1229, 1734
    unconstitutionality, 406, 579, 627, 1229–1230, 1458
    Wagner (Robert F.) role, 2092
National Institute for Dental Research, 955
National Institute of Alcohol Abuse and Alcoholism, 47, 48, 1632
National Institute of Health. See National Institutes of Health
National Institute of Health Act of 1930, 958

National Institute of Mental Health, 46, 48, 954, 957, 958
National Institute on Aging, 18
National Institute on Alcoholism and Alcohol Abuse, 46, 47, 48
National Institutes for Standards and Technology, 1768
National Institutes of Health, 18, 48, 953, 955–956, 959, 960, 963, 1318, 1764–1765
National Institutes of Health Revitalization Act of 1993, 2146
National Intelligencer, 608, 1612, 1685
Nationalism. *See under* History of Congress
Nationality Act of 1940, 347
National Journal, 499, 500, 501, 530
National Labor Relations Act of 1935. *See* Wagner-Connery National Labor Relations Act of 1935
National Labor Relations Act of 1947. *See* Taft-Hartley Labor Management Relations Act of 1947
National Labor Relations Board, 676, 681, 1230–1231, 1233, 1238, 1698, 2093, 2094
    Taft-Hartley Labor Management Relations Act of 1947, 1908
National Labor Relations Board v. Jones & Laughlin Steel Corporation (1937), 407, 459, 552, 756, 817, 2015
National League of Cities, 824, 2025
National League of Cities v. Usery (1976), 408, 459, 563, 564
National Library of the United States (proposed), 1292
National Library Service for the Blind and Handicapped, 1288–1289
National Mass Transportation Assistance Act of 1974, 1974–1975
National Medal of Arts, 110
National Mental Health Act of 1946, 954, 958
National Military Establishment, 88, 93, 95, 1449, 1454; *see also* Defense, Department of
National Monetary Commission, 134, 599, 829
National monuments. *See* National cemeteries, monuments, and battlefields
National Museum, 1761
National Museum Services Board, 1444
National Neuropsychiatric Institute, 954
National Newspaper Index, 498
National Oceanic and Atmospheric Administration, 737
National Ocean Policy Study Subcommittee, Senate, 389
National Organization for Women, 2143
National Organ Transplant Act of 1984, 1307

Nixon, Richard M., *continued*
  foreign policy, 894, 1472, 1473, 1985
  government custody of papers, 167
  government growth, 1305
  health policy, 959–960
  House Un-American Activities
    Committee, 2007
  housing policy, 1070–1071
  impeachment proceedings, 198, 554,
    1037, 1103–1104, 1106
  impoundments, 209, 214, 503, 624,
    791, 793, 1107–1108, 1724
  "law and order" policy, 586–587
  New Federalism, 819, 823, 1472,
    1581, 1888
  nuclear weapons policy, 1483, 1486
  Panama Canal treaty, 1520
  presidency, 858, 1034, 1035–1036,
    1471–1473, 1558, 1581, 1593, 1596,
    1699
  presidential campaigns, 1086, 1212,
    1360, 1602, 1673, 1997
  resignation from presidency, 306, 554,
    555, 667, 916, 1037, 1473, 1999
  roll-call vote successes, 235, *1035*
  science policy, 1766
  Senate investigative committees, 1148
  urban programs, 2019, 2021
  usurpation of congressional powers,
    2048
  vetoes, 393, 622, 638, 805, 870, 1037,
    1169, 1428, 1472, 1726, 2052–2053,
    2098, 2100, 2144
  vice presidency, 179, 1470–1471, 1999
  vice presidential choices, 555
  Vietnam War policy, 392–393, 528,
    1036, 1037, 1349, 1584, 1586, 1967,
    2055–2057, 2058
  war powers, 1428, 1726, 2098, 2100
  Watergate scandal. *See* Watergate;
    Watergate Committee
  welfare reform, 1848
  White House conference on aging, 17
Nixon, Walter L., Jr., 1102, 1105, 1775
Nixon Doctrine, 1472
*Nixon v. Administrator of General
    Services* (1977), 167
Nixon v. United States, 554
NLRB. *See* National Labor Relations
    Board
NMC. *See* National Monetary
    Commission
Noble, John W., 758
Noell, John W., 372
Nolan, Mae E., *1021*, 2136, 2139
No Net Cost Tobacco Program Act of
    1982, 1965
Nongermane amendment, 1253,
    1792–1793, 2194
Non-Legislative and Financial Services,
    Director of, 1121, **1473–1474**, 1860
  House reform, 1715
  patronage employees, 1529

Nonpartisan League, 1481
Nonprofit organizations, 105–106
Non-Proliferation Treaty. *See* Nuclear
    Non-Proliferation Treaty
Nonstatutory controls, **1474–1475**
Nonvoting delegates. *See* Delegates,
    nonvoting
NORAD. *See* North American Air
    Defense Command
Norbeck, Peter, 1854
Noriega, Manuel, 235, 1520
Norrell, Catherine D., 2136
Norris, Frank, 1301
Norris, George W., 182, 808, 1022, 1161,
    1243, 1455, **1475–1478**, 1481
  on Borah, William E., 192
  Cannon revolt leadership, 180,
    268–269, 374, 1019
  committee reform, 1796
  energy projects, 181, 573, 765, 963
  Hoover (Herbert) presidency, 1050
  progressive movement, 1284, 1285,
    1630, 1722, 1746
  Rural Electrification Act, 1748
  Tennessee Valley Authority, 1459,
    1941–1943
  Twentieth Amendment, 1994–1995
Norris, George W. (grocery clerk), 1478
Norris-Doxey Farm Forestry Act of
    1937, 1478
Norris-LaGuardia Anti-Injunction Act of
    1932, 1230, 1232, 1243, 1467, 1475,
    1478, 2093
Norris-Rayburn Rural Electrification
    Act of 1936. *See* Rural
    Electrification Act of 1936
Norris-Sinclair bill, 1477–1478
North, Oliver, 188, 620, 1156, 1159,
    1160, 1409, 2134–2135
North American Air Defense Command,
    264
North American Free Trade Agreement
    (1993), 236, 264, 384, 521, 797,
    1236, 1308, 1396, 1920, 1921, 1922,
    1923, 2117
North American Free Trade Agreement
    Implementation Act of 1933, 1920
North Atlantic Treaty (1949), 632, 880,
    1479–1480, 1981, 1990
North Atlantic Treaty Organization, 864,
    874, 1586, 1906
North Carolina, **1480–1481**
  charter, 1945
  constitutional ratification, 162
  Doughton, Robert L. (Muley), 661
  elector dispute, 1602
  Ervin, Samuel J., Jr., 773–774
  Kitchin, Claude, **1218–1219**
  Macon, Nathaniel, 1339–1340
  populism, 1569
  primary system, 707
  secession, 1774
  statues in Capitol, 293

  tobacco regulation opposition, 1966
  voter qualifications, 2072
North Dakota, 1319, **1481–1482**
  Nye, Gerlad P., 1487–1488
  primary system, 707
  statehood, 1413, 1853, 2105
  statues in Capitol, 293
  term limitations, 1944
  voter qualifications, 2080
Northeast-Midwest Advancement
    Coaliton, 1781, 1881
Northern Ohio Boundary bill, 1397
Northern Pacific Railroad, 396, 672
Northern Pacific Railway Act of 1864.
    See Pacific Railroad Acts of 1862
    and 1864
*Northern Pipeline Construction Co. v.
    Marathon Pipeline Company* (1982),
    1194
North Korea, 307; *see also* Korean War
North Pole, 798–799
Northwest Ordinances of 1785, 1787,
    460, 626, 682–683, 1633, 1829
  reenactment (1789), 1705
  slavery prohibition, 1828, 1946, 1959
  state admission process, 1883, 1951
  territory boundaries, 1397
Northwest Territory, 1499, 1634, 2133
Norton, Eleanor Holmes, 648, 702,
    2135, 2137, 2139
Norton, Mary T., **1482**, 2139
Norton, Philip, *as contributor*, 485–490
Norvell, John, 1397
Norway, 699, 1479
Notations of the Americans (Cooper),
    593
*Notes on Debate in the Federal
    Convention of 1787* (Madison),
    1785
Not voting, 2194
Novak, Robert, 1265
Novels. *See* Literature on Congress
NOW. *See* National Organization for
    Women
Noyes, Theodore W., 1997
NPL. *See* Nonpartisan League
NPT. *See* Nuclear Non-Proliferation
    Treaty (1968)
NRA. *See* National Recovery
    Administration; National Rifle
    Association
NRC. *See* Nuclear Regulatory
    Commission
NRCC. *See* National Republican
    Congressional Committee
NRPB. *See* National Resources Planning
    Board
NRSC. *See* National Republican
    Senatorial Committee
NRTA. *See* National Retired Teachers
    Association
NSA. *See* National Security Agency
NSC. *See* National Security Council

floor leadership, 830, 849, 1257, 1358, 1359, 1365, 1860, 1863, 1864
House ethics reforms, 779
House speakership, 234, 1043, 1059
House television rules, 201
humor, 1246
on politics, 1717
Reagan (Ronald) relationship, 1673, 1674
task forces, 1527
O'Neill House Office Building, 513
One-minute speeches, 201, 1060, **1505–1506**
One person, one vote doctrine, 605, 1034
Baker v. Carr (1962), 62, **127–128**
One-vote-per-state principle, 625
ONR. *See* Office of Naval Research
On the Waterfront (film), 1425
Open rule, 1252, 1742, 2194
OPIC. *See* Overseas Private Investment Corporation
Opium Exclusion Act of 1909, 1434
OPM. *See* Office of Personnel Management
Oppenheimer, Bruce I., as contributor, 385–386, 654–659, 833–835
Oppenheimer, J. Robert, 116
Oratory. *See* Debate and oratory
Order of business resolution. *See* Rule, special
Orders, **1506–1507**
Ordinance of 1784, 626, 1951
Ordway, Nathaniel G., 1801
Oregon, **1507**
  boundary dispute, 1949
  direct primaries, 1413, 2075
  Green, Edith S., 933
  McNary, Charles L., 1337–1339
  Morse, Wayne L., 1418–1419
  primary system, 707
  shadow senators, 1812
  slavery issue, 1824
  Spanish claims, 1948
  statehood, 249, 1884
  statues in Capitol, 293
  term limitations, 1944
  territory, 153, 206, 664, 798, 1952, 2105
  woman suffrage, 1468
Oregon system (direct primaries), 2075
Oregon v. Mitchell (1970), 561, 1188, 1196, 2000, 2079
Organic Act of 1848, 1507
Organic Act of 1868, 2157
Organic Act of Guam of 1950, 1954
Organization for Economic Cooperation and Development, 864
Organization of American States, 178, 1143
Organization of Congress Committee, Joint, 513, 796, 1039–1040, 1045, 1197, 1279–1280, 1281, 1405, 1413,

1508–1510, 1713, 1716, 1744, 1879
  authorization separation from appropriation, 120
  creation of, 1039–1040
  ethics recommendations, 784, 787
Organization of the Executive Branch, Commissions on. *See* Hoover Commission
Organizations That Rate Members of Congress on Their Voting Records, 499
Organization, Study, and Review Committee, House, 1040
Organized crime
  commerce clause application, 407, 584, 585–587
  Kefauver investigations, 198, 199, 200, 585–586, **1208–1209**
  Racketeer Influenced and Corrupt Organizations Act (RICO) of 1987, 587–588, 1659
  Senate Rackets Committee investigation, 1213–1214
Organized Crime Control Act. *See* Racketeer Influenced and Corrupt Organizations Act
Organized Crime Control Act of 1970, 587; *see also* Racketeer Influenced and Corrupt Organizations Act (RICO) of 1970
Organized Crime in Interstate Commerce Committee, Senate Special. *See* Kefauver Crime Committee
Organized labor. *See* Labor
Organ transplant legislation, 1307
Original bill, 1250
Origins of the House of Representatives, The: A Documentary Record, 1917–1989, 157
Orlando v. Laird (1971), 2058
Orleans Territory, 1318, 1319
Orleans Territory Act of 1811, 1318
Ornstein, Norman J., 891, 1274
  as contributor, 775–785, 1131–1138
Orphan drugs, 1239
Orr, James L., 1522, 1852, 1862
Ortega, Daniel, 2156
Ortiz, Solomon P., 965
Osborn, Shari L., as contributor, 2092–2093
OSHA. *See* Occupational Safety and Health Act of 1970; Occupational Safety and Health Administration
Oshinsky, David M., as contributor, 103–104, 1325–1328
Osmeña, Sergio, 1543
OSR. *See* House Democratic Committee on Organization, Study, and Review
OSRD. *See* Office of Scientific Research and Development

OSS. *See* Office of Strategic Services
Ostend Manifesto, 206
Oswald, John H., 380
Oswald, Lee Harvey, 1210
OTA. *See* Office of Technology Assessment
Otero, Miguel A., 964
Other America, The (Harrington), 1846
Otis, James, 971
Otis, Samuel Allyne, 1777, 1778
Ottinger, Richard L., *750*
Ouachita River exploration, 797
Oulahan, Richard, 1619
Outdoor Recreation Resources Review Commission, 1447
Outer Continental Shelf Lands Act of 1953, 742, 746
Outer Continental Shelf Lands Amendments of 1978, 743
Outlays, 2194
Outreach. *See* Constituency outreach
Overman, Lee S., 574
Overman Act of 1918, 2148
Overman Subcommittee, Senate, 445
Override, 2195; *see also* Veto override
Overseas Private Development Corporation, 864
Overseas Private Investment Corporation, 864
Oversight, **1510–1513**
  accountability, 3
  of bureaucracy, 225, 229, 231–232, 242, 538
  committee role, 3, 225, 413, 2195
  congressional history, 986, 993
  Congressional Research Service support, 518
  constituent complaints and, 538, 545
  executive privilege, **794–795**
  General Accounting Office, 901–904
  government corporations, 921–922
  House Foreign Affairs Committee, 861
  House Ways and Means Committee, 985
  impact, 1512
  Inspector General of the House, **1121**
  inspectors general, **1121**
  of intelligence operations, 321, 345, 394, 618, 1122–1126, 1127–1130
  investigations, **1147–1153, 1159–1160**
  investigative power, **1154–1158**
  legislative reorganization, 1280, 1281
  of Postal Service, 1574
  regulatory agencies, 1699–1700
  Senate Governmental Affairs Committee, 917–920
  sunset laws, 1899
  see also Investigations
Oversight committee, 2195
Overstreet, Jesse, 267
Overton, John H., 1645

Price-Anderson Act of 1957, 746, 748
Price controls. *See* Wage and price controls
Price Waterhouse v. Hopkins (1989), 1196
Priest, J. Percy, 952, 954
Priestly, Joseph, 609
Prigg v. Pennsylvania (1842), 891, 1820
Primary systems, 706–707, 708, 2073, 2074, 2077, 2105
"Prime Time Live" (TV program), 1979
Princeton (ship), 507
Princeton University, 2129
Principle of rotation *See* Term limitation
Printing Act of 1895, 926, 1623
Printing Committee, Joint, 434, 509, 516, 800, 1052, **1623**
Printing of bills, 1247
Prior year (budget term), 845
Prisoner of War Medal, 122
Pritchard, Jeter C., 758, 759
Privacy, **1623–1626**
    landmark legislation, 1624–1625
Privacy Act of 1974, 366, 1623, 1624
Privacy Protection Act of 1980, 351, 354, 1190, 1625
Private bill, 243, 1063, 1248, **1626–1627**, 2179
    presidential veto, 2051
    veterans' benefits, 2037, 2038, 2046
Private Calendar (House), 243, 244, 1061, 1251, 1252, 1491
Private utilities. *See* Energy and natural resources
Privatization, 2197; *see also* Regulation and deregulation
Privilege, **1627–1628**
    constitutional provisions, 551
    recognition, 1676
Privileged bills, 246, 1063, 1066
Privileged matter, 2197
Privileges and Elections Subcommittee, Senate, 777, 1046, 1153, 1467
Prizes. *See* Awards and prizes
Procedure in the United States House of Representatives (Deschler and Brown), 1063, 1350, 1577
Proceed, motion to, 1420
Process of Government, The (Bentley), 424, 1134
Proclamation of Amnesty and Reconstruction (1863), 1679–1680
Proclamations, commemorative, 399
Procter, Ben, *as contributor*, 1400, 1672
Proctor, Redfield, **1628**, 1856
Proctor, Samuel, *as contributor*, 2121–2122
Pro-family policies, 803
Professional Standards Review Organizations, 959
Profiles in Courage (Kennedy), 951, 1211, 1741

Pro forma amendment or motion, 1253, 2197
Pro forma session, 2197
Program Evaluation and Methodology Division, 902
Progressive movement, 1284–1285, **1628–1631**
    Arizona, 86
    budget process reforms, 208
    Bull Moose party, 375, 1017
    California politics, 251
    child labor laws, 339–340
    civil service reform, 1532
    conservationism, 762, 1633
    Democratic alliance, 375, 631
    development, 1559
    executive budget support, 1493
    farm bloc, 181
    impact on Congress, 1017–1020
    labor legislation, 1227, 1228
    La Follette, Robert M., 1240–1242
    La Follette, Robert M., Jr., 1242
    landmark legislation, 1629
    literature and, 1301
    lobbying reform, 1303–1304
    Montana politics, 1413
    muckraking, **1426–1427**
    New Nationalism program, 1461, 1462
    presidential activism, 1587
    prominent members, 180, 595
    public health, 952, 954
    Republican party and, 154, 180, 182, 267, 268, 1561, 1562, 1630, 1721–1722
    Roosevelt, Theodore, 1177
    sectional alignment, 1779–1780
    social welfare programs, 1842
    statute law development, 150
    strength, 1563
    two factions, 180–181
    veterans' benefits, 2038
    voting reform, 2073–2074
    Washington state politics, 2105
    Wheeler, Burton K., 2124
    Wilson, Woodrow, 2129
    Wisconsin politics, 1796, 2133
    woman suffrage impetus, 2076
Progressive party. *See* Progressive movement
Progressivism. *See under* History of Congress
Progress of Civilization (pediment), 289
Prohibition, **1631–1632**
    Bryan (William Jennings) support, 205
    congressional debate on, 47, 60–61, 694
    constitutional amendment enactment, 46, **694–695**, 1019, 2172
    Democratic party faction, 181
    enforcement on Capitol Hill, 44
    interest groups, 694, 1020

legislation, 46, 47, 584, 587, 694, 695
    religious influence, 1707
    repeal, 46, 47–48, 694, 695, **1995–1996**, 2173
    Treasury Department enforcement, 584
    woman suffrage impact, 2076
    see also Anti-Saloon League; Eighteenth Amendment; National Prohibition Act of 1919; Twenty-first Amendment
Prohibition party, 46
Pro-Life Caucus, 182
Proportional representation
    comparative systems, 699–700
    districts, 654
    Huntingdon congressional formula, 61, 62
    single member, simple plurality (SMSP) rules, 64, 65
    Supreme Court ruling, 606
    Virginia Plan (1787), 980
    Voting Rights Act of 1965, 64, 66
Prostitution, 583, 584, 587, 2128, 2140
Protectionism, 1011, 1210, 1218, 2026
    Aldrich (Nelson) advocacy, 49, 50, 180
    bipartisanship, 1010
    Cannon (Joseph G.) advocacy, 266, 268
    Civil War, 373
    Clay (Henry) advocacy, 376, 377, 670–671
    as dominant policy, 1912–1914
    enactment of first bill (1816), 670
    during Great Depression, 1914
    McKinley bill, 305
    1920s, 1022
    nineteenth century, 252, 670–671
    party divisions, 1739, 1814, 1910–1912, 1912–1913, 1921–1922
    philosophical basis, 1910
    Randall, Samuel J., 1666, 1667
    southern opposition, 671
    see also Hawley-Smoot Tariff Act of 1930; Nullification; Payne-Aldrich Tariff of 1909
Protestantism
    cultural hegemony, 1706, 1707
    Indian sectarian schools, 1707
    members of Congress, 1372–1373
    parochial school aid issue, 1708, 1710
Protests
    Bonus march, **190–191**
    Civil Rights March on Washington (1963), *357*, 1213
    Coxey's army, **582**
    farm bloc, *808*
    as interest group tactic, 1306
    Poor People's March on Washington (1968), *1847*, 1889
Protocol (film), 1424
Protocol (treaty amendment), 1987
Provision of privileges, 2084

X

Y

Z